THE COLLEGE OF LAW
MCR
M1 4BD

THE UNIVERSITY OF LAW
WITHDRAWN

Manchester and Salter on Exploring the Law:
The Dynamics of Precedent and Statutory Interpretation

D1471302

L A B

(ELSM)
Man
std

The College of Law, Manchester
N02042

Manchester and Salter on Exploring the Law: The Dynamics of Precedent and Statutory Interpretation

4th edition

by

Colin Manchester, LL.B., Ph.D.
Professor of Licensing Law, University of Warwick

David Salter, LL.B., Solicitor
Reader in Law, University of Warwick

RECEIVED

2 9 MAY 2011

SWEET & MAXWELL

THOMSON REUTERS

Reprinted 1998
Second Edition 2000
Third Edition 2006

Published in 2011 by Sweet & Maxwell, 100 Avenue Road, London NW3 3PF
Part of Thomson Reuters (Professional) UK Limited
(Registered in England & Wales, Company No 1679046.
Registered Office and address for service: Aldgate House,
33 Aldgate High Street, London EC3N 1DL

For further information on our products and services, visit www.sweetandmaxwell.co.uk

Typeset by YHT Ltd, London
Printed in the UK by TJ International Ltd, Padstow, Cornwall

No natural forests were destroyed to make this product;
only farmed timber was used and re-planted.

British Library Cataloguing in Publication Data

A CIP catalogue record for this book
is available from the British Library

ISBN 978 0 41404 185 1

Crown Copyright material is reproduced with the permission of
the Controller of HMSO and the Queen's Printer for Scotland.

All rights reserved. No part of this publication may be reproduced or transmitted, in any
form or by any means, or stored in any retrieval system of any nature, without prior written
permission, except for permitted fair dealing under the Copyright, Designs and Patents Act
1988, or in accordance with the terms of a license issued by the Copyright Licensing
Agency in respect of photocopying and/or reprographic reproduction. Application for
permission for other use of copyright material including permission to reproduce extracts
in other published works shall be made to the publishers. Full acknowledgment of author,
publisher and source must be given.

Sweet & Maxwell® is a registered trademark of
Thomson Reuters (Professional) UK Limited.

© 2011 Colin Manchester and David Salter

PREFACE TO THE 4TH EDITION

When this book first appeared in 1996, we wondered how the book would fare. The idea behind the book was a new one—as far as we were aware, nothing quite like it had been previously attempted—and the approach that we had taken was a novel one. New ideas and novel approaches are sometimes well received and prosper, whilst on other occasions they are not and make no impact. Into which category would our work fall? Would the book sell well or would it be a spectacular sales flop? We ourselves believed in the value of the work, in which we had invested a considerable amount of time and effort, so we retained a cautious optimism. Nevertheless we awaited peer reaction and sales figures with more than a hint of apprehension. Early reaction, gauged from inspection copy comments received by the publishers, was encouraging, as were sales figures in the first few months. Further, we were delighted to receive, in particular, two subsequent endorsements of it. One was a favourable review of the book in the *Law Teacher*, which appeared in the December 1997 issue, and the other was a personal letter, dated June 11, 1996, from the late Professor Glanville Williams, which is reproduced below.

Dear Colin

I acknowledged the copy of your book upon its receipt from the publishers. Having now found time to read it, I am enthusiastic. It admirably fills several large holes in the literature. You are all to be warmly congratulated.

Yours ever (or whatever my constantly shrinking years may be read into that expression),

Glanville

The book's initial promise was sustained, for it continued to sell well after its publication and was adopted for use on a number of degree and other courses, such as the Common Professional Examination. In due course, a second edition of the book appeared in 2000 and a third edition in 2006. These were generally well received and sales continued to be encouraging.

The basic format of this fourth edition remains essentially unchanged, comprising three sections as in previous editions: Principles in Part 1, Selected Case Studies in Part 2 and Tracing the Evolution of Law in Selected Fields in Part 3. The most significant change in this edition is the introduction of a new chapter on courts and tribunals. The book has always included material on courts, tribunals and the court/tribunal hierarchy, which is of crucial importance in relation to binding and persuasive precedents, but the information provided was only such as was considered necessary for an understanding of the precedent system. In particular, no details were provided on the composition of courts, tribunals or their jurisdiction, whether present day courts/tribunals or courts/tribunals no longer in existence which feature in some of the case studies.

The opportunity has now been taken to provide this information, which seems particularly apt in view of the establishment of the Supreme Court as the final domestic court of appeal in place of the House of Lords and significant reforms to the tribunals system. There is appropriate cross-referencing in this chapter to Chapter 1 and other chapters in which particular courts are mentioned, and it is hoped that this will provide an enhanced understanding of the structure and hierarchy of courts and tribunals. This chapter has been included as Chapter 2 as a replacement for the chapter on *Pepper v Hart*. Although *Pepper v Hart* remains important on the extent to which statements in *Hansard* can be taken into account as an external aid to the interpretation of statutes, we have come to the view that this no longer justifies inclusion as a separate chapter in the book and a less detailed section on this area appears in Chapter 1 alongside other external aids to statutory interpretation.

Further reading has also been included at the end of each of the case studies in Parts 2 and 3 of the book, which provides an opportunity to supplement the case studies by looking at case notes, articles and other material pertaining to the case studies in question.

In other respects, the new edition incorporates important developments since publication of the third edition that have impacted on Principles in Part 1 (e.g. changes introduced by the Treaty of Lisbon to EU law in Chapter 4), and on the case studies in Parts 2 (e.g. the case of *R. v L* in Chapter 12) and 3 (e.g. the case of *Grieves* in Chapter 15).

We would like to thank all those who have helped us in different ways during the preparation of this edition. We are particularly indebted to Sarah Brown for her help in collecting and collating material since the publication of the previous edition. Needless to say, any errors remain our sole responsibility. We are also grateful to our publishers and to Constance Sutherland in particular for allowing us the extra time that we felt was needed to complete the manuscript. Last, but by no means least, our thanks go to our respective families for their continuing interest and support.

Colin Manchester and David Salter
University of Warwick

October 9, 2010

CONTENTS

Preface to the 4th Edition   v
Table of Cases   ix
Table of Statutes   xvii
Table of Statutory Instruments   xxi
Table of Treaties   xxiii
Glossary of Abbreviations   xxv
Acknowledgments   xxxi
Content, Format and Use of the Book   xxxiii

PART 1: PRINCIPLES

1. Precedent and Statutory Interpretation: An Outline and Guide   3
2. Courts and Tribunals   69
3. The Incoming Tide: European Influences on Statutory Interpretation
    and the Doctrine of Precedent   84
4. The European Union Legal Order: Influence on Statutory Interpretation
    and the Doctrine of Precedent   87
5. The European Convention on Human Rights and the Human Rights
    Act 1998: Influence on Statutory Interpretation and the Doctrine of
    Precedent   138

PART 2: SELECTED CASE STUDIES

6. Contractual Obligations Arising out of an Invitation to Tender   173
7. Existing Obligations as Consideration in Contract   188
8. The Right to Sue in the Tort of Private Nuisance   201
9. False Imprisonment, "Detention" and the Mental Health Act 1983   225
10. Video Cassettes as Obscene Articles   254
11. The Regulation of Abortion   263
12. Wives as Prosecution Witnesses   293
13. Succession Rights under the Rent Act 1977   312
14. Equal Pay   324

PART 3: TRACING THE EVOLUTION OF LAW IN SELECTED FIELDS

15. Nervous Shock or Psychiatric Injury   365
16. Marital Rape   432
17. Appropriation in Theft   466

Index   499

TABLE OF CASES

A v National Blood Authority (No.1) [2001] 3 All E.R. 289; [2001] Lloyd's Rep. Med. 187, QBD 4–040
A v Secretary of State for the Home Department [2004] UKHL 56; [2005] 2 A.C. 68; [2005] 2 W.L.R. 87 1–046
AS (Somalia) v Entry Clearance Officer (Addis Ababa) [2009] UKHL 32; [2009] 1 W.L.R. 1385; [2009] 4 All E.R. 711 5–015
Actavis UK Ltd v Merck & Co Inc [2008] EWCA Civ 444; [2009] 1 W.L.R. 1186; [2009] Bus. L.R. 573 .... 1–008, 1–021
Adam Opel GmbH v Mitras Automotive (UK) Ltd, Renault S.A.[2007] EWHC 3481 (QB) 1–020, 1–055, 7–006
Alcock v Chief Constable of South Yorkshire [1992] 1 A.C. 310; [1991] 3 W.L.R. 1057, HL 1–009, 1–012, 1–029, 1–058, 9–007, 15–009–15–011, 15–014, 15–018, 15–019
Amministrazione delle Finanze dello Stato v Simmenthal SpA (106/77) [1978] E.C.R. 629; [1978] 3 C.M.L.R. 263, ECJ 4–018, 4–023, 14–005
Anandarajah v Lord Chancellor's Department [1984] I.R.L.R. 130, EAT 1–041
Anangel Atlas Compania Naviera SA v Ishikawajima-Harima Heavy Industries Co (No.2) [1990] 2 Lloyd's Rep. 526, QBD 1–055, 7–001, 7–006
Aston Cantlow and Wilmcote with Billesley Parochial Church Council v Wallbank [2003] UKHL 37; [2004] 1 A.C. 546; [2003] 3 W.L.R. 283 5–010
Attorney General's Reference (No.5 of 1980), Re [1981] 1 W.L.R. 88; [1980] 3 All E.R. 816, CA (Crim Div) 1–013, 1–073, 1–093, 10–001–10–004
Attorney General v HRH Prince Ernest Augustus of Hanover [1957] A.C. 436; [1957] 2 W.L.R. 1, HL 1–076
Attorney General for Jersey v Holley [2005] UKPC 23; [2005] 2 A.C. 580; [2005] 3 W.L.R. 29 .... 1–031, 1–046, 2–022
B v Forsey, 1988 S.C. (H.L.) 28; 1988 S.L.T. 572, HL 1–010, 1–033, 1–055, 1–056, 9–007, 9–010
Barber v Somerset CC [2002] EWCA Civ 76; [2002] 2 All E.R. 1; [2002] I.C.R. 613 15–021
Becke v Smith (1836) 2 M. & W. 191 1–068
Bell v Great Northern Railway Co of Ireland (1890) 26 L.R.Ir. 428 .... 1–033, 15–003, 15–006
Best v Hill (1872–73) L.R. 8 C.P. 10, CCP 2–016
Beswick v Beswick [1968] A.C. 58; [1967] 3 W.L.R. 932, HL 1–084
Birmingham City Council v Doherty. See Doherty v Birmingham City Council
Black Clawson International Ltd v Papierwerke Waldhof-Aschaffenburg AG [1975] A.C. 591; [1975] 2 W.L.R. 513, HL 1–084, 1–086, 17–008
Blackpool and Fylde Aero Club v Blackpool BC [1990] 1 W.L.R. 1195; [1990] 3 All E.R. 25, CA (Civ Div) 1–009, 1–012, 1–013, 1–055, 1–090, 6–001–6–010
Boardman v Sanderson [1964] 1 W.L.R. 1317; (1961) 105 S.J. 152, CA 1–056, 15–008, 15–009
Borgers v Belgium (A/214) (1993) 15 E.H.R.R. 92, ECHR 5–007
Bourhill v Young [1943] A.C. 92; [1942] 2 All E.R. 396, HL 1–010, 1–049, 1–055, 15–005–15–007, 15–009
Boys v Chaplin [1968] 2 Q.B. 1; [1968] 2 W.L.R. 328, CA (Civ Div) 1–021
Brannigan v United Kingdom (14553/89) (1994) 17 E.H.R.R. 539, ECHR 5–010
British Amusement Catering Trades Association (BACTA) v Westminster City Council [1989] A.C. 147; [1988] 2 W.L.R. 485, HL 1–080
Brown v Rentokil Ltd (C–394/96) [1998] All E.R. (EC) 791; [1998] E.C.R. I–4185 4–018
Butcher Robinson & Staples Ltd v London Regional Transport (2000) 79 P. & C.R. 523; [1999] 3 E.G.L.R. 63, QBD 8–007
C (A Minor) v DPP [1996] A.C. 1; [1995] 2 W.L.R. 383, HL 1–007, 1–055, 2–006, 16–011
CR v United Kingdom. See SW v United Kingdom
Caparo Industries Plc v Dickman [1990] 2 A.C. 605; [1990] 2 W.L.R. 358, HL 6–009
Carter v Bradbeer [1975] 1 W.L.R. 1204; [1975] 3 All E.R. 158, HL 1–080
Chadwick v British Railways Board [1967] 1 W.L.R. 912; [1967] 2 All E.R. 945, QBD 1–010, 15–009, 15–012, 15–018

Table of Cases

Chartbrook Ltd v Persimmon Homes Ltd [2009] UKHL 38; [2009] 1 A.C. 1101; [2009] 3 W.L.R.
267 1–026
Chief Adjudication Officer v Foster [1993] A.C. 754; [1993] 2 W.L.R. 292, HL 1–084
Chief Constable of the West Midlands v Marsden (1995) 159 J.P. 405; (1995) 159 J.P.N. 407,
QBD 1–021
Chief Supplementary Benefit Officer v Leary [1985] 1 W.L.R. 84; [1985] 1 All E.R. 1061, CA (Civ
Div) 1–039
Colchester Estates (Cardiff) v Carlton Industries Plc [1986] Ch. 80; [1984] 3 W.L.R. 693, Ch D 1–026
Commission of the European Communities v United Kingdom (61/81) [1982] E.C.R. 2601; [1982]
3 C.M.L.R. 284, ECJ 14–002, 14–014, 14–021
Commission of the European Communities v United Kingdom (165/82) [1984] 1 All E.R. 353;
[1983] E.C.R. 3431, ECJ 14–002
Commission of the European Communities v United Kingdom (C–246/89 R) [1989] E.C.R.
3125; [1989] 3 C.M.L.R. 601, ECJ 4–018
Commission of the European Communities v United Kingdom (C–300/95) [1997] All E.R. (EC)
481; [1997] E.C.R. I–2649, ECJ 4–040
Coote v Granada Hospitality Ltd [1999] 3 C.M.L.R. 334; [1999] I.C.R. 942, EAT 4–038
Coppen v Moore (No.2) [1898] 2 Q.B. 306, QBD 2–006
Corocraft Ltd v Pan American Airways Inc [1969] 1 Q.B. 616; [1968] 3 W.L.R. 1273, CA (Civ
Div) 1–065
Cossey v United Kingdom (10843/84) [1991] 2 F.L.R. 492; [1993] 2 F.C.R. 97, ECHR 5–007
Costa v Ente Nazionale per l'Energia Elettrica (ENEL) (6/64) [1964] E.C.R. 585; [1964] C.M.L.R.
425, ECJ 4–018, 4–023
Coventry & Solihull Waste Disposal Co Ltd v Russell (Valuation Officer) [1999] 1 W.L.R. 2093;
[2000] 1 All E.R. 97, HL 1–079
Criminal Proceedings against Pupino (C–105/03) [2006] Q.B. 83; [2005] 3 W.L.R. 1102,
ECJ 4–023, 4–035
Customs & Excise Commissioners v ApS Samex [1983] 1 All E.R. 1042 4–026
Da Costa en Schaake NV v Nederlandse Belastingadministratie (28/62) [1963] E.C.R. 31; [1963]
C.M.L.R. 224, ECJ 4–018
Death v Harrison (1870–71) L.R. 6 Ex. 15, Exch Ct 2–017
Defrenne v Sabena (80/70) [1971] E.C.R. 445; [1974] 1 C.M.L.R. 494, ECJ 4–014, 4–016, 4–028,
4–040, 14–001, 14–004, 14–005,
14–006, 14–012, 14–018
Delcourt v Belgium (A/11) (1979–80) 1 E.H.R.R. 355, ECHR 5–007
Derbyshire CC v Times Newspapers Ltd [1992] Q.B. 770; [1992] 3 W.L.R. 28 5–012
Derrick v Customs and Excise Commissioners [1972] 2 Q.B. 28; [1972] 2 W.L.R. 359, DC 2–006,
10–003
Dillon v Cunningham (1872–73) L.R. 8 Ex. 23, Exch Ct 2–017
Dillon v Legg (1968) 29 A.L.R. 3d 1316 15–011
DPP v Gomez (Edwin) [1993] A.C. 442; [1992] 3 W.L.R. 1067, HL 1–003, 1–010, 1–012, 1–013,
1–020, 1–027, 1–029, 1–035, 1–055, 1–068,
1–077, 1–087, 17–001, 17–006–17–018
DPP for Northern Ireland v Lynch [1975] A.C. 653; [1975] 2 W.L.R. 641, HL 16–011
Dobson v General Accident Fire and Life Assurance Corp [1990] 1 Q.B. 274; [1989] 3 W.L.R.
1066, CA (Civ Div) 17–002, 17–005, 17–006, 17–007
Dobson v Thames Water Utilities Ltd [2009] EWCA Civ 28; [2009] 3 All E.R. 319; [2009] B.L.R.
287 .... 5–010, 8–007
Doherty v Birmingham City Council [2008] UKHL 57; [2009] 1 A.C. 367; [2008] 3 W.L.R.
636 5–010
Donoghue v Stevenson [1932] A.C. 562; 1932 S.C. (H.L.) 31, HL 15–006
Dooley v Cammell Laird & Co Ltd [1951] 1 Lloyd's Rep. 271, Assizes 1–055, 15–007
Dudgeon v United Kingdom (A/45) (1982) 4 E.H.R.R. 149, ECHR 5–008, 5–009
Duke v GEC Reliance Ltd [1988] A.C. 618; [1988] 2 W.L.R. 359, HL 4–021, 4–036, 14–021
Dulieu v White & Sons [1901] 2 K.B. 669, KBD 1–014, 1–029, 1–031, 1–033, 1–035,
2–006, 2–022, 15–001–15–006, 15–009
E Hulton & Co v Jones [1910] A.C. 20, HL 1–050
EBR Attridge Law LLP (formerly Attridge Law) v Coleman [2010] 1 C.M.L.R. 28; [2010] I.C.R.
242, EAT 4–036
Ealing LBC v Race Relations Board [1972] A.C. 342; [1972] 2 W.L.R. 71, HL 1–094
Easterbrook v Barker (1870–71) L.R. 6 C.P. 1, CCP 2–016

Eddy v Niman (1981) 73 Cr. App. R. 237; [1981] Crim. L.R. 502, DC 17–005
F (Mental Patient: Sterilisation), Re. [1990] 2 A.C. 1; [1989] 2 W.L.R. 1025, HL 9–007, 9–010
Faccini Dori v Recreb Srl (C–91/92) [1995] All E.R. (E.C.) 1; [1994] E.C.R. I–3325, ECJ 4–016
Fielden v Morley Corp [1899] 1 Ch. 1, CA 1–076
Fitzpatrick v Sterling Housing Association Ltd [2001] 1 A.C. 27; [1999] 3 W.L.R. 1113, HL 1–015,
13–002, 13–003, 13–005
Fleming (t/a Bodycraft) v Customs and Excise Commissioners [2008] UKHL 2; [2008] 1 W.L.R.
195; [2008] 1 All E.R. 1061 .... 4–031, 5–010
Foakes v Beer (1883–84) L.R. 9 App. Cas. 605, HL 7–002, 7–006
Ford v Boon (1871–72) L.R. 7 C.P. 150, CCP 2–016
Fortescue v St Matthew's Vestry, Bethnal Green [1891] 2 Q.B. 170, QBD 1–021
Foster v Warblington Urban DC [1906] 1 K.B. 648, CA 8–004
Fothergill v Monarch Airlines Ltd [1978] Q.B. 108; [1977] 3 W.L.R. 885, QBD 1–088
Fowell v Tranter, 159 E.R. 610; (1864) 3 Hurl. & C. 458, KB 1–068
Galt v British Railways Board (1983) 133 N.L.J. 870 1–055
Garland v British Rail Engineering Ltd (12/81) [1982] 2 All E.R. 402; [1982] E.C.R. 359,
ECJ 4–014, 4–019, 4–026, 14–001, 14–002, 14–012–14–013
Garland v British Rail Engineering Ltd [1983] 2 A.C. 751; [1982] 2 W.L.R. 918, HL 1–018, 4–026,
4–027, 4–031, 4–039, 4–041, 14–001,
14–002, 14–008–14–013, 14–018
Garrett v Camden LBC [2001] EWCA Civ 395 15–021
Ghaidan v Godin-Mendoza [2004] UKHL 30; [2004] 2 A.C. 557; [2004] 3 W.L.R. 113 1–003,
1–015, 1–064, 1–072, 1–091, 1–093, 4–036,
4–041, 5–014, 5–015, 13–001–13–005
Golder v United Kingdom (A/18) (1979–80) 1 E.H.R.R. 524, ECHR 5–006
Goodwin v United Kingdom (28957/95) [2002] I.R.L.R. 664; [2002] 2 F.L.R. 487, ECHR 5–006,
5–007
Grieves v FT Everard & Sons Ltd [2007] UKHL 39; [2008] 1 A.C. 281; [2007] 3 W.L.R. 876 .. 1–033,
1–035, 1–055, 1–056, 15–012, 15–020, 15–021
HL v United Kingdom (45508/99) (2005) 40 E.H.R.R. 32; 17 B.H.R.C. 418, ECHR 2–023, 9–012
HP Bulmer Ltd v J Bollinger SA (No.2) [1974] Ch. 401; [1974] 3 W.L.R. 202, CA (Civ Div) 1–006,
4–011, 4–012, 4–021, 4–026
Hadjianastassiou v Greece (A/252–A) (1993) 16 E.H.R.R. 219, ECHR 5–017
Hambrook v Stokes Bros [1925] 1 K.B. 141, CA 1–014, 1–029, 1–049, 1–055, 15–005,
15–006, 15–007, 15–009
Handels- og Kontorfunktionaerernes Forbund i Danmark v Dansk Handel & Service (C–400/
95) [1997] E.C.R. I–2757; [1997] 2 C.M.L.R. 915, ECJ 4–018
Harmon CFEM Facades (UK) Ltd v Corporate Officer of the House of Commons (1999) 67 Con.
L.R. 1; (2000) 2 L.G.L.R. 372, QBD 1–055, 6–010
Harris v Nickerson (1872–73) L.R. 8 Q.B. 286, QBD 2–015, 6–002, 6–010
Harris v Watson, 170 E.R. 94; (1791) Peake 102, Assizes 2–015, 7–002
Hatton v Sutherland. *See* Barber v Somerset CC
Heydon's Case (1584) 3 Co. Rep. 7a 1–069, 2–017
Hinz v Berry [1970] 2 Q.B. 40; [1970] 2 W.L.R. 684, CA (Civ Div) 15–009
Hiro Balani v Spain (A/303–B) (1995) 19 E.H.R.R. 566, ECHR 5–017
Hoskyn v Commissioner of Police of the Metropolis [1979] A.C. 474; [1978] 2 W.L.R. 695,
HL 1–003, 1–010, 1–013, 1–025, 1–027, 1–029, 1–033, 1–035,
1–044, 1–046, 1–051, 1–055, 1–056, 1–058, 12–001–12–008
Housden v Conservators of Wimbledon and Putney Commons [2008] EWCA Civ 200; [2008] 1
W.L.R. 1172; [2008] 3 All E.R. 1038 1–043
Huddersfield Police Authority v Watson [1947] K.B. 842; [1947] 2 All E.R. 193, KBD 1–021,
2–006, 2–019
Hunter v Canary Wharf Ltd [1997] A.C. 655; [1997] 2 W.L.R. 684, HL 1–002, 1–008, 1–011,
1–022, 1–025, 1–033, 1–035, 1–037, 1–049, 1–056,
1–058, 1–063, 1–068, 8–001–8–007
Inland Revenue Commissioners v Hinchy [1960] A.C. 748; [1960] 2 W.L.R. 448, HL 1–076
Jaensch v Coffey (1984) 155 C.L.R. 549 15–011
James Buchanan & Co Ltd v Babco Forwarding & Shipping (UK) Ltd [1978] A.C. 141; [1977] 3
W.L.R. 907, HL 1–088, 4–016, 4–037
Jenkins v Kingsgate (Clothing Productions) Ltd (96/80) [1981] 1 W.L.R. 972; [1981] E.C.R. 911,
ECJ 1–022, 4–028, 4–040, 14–001

Table of Cases

Johnson v Barnes (1871–72) L.R. 7 C.P. 592, CCP 2–016
Kay v Lambeth LBC [2006] UKHL 10; [2006] 2 A.C. 465; [2006] 2 W.L.R. 570 .... 1–023, 5–017
Khorasandjian v Bush [1993] Q.B. 727; [1993] 3 W.L.R. 476, CA (Civ Div) 1–002, 1–008,
 1–011, 1–022, 1–025, 1–049, 1–063, 8–001,
 8–004, 8–005, 8–006, 8–007
King v Phillips [1953] 1 Q.B. 429; [1953] 2 W.L.R. 526, CA 1–007, 1–031, 1–033,
 1–055, 15–006—15–008, 15–021
Kruse v Johnson [1898] 2 Q.B. 91, QBD 1–021
Laroche v Spirit of Adventure (UK) Ltd [2008] EWHC 788 (QB); [2008] 4 All E.R. 494; [2008] 2
 All E.R. (Comm) 1076 1–088
Larsson v Fotex Supermarked. See Handels– og Kontorfunktionaerernes Forbund i Danmark v
 Dansk Handel & Service (C–400/95)
Lawrence v Commissioner of Police of the Metropolis [1972] A.C. 626; [1971] 3 W.L.R. 225,
 HL 1–003, 1–013, 1–027, 1–071, 17–002, 17–003, 17–004, 17–005,
 17–006, 17–007, 17–009, 17–010, 17–012, 17–013, 17–017, 17–018
Leach v R. [1912] A.C. 305; (1912) 7 Cr. App. R. 157, HL 1–003, 1–010, 1–013, 1–027, 1–029,
 1–050, 1–051, 12–002, 12–004
Litster v Forth Dry Dock & Engineering Co Ltd [1990] 1 A.C. 546; [1989] 2 W.L.R. 634, HL .. 4–021,
 4–036, 5–015, 5–019
London Street Tramways Co Ltd v London CC [1898] A.C. 375, HL 1–026
Loutchansky v Times Newspapers Ltd (No.2) [2001] EWCA Civ 1805; [2002] Q.B. 783; [2002] 2
 W.L.R. 640 5–018
Lune Metal Products Ltd (In Administration), Re [2006] EWCA Civ 1720; [2007] Bus. L.R. 589;
 [2007] B.C.C. 217 1–026
M v Home Office [1994] 1 A.C. 377; [1993] 3 W.L.R. 433, HL 4–037
Macarthys Ltd v Smith (C–129/79) [1980] E.C.R. 1275; [1980] 2 C.M.L.R. 205, ECJ 4–014, 4–017,
 4–019, 4–026, 14–001, 14–006—14–007, 14–018
Macarthys Ltd v Smith [1981] Q.B. 180; [1980] 3 W.L.R. 929, CA (Civ Div) 1–018, 4–024,
 4–026, 4–027, 4–031, 4–032, 4–033, 4–035,
 4–039, 4–040, 4–041, 14–001—14–007, 14–011
McKenna v British Aluminium Ltd [2002] Env. L.R. 30, Ch D 8–007
McKerr's Application for Judicial Review, Re [2004] UKHL 12; [2004] 1 W.L.R. 807; [2004] 2 All
 E.R. 409 5–009
McLoughlin v O'Brian [1983] 1 A.C. 410; [1982] 2 W.L.R. 982, HL 1–009, 1–057, 1–058,
 15–009, 15–010, 15–011, 15–014
Malone v Laskey [1907] 2 K.B. 141, CA 1–008, 1–011, 1–022, 1–025,
 1–056, 8–001, 8–004, 8–005, 8–006
Marleasing SA v La Comercial Internacional de Alimentacion SA (C–106/89) [1990] E.C.R. I–
 4135; [1993] B.C.C. 421, ECJ 4–021, 4–023, 4–035, 4–036, 5–014
Marshall v Southampton and South West Hampshire AHA (152/84) [1986] Q.B. 401; [1986] 2
 W.L.R. 780, ECJ 4–016, 4–018, 4–023, 4–026
Maunsell v Olins [1975] A.C. 373; [1974] 3 W.L.R. 835, HL 1–065
Meering v Grahame-White Aviation Co Ltd (1919) 122 L.T. 44 .... 9–003, 9–006, 9–009
Milch-, Fett- und Eierkontor GmbH v Hauptzollamt Saarbrucken (29/68) [1969] E.C.R. 165;
 [1969] C.M.L.R. 390, ECJ 4–038, 4–039
Ministre de l'Intérieur v Oteiza Olazabal (C–100/01) [2002] E.C.R. I–10981; [2005] 1 C.M.L.R.
 49, ECJ 4–018
Mirehouse v Rennell. See Thomas Henry Mirehouse, and William Squire Mirehouse v Frances
 Henrietta Rennell, Widow and Administratrix of Thomas Rennell, Clerk, deceased
Mitchell v Rochester Ry Co (1896) 151 N.Y. 107 15–004
Motherwell v Motherwell (1976) 73 D.L.R. (3d) 62 .... 8–004, 8–006
Mount Isa Mines Ltd v Pusey (1970) 125 C.L.R. 383 15–011
Murray v Ministry of Defence [1988] 1 W.L.R. 692; [1988] 2 All E.R. 521, HL 9–006
NMB (Deutschland) GmbH v Commission of the European Communities (C–188/88) [1992]
 E.C.R. I–1689; [1992] 3 C.M.L.R. 80, ECJ 4–019
NMB France Sarl v Commission of the European Communities (T–162/94) [1996] E.C.R. II–427;
 [1997] 3 C.M.L.R. 164, CFI 4–019
NV Algemene Transport- en Expeditie Onderneming van Gend en Loos v Nederlandse
 Administratie der Belastingen (26/62) [1963] E.C.R. 1; [1963] C.M.L.R. 105, ECJ 4–016,
 4–018, 4–023
Norris v Southampton City Council [1982] I.C.R. 177; [1982] I.R.L.R. 141, EAT 1–041

O'Brien v Sim-Chem Ltd [1980] 1 W.L.R. 734; [1980] C.M.L.R. 555, CA 1–022, 1–040, 4–040, 14–015, 14–019

Overseas Tankship (UK) Ltd v Miller Steamship Co Pty Ltd (The Wagon Mound) [1967] 1 A.C. 617; [1966] 3 W.L.R. 498, PC (Aus) 1–031, 1–035, 15–011

Page v Smith (No.2) [1996] 1 W.L.R. 855; [1996] 3 All E.R. 272, CA (Civ Div) 1–010, 1–014, 1–031, 1–033, 1–035, 1–055, 1–056, 1–058, 15–011, 15–012, 15–014, 15–016, 15–020, 15–021

Pepper (Inspector of Taxes) v Hart [1993] A.C. 593; [1992] 3 W.L.R. 1032, HL 1–084, 2–004, 2–012, 16–009, 17–008

Perrin v Northampton BC [2007] EWCA Civ 1353; [2008] 1 W.L.R. 1307; [2008] 4 All E.R. 673 1–062

Pfeiffer v Deutsches Rotes Kreuz Kreisverband Waldshut eV (C–397/01) [2004] E.C.R. I–8835; [2005] 1 C.M.L.R. 44, ECJ 4–023

Pickstone v Freemans Plc [1989] A.C. 66; [1988] 3 W.L.R. 265, HL 1–022, 1–040, 1–070, 1–085, 4–027, 4–028, 4–029, 4–033, 4–035, 4–040, 4–041, 5–015, 5–019, 14–001, 14–002, 14–013–14–021

Pinnell's Case, 77 E.R. 237; (1602) 5 Co. Rep. 117a, QB 7–002

Police Authority for Huddersfield v Watson. *See* Huddersfield Police Authority v Watson

Politi Sas v Ministero delle Finanze (43/71) [1971] E.C.R. 1039; [1973] C.M.L.R. 60, ECJ 4–018, 4–023

Popkin v Popkin, cited in 1 Hagg.Eccl.Rep. 767 16–003

Poplar Housing & Regeneration Community Association Ltd v Donoghue [2001] EWCA Civ 595; [2002] Q.B. 48; [2001] 3 W.L.R. 183 5–014

Practice Direction (Crown Ct: Allocation of Business) (No.1) [1995] 1 W.L.R. 1083; [1995] 2 All E.R. 900, CA (Crim Div) 2–007

Practice Statement (HL: Judicial Precedent) [1966] 1 W.L.R. 1234; [1966] 2 Lloyd's Rep. 151, HL 17–009

Pugh v London Brighton & South Coast Railway Co [1896] 2 Q.B. 248, CA 1–055, 15–005

R. v A (Complainant's Sexual History) [2001] UKHL 25; [2002] 1 A.C. 45; [2001] 2 W.L.R. 1546 .... 5–014, 5–015

R. v Bourne [1939] 1 K.B. 687, CCC 1–046, 1–081, 1–083, 2–019, 11–001–11–002

R. v Bournewood Community and Mental Health NHS Trust Ex p. L [1999] 1 A.C. 458; [1998] 3 W.L.R. 107 .... 1–004, 1–005, 1–010, 1–033, 1–035, 1–055, 1–056, 1–068, 1–070, 1–077, 1–081, 1–085, 1–087, 1–091, 1–093, 9–001–9–012

R. v Bow Street Metropolitan Stipendiary Magistrate Ex p. Pinochet Ugarte (No.1) [2000] 1 A.C. 61; [1998] 3 W.L.R. 1456, HL 1–001

R. v Bow Street Metropolitan Stipendiary Magistrate Ex p. Pinochet Ugarte (No.2) [2000] 1 A.C. 119; [1999] 2 W.L.R. 272, HL 1–001

R. v C (Barry) [2004] EWCA Crim 292; [2004] 1 W.L.R. 2098; [2004] 3 All E.R. 1 .... 1–055, 16–011

R. v C (Rape: Marital Exemption) [1991] 1 All E.R. 755; [1991] Crim. L.R. 60, Crown Ct 2–007, 16–006, 16–007

R. v Chapman (Frank) [1959] 1 Q.B. 100; [1958] 3 W.L.R. 401, CCA 1–081, 2–013, 16–008

R. v Clarence (Charles James) (1889) L.R. 22 Q.B.D. 23, CCR 2–014, 16–002–16–004, 16–008, 16–009

R. v Clarke (James) [1949] 2 All E.R. 448; (1949) 33 Cr. App. R. 216, Assizes 1–010, 2–019, 16–004

R. v Clarke (Joseph) [2009] EWCA Crim 1074; [2010] 1 W.L.R. 223; [2009] 4 All E.R. 298 ... 1–021

R. v Clegg (Lee William) [1995] 1 A.C. 482; [1995] 2 W.L.R. 80 16–011

R. v Colyer [1974] Crim. L.R. 243, DC 1–021, 10–003

R. v DPP Ex p. Kebeline [2000] 2 A.C. 326; [1999] 3 W.L.R. 972, HL 5–008, 5–014

R. v Fellows (Alban) [1997] 2 All E.R. 548; [1997] 1 Cr. App. R. 244, CA (Crim Div) .. 1–071, 10–004

R. v Fritschy [1985] Crim. L.R. 745, CA (Crim Div) 17–005

R. v G [2003] UKHL 50; [2004] 1 A.C. 1034; [2003] 3 W.L.R. 1060 1–072

R. v Gallasso (Lesley Caroline) (1994) 98 Cr. App. R. 284; [1993] Crim. L.R. 459, CA (Crim Div) 17–013

R. v Henn (Maurice Donald) [1981] A.C. 850; (1980) 71 Cr. App. R. 44, HL 4–028, 4–040

R. v Hinks (Karen Maria) [2001] 2 A.C. 241; [2000] 3 W.L.R. 1590, HL 1–002, 1–010, 1–022, 1–035, 1–053, 1–071, 1–077, 1–087, 1–093, 17–017–17–018

R. v HM Coroner for Greater Manchester Ex p. Tal [1985] Q.B. 67; [1984] 3 W.L.R. 643, QBD 1–021

R. v Horncastle (Michael Christopher) [2009] UKSC 14; [2010] 2 A.C. 373; [2010] 2 W.L.R. 47 .... 1–023, 2–004, 5–017, 5–019

R. v Inhabitants of All Saints, Worcester, 105 E.R. 1215; (1817) 6 M. & S. 194, KB 1–029,
1–046, 1–055, 1–056, 2–015, 12–002—12–003
R. v International Stock Exchange of the United Kingdom and the Republic of Ireland Ltd Ex p.
Else (1982) Ltd [1993] Q.B. 534; [1993] 2 W.L.R. 70 4–026
R. v Ireland (Robert Matthew) [1998] A.C. 147; [1997] 3 W.L.R. 534, HL 1–072
R. v J (Rape: Marital Exemption) [1991] 1 All E.R. 759, Crown Ct 2–007, 16–006, 16–007
R. v James (Leslie) [2006] EWCA Crim 14; [2006] Q.B. 588; [2006] 2 W.L.R. 887 1–031
R. v Kendrick (Kathleen) [1997] 2 Cr. App. R. 524; [1997] Crim. L.R. 359, CA (Crim Div) 1–055,
1–056, 17–016, 17–017
R. v Kirklees MBC Ex p. C (A Minor) [1993] 2 F.L.R. 187; [1993] 2 F.C.R. 381, CA (Civ Div) 9–007
R. v L (Graham) [2003] EWCA Crim 1512 .... 1–055, 1–085, 16–011
R. v L [2008] EWCA Crim 973; [2009] 1 W.L.R. 626; [2008] 2 Cr. App. R. 18 .... 1–012, 12–008
R. v Lambert (Steven) [2001] UKHL 37; [2002] 2 A.C. 545; [2001] 3 W.L.R. 206 ...... 5–014, 5–015
R. v Lapworth (John Henry) [1931] 1 K.B. 117; (1931) 22 Cr. App. R. 87, CCA 1–025, 1–044,
1–046, 2–013, 12–001, 12–002, 12–003,
12–005, 12–006, 12–007
R. v Lord Audley, 123 E.R. 1140; (1631) 3 St. Tr. 401 12–001
R. v McHugh (Eileen Cecilia) (1989) 88 Cr. App. R. 385, CA (Crim Div) 17–005
R. v Magro (Anthony) [2010] EWCA Crim 1575; [2010] 3 W.L.R. 1694; [2010] 2 Cr. App. R.
25 1–021
R. v Mazo (Ellen) [1997] 2 Cr. App. R. 518; [1996] Crim. L.R. 435, CA (Crim Div) 1–002, 1–010,
1–022, 1–053, 1–055, 17–015, 17–016, 17–017
R. v Miller (Peter) [1954] 2 Q.B. 282; [1954] 2 W.L.R. 138, Assizes 1–010, 2–019, 16–004
R. v Ministry of Agriculture, Fisheries and Food Ex p. Federation Europeene de la Sante
Animale (FEDESA) (C–331/88) [1990] E.C.R. I–4023; [1991] 1 C.M.L.R. 507, ECJ 4–020
R. v Montila (Steven William) [2004] UKHL 50; [2004] 1 W.L.R. 3141; [2005] 1 All E.R. 113 .. 1–076,
1–079
R. v Morris (David Alan) [1984] A.C. 320; [1983] 3 W.L.R. 697, HL 1–012, 1–020, 1–029,
17–004, 17–005, 17–006, 17–007,
17–010, 17–012, 17–013
R. v O'Brien (Edward Vincent) [1974] 3 All E.R. 663, Crown Ct 2–007, 16–004
R. v Philippou (Christakis) (1989) 5 B.C.C. 665; (1989) 89 Cr. App. R. 290, CA (Crim Div) ... 17–005
R. v Phillips [1922] S.A.S.R. 276 12–006
R. v R (Rape: Marital Exemption) [1992] 1 A.C. 599; [1991] 3 W.L.R. 767, HL .. 1–007, 1–033, 1–035,
1–044, 1–047, 1–055, 1–058, 1–071, 1–081, 1–085, 1–093,
2–005, 16–001, 16–002, 16–006—16–011
R. v Rollins (Neil) [2010] UKSC 39; [2010] 1 W.L.R. 1922; [2010] Bus. L.R. 1529 1–048
R. v Secretary of State for the Home Department and the Parole Board Ex p. Norney (1995) 7
Admin. L.R. 861; [1996] C.O.D. 81, QBD 5–012
R. v Secretary of State for Transport Ex p. Factortame Ltd (No.1) [1990] 2 A.C. 85; [1989] 2
W.L.R. 997, HL 4–024, 4–037
R. v Secretary of State for Transport Ex p. Factortame Ltd (No.2) [1991] 1 A.C. 603; [1990] 3
W.L.R. 818, HL 4–023, 4–037
R. v Secretary of State for Transport Ex p. Factortame Ltd (C–221/89) [1992] Q.B. 680; [1992] 3
W.L.R. 288, ECJ 4–018
R. v Simpson (Ian McDonald) [2003] EWCA Crim 1499; [2004] Q.B. 118; [2003] 3 W.L.R. 337,
CA (Crim Div) 1–021
R. v Skipp [1975] Crim. L.R. 114, CA (Crim Div) 17–003, 17–004, 17–005
R. v Smith (Morgan James) [2001] 1 A.C. 146; [2000] 3 W.L.R. 654, HL 1–031
R. v Spencer (Alan Widdison) [1985] Q.B. 771; [1985] 2 W.L.R. 197, CA (Crim Div) 1–021
R. v Stafford Crown Court Ex p. Shipley [1998] 1 W.L.R. 1438; [1998] 2 All E.R. 465, CA (Civ
Div) 1–021
R. v Steele (Peter Edward) (1977) 65 Cr. App. R. 22; [1977] Crim. L.R. 290, Crim Div 16–004,
16–006
R. v Warwickshire CC Ex p. Johnson [1993] A.C. 583; [1993] 2 W.L.R. 1, HL 1–084
R. v Zafar [2008] EWCA Crim 1323 1–062
R. (on the application of Anderson) v Secretary of State for the Home Department [2002]
UKHL 46; [2003] 1 A.C. 837; [2002] 3 W.L.R. 1800 5–014
R. (on the application of Ashton) v Bolton Combined Court [2001] EWHC Admin 703 1–034
R. (on the application of Black) v Secretary of State for the Home Department [2009] UKHL 1;
[2009] 1 A.C. 949; [2009] 2 W.L.R. 282 .... 5–013, 5–014

R. (on the application of Confederation of Passenger Transport UK) v Humber Bridge Board
[2003] EWCA Civ 842; [2004] Q.B. 310; [2004] 2 W.L.R. 98 1–079
R. (on the application of Countryside Alliance) v Attorney General [2007] UKHL 52; [2008] 1
A.C. 719; [2007] 3 W.L.R. 922 5–014
R. (on the application of Holding & Barnes Plc) v Secretary of State for the Environment,
Transport and the Regions [2001] UKHL 23; [2003] 2 A.C. 295; [2001] 2 W.L.R. 1389 ... 1–023
R. (on the application of IDT Card Services Ireland Ltd) v Customs and Excise Commissioners
[2006] EWCA Civ 29; [2006] S.T.C. 1252; [2006] B.T.C. 5175 .... 4–036, 5–014
R. (on the application of Kadhim) v Brent LBC Housing Benefit Review Board [2001] Q.B. 955;
[2001] 2 W.L.R. 1674, CA (Civ Div) 1–021, 1–022
R. (on the application of M) v Secretary of State for Work and Pensions [2008] UKHL 63;
[2009] 1 A.C. 311; [2008] 3 W.L.R. 1023 5–017
R. (on the application of RJM) v Secretary of State for Work and Pensions. *See* R. (on the
application of M) v Secretary of State for Work and Pensions
R. (on the application of Smith) v Oxfordshire Assistant Deputy Coroner [2010] UKSC 29;
[2010] 3 W.L.R. 223; [2010] 3 All E.R. 1067 .... 1–046, 2–004
R. (on the application of Smith) v Secretary of State for Defence. *See* R. (on the application of
Smith) v Oxfordshire Assistant Deputy Coroner
R. (on the application of Spath Holme Ltd) v Secretary of State for the Environment, Transport
and the Regions [2001] 2 A.C. 349; [2001] 2 W.L.R. 15, HL 1–084
R. (on the application of Westminster City Council) v National Asylum Support Service [2002]
UKHL 38; [2002] 1 W.L.R. 2956; [2002] 4 All E.R. 654 1–079
R. (on the application of Wright) v Secretary of State for Health [2009] UKHL 3; [2009] 1 A.C.
739; [2009] 2 W.L.R. 267 .... 1–074, 5–010
Reynolds v Times Newspapers Ltd [2001] 2 A.C. 127; [1999] 3 W.L.R. 1010, HL 5–018
Rheinmühlen-Düsseldorf v Einfuhr- und Vorratsstelle für Getreide und Futtermittel (166/73)
[1974] E.C.R. 33; [1974] 1 C.M.L.R. 523, ECJ 4–038
Rickards v Rickards [1990] Fam. 194; [1989] 3 W.L.R. 748, CA (Civ Div) 1–021
Riddle v R. (1911) 12 C.L.R. 622 12–006
River Wear Commissioners v Adamson (1876–77) L.R. 2 App. Cas. 743, HL 1–068
Robertson v Forth Road Bridge Joint Board (No.2) 1995 S.C. 364; 1996 S.L.T. 263, IH (1 Div) 15–014
Ross v Counters [1980] Ch. 297; [1979] 3 W.L.R. 605, Ch D 6–009
Royal College of Nursing of the United Kingdom v Department of Health and Social Security
[1981] A.C. 800; [1981] 2 W.L.R. 279, HL 1–046, 1–060, 1–072, 1–077,
1–081, 1–093, 11–001—11–017
Royal Crown Derby Porcelain Co v Russell [1949] 2 K.B. 417; [1949] 1 All E.R. 749, CA 1–080
Rutili v Ministre de l'Intérieur (36/75) [1975] E.C.R. 1219; [1976] 1 C.M.L.R. 140, ECJ 4–018
S v HM Advocate, 1989 S.L.T. 469; 1989 S.C.C.R. 248 .... 1–033, 16–005, 16–007, 16–008
S (Children) (Care Order: Implementation of Care Plan), Re [2002] UKHL 10; [2002] 2 A.C. 291;
[2002] 2 W.L.R. 720 .... 5–013, 5–014, 5–015
S-C (Mental Patient: Habeas Corpus), Re [1996] Q.B. 599; [1996] 2 W.L.R. 146, CA (Civ
Div) 9–007
SW v United Kingdom (A/355–B) [1996] 1 F.L.R. 434; (1996) 21 E.H.R.R. 363, ECHR 16–001,
16–010
Salomon v Customs and Excise Commissioners [1967] 2 Q.B. 116; [1966] 3 W.L.R. 1223, CA 1–088
Scottish Provident Institution v Inland Revenue Commissioners [2004] UKHL 52; [2004] 1
W.L.R. 3172; [2005] 1 All E.R. 325 1–048
Secretary of State for the Home Department v MB [2007] UKHL 46; [2008] 1 A.C. 440; [2007]
3 W.L.R. 681 5–014
Selectmove Ltd, Re [1995] 1 W.L.R. 474; [1995] 2 All E.R. 531, CA (Civ Div) ... 1–055, 7–001, 7–006
Selmouni v France (25803/94) (2000) 29 E.H.R.R. 403; 7 B.H.R.C. 1, ECHR 5–006
Sheffield (Kristina) v United Kingdom (22985/93) [1998] 2 F.L.R. 928; [1998] 3 F.C.R. 141,
ECHR 5–007
Simpson v Smith (1870–71) L.R. 6 C.P. 87, CCP 2–016
Smith v Johnson & Co, Unreported, 1896, QBD 1–055, 15–005
Smith v Secretary of State for Work and Pensions. *See* Smith v Smith
Smith v Smith [2006] UKHL 35; [2006] 1 W.L.R. 2024; [2006] 3 All E.R. 907 .... 1–062, 1–094
Snoxell v Vauxhall Motors Ltd [1978] Q.B. 11; [1977] 3 W.L.R. 189, EAT 14–004
Soering v United Kingdom (A/161) (1989) 11 E.H.R.R. 439, ECHR 5–006
South Caribbean Trading Ltd v Trafigura Beheer BV [2004] EWHC 2676 (Comm); [2005] 1
Lloyd's Rep. 128 .... 1–055, 7–006

Spade v Lynn and Boston Rail Road (1897) 60 Am.St.Rep. 393 15–004
Spencer v Harding (1869–70) L.R. 5 C.P. 561, CCP 2–016, 6–002, 6–010
Stilk v Myrick, 170 E.R. 1168; (1809) 2 Camp. 317, Assizes 1–025, 1–044, 2–015, 7–001,
7–002, 7–003, 7–005
Sunday Times v United Kingdom (A/30) (1979–80) 2 E.H.R.R. 245; (1979) 76 L.S.G. 328,
ECHR 5–009, 16–010
Sutherland v United Kingdom (25186/94) (1996) 22 E.H.R.R. CD182; (1997) 24 E.H.R.R. CD22,
Eur Comm HR 5–008
Thoburn v Sunderland City Council [2002] EWHC 195 (Admin); [2003] Q.B. 151; [2002] 3
W.L.R. 247, DC 1–084, 4–024
Thomas Henry Mirehouse, and William Squire Mirehouse v Frances Henrietta Rennell, Widow
and Administratrix of Thomas Rennell, Clerk, deceased, 6 E.R. 1015; (1833) 1 Cl. & F. 527,
HL 1–001
Three Rivers DC v Bank of England (No.2) [1996] 2 All E.R. 363, QBD 1–084
Tyrer v United Kingdom (A/26) (1979–80) 2 E.H.R.R. 1, ECHR 5–006
Unilin Beheer BV v Berry Floor NV [2007] EWCA Civ 364; [2007] Bus. L.R. 1140; [2008] 1 All
E.R. 156 1–001
Vacher & Sons Ltd v London Society of Compositors [1913] A.C. 107, HL 1–076
Van Duyn v Home Office (41/74) [1975] Ch. 358; [1975] 2 W.L.R. 760, ECJ 4–018, 4–023
Victorian Railway Commissioners v Coultas (1888) L.R. 13 App. Cas. 222, PC (Aus) 1–031,
1–035, 15–004
Vodafone 2 v Revenue and Customs Commissioners [2009] EWCA Civ 446; [2010] Ch. 77;
[2010] 2 W.L.R. 288 .... 4–036, 4–041, 5–014
Von Colson v Land Nordrhein-Westfahlen (C–14/83) [1984] E.C.R. 1891; [1986] 2 C.M.L.R. 430,
ECJ 4–023
Wagon Mound, The. *See* Overseas Tankship (UK) Ltd v Miller Steamship Co Pty Ltd
Walker v Northumberland CC [1995] 1 All E.R. 737; [1995] I.C.R. 702, QBD 15–021
Walter Rau Lebensmittelwerke v De Smedt Pvba (261/81) [1982] E.C.R. 3961; [1983] 2 C.M.L.R.
496, ECJ 4–020
Walton, Ex p. (1881) L.R. 17 Ch. D. 746; (1881) 50 L.J. Ch. 657, CA 1–068
Ward v James (No.2) [1966] 1 Q.B. 273; [1965] 2 W.L.R. 455, CA 2–005
Warwickshire CC Ex p. Johnson. *See* R. v Warwickshire CC Ex p. Johnson
Webb v EMO Air Cargo (UK) Ltd (Reference to ECJ) [1993] 1 W.L.R. 49; [1992] 4 All E.R. 929,
HL 4–026, 4–036, 4–037, 14–021
White v Chief Constable of South Yorkshire [1999] 2 A.C. 455; [1998] 3 W.L.R. 1509, HL 1–010,
1–012, 1–014, 1–029, 1–033, 1–035, 1–051,
1–055, 1–057, 1–058, 9–007, 15–012–15–021
Wigg v British Railways Board, *The Times*, February 4, 1986, QBD 1–055
Wilkinson v Downton [1897] 2 Q.B. 57, QBD 1–055, 15–001, 15–005
Williams v Roffey Bros & Nicholls (Contractors) Ltd [1991] 1 Q.B. 1; [1990] 2 W.L.R. 1153, CA (Civ
Div) 1–025, 1–029, 1–044, 1–046, 1–055, 7–001–7–006
Wilson v First County Trust Ltd (No.2) [2003] UKHL 40; [2004] 1 A.C. 816; [2003] 3 W.L.R.
568 1–084
Woking Urban DC (Basingstoke Canal) Act 1911, Re [1914] 1 Ch. 300, CA 1–076
Woodhouse AC Israel Cocoa SA v Nigerian Produce Marketing Co Ltd [1972] A.C. 741; [1972] 2
W.L.R. 1090, HL 1–029
Worringham v Lloyds Bank Ltd (69/80) [1981] 1 W.L.R. 950; [1981] 2 All E.R. 434, ECJ 4–014,
4–040
Young v Bristol Aeroplane Co Ltd [1944] K.B. 718; (1945) 78 Ll. L. Rep. 6, CA 1–021,
14–019, 17–017
Younghusband v Luftig [1949] 2 K.B. 354; [1949] 2 All E.R. 72, DC 1–021, 2–006

TABLE OF STATUTES

1833 Judicial Committee Act (3 & 4
       Will.4 c.41) 2–022
1834 Central Criminal Court Act (4 & 5
       Will.4 c.36) 2–019
1837 Wills Act (7 Will.4 & 1 Vict. c.26)
       s.15 6–009
1846 County Courts Act (9 & 10 Vict.) .. 2–008
       Fatal Accidents Act (9 & 10 Vict.
       c.93) 15–005
1848 Administration of Criminal Law
       (Amendment) Act (11 & 12
       Vict.) 2–014
       Crown Cases Act (11 & 12 Vict.
       c.78) 2–014
1861 Offences Against the Person Act
       (24 & 25 Vict. c.100) 11–004
       s.20 16–003
       s.47 16–003
       s.58 .... 1–081, 1–083, 11–001,
                           11–002, 11–004
1869 Bankruptcy Act (32 & 33 Vict. c.71)
       s.23 1–068
1873 Supreme Court of Judicature Act
       (36 & 37 Vict. c.66) 2–005,
                           2–006, 2–015, 2–016,
                           2–017, 2–018
1876 Customs Consolidation Act (39 &
       40 Vict. c.36)
       s.42 4–028
       Appellate Jurisdiction Act (39 &
       40 Vict. c.59) 2–005
1898 Criminal Evidence Act (61 & 62
       Vict. c.36)
       s.4(1) 12–004
       (2) 12–004
1907 Criminal Appeal Act (7 Edw.7
       c.23) 2–013
1909 Cinematograph Act (9 Edw.7 c.30)
       s.1(3) 1–080
1911 Official Secrets Act (1 & 2 Geo.5
       c.28) 2–007
1916 Larceny Act (6 & 7 Geo.5 c.50)
       s.1(1) 17–002
1929 Infant Life (Preservation) Act (19 &
       20 Geo.5 c.34) 1–081, 11–002
1956 Sexual Offences Act (4 & 5 Eliz.2
       c.69)
       s.1 16–005
       s.19 .... 1–071, 1–081, 16–008
1959 Obscene Publications Act (7 & 8
       Eliz.2 c.66)
       s.1(2) 1–073, 1–090, 10–001,
                           10–003, 10–004
       (3) 1–013, 10–003, 10–004

       (b) 10–003
       s.2 .... 1–013, 10–001
       Mental Health Act (7 & 8 Eliz.2
       c.72)
       s.5(1) 1–081, 1–091, 9–007, 9–010
1963 London Government Act (c.33) ... 2–019
1965 Carriage of Goods by Road Act
       (c.37)
       s.1 4–036
1966 Criminal Appeal Act (c.31) 2–005
1967 Criminal Law Act (Northern Ire-
       land) (c.18)
       s.3(1) 16–011
       Sexual Offences Act (c.60) 5–008
       Abortion Act (c.87) 1–060,
                           11–001–11–11–017
       s.1 .... 11–005, 11–006
       (1) 1–071, 1–077, 1–081, 1–093,
                           11–001, 11–003, 11–004,
                           11–005, 11–007, 11–008,
                           11–009, 11–010, 11–011,
                           11–012, 11–013, 11–014,
                           11–015, 11–016, 11–017
       (3) 11–001, 11–005, 11–011
       (4) 11–001
       s.3 11–011
       (1) 11–005
       s.4 11–011
1968 Theft Act (c.60) 1–068
       s.1 17–008
       (1) 1–035, 1–071, 1–077, 1–087,
                   1–091, 17–001, 17–002, 17–004,
                           17–007, 17–008, 17–009,
                                               17–012
       ss.1–6 1–077
       s.2 17–008
       s.3 17–008
       (1) 17–001, 17–004, 17–008
       s.4 17–008
       s.6 17–008
1970 Administration of Justice Act
       (c.31) 2–006
       Equal Pay Act (c.41) 14–002, 14–008
       s.1 .... 1–061, 4–015, 14–003
       (1) 14–002
       (2) 4–035, 14–002, 14–004,
                           14–006, 14–007
       (a) 14–004, 14–005, 14–014,
                           14–016, 14–017
       (b) 14–014, 14–017
       (c) 1–070, 1–085, 4–028,
                           4–035, 4–040, 14–014,
                           14–015, 14–016, 14–017,
                           14–020, 14–021

(4) 4–035, 14–002, 14–004,
14–007
1971 Courts Act (c.23) 2–007, 2–019
1972 European Communities Act
(c.68) 1–084, 1–088, 3–001,
4–014, 14–007, 14–019
s.2 ..... 4–021, 4–022, 4–024, 4–025,
4–032, 4–034, 4–038, 5–013,
14–004, 14–005, 14–015
(1) 4–024, 4–025, 4–035
(4) 4–024, 4–025, 4–032,
4–035, 5–013, 5–014, 5–015
s.3 ..... 4–021, 4–022, 4–024, 4–025,
4–028, 4–032, 4–034,
4–038, 5–013, 14–004
(1) 4–025, 4–026, 4–028,
4–032, 4–034, 4–038
(2) 4–025
(3) 4–025
Criminal Justice Act (c.71)
s.36 10–001
1975 Sex Discrimination Act (c.65) 4–036,
14–002, 14–004, 14–008
s.6(2) 14–008, 14–009, 14–010,
14–013
(4) 4–039, 14–008, 14–009,
14–010, 14–013
(6) 14–004
1976 Sexual Offences (Amendment)
Act (c.82) 16–006, 16–007,
16–008, 16–009
s.1(1) 1–081, 1–093, 16–005
(a) 16–006
s.7(6) 16–005
1977 Rent Act (c.42) .... 13–001—13–005
s.70 .... 13–001, 13–004
Sch.1 1–072
para.2 .... 1–064, 5–015, 13–001,
13–002, 13–003, 13–004
(1) 13–001, 13–002
(2) 13–002, 13–004
para.3 13–001
(1) 13–001, 13–002
1981 Senior Courts Act (c.54)
s.31(2) 4–037
Supreme Court Act. *See* Senior
Courts Act
1983 Mental Health Act (c.20) .. 9–001—9–010
s.3 9–001
s.131 .... 1–085, 1–087, 1–091,
1–093, 9–001, 9–004, 9–007,
9–010
(1) 1–077, 1–081, 9–004,
9–007, 9–010
(2) 1–077, 9–007, 9–010
1984 Mental Health (Scotland) Act
(c.36) 9–007
Police and Criminal Evidence Act
(c.60)
Pt VI 1–059
s.29 9–003

s.80 12–008
1987 Consumer Protection Act (c.43) .. 4–040
1988 Merchant Shipping Act (c.12)
Pt II 4–024, 4–037
1994 Criminal Justice and Public Order
Act (c.33) 16–009
Sch.9 para.3 10–004
1997 Protection from Harassment Act
(c.40) 1–063, 8–004
1998 Employment Rights (Dispute
Resolution) Act (c.8)
s.1 .... 1–016, 2–010
Human Rights Act (c.42) 1–015,
1–065, 1–068, 1–088, 2–004,
3–001, 5–001—5–019
s.1(1) 5–010
(2) 5–010
(3) 5–010
s.2 .... 5–016, 5–017, 5–018
(1) ... 1–023, 5–005, 5–010, 5–012,
5–017
(a) 5–010
(b) 5–010
(c) 5–010
(d) 5–010
s.3 ...... 1–064, 5–010, 5–014, 13–001,
13–002, 13–003, 13–004
(1) 1–063, 1–074, 4–036, 4–041,
5–010, 5–011, 5–013, 5–014,
5–015, 5–016, 5–017, 5–018,
5–019, 13–002, 13–005
(2) 1–074, 5–010, 5–018
(a) 5–013
(b) 5–013
(c) 5–013
s.4 .... 1–063, 1–074, 5–010,
5–012, 5–014
(2) 5–016
(5) 5–010
(6) 5–010
s.6 .... 5–010, 5–018, 8–007
(1) 5–010, 5–012, 5–016,
5–017, 5–018
(2) 5–010
(3) 5–010
(a) 5–012, 5–016, 5–018
s.7 .... 5–010, 5–017, 5–018
(1) 5–010, 5–016
(a) 5–016
(b) 5–018
(7) 5–010
s.8 .... 5–010, 8–007
(3) 5–010
s.10 .... 1–074, 5–014, 5–017
(1)(a) 5–010
(2) 5–010
s.12 5–011
s.13 5–011
(1) 5–011
s.14 5–010
s.15 5–010

s.22(3) 5–010
1999 Access to Justice Act (c.22)
s.59 2–005
2000 Sexual Offences (Amendment)
Act (c.44) 5–008
2003 Sexual Offences Act (c.42)
s.1(1) 16–001
Criminal Justice Act (c.44)
s.114 12–008
2004 Civil Partnership Act (c.33) 13–005
2005 Constitutional Reform Act (c.4)
Pt 3 2–004
s.42(1) 2–004
s.59(1) 2–005

Income Tax (Trading and Other
Income) Act (c.5) 1–080
Mental Capacity Act (c.9)
s.4A 9–012
s.4B 9–012
s.5 9–012
Sch.A1 9–012
2006 Government of Wales Act (c.32)
Pt 3 1–059
2007 Tribunals, Courts and Enforcement Act (c.15) 1–016, 2–020
Pt 1 2–010
s.13(6) 2–010
2010 Equality Act (c.15) 14–002

TABLE OF STATUTORY INSTRUMENTS

1955 Cinematograph (Safety) Regula-
      tions (SI 1955/1129) 1–080
1968 Abortion Regulations (SI 1968/
      390) 11–007
1981 Transfer of Undertakings (Protec-
      tion of Employment) Regula-
      tions (SI 1981/1794) 4–036
1982 Homosexual Offences (Northern
      Ireland) Order (SI 1982/
      1536) 5-008

1983 Equal Pay (Amendments) Reg-
      ulations (SI 1983/1794) 1–085,
                               14–002, 14–014
1991 Public Works Contracts Regula-
      tions (SI 1991/2680) 6–010
2003 Equal Pay Act 1970 (Amendment)
      Regulations (SI 2003/1656) .. 14–002
2004 Equal Pay Act 1970 (Amend-
      ment) Regulations (SI 2004/
      2352) 14–002

TABLE OF TREATIES

1948 Universal Declaration of Human Rights
     art.12 1–037
1950 European Convention on Human Rights .... 1–003, 1–015, 1–063, 1–074, 1–088, 1–094, 2–023, 3–001, 4–010, 4–020, 4–036, 4–041, 5–001—5–019, 8–007
     art.1 .... 2–004, 5–010
     art.2 2–004
     art.3 .... 5–004, 5–006
     art.4 5–004
     art.5 9–012
       (1)(e) 9–012
         (f) 1–046
     art.6 ... 1–023, 5–004, 5–006, 5–007
       (1) 5–017
     art.7 .... 16–001, 16–010
       (1) 16–010
     art.8 .... 1–064, 5–004, 5–006, 5–008, 8–007, 13–003, 13–004
       (1) 5–015
       (2) 5–004
     art.9 5–004
     art.10 ... 5–008, 5–010, 5–012, 5–018
     art.11 .... 5–008, 5–010
     art.13 5–010
     art.14 .. 1–064, 5–008, 5–010, 5–015, 13–002, 13–003, 13–004
     art.15 5–004
     art.16 5–010
     arts 16–18 5–010
     art.17 5–010
     art.18 5–010
     art.26 5–010
     art.27(2) 5–010
     art.31 5–010

     art.32 5–003
     art.34 .... 5–002, 5–010
     art.35 5–002
     art.46 5–010
     Protocol 4 art.1 5–010
     Protocol 11 ..... 5–001, 5–003, 5–005
1951 Treaty Establishing the European Coal and Steel Community .. 4–009, 4–010

1956 Convention on the Contract for the International Carriage of Goods by Road 4–037
1957 EC Treaty. *See* Treaty on the Functioning of the European Union
1965 Merger Treaty 4–009, 4–010
1969 Vienna Convention on the Law of Treaties 5–006
1986 Single European Act 4–010
1989 Convention on the Rights of the Child (United Nations) 8–007
     art.16 1–037
1992 Treaty on European Union 1–001, 4–009, 4–010
     art.19 4–011
1997 Treaty of Amsterdam 4–001, 4–010
2000 Charter of Fundamental Rights .. 4–010, 5–019
2001 Treaty of Nice 4–010
2008 Treaty on the Functioning of the European Union 1–088, 4–001
     art.3 .... 4–010, 4–023
     art.34 4–028
     art.157 ... 1–040, 1–061, 4–011, 4–014, 4–017, 4–028, 4–029, 4–035, 4–039, 4–040, 14–001, 14–002, 14–004, 14–005, 14–006, 14–007, 14–008, 14–010, 14–011, 14–012, 14–013, 14–014, 14–015, 14–016, 14–018—14–020
       (1) 4–028, 14–002
       (2) 4–028, 14–002
     art.234 4–039
     arts 263—264 4–011
     art.267 ... 1–016, 4–011, 4–017, 4–018, 4–023, 4–024, 4–025, 4–026, 4–027, 4–028, 4–033, 4–036, 4–038, 4–039, 4–040, 5–011, 14–002, 14–004, 14–005, 14–011, 14–018, 14–019
     art.288 .... 4–012, 4–016, 4–023
2009 Treaty of Lisbon (Reform Treaty) .. 2–003, 4–001, 4–009, 4–010

GLOSSARY OF ABBREVIATIONS

Actavis	*Actavis UK Ltd v Merck & Co Inc* [2008] EWCA Civ 444
Adam Opel GmbH	*Adam Opel GmbH, Renault S.A. v Mitras Automotive (UK) Limited* [2007] EWHC 3481 (QB)
Alcock	*Alcock v Chief Constable of South of Yorkshire* [1992] A.C. 310, HL
All Saints, Worcester	*R. v Inhabitants of All Saints, Worcester* (1817) 6 M. & S. 194
Anangel	*Anangel Atlas Cornpania Naviera S.A. v Ishikwajirna-Harima Heavy Industries Co Ltd* [1990] 2 Lloyds Rep. 526
Bell	*Bell v Great Northern Railway Company of Ireland* (1890) 26 L.R.Ir. 428
Blackpool	*Blackpool and Fylde Aero Club Ltd v Blackpool Borough Council* [1990] 3 All E.R. 25, CA
Boardman	*Boardman v Sanderson* [1964] 1 W.L.R. 1317, CA
Bourhill	*Bourhill v Young* [1943] A.C. 92, HL
Bourne	*R. v Bourne* [1939] 1 K.B. 687
Bournewood	*R. v Bournewood Community and Mental Health N.H.S. Trust, ex parte L.* [1999] 1 A.C. 458, HL
BREL	British Rail Engineering Ltd
Bulmer	*H.P. Bulmer Ltd v J. Bollinger S.A.* [1974] Ch. 401, CA
C. (A Minor)	*C. (A Minor) v Director of Public Prosecutions* [1996] 1 A.C. 1, HL
CEA 1898	Criminal Evidence Act 1898
CFI	European Court of First Instance in Luxembourg (as the General Court was formerly known)
CJ	Court of Justice in Luxembourg (formerly known as the European Court of Justice)
CJ interpretative techniques	Techniques which focus on giving effect to the underlying aims of legislative provisions, rather than seeking to give a meaning to the particular words used, and, in doing so, adopting schematic and/or teleological approaches to interpretation, using general principles, having recourse to a body of case law (*jurisprudence constante*), and engaging in "gap filling".
Chadwick	*Chadwick v British Railways Board* [1967] 1 W.L.R. 912
Clarence	*R. v Clarence* (1888) 22 Q.B.D. 23, CCR
Clarke	*R. v Clarke* [1949] 2 All E.R. 448

Clegg	*R. v Clegg* [1995] 1 A.C. 482, HL
Convention	European Convention on Human Rights and Fundamental Freedoms (including Protocols to the Convention)
Costa	*Costa v ENEL* (C-6/64) [1964] E.C.R. 585, ECJ
Coultas	*Victorian Railway Commissioners v Coultas* (1888) 13 App. Cas. 222, PC
CPA 1987	Consumer Protection Act 1987
CRA 2005	Constitutional Reform Act 2005
Defrenne	*Defrenne v Sabena* (80/70) [1971] E.C.R. 445, ECJ
Derbyshire	*Derbyshire County Council v Times Newspapers Ltd* [1992] 3 All E.R. 65, CA; [1993] 1 All E.R. 1011, HL
Derrick	*Derrick v Customs and Excise Commissioners* [1972] 2 Q.B. 28
DHSS	Department of Health and Social Security
Dobson	*Dobson v General Accident Fire and Life Assurance Corporation Plc* [1990] 1 Q.B. 274, CA
Duke	*Duke v GEC Reliance Ltd* [1988] A.C. 618, HL
Dulieu	*Dulieu v White and Sons* [1901] 2 K.B. 669
EAT	Employment Appeal Tribunal
EC	European Community
ECA 1972	European Communities Act 1972
ECJ	European Court of Justice in Luxembourg (as the Court of Justice was formerly known)
EC Treaty	European Community Treaty, i.e. the Treaty of Paris of 1951 and the Treaties of Rome of 1957, as amended
EU	European Union
EPA 1970	Equal Pay Act 1970
equal pay directive	Directive 75/117 on "The approximation of the laws of the Member States relating to the application of the principle of equal pay for men and women"
Fitzpatrick	*Fitzpatrick v Sterling Housing Association* [2001] 1 A.C. 27, HL
Foster	*Foster v Warblington Urban District Council* [1906] 1 K.B. 648
Fritschy	*R. v Fritschy* [1985] Crim. L.R. 745, CA
Gallasso	*R. v Gallasso* (1992) 98 Cr. App. R. 284, CA
Garland	*Garland v British Rail Engineering Ltd* [1978] 2 All E.R. 789, EAT; [1979] 2 All E.R. 1163, CA; [1982] 2 All E.R. 402, HL; Case 12/81 [1982] E.C.R. 359, ECJ; [1982] 2 All E.R. 413, HL

GC	General Court in Luxembourg (formerly known as the European Court of First Instance)
Ghaidan	*Ghaidan v Godin-Mendoza* [2004] 3 All E.R. 411, HL
Gomez	*Director of Public Prosecutions v Gomez* [1993] A.C. 442, HL
Grieves	*Grieves v F T Everard & Sons Ltd* [2008] 1 A.C. 281
Hambrook	*Hambrook v Stokes Brothers* [1925] 1 K.B. 141, CA
Harmon	*Harmon CFEM Facades (UK) Ltd v The Corporate Officer of the House of Commons* (1999) 67 Con.L.R.1
Harris	*Harris v Nickerson* (1873) L.R. 8 Q.B. 286
Hatton	*Hatton v Sutherland* [2002] 2 All E.R. 1, CA
Henn	*Henn and Darby v Director of Public Prosecutions* [1981] A.C. 850, HL
Hinks	*R. v Hinks* [2001] 2 A.C. 241, HL
Holley	*Att Gen for Jersey v Holley* [2005] 2 A.C. 580, PC
Horncastle	*R. v Horncastle and others* [2009] UKSC 14
Hoskyn	*Hoskyn v Metropolitan Police Commissioner* [1978] 2 All E.R. 136, HL
Huddersfield	*Police Authority for Huddersfield v Watson* [1947] K.B. 842
HRA 1998	Human Rights Act 1998
Hunter	*Hunter v Canary Wharf Ltd* [1997] A.C. 655, HL
IDT Card Services	*Revenue and Customs Commissioners v IDT Card Services Ireland Ltd* [2006] EWCA Civ 29, CA
ITCs	International treaties and conventions
James Buchanan	*James Buchanan & Co Ltd v Babco Forwarding and Shipping (UK) Ltd* [1977] Q.B. 208, CA
Jenkins	*Jenkins v Kingsgate (Clothing Productions) Ltd* (C-96/80) [1981] 1 E.C.R. 911, ECJ
Kay	*Lambeth LBC v Kay* [2006] UKHL 10
Kadhm	*R. (on the application of Kadhm) v Brent London Borough Council Housing Benefit Review Board* [2001] Q.B. 955, CA
Kendrick and Hopkins	*R. v Kendrick and Hopkins* [1997] 2 Cr. App. R. 524, CA
Khorasandjian	*Khorasandjian v Bush* [1993] 3 All E.R. 669, CA
King	*King v Phillips* [1953] 1 Q.B. 429, CA
Kirklees	*R. v Kirklees Metropolitan Borough Council, Ex p. C.* [1993] 2 F.L.R. 187, CA
Lambert	*R. v Lambert* [2001] 3 W.L.R. 206, HL
Lapworth	*R. v Lapworth* [1931] 1 K.B. 117, CA
Lawrence	*Lawrence v Metropolitan Police Commissioner* [1972] A.C. 626, HL

Leach	*Leach v R.* [1912] A.C. 305, HL
Litster	*Litster v Forth Dry Dock and Engineering Co Ltd* [1990] 1 A.C. 546, HL
Macarthys	*Macarthys Ltd v Smith* [1978] 2 All E.R. 746, EAT; [1979] 3 All E.R. 325, CA; Case 129/79 [1980] E.C.R. 1275, ECJ; [1981] 1 All E.R. 111, CA
McKenna	*McKenna v British Aluminium Limited* [2002] Env. L.R. 30
McLoughlin	*McLoughlin v O'Brien* [1983] A.C. 410, HL
Magro	*R. v Magro and others* [2010] EWCA Crim 1575
Malone	*Malone v Laskey* [1907] 2 K.B. 141, CA
Marleasing	*Marleasing SA v La Commercial de Alimentation SA* (C-106/89) [1990] E.C.R. 1-4135, ECJ
Marshall	*Marshall v Southampton and South-West Hampshire Area Health Authority* (C-152/84) [1986] 1 E.C.R. 723, ECJ
Mazo	*R. v Mazo* (1997) 2 Cr. App. R. 518, CA
Meering	*Meering v Grahame-White Aviation Co Ltd* (1919) 122 LT 44, CA
Milchkontor	*Milchkontor v Hauptzollamt Saarbrucken* (C-29/68) [1969] E.C.R. 165, ECJ
Miller	*R. v Miller* [1954] 2 Q.B. 282
Morris	*R. v Morris* [1984] A.C. 320, HL
Motherwell	*Motherwell v Motherwell* (1976) 73 D.L.R. (3d) 62
OAPA 1861	Offences Against the Person Act 1861
O'Brien	*O'Brien v Sim-Chem Ltd* [1980] 2 All E.R. 307, CA
OPA 1959	Obscene Publications Act 1959
Pepper	*Pepper v Hart* [1993] 1 All E.R. 42, HL
Pickstone	*Pickstone v Freemans Plc* [1986] I.R.L.R. 335, EAT; [1987] 3 All E.R. 756, CA; [1988] 2 All E.R. 803, HL
Politi	*Politi v Italian Ministry of Finance* (C-43/71) [1971] E.C.R. 1039, ECJ
Pugh	*Pugh v London, Brighton and South Coast Rly Co* [1896] 2 Q.B. 248
Pupino	*Maria Pupino* [2005] E.C.R. I-5285
RCN	Royal College of Nursing
R. v A.	*R. v A.(No. 2)* [2001] 2 W.L.R. 1546, HL
Re F.	*Re F. (Mental Patient: Sterilisation)* [1990] 2 AC. 1, HL
Re S.	*Re S. (minors)(care order: implementation of care plan)* [2002] 2 W.L.R. 720, HL

Re S.-C.	*Re S.-C. (Mental Patient: Habeas Corpus)* [1996] Q.B. 599, CA
Reynolds	*Reynolds v Times Newspapers Ltd* [1999] 3 W.L.R. 1010, HL
RMP	Registered medical practitioner
Royal College	*Royal College of Nursing of the United Kingdom v Department of Health & Social Security* [1981] AC. 800, CA, HL
SDA 1975	Sex Discrimination Act 1975
Selectmove	Re Selectmove Ltd [1995] 1 W.L.R. 474, CA
Simmenthal	*Amministrazione delle Finanze Della Stato v Simmenthal* (C-106/77) [1978] E.C.R. 629, ECJ
Skipp	*R. v Skipp* [1975] Crim. L.R. 114, CA
Smith	*Smith v Johnson & Co* (1896), unreported
SOAA 1976	Sexual Offences (Amendment) Act 1976
Spencer	*Spencer v Harding* (1870) L.R. 5 C.P. 561
Steele	*R. v Steele* (1976) 65 Cr.App.R. 22, CA
Stilk	*Stilk v Myrick* (1809) 2 Camp. 317
Strasbourg Court	European Court of Human Rights in Strasbourg
TCEA 2007	Tribunals, Courts and Enforcement Act 2007
TFEU	Treaty on the Functioning of the European Union
Thoburn	*Thoburn v Sunderland City Council* [2003] Q.B. 151
Trust	Bournewood Community and Mental Health NHS Trust
UK	United Kingdom
Van Duyn	*Van Duyn v Home Office* (C-41/74) [1974] E.C.R. 1337, ECJ
Van Gend en Loos	*Van Gend en Loos v Nederlandse Administratie der Belastingen* (C-26/62) [1963] E.C.R. 1, ECJ
Vodafone 2	*Vodafone 2 v The Commissioners for Her Majesty's Revenue & Customs* [2009] EWCA Civ 446
Webb	*Webb v EMO Air Cargo (UK) Ltd* [1992] 4 All E.R. 929, HL
White	*White and others v Chief Constable of South Yorkshire* [1998] 3 W.L.R. 1507, HL
Wilkinson	*Wilkinson v Downton* [1897] 2 Q.B. 57
Williams	*Williams v Roffey Bros & Nicholls (Contractors) Ltd* [1990] 1 All E.R. 512, CA
Worringham	*Worringham v Lloyds Bank Ltd* (C-69/80) [1981] E.C.R. 796, ECJ
Young	*Young v Bristol Aeroplane Co Ltd* [1944] K.B. 718, CA
Younghusband	*Younghusband v Luftig* [1949] 2 K.B. 354

ACKNOWLEDGMENTS

We are most grateful to all those copyright holders who gave permission for extracts from various materials to be included in this book and wish to record and express our thanks to the following publishers:

Cambridge University Press for permission to reproduce extracts from *The Law-Making Process* by Michael Zander (6th edn., 2004)

Informa Law for permission to reproduce extracts from *Lloyd's Law Reports*

LexisNexis for permission to reproduce extracts from *Construction Law Reports*

Oxford University Press for permission to reproduce extracts from *The European Union and its Court of Justice* by Anthony Arnull (p.637, 2nd edn., 2006) and *Medical Law* by Ian Kennedy and Andrew Grubb (pp. 1478 and 1479, 3rd edn., 2005)

Penguin Books Ltd for permission to reproduce extracts from *Medicine, Patients and the Law* by Margaret Brazier (1992)

Wolters Kluwer Law & Business (Aspen Publishers: www.aspenpublishers.com) for permission to reproduce an extract from "Owning Up to Fallibility: Precedent and the Court of Justice" by Anthony Arnull in *Common Market Law Review* (p.248, Vol. 30, 1993).

While every care has been taken to establish and acknowledge copyright, and contact the copyright owners, the publishers tender their apologies for any accidental infringement. They would be pleased to come to a suitable arrangement with the rightful owners in each case.

CONTENT, FORMAT AND USE OF THE BOOK

One of the problems associated with the teaching of law to undergraduates is that pressures, which are often not academic, lead to the teaching of the subject in compartments. Not only is this unreal in the sense that legal problems often involve a multiplicity of issues and do not usually present themselves in a "compartmentalised" form, but this also has ramifications for the teaching of subjects which are variously described as legal method/introduction to law. Such subjects, by virtue of the fact that they do not comprise a self-contained substantive body of law, are often perceived by students as peripheral to mainstream ("compartmentalised") legal subjects. As a consequence, in our view, legal method/introduction to law as a subject tends not to be given the prominence it deserves, especially in view of the fact that many of the subject areas that may be covered, in particular, statutory interpretation and the doctrine of precedent, are essential to a proper understanding of substantive law.

In this book, our prime objective has been to seek to overcome this problem by endeavouring to impress upon, in particular, first year undergraduates, the importance of the core elements of statutory interpretation and precedent. Our approach aims to encourage students to see these core elements as an integral and vibrant part of the law itself, as part of the subject area(s) of substantive law which they are studying, rather than as abstract, artificial topics. Accordingly, case studies, drawn principally (though not exclusively) from some areas of law commonly encountered by students in their first year studies, are used to forge a link between the mechanics of precedent and statutory interpretation and substantive law. There are two types of case studies used, the choice of which has inevitably been subjective.

In the first type (see Chapters 6–14), the focus is primarily on individual cases, examined for the most part in isolation, with particular aspects of precedent and statutory interpretation being considered and examined in the context of those cases. Reference is made in the Introduction section at the start of each of the case studies to the particular aspects illustrated in a paragraph which is initially set out in bold type and begins with the words "**This case study illustrates . . .**". Clearly no single case study covers more than a limited number of such aspects but each study is a self-contained examination of an area of substantive law and can be read as such, although it is not necessarily exhaustive, since its primary purpose, in the context of the book, is as part of the composite picture demonstrating the major features of precedent and statutory interpretation.

The first type of case studies, with their focus primarily on individual cases, necessarily presents only a "snapshot" of development of the law on the topic in question but in the second type (see Chapters 15–17) the emphasis is on providing an understanding of how legal rules and principles might develop cumulatively over a period of time through a series of judicial decisions and/or legislation. Three areas have been selected. The first is *"Nervous shock or psychiatric injury"*, where the development of legal rules and principles has been entirely through case law, with the law developing through a series of cases to move from one particular position to another. The second is *"Marital rape"*, where the development has been initially through case law, then subsequently through legislation and its inter-pretation by the courts. Here again the law has developed, in this instance through a series of cases and through statutory provisions, to move from one particular position to another. The third is *"Appropriation in theft"*, where the development has been entirely statutory, with the courts interpreting the relevant provisions in the Theft Act 1968. In this instance the law has not so much moved from one particular position to another but rather the development of the law has been characterised by a "yo-yo" or "pendulum" effect. Essentially, the law has oscillated between two opposing positions and, at different periods of time, different view-points have prevailed. In the end, however, as will be seen, the "yo-yo" or "pen-dulum" seems to have returned to its starting point, with the law ultimately appearing to have come a full circle. Again, reference is made in the Introduction section at the start of each of these case studies in Part 3 to the particular aspects of precedent and statutory interpretation illustrated in a paragraph commencing in bold type and beginning with the words **"This case study illustrates . . .".**

It is intended that the aspects of precedent and statutory interpretation illustrated in all of the case studies will be enhanced by Chapter 1, which provides an outline and guide to these major features. This chapter is central to the book in that it provides a means by which the student can explore these features in some depth through the case studies. This is achieved by the inclusion in this "map" chapter of extensive cross-referencing to the case studies through **Illustrative references**. So, for instance, if a student wished to consider the extent to which the Court of Appeal is bound to follow its previous decisions the position is explained at section 1–021 in Chapter 1 and examples of how these rules operate are provided in the **Illustrative references** at 1–022, which direct the student to the relevant sections in Chapters 8 (8–001), 14 (14–019) and 17 (17–017).

The treatment of precedent and statutory interpretation would be incomplete without consideration of the growing influence of the European Union legal order and the European Convention on Human Rights and Fundamental Freedoms. The importance of the latter has increased considerably following the enactment of the Human Rights Act 1998, which seeks to give "further effect" (i.e. greater protection) to Convention rights in the UK. These matters are addressed in Chapters 3–5, which examine generally this "European dimension". Some aspects of these areas are considered in detail in the case studies in Chapters 13 and 14, which respec-tively contain a case study on Succession Rights under the Rent Act 1977 and a case study on Equal Pay.

In previous editions, a separate chapter, Chapter 2, was devoted to *"Statutory Interpretation and Pepper v Hart"*, focusing on the extent to which use might be made by the courts of parliamentary material contained in *Hansard* (the reports of proceedings in either House of Parliament) as an external aid to the construction of statutes following the House of Lords' decision in *Pepper v Hart* [1993] 1 All E.R. 42 (*Pepper*). Since that decision, at least some members of the judiciary have voiced criticism of *Pepper* and the reception of ministerial statements in Parliament as an aid to construction. Lord Steyn, writing extra-judicially in *"Pepper v Hart*; A Re-examination" (2001) 21 O.J.L.S. 59, was particularly critical, indicating that courts might place reliance on the Explanatory Notes that have accompanied primary legislation since 1998 (which they have done—see below, 1–079), and, as a result, "it is likely that the disinclination of judges to delve into *Hansard* will increase". Whilst *Pepper* has not ceased to be important, we have come to the view that it no longer merits an individual chapter in its own right and the principles laid down in *Pepper* are now covered in Chapter 1 (at 1–084), along with other extrinsic material to which courts may have regard when interpreting legislation.

This has provided the opportunity in this edition to introduce a new Chapter 2, *"Courts and Tribunals"*, which enables, in particular, account to be taken of the establishment of the Supreme Court and recent reforms to the tribunal system. In previous editions, reference has always been made to courts and tribunals in Chapter 1 in the context of binding and persuasive precedents, and this section (see 1–015—1–041) continues largely unchanged. In previous editions, however, no additional information on the composition of courts and tribunals was provided. Provision of further information in this new chapter in relation to courts and tribunals, particularly as to their structure and composition, will, it is hoped, assist in obtaining a better understanding of the doctrine of precedent when it is encountered in subsequent chapters.

Chapter 2 therefore seeks to provide information on the composition of particular courts and the number of judges ordinarily, or exceptionally, sitting in particular courts, since this may well affect precedential strength (see below, 1—045—1—046). It also includes reference both to courts within the current court hierarchy and courts previously within the hierarchy but no longer in existence, e.g. the Appellate Committee of the House of Lords which in 2009 was replaced by the Supreme Court as the final domestic court of appeal. The decisions of courts that have ceased to exist will be encountered within the case studies and they continue to form precedents, so knowledge of the position of these courts in the hierarchy will assist in understanding the status that their decisions may have as precedents. Where a decision of such a court is encountered in a case study, there is a cross-reference to the relevant section in Chapter 2 to that particular court.

It will be apparent from what has been said above that the approach adopted in the book is a novel one and that there may be no directly comparable work. It is envisaged that the work itself may be used in various ways. Students might, when initially using it, familiarise themselves with the substance of the topics of precedent and statutory interpretation by reading the outline provided in Chapter 1. In the course of doing so, or after doing so, they might seek to obtain a more detailed understanding of particular aspects of these topics. This can be done by looking to the relevant section(s) and chapter(s) specified in the ***Illustrative reference(s)*** in respect of the aspects in question. It may be apparent from consulting the section(s) specified how the case study in question illustrates the particular aspects, although in some instances, in order to obtain a full understanding, it may be necessary to read a more substantial part of the case study or even the whole case study itself. Alternatively, since each of the case studies is self-contained, each can be read *in toto*, independently of the other chapters in the book, including Chapter 1, for (as indicated above) mention is made in the Introduction section of each case study of the main aspects of precedent and statutory interpretation illustrated in that case study.

Hopefully, when using the book in any or all of the ways, students will develop an appreciation of the integration of principles of precedent and statutory interpretation within the context of substantive law. If so, this should lead to an enhanced understanding of substantive law itself as well as providing a sound basis from which to engage in constructive criticism of that law.

Finally, where cases are reported in more than one set of law reports we have not given preference to any particular series. Nor in relation to cases reported since 2001 have we invariably adopted the form of neutral citation introduced in that year to facilitate reference to cases reported electronically whereby a unique number is allocated to cases from the particular court, e.g. for [2006] EWCA Civ 29, where the court is the (England and Wales) Court of Appeal (Civil Division) and the unique number is 29. Paragraphs in the judgments of cases reported in this way are numbered sequentially and reference is made to the paragraphs in square brackets (e.g. [2006] EWCA Civ 29 at [54]). Details of this practice can be found in the Practice Direction (Supreme Court Judgments: Format and Citation) at [2001] 1 W.L.R. 194. Paragraph numbering has now become an established feature of court judgments, and it is common for referencing in law reports to be to the paragraph number(s) as an alternative to the page number(s) of the report. However, either of these methods of citation, i.e. reference to either paragraph or page numbers, seems to be accepted. It will be apparent that no one method has been employed in this book, although where the neutral citation for a case is used references are to paragraph numbers. In the case of pre-2001 cases references are to the page numbers of the report.

PART 1

PRINCIPLES

1 PRECEDENT AND STATUTORY INTERPRETATION: AN OUTLINE AND GUIDE

CASE LAW AND PRECEDENT

▶ ## 1. Introduction

▷ ### (a) The formulation of legal rules

Traditionally, there are said to be two main sources of English law, common law **1-001** and statute. However, since entry by the United Kingdom (UK) into the European Community on January 1, 1973, and the signing of the Treaty of European Union at Maastricht in 1992, the Treaties and legislation of the European Union (EU) together with judicial decisions of the Court of Justice (CJ), previously the European Court of Justice (ECJ), provide an additional important source of law.

The significant impact of membership of the EU on the English legal system is mentioned in outline below (see 1–006 and 1–059—1–063) and considered in detail in Chapter 4. As to the two traditional sources, common law consists of legal rules established entirely by judicial decisions, i.e. rules originating in the statements of judges made when deciding cases heard before them, whilst statute law comprises legal rules contained in legislation passed by Parliament. However, since it is the function of judges to interpret legislation, there will also be legal rules established by judges when interpreting statutes in cases heard before them. It is customary to use the term "case law" to cover legal rules established by judicial decisions either at common law or when interpreting statutes.

Since legal rules are established by judges when deciding cases, it is important to become familiar with how these rules are formulated. The rules will be contained in the judgment(s) delivered by the court. The court's judgment and the decision in the case will be important to the parties and be binding upon them, a principle known as res judicata (see, for example, *Unilin Baheer v Berry Floor* [2007] EWCA Civ 364). Exceptionally, there may be instances where a judgment is not binding, e.g. the decision of the House of Lords in *R. v Bow Street Metropolitan Stipendiary Magistrate Ex p. Pinochet Ugarte* [1998] 4 All E.R. 897 that General Pinochet, the former Head of State of Chile, was not immune from extradition proceedings. This was because Amnesty International had been joined as a party to the proceedings and links with that organisation on the part of one member of the House, Lord Hoffmann, created a real danger of the perception of bias. In consequence, the court was regarded as improperly constituted and there was a rehearing of the case, in *R. v Bow Street Metropolitan Stipendiary Magistrate Ex p. Pinochet Ugarte (No. 2)* [1999] 1 All E.R. 577, before a differently constituted court.

From a lawyer's viewpoint, however, it is not the court's judgment and the decision in the case that is important. What is important is what is known as the ratio decidendi (usually shortened to ratio) of the case. Although there is no agreed definition of the ratio, Zander (*The Law-Making Process* (6th ed., 2004), p.269) has described it as "a proposition of law which decides the case, in the light or in the context of the material facts". As well as parts of the judgment(s) which comprise the ratio of the case, there may be parts which have legal significance which are not essential for the decision and which are known as obiter dicta (usually shortened to obiter).

A legal rule established by the ratio of a case forms a precedent for application in future cases. The precedent may be binding or persuasive, depending on the relative positions in the hierarchy of the court which established the legal rule and the court which is now considering its application. To form a binding precedent, it will be necessary for the legal rule to have been established by a court at a higher level in the court hierarchy, although in some instances a precedent is binding where the legal rule is established by a court at the same level in the court hierarchy. Otherwise, a legal rule established by the ratio of a case will form only a persuasive precedent.

Any statements which are obiter will strictly form only a persuasive precedent, irrespective of the court deciding the case and its position in the court hierarchy. However, in practice, if, for example, a higher court deliberately sets out guidelines with regard to the manner in which a particular matter should be approached, it is highly unlikely that a lower court in a subsequent case will not follow such guidelines, even if technically obiter, if they are considered relevant to the matter before it. Indeed, generally speaking, courts are reluctant to depart from previous precedents, whether binding or persuasive, since adherence to them promotes consistency and a degree of certainty. As Parke J., in one of the earliest statements of the rationale underpinning the doctrine of precedent, stated in *Mirehouse v Rennell* (1833) 1 Cl. & F. 527 at 546:

"Our common law system consists in the applying to new combinations of circumstances those rules of law which we derive from legal principles and judicial precedents; and for the sake of attaining uniformity, consistency and certainty, we must apply those rules, where they are not plainly unreasonable and inconvenient, to all cases which arise; and we are not at liberty to reject them, and to abandon all analogy to them, in those to which they have not yet been judicially applied, because we think that the rules are not as convenient and reasonable as we ourselves could have devised."

Where a (binding or persuasive) precedent is considered relevant to the case in hand and is applied by a subsequent court, the court is said to follow the precedent established in the earlier case. Conversely, if a precedent is not applied, the court is said not to follow the precedent established in the earlier case. A subsequent court, however, may go further and disapprove or overrule the precedent. If a precedent is disapproved, the legal rule established in the earlier case may retain its status as a precedent (although it may be unlikely it will be followed in future cases), but where a precedent is overruled, any legal rule established in the earlier case ceases to have effect. (Overruling of a precedent in an earlier case should not be confused with reversing a decision in a case, which is where a higher court *in the same case* comes, on appeal, to a different decision to that reached by a lower court.) It may not always be easy to ascertain whether a precedent has been disapproved or overruled.

1–002

Illustrative references

See: Chapter 8: *"The right to sue in the tort of private nuisance"* (8–004 and 8–006), where in *Hunter v Canary Wharf Ltd* (*Hunter*) the House of Lords expressed differing opinions about the Court of Appeal decision in *Khorasandjian v Bush* (*Khorasandjian*), with Lords Goff and Lloyd stating that it should be overruled; Lord Hope, remarking that it was "open to criticism", appearing to disapprove it; Lord Hoffmann stating that he was not prepared to accept that it was wrongly decided (and hence should be overruled), because it was a case concerned with intentional harassment not nuisance; and Lord Cooke, in his dissenting judgment (see below), supporting the decision.

Chapter 17: *"Appropriation in theft"* (17–017), where it is unclear whether the Court of Appeal's decision in *R. v Mazo* (*Mazo*) was simply disapproved by a later Court of Appeal in *R. v Hinks* (*Hinks*) or whether *Mazo* should be regarded as overruled by that case.

On the other hand, a precedent may not be considered relevant to the case in hand, in which case the precedent is said to be distinguishable. It may not be considered relevant either because there is one or more material facts in the previous case (considered necessary for the operation of the legal rule) which are absent in the present case or because there is one or more material facts in the present case which are absent in the previous case.

Where a precedent, whether potentially binding or persuasive, is considered not to be relevant, it is said to be distinguishable and, where this view is taken, the precedent will not have application. Where a court distinguishes a precedent, rather than not following, disapproving or overruling it, the correctness of the precedent is not called into question and the precedent remains good law. It is simply that the requirements for the operation of the legal rule established by the precedent are not considered to be met in the case under consideration.

There may well be a number of previous precedents considered by a court. The court might decide that some of these have application and they may be followed (or, alternatively, not be followed, be disapproved or be overruled), whilst it might be felt that others are not relevant and they may be distinguished. Since the court may consider a number of precedents and may subject at least some of them to detailed analysis, it follows that a judgment in a case may well be of considerable length. Further, there may be a number of judgments delivered, with a detailed analysis undertaken by more than one judge. Whilst judges may take the same view of the ratio of previous cases and reach the same decision as to the outcome of the case in question, it cannot necessarily be assumed that judges will agree on the law to be applied and/or the outcome of the case. Since judges may not agree, there may be what are described as one or more dissenting judgments delivered in the case.

1–003

Illustrative references

See: Chapter 12: *"Wives as prosecution witnesses"* (12–001 and 12–002), where in *Hoskyn v Metropolitan Police Commissioner (Hoskyn)* four out of five members of the House of Lords delivered judgments, in which reference was made in all to 19 cases, three of which were subject to detailed analysis; (12–004), where not all members of the House took the same view of the ratio of one of these three cases, *Leach v R. (Leach)*; and (12–003–12–005), where one member of the House delivered a dissenting judgment.

Chapter 13: *"Succession Rights Under The Rent Act 1977"* (13–004), where in *Ghaidan v Godin-Mendoza (Ghaidan)* four out of five members of the House of Lords were willing to read words into para.2 of Sch.1 to the Rent Act 1977 in order to ensure its compatibility with rights under the European Convention on Human Rights and Fundamental Freedoms (Convention) but Lord Millett, dissenting, was not prepared to do so.

Chapter 17: *"Appropriation in theft"* (17–007), where in *Director of Public Prosecutions v Gomez (Gomez)*, three out of five members of the House of Lords delivered judgments, one of which was a dissenting judgment; and (17–009), where the member of the House delivering the dissenting judgment took a different view from other members of the ratio of *Lawrence v Metropolitan Police Commissioner (Lawrence)*.

There may, conversely, be cases, perhaps arising only occasionally, where a court is required to formulate a legal rule where there are no previous precedents on which reliance can be placed. Such cases may be described as novel cases or cases of first impression. One way in which such cases may be determined is by having regard to any general principle(s) which may be felt to be applicable. This could include having regard to analogous areas of law when considering the legal rule that should be adopted, although having regard to analogous areas need not necessarily be confined to cases where there are no previous precedents on which reliance can be placed.

Illustrative reference

See: Chapter 9: *"False imprisonment, "detention" and the Mental Health Act 1983"* (9–003), where in *R. v Bournewood Community and Mental Health NHS Trust Ex p. L.* [1999] 1 A.C. 458 (*Bournewood*) Owen J. in the High Court, when considering whether there had been "detention" of a mental patient kept in hospital, drew an analogy with the position of a suspect attending a police station to "help with police inquiries".

1–004

Alternatively, although there may be no previous precedent(s), this does not necessarily mean that the matter in question may not have been considered, for views may have been expressed as to what would be the appropriate legal rule by learned authors in textbooks or articles and, perhaps, by judges extra-judicially. Where this is the case, a court may or may not have regard to such views, if drawn to its attention, when reaching its decision.

Illustrative reference

See: Chapter 11: *"The regulation of abortion"* (11–002), where in *R. v Bourne* (*Bourne*) at the Central Criminal Court (see below, 2–019) Macnaughten J. in his summing up to the jury stated that, for the crime of abortion to be committed, the act terminating pregnancy had to be done not in good faith for the purpose of preserving the mother's life, although there was no previous supporting precedent on which reliance could be placed; and where views in textbooks had been expressed on this matter, although no reference was made to these by the court.

1–005

▷ *(b) The impact of membership of the European Union*

The above outline provides some indication of how legal rules have traditionally been formulated by English judges, but membership of the EU has had some impact on this approach as English judges have considered and given effect to cases decided by the CJ. Such cases are decided by the CJ in a way that is quite different from the approach described above. The decision in a case in the CJ, although binding on the parties to the case (res judicata), does not contain a ratio decidendi and thus does not establish a specific legal rule for application in future cases in the same way as does a decision of an English court. Nevertheless, in the interests of legal certainty, the CJ, in practice, generally does follow its own previous decisions and in doing so may develop a consistent body of case law (*jurisprudence constante*), which can provide a guide for judges in future cases as to relevant general principles of law to be applied. Despite this, however, because decisions only bind parties to the case and do not contain a ratio decidendi, courts

1–006

in future cases are free to depart from a single previous decision or from a body of previous case law. Thus decisions do not constitute binding precedents nor do they need to be distinguished in the same way as in the English legal system.

Accordingly, the form of judgments delivered by the CJ differ from those in English cases (see above, 1–002) in that only one judgment will be delivered, with no dissent, and judgments are much more succinct. Previous case decisions may well not be referred to at all or, if they are, will not be subject to any detailed analysis. Although in more recent years previous cases have tended to be dealt with more fully by the CJ, analysis of them nevertheless remains cursory compared with judgments in English cases. The focus, to a much greater extent, continues to be on aims, objectives and general principles.

With the Treaties and legislation of the EU constituting a source of English law together with decisions of the CJ, English judges have been exposed to, and been influenced by, this different approach. Perhaps inevitably, some judges have embraced what Lord Denning, M.R. in *H.P. Bulmer Ltd v J. Bollinger S.A.* [1974] Ch. 401 at 425 described as "the European way" with greater enthusiasm than others. Nevertheless, the traditional English approach continues to flourish and ratio decidendi and obiter dicta remain fundamental concepts in English law, as do the notions of binding and persuasive precedents. These fundamental concepts are considered in further detail in the following sections.

▶ 2. Ratio Decidendi and Obiter Dicta

1–007   Although the most important part of a case is the ratio, there is no agreed way of discovering the ratio and no simple mechanical procedure for doing so. When a case (case A) is decided by a court, whether comprising a single judge or several judges, the judge or judges will examine relevant previous cases (if any) and their rationes with a view to determining the outcome of case A. Where there is a single judge, obviously only one judgment will be delivered but, where there are several judges, there may be either a single judgment or a number of judgments delivered. A single judgment is likely where all judges are in agreement, but in other cases, notably where there is disagreement as to the rationes of previous decisions, separate judgments may be delivered.

Whether there is a single judgment or separate judgments, it will not be possible at the time when case A is decided to give a definitive answer as to what is the ratio of that case, not least because judges themselves do not identify the ratio of a case when deciding it. A tentative view, however, can be stated, as it will be by the law reporter in the headnote to the case in the law reports, although what is recorded in the headnote may differ and depends on which particular law report is read (see, e.g. *C. (A Minor) v DPP* [1996] A.C. 1, referred to below at 16–011, in respect of whether the decision in *R. v R.* [1992] 1 A.C. 599 was distinguished in that case).

Moreover, the reliability of headnotes might be questioned, for they may, on occasions, not accurately record what is stated in the case (see, e.g. *King v Phillips* [1953] 1 Q.B. 429, which is considered in Chapter 15 (at 15–007), *"Nervous shock or psychiatric injury"*, where the headnote (at 429) does not accurately reflect what was stated by Denning L.J. in the case at 439–440).

Although the headnote will state a tentative view of the ratio of case A, it will only be when case A has been considered in subsequent cases (cases B, C, D, etc.) that a more definitive view of its ratio may be stated. It will be subsequent cases which seek to clarify the ratio of case A (although, as will be seen from some of the case studies, not always successfully!). In cases B, C, D, etc. counsel may be arguing for and against different understandings of the ratio of case A and these arguments may or may not be accepted by the courts in those cases. Ultimately, each judge in each of those cases will need to determine what, in his view, is the ratio of case A. Although only one judgment may have been delivered in case A, and obviously the ratio must be contained within that judgment, there may well be a divergence of views in respect of the ratio of case A on the part of judges in cases B, C, D, etc.

If there was more than one judgment in case A, ascertaining the ratio may well be more complicated. In particular, this is likely to be the case if there was a lack of unanimity in approach on the part of judges in case A. In this instance, the ratio of case A can be said to be whatever proposition of law is considered (by the judges in cases B, C, D, etc.) to have been adopted by a majority of the judges in case A to decide that case, in the light or in the context of the facts of case A determined to be material by the judges in cases B, C, D, etc. This, of course, assumes that judges in cases B, C, D, etc. all agree as to what constitutes the ratio of case A!

So far it has been assumed that there has been only one proposition of law which decided the case, in the light or in the context of that proposition's related material facts. Where this is so, the case will have only a single ratio. It is conceivable, however, that, in some instances, that ratio might conflict with the ratio in some other case, in which case a subsequent court may have to choose between the two competing rationes.

Illustrative reference

1–008

See: Chapter 8: *"The right to sue in the tort of private nuisance"* (8–004), where in *Hunter* the House of Lords had to choose between two competing Court of Appeal decisions, *Malone v Laskey* (*Malone*) and *Khorasandjian*, in respect of whether an interest in land was necessary to sue in the tort of private nuisance.

However, in any given case, there could be more than one proposition of law, each with its related material facts, on which that decision was based. In this instance, the case will have more than one ratio. Conversely, there may be "cases where there is simply no *ratio*" (*Actavis UK Ltd v Merck & Co Inc* [2008] EWCA Civ 444

(*Actavis*) at [79], per Jacob L.J.). Although there will be a ratio in respect of each judgment delivered, there may be so little common ground between each of the judgments that there cannot be said to be any single combination of a proposition of law and related material facts on which there is majority agreement.

1–009

Illustrative references

See: Chapter 6: *"Contractual obligations arising out of an invitation to tender"* (6–005), where in *Blackpool and Fylde Aero Club Ltd v Blackpool Borough Council* (*Blackpool*) there may be a number of possible ratio*nes* of the Court of Appeal's decision.

Chapter 15: *"Nervous shock or psychiatric injury"* (15–009), where in *McLoughlin v O'Brian* (*McLoughlin*) there may be two possible ratio*nes* of the case and (15–010), where in the later case of *Alcock v Chief Constable of South Yorkshire* (*Alcock*) the uncertainty surrounding the ratio of *McLoughlin* was not decisively resolved.

As stated, there may be different views on the part of judges in cases B, C, D, etc. as to the ratio of case A. This may be due to judges in cases B, C, D, etc. taking different views as to which facts in case A were material facts. If only relatively few facts were considered to have been material, the ratio of case A, which may be described as a broad one, may have application to a wide variety of fact situations. If, however, a significant number of facts was considered to have been material, the ratio of case A, which may be described as a narrow one, may have application only in a limited range of fact situations, i.e. only in cases where all those material facts are present.

1–010

Illustrative references

See: Chapter 9: *"False imprisonment, "detention" and the Mental Health Act 1983"* (9–010), where in *Bournewood* a broader view of the ratio of *B v Forsey* was taken by the Court of Appeal than by Lord Goff in the House of Lords.

Chapter 12: *"Wives as prosecution witnesses"* (12–004), where in *Hoskyn* a broader view of the ratio of *Leach* was taken by Lord Salmon than by Viscount Dilhorne and Lords Wilberforce and Keith.

Chapter 15: *"Nervous shock or psychiatric injury"* (15–011), where in *Page v Smith* (*Page*) a broader view of the ratio of *Bourhill v Young* (*Bourhill*) and subsequent cases was taken by Lord Lloyd, delivering the majority judgment, than Lords Keith and Jauncey, dissenting; and (15–018), where in *White v Chief Constable of South Yorkshire Police* (*White*) Lords Hoffmann and Steyn took a broader view of the ratio of *Chadwick v British Railways Board* than Lords Goff and Griffiths.

Chapter 16: *"Marital rape"* (16–004), where in *R. v Miller* a broader view of the ratio of *R. v Clarke* was taken by counsel for the prosecution than by counsel for the defendant and the court, in the event, took an intermediate view.

Chapter 17: *"Appropriation in theft"* (17–017), where in *Hinks* a broader view of the ratio of *Gomez* was taken than in *Mazo*.

Which facts are considered to be material is thus a crucial factor in determining the scope and development of legal rules. There is not, however, any recognised method (nor is it easy to envisage there being one) for determining which facts are material. There is, therefore, a large measure of judicial discretion with regard to determining which facts are material and what constitutes the ratio(nes) of previous cases. This means that, in turn, there is a large measure of judicial discretion in determining the application of legal rules and consequently the outcome of particular cases.

Accordingly, there is ample scope for judges to take into account policy considerations (e.g. social, political and economic implications of the decision beyond the boundaries of the case itself) and to determine what is the best policy for the law to adopt. Indeed, courts are not necessarily precluded from taking into account such considerations even where there are binding precedents which cannot realistically be distinguished by finding differences in material facts between them and the case in question. Instances do occur where binding precedents, which are not distinguished (or perhaps distinguishable), are not followed by courts.

Illustrative reference

1–011

See: Chapter 8: *"The right to sue in the tort of private nuisance"* (8–004), where in *Hunter* the House of Lords acknowledged that the Court of Appeal in *Khorasandjian* had been bound by its previous decision in *Malone*, although *Malone* had not been followed by the majority in *Khorasandjian* "in the light of changed social conditions".

Any parts of the judgment(s) in the case which do not form part of the ratio will be obiter. These parts do not establish legal rules and are not capable of becoming binding precedents but may be persuasive, particularly if made in judgments in the Supreme Court or House of Lords or Court of Appeal (see below, 1–028). In some cases, there may be little doubt that statements do not form part of the ratio of a case and are only obiter. Judges themselves may make this clear in the course of delivering their judgments in the case in question, either by expressly declaring a statement to be obiter or, more frequently, by indicating that a statement is unnecessary for the decision in the case. Alternatively, judges in later cases may indicate that statements in earlier cases were obiter. It may be, however, that no mention is made by judges in the case in question or by judges in later cases of this issue, although it may be readily apparent that a statement can only be obiter, since it was clearly not essential to the decision in the case in question.

1–012

Illustrative references

See: Chapter 6: *"Contractual obligations arising out of an invitation to tender"* (6–009), where in *Blackpool* the Court of Appeal stated tentatively that the claim in that case could succeed in the tort of negligence, although indicating that it was unnecessary to decide the matter since it had already been decided that the claim could succeed in contract.

Chapter 12: *"Wives as prosecution witnesses"* (12–008), where in *R. v L* in the Court of Appeal Lord Phillips C.J., having decided that there was no requirement that the defendant's wife should have been advised by the police that she could not be compelled to give evidence against her husband, went onto observe, obiter, that *"it does not follow that there may not be circumstances in which the police will be well advised to make it plain to a wife that she need not make a statement that implicates her husband"*.

Chapter 15: *"Nervous shock or psychiatric injury"* (15–018), where in *White* in the House of Lords statements by Lord Oliver in an earlier House of Lords' case, *Alcock*, were expressly declared by Lord Hoffmann to be obiter and were similarly regarded by Lord Steyn, who described them as *"general observations"*.

Chapter 17: *"Appropriation in theft"* (17–010), where in *Gomez* the House of Lords indicated that statements by Lord Roskill in an earlier House of Lords' case, *R. v Morris* (*Morris*), were obiter.

On the other hand, there may be uncertainty as to whether statements form part of the ratio or are obiter. Uncertainty may be apparent from an examination of the case and/or because of judicial disagreement on this matter when the case is considered by a later court.

1–013

Illustrative references

See: Chapter 6: *"Contractual obligations arising out of an invitation to tender"* (6–004–6–005), where it is uncertain whether Stocker L.J.'s statements in *Blackpool* that contractual obligations arose from the circumstances surrounding the sending out of an invitation to tender and from the express words of the tender were ratio or obiter.

Chapter 10: *"Video cassettes as obscene articles"* (10–003), where it is uncertain whether the Court of Appeal's statement in *Att-Gen's Reference (No.5 of 1980)*, that a video cassette was an *"other record of a picture or* pictures" under s.2 of the Obscene Publications Act 1959 which was capable of being published because it could be "projected" under s.1(3) of the Act, was ratio or obiter.

Chapter 12: *"Wives as prosecution witnesses"* (12–004), where differing views were expressed in *Hoskyn* as to whether the statements in *Leach* that a wife was not a compellable witness against her husband on a charge of personal violence by him on her were ratio or obiter, with Lord Salmon considering these statements to have been part of the ratio but other members of the House considering them to have been obiter.

Chapter 17: *"Appropriation in theft"* (17–017), where differing views were expressed by Lords Keith and Lowry in *Gomez* as to whether the statements of the House of Lords in *Lawrence* on the meaning of appropriation were ratio or obiter.

Even if statements are only obiter and not binding, judges in subsequent cases may be influenced by such statements and may adopt them as part of the legal reasoning of their judgments. When doing so, the obiter statements will then become part of the ratio of the judgment. In the case of a single judgment or a judgment which represents the reasoning of the majority, this will then become part of the ratio of the case.

Illustrative reference

See: Chapter 15: *"Nervous shock or psychiatric injury"* (15–005), where in *Hambrook v Stokes Brothers* (*Hambrook*) in the Court of Appeal Sargant L.J., dissenting, adopted as the ratio of his judgment a statement made obiter by Kennedy J. in *Dulieu v White & Sons* (*Dulieu*); and (15–014), where in *White* in the House of Lords, Lords Steyn and Griffiths adopted as the ratio of their judgments a statement made obiter by Lord Lloyd in *Page*.

1–014

▶ 3. Binding and Persuasive Precedents

▷ *(a) Introduction*

Except in the case of the CJ, the decisions and rulings of which may form binding **1–015** precedents, it is only the ratio of a case which is capable of being binding. Whether the ratio is binding will depend upon the position in the court hierarchy of the court that decided the case and the court that is now considering the case.

Courts will be bound by the ratio of cases determined by courts at a higher level in the court hierarchy and, in some instances, by cases determined by the same court, e.g. the Court of Appeal. This is sometimes known as the doctrine of stare decisis, which means standing by what has been decided, i.e. being bound by previous decisions. Conversely, the ratio of cases determined by courts at a lower level in the court hierarchy will not bind higher courts nor, in general, bind courts at the same level in the court hierarchy. Further, statements which are obiter can never form a binding precedent, although they might be very persuasive and in practice may well be followed.

However, since the coming into force of the Human Rights Act 1998 on October 2, 2000, the above needs to be read subject to the qualification that, if a statute was interpreted before this date, this interpretation will not be binding on a court after the Act came into force if this results in violation of a right under the European Convention on Human Rights.

Accordingly, a precedent on the interpretation of the legislation that is inconsistent with the Convention which might otherwise be binding will cease to be so and a court which seeks a consistent interpretation will not be bound by the previous inconsistent interpretation. This will be so irrespective of how authoritative that previous interpretation might otherwise have been. Perhaps an instance of where this has occurred is in *Ghaidan* where the Court of Appeal apparently disregarded a previous, otherwise binding, House of Lords' decision in *Fitzpatrick v Sterling Housing Association* [2001] 1 A.C. 27 (see below, 13–002).

▷ *(b) Court hierarchy and appellate structure*

1–016 Set out below is an outline of the hierarchy of the principal civil and criminal courts, which also indicates the courts to which appeals may be made. It is this court hierarchy which determines whether or not precedents may be binding. A more detailed, composite diagram, covering both civil and criminal courts, is set out in Chapter 2, at 2–002, to which reference should also be made. The outline below is included here in this section for ease of reference when considering binding and persuasive precedents.

Courts Exercising Civil Jurisdiction

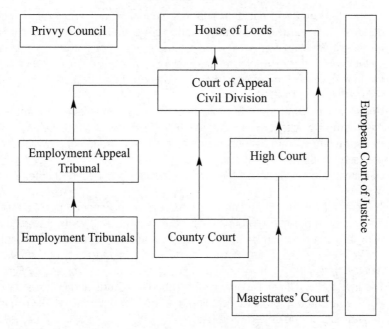

Courts Exercising Criminal Jurisdiction

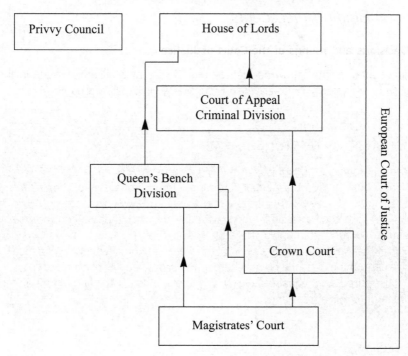

Notes

1.   These diagrams set out the principal courts in a hierarchical structure designed to illustrate their relative standing with regard to the application of precedent and illustrate the principal routes of appeal through the court system, which, for convenience, are indicated by arrows. For an exposition of the inter-relationship between these various courts and tribunals, see below, 1–017–1–031 and 1–038–1–041.

2.   Under Article 267 of the TFEU (ex 234 of the EC Treaty)—for an explanation of this method of citation, see Chapter 4, 4–001)—the CJ (see below, 2-003) hears references from national courts on the interpretation of provisions of EU law (see Chapter 4, 4–011).

3.   Details on the jurisdiction of the Privy Council are included in Chapter 2, at 2–022.

4.   The diagram of the civil courts includes the Employment Appeals Tribunal (EAT) and Employment Tribunals (or Industrial Tribunals as they were known prior to being renamed by s.1 of the Employment Rights (Dispute Resolution) Act 1998), since these are referred to in Chapter 14. Most tribunals have been amalgamated into a new unified two-tier structure comprising a First-tier Tribunal and an Upper Tribunal by the Tribunals, Courts and Enforcement Act 2007 but some tribunals, including the EAT and Employment Tribunals, remain outside the system (see below, 2–010).

▷   *(c) Binding precedents*

(i) Decisions and rulings of the Court of Justice

1–017   Simply stated, points of law decided by the CJ may bind all other courts in the English legal system, a matter which is considered in detail in Chapter 4.

1–018

Illustrative reference

See: Chapter 14: *"Equal pay"* (14–007), where in *Macarthys Ltd v Smith* (*Macarthys*) the Court of Appeal, following reference of a case to the ECJ for a ruling whether women were entitled to equal pay with men even if not employed at the same time, applied the ECJ's ruling (that women were so entitled) when determining the appeal; and (14–013), where in *Garland v British Rail Engineering Ltd* (*Garland*), the House of Lords following reference of a case to the ECJ for a ruling whether free travel benefits constituted "pay" for the purposes of equal pay legislation, applied the ECJ's ruling (that it did) when determining the appeal.

(ii) Ratio of decisions of higher courts

The ratio of a case decided by the Supreme Court or House of Lords (or, strictly **1–019** speaking the Appellate Committee of the House of Lords) will bind all courts except the CJ (although, exceptionally a Privy Council decision may be regarded as equivalent to a decision of the Supreme Court or House of Lords and may be followed in preference to the ratio of a decision of the Supreme Court or House itself—see below, 1–031). The ratio of a case decided by the Court of Appeal will bind the High Court and the Crown Court, and county courts and magistrates' courts, but not the Supreme Court or the CJ. The ratio of a High Court case will bind only county courts and magistrates' courts.

In principle, magistrates' courts should also be bound by decisions of the Crown Court, which is in a superior position in the court hierarchy, but there is some doubt whether this is so. Crown Court cases are not decided in the same way as in other courts, for Crown Court judges do not decide the case and deliver a judgment from which the ratio can be extracted. A Crown Court judge sums up the law for the jury, which then reaches a decision that determines the outcome of the case. Whilst there may be rulings on points of law given by judges in the course of their summing up, which may occasionally be reported (e.g. in the *Criminal Law Review*), there is no system of regular reporting of Crown Court rulings. They are not included as a matter of course in any series of law reports in daily use and the hierarchical principle of binding judicial precedent is accordingly likely to be ineffective, for there may well be contrary rulings which happen not to have been reported. It may be, therefore, that Crown Court rulings on points of law should not be regarded as binding on magistrates' courts and should be regarded as an exception to the general rule of stare decisis (see "The Binding Effect of Crown Court Decisions" [1980] Crim. L.R. 402–403).

Illustrative reference

See: Chapter 7: *"Existing obligations as consideration in contract"* (7–006), **1–020** where in *Adam Opel GmbH* David Donaldson QC, sitting as a Deputy High Court Judge, stated that *"Williams v Roffey* would seem to permit any variation of a contract, even if the benefits and burdens of the variation move solely in one direction, and I am bound to apply the decision accordingly, whatever view I might take of its logical coherence".

Chapter 17: *"Appropriation in theft"* (17–006), where in *Gomez* the Court of Appeal stated that the House of Lords' decision in *Morris* was (per Lord Lane C.J.) a "decision which we must follow".

(iii) Ratio of decisions of the same court

Most courts are not in fact bound by their own previous decisions, the only **1–021** exceptions being the Court of Appeal and the High Court when sitting as a

Divisional Court. This is where the High Court is sitting not as a trial court, with a single judge hearing a case, but as a court consisting usually of two or three judges which, broadly speaking, is exercising appellate or supervisory jurisdiction. When sitting in this capacity, the court is often referred to as "the Divisional Court", although it may be described as "a Divisional Court".

It was established in *Young v Bristol Aeroplane Co Ltd* [1944] K.B. 718 (*Young*) that the Court of Appeal (Civil Division) is bound by its own previous decisions, although three exceptional instances were recognised where the court could depart from one of its previous decisions:

(a) where there are two conflicting decisions, the court may choose which one to follow, the decision not followed being deemed to be overruled;
(b) where a previous Court of Appeal decision, although not expressly overruled, cannot stand with a subsequent House of Lords' decision; and
(c) where a previous Court of Appeal (or House of Lords) decision was reached per incuriam, i.e. through want of care, which may arise, for example, if a relevant authority has not been cited to and considered by the court.

In the light of the UK's membership of the EU, the second exception identified would seem also to encompass cases where a previous Court of Appeal decision cannot stand with and is inconsistent with a subsequent decision of the CJ. Lord Greene, M.R. in *Young* regarded the above instances as being the only exceptions to the rule, but other exceptions have subsequently been recognised. Thus in *Boys v Chaplin* [1968] 2 Q.B. 1 the Court of Appeal held that it was not bound by an interlocutory decision (i.e. an interim decision which is not final but which has immediate effect) of two Lord Justices (although some subsequent judicial pronouncements as to the effect and application of this "exception" have been questioned—see T. Prime and G. Scanlan, "*Stare Decisis* and the Court of Appeal; Judicial Confusion and Judicial Reform?" (2004) 23 C.J.Q. 212).

Similarly, in *Rickards v Rickards* [1989] 3 All E.R. 193 the Court of Appeal held that, in rare and exceptional cases concerning the jurisdiction of the court where no review by the House of Lords was possible, it was not bound by an earlier decision which it was satisfied was wrongly decided, even if strictly it might not fall within the category of a decision reached per incuriam. The Court of Appeal in this case nevertheless re-affirmed the significance of the rule laid down in *Young*. Lord Donaldson, M.R. stated (at 198–199):

"The importance of the rule of stare decisis in relation to the Court of Appeal's own decisions can hardly be overstated. We now sometimes sit in eight divisions and, in the absence of such a rule, the law would quickly become wholly uncertain. However, the rule is not without exceptions, albeit very limited . . . Nevertheless, this court must have very strong reasons if any departure from its own previous decisions is to be justifiable."

Neither of these decisions were referred to by the Court of Appeal in *R. (on the application of Kadhim) v Brent London Borough Council Housing Benefit Review Board* [2001] Q.B. 955 (*Kadhim*) where the court recognised an additional exception to the three identified in *Young*, i.e. where a proposition of law, although part of the ratio of an earlier decision, had been assumed to be correct by the earlier court but had not been the subject of argument before, or consideration by, that court. Recently, a further "specialist and very limited exception" was identified in *Actavis* that the court may depart from an earlier decision where it is satisfied that the European Patents Office Boards of Appeal have formed a settled view of European Patent Law which is inconsistent with that earlier decision. As to the rule in *Young* and the exceptions to it, Jacob L.J. stated (at [92]):

> ". . . ultimately it is for this court, exercising its powers in favour of legal certainty, to rule on whether there can and should be further exceptions to the rule. That can only be done by considering all the circumstances and practicalities of a proposed exception."

The Court of Appeal (Criminal Division) is generally bound by the same principles, save that where the liberty of the subject is at stake it might be necessary in the interests of justice for the court to decline to follow one of its previous decisions. As May L.J. stated in *R. v Spencer* [1985] Q.B. 771 at 779:

> "As a matter of principle we . . . find it difficult to see why there should in general be any difference in the application of the principle of stare decisis between the Civil and Criminal Divisions of this Court, save that we must remember that in the latter we may be dealing with the liberty of the subject and if a departure from authority is necessary in the interests of justice to an appellant, then this court should not shrink from so acting."

Notwithstanding that the Court of Appeal (Criminal Division) is generally bound by its previous decisions, it was subsequently established in *R. v Simpson* [2004] Q.B. 118 that a general discretion was available to a five member court to decide that a previous decision of the court should not be treated as a binding decision when it is wrong. A subsequent five member court in *R. v Magro and others* [2010] EWCA Crim 1575 (*Magro*), however, made it clear that "[w]hat *Simpson* does not establish . . . is that a five judge constitution is entitled to disregard or deprive the only previous decision of the three judge constitution of the court of its authority on a distinct and clearly identified point of law, reached after full argument and close analysis of the relevant legislative provisions". In such circumstances, the court would be bound by the previous decision and the court in *Magro* regarded itself as bound by its earlier decision in *R. v Clarke* [2009] EWCA Crim 1074 that the Crown Court had no power to make a confiscation order where a defendant received an absolute or conditional discharge for an offence. Lord Judge C.J. stated (at [31]):

> "The court in *Clarke* was fully appraised of all the relevant legislative provisions. There was no relevant information available to us which was not made

available for consideration in *Clarke*. It was the first occasion when the question arose for decision in the Court of Appeal Criminal Division. There was no actual or perceived possibility of a conflict of or inconsistencies between the authorities, or a decision or decisions based on a misunderstanding of earlier decisions. *Clarke* itself followed careful investigation by the court into the historic development of the law relating to discharges. It was a reserved judgment. It is plain from the terms of the judgment itself that it was con- sidered in meticulous detail, and given the closest possible attention. If we were to extend the principle in *Simpson* to the present situation, we should be going further than the decision itself justified, and it is not open to us to do so."

The principles laid down by the Court of Appeal in *Young* were subsequently adopted a few years later by the High Court, when sitting as a Divisional Court, in *Police Authority for Huddersfield v Watson* [1947] K.B. 842 (*Huddersfield*). Hearing an appeal from Quarter Sessions (see below, 2–019) in a civil case (concerning a constable's entitlement to a police pension), the High Court in this case took the view that it was bound by previous Divisional Court decisions. The court regarded the rule established in *Young* and the exceptions recognised in that case as having equal application to Divisional Court decisions and this was re-affirmed by a full Divisional Court of five judges in *Younghusband v Luftig* [1949] 2 K.B. 354 (*Younghusband*). In this case, where the court was hearing an appeal by case stated in a criminal case, Lord Goddard C.J. stated (at 361):

"This court is bound by its own decisions as is the Court of Appeal whatever the number of judges that may constitute it: see *Police Authority for Hud- dersfield v Watson* [1947] K.B. 842, 847. The principles of *Young v Bristol Aeroplane Co. Ltd* [1994] K.B. 718 apply equally to this court."

A subsequent Divisional Court in *R. v Greater Manchester Coroner Ex p. Tal* [1985] Q.B. 67, when exercising its supervisory jurisdiction by hearing an application for judicial review, has held that previous decisions of the Divisional Court are not binding on it and it can depart from decisions that it feels are wrong. In this case, unlike in *Huddersfield* and *Younghusband*, the court was not exercising appellate jurisdiction (i.e. hearing an appeal from another court) and was hearing a case at first instance. Although there was some criticism in *Tal* of these two cases, based partly on previous decisions (*Fortescue v Vestry of St Matthew, Bethnal Green* [1891] 2 Q.B. 170 and *Kruse v Johnson* [1898] 2 Q.B. 91) not being brought to those courts' attention and partly on the Divisional Court no longer being a final court of appeal (following s.1 of the Administration of Justice Act 1960, which provided a right of appeal to the House of Lords), it seems that the cases were distinguished rather than overruled. This was certainly the view taken by the headnote writer in the law report. If this is correct, the decisions in *Huddersfield* and *Younghusband* remain good law and it continues to be the case that the Divisional Court is bound by its previous decisions when exercising appellate jurisdiction. The case of *Tal*, when the Divisional Court is exercising supervisory jurisdiction, constitutes an exception to this. This is the view which has been taken in previous editions of this work and this view is re-iterated here. An alternative view, however, may be that *Tal* decides that the Divisional Court is not bound by its previous decisions, whatever jurisdiction is being exercised, in which case *Huddersfield* and *Younghusband* may no longer be good law. Thus appears to be the view taken in Glanville Williams *Learning the Law*, 13th edn (2006), where Professor A.T.H. Smith states:

> "The Divisional Court formerly used to be regarded as binding itself. In *R. v Greater Manchester Coroner, ex p. Tal*, however, it was decided that (as is the case with the High Court) it was not bound, but would follow the decision of another judge unless convinced that this was wrong . . ."

It is thought that the better view is that *Huddersfield* and *Younghusband* remain good law and that *Tal* constitutes an exception to the rule that the Divisional Court is bound by its previous decisions rather than a reversal of that rule.

Some uncertainty exists as to whether Divisional Court decisions are binding on other courts of comparable status in the court hierarchy, such as the High Court sitting as a trial court, with a single judge hearing a case at first instance, or the Crown Court where a case is heard before a judge and jury. In *Huddersfield*, Lord Goddard C.J. (at 848) regarded a High Court judge as bound by Divisional Court decisions and in *R. v Stafford Crown Court Ex p. Shipley* [1998] 2 All E.R. 465 at 468, the Court of Appeal stated (without comment) that the Crown Court in the present case had ruled that it was bound by the Divisional Court's decision in *Chief Constable of West Midlands Police v Marsden* (1995) 159 J.P. 405.

In *R. v Colyer* [1974] Crim.L.R. 243, however, a Crown Court judge declined to follow a decision of the Divisional Court, considering the decision to be of only persuasive authority. As a Crown Court ruling, however, this itself may have no more than persuasive authority and the point appears not to have been authoritatively considered at appellate level.

Illustrative references

1–022

See: Chapter 8: *"The right to sue in the tort of private nuisance"* (8–001), where in *Hunter* the House of Lords had to decide whether to follow the Court of Appeal's decision in *Malone* or its later decision in *Khorasandjian*, where a majority of the court had not followed *Malone*, although not, it would appear, in accordance with any of the recognised exceptions to the rule that the Court of Appeal is bound by its previous decisions.

Chapter 14: *"Equal pay"* (14–019), where in *Pickstone v Freemans Plc* (*Pickstone*) the Court of Appeal declined to follow the previous Court of Appeal decision in *O'Brien v Sim Chem Ltd* (*O'Brien*) on the basis that that decision was inconsistent with subsequent decisions of the ECJ in *Jenkins v Kingsgate (Clothing Productions) Ltd* and *Worringham v Lloyds Bank Ltd*.

Chapter 17: "*Appropriation in theft*" (17–017), where in *Hinks* the Court of Appeal declined to follow the previous Court of Appeal decision in *Mazo* which might be justified in accordance with the exception recognised in *Kadhim*, although no reference was made to this decision.

▷ (d) Persuasive precedents

(i) Decisions of the European Court of Human Rights

1–023 Under s.2(1) of the Human Rights Act 1998 (HRA 1998) courts or tribunals, when determining questions arising under the Act in connection with a Convention right, are required to "take into account" decisions of the European Court of Human Rights (Strasbourg Court), so it is clear these are only persuasive (see below 5–017). In most cases, courts are likely to follow such decisions and, according to Lord Slynn in *R. (Alconbury Developments Ltd) v Secretary of State for the Environment, Transport and the Regions* [2003] 2 A.C. 295 (at [27]), "[i]n the absence of some special circumstances . . . the court should follow any clear and constant jurisprudence of the European Court of Human Rights". However, a departure from the jurisprudence of the Strasbourg Court did occur in the case of *R. v Horncastle and others* [2009] UKSC 14 (*Horncastle*). In that case, the Supreme Court declined to follow the approach adopted by the Strasbourg Court in relation to a matter of criminal procedure that was germane to Article 6 of the Convention (the right to a fair trial). In the course of delivering the Supreme Court's judgment, with which all its members agreed, Lord Phillips, the President of the Supreme Court, stated (at [11]):

"The requirement to 'take into account' the Strasbourg jurisprudence will normally result in this Court applying principles that are clearly established by the Strasbourg Court. There will, however, be rare occasions where this court has concerns as to whether a decision of the Strasbourg Court sufficiently appreciates or accommodates particular aspects of our domestic process. In such circumstances it is open to this court to decline to follow the Strasbourg decision, giving reasons for adopting this course. This is likely to give the Strasbourg Court the opportunity to reconsider the particular aspect of the decision that is in issue, so that there takes place what may prove to be a valuable dialogue between this court and the Strasbourg Court. This is such a case."

Further, in *Lambeth LBC v Kay* [2006] UKHL 10 (*Kay*), the House of Lords held that the lower courts are bound by a House of Lords' decision (and, presumably, now by a decision of the Supreme Court) even if it is inconsistent with a subsequent, albeit persuasive, decision of the Strasbourg Court.

(ii) Ratio of decisions of lower courts

The ratio of a decision of a lower court in the court hierarchy is only a persuasive **1-024**
precedent. It may be followed by the court considering it or it may not be followed,
may be disapproved or may be overruled.

Illustrative references

1-025

See: Chapter 7: *"Existing obligations as consideration in contract"* (7–002),
where in *Williams v Roffey Bros & Nicholls (Contractors) Ltd* (*Williams*) the
Court of Appeal followed the *ratio* of *Stilk v Myrick* (*Stilk*), a first instance
decision of long standing which it was not prepared to overrule "except on
the strongest possible grounds".

Chapter 8: *"The right to sue in the tort of private nuisance"* (8–004), where in
Hunter a majority of the House of Lords, when faced with conflicting decisions of the Court of Appeal in *Malone* and *Khorasandjian*, chose to follow
the former and earlier decision.

Chapter 12: *"Wives as prosecution witnesses"* (12–005), where in *Hoskyn* the
House of Lords overruled the Court of Appeal decision in *R. v Lapworth*
(*Lapworth*), the ratio of which had been established law for over 50 years.

(iii) Ratio of decisions (or rulings) of the same court

These are generally only persuasive precedents. Thus rulings of the CJ are only **1-026**
persuasive in subsequent cases heard by the CJ and similarly the ratio of a decision
of the Supreme Court, or its predecessor, the House of Lords, is only persuasive in
subsequent cases heard by the Supreme Court. Until 1966, however, the House of
Lords did regard itself as bound by its own previous decisions (*London Tramways v
London County Council* [1898] A.C. 375), but in that year a Practice Statement
issued by Lord Gardiner L.C., on behalf of himself and all the other Law Lords,
indicated that the House would in future regard itself as free to depart from its
own previous decisions.

Lord Gardiner L.C. stated that their Lordships would "while treating former decisions of this House as normally binding . . . depart from a previous decision when
it appears right to do so" and "in this connection they will bear in mind the danger
of disturbing retrospectively the basis on which contracts, settlements of property
and fiscal arrangements have been entered into and also the especial need for
certainty in the criminal law" ([1966] 1 W.L.R. 1234). In practice, the House has
rarely departed from its previous decisions. Moreover, in the case of *Chartbrook Ltd
v Persimmon Homes Ltd* [2009] EWHL 38, the House reaffirmed that the Practice
Statement was only a limited exception to its foremost obligation to follow its
previous decisions. Lord Hoffmann stated (at [41]) that the Practice Statement was
intended to apply in "a small number of cases" where previous decisions were
thought to be "impeding the law's development" or where they had led to "results

that were unjust or contrary to public policy". It is likely that the Supreme Court will continue to follow this approach.

The ratio of a decision of the High Court when sitting as a trial court is also only persuasive in subsequent cases heard by the High Court when sitting as a trial court. However, where a decision of the High Court has been fully considered and not followed, the second decision should be regarded as having settled the issue and in a later case a High Court judge should follow the second of the two conflicting decisions. This is except in rare cases where the judge in the later case is convinced that the judge in the second case was wrong not to have followed the first decision, as where some relevant authority had not been cited in either of the first two cases: *Colchester Estates (Cardiff) v Carlton Industries Plc* [1984] 2 All E.R. 601, approved by the Court of Appeal in *Re Lune Metal Products Ltd (In Administration)* [2006] EWCA Civ 1720 (at [9]). A ruling on a point of law by a judge in the Crown Court similarly seems to be of only persuasive authority in subsequent Crown Court cases, for the same reasons that such rulings may not be binding on magistrates' courts (see above, 1–019), and such rulings are not binding precedents. Nor are the county courts or magistrates' courts, neither of whose decisions are reported, bound by their own previous decisions, which are persuasive only.

1–027

Illustrative references

See: Chapter 12: *"Wives as prosecution witnesses"* (12–004), where in *Hoskyn* in the House of Lords Lord Salmon regarded statements in a previous House of Lords' case, *Leach*, as part of the ratio of that case and followed the decision; where Viscount Dilhorne and Lords Keith and Wilberforce, although considering the statements to have been obiter, nevertheless followed that decision; and where Lord Edmund-Davies similarly considered the statements to have been obiter but declined to follow that decision.

Chapter 17: *"Appropriation in theft"* (17–009), where in *Gomez* a majority of the House of Lords followed (what they regarded as) the ratio of a previous House of Lords' decision, *Lawrence*; and where Lord Lowry, dissenting, although regarding the statements in *Lawrence* as obiter, indicated he would have departed from that decision in accordance with the *Practice Statement* if those statements were accepted as ratio.

(iv) Obiter statements of any court

1–028 Such statements are persuasive as precedents, but may be particularly influential when made in the Supreme Court or House of Lords and in the Court of Appeal. Statements which are obiter may be followed and approved in subsequent cases or equally may be disregarded, either being ignored or disapproved.

Illustrative references

See: Chapter 7: *"Existing obligations as consideration in contract"* (7–004), **1–029**
where in *Williams* Purchas L.J. in the Court of Appeal followed an obiter
statement of Lord Hailsham L.C. in the House of Lords in *Woodhouse A.C.
Israel Cocoa Ltd S.A. v Nigerian Produce Marketing Co Ltd.*

Chapter 12: *"Wives as prosecution witnesses"* (12–004), where in *Hoskyn*
Viscount Dilhorne and Lords Keith and Wilberforce, but not Lord Edmund-
Davies, followed what they perceived to be obiter statements of the House of
Lords in *Leach* and (12–003), where Lord Salmon regarded a statement
made obiter by Bayley J. in *R. v Inhabitants of All Saints, Worcester* (*All Saints,
Worcester*), although in a case decided at first instance, as "being of the
highest persuasive authority", whilst (12–003) Lord Edmund-Davies disregarded this statement, feeling that the case had "nothing to do with the
compellability of a witness competent at common law" (which was the point
at issue in *Hoskyn*).

Chapter 15: *"Nervous shock or psychiatric injury"* (15–005), where in *Hambrook* Bankes L.J. disapproved a dictum of Kennedy J. in *Dulieu* which, being
"laid down in quite general terms in that case, cannot be accepted as good
law applicable in every case", and (15–018), where in *White* Lords Steyn and
Hoffmann in the House of Lords declined to follow an *obiter* statement of
Lord Oliver in the House of Lords in *Alcock*.

Chapter 17: *"Appropriation in theft"* (17–010) where in *Gomez* Lord Lowry in
the House of Lords followed an obiter statement of Lord Roskill in the House
of Lords in *Morris*.

**(v) Ratio of decisions or obiter statements of the Judicial Committee of the
Privy Council**

The Judicial Committee of the Privy Council is the final appeal court of those **1–030**
Commonwealth countries which have not abolished the right of appeal to it and
also, domestically, for Jersey, Guernsey and the Isle of Man (see below, 2–022). Its
decisions are, strictly, not binding on any English court and it is open to any court
to decline to follow Privy Council decisions.

Illustrative reference

See: Chapter 15: *"Nervous shock or psychiatric injury"* (15–004), where in **1–031**
Dulieu the Divisional Court declined to follow the Privy Council decision in
Victorian Railways Commissioners v Coultas (*Coultas*), which had decided that
damages could not be recovered for nervous shock sustained but unac-
companied by any physical injury; and (15–011), where in *Page* in the House of
Lords Lord Lloyd remarked that a statement of the Privy Council in *The*

Wagon Mound approving a dictum of Denning L.J. in *King* was "perhaps the strongest authority supporting the view taken by the Court of Appeal" in the court below, although Lord Lloyd took the view that the Privy Council's approval should not be regarded as endorsing general application of the dictum.

However, since members of the Privy Council are usually Justices who sit in the Supreme Court, its decisions are considered particularly persuasive. Indeed, they may be regarded in some circumstances as equivalent to a decision of the Supreme Court and, for all practical purposes, as binding, to be followed even in preference to a decision of the Supreme Court itself. This was the view taken by the Court of Appeal in *R. v James, R. v Karimi* [2006] 1 All E.R. 759 in respect of the Privy Council's decision in *Att Gen for Jersey v Holley* [2005] 2 A.C. 580. The Privy Council in that case, in an appeal heard, unusually, by 9 of the 12 Law Lords then sitting in the House of Lords, decided by a 6–3 majority that the House of Lords' decision in *R. v Smith (Morgan)* [2001] 1 A.C. 146, dealing with the standard of self-control in the provocation defence for murder, was wrongly decided. Under established principles of precedent it was not open to the Privy Council to overrule a House of Lords' decision, although, as the Court of Appeal recognised, these principles had not been adhered to in this instance. Lord Phillips C.J., delivering the Court of Appeal's judgment, stated (at [41]):

"Putting on one side the position of the European Court of Justice, the Lords of Appeal in Ordinary [*law lords*] have never hitherto accepted that any other tribunal could overrule a decision of the [*House of Lords'*] Appellate Committee. Uniquely a majority of the Law Lords have on this occasion [*in Holley*] decided that they could do so and have done so in their capacity as members of the Judicial Committee of the Privy Council. We do not consider that it is for this court to rule that it was beyond their powers to alter the common law rules of precedent in this way."

Accordingly, the Court of Appeal followed the Privy Council decision in *Holley* in preference to the House of Lords' decision in *Smith (Morgan)*, justifying this by reference to the following "exceptional features": (i) All nine law lords sitting in *Holley* agreed in the course of their judgments that the result reached by the majority clarified definitively English law on the issue in question; (ii) the majority in *Holley* constituted half the Appellate Committee of the House of Lords, although "we do not know whether there would have been agreement that the result was definitive had the members of the Board divided five/four" (at [43]); and (iii) in the circumstances, the result of any appeal on the issue to the House of Lords is a foregone conclusion. As if to emphasise the exceptional nature of the course of action being taken, the Court of Appeal went on to state that "our decision should not be taken as a licence to decline to follow a decision of the House of Lords in any other circumstances" and it is expected that the Court of Appeal will follow a similar approach in relation to the Supreme Court.

(vi) Decisions, rulings and statements of courts of other jurisdictions

These are persuasive as precedents. Cases from a range of jurisdictions might be **1–032** considered, including Scotland and Northern Ireland (which are separate jurisdictions, although they have a common system of appeal to the Supreme Court), the Irish Republic and Commonwealth and other countries (e.g. United States, Australia) whose legal systems are based on English law. In some cases, such decisions may be considered particularly persuasive, although in other cases they may be regarded as having little or no persuasive strength.

Illustrative references

1–033

See: Chapter 8: *"The right to sue in the tort of private nuisance"* (8–005), where in *Hunter* Lord Goff did not derive any assistance from certain (unspecified) American cases which his Lordship described as a "slender and inconclusive line of authority"; whilst, on the other hand, (8–006) Lord Cooke, in his dissenting judgment, placed particular reliance upon North American case law.

Chapter 9: *"False imprisonment, "detention" and the Mental Health Act 1983"* (9–007), where in *Bournewood* the Court of Appeal adopted the reasoning in a Scottish case, *B v Forsey*, although (9–010) Lord Goff in the House of Lords distinguished (see below, 1–054) this case.

Chapter 12: *"Wives as prosecution witnesses"* (12–006), where in *Hoskyn* Viscount Dilhorne referred in passing to two Australian cases and Lord Wilberforce, in a brief concluding paragraph to his judgment in which various cases were cited, referred to having "taken into account the position, so far as it has been made clear, in other jurisdictions".

Chapter 15: *"Nervous shock or psychiatric injury"* (15–003), where in *Dulieu* the Divisional Court placed reliance on an Irish decision, *Bell v Great Northern Railway Company of Ireland*, and (15–004) made reference to two American decisions; (15–011), where in *Page* the House of Lords, when considering a dictum of Denning L.J. in *King*, referred to approval of the dictum in two Australian decisions and where Lord Jauncey (who also referred to an American decision), when doing so, remarked that "as is often the case in the field of negligence valuable contributions to the discussion are to be found in judgments of the High Court of Australia"; (15–014), where in *White* Lord Hoffmann attached little importance to the view of one of five judges in an Australian case, but, along with Lord Goff (15–016), adopted the reasoning of a Scottish case; and (15–020) where in *Grieves* Lord Phillips C.J. in the Court of Appeal made reference to two decisions of the U.S. Supreme Court.

Chapter 16: *"Marital rape"* (16–008), where in *R. v R.* the House of Lords paid particular attention to a Scottish case, *S v HM Advocate*, in which marital rape had been held to be an offence known to the law.

(vii) Views of authors and law reform bodies

1–034 These do not, strictly speaking, form a persuasive precedent in the same way as judicial statements in cases. However, they may be taken into account by courts and considered to be persuasive in a general sense as reinforcing the decision or conclusion which the court has reached. Views expressed by law reform bodies such as the Law Commission may be considered particularly persuasive. So also might views expressed by authors in legal treatises and textbooks of recognised authority, especially if written by authors of particular eminence. This will include works written by those who are or may have been members of the judiciary themselves, e.g. Coke and Hale (both of whom held the office of Chief Justice and whose works are generally regarded as authoritative). Views expressed in articles in learned legal journals may also be considered. Indeed, courts, on occasions, may have regard to all these sources. Nor do courts confine themselves to considering legal materials. They may have regard to textbooks or articles in other disciplines, which might better inform the court of the policy considerations and possible implications of any decision (see below, 1–057) that it might reach.

Similarly they may have regard to guides dealing with the practical application of the law, e.g. in *R. (on the application of Ashton) v Bolton Combined Court* (2001) 47 Licensing Review 25, the Divisional Court had regard to the *Good Practice Guide* prepared by the Magistrates' Association and the Justices' Clerks' Society, which gave guidance to licensing committees of justices on how to approach the grant of licences for the sale of intoxicating liquor, when deciding that a licence could not be granted with a condition attached precluding the licensee from applying for a special hours certificate for late night drinking. Sir Christopher Bellamy, delivering the court's judgment, stated (at [29]): "Although . . . this Guide has no statutory authority, I do, for my part, consider that it is a persuasive source of information to which the court can legitimately have regard".

While the views of authors may be considered persuasive in some cases, they may not in other instances. Indeed, they may, on occasions, be regarded as expressing an incorrect statement of the law and they may be expressly disapproved.

Illustrative references

1–035 See: Chapter 8: *"The right to sue in the tort of private nuisance"* (8–003), where in *Hunter* Lord Goff approved the view of Professor Newark in an article entitled "The Boundaries of Nuisance" that the tort of private nuisance applied only to interference with the plaintiff's use and enjoyment of his rights in the land, and (8–005) also disapproved other academic writings upon which Lord Cooke relied, in his dissenting judgment, to support the proposition that such right to sue should not be so restricted.

Chapter 9: *"False imprisonment, "detention" and the Mental Health Act 1983"* (9–006), where in *Bournewood* the Court of Appeal disapproved statements in Hoggett's *Mental Health Law* and Jones' *Mental Health Act Manual* which indicated that mental patients could be informally admitted to hospital for treatment for mental disorder where they were incapable of consenting to admission; and (9–011) where Lord Steyn in the House of Lords referred to two textbooks by American psychiatrists and an article in the *Journal of Applied Philosophy* when considering the importance of safeguards for the detention of mental patients.

Chapter 12: *"Wives as prosecution witnesses"* (12–003), where in *Hoskyn* Lord Wilberforce referred to the views of *Taylor on Evidence* (as did Viscount Dilhorne), *Phillips and Anderson on Evidence*, and Roscoe's *Digest* when considering whether a wife could be a compellable witness against her husband on a charge of personal violence by him on her.

Chapter 15: *"Nervous shock or psychiatric injury"* (15–004), where in *Dulieu* Kennedy J. referred to the unfavourable reviews in *Sedgewick On Damages*, Pollock's *The Law of Torts* and Bevan's *Negligence in Law* of the Privy Council's decision in *Coultas* that no action could be brought for nervous shock unaccompanied by physical injury, when declining to follow that decision; (15–011), where in *Page* Lord Lloyd referred to a journal article and to *Clerk and Lindsell on Torts* when considering *The Wagon Mound* decision; (15–014), where in *White* Lords Steyn, Hoffmann and Goff referred to a number of academic works, including books and articles, and the Law Commission Report on *Liability for Psychiatric Illness*; and (15–020) where in *Grieves* Lord Hope referred to a journal article.

Chapter 16: *"Marital rape"* (16–002), where, until *R. v R.*, courts had taken the view that marital rape was not an offence known to the law, on the basis of a statement by Hale in his book *Pleas of the Crown* published in the 18th century.

Chapter 17: *"Appropriation in theft"* (17–008), where in *Gomez* Lord Lowry, when considering the meaning of "appropriates" in s.1(1) of the Theft Act 1968, referred to the Criminal Law Revision Committee's Eighth Report which preceded the Act, and (17–011) to the increasing willingness of the courts to entertain submissions from counsel based upon academic decision or comment; and (17–017), where in *Hinks* Rose L.J. made references to *Criminal Law Review* articles by Professor Sir John Smith QC.

(viii) International standards

International standards relating to matters under consideration in a case, espe- **1–036** cially those derived from treaties which the United Kingdom has ratified, may be persuasive when a court is seeking to develop the law.

1–037

Illustrative reference

See: Chapter 8: *"The right to sue in the tort of private nuisance"* (8–006), where in *Hunter* Lord Cooke had regard to the art.16 of the United Nations Convention on the Rights of the Child, which is based on art.12 of the Universal Declaration of Human Rights and Fundamental Freedoms, when considering who should have the right to sue in the tort of private nuisance, and stated: "International standards such as this may be taken into account in shaping the common law".

> ## (e) Tribunals

1–038 In some areas of law, such as employment and social security, matters are generally dealt with by tribunals rather than courts. The doctrine of stare decisis has application here, so that court decisions may act as binding precedents for tribunals and, in some instances, decisions of tribunals themselves may form binding precedents.

(i) Court decisions as binding precedents for tribunals

1–039 All tribunals will be bound by rulings of the CJ and the ratio of decisions of the Supreme Court or House of Lords and the Court of Appeal. Some tribunals may be bound by decisions of the High Court, sitting either as a Divisional Court or as a trial court, whilst others may not be. Since county courts and magistrates' courts are regarded as bound by High Court decisions, tribunals which seem to be comparable in status to these courts, such as the First-tier Tribunal and other tribunals not incorporated into it e.g. Employment Tribunals (see below 2–010), may similarly be bound by High Court decisions.

However, tribunals whose status is comparable to the High Court, such as the Upper Tribunal and other tribunals not incorporated into it e.g. the Employment Appeals Tribunal (EAT), to which there is a right of appeal from the First-tier Tribunal and Employment Tribunals respectively, may not be bound by High Court decisions where the High Court was sitting as a trial court. Since the High Court itself is not bound by such decisions (see above, 1–026), it might be expected that the position would be the same for tribunals of comparable status to the High Court. Less clear is whether such tribunals are bound when the High Court is sitting as a Divisional Court. There is some authority to indicate that they are, for the Court of Appeal stated *obiter* in *Chief Supplementary Benefit Officer v Leary* [1985] 1 W.L.R. 84 at 89, in relation to Social Security Commissioners, a tribunal which previously existed prior to its incorporation as part of the Upper Tribunal and which had comparable status to the High Court, that "decisions of the High Court exercising its supervisory jurisdiction [*as a Divisional Court*] . . . are, and always have been, binding on Commissioners". Whether the Upper Tribunal and other tribunals not incorporated into it such as the EAT will regard themselves as bound by Divisional Court decisions remains to be seen.

Illustrative reference

See: Chapter 14: *"Equal pay"* (14–015), where in *Pickstone* the EAT decided that art.141 of the EC Treaty (now art.157 of the TFEU) had no application to the case in question in view of the decision of the Court of Appeal in *O'Brien*.

1–040

(ii) Tribunal decisions as binding precedents

Decisions of tribunals whose status is comparable to the High Court may form **1–041** binding precedents for inferior tribunals. Thus decisions of the Upper Tribunal must be followed by the First-tier Tribunal and decisions of the EAT must be followed by Employment Tribunals. However, tribunals are not bound by their own previous decisions. The EAT has in a number of instances departed from its previous decisions (e.g. *Norris v Southampton CC* [1982] I.C.R. 177) and the Upper Tribunal may well follow a similar approach. Nor are Employment Tribunals bound by their previous decisions. As Waite J. observed in the EAT in *Anandarajah v Lord Chancellor's Department* [1984] I.R.L.R. 131 at 132:

> "Sometimes the judgment in a particular case will be found to express, in concise and helpful language, some concept which is regularly found in this field of inquiry and it becomes of great illustrative value. But . . . Industrial Tribunals are not required, and should not in our view be invited, to subject the authorities to the same analysis as a court of law searching in a plethora of precedent for binding or persuasive authority."

It is thought that these words will not be confined in scope to the employment field but will have application to tribunal decisions generally and it might be expected therefore that the First-tier Tribunal (and any other tribunal) will not regard itself as bound by its previous decisions.

▶ 4. Precedential Strength

Whilst the status of a precedent is determined by whether it is ratio or obiter and **1–042** by the position of the court determining the case in the court hierarchy, there are, in practice, a number of other factors which affect the strength of a precedent. These include:

▷ (a) The age of a precedent

Generally, a court will be reluctant to disregard a long established precedent, since **1–043** this reflects well-settled law. This may be the case even in circumstances where without such a precedent a court might have contemplated a different course (see, for example, *Housden v Conservators of Wimbledon and Putney Commons* [2008] EWCA Civ 200).

Such a long established precedent, which will either have remained unchallenged or have resisted challenges to its authority, is usually regarded as having considerable precedential strength. However, courts on occasions depart from long established precedents if they are considered no longer suitable for modern conditions.

Illustrative references

1–044

See: Chapter 7: *"Existing obligations as consideration in contract"* (7–002), where in *Williams* the Court of Appeal followed the *ratio* of *Stilk*, a first instance decision of long standing, which it was not prepared to overrule "except on the strongest possible grounds".

Chapter 12: *"Wives as prosecution witnesses"* (12–005), where in *Hoskyn* the House of Lords overruled the Court of Appeal decision in *Lapworth*, the ratio of which had been established law for over 50 years.

Chapter 16: *"Marital rape"* (16–008), where in *R. v R.* the House of Lords decided that the long established rule that marital rape was not an offence known to the law could no longer be justified in modern society.

▷   *(b) The composition of the court*

1–045 The strength of a precedent must be considered greater if the judge or judges deciding the case are regarded as especially eminent. As Zander, *The Law-Making Process* (6th ed., 2004), p.278, states, "all judges are equal but some are a little more equal than others". Judges generally regarded as especially eminent include Lord Blackburn, Lord Atkin, Lord Reid, Lord Wilberforce, Lord Diplock and Scrutton L.J. Even if particular judges might not generally be regarded as especially eminent, courts might nevertheless place emphasis on their reputation in a particular field if they wish to accord weight to one of their decisions or statements. Conversely, it may be that statements of certain judges are not held in high regard.

Illustrative references

1–046

See: Chapter 7: *"Existing obligations as consideration in contract"* (7–002), where in *Williams* Purchas L.J. in the Court of Appeal stated that: "I would not be prepared to overrule two cases of such veneration [*Harris v Watson* (1791) *and Stilk* (1809)] involving judgments of judges of such distinction [*Lord Kenyon C.J. and Lord Ellenborough C.J.*] except on the strongest possible grounds since they form a corner-stone of the law of contract".

Chapter 11: *"The regulation of abortion"* (11–010), where in *Royal College of Nursing v Department of Health and Social Security* (*Royal College*) Lord Diplock made the following comment about the summing up to the jury of Macnaughten J. in *Bourne*: "No disrespect is intended to that eminent judge and head of my former chambers if I say that his reputation is founded more upon his sturdy common sense than upon his lucidity of legal expression".

Chapter 12: *"Wives as prosecution witnesses"* (12–003), where in *Hoskyn* Lord Salmon referred to a pronouncement of Bayley J. in *All Saints, Worcester* as "no doubt, obiter, but coming from such a master of the common law it deserves to be treated with the greatest respect: I regard it as being of the highest persuasive authority"; and (12–005), where Lord Edmund-Davies, expressing support for *Lapworth*, stated that "the reputation of few criminal judges this century stands as high as Avory J, who gave the judgment of the court".

Further, if there are more judges sitting than is usual—perhaps five in the Court of Appeal rather than the normal three, or seven in the Supreme Court rather than the normal five—this may reflect the importance attached to the case and the decision may be given correspondingly greater weight. Indeed, in particularly important cases nine Justices may sit in the case in the Supreme Court. This occurred, for instance in *R. (on the application of Smith) (FC) v Secretary of State for Defence and another* [2010] UKSC 29 (see below, 2–004). A similar number had, on previous occasions, sat in the House of Lords e.g. in *A v Secretary of State for the Home Department* [2005] 2 A.C. 68, where the House considered whether anti-terrorist legislation which derogated from the right to liberty provided by art.5(1)(f) [a] of the European Convention on Human Rights (see below, 5–010) could be justified. A similar number of Law Lords sat in the Privy Council in *Att Gen for Jersey v Holley* [2005] 2 A.C. 580 (see above, 1–031) and it is readily apparent that that decision was intended to be given great weight, even to the extent of taking precedence over a decision of the House of Lords.

Illustrative reference

See: Chapter 16: *"Marital rape"* (16–007), where in *R. v R.* a full Court of Appeal of five judges considered whether to uphold the long established rule that marital rape was not an offence known to the law.

1–047

▷ *(c) The existence of dissent*

An appellate court decision will have greater precedential strength if it is unan- **1–048** imous. Moreover, the strength of a precedent will be enhanced if there is unanimity as to both the decision reached and the reasons given for that decision. In some cases, courts deliver only one judgment which is stated to be the judgment of the court (see, e.g., the Supreme Court's decision in *R. v Rollins* [2010] UKSC 39). There may or may not be an indication that this is a judgment to which each member of the court has contributed (for an example of where there is such an indication, see the House of Lords' decision in *Inland Revenue Commissioners v Scottish Provident Institution* [2004] 1 W.L.R. 3172).

Where, however, one or more dissenting judgment is delivered this may be done with some reluctance, and diffidence may be expressed about disagreeing with the majority approach, since a judge may be conscious that such a judgment could affect the precedential strength of the decision. On occasions, however, it may be that dissenting judgments are seen as persuasive in subsequent cases and, indeed, may be adopted in preference to the majority view.

Illustrative reference

1–049

See: Chapter 8: *"The right to sue in the tort of private nuisance"* (8–004), where in *Hunter* Lord Lloyd followed a dissenting judgment, stating: "for the reasons given by Peter Gibson L.J. [sic] in his dissenting judgment in *Khoransandjian v Bush*, with which I agree, I would hold that that case was wrongly decided, and should be overruled".

Chapter 15: *"Nervous shock or psychiatric injury"* (15–006), where in *Bourhill* Lord Macmillan seemed to regard the "powerful dissent" of Sargant L.J. in *Hambrook*, who was of the view that nervous shock was actionable only if arising from a reasonable fear of immediate personal injury to oneself, as weakening the strength of the decision in that case that nervous shock was actionable if it arose from fear for another person's safety.

▷ *(d) The reserving of decision*

1–050 A reserved decision, indicated in law reports by the abbreviation *cur. adv. vult*, which is short for *curia advisari vult*, meaning that the court wishes to deliberate before delivering judgment, may, perhaps, be of greater precedential strength than an unreserved (ex tempore) decision where the court pronounces judgment immediately at the conclusion of the case.

A reserved decision will be a more considered decision, given after some reflection and with the opportunity to take account of possible implications of the decision that may be reached. In the case of appeals, which will involve more than one judge, different members of the court will also have had the opportunity to discuss the case and ascertain the extent of their agreement prior to delivering judgment. Certainly the value of judgments ought to be enhanced where the court has reserved decision. However, there seems little authority to indicate that reserved judgments should be accorded greater precedential strength, although some support for this might be found in views expressed extra-judicially by Russell L.J. in a lecture in 1969 (Sir Charles Russell, "Behind the Appellate Curtain", *Holdsworth Club Lecture*, University of Birmingham, 1969, pp.3 and 8):

> "It is important in considering appellate judgments to differentiate between reserved judgments and unreserved judgments. The quality of the former is, or should be, better than that of the latter . . . in the case of unreserved judgments weight should be attached only to pronouncements [*by one judge*] that in express terms approve of other pronouncements [*of other judges*], and with particularity rather than generality. All else should be suspect in terms of value. . ."

In a high proportion of cases, however, judgments are unreserved, including judgments in the Court of Appeal. In contrast, the House of Lords almost invariably reserved judgment, a rule of practice apparently adopted following its (much criticised) decision in *Hulton v Jones* [1910] A.C. 20 (see *Salmond & Heuston on The Law of Torts* (21st ed., 1996), p.143, n.61). This practice was not, however, universally followed from that time since, as can be seen from the first **Illustrative reference** below, extempore judgments were delivered by the House in *Leach*, which was decided a couple of years after *Hulton v Jones*. It seems likely that the practice of generally reserving judgments, previously adopted by the House of Lords, will be followed by the Supreme Court.

Illustrative references

1–051

See: Chapter 12: *"Wives as prosecution witnesses"* (12–004), where in *Hoskyn* Lord Edmund-Davies, expressed reservations about an earlier House of Lords' decision, *Leach*, stating that "there are features of the undoubtedly extempore views expressed in the . . . case which require the closest scrutiny".

Chapter 15: *"Nervous shock or psychiatric injury"* (15–014), where in *White* Lord Hoffmann in the House of Lords, when assessing three decisions relied upon by the plaintiffs, stated: "All appear to have been extempore first instance judgments given on circuit".

▷ *(e) Absence of argument*

Not all points that arise in cases are disputed. Some points may be conceded and **1–052** some issues may be agreed by the parties. A conceded or agreed point may (but need not) be accepted by the court and may form part of the court's decision. Where such a point has been accepted without argument, but might nevertheless be arguable, it may have less precedential strength than a point determined by the court following detailed argument.

1–053

Illustrative reference

See: Chapter 17: *"Appropriation in theft"* (17–015), where in *Mazo* it was agreed by both counsel and accepted by the Court of Appeal that, where there were valid gifts, there could be no appropriation and that in such a case the jury needed a direction as to the validity of the gifts; and (17–017) where a later Court of Appeal in *Hinks* stated that these concessions by prosecuting counsel were wrongly made and had led the court in *Mazo* into error.

▶ 5. Distinguishing Precedents

1–054 Whether binding or persuasive, precedents must be relevant to the facts of the case. If not considered relevant, precedents are said to be distinguishable. This differs from refusing to follow a previous decision, where the correctness of the earlier decision is called into question. When a court distinguishes a previous decision, it recognises it to be good law and does not question its correctness, but finds certain factual differences which justify not following that previous decision. In essence, it finds that the ratio of the previous decision is inapplicable. This may be because of some material fact or facts in the previous case which are absent in the present case or because of some material fact or facts in the present case which were absent in the earlier case.

The process of distinguishing, which enables a court to avoid following either a binding or persuasive precedent, is an important one. As Zander, *The Law-Making Process* (6th ed., 2004), p.275, states:

"Distinguishing between factual situations and applying the appropriate rule of law is one of the lawyer's and judge's most crucial functions. It is the business of drawing lines, or seeing how far to take a particular rule and of expanding or contracting the scope of rules to meet new circumstances. The question is always the same, are there any material differences between the facts of the present case and the facts of the precedents to warrant the rule being different?"

The question posed by Zander is not, however, one to which there will always be a clear answer, for there is no inevitable logic to the process. Opinions may differ as to which facts are material.

A court may decide that there is a single material fact or that there are several material facts which distinguish the present case from the previous case. In the latter instance, this may make it difficult to predict the outcome in future cases in which some but not all of the material facts are present. If, for instance, the court in case A decided that there were four material facts present in case B which were absent in case A and accordingly distinguished case B, what would be the position in case C if two of the four material facts from case B were present but two were absent? Would the court in case C also distinguish case B, on the basis that two of the four material facts were absent, and follow case A? Or would the court in case C follow case B, not regard it as distinguishable and effectively distinguish case A? These questions are not ones which admit of any ready answer.

Illustrative references

1–055

See: Chapter 6: "*Contractual obligations arising out of an invitation to tender*" (6–010), where in *Harmon*, the High Court distinguished the case of *Blackpool*.

Chapter 7: "*Existing obligations as consideration in contract*" (7–006), where in *Anangel Atlas Compania Naviera S.A. v Ishikawajima-Harima Heavy Industries Co Ltd (No. 2)* and *Adam Opel GmbH*, the High Court declined to distinguish *Williams*; but where in *Re Selectmove Ltd* and in *South Caribbean Trading Ltd v Trafigura Beheer BV* the Court of Appeal and High Court respectively did distinguish *Williams*.

Chapter 9: "*False imprisonment, "detention" and the Mental Health Act 1983*" (9–010), where in *Bournewood* in the House of Lords Lord Goff distinguished the case of *B v Forsey*, although (9–007) the Court of Appeal, appearing to regard the ratio of that case as applicable, had not done so.

Chapter 12: "*Wives as prosecution witnesses*" (12–003), where in *Hoskyn* Lord Edmund-Davies regarded the case of *All Saints, Worcester*, although not a binding precedent, as distinguishable on a number of grounds.

Chapter 15: "*Nervous shock or psychiatric injury*" (15–005), where in *Hambrook* different views were expressed by members of the Court of Appeal as to whether the cases of *Smith v Johnson & Co, Pugh v London, Brighton and South Coast Rly Co* and *Wilkinson v Downton* were distinguishable; (15–007), where in *King v Phillips (King)* the Court of Appeal distinguished *Hambrook*; (15–008), where in *Boardman v Sanderson* the Court of Appeal distinguished *King*; (15–011), where in *Page* a majority of the House of Lords distinguished *Bourhill* and subsequent decisions where a person suffered nervous shock through fear for another's safety, although the minority did not regard these cases as distinguishable; (15–014), where in *White* Lord Hoffmann distinguished the cases of *Dooley v Cammell Laird & Co Ltd and Mersey Insulation Co Ltd, Galt v British Railways* and *Wigg v British Railways Board*; and (15–020) where in *Grieves* both the Court of Appeal and the House of Lords distinguished *Page*.

Chapter 16: "*Marital rape*" (16–011), where in *R. v C (Barry)* the Court of Appeal declined to distinguish its earlier decision in *R. v Graham L.*

Chapter 17: "*Appropriation in theft*" (17–015), where in *Mazo* the Court of Appeal distinguished *Gomez*; and (17–016), where in *R. v Kendrick and Hopkins (Kendrick)* the Court of Appeal distinguished *Mazo*.

In some instances, it may be obvious that a court has distinguished a previous precedent, for the court may in the course of its judgment give a clear indication that it is doing so. The court may expressly state that a previous precedent is distinguishable or this may clearly be inferred. A clear inference can be drawn where the court states that there are material differences between the present case and the previous precedent or where it states that a previous precedent is not in point.

In other cases, however, there may be no express statement or clear inference that can be drawn and the position may be less certain. As with the ratio of a case (see above, 1–007), a tentative view may be expressed by the law reporter in the headnote to the case in the law reports. However, what is recorded in the headnote may depend on which particular law report is read. Thus the headnote in one report may state that a previous case has been distinguished, whilst the headnote in another report may state, more neutrally, that that case has been "considered" or may make no mention of the case, e.g. in *C (A Minor) v DPP*, considered in Chapter 16 at 16–011, the headnote in some law reports ([1996] A.C. 1; [1995] 2 W.L.R. 383; [1995] 2 Cr. App. R. 166; and [1995] R.T.R. 261) records that the House of Lords distinguished its earlier decision in *R. v R.* [1992] 1 A.C. 599, although the headnote in other law reports ([1995] 2 All E.R. 43; [1995] 1 F.L.R. 933; and (1995) 159 J.P. 269) makes no mention of this case being distinguished.

1–056

Illustrative references

See: Chapter 8: *"The right to sue in the tort of private nuisance"* (8–006), where in *Hunter* Lord Cooke, dissenting, stated that *Malone* was "not directly in point".

Chapter 9: *"False imprisonment, "detention" and the Mental Health Act 1983"* (9–010), where in *Bournewood* Lord Goff stated that *B v Forsey* "was concerned with the invocation of the common law to supplement the statutory power of compulsory detention . . . [and] has no relevance in the present case which is concerned with informal admission".

Chapter 12: *"Wives as prosecution witnesses"* (12–003), where in *Hoskyn* Lord Edmund-Davies stated that in *All Saints, Worcester* "the facts were widely different from those of the present case".

Chapter 15: *"Nervous shock or psychiatric injury"* (15–008), where in *Boardman* Ormrod L.J. expressly stated that "this case is distinguishable from *King v. Phillips"*; (15–011), where in *Page* Lord Lloyd stated that "the cases following on from *Bourhill v. Young*, are not in point"; and (15–020), where in *Grieves* Lord Hope expressly stated that "[o]n the facts of Mr Grieves's case, *Page v Smith* is distinguishable", Lord Scott expressly stated that "I am in agreement with Mr Kent [*counsel for the claimant*] that *Page v Smith* is distinguishable" and Lord Mance expressly stated that "I agree that it [*Page*] can and should be distinguished on its facts".

Chapter 17: "*Appropriation in theft*" (17–016), where in *Kendrick* Ebsworth J. stated that the present case was "very different on its facts from *Mazo*".

▶ 6. Policy Considerations

Where there is only a persuasive precedent, judges can decide whether or not to **1–057** follow it and, in reaching their decision, will inevitably be influenced by their own views as to what the legal rule and outcome of the case should be. The case may be determined by reference to what is considered to be the best policy for the law to adopt: a declaration of what the law is will, in essence, be determined by views as to what the law should be.

Judges may have differing views as to what is the best policy for the law to adopt. It may be, therefore, that the composition of the court could determine the direction that the law will take, a point which appears to be acknowledged by Lord Hoff-mann in *White* (on which, see 15–014). In this case his Lordship remarked ([1998] 3 W.L.R. 1507 at 1549) that the House of Lords' previous decision in *McLoughlin* was "one of those cases in which one feels that a slight change in the composition of the Appellate Committee would have set the law on a different course". (Reference might also be made to Robertson, *Judicial Discretion in the House of Lords* (1998), the main theme of which is that the Law Lords enjoy and fully utilise far more discretion than is normally admitted, and that much depends on exactly which judges happen to hear a case.)

In some cases, policy considerations (e.g. the social, political and economic implications of the decision beyond the boundaries of the case itself) might be examined explicitly by judges. In other cases there may be no mention of policy at all, although in such cases policy considerations may nevertheless have been taken into account by judges when reaching their decisions.

There may be policy considerations implicit in and underlying decisions which, although not overtly referred to, have been influential in the reaching of those decisions. Although judges may follow a traditional approach of referring only to previous authorities, it may be that there are policy considerations in the back-ground which govern the choice of which authorities should be followed. The extent to which policy considerations are taken into account or are recognised explicitly will vary, with some judges more active and open in taking them into account than others.

In taking account of policy considerations, whether overtly or not, judges may seek to expand or to limit the scope of liability. A good example is in the field of nervous shock or psychiatric injury (see Chapter 15). For much of the last century, the courts sought to expand the scope of liability, for the most part without overt reference to policy considerations, although in recent years such considerations have been explicitly examined and a more restrictive approach has generally been adopted. As Lord Steyn observed in *White*, "since *McLoughlin*'s case [1983] 1 A.C. 410 the pendulum has swung and the House of Lords have taken greater account of policy considerations . . . in regard to . . . psychiatric injury".

Even where there is binding authority, this does not mean that policy considerations may not be taken into account. If a binding authority is contrary to what the court feels is the best policy for the law to adopt, the court may distinguish that authority, examine the policy considerations and reach a decision in keeping with its perception of the appropriate legal rule.

1–058

Illustrative references

See: Chapter 8: *"The right to sue in the tort of private nuisance"* (8–005), where in *Hunter* the policy considerations for and against restricting the right to sue to persons with an interest in land were considered expressly by the House of Lords, and (8–006) where Lord Cooke's views differed markedly from those of the other members of the House.

Chapter 12: *"Wives as prosecution witnesses"* (12–007), where in *Hoskyn* the arguments and policy considerations for and against making a wife a compellable witness against her husband on a charge of personal violence by him on her were considered expressly by the House of Lords.

Chapter 15: *"Nervous shock or psychiatric injury"* (15–009), where in *McLoughlin* and (15–010) in *Alcock* the House of Lords considered the policy arguments for limiting recovery for nervous shock; (15–011), where in *Page* the House of Lords decided that the policy arguments for limiting recovery did not apply where primary victims who were injured in an accident sustained nervous shock; and (15–015, 15–016 and 15–019), where in *White* the House of Lords considered the policy arguments for and against allowing recovery of damages by police officers who sustained nervous shock whilst acting in the course of their employment and whilst acting as rescuers.

Chapter 16: *"Marital rape"* (16–008), where in *R. v R.* the House of Lords, in examining the long history of the rule that a man could not be guilty of raping his wife, indicated a readiness to consider contemporary policy issues when stressing that "the common law is . . . capable of evolving in the light of changing social, economic and cultural developments".

STATUTORY INTERPRETATION

▶ ## 1. Introduction

▷ ### *(a) Legislation*

As a consequence of membership of the EU, both English and EU legislation are **1–059** sources of English law. Such legislation is not, however, uniform in nature and can take various forms.

The most common form of English legislation is statute law, whereby Bills introduced in Parliament become Acts of Parliament. Such Acts can be either Public General Acts, which affect the whole public, or Personal or Local Acts (sometimes known collectively as Private Acts), which affect only some particular person or body of persons or some particular locality. Acts of Parliament are sometimes known as primary legislation. It might be added, in passing, that the nomenclature, primary legislation, is also apposite to describe those Acts that fall within the devolved law making powers of the Northern Ireland Assembly and of the Scottish Parliament, whilst the Assembly Measures passed by the National Assembly of Wales might be categorised as quasi-primary legislation (see, the Government of Wales Act 2006, Part 3).

Primary legislation should be distinguished from another form of legislation, which is known variously as secondary or subordinate or (more usually) delegated legislation. Delegated legislation occurs where in Acts of Parliament a power is given to somebody else, often the Minister of a Government Department, to make law in the appropriate area. Whilst the Act will specify the area in which the law can be made and perhaps contain provisions as regards content, the details of the law will be left to the person to whom legislative power is delegated (subject to a requirement normally for such provisions to be laid before Parliament before becoming effective). These details will usually be published in the form of a statutory instrument. Whilst detailed provisions can be contained in a statutory instrument, such provisions can also be incorporated in the Act of Parliament itself. Indeed, detailed provisions, which purport to be comprehensive in coverage, specific in nature and formulated with a degree of precision, are a predominant characteristic of (the drafting style of) English legislation.

Delegated legislation introduced by the Minister of a Government Department needs to be carefully distinguished from Ministerial circulars, directives, letters or other similar official communications issued by Government Departments, which are not a form of legislation and have no legal effect. Such circulars may bind the persons to whom they are addressed to behave in a certain way, or may state what is considered to be the legal position on a particular matter, but they are not legally binding. What is stated to be the legal position in a circular, however, may in fact subsequently be held by a court to correctly represent the law, although equally it may be held not to do so. Similarly, Codes of Practice which are issued, but which do not form part of a statute or statutory instrument, have no legal effect. This is so even if they are issued pursuant to some statutory provision, as for instance, is the case under Pt VI of the Police and Criminal Evidence Act 1984, which refers to Codes of Practice which the Secretary of State (for the Home Department) is required to issue in relation to a number of matters (e.g. search of premises and seizure of property found).

Illustrative reference

1–060   See: Chapter 11: *"The regulation of abortion"* (11–008), where in *Royal College* the House of Lords held that a statement in a Department of Health and Social Security Circular, that nurses assisting in the carrying out of an abortion under the Abortion Act 1967 committed no offence, whilst of no legal effect, was a correct statement of the law.

EU legislation can take a number of forms, e.g. regulations and directives, and these contain further instructions as to the methods by which the broad objectives of the Treaties, which constitute the foundations of the EU, are to be realised and implemented. However, there is a fundamental difference in drafting style between EU legislation and English legislation. EU legislation is drafted in broad, abstract terms and is often expressed in the language of general principles. It is, in general, markedly less detailed than English primary or secondary legislation.

Illustrative reference

1–061   See: Chapter 14: *"Equal pay"* (14–002 and 14–003), for extracts from art.157 of the TFEU (ex 119 of the EC Treaty) and from Directive 2006/54, which may be contrasted with extracts from s.1 of the (English) Equal Pay Act 1970 (EPA 1970).

▷ *(b) Interpretation of legislation*

1–062   An important function of judges is to interpret legislative provisions and the majority of cases heard by appellate courts concern statutory interpretation (see, *Smith v Secretary of State for Work and Pensions* [2006] UKHL 35 at [79] per Lord Carswell). In interpreting statutes judges rarely articulate the rules or principles which they are using and this in turn makes it difficult, first, to extrapolate rules or principles from court decisions, and secondly, to define with any precision the parameters of those rules or principles. Courts, particularly in modern times, have frequently declared that, when interpreting (English) legislation, they are seeking to give effect to the intention of Parliament.

The words used in statutory provisions are taken to reflect Parliament's intention and courts have been primarily concerned with attributing a meaning to those words. A matter of crucial significance therefore is what should be taken into account by the courts in their search for the meaning of the words used. Should they confine themselves to a consideration of the words alone, or (because of the possible ambiguity of words) should they seek assistance from a range of external sources and, if so, which sources? The courts have used various means to assist in the process of ascribing a meaning to the words used, some of which have been described as "rules", and these "rules" and other aids to interpretation are considered in the following section.

These "rules" and aids are all directed to ascertaining the meaning of the words used, which remains the principal objective of the court. In achieving this objective, the primary focus is on the words used and in giving them a meaning which they are reasonably capable of bearing. This is a distinctive feature of the approach of English courts to the interpretation of legislation and a consequence of this is that, if, on the wording of the legislation, a particular situation appears not to be covered, many judges traditionally have been reluctant to engage in "gap filling" by reading in or implying words to bring that particular situation within the scope of the legislation. This is because, to do so could be regarded as beyond the scope of the proper judicial role and more akin to a "legislative" act on the part of the courts (see *Perrin v Northampton BC* [2007] EWCA Civ 1353 and *R. v Zafar* [2008] EWCA Crim 1323 for examples of the permissible limits of interpretation). Parliament itself, of course, may choose through legislation to fill a "gap" identified by a decision of the courts.

Illustrative reference

1-063

See: Chapter 8, *"The right to sue in the tort of private nuisance"* (8–004), where in *Hunter* Lord Hoffmann referred to the case of *Khorasandjian* as having identified a gap in the common law, in that it provided no remedy for harassment of persons, and this gap was subsequently filled by the enactment of the Protection from Harassment Act 1997.

The CJ, when interpreting EU law, has accorded itself the task of ascertaining and furthering the fundamental aims and purposes of the EU. These will not necessarily be articulated in or be apparent from the words used in provisions in EU legislation, since these often contain broad, general language and are expressed in terms of general principles.

When interpreting legislation, the CJ does not focus primarily on the words used but on the aims and purposes of the legislation. Although the initial focus may be on the words, the court is not simply seeking to give a meaning to the particular words used in accordance with any perceived legislative intention. Rather it is seeking to interpret the words in a way which will give effect to the CJ's view of the spirit and objectives of both the legislation and of the EU generally. Since the focus is on spirit and objectives, if a particular situation appears not to fall within the wording of a legislative provision but is considered to fall within its aims and purpose, CJ judges may engage in "gap filling" in order to bring that situation within the scope of the provision.

When interpreting legislation, the CJ, like English courts, has regard to a range of materials as aids to interpretation, e.g. provisions in the TFEU and general principles regarded as underlying EU law such as proportionality and respect for fundamental human rights. Taking into account these matters, the CJ uses a combination of various "techniques" when interpreting legislation, all of which are directed towards the end of ensuring that the legislative provision in question furthers the fundamental aims and purposes of the EU. The matters to which recourse may be had when interpreting legislation and the "techniques" of interpretation employed are considered in Chapter 4. English judges, as will be seen in that chapter (see 4–028—4–037), have increasingly followed a similar approach to CJ judges when interpreting EU legislation and also, in the case of some (English) judges at least, when interpreting English legislation to ensure compliance with EU law.

Further, English courts have an "interpretative obligation" under s.3(1) of the HRA 1998 to "read and give effect to" (i.e. interpret) both existing and future legislation in a manner that is compatible with (certain) rights under the European Convention on Human Rights, so far as it is possible to do so (see Chapter 5). Broadly, therefore, when discharging this obligation, courts are required to interpret the legislation, if possible, in a way which will give effect to the rights and freedoms which the Convention seeks to protect and courts may adopt any of a number of different techniques (on which, see 5–015) in order to do so. As with the interpretation of EU law, this may include reading in words and engaging in "gap filling". However, there are limits to the extent to which courts can go and, if it is not possible to interpret the legislation compatibly, a declaration of incompatibility may be made under s.4 of the Act. The onus is then on Parliament to decide whether any remedial action in the way of amending legislation should be taken.

1–064

Illustrative reference

See: Chapter 13: *"Succession Rights Under The Rent Act 1977"* (13–004), in *Ghaidan* where the House of Lords, in exercise of the interpretative obligation under s.3 of the HRA 1998, read words into para.2 of Sch.1 to the Rent Act 1977 in order to ensure its compatibility with arts 8 and 14 of the Convention.

▶ 2. Ascertaining the Intention of Parliament

▷ (a) Meaning of words

When courts are interpreting legislation, it is necessary to attribute a legal **1–065** meaning to the words as used in the particular legislation under consideration. In doing so, as stated above, courts often profess to be giving effect to the intention of Parliament. As Donaldson J. remarked in *Corocraft Ltd v Pan American Airways Inc* [1969] 1 Q.B. 622 at 638:

> "The duty of the courts is to ascertain and give effect to the will of Parliament as expressed in its enactments. In the performance of this duty the judges do not act as computers into which are fed the statutes and the rules for the construction of statutes and from whom issue forth the mathematically correct answer. The interpretation of statutes is a craft as much as a science and the judges, as craftsmen, select and apply the appropriate rules as the tools of their trade. They are not legislators, but finishers, refiners and polishers of legislation which comes to them in a state requiring varying degrees of further processing."

Thus, the process of interpretation is not a mechanical one and there will inevitably be uncertainty as to the way in which a court in any given case will attribute a meaning to the words used in the legislation. In some instances, a definition of words may be provided in the Act, to which the courts will have regard, but even where that is the case it will still be necessary for a court to give a meaning to the words used in the definition!

The words used in legislation may have one or more meanings. If a court is of the view that the words, in the context of the Act, can have only one meaning, then it will give effect to that meaning (and this will become the legal meaning of those words for the purposes of the particular statutory provision in question). This is unless it feels that this is clearly contrary to what the court perceives to be the intention of Parliament in enacting those words (a matter to which further reference is made below at 1–068) and subject to the court fulfilling, where appropriate, its respective interpretive obligations in respect of EU law or under the HRA 1998 (see below, 1-074). However, it is more likely that, because language is inherently imprecise and equivocal, even words which might be thought to have an obvious meaning can in fact have a number of different meanings. In such circumstances, in order to give a legal meaning to the words, the court will be obliged to decide which meaning to adopt.

The court may seek to resolve the ambiguity of meaning in a number of ways. How it is resolved will depend to a large extent on, to use the words of Donaldson J. above, which "tools of their trade" judges opt to select and apply. It is generally accepted that these "tools" include, inter alia, a number of so-called "rules", although these are not rules in the strict sense, as indicated by Lord Reid in *Maunsell v Olins* [1975] A.C. 373 at 382:

> ". . . rules of construction . . . are not rules in the ordinary sense of having some binding force. They are our servants not our masters. They are aids to construction . . . Not infrequently, one "rule" points in one direction, and another in a different direction. In each case we must look at all relevant circumstances and decide as a matter of judgment what weight to attach to any particular "rule"."

Moreover, it is rare for judges to state which rule(s) they are applying in a particular case and there is no hierarchy which governs their application. These rules are considered in outline below, in an order of presentation adopted purely as a matter of convenience, and, for further and more detailed treatment, reference may be made to Bennion, *Statutory Interpretation*, 5th edn (2008); and Cross, *Statutory Interpretation*, 3rd edn (1995).

▷ *(b) The traditional "rules"*

1–066 It is important to reiterate that, whichever rule(s) may be applied by the court, the basic task will be always be to give a meaning to the particular words used in the statute in question. Each "rule" is simply a means by which that may be achieved.

(i) The literal rule and the golden rule

1–067 The literal rule seeks to give the words a meaning which equates with their ordinary meaning in the context of the Act, whether that is a popularly understood meaning or a technical meaning. Cases abound with references by judges to the need, wherever possible, to give words their ordinary meaning. Judges may use their own understanding of the meaning of words or their understanding of how words are comprehended by the population generally or by particular groups of persons. Alternatively, or in addition, the courts may have recourse to a dictionary definition of words (as indeed they may do when considering the meaning of words which do not appear in statutory provisions) and may (or may not) refer to the particular dictionary from which the definition was taken, e.g. the *Oxford English Dictionary*.

Illustrative references

1–068 See: Chapter 8: *"The right to sue in the tort of private nuisance"* (8–006), where in *Hunter* Lord Cooke referred to the *Concise Oxford Dictionary* definition of "occupy".

Chapter 9: *"False imprisonment, "detention" and the Mental Health Act 1983"* (9–003), where in *Bournewood* Owen J. in the High Court referred to the *Oxford English Dictionary* definition of "detention".

Chapter 17: *"Appropriation in theft"* (17–008), where in *Gomez* Lord Lowry, when considering the meaning of the word "appropriates" in the Theft Act 1968, referred (without identifying any particular dictionary) to the "primary dictionary meaning" of the term.

However, although the courts will generally give words their ordinary meaning, they will not do so if it is perceived not to be in conformity with the intention of Parliament (see above, 1–065), and may not do so if the ordinary meaning is either inconsistent with EU law or incompatible with Convention rights under the HRA 1998 (see below, 1–074). In the former respect, such a departure from the ordinary meaning may be justified by adopting what has been described as the golden rule, a term which seems to have had its origins in judgments in the mid-19th century, in particular those of Parke B., later Lord Wensleydale (perhaps uncharitably described by Pollock C.B. as "the greatest legal pedant that I believe ever existed": Hanworth, *Lord Chief Baron Pollock* (Murray, 1929), p.198). In *Becke v Smith* (1836) 2 M. & W. 191 at 195, Parke B. stated:

"It is a very useful rule, in the construction of a statute, to adhere to the ordinary meaning of the words used, . . . unless that is at variance with the intention of the legislature, to be collected from the statute itself, or leads to any manifest absurdity or repugnance, in which case the language may be varied or modified, so as to avoid such inconvenience, but no further."

Similar remarks were made by his Lordship, as Lord Wensleydale, in *Grey v Pearson* (1857) 6 H.L.Cas. 61 at 106 and we find Lord Blackburn in *River Wear Commissioners v Adamson* (1877) 2 App. Cas. 743 at 764–765 stating:

"I believe that it is not disputed that what Lord Wensleydale used to call the golden rule is right, viz., that we are to take the whole statute together, and construe it all together, giving the words their ordinary signification, unless when so applied they produce an inconsistency, or an absurdity or inconvenience so great as to convince the Court that the intention could not have been to use them in their ordinary signification, and to justify the Court in putting on them some other signification, which, though less proper, is one which the Court thinks the words will bear."

Although other formulations of the golden rule have not been expressed in identical terms (e.g. by Bramwell B. in *Fowell v Tranter* (1864) 3 H. & C. 458 at 461), the common and overriding feature of all formulations appears to be that courts will, under the golden rule, depart from the ordinary meaning of words only when convinced that it is necessary to do so to give effect to the intention of Parliament. Therefore, in any given case, the question of whether a meaning is attributed to words other than their ordinary one will depend on first, whether in the court's view the words, if given their ordinary meaning, will give rise to an inconsistency, absurdity or inconvenience (or such other nomenclature as may be employed), and secondly, if so, whether such inconsistency, etc. is so great that the intention of Parliament could not have been to use them in their ordinary sense.

The case of *In re Levy* [1881] L.R. 17 Ch.D 746 provides an illustration. Here the Court of Appeal was concerned with the interpretation of s.23 of the Bankruptcy Act 1869, under which, although the property of a bankrupt person vested in his trustee in bankruptcy, the trustee could disclaim onerous or burdensome property. A literal interpretation of s.23 would enable a trustee to disclaim property even though this might affect the rights of third parties in the property, which the court felt could not have been intended by Parliament. The court accordingly held (at 751–752) that the section must be read as meaning that the property is to be disclaimed so as not to interfere with third party rights:

> "It was manifestly the intention of the Legislature that the trustee should not be compelled to acquire the bankrupt's property subject to . . . liabilities, and . . . when he finds that the property will not produce a surplus beyond the value of the liability affecting it, he may be able to disclaim it, and so get rid of the property and the liability together . . . This was the object of the Legislature, and . . . it never could have been their intention to confiscate the property of any man without urgent reason for doing so. A construction of the section which would lead to such a result might well be, to use the words of Lord Wensleydale [*in Grey v Pearson (1857) 6 H.L.Cas. 61 at 106*], described as an absurdity."

(ii) The mischief rule and the purposive approach

1–069 The mischief rule and the purposive approach are similarly seeking to establish the legal meaning of words used in a statutory provision, i.e. the meaning which Parliament intended the words to have. In the case of the literal rule and the golden rule, the emphasis is on the words themselves in their immediate statutory context as a means of establishing what meaning Parliament intended the words to have (see above, 1–065), but, in the case of the mischief rule and the purposive approach, the emphasis is on the underlying purpose of the legislation as a means of establishing what meaning Parliament intended the words to have.

The purposive approach recognises that the "real" intention of Parliament may not always be adequately expressed in the words themselves, because every situation cannot be foreseen and drafting provisions so that they cover every possibility is virtually impossible to achieve.

Historically, the common law and not legislation was the major source of law and legislation was concerned in large measure with supplementing the common law, either by restricting or enlarging its scope. Accordingly, when looking to legislative purpose, courts would essentially be having regard to the "mischief" or defect in the common law which the statute was seeking to remedy and could be said to be applying a "mischief rule" when seeking to ascertain what meaning Parliament intended the words to have. The classic statement of the "mischief rule" was that given by the Barons of the Court of Exchequer (see below, 2–017) in *Heydon's* case (1584) 3 Co. Rep. 7a:

"And it was resolved by them, that for the sure and true interpretation of statutes in general (be they penal or beneficial, restrictive or enlarging of the Common Law), four things are to be discerned and considered:

1st. What was the Common Law before the making of the Act,

2nd. What was the mischief and defect for which the Common Law did not provide,

3rd. What remedy the Parliament hath resolved and appointed to cure the disease of the commonwealth,

And 4th. The true reason of the remedy; and then the office of all the Judges is always to make such construction as shall suppress the mischief, and advance the remedy, and to suppress subtle inventions and evasions for continuance of the mischief, and *pro privato commodo*, and to add force and life to the cure and remedy, according to the true intent of the makers of the Act, *pro bono publico*."

There is no indication in the above statement that the mischief rule should have application only in cases where there is some ambiguity in the meaning of words used, although courts in some subsequent cases seem to have regarded the rule as being so limited.

In more recent times, however, legislation has become the major source of law and is no longer concerned primarily with supplementing the common law. Legislation may still be concerned, at least in part, with remedying specific "mischiefs," but much of it is concerned with seeking to promote in a general sense positive social, economic and/or political objectives. In consequence, courts, in considering legislative purpose as a means of establishing what meaning Parliament intended words to have, have not restricted themselves to a consideration of mischiefs to be remedied but have looked to the general legislative purpose. In looking to general legislative purpose as well as mischiefs, courts may be said to be adopting a "purposive approach" when determining what meaning Parliament intended the words to have.

For present purposes, the essential difference between the mischief rule and the purposive approach is encapsulated in the following extract from the Law Commission's Report on *The Interpretation of Statutes* (Law Com. No. 21, 1969):

"Even for the lawyer the expression [*the mischief rule*] is unsatisfactory. It tends to suggest that legislation is only designed to deal with an evil and not to further a positive social purpose. Furthermore, it seems too narrow to speak of the "mischief of the statute". The general legislative purpose underlying a provision may emerge from a series of statutes dealing with the same subject matter . . . or from other indications of that purpose [afforded by information relating to legal, social, economic and other aspects of society of which a judge is able to take judicial notice]."

Illustrative references

1–070

See: Chapter 9: *"False imprisonment, "detention" and the Mental Health Act 1983"* (9–010), where in *Bournewood* Lord Goff, considering a Royal Commission Report on which legislation was subsequently based, referred to "a central recommendation of the . . . Commission and the mischief which it was designed to cure".

Chapter 14: *"Equal pay"* (14–017), where in *Pickstone* Nicholls L.J. in the Court of Appeal referred to "the mischief which the introduction of para (c) into s1(2)(c) of the Equal Pay Act 1970 was intended to cure"; and (14–021) where the House of Lords focused on the purpose of s.1(2)(c) which, as its legislative background demonstrated, was to ensure that the provisions of the EPA 1970 complied with EU law.

In order to give a meaning to words in accordance with the above rules, it may be necessary for courts to read a word (or words) into a legislative provision if this is thought to be necessary to give effect to Parliament's intention in relation to other words used in the provision. When judges adopt any of the traditional "rules", words are likely to be read into a provision only in limited circumstances, although there are well-established instances where this might be done, e.g. reading in a word requiring a mental element for a criminal offence, such as "knowingly", since there is a presumption that statutes creating criminal offences require a blameworthy state of mind (mens rea). This presumption is one of the aids to ascertaining meaning when interpreting statutes (see below, 1–090). However, whilst courts might read words into statutes, they may equally decline to do so, perhaps, in the latter respect, because this could be seen as "legislating" rather than "interpreting" (see above, 1–062). Conversely, courts might read out a word (or words) if considered surplusage and not capable of being given any satisfactory meaning.

Illustrative references

1–071

See: Chapter 11: *"The Regulation of Abortion"* (11–007), where in *Royal College* Sir George Baker in the Court of Appeal and (11–014) Lords Wilberforce and Edmund-Davies in the House of Lords declined to read in the words "by a registered medical practitioner" into s.1(1) of the Abortion Act 1967.

Chapter 16 *"Marital rape"* (16–007), where in *R. v R.* the House of Lords considered that no satisfactory meaning could be ascribed to the word "unlawful" in s.19 of the Sexual Offences Act 1956 and effectively read the word out of the section.

Chapter 17: *"Appropriation in theft"* (17–002), where in *Lawrence* the House of Lords declined to read the words "without the consent of the owner" into the definition of theft in s.1(1) of the Theft Act 1968, taking the view that their omission was not inadvertent and that Parliament had intended to relieve the prosecution of the burden of establishing that an appropriation was without the owner's consent; and (17–017), where in *Hinks* the House of Lords declined to read in the word "unlawfully" prior to the word "appropriates" in s.1(1) of the Theft Act 1968.

It is important to appreciate that any of the above rules—the literal rule, the golden rule, the mischief rule and the purposive approach—and reading words into or out of a statute may be used by courts to ascertain what meaning Parliament intended the words to have in a particular statutory provision. It will not be possible, however, to predict which rule or approach will be adopted in any particular case. As Evans L.J. remarked, delivering the judgment of the Court of Appeal in *R. v Fellows and Arnold* [1997] 2 All E.R. 548 at 554, "whilst the court's decision in a particular case may indicate what can be described as a 'purposive' as distinct from a 'literal' approach, it would be wrong in our view to say that one or other of these two methods should be pre-determined or is correct".

Finally, it should be mentioned that, irrespective of the rule or approach adopted, in seeking to give the words a meaning which Parliament intended them to have, the courts may attribute a meaning to the words as they would be understood at the time the legislation was passed or which reflects any recurrent theme felt to be present initially in the legislation and any subsequent amendments of it.

Illustrative reference

1–072

See: Chapter 13: *"Succession Rights Under The Rent Act 1977"* (13–004), where in *Ghaidan* Lord Millett felt that the language of para.2 of Sch.1 to the Rent Act 1977 and its legislative history showed that a recurrent theme and the essential feature of the relationship which Parliament had in contemplation was an open relationship between persons of the opposite sex and not the same sex.

However, this does not mean that words cannot be taken to encompass matters which could not have been within the contemplation of Parliament at the time of enacting the legislation. Taking account of subsequent changes and developments when interpreting legislation is sometimes described as "ambulatory" interpretation and is a recognised technique of statutory interpretation. As Lord Steyn stated in *R. v Ireland* [1998] A.C. 147 at 158:

> "Bearing in mind that statutes are usually intended to operate for many years it would be most inconvenient if courts could never rely in difficult cases on the current meaning of statutes. Recognising the problem Lord Thring, the great Victorian draftsman of the second half of the last century, exhorted draftsmen to draft so that "An Act of Parliament should be deemed to be always speaking." . . . In cases where the problem arises it is a matter of interpretation whether a court must search for the historical or original meaning of a statute or whether it is free to apply the current meaning of the statute to present day conditions. Statutes dealing with a particular grievance or problem may sometimes require to be historically interpreted. But the drafting technique of Lord Thring and his successors have [*sic*] brought about the situation that statutes will generally be found to be of the "always speaking" variety: see *Royal College of Nursing of the United Kingdom v. Department of Health and Social Security* [1981] A.C. 800 for an example of an "always speaking" construction in the House of Lords."

Thus, for instance, medical or technological developments which had not taken place when the legislation was introduced, as occurred in the *Royal College* case to which Lord Steyn referred (and on which see Chapter 11), might nevertheless be held to fall within the meaning of the words used. But whilst the meaning of the words might extend to matters not contemplated by Parliament at the time, the meaning itself will remain unchanged, as Lord Bingham recognised in *R. v G* [2003] 4 All E.R. 765 (at [29]): "Since a statute is always speaking, the context or application of a statutory expression may change over time, but the meaning of the expression itself cannot change".

Illustrative reference

1-073

See: Chapter 10: *"Video cassettes as obscene articles"* (10–003), where in *Attorney General's Reference (No. 5 of 1980)* the Court of Appeal interpreted words in s.1(2) of the Obscene Publications Act 1959 "in the ways in which they would have been understood by ordinary literate persons at the material time, namely in 1959" and held that, even if video cassettes had not been within Parliament's contemplation in 1959 (which the court doubted), they fell within the meaning of the words used.

(iii) Departures from the traditional "rules"

1-074 In recent years, the courts have deviated from the traditional "rules" first, when interpreting EU and (sometimes) English legislation, and, secondly, when fulfilling their "interpretative obligation" under s.3(1) of the HRA 1998. In relation to the former, the courts have shown an increasing tendency to adopt techniques of interpretation employed by the CJ which focus on aims and purposes (see above, 1–063 and Chapter 4, 4–028—4–037), and there has been a move away from focusing on the words used and giving them a meaning which they might ordinarily be regarded as bearing. In some cases, it may not be possible to interpret EU legislation, and to interpret English legislation to ensure that it complies with EU law, using the traditional "rules". These "rules" may need to be eschewed, therefore, in favour of "rules" adopted by the CJ which focus on giving effect to the underlying aims of the legislative provisions rather than on the particular words used. This may require courts to read words into or "read down" legislative provisions by narrowing the scope of provisions in order to ensure compliance. Although words might to a limited extent be read into legislative provisions under the traditional "rules" (see above, 1–070), there has been an increasing willingness over the years on the part of the courts to do so, along with "reading down" legislative provisions to narrow their application.

Secondly, under the HRA 1998, courts are required, under s.3(1), to "read and give effect to" (i.e. interpret) all legislation, both existing and future, in a way which is compatible with (certain) rights under the European Convention on Human Rights, so far as it is possible to do so (see Chapter 5). This is the "interpretative obligation" referred to above (see above, 1–063). Again, it may not be possible to interpret either the Convention, or English legislation to ensure that it is compatible with the Convention, using the traditional "rules" and so other "rules", such as those adopted by the European Court of Human Rights (the Strasbourg Court), which are similar to those used by the CJ, may be employed. A compatible interpretation may not, of course, be possible in all cases, even employing such techniques. If this is the case, courts (or tribunals) are not required to produce an implausible or incredible meaning, for s.3(1) requires a compatible interpretation only "so far as it is possible to do so". Under s.3(2), failure to achieve a compatible interpretation does not invalidate primary legislation, although delegated (secondary) legislation does become invalid and ineffective unless the primary legislation under which it is made prevents removal of the incompatibility.

Where a compatible interpretation cannot be achieved, it is, under s.4, open to certain courts to issue a declaration of incompatibility. Such a declaration should identify the incompatibility in sufficient detail to enable the Government Minister/ Secretary of State to determine what amending legislation in the form of a remedial order under s.10 is necessary in order to achieve compatibility (see *R. (on the application of Wright) v Secretary of State for Health* [2007] EWCA Civ 999). These matters, including the exercise by the courts of their "interpretative obligation" under s.3(1), are considered in detail in Chapter 5.

To produce an interpretation consistent with EU law or one that is compatible with Convention rights, courts may have to examine a range of possible meanings before they can adopt a meaning that is consistent or compatible. There will not be one legal meaning that the words are capable of bearing, but rather a range of meanings, and whichever meaning is adopted will become the legal meaning of the words in the particular legislation under consideration. Further, the meaning adopted will remain the legal meaning only in so far it continues to be consistent with EU law or compatible with Convention rights. EU law and Convention rights are not static and inflexible, but dynamic and developmental, and it may be that in time the meaning adopted as the legal meaning ceases to be consistent or compatible. If this is the case, the legal meaning will require reassessment and another, different, meaning may need to be adopted as the legal meaning which achieves consistency or compatibility.

▷ *(b) Aids to ascertaining meaning*

1–075 Courts, when attributing a meaning to the words of a particular statutory provision, can take into account not only certain intrinsic material within the statute itself but also certain extrinsic material outside the statute. Intrinsic material might include, e.g. other provisions in the statute and extrinsic material might include Explanatory Notes which, in more recent years, have accompanied the passage of legislation. Explanatory Notes, although not part of the legislation itself, are intended to make the legislation more comprehensible and, as will be seen, have been used by courts as an aid to ascertaining the meaning of the legislation (see below, 1–079).

(i) Intrinsic material

1–076 When examining the meaning of words contained in any particular part of a statute, the court can look at the whole of the statute. As Lord Reid remarked in *IRC v Hinchy* [1960] A.C. 748 at 766:

> "It is no doubt true that every Act should be read as a whole, but that is, I think, because one assumes that in drafting one clause of a Bill the draftsman had in mind the language and substance of other clauses, and attributes to Parliament a comprehension of the whole Act."

Thus, for example, regard may be had to the wording of other subsections within the same section or other sections in the statute which, by way of comparison or contrast, may cast light on the meaning of words used in the particular statutory provision in question.

The court may also look at what have traditionally been marginal notes (or sidenotes) to statutory provisions in an Act, so called because they have appeared as a note in the margin to (or at the side of) the provision, although notes no longer appear in this form. Following a change in practice in 2001 by the Parliamentary Counsel Office, they now appear in bold type as headings to each provision in the statute.

Historically, there has been some ambivalence on the part of the courts as to whether such notes, which unlike the provisions themselves are not subject to Parliamentary amendment, can be considered as an aid to interpreting a statute.

Views have sometimes been expressed that they should not (e.g. by Phillimore L.J. in *Woking Urban District (Basingstoke Canal) Act 1911 Re* [1914] 1 Ch. 300 at 322), although, as can be seen in the **Illustrative references** below, courts have on occasions used such notes as an aid to construction. That such notes can be taken into account was acknowledged in *R. v Montila* [2005] 1 All E.R. 113 where the House of Lords disapproved earlier statements to the contrary, which it felt (at [33]) were "out of keeping with the modern approach to the interpretation of statutes". The House observed (at [34]) that account must be taken of the fact that these components were included "not for debate but for ease of reference", indicating that "less weight can be attached to them than to the parts of the Act that are open for consideration and debate in Parliament", but "they ought to be open to consideration as part of the enactment when it reaches the statute book". The House went on to state (at [35–36]) that headings and sidenotes, like Explanatory Notes (on which, see below, 1–079) could be taken into account:

> "It has become common practice for their Lordships to ask to be shown the explanatory notes when issues are raised about the meaning of words used in an enactment. The headings and sidenotes are as much part of the contextual scene as these materials, and there is no logical reason why they should be treated differently."

Other parts of a statute may also be admissible as an aid to interpretation, such as the long title (*Fielding v Morley Corporation* [1899] 1 Ch. 1 at 3) or the preamble (*Attorney General v Prince Ernest of Hanover* [1957] A.C. 460). The only part of a statute that it seems may not be considered is the short title, which is given to the Act solely for the purpose of reference and identification, not description. In the view of Lord Moulton in *Vacher & Sons Ltd v London Society of Compositors* [1913] A.C. 107 at 128, it is a "statutory nickname" to obviate the necessity of always referring to the Act under its full and descriptive title, and it is not legitimate to use it to ascertain the scope of the Act.

Illustrative references

1–077

See: Chapter 9: *"False imprisonment, "detention" and the Mental Health Act 1983"* (9–007 and 9–010), where in *Bournewood* (i) the Court of Appeal, but not Lord Goff in the House of Lords, placed reliance upon s.131(2) of the Mental Health Act 1983 when interpreting s.131(1) of the Act; and (ii) (9–010) Lord Steyn in the House of Lords referred to the marginal note (or sidenote) to s.131 of the Mental Health Act 1983 when considering the meaning of that section.

Chapter 11: *"The regulation of abortion"* (11–011), where in *Royal College* in the House of Lords (i) Lord Roskill compared the terminology of s.1(1) of the Abortion Act 1967, where the phrase "a pregnancy is terminated" is used, with the phrase "treatment for the termination of pregnancy" in other sections of the same Act; (ii) (11–013) Lord Edmund-Davies referred to the preamble to the Act; (iii) (11–008) Lord Keith made use of the marginal note (or sidenote) to s.1(1) when considering the meaning of the same phrase in the section; (iv) (11–010) Lords Diplock and Roskill referred to the long title to the Act; and (v) (11–007) in the Court of Appeal Sir George Baker referred both to the marginal note (or sidenote) to s.1(1) and to the long title to the Act.

Chapter 17: "*Appropriation in theft*" (17–008), where in *Gomez* Lord Lowry referred to ss.1 to 6 of the Theft Act 1968 when considering the meaning of "appropriates" in s.1(1) of the Theft Act 1968; and (17–017) where in *Hinks* Lord Hobhouse made similar reference to these sections and focused on the importance of looking at the statute as a whole.

When examining the meaning of words contained in delegated legislation, the court can (presumably) look similarly at the whole of the statutory instrument containing the provisions and (presumably) the statute itself under which the delegated legislation was made. However, unlike statutes, there are no other parts, such as long titles and preambles, in statutory instruments which may act as an aid to construction. Although there is frequently an Explanatory Note at the end of the instrument, the Note expressly provides that this is not part of the instrument itself. The Note may, however, be considered as extrinsic material (see below, 1–079) aiding implementation.

(ii) Extrinsic material

1–078 Extrinsic material, which the courts have taken into account, includes:

(1) Explanatory Notes

1–079 Delegated legislation contained in a statutory instrument has for some years had an Explanatory Note appended at the end, which does not form part of the statutory instrument (see above, 1–077), and the courts have shown a willingness to take this into account when ascertaining meaning. As Lord Hope (with whose judgment Lords Cooke, Millett and Steyn expressed agreement) stated in *Coventry and Solihull Waste Disposal Co Ltd v Russell* [1999] 1 W.L.R. 2093 at 2103:

> "In my opinion an explanatory note may be referred to as an aid to con-struction where the statutory instrument to which it is attached is ambiguous. In *Pickstone v Freemans Plc* [1989] A.C. 66, 127 Lord Oliver of Aylmerston said that the explanatory note attached to the statutory instrument, although it was not of course part of the instrument, could be used to identify the mischief it was attempting to remedy."

Courts have followed the same approach in respect of Explanatory Notes which have been issued to accompany primary legislation. Such Notes, prepared by the relevant Government Department under whose remit the legislation falls, have been published for all primary legislation enacted since November 24, 1998.

They are published to accompany the legislation, both when the provisions are in Bill form and when they become an Act of Parliament. (When a Bill is drafted and introduced into one House of Parliament, Explanatory Notes are published, as a separate document, explaining why it is being introduced and the purpose(s) of its clauses; new Explanatory Notes are published when the Bill begins its passage through the other House of Parliament; and, when the Bill receives the Royal Assent, another set of Explanatory Notes is issued with the Act of Parliament.) The Explanatory Notes are to facilitate understanding of the legislation but, as with delegated legislation, do not form part of the Act. This is made clear from the Introduction section in the Explanatory Notes, a typical example of which is set out below:

> "**INTRODUCTION**
>
> 1. These explanatory notes relate to the Youth Justice and Criminal Evidence Act 1999. They have been prepared by the Home Office in order to assist the reader in understanding the Act. They do not form part of the Act and have not been endorsed by Parliament.
> 2. The notes need to be read in conjunction with the Act. They are not, and are not meant to be, a comprehensive description of the Act. So where a section or part of a section does not seem to require any explanation or comment, none is given."

Although intended to assist the "reader" of the Act in understanding it, the courts have recognised that judges can have recourse to them when interpreting statutes. In *Westminster City Council v National Asylum Support Service* [2002] UKHL 38 at [5] Lord Steyn in the House of Lords stated, obiter: "Insofar as the Explanatory Notes cast light on the objective setting or contextual scene of the statute, and the mischief at which it is aimed, such materials are . . . admissible aids to construction . . .", although his Lordship went on to say at [6]: "What is impermissible is to treat the wishes and desires of the Government about the scope of the statutory language as reflecting the will of Parliament. The aims of the Government in respect of the meaning of clauses as revealed in Explanatory Notes cannot be attributed to Parliament. The object is to see what is the intention expressed by the words enacted". Although no other members of the House in this case made reference to the use of Explanatory Notes, the Court of Appeal in *R. (on the application of the Confederation of Passenger Transport UK) v Humber Bridge Board* [2004] 2 W.L.R. 98, when having regard to an Explanatory Note to a statutory instrument to decide whether any words had been omitted from the instrument by mistake, stated (per Clarke L.J. at [50]) that this was "entirely consistent" with the views expressed by Lord Steyn in the above case (see also, Lord Steyn's extra-judicial observations about the use of Explanatory Notes in *"Pepper v Hart*; A Re-examination" (2001) 21 O.J.L.S. 59, 71–72). Indeed, the House of Lords in *R. v Montila* [2005] 1 All E.R. 113 has recognised (at [35]) that it "has become common practice for their Lordships to ask to be shown the explanatory notes when issues are raised about the meaning of words used in an enactment" and these should be considered "part of the contextual scene" (see above, 1–076).

(2) Other statutory provisions

1-080 When ascertaining the meaning of words, courts may have regard to earlier statutory provisions in which the words in question appear, for these earlier provisions and judicial decisions on their interpretation may provide guidance on the meaning of the words. These statutory provisions may be earlier ones dealing with the same subject-matter or (less likely) earlier statutory provisions in a different area in which the same words appear.

Courts are not, however, obliged to follow judicial decisions interpreting words which appear in earlier statutory provisions. This is so whether the same words appear in an earlier statute dealing with a different area (*Carter v Bradbeer* [1975] 3 All E.R. 158 at 161) or where the words appear in an earlier statute dealing with the same subject-matter, although in the latter instance judicial decisions interpreting the words will generally be followed (*Royal Crown Derby Porcelain Co Ltd v Raymond Russell* [1949] 2 K.B. 417 at 429). Such decisions nevertheless, strictly, do not form binding precedents and courts may choose not to follow them. Whilst it will normally be earlier provisions in which the words appear to which courts will have regard, courts are not restricted to this and may also consider later statutory provisions in which the words appear, along with judicial decisions on their interpretation.

Further, courts are not confined to examining statutory provisions in which the particular words in question appear. Similar or related words which appear in other earlier statutory provisions, which may contrast with or clarify the meaning of the particular words in question, may be taken into account and considered as providing assistance in ascertaining the meaning of those words. This may occur in cases in which a court has to interpret a provision in a statute, e.g. the Income Tax (Trading and Other Income) Act 2005 which is a rewrite of earlier legislation. Such rewritten tax legislation is based on the work of the Tax Law Rewrite Project, which was set up in the mid 1990s with a view to rewriting the UK's primary direct tax legislation in clearer and easier to use language but without *changing the law* (other than in minor respects).

In addition, courts can have regard to statutory provisions in delegated (secondary) legislation made under primary legislation in order to interpret the meaning of the primary legislation itself. Thus in *British Amusement Catering Trades Association v Westminster CC* [1988] 1 All E.R. 740 the House of Lords, when deciding that the expression "exhibition of moving pictures" in s.1(3) of the Cinematograph Act 1909 denoted the showing of moving pictures to an audience rather than a display of moving objects on a (video) screen, had regard to the Cinematograph (Safety) Regulations 1955 (SI 1955/1129) made under that Act. Lord Griffiths stated (at 745):

". . . these regulations are inapt to cover amusement arcades and other places where video games are normally located. The regulations only make sense if the 'cinematograph exhibitions' referred to in the regulations are understood in the sense of a show to an audience for example, there are frequent references to the auditorium, of which the definition in the Shorter Oxford English Dictionary is: 'The part of a public building occupied by the audience . . .' The regulations are dealing with the precautions necessary to protect an audience at a film show. Parliament having used the phrase 'cinematograph exhibition' in the sense of a film show in the regulations must in my view have intended to use the phrase in the same sense in the . . . Act in which it adopted the regulations."

Illustrative references

1–081

See: Chapter 9: *"False imprisonment, "detention" and the Mental Health Act 1983"* (9–007 and 9–010), where in *Bournewood* both the Court of Appeal and the House of Lords, when interpreting s.131(1) of the Mental Health Act 1983, considered the earlier identically-worded provision in s.5(1) of the Mental Health Act 1959.

Chapter 11: *"The regulation of abortion"* (11–002), where in *Bourne* Macnaughten J. referred to the words "acting in good faith for the purpose of preserving the mother's life" in the Infant Life (Preservation) Act 1929 (which created the offence of child destruction) to assist in the interpretation of the word "unlawful" in s.58 of the Offences Against the Person Act 1861 (under which abortion was an offence); and (11–007 and 11–008) where in *Royal College* Lord Denning, M.R. and Sir George Baker in the Court of Appeal, and Lord Wilberforce in the House of Lords, with a view to determining the meaning of the words used in s.1(1) of the Abortion Act 1967 ("terminated by a registered medical practitioner"), contrasted those words with the words used in other earlier and later statutes (e.g. "by a registered medical practitioner or by a person acting in accordance with the directions of any such practitioner").

Chapter 16: *"Marital rape"* (16–008), where in *R. v R.* the House of Lords examined the meaning of the word "unlawful" in s.19 of the Sexual Offences Act 1956, as considered in *R. v Chapman*, when considering what meaning should be given to the same word in s.1(1) of the Sexual Offences (Amendment) Act 1976.

(3) Common law

Courts may also have regard to established and relevant common law principles **1–082** when attributing a meaning to the words used in a statutory provision.

1–083

Illustrative reference

See: Chapter 11: *"The regulation of abortion"* (11–002), where in *Bourne* Macnaughten J., when considering whether there may be justification for the act of abortion under s.58 of the Offences Against the Person Act 1861 so as not to constitute a crime, referred to the fact that in cases of homicide (under the common law) there may be justification for the act which prevents the act constituting a crime.

(4) Parliamentary materials

1–084 Until 1993, it was not generally permissible to look at Parliamentary debates and other Parliamentary materials when attributing a meaning to the words used in a statutory provision; a rule based principally on constitutional and on practical grounds.

In the former respect, the exclusionary rule, as it was known, was justified on two grounds. First, it was opined that it was contrary to principle for the courts to accept what might be said in Parliament as to the intended meaning of a particular provision in an Act as to do so would nullify the judicial role in the interpretative process (see, for example, Lord Wilberforce in *Black-Clawson Ltd v Papierwerke Waldhof-Aschaffenburg A.G.* [1975] A.C. 591, at 629–630). Secondly, a further constitutional justification for the exclusionary rule was based on the relationship between the courts and Parliament and, in particular, on the need for comity, or mutual respect, between the courts and the legislature. As Lord Hailsham of St Marylebone L.C. observed in the course of his Hamlyn Lectures (*Hamlyn Revisited: The British Legal System Today*) in 1983:

> "From the constitutional viewpoint, I do not think it appropriate with a view to the comity between the different branches of Government, and the independence of each from the other, that the actual proceedings in Parliament should be the subject of discussion (and thereby inevitably criticism) in the courts both from the Bench and by counsel. . . [*It*] would be constitutionally most undesirable."

The perceived practical difficulties associated with permitting recourse to parliamentary material as an aid to statutory interpretation focused on the increased time, effort and expense to which a practitioner might be put, to the lack of familiarity of lawyers with parliamentary procedure and to the consequent increase in the costs of litigation. Further, as Lord Reid pointed out in *Beswick v Beswick* [1968] A.C. 58 at 74:

> "For purely practical reasons we do not permit debates in either House to be cited: it would greatly add to the time and expense involved in preparing cases involving the construction of a statute if counsel were expected to read all the debates in Hansard, and would often be impracticable for counsel to get

access to at least the older reports of debates in select committees of the House of Commons; moreover, in a very large proportion of cases such a search, even if practicable, would throw no light on the question before the court."

However, notwithstanding these justifications for the exclusionary rule, the House of Lords, by a 6–1 majority (Lord Mackay of Clashfern L.C. dissenting), decided in *Pepper v Hart* [1993] 1 All E.R. 42 (*Pepper*), that whilst the exclusionary rule should not be abandoned it might be relaxed to enable limited recourse to Parliamentary materials as an aid to statutory interpretation in the following circumstances:

(a) the legislation is ambiguous or obscure or its literal meaning leads to an absurdity;
(b) the material relied on consists of one or more statements by a Minister or other promoter of the Bill together, if necessary, with such other parliamentary material as was necessary to understand such statements and their effect; and
(c) the statements relied upon are clear.

Various aspects of each of these three conditions have been explored in subsequent cases, and it is clear that some issues are problematic, for example, there is a degree of uncertainty surrounding the question of when a statutory provision may be regarded as ambiguous (as to which, see the differing opinions expressed by Lord Nicholls and Lord Hutton in *R. (on the application of Spath Holme Ltd) v Secretary of State for the Environment, Transport and the Regions* [2001] 2 A.C. 349). Moreover, it is also apparent that judges have in a manner that was not necessarily anticipated had recourse to Parliamentary materials to confirm their understanding of a statutory provision even though the above conditions may not have been met (see, for example, *Warwickshire CC v Johnson* [1993] 1 All E.R. 299 and *Chief Adjudication Officer v Foster* [1993] 1 All E.R. 705).

The relaxation of the exclusionary rule has also led to a division of opinion between senior members of the judiciary as to its legitimacy and/or utility (compare, in this respect, the contrasting extra-judicially expressed views of Lord Steyn in *"Pepper v Hart*: A Re-examination" (2001) O.J.L.S. 59 and Lord Cooke in "The Road Ahead for the Common Law" (2004) 53 I.C.L.Q. 273).

Finally, there are three cases after *Pepper* which, notwithstanding the relaxation of the exclusionary rule in *Pepper*, may also have an important bearing on the circumstances in which recourse may be had for interpretative purposes to parliamentary materials in *Hansard*. First, in *Three Rivers DC v Bank of England (No. 2)* [1996] 2 All E.R. 363 Clark J. suggested that a more flexible approach to the admissibility of parliamentary material than that permitted by *Pepper* might be required where a court is attempting to interpret a statute purposively and consistently with EU law or where the purpose of the statute is to introduce into English law the provisions of an international convention or EU Directive. Secondly, in *Thoburn v Sunderland CC* [2003] Q.B. 151, Laws L.J., sitting in the Divisional

Court (QBD), stated that there should be *no* recourse to parliamentary materials in *Hansard* pursuant to *Pepper* in cases where a court is required to construe a statutory provision that purports to repeal or amend, significantly, a "constitutional statute", e.g. the European Communities Act 1972 (see below, Chapters 3 and 4). In such instances, the importance attributed to the provisions of "constitutional" statutes, as opposed to "ordinary" statutes, meant that repeal or amendment could only be brought about by *unambiguous* words. Thirdly, in *Wilson v First County Trust Ltd (No. 2)* [2003] 4 All E.R. 97, the House of Lords determined that in deciding whether a statutory provision may be regarded as compatible with Convention rights (see below, Chapter 5) a court may look at parliamentary material only to a "limited extent", i.e. to the extent that it is background information "tending to show, for instance, the likely practical impact of the statutory measure and why the course adopted by the legislature is or is not appropriate" (per Lord Nicholls at 118) and where this leads to a court being in a better position to understand the statutory provision.

Illustrative references

1–085

See: Chapter 9: *"False imprisonment, "detention" and the Mental Health Act 1983"* (9–010), where in *Bournewood* Lord Goff in the House of Lords had regard to ministerial statements made in Parliament when interpreting s.131 of the Mental Health Act 1983.

Chapter 14: *"Equal pay"* (14–021), where in *Pickstone* Lord Keith in the House of Lords, when construing s.1(2)(c) of the EPA 1970, which had been incorporated into that Act by the Equal Pay (Amendments) Regulations 1983, stated that "I consider it to be entirely legitimate for the purpose of ascertaining the intention of Parliament to take into account the terms in which the draft [of the regulations] was presented by the responsible Minister" in view of the fact that "the draft regulations were not subject to the [usual] parliamentary process of consideration and amendment", thereby recognising a pre-*Pepper v Hart* exception to the exclusionary rule.

Chapter 16: *"Marital rape"* (16–011), where in *R. v Graham L* Pill L.J. in the Court of Appeal had regard to ministerial statements made in Parliament when deciding whether the House of Lords in *R. v R.* had acted ultra vires and exceeded its powers by deciding to change the law in its judicial capacity when Parliament in its legislative capacity had decided against doing so.

(5) Pre-Parliamentary publications

1–086 Courts may have recourse to official publications that precede and form the basis for legislation, e.g. Government White Papers and reports of bodies such as Royal Commissions, the Law Commission and the Criminal Law Revision Committee, when attributing a meaning to the words used in a statutory provision. The precise extent to which pre-Parliamentary publications might be taken into account when interpreting a statutory provision was subject to differing views in the House of Lords in *Black-Clawson Ltd v Papierwerke Waldhof-Aschaffenburg SG* [1975] A.C. 591 (to which further reference is made in Chapter 17, 17–008).

Illustrative references

1-087

See: Chapter 9: *"False imprisonment, "detention" and the Mental Health Act 1983"* (9–007 and 9–010), where in *Bournewood* both the Court of Appeal and the House of Lords had regard to Government White Papers when interpreting s.131 of the Mental Health Act 1983.

Chapter 17: *"Appropriation in theft"* (17–008), where in *Gomez* Lord Lowry, when considering the meaning of "appropriates" in s.1(1) of the Theft Act 1968, had regard to the Criminal Law Revision Committee's Eighth Report and the draft Bill attached to it which was passed by Parliament, substantially unchanged, as the Theft Act 1968; (17–008) where in *Gomez* Lord Keith declined to have regard to this Report; and (17–017) where in *Hinks* the Court of Appeal similarly declined to have regard to it.

(6) International treaties and conventions

International treaties and conventions (ITCs), under which obligations are entered **1-088** into by governments, do not become part of English law unless Parliament so enacts. Nevertheless, when not part of English law, courts may have recourse to them when attributing a meaning to the words used in a statutory provision.

As will be seen, there is a presumption that, when enacting legislation, Parliament intends the legislation to comply with the UK's obligations under ITCs, even if the legislation was not specifically enacted to give effect to those obligations (see below, 1–090). Accordingly, where there is ambiguity or uncertainty as to the meaning of words in a statutory provision, it is permissible to have regard to ITCs to resolve the ambiguity or uncertainty in a way which is consistent with the UK's obligations. By doing so, a meaning can be attributed to the words which accords with what is perceived to be the intention of Parliament. As Diplock L.J. has observed in *Salomon v Commissioners of Customs and Excise* [1966] 3 All E.R. 871 at 875:

"If the terms of the legislation are not clear . . . but are reasonably capable of more than one meaning, the Treaty itself becomes relevant, for there is a prima facie presumption that Parliament does not intend to act in breach of international law, including therein specific treaty obligations; and if one of the meanings which can reasonably be ascribed to the legislation is consonant with the treaty obligations and another or others are not, the meaning which is consonant is to be preferred. Thus, in case of lack of clarity in the words used in the legislation, the terms of the treaty are relevant to enable the court to

> make its choice between the possible meanings of these words by applying this presumption."

As well as having regard to ITCs themselves, courts can consider preparatory materials leading up to them (*travaux préparatoires*), since in most jurisdictions preparatory materials are admissible in evidence, even when interpreting domestic legislation, and it is desirable for courts in different countries to achieve uniformity in their approach to the same issues (*Fothergill v Monarch Airlines* [1978] 1 Q.B. 108). Indeed, with regard to achieving uniformity of approach, where English legislation has been specifically enacted to give effect to obligations under ITCs, English courts may be prepared to construe the statutory provisions in a manner, to use the words of Lord Wilberforce in *James Buchanan & Co Ltd v Babco Forwarding & Shipping (UK) Ltd* [1977] 3 All E.R. 1048 at 1052, "unconstrained by technical rules of English law, or by English legal precedent". Regard can be had to *travaux préparatoires* only where material is publicly available and clearly points to a definitive intention (see *Laroche v Spirit of Adventure (UK) Ltd* [2009] EWCA Civ 12).

Instances of ITCs to which reference has been made earlier are the EC Treaty ((now the TFEU) and the European Convention on Human Rights. The former, which is part of EU law, was incorporated into and become part of English law by the ECA 1972. The latter has not been incorporated, although "further effect" (i.e. greater protection) is to be given to rights and freedoms guaranteed under the Convention following the passage of the HRA 1998. The TFEU and the Convention, and their impact, are considered in Chapters 4 and 5 respectively.

(iii) Presumptions of form and substance

1–089   There are several presumptions to which courts may have recourse when attributing a meaning to the words used in a statutory provision. Sometimes, presumptions may be accorded considerable weight, although on other occasions courts may pay little or no regard to them. It is not possible to predict when a court will have recourse to presumptions and, when it does, the extent to which it may be influenced by them in reaching its decision as to the meaning of the words used. Presumptions fall broadly into two categories, ones relating to matters of form such as language and syntax, and ones relating to the substance of legal rules.

Examples of presumptions relating to matters of form include a presumption that:

(a)   where general words follow a list of particular words in a statutory provision, the general words should be attributed a meaning which is of the same kind or nature as the particular words listed. Where this presumption is applied, the court is said to adopt a *ejusdem generis* (same kind or nature) construction of the statutory provision.

(b)   where one matter or thing is mentioned within a class, this by implication excludes other matters or things within the same class, or, in the words of the Latin maxim, *expressio unius exclusio alterius*.

Illustrative references

1–090

See: Chapter 6: *"Contractual obligations arising out of an invitation to tender"* (6–006), where in *Blackpool* the Court of Appeal referred to the concept of *expressio unius exclusio alterius*, although not in the context of statutory interpretation but, rather unusually, in the context of construction of the terms of a commercial document.

Chapter 10: *"Video cassettes as obscene articles"* (10–003), where in *Attorney General's Reference (No. 5 of 1980)* the Court of Appeal stated that the trial judge in the case had been wrong to adopt an *ejusdem generis* construction of the words "other record of a picture or pictures" in s.1(2) of the Obscene Publications Act 1959.

Examples of presumptions relating to the substance of legal rules include a presumption that:

(a) statutes creating criminal offences require a blameworthy state of mind (mens rea) on the part of the defendant;
(b) penal statutes should be construed strictly in favour of the individual;
(c) a statutory provision is not intended to make changes in the existing law beyond those expressly stated, or arising by necessary implication, from the language of the statute; and
(d) a statute complies with the UK's obligations under ITCs.

Illustrative references

1–091

See: Chapter 9: *"False imprisonment, "detention" and the Mental Health Act 1983"* (9–010), where in *Bournewood* the House of Lords took the view that s.131 of the Mental Health Act 1983, which re-enacted verbatim the provision in s.5(1) of the Mental Health Act 1959, had not intended to effect any change in the existing law.

Chapter 13: *"Succession Rights Under The Rent Act 1977"* (13–004), where in *Ghaidan* Lord Millett recognised that ordinary principles of statutory interpretation "include a presumption that Parliament does not intend to legislate in a way that would put the United Kingdom in breach of its international obligations".

Chapter 17: *"Appropriation in theft"* (17–008), where in *Gomez* Lord Lowry in the House of Lords invoked the presumption against alteration in the existing law when considering the meaning of "appropriates" in s.1(1) of the Theft Act 1968.

> ### *(c) Policy considerations*

1–092   Judges, when deciding cases and establishing legal rules, whether the rules being established are ones derived from the common law or are ones resulting from the interpretation of statutory provisions, may be influenced by policy considerations and their own view as to what would be the best policy for the law to adopt (see above, 1–057). This is notwithstanding that there is previous authority on the point in question; where there is previous authority and it is persuasive, it need not be followed and, if it is binding, it need not be followed provided it can be distinguished.

It may be, of course, that there is no previous authority on the point in question and the court is concerned with interpreting a statutory provision which has not previously been judicially considered. Where this is the case, judges may similarly be influenced by policy considerations in deciding what meaning should be attributed to words used in the statutory provision. There may also be cases where judges feel constrained to adopt a particular interpretation of a statutory provision, although of the view that this would not be the best policy for the law to adopt.

In some cases, it may not be obvious what is the best policy for the law to adopt, for there may be competing policy considerations. Some policy considerations might favour the adoption of one interpretation of a statutory provision (or the adoption of one rule at common law), whereas others may favour the adoption of a different interpretation (or rule). In such cases, it will be necessary for judges to decide which of the competing policy considerations should be regarded as paramount.

1–093   ## Illustrative references

See: Chapter 9: *"False imprisonment, "detention" and the Mental Health Act 1983"* (9–011), where in *Bournewood* the House of Lords considered the competing policy considerations involved in deciding whether patients suffering from mental disorder might be informally admitted to hospital where they were incapable of consenting to admission and treatment; and (9–011) where Lord Steyn adopted an interpretation of s.131 of the Mental Health Act 1983 which did not accord with his view as to what would be the best policy for the law to adopt (". . . I would have wished to uphold the judgment of the Court of Appeal if that were possible. But as the issues were extensively probed in oral argument it became clear to me that, on a contextual interpretation of the Act of 1983, this course was not open to the House").

Chapter 10: *"Video cassettes as obscene articles"* (10–003), where in *Attorney General's Reference (No. 5 of 1980)* the Court of Appeal, although not referring overtly to policy considerations, may have been influenced in its view that video cassettes were an "other record of a picture or pictures" which could be published by being "played" or "projected" by the fact that, to have decided otherwise, would have frustrated the policy of the legislation of seeking to regulate all forms of obscene material.

Chapter 11: *"The regulation of abortion"* (11–010 and 11–013), where in *Royal College* the House of Lords referred to the policy behind the Abortion Act 1967 when interpreting the words "terminated by a registered medical practitioner" in s.1(1) of the Act.

Chapter 13: *"Succession Rights Under The Rent Act 1977"* (13–004), where in *Ghaidan* the House of Lords made reference to the social policy underlying the Rent Act 1977 (as amended) in respect of the greater security of tenure provided for surviving spouses as distinct from other family members.

Chapter 16: *"Marital rape"* (16–008), where in *R. v R.* the House of Lords, when considering the meaning of "unlawful" sexual intercourse without consent in the offence of rape in s.1(1) of the Sexual Offences (Amendment) Act 1976 and deciding that intercourse must be "unlawful" if it took place within the marital relationship, was clearly influenced by its recognition of the need to adopt a policy in keeping with modern social conditions.

Chapter 17: *"Appropriation in theft"* (17–017), where in *Hinks* Lord Steyn, although not referring overtly to policy considerations, had regard to the perceived social consequences of taking a broad view of the meaning of "appropriation", taking the view that this was necessary so that dishonest persons who should be found guilty of theft were not placed beyond the reach of the criminal law and that the mental requirements of theft were an adequate protection against injustice.

CONCLUSION

It will be appreciated from the contents of this chapter that ascertaining the law in many instances admits of no ready answer. As regards case law and precedent, there is no agreed definition of the ratio of a case and, whatever definition is adopted, it may be difficult to predict with any degree of certainty what will be held by a subsequent court to be the ratio of any particular case. Even after a subsequent court has purported to ascertain the ratio of a particular case, this does not necessarily mean that it will be followed by the court in that later case, either because the ratio may not be binding on the court or, if it is, the case may be distinguished by finding certain (material) factual differences which justify not following it. Irrespective of whether or not the purported ratio is followed by the subsequent court, this does not necessarily mean that the view of the ratio taken by that court will itself be followed in later cases!

1–094

As regards statutory interpretation, it is necessary for courts to attribute a legal meaning to the words used in the context of the statute and, in doing so, to give effect to what they perceive to be the intention of Parliament. The intention of Parliament is, however, a rather artificial and elusive concept, since there cannot be said to be a collective intention on the part of numerous individual members of Parliament. Accordingly, there have been suggestions (e.g. by Lord Simon in *Ealing LBC v Race Relations Board* [1972] A.C. 342 at 360) that it may be more appropriate to refer to the intention of the draftsman of the legislation, for the draftsman will be aware of the intention of the initiator of the legislation (normally the Government Minister with responsibility for its passage) and will seek to give effect to that intention when drafting the legislation. This does not, of course, mean that the task of ascertaining the meaning of the words used is necessarily any easier!

The courts will therefore be involved in a process of constructing an intention which can be attributed to Parliament. This process is further complicated by the fact that there are various "tools of the trade", in particular the so-called "rules" of statutory interpretation, which can be selected and applied by the courts as and when they are felt to be appropriate. These "rules" include not only those which have traditionally been applied by courts but also departures from those rules to enable legislation to be interpreted consistently with EU law and compatibly with rights under the European Convention on Human Rights (see above, 1–074), thereby increasing the range of "tools" that might be employed. Since judges can decide which "tool(s)" to select from an increasingly wide range, it may be difficult, in any given case, to predict which will actually be chosen and, moreover, where there is more than one judge hearing a case, there is no guarantee that each judge will choose the same "tool(s)". It is scarcely surprising, therefore, that ascertaining the law can be an elusive and difficult task. As observed by Lord Carswell in *Smith v Secretary of State for Work and Pensions* [2006] UKHL 35 at [79]:

> "In a judicial utopia every statute or statutory instrument would be expressed with such clarity and would cover every contingency so effectively that interpretation would be straightforward and the only task of the courts would be to apply their terms. Utopia has not yet arrived . . ."

2 COURTS AND TRIBUNALS

▶ ## 1. Introduction

As indicated in Chapter 1, whether the ratio of a case can form a binding precedent **2-001** depends on the position in the court hierarchy of the court that decided the case and the court that is now considering the case (see above, 1–015). Further, in the case of statements which are obiter and which form persuasive precedents, the position in the court hierarchy of the court making the statement will affect how persuasive the precedent is (see above, 1–028). Similarly, court decisions may act as binding or persuasive precedents for tribunals and, in some instances, decisions of tribunals themselves may form binding or persuasive precedents (see above, 1–038—1–041). Chapter 1 has provided some guidance on these matters in respect of current courts and tribunals and their position in the hierarchy, but the provision of further information in this chapter in relation to courts and tribunals, particularly as to their structure and composition, will, it is hoped, assist in obtaining a better understanding of the doctrine of precedent when it is encountered in subsequent chapters.

The composition of a court and the number of judges sitting may well affect precedential strength (see above, 1–046), so Chapter 2 includes details of the number of judges ordinarily, or exceptionally, sitting in particular courts. The court structure and hierarchy to which reference has been made in Chapter 1 is the current one, with present-day courts, but, over the years, there have been changes to the court structure and some courts previously within the structure no longer exist. Decisions of these courts, however, may still constitute precedents and these decisions may have comparable status to certain courts within the current court structure and hierarchy. Examples of cases heard in these courts will be encountered in the case studies and knowledge of the position of these courts in the hierarchy will assist in understanding the status that their decisions may have as precedents. The latter part of this chapter deals with the salient characteristics of these courts.

The current structure and hierarchy is set out in diagrammatic form on Her **2-002** Majesty's Court Service website (*http://www.hmcourts-service.gov.uk/aboutus/ structure/index.htm*) and the diagram gives a brief indication of the nature of the jurisdiction of each court. This diagram is reproduced below:

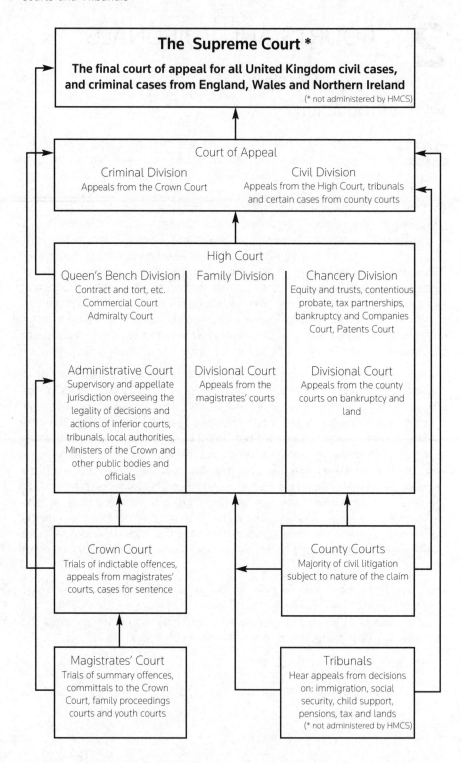

The Supreme Court *

The final court of appeal for all United Kingdom civil cases, and criminal cases from England, Wales and Northern Ireland

(* not administered by HMCS)

Court of Appeal

Criminal Division
Appeals from the Crown Court

Civil Division
Appeals from the High Court, tribunals and certain cases from county courts

High Court

Queen's Bench Division
Contract and tort, etc.
Commercial Court
Admiralty Court

Family Division

Chancery Division
Equity and trusts, contentious probate, tax partnerships, bankruptcy and Companies Court, Patents Court

Administrative Court
Supervisory and appellate jurisdiction overseeing the legality of decisions and actions of inferior courts, tribunals, local authorities, Ministers of the Crown and other public bodies and officials

Divisional Court
Appeals from the magistrates' courts

Divisional Court
Appeals from the county courts on bankruptcy and land

Crown Court
Trials of indictable offences, appeals from magistrates' courts, cases for sentence

County Courts
Majority of civil litigation subject to nature of the claim

Magistrates' Court
Trials of summary offences, committals to the Crown Court, family proceedings courts and youth courts

Tribunals
Hear appeals from decisions on: immigration, social security, child support, pensions, tax and lands
(* not administered by HMCS)

▶ ## 2. Composition of courts and tribunals within the current structure and hierarchy

▷ ### (a) (European) Court of Justice and General Court

The Court of Justice (CJ), known as the European Court of Justice prior to the **2-003** ratification of the Treaty of Lisbon in 2009 (see below, 4–001), sits in Luxembourg and comprises a senior judge from each Member State of the European Union. It determines matters of EU law and, in particular, provides preliminary rulings for Member States on uncertain aspects of EU law (see below, 4–011), and traditionally has sat as a Grand Chamber of 13 judges. However, with an increasing workload (not entirely offset by the creation of the Court of First Instance in 1989 with jurisdiction in certain areas, e.g. competition law), there has been a growing tendency for cases to be heard before a chamber of three or five judges.

The judges in the CJ are assisted by several Advocates General and their responsibilities include preparation for the court of a report with detailed analysis of issues of fact and law which are relevant to the case which the court is hearing. The legal analysis may well be more detailed than that produced by the parties in argument. The report will include recommendations, which themselves may form persuasive precedents, even if the court chooses not to follow the recommendations. The Court of First Instance, which since ratification of the Treaty of Lisbon in 2009, has been known as the General Court, does not have any permanent Advocates General but the work normally undertaken by an Advocate General may, in exceptional circumstances, be carried out by a judge of the court.

Decisions of the CJ sitting as Grand Chamber of 13 judges are likely to be particularly influential as precedents. Such sittings are, however, now increasingly rare and are likely to be confined to instances where treaties so require or where the issues raised are considered to be of exceptional importance.

▷ ### (b) Supreme Court

The Supreme Court was created by Part 3 of the Constitutional Reform Act 2005 **2-004** (CRA 2005) which came into effect in 2009. It replaces the House of Lords, or, strictly speaking, as was seen in Chapter 1 (at 1–019), the Appellate Committee of the House of Lords. The Lords of Appeal in Ordinary, more commonly known as Law Lords, who sat as the Appellate Committee in the House of Lords until its abolition, have been appointed as the first Justices of the Supreme Court. Presently, there are 12 members of the Supreme Court, one of whom acts as the President of the Court.

Under s.42(1) of the CRA 2005, the Supreme Court is required to sit with an uneven number of judges, with a minimum of three and with more than half the judges being permanent judges (as distinct from acting judges from the Court of

Appeal and equivalent courts in Scotland and Northern Ireland, who may sit if requested to do so by the President of the Supreme Court). There was no statutory requirement for the House of Lords to sit with an uneven number of judges and a minimum number, although in practice the House did sit with an uneven number of judges, usually five members, and this practice of sitting with five members seems to have largely been followed in the Supreme Court.

In cases of particular importance e.g. where the decision is considered to have wide-ranging implications, however, a "full court" of seven or nine members may sit and this may increase the precedential strength of the decision, particularly if the decision is unanimous (see, for example, *Horncastle* (above, 1–023) in which seven Justices of the Supreme Court unanimously decided, inter alia, not to follow the approach of the Strasbourg Court in relation to a matter of criminal procedure that was relevant to art.6 of the Convention (the right to a fair trial). Even decisions which are not unanimous may nevertheless form strong precedents in future cases. Thus, in *Pepper* seven law lords heard the case in the House of Lords and a 6–1 majority decided that the exclusionary rule prohibiting access to parliamentary material as an aid to the construction of statutory provisions should not be abandoned but relaxed in certain circumstances (see 1–084). Further, a "full court" may in a particular case be unanimous in its resolution of one issue whilst divided on another. Hence, the nine Justices of the Supreme Court who heard *R. (on the application of Smith) (FC) v Secretary of State for Defence and another* [2010] UKSC 29, found (by a 6–3 majority) that a soldier who died from heat exhaustion on active service abroad outside of his military base in a location over which the armed forces did not have exclusive control was not within the jurisdiction of the UK for the purposes of art.1 of the Convention and was not therefore subject to the protection of the HRA 1998. However, the Supreme Court unanimously expressed the view (obiter) that, on the assumption the deceased had been within the jurisdiction for the purposes of art.1, there was an arguable breach of the obligation under art.2 of the Convention (the right to life) through a possible systemic failure by the military authorities to protect soldiers from the risk posed by the extreme temperatures in which they had to serve and to hold an inquiry which complied with art.2 requirements.

▷ (c) Court of Appeal

2–005 The Court of Appeal was established, with jurisdiction in civil matters, by the Judicature Act 1873. This Act created a new court structure, the Supreme Court of Judicature, which comprised the Court of Appeal and the High Court of Justice (more commonly known simply as the High Court). At one time, it had been intended that the Court of Appeal would be the final appeal court, replacing the House of Lords which would be abolished as an appeal court, but a change of government led to the introduction of the Appellate Jurisdiction Act 1876 which reinstated the House as the final appeal court. Now that the House of Lords has been replaced by the Supreme Court (see above, 2–004), the Court of Appeal and

High Court, along with the Crown Court, are collectively known as the Senior Courts of England and Wales (see s.59(1) of the CRA 2005).

A separate Court of Criminal Appeal (see below, 2–013), to replace the Court for Crown Cases Reserved (see below, 2–014), was established in 1907 to hear appeals in criminal cases from Assizes, Quarter Sessions and the Central Criminal Court (see below, 2–019) and, following their abolition by the Courts Act 1971, from the Crown Court (see below, 2–007) which replaced them. The Court of Criminal Appeal itself was replaced, under the Criminal Appeal Act 1966, by the Court of Appeal (Criminal Division) and the civil jurisdiction of the Court of Appeal since then has been exercised by the Court of Appeal (Civil Division).

Court of Appeal judges are Lord Justices of Appeal, more commonly known simply as Lord Justices, and they may sit in either civil or criminal cases.

The Court of Appeal (Civil Division) is headed by the Master of the Rolls and the court traditionally has sat with three members. The court's composition has been either the Master of the Rolls and two Lord Justices, or three Lord Justices, although others who may sit include the President of the Family Division of the High Court, the Chancellor of the High Court (formerly the Vice-Chancellor of the Chancery Division of the High Court), and High Court judges. The court will not necessarily sit with three members, for provision was made in s.59 of the Access to Justice Act 1999 for it to sit with one or more judges. The introduction of this greater flexibility enabled the court to sit with one or two members in cases regarded as being of lesser importance and complexity. Conversely, in cases of particular importance e.g. where the decision is considered to have wide-ranging implications, a "full court" of five members may sit (see, e.g., *Ward v James (No 2)* [1966] 2 Q.B.273).

The Court of Appeal (Criminal Division) is headed by the Lord Chief Justice and includes, as well as Lord Justices, the Vice-President of the Criminal Division, High Court judges from the Queen's Bench Division of the High Court and some circuit judges from the Crown Court specially nominated by the Lord Chief Justice. It also usually sits with three judges, often with a single Lord Justice who is accompanied by either two High Court judges or one High Court judge and one circuit judge. It can similarly sit as a "full court" of five members in cases of particular importance, as it did, e.g., in *R. v R.* [1992] 1 A.C. 599 (see below, 16–007) on marital rape.

▷ *(d) High Court*

The High Court was established as part of the court structure, the Supreme Court **2–006** of Judicature, created by the Judicature Act 1873 (see above, 2–005). Currently, it has three divisions, Queen's Bench, Chancery and Family. The first two divisions have been part of the High Court since its inception, whilst the Family Division has its origins in the Administration of Justice Act 1970. It replaced the previous Probate, Divorce and Admiralty Division in that year, when Probate work was assigned to the Chancery Division and Admiralty work to the Queen's Bench

Division. As seen above (2–005), the High Court is now a Senior Court of England and Wales.

The Queen's Bench Division, which is by far the largest of the three divisions, is headed by the Lord Chief Justice; the Chancery Division is headed by the Chancellor of the High Court (previously known as the Vice-Chancellor until the title was changed by the CRA 2005); and the Family Division is headed by the President.

High Court judges, normally addressed as "Mr Justice" (e.g. Mr Justice Saunders), are assigned to one of the three divisions and usually sit alone when hearing cases at first instance i.e. when cases are being heard for the first time. In addition to cases heard by full-time High Court judges, cases may be heard by lawyers sitting part-time as Deputy High Court judges. Each of the divisions also has jurisdiction to hear appeals from other courts in certain cases and, when doing so, the court is said to be sitting as a Divisional Court. A Divisional Court usually has two or three judges, although a "full court" of five or more members may occasionally sit e.g. in *Younghusband* (see above, 1–021) there was a court of five judges and in *Coppen v Moore (No. 2)* [1898] 2 Q.B. 306 there was a court of six judges.

The Queen's Bench Divisional Court has the most wide-ranging appellate jurisdiction and it is often referred to simply as "the Divisional Court", an approach which has been adopted in this book. A number of instances will be encountered in the book of decisions by this court e.g. *Huddersfield* (at 1–021), *Derrick v Customs and Excise Commissioners* (at 10–003), *Dulieu* (at 15–002) and *C (A Minor) v DPP* (at 16–011). There are, in addition, a number of "specialist" courts within the High Court e.g. the Administrative Court in the Queen's Bench Division, which hears applications for judicial review, and the Companies Court in the Chancery Division, which mainly deals with matters of company insolvency.

▷ (e) Crown Court

2–007 The Crown Court was established by the Courts Act 1971 and it replaced Courts of Assize and Quarter Sessions which had hitherto been the main criminal courts. The Crown Court is where the more serious criminal trials are held before a single judge and a jury (or, exceptionally, without a jury) and the court's jurisdiction is overwhelmingly criminal. It also hears appeals from magistrates' courts in criminal cases, which are usually heard by a single circuit judge and two magistrates. In addition, the Crown Court hears some civil cases e.g. taxi licensing appeals. As seen above (2–005), it is now a Senior Court of England and Wales.

It is a single court which sits in a number of different centres in England and Wales and the centres are divided into three tiers, which reflect the nature of the cases heard and the type of judges who may hear them. First tier centres are ones visited by High Court judges to hear serious criminal cases and also civil cases. Second tier centres are ones visited by High Court judges to hear only criminal cases. Third tier centres are ones not normally visited by High Court judges and here circuit judges, recorders and assistant recorders (who sit at all three centres) hear only criminal cases.

Criminal offences, according to their gravity, are divided into four classes and High Court judges, although they can try cases in all four classes, are likely to hear only cases in Classes 1 and 2. Some cases in Class 1, the most serious category, can be tried only by a High Court judge e.g. an offence under the Official Secrets Act 1911, although others, including murder, can be released for trial by a circuit judge. All cases in Class 2, which covers serious offences such as manslaughter and rape, can also be similarly released, although like Class 1 cases they are generally tried by a High Court judge. Cases in Class 3, which includes offences that are indictable only e.g. robbery, may be tried by a High Court judge but are normally tried by a circuit judge or recorder. Cases in Class 4, the least serious category, can be tried by a High Court judge, although this would be exceptional, and usually they are tried by a circuit judge, recorder or assistant recorder. Further details can be found in *Practice Direction (Crown Court: Allocation of Business)* [1995] 1 W.L.R. 1083, as amended by *Practice Direction (Crown Court: Allocation of Business) (No. 2)* [1998] 1 W.L.R. 1244.

Several instances will be encountered in this book of decisions by the Crown Court e.g. *R. v O'Brien* (at 16–004), *R. v R.* (at 16–006), *R. v C (Rape: Marital Exemption)* (at 16–006), and *R. v J (Rape: Marital Exemption)* (at 16–006).

▷ (f) County Courts

2–008 County courts were established by the County Courts Act 1846 and enable relatively small-scale and inexpensive civil disputes to be resolved locally as an alternative to proceedings in the High Court. The more complex cases are heard by circuit judges and other cases are heard either by District Judges or recorders, who both sit part-time. All are qualified, experienced lawyers and normally sit alone. Judgments are only occasionally reported in law reports or law journals; they are only persuasive precedents and have little precedential value (see above, 1–026).

▷ (g) Magistrates' Courts

2–009 Magistrates, or justices of the peace, have a long history, dating back to the 12th century, when "keepers of the peace" were appointed to maintain order. Magistrates' courts, previously known as petty sessions and police courts, deal with the vast majority of criminal offences and also some civil matters such as adoption proceedings, family maintenance relating to spouses and children, and council tax recovery. Magistrates, who are lay persons, hear cases as a bench of two or three persons and have a legal adviser (traditionally known as the justices' clerk) to advise them on the law. Cases are also heard in magistrates' courts by District Judges (formerly known as stipendiary magistrates) or Deputy District Judges, who normally sit alone and are qualified, experienced lawyers. Although judgments may be delivered by District or Deputy District Judges on points of law, they are only occasionally reported in law reports or law journals; they are only persuasive precedents and have little precedential value (see above, 1–026).

▷ *(h) Tribunals*

2–010   Over the years, a large number of tribunals were created, for the most part on an ad hoc basis, resulting in a mainly fragmented system which lacked any consistency and common standards. Part 1 of the Tribunals, Courts and Enforcement Act 2007 (TCEA 2007) introduced a new, more streamlined system of tribunals (for the development of modern tribunals and the features of the new system, see Jacobs, "Something Old, Something New: The New Tribunal System" (2009) 38 *Industrial Law Journal* 417). The TCEA 2007 created a new unified two-tier structure comprising a First-tier Tribunal and an Upper Tribunal. This structure was intended to better accommodate users' needs and accessibility, to be a more efficient use of judicial and administrative resources, and to make provision for greater use and exploration of "proportionate dispute resolution". The First-tier Tribunal is the first instance tribunal in most cases. It is a generic tribunal with jurisdiction over appeals formerly heard by a range of different tribunals and it is divided into six different chambers: the General Regulatory Chamber; the Immigration and Asylum Chamber; the Health, Education and Social Care Chamber; the Social Entitlement Chamber; the Tax Chamber; and the War Pensions and Armed Forces Compensation Chamber. Those hearing cases in the First-tier Tribunal are known as judges and cases are usually heard by a judge sitting alone. Most tribunals have now been incorporated into the First-tier Tribunal but not all have e.g., Employment Tribunals (or Industrial Tribunals as they were known prior to being renamed by s.1 of the Employment Rights (Dispute Resolution) Act 1998). Reference is made in Chapter 14 to these tribunals and also to the Employment Appeals Tribunal, to which appeals are made from Employment Tribunals. The Employment Appeals Tribunal also continues to exist as a separate tribunal.

The Upper Tribunal deals with appeals on a point of law from the First-tier Tribunal, decides certain cases that do not go through the First-tier Tribunal, exercises powers of judicial review in certain circumstances and enforces the First-tier Tribunal's decisions. The Upper Tribunal is also divided into different chambers, of which there are four: the Administrative Appeals Chamber; the Immigration and Asylum Chamber; the Lands Chamber; and the Tax and Chancery Chamber. As with the First-tier Tribunal, those hearing cases are known as judges (or, in some cases, members) and usually sit alone. In complex cases, however, there may be more than a single judge sitting with one or more expert members if required. High Court judges can also sit as full-time or part-time judges in the Upper Tribunal. The Upper Tribunal has the same standing as the High Court, and so its decisions cannot be challenged in or reviewed by the High Court. A right of appeal from the Upper Tribunal to the Court of Appeal may be exercised where either the Upper Tribunal or the Court of Appeal consider that the appeal would "raise some important point of principle or practice" or "there is some other compelling reason" for an appeal (see s.13(6) of the TCEA 2007).

The structure and hierarchy of the tribunal system is set out in diagrammatic form below, with routes of appeal through the system indicated by arrows.

Composition of courts and tribunals within the current structure and hierarchy

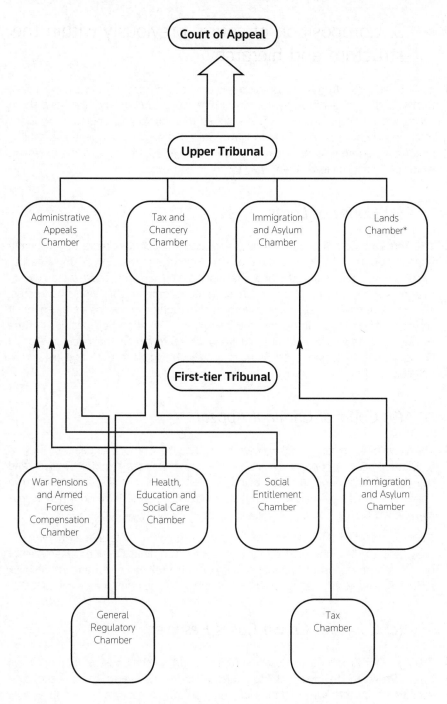

* The Lands Chamber hears appeals from various tribunals which are outside the
First-tier Tribunal e.g. Leasehold Valuation Tribunals, Residential Property Tribunals.

▶ 3. Composition of courts previously within the structure and hierarchy

2–011 It will be apparent from the preceding section that a number of courts have ceased to exist and no longer form part of the current court structure and hierarchy. These courts will be encountered at various points throughout this book and decisions made by them may continue to form precedents in subsequent cases. It is important therefore to have some awareness of these courts and the extent to which decisions made by them may form binding precedents.

▷ *(a) House of Lords*

2–012 The Appellate Committee of the House of Lords was, until its replacement by the Supreme Court in 2009 when the provisions of Part 3 of the CRA 2005 came into force, the final appeal court and the highest court in the court hierarchy. Its members were Lords of Appeal in Ordinary, more commonly known as Law Lords. The House normally sat with five members, although on occasions a "full court" of seven members sat, as in *Pepper* (see 2–004 and 1–084 above). Decisions of the House of Lords will be encountered frequently throughout the book, in Parts 1 (Principles), 2 (Selected Case Studies) and 3 (Tracing the Evolution of Law in Selected Fields).

▷ *(b) Court of Criminal Appeal*

2–013 The Court of Criminal Appeal was established by the Criminal Appeal Act 1907 as a court for hearing appeals in criminal cases from Assizes, Quarter Sessions and the Central Criminal Court (see below, 2–019). It replaced the Court for Crown Cases Reserved (see below, 2–014) and ceased to exist in 1966 when it was superseded by the Court of Appeal (Criminal Division) (see above, 2–005).

Decisions of the Court of Criminal Appeal have comparable status in terms of precedent to decisions of the Court of Appeal (Criminal Division). Examples of decisions of the Court of Criminal Appeal to which reference is made in this book include *R. v Lapworth* (see below, 12–005) and *R. v Chapman* (see below, 16–008).

▷ *(c) Court for Crown Cases Reserved*

2–014 The Court for Crown Cases Reserved (or the Court for the Consideration of Crown Cases Reserved, to give it its full title, which rarely seems to be used) was established by the Administration of Criminal Law (Amendment) Act 1848 as a court for hearing appeals in criminal cases. Only appeals on points of law could be heard by the court and there was no general right of appeal to it, although under the Crown Cases Reserved Act 1848 there was a limited right of appeal from decisions of the Central Criminal Court (see below, 2–019). Apart from appeals from the Central Criminal Court, the court heard appeals from Assizes and Quarter Sessions (see below, 2–019), which were discretionary on reference to the court by the trial judge who was hearing the case.

The Court for Crown Cases Reserved was presided over by judges of the High Court who sat as and when cases were referred to it for a ruling. The court's jurisdiction was taken over by the Court of Criminal Appeal in 1907 (see above, 2–013) and the court ceased to exist the following year. The court usually sat with five members, although larger numbers were sometimes in attendance, as was the case in *R. v Clarence* (see below, 16–003), where there was a court of 13 members. The status of the court's decisions in terms of precedent is equivalent to decisions of the Court of Appeal (Criminal Division).

▷ *(d) Court of King's (or Queen's) Bench*

This court, whose name was dependent upon whether the reigning monarch was a **2–015** king or queen, dates back to the 13th century and was headed by the Lord Chief Justice. Cases would normally be heard by Lord Chief Justice sitting with two other Justices or by three Justices sitting together. The court was one of the three common law courts at Westminster that existed prior to the enactment of the Judicature Act 1873, the others being the Court of Common Pleas, whose jurisdiction was focused on private civil actions between individuals (in which the king or queen had no interest), and the Court of Exchequer, whose jurisdiction was concerned, principally, with revenue matters. The Court of King's (or Queen's) Bench exercised criminal jurisdiction and such other civil jurisdiction as was not exercised by the other two courts.

The court was abolished by the Judicature Act 1873 and its jurisdiction was transferred to the Queen's Bench Division of the High Court. Cases heard by the court, to which reference is made in this book, include *Harris v Watson* and *Stilk v Myrick* (see below, 7–002) (both Court of King's Bench), *R. v Inhabitants of All Saints, Worcester* (see below, 12–003) (Court of King's Bench) and *Harris v Nickerson* (see below, 6–002) (Court of Queen's Bench).

▷ *(e) Court of Common Pleas*

Like the Court of King's (or Queen's) Bench, the Court of Common Pleas dates **2–016** back to the 13th century and was headed by a Chief Justice. Cases would normally be heard by the Chief Justice sitting with two other Justices or by three Justices sitting together, although on occasions only two Justices would sit (e.g. *Johnson v Barnes* (1871–72) L.R. 7 C.P. 592). It also seems not to have been uncommon for the court to sit with four members and numerous examples can be found in the law reports. The four members might consist of the Chief Justice and three Justices (for examples, see *Simpson v Smith* (1870–71) L.R. 6 C.P. 87 and *Best v Hill* (1872–73)

L.R. 8 C.P. 10) or four Justices sitting together (for examples, see *Easterbrook v Barker* (1870–71) L.R. 6 C.P. 1 and *Ford v Boon* (1871–72) L.R. 7 C.P. 150). As seen above (2–015), the court's jurisdiction was focused on private civil actions between individuals, e.g. actions in contract, in which the king or queen had no interest.

The court was abolished by the Judicature Act 1873 and its jurisdiction was transferred to the Common Pleas Division of the High Court and subsequently (in 1880) to the Queen's Bench Division of the High Court which took over the work of the Common Pleas Division in that year. A case decided by the Court of Common Pleas, *Spencer v Harding*, can be found in Chapter 6 of the book (see below, 6–002).

▷ *(f) Court of Exchequer*

2–017 The Court of Exchequer, along with the Courts of King's (or Queen's) Bench and Common Pleas, was the third of the three common law courts dating back to the 13th century (see above, 2–015). Judges who sat in the Court of Exchequer were known as Barons and the head of the court was the Chief Baron. Cases would normally be heard by the Chief Baron sitting with two other Barons or by three Barons sitting together, although on occasions only two Barons would sit (e.g. *Death v Harrison* (1870–71) L.R. 6 Ex. 15). As with the Court of Common Pleas, it also seems not to have been uncommon for the court to sit with four members (see, e.g., *Dillon v Cunningham* (1872–73) L.R. 8 Ex. 23). As indicated above (2–015), the court's jurisdiction was focused on revenue matters and included both common law and equity, with a variable balance between the two operating at different points in the court's history.

The court was abolished by the Judicature Act 1873 and its jurisdiction was transferred to the Exchequer Division of the High Court and subsequently (in 1880) to the Queen's Bench Division of the High Court which took over the work of the Exchequer Division in that year. The Court of Exchequer featured prominently in *Heydon*'s case (1584) 3 Co. Rep. 7a, where Barons of the court formulated the classic statement of what is known as the "mischief rule" of statutory interpretation, which is considered in Chapter 1 (see above, 1–069).

▷ *(g) Court of Chancery*

2–018 The Court of Chancery exercised equitable jurisdiction and, although no further reference to this court is made in this book, it is mentioned here because of its early role in the recognition of equitable principles. The court was headed by the Lord Chancellor, who was assisted by 12 Masters (Clerks) in Chancery; the chief of these was the Master of the Rolls, who acted as the Lord Chancellor's deputy and also heard cases. Long delays were not uncommon and various reforms were instituted in the early nineteenth century, including the appointment of a Vice-Chancellor to deal with matters delegated to him by the Lord Chancellor. The

Court of Chancery was abolished by the Judicature Act 1873 and its jurisdiction was transferred to the Chancery Division of the High Court. The Master of the Rolls moved to become head of the newly-created Court of Appeal (see above, 2–005) and the Vice-Chancellor (now the Chancellor of the High Court) became head of the Chancery Division of the High Court (see above, 2–006).

▷ (h) Assizes, Quarter Sessions and the Central Criminal Court

Courts of Assize, more commonly known as Assizes, were courts held periodically **2–019** in the main county towns in England and Wales from the 13th century onwards, initially to hear property disputes, but subsequently hearing the more serious criminal cases. Assizes were held at different times of the year and cases were tried by visiting judges from the higher courts based in London such as the High Court. Assizes continued to exist until their abolition and replacement by the Crown Court under the Courts Act 1971 (see above, 2–007). Cases heard at Assizes, to which reference is made in this book, include *R. v Clarke* and *R. v Miller* (see below, 16–004).

Courts of Quarter Sessions, more commonly known as Quarter Sessions, were courts held periodically—quarterly each year—in all county areas and county boroughs in England and Wales. The courts had jurisdiction in some administrative/civil matters (e.g. highways)—for an instance of an appeal from Quarter Sessions heard in the Divisional Court, see *Huddersfield* (above, 1–021)—and in criminal cases where crimes could not be tried summarily (i.e. without a jury) in magistrates' courts. In county areas, cases at Quarter Sessions were heard by a jury and two or more magistrates, with a chairman presiding. In county boroughs, instead of a bench of magistrates, there was a single Recorder, normally a senior local practitioner at the Bar, who sat part-time. The criminal cases heard by Quarter Sessions would not include the most serious criminal offences, which would be heard by judges at Assizes. Quarter Sessions, like Assizes, continued to exist until their abolition and replacement by the Crown Court under the Courts Act 1971 (see above, 2–007).

The Central Criminal Court, more commonly known as the Old Bailey, was established by the Central Criminal Court Act 1834 for the trial of treasons, murders, and other offences committed in London and Middlesex and certain parts of Essex, Kent and Surrey. The case of *R. v Bourne* (see below, 11–002), where the defendant was charged with carrying out an unlawful abortion at St Mary's Hospital, London, was heard in this court. The court was also empowered to try offences committed on the high seas or elsewhere abroad previously tried at the Admiralty Sessions. Its jurisdiction was subsequently extended to cases outside its ordinary jurisdiction e.g., to ensure a fair trial where local prejudice existed and, following the creation of the area of Greater London by the London Government Act 1963, the court's jurisdiction was subsequently redefined as being the Greater

London area. The most senior permanent full-time judge at the court is the Recorder of London and other judges who may sit part-time include High Court judges, circuit judges and recorders. The Central Criminal Court was not abolished when the Crown Court was created by the Courts Act 1971. The Crown Court sits at various centres in England and Wales and the Central Criminal Court was retained as the name for the Crown Court centre in the City of London. As with other Crown Courts, cases are heard before a single judge and a jury.

▷ (i) Tribunals

2–020 There are a number of tribunals which have ceased to exist since the TCEA 2007 created a new unified two-tier structure comprising a First-tier Tribunal and an Upper Tribunal e.g., the work of the Mental Health Review Tribunal is now undertaken by the Health, Education and Social Care Chamber of the First-tier Tribunal and the work of the Social Security & Child Support Commissioners is now undertaken by the Administrative Appeals Chamber of the Upper Tribunal.

Further details can be found in Annex A to the Tribunals Service, *Annual Report & Accounts 2009–10*, pp.136–137. This can be accessed at the following website link: *http://www.tribunals.gov.uk/Tribunals/Documents/Publications/TS-AR-09-10-WEB-final.pdf*

▶ 4. Other courts outside the current structure and hierarchy

2–021 There are other courts which fall outside the current structure and hierarchy which will be encountered in the course of the book, notably the Privy Council and the European Court of Human Rights, and details of these courts are set out below.

▷ (a) Privy Council

2–022 The Judicial Committee of the Privy Council was established by the Judicial Committee Act 1833 to hear appeals from courts in the Dominions and these include both criminal and civil cases (see above, 1–030). Normally referred to simply as "the Privy Council", its principal jurisdiction continues to be the hearing of appeals from certain countries of the Commonwealth, although it also hears appeals domestically for Jersey, Guernsey and the Isle of Man. For the most part, the Privy Council does not have jurisdiction to hear cases from courts or tribunals in England and Wales (although there are exceptions e.g., appeals can be made to it from the Royal College of Veterinary Surgeons' Disciplinary Committee). Essentially, therefore, it falls outside the court structure for England and Wales and so does not appear in the diagram on Her Majesty's Court Service website (see above, 2–002).

The Judicial Committee consists of those individuals who currently hold, or have previously held, high judicial office. These will normally be Justices of the Supreme Court or their predecessors, Law Lords in the House of Lords (see above, 2–004). In practice, the Privy Council usually sits with five members, although exceptionally it may sit with a higher number than this, as it did, e.g., in *Att Gen for Jersey v Holley* (see above, 1–031), where there were nine members sitting. Although its decisions are only persuasive precedents, they are particularly persuasive because of the authority accorded to the statements of those hearing the case. It is nevertheless open to any court to decline to follow a decision of the Privy Council and an instance of the High Court declining to do so can be seen in *Dulieu* (see below, 15–004).

▷ *(b) European Court of Human Rights*

The European Court of Human Rights in Strasbourg (Strasbourg Court) was **2–023** established as a full-time court in 1998, following amalgamation of the previous part-time court and the European Commission on Human Rights, and it interprets and enforces the Convention for those Member States that have signed and ratified it. Complaints of violations of the Convention by Member States are filed with the court and are assigned to one of its sections. A committee of three judges examines the complaint to determine whether it should go forward for hearing by the court. If it does go forward and the court finds a breach of the Convention, the Member State is legally obliged to make reparation for the consequences of the violation.

The court consists of the President, Vice-President and judges who are selected from Member States of the Council of Europe (all of whom are required to sign and ratify the Convention). Judges sit for a period of six years and the Court sits in Chambers of seven or exceptionally as a Grand Chamber of 17 judges where a case raises a serious issue of interpretation of Convention law or where there is a risk of departing from existing case law. Particular mention is made of the court in Chapter 5, which examines the influence of the Convention on statutory inter-pretation and the doctrine of precedent, although a decision of the court in *HL v UK* is also mentioned in Chapter 9 (see below, 9–012).

3 THE INCOMING TIDE: EUROPEAN INFLUENCES ON STATUTORY INTERPRETATION AND THE DOCTRINE OF PRECEDENT

▶ 1. Developments in Europe and European Influences

3–001 Judicial techniques traditionally employed by English courts in relation to statutory interpretation and precedent, as outlined in Chapter 1, involve close adherence to a system of binding precedent based on the doctrine of stare decisis and (in deference to the recognised legislative supremacy of Parliament) close adherence to the language used by Parliament when enacting statutory provisions. In recent years, there have been some modifications to these techniques because of developments in Europe during the post-Second World War period.

Closer European co-operation has had a considerable impact on English economic and political life, but, from a legal standpoint, the two most significant events have been the ratification, on March 8, 1951, of the European Convention on Human Rights and Fundamental Freedoms (Convention) and entry, on January 1, 1973, into the European Community (which has now become part of the European Union). These events have led to the establishment of distinctive legal orders with their own legislative and institutional framework. Each has a judicial arm; in the case of the Convention, the European Court of Human Rights in Strasbourg (Strasbourg Court) and, in the case of the European Union (EU), the Court of Justice (CJ) and the General Court (GC) in Luxembourg. The judiciaries of these courts have developed their own techniques for interpreting legislation and dealing with previous case law. In the case of the Convention, these techniques have been influenced both by practices in international courts and by the common law and civil law traditions of the signatory States, whilst judicial techniques in the CJ and GC bear the distinctive stamp of the civil law systems of the founding States (i.e. France, Germany, Italy, Luxembourg, Belgium and the Netherlands) and the Continental legal tradition underpinning those systems. In both instances, however, the judicial techniques employed share common characteristics: creative interpretation of broadly drafted legislative codes by reference to their purpose and context; the use of broad, general principles both as an aid to interpretation of legislative codes and as a residual source of law; and a much less rigid reliance on previous case law. These judicial techniques are quite distinct from those traditionally employed by English courts.

English judicial practice in the areas of statutory interpretation and precedent has been influenced by participation in these two European legal orders. Of the two orders, the EU has had the greater impact. This is because entry into the European Community by the United Kingdom (UK) required incorporation of its legal order into the English legal system. This was effected by the European Communities Act 1972 (ECA 1972), since when it has become necessary to ensure that English law, in relevant circumstances, complies with EU law. The Convention has not, however, been similarly incorporated and rights and freedoms guaranteed under it have not become part of English law. This remains the case even after the passing of the Human Rights Act 1998 (HRA 1998). The HRA 1998 seeks to give "further effect" to rights and freedoms guaranteed under the Convention but does not incorporate them directly into English law. Consequently the influence of the Convention has been, and may well continue to be, more subtle and less direct than the EU legal order.

▶ 2. Assessment of European Influences

Both legal orders have undoubtedly influenced English judicial practice in the areas of statutory interpretation and precedent as the impact of the two legal orders continues to evolve. The following two chapters seek to give an indication of the effects of these two orders on the doctrines of statutory interpretation and precedent. Chapter 4 covers the EU legal order and Chapter 5 the Convention and the HRA 1998, and throughout these chapters the following abbreviations are used: **3–002**

CFI	European Court of First Instance in Luxembourg (as the General Court was formerly known).
CJ	Court of Justice in Luxembourg (formerly known as the European Court of Justice).
CJ interpretative techniques	Techniques which focus on giving effect to the underlying aims of legislative provisions, rather than seeking to give a meaning to the particular words used, and, in doing so, adopting schematic and/or teleological approaches to interpretation, using general principles, having recourse to a body of case law (*jurisprudence constante*), and engaging in "gap filling."
Convention	European Convention on Human Rights and Fundamental Freedoms (including Protocols to the Convention).
ECJ	European Court of Justice in Luxembourg (as the Court of Justice was formerly known).
EC	European Community.
EC Treaty	European Community Treaty, i.e. the Treaty of Paris of 1951 and the Treaties of Rome of 1957, as amended.

ECA 1972	European Communities Act 1972.
EPA 1970	Equal Pay Act 1970 (as amended).
EU	European Union.
GC	General Court in Luxembourg (formerly known as the European Court of First Instance).
HRA 1998	Human Rights Act 1998.
Strasbourg Court	European Court of Human Rights in Strasbourg.
TFEU	Treaty on the Functioning of the European Union.
UK	United Kingdom.

4 THE EUROPEAN UNION LEGAL ORDER: INFLUENCE ON STATUTORY INTERPRETATION AND THE DOCTRINE OF PRECEDENT

This chapter is divided into three parts. Part 1 examines, with a view to providing **4-001** the necessary background, the key features of the Continental legal tradition and Continental judicial techniques in respect of legislation and case law. Part 2 examines the key features of the EU legal order and judicial techniques of its courts in respect of legislation and case law. These are the Court of Justice (CJ), previously the European Court of Justice (ECJ), and the General Court (GC), previously the European Court of First Instance (CFI)—see 3-001 above. Part 3 contains an assessment of the impact of the EU legal order on the doctrines of statutory interpretation and precedent in English law. In Parts 2 and 3, illustrative references are made to Chapter 14 on *"Equal pay"*, where appropriate. A list of abbreviations used throughout this chapter can be found at the end of Chapter 3 at 3–002.

Following ratification in 2009 of the European Reform Treaty, usually known as the Treaty of Lisbon, the EC Treaty has been amended and renamed the "Treaty on the Functioning of the European Union" (TFEU) and there has been a renumbering of articles in the Treaty (and some textual changes made to them). With this renumbering, the following method of citation has been adopted. When referring to current Treaty provisions, the new number of the relevant article has been used, with a reference thereafter in brackets to the old number, preceded by the word "ex", e.g. art.267 (ex 234). When referring to previous cases, however, the old number of the relevant article, current at the time of the particular case, has been used, with a reference thereafter in brackets to the new number, preceded by the word "now", e.g. art.234 (now 267) or art.177 (now 267). That the article currently numbered 267 might previously have been numbered art.234 or art.177 reflects the fact that (most of) the articles in the EC Treaty were renumbered as a result of the Treaty of Amsterdam in 1997. It was at that time that the original art.177 was renumbered art.234 and, depending on whether cases were decided after or before that time, the reference would be art.234 (now 267) or art.177 (now 267). In the case of quotations from previous cases, square brackets containing italicised text have been used (as they have throughout the book in order to denote an insertion), e.g. art.177 [*now 267*].

PART 1: THE CONTINENTAL LEGAL TRADITION

▶ 1. Introduction

4–002 Whilst there are inevitably differences between western European countries in their approach to the interpretation of legislation and to their use of previous cases, it is nevertheless possible to identify certain characteristics common to many, if not all, such European legal orders and to identify a general pattern of interpretative and case law techniques which form a coherent tradition which historically has been unfamiliar to the English lawyer. The following sections examine these issues, drawing on the French and German legal systems for illustrative examples.

▶ 2. Key Features of the Continental Legal Tradition

▷ *(a) Constitutions*

4–003 The constitutional structure of many western European countries differs dramatically from that with which the English lawyer is familiar. There is no doctrine of Parliamentary sovereignty operating as the ultimate guarantee of democracy, but rather a written constitution which usually seeks to protect democratic rights by establishing a governmental framework based on a formal separation of powers and by securing certain fundamental rights and liberties in a Bill of Rights. The written constitution may be contained in several different legislative texts or codes and these will normally enjoy priority over any other legal provisions. Such legislative texts or codes may be referred to as "constitutional legislation" and as being "entrenched". Typically, these legislative texts or codes are not, like English legislation, specific in nature but are drafted in broad, general language and expressed in terms of general principles rather than rules. A supreme or special constitutional court is often entrusted with guardianship of the written constitution and has jurisdiction to review "ordinary legislation" (i.e. legislation not forming part of what might be regarded as the written constitution) to ensure that it is valid in accordance with the written constitution. Any conflict with the constitution can result in "ordinary legislation" being declared invalid or "unconstitutional". France and Germany provide examples of such a model.

The French Constitution is based on constitutional legislation dating back to the 1789 Revolution, including the *Declaration de 1789* and the Constitution establishing the Fifth Republic in 1958. The language of this constitutional legislation is characteristically broad, e.g. art.2 of the 1958 Constitution states only that "France is an indivisible, lay, democratic and social Republic" and the role of constitutional guardian is performed by the *Conseil Constitutionnel*, which has jurisdiction to review the constitutionality of "ordinary legislation" prior to it coming into force. In

Germany, the written constitution, the *Grundgesetz* or "basic law", came into existence after the Second World War and is also broadly drafted. Thus, art.1 provides:

> "(1) The dignity of man shall be inviolable. To respect and protect it shall be the duty of all state authority.
>
> (2) The German people therefore acknowledge inviolable and inalienable human rights as the basis of every community, of peace and of justice in the world."

The role of constitutional guardian is performed by the Federal Constitutional Court, which interprets the *Grundgesetz* to ensure uniformity and consistency for all other courts and organs of state and government.

▷ *(b) Codification*

4–004 Another significant feature of Continental legal systems is codification in most areas of substantive law. Such codification encompasses a comprehensive body of substantive law in a particular area, e.g. criminal law, and contains general and abstract principles in addition to specific legal rules. Both "constitutional legislation" and "ordinary legislation" might be so drafted and may collectively be referred to either as "codified law" or as "a code". Thus in France private law is contained in the *Code Civil* and criminal law in the *Code Pénal*. In Germany, the same areas of law are contained in the *Burgerliches Gesetzbuch* and in the *Strafgesetzbuch*.

The contrast between codified law in Continental systems and legislative provisions in the English legal system has been described by Foster (*German Legal System and Laws*, 3rd ed., 2002, p.5):

> "Codification is more than simple assimilation or compilation or, as in the UK, the consolidation of a number of statutes in particular areas of law. It is the presentation of these laws in a complete and systematic form, free of contradictions and complete with general and specific principles. The very many statutes and case decisions that exist in a particular area of law are completely reviewed, and the general principles that exist are filtered out and presented at the beginning of the code with the specific rules in following books of the code. The style of codified law differs greatly from UK law. It is an attempt to present an area of law as a unified whole, to contain not only the specific rules but also the general and abstract rules and principles which apply to all of the specific circumstances."

▷ *(c) Judicial function*

4–005 The function of judges is to determine the application of the law to the facts before them. In order to do so, judges have to ascertain what the law is and, in the case of codified law, it is assumed that the law will be contained in the code, since codes are intended to be comprehensive statements of the law. Judges will, therefore, be concerned with interpretation of the relevant provisions of the code. Whilst it might appear that there is little scope for developing propositions of law, this is not the case. Indeed, judges in Continental systems are often said to be acting in a "quasi-legislative" capacity and creating law when interpreting codes, a proposition derived from the important constitutional position of judges and the common practice of drafting codes in broad, general language, with propositions of law formulated as abstract statements of principle. Thus judges, as guardians of the constitution, may, when interpreting legislation, need to depart from its wording in order to ensure that the legislation accords with the principles of the written constitution. Further, judges may be required constitutionally to expound a proposition of law to determine cases where codified law makes no provision or produces uncertainty or injustice, e.g. in France, art.4 of the *Code Civil* prohibits a judge from failing to reach a decision on grounds of the silence, lack of clarity or insufficiency of the written codified law. Further, the use of broad, general language means that, in a given case, there may be a degree of vagueness in the relevant provision(s) in the code or may not be any relevant provision in the code which could have application, i.e. there may be a "gap" in the code.

Judges in Continental systems, when determining the law to be applied to the factual situation before them, may engage in various practices not traditionally adopted, at least to the same degree, by their English counterparts. These include:

(i) Inquiring into the constitutional validity of "ordinary legislation" in order to decide whether that legislation should have application to the case in question.

(ii) Determining, through decisions in cases, the scope of propositions of law from the abstract statements of principle contained in code provisions.

(iii) Filling in any "gap" in a code and expounding the proposition of law required to fill the "gap". Such a proposition may, like provisions in the codes, be expressed as an abstract statement of principle and, if so, the scope of such a proposition may then be clarified through decisions in later cases.

(iv) Contributing to and having regard to a body of case law (and the principles which may have been formulated and developed therefrom) which has evolved as a result of earlier courts supplementing a code by determining the scope of provisions in codes and filling "gaps". It may be that judicial supplementation of codified law in this way is anticipated and sanctioned by codes themselves, on the basis that legislative enactment cannot cover every eventuality. Thus the drafters of the original *Code Civil* in France provided: "We leave to the case law the rare and extraordinary cases that do not enter into the plan of a rational legislation . . . it is for experience to fill in gradually the gaps".

(v) Making extensive use of general principles, both as propositions of law (see (b) and (c) above) and as aids to interpretation, in determining the law to be applied to particular facts. In identifying general principles which may be so applied, courts may have recourse to several sources, including abstract statements of general principles contained in codified law; principles which have been formulated and developed by courts over a period of time through a body of case law (see (d) above); principles taken from other legal systems; or principles considered to be of application in legal systems generally (e.g. fairness and justice).

(vi) Adopting a general approach which focuses on effecting the underlying aims of provisions rather than seeking a meaning to the particular words used. This approach has required judges to employ a variety of techniques and to have recourse to a broad range of factors, to which different weight may be given, when ascertaining the final meaning (see Bredimas, *Methods of Interpretation and Community Law* (North-Holland Publishing Company, 1978), p.9).

▶ 3. Continental Judicial Techniques

▷ *(a) Interpreting codified law*

As mentioned in (vi) above, judges have employed various techniques of inter- **4–006**
pretation. Code provisions have been interpreted not only by reference to the language used (a textual approach) but also by reference to the underlying purpose of a provision (a purposive or teleological approach). This underlying purpose might be ascertained by reference to several factors. These might include general matters such as the spirit of the code in general and general principles of law, either articulated in codified law within the system or which emanate from fundamental notions of equity and justice. More particularly, they might include the legislative context in which the provision is set (a contextual approach) and legislative intention in respect of the provision. As regards the latter, reference might be made to materials from which the legislator's actual intention, at the time of enactment of the code, can be ascertained, e.g. in France pre-legislative materials, known as *travaux préparatoires* (see below). Alternatively, intention might be determined objectively in the light of contemporary social conditions (a popular approach in Germany), with a notional rather than actual intention attributed to the legislator.

No one technique of interpretation has dominated in Europe; rather a flexible combination of techniques, often with differences in emphasis rather than substance, has been used. Thus in Germany, there is a preference for an objective approach as a starting point, with the process of interpretation consisting of an examination of the literal meaning of the language, together with consideration of the legislative context within which the provision is placed, both in the particular code in question and in other codes in the general field. In situations of uncertainty, recourse may be had to a teleological approach in an attempt to ascertain the underlying purpose of the particular provision. However, use may also be made of a subjective (or historical) approach, which seeks to establish the aim of the legislator at the time of drafting, and which allows reference to be made to preparatory documents. Further, a comparative approach may be used, with examination of similar situations in other jurisdictions, often the Swiss or Austrian systems.

In France, interpretation is generally more subjective. When examining the language used in a provision and in the code in which it appears, considerable use is made of *travaux préparatoires*, including draft bills, reports presented to Parliament and parliamentary debates. However, alongside these methods French judges also adopt a teleological approach, under which they take into account the purpose of the code in its modern context and interpret provisions in the light of contemporary social conditions and values.

▷ (b) Using previous cases

4–007   As stated (see above, 4–005), judges may have regard to a body of case law when interpreting provisions in codes, but previous decisions are accorded much less significance than in the English system. This is because codes are intended to be comprehensive statements of the law in a given area and therefore the judicial function is restricted to interpretation, albeit creative interpretation, of the legislative language. Thus decisions in individual cases, although binding on the parties to those cases, do not establish legal rules which may be binding in future cases, as they may do in the English system. Indeed, both French and German judges are prohibited from making decisions which will create a general rule of law when deciding cases (by art.5 of the *Code Civil* and arts 20(3) and 97(1) of the *Grundgesetz* respectively). Hence no doctrine of precedent, with its emphasis on stare decisis, is found in Continental systems. As a consequence, judges are not required to engage in the process of applying, distinguishing and overruling earlier decisions nor do their judgments include lengthy analyses of previous cases. In addition, whilst English decisions may contain several judgments, including dissenting ones, the decisions made by Continental courts are likely to contain only one judgment, that being the judgment of the whole court rather than an individual judge, with no dissenting judgments given.

Despite the absence of a doctrine of binding precedent, however, judicial decisions in civil law systems might be described (from an English perspective) as having persuasive authority in that they may be important as sources of guidance for a court in determining the law to be applied in a particular case. When provisions in codes are interpreted by courts, a series of decisions may emerge over a period of time on the scope of those provisions or in respect of any "gap" to be filled. These decisions are likely to be consistent with each other (since certainty and rationality are important precepts in any legal system) and comprise a body of law which may supplement the code and be a source of guidance for courts in future cases. This body of law may provide guidance not only for courts considering future cases involving some provision or "gap" but also for courts seeking general principles when considering other provisions or "gaps" in the code. In this context, some cases within that body of law may carry greater weight than others, e.g. in France cases confirmed by a significant series of later decisions and cases decided by higher courts, and, in Germany, decisions of higher courts and recent decisions. Previous cases thus constitute an important source of guidance for courts, to which recourse should be had, and judges who disregard such case law are likely to find their decisions reversed on appeal.

▷ (c) Using general principles

As stated (see above, 4–005), judges may make extensive use of general princi- **4–008**
ples, derived from a number of sources, not only as propositions of law but also as aids to interpretation. An example of a general principle in a code is art.1 of the *Grundgesetz* (see above, 4–003), which accords protection to human dignity. Examples of general principles, not contained in a code, but developed by courts, include, in Germany, legal certainty (*Bestimmtheit*) and proportionality (*Verhält-nismässigkeit*), under which a measure taken by a public body or a penalty imposed must bear a reasonable and proportionate relationship to the intended objective, whilst in France the constitutional court, the *Conseil Constitutionnel*, has evolved *Principes Fondamentaux* for use in the constitutional sphere and other courts have developed *Principes Généraux* for general use in the private and administrative law domains.

However, it should not be assumed that use of general principles is confined to Continental systems, for such principles may also be used in common law systems in the English tradition, although perhaps to a more limited extent. The more detailed propositions of law usually found in common law systems, contained in either legislation or in the rationes of cases, reduce the need for recourse to general principles.

PART 2: THE EUROPEAN UNION LEGAL ORDER

▶ 1. Introduction

In the aftermath of the Second World War, a variety of inter-state initiatives **4–009**
intended to ensure peaceful co-existence and co-operation between European nations emerged. The European Coal and Steel Community, established by the Treaty of Paris in 1951 by France, Germany, Italy, Luxembourg, Belgium and the Netherlands, aimed to create a single market in coal and steel in order to prevent any nation acquiring dominance over the materials of war. This organisation formed the prototype for the European Economic and European Atomic Energy Communities established by the twin Treaties of Rome in 1957 by the same six States.

At the same time, there was a move towards a unified structure for the three Communities, with the establishing of a single European Parliament and a

European Court of Justice with jurisdiction in respect of all three Communities. This was continued under the Merger Treaty in 1965 with the establishing of a single Council of Ministers and a single European Commission, again with jurisdiction in respect of all three Communities. Of the three Communities, the European Economic Community subsequently became the dominant entity, primarily because its sphere of competence was significantly wider than the other two, encompassing, in addition to economic objectives, social, cultural and political goals. This in due course came to be known as the European Community and was formally known as such since the Treaty on European Union in 1992 (see below).

The European Community has, since emerging, made a number of advances. First, its institutions, the Commission, the Parliament and the Council of Ministers, which, broadly speaking, are concerned respectively with the initiation, consideration and enactment of legislation (although the Parliament itself does have some powers to enact legislation) and the Court of Justice, which is concerned with the validity and interpretation of EU law, have evolved into established and powerful bodies. Secondly, its membership expanded considerably over the years and the current number of Members States is now 27, following the accession of the UK, Ireland and Denmark in 1973; Greece in 1981; Portugal and Spain in 1986; Austria, Finland and Sweden in 1995; Cyprus, Malta and a number of former "Eastern bloc" States (Czech Republic, Estonia, Hungary, Latvia, Lithuania, Poland, Slovakia and Slovenia) in 2004; and Bulgaria and Romania in 2007. Thirdly, major steps were taken towards the harmonisation of Member States' laws, the creation of a single internal market and, most significantly in the context of this chapter, the development of a sophisticated legal order with a distinctive legislative style and techniques of interpretation.

The European Community, following the Treaty on European Union signed at Maastricht in 1992, became part of a wider European Union. Under this Treaty, Member States made mutual commitments in two areas: (a) common foreign and security policy; and (b) justice and home affairs (which, following the Treaty of Amsterdam in 1997, was revised to constitute police and judicial co-operation in criminal matters, and this took on a more supranational character). The Union thus became an "umbrella" organisation, encompassing these two areas in addition to the third area of the EC. The EU thus comprised three "pillars", of which the EC was one component, albeit the most significant and highly developed. From this point onwards, it became more appropriate to talk of EU law and an EU legal order rather than EC law and an EC legal order. The three "pillars" themselves in fact now no longer form separate aspects of the EU and have, following the Treaty of Lisbon in 2009, been unified into a single structure. The EC has thus now ceased to exist as a separate entity and has been subsumed into the EU, with the EC Treaty being amended and renamed the Treaty on the Functioning of the European Union (see above, 4–001). All references to "European Community" or "European Communities" now disappear and are replaced by "European Union". Notwithstanding this, it has been necessary to make reference to the EC rather than the EU at various points in the chapter e.g. when referring to case law decided before the creation of the EU, although the term "European Union" has therefore (for the most part) been employed in this chapter.

▶ 2. Key Features of the European Union Legal Order

▷ (a) "Constitution"

The fundamental principles and institutional framework upon which the EU is **4–010** founded are set out in written form in a series of Treaties and Acts, which might be considered to form the "constitution" of the EU. They include the Treaty of Paris in 1951 and the two Treaties of Rome in 1957, the Merger Treaty of 1965, the Single European Act of 1986, the Treaty on European Union of 1992, the Treaty of Amsterdam of 1997, the Treaty of Nice of 2001 and the Treaty of Lisbon 2009. They also include the Charter of Fundamental Rights of the European Union, drawn up in 2000 and given the same legally binding status by the Treaty of Lisbon 2009 as the preceding provisions. The Charter, which is based on the fundamental rights and freedoms recognised by the European Convention on Human Rights (see below, 5–010), sets out in a single document the range of civil, political, economic and social rights of EU citizens and persons resident in EU member states. These rights are divided into six sections, which comprise Dignity, Freedoms, Equality, Solidarity, Citizens' rights and Justice.

Although not strictly constituting legislation, Treaty provisions might be regarded as the constitutional "legislation" of the EU. In typical Continental style, such provisions, which contain the fundamental objectives upon which the EU legal order is founded, are drafted in broad, general language and expressed in terms of general principles rather than rules. Thus art.3 of the TFEU provides:

> "1. The Union's aim is to promote peace, its values and the well-being of its peoples.
>
> 2. The Union shall offer its citizens an area of freedom, security and justice without internal frontiers in which the free movement of persons is ensured in conjunction with respect to external border controls, asylum, immigration and the prevention and combating of crime.
>
> 3. It shall work for the sustainable development of Europe based on balanced economic growth and price stability, a highly competitive social market economy, aiming at full employment and social progress, and a high level of protection and improvement of the quality of the environment. It shall promote scientific and technological advance.
>
> It shall combat social exclusion and discrimination, and shall promote social justice and protection, equality between women and men, solidarity between generations and protection of the rights of the child.

It shall promote economic, social and territorial cohesion, and solidarity among Member States.

It shall respect its rich cultural and linguistic diversity, and shall ensure that Europe's cultural heritage is safeguarded and enhanced.

4. The Union shall establish an economic and monetary union whose currency is the euro.

5. In its relations with the wider world, the Union shall uphold and promote its values and interests and contribute to the protection of its citizens. It shall contribute to peace, security, the sustainable development of the Earth, solidarity and mutual respect among peoples, free and fair trade, eradication of poverty and the protection of human rights, in particular the rights of the child, as well as to the strict observance and the development of international law, including respect for the principles of the United Nations Charter.

6. The Union shall pursue its objectives by appropriate means commensurate with the competences which are conferred upon it in the Treaties."

Illustrative reference

4–011 See: Chapter 14: *"Equal pay"* (14–002), for an example of an EC Treaty provision, art.141 (now 157), which is drafted in typical Continental style.

Such provisions are in marked contrast to English legislation. As Lord Denning, M.R. observed in *H.P. Bulmer Ltd v J. Bollinger S.A.* [1974] Ch. 401 at 425 (*Bulmer*):

"The . . . Treaty is quite unlike any of the enactments to which we have become accustomed . . . It lays down general principles. It expresses its aims and purposes. All sentences are of moderate length and commendable style. But it lacks precision. It uses words and phrases without defining what they mean. An English lawyer would look for an interpretation clause, but he would look in vain. There is none. All the way through the Treaty there are gaps and lacunae. These have to be filled in by the judges, or by Regulations or directives. It is the European way . . .".

Typical again of the Continental tradition is the role given to the CJ of guardian of the "constitution" and supreme interpreter of EU law. This role is conferred by the following provisions: art.19 of the TEU, which requires the CJ to ensure that in the interpretation and application of the Treaties the law is observed; arts 263–264 (ex 230–231) of the TFEU, which give the CJ power to annul an unlawful act; and art.267 (ex 234) of the TFEU, which enables the CJ to interpret the Treaty, legislation (the meaning of which is explained immediately below) and administrative acts of the other EU institutions, namely the Commission, the Council of Ministers and the Parliament. The power under art.267 (ex 234) arises following a reference to the CJ by a Member State court, which can refer if it considers that a decision on the matter referred is "necessary to enable it to give judgment" and request that the CJ give a preliminary ruling in answer to a question on the meaning of EU law. Through this procedure, the CJ has the opportunity, not only to interpret EU law, but, in doing so, to provide, indirectly, an indication of where the national law of Member States is failing to conform with EU law. All Member States accept an obligation to conform with EU law so, if when interpreting EU law it appears that the national law of a Member State is in conflict with EU law, the CJ by implication can determine that national law cannot have application. Hence the CJ performs the role of guardian of the "constitution" in two senses: by reviewing the validity of EU law in general by reference to the "constitutional" legislation, i.e. the TEU and TFEU, and by effectively reviewing the applicability of national laws by reference to the superior legal authority of EU law.

▷ *(b) Legislation*

Under various provisions in the TFEU, the Council of Ministers and the European Commission can draft and enact legislation containing further instructions as to the methods by which the broad objectives of the Treaties are to be realised and implemented. Such legislation includes regulations (which are the most numerous), directives and decisions. Regulations seek to (uniformly) govern activities in Member States, e.g. in agriculture and health and safety; directives seek to harmonise national laws to meet community objectives, whilst leaving the form of legislation to national governments; and decisions are addressed to individual Member States or community sectors. All of these forms of legislation have binding legal force under art.288 (ex 249), which provides:

4–012

> "A regulation shall have general application. It shall be binding in its entirety and directly applicable in all Member States.
>
> A directive shall be binding as to the result to be achieved, upon each Member State to which it is addressed, but shall leave to the national authorities the choice of form and methods.
>
> A decision shall be binding in its entirety on those to whom it is addressed."

Opinions and recommendations, in contrast, do not have such force and cannot properly be called legislation. As the function of legislation is to embellish the bare provisions of the TFEU, their provisions are usually more specific and precise than TFEU provisions. They are nevertheless often less comprehensive and technical than either English Acts of Parliament or English secondary legislation in the form of statutory instruments. As Lord Denning, M.R. remarked in *Bulmer* (at 425–426):

> ". . . the Regulations and directives . . . are enacted by the Council [*of Ministers*] sitting in Brussels for everyone to obey. They are quite unlike our statutory instruments. They have to give the reasons on which they are based: article 190 of the EEC Treaty [*now Article 296 of the TFEU*]. So they start off

> with pages of preambles, "whereas" and "whereas" and "whereas." These show the purpose and intent of the Regulations and directives. Then follow the provisions which are to be obeyed. Here again words and phrases are used without defining their import . . . In case of difficulty, recourse is had to the preambles. These are useful to show the purpose and intent behind it all. But much is left to the judges. The enactments give only an outline plan. The details are to be filled in by the judges."

Whilst these remarks may still be true in respect of some regulations and directives, it should be said that many of them are now more detailed than perhaps Lord Denning M.R.'s remarks suggest.

▷ *(c) Judicial function*

4–013   The function of judges in the CJ is broadly comparable to that of judges in Continental systems generally (see above, 4–005). Thus judges in these courts are concerned with interpreting broadly drafted provisions in codified law. Relatively little indication of the scope of these provisions may be provided at the time of their enactment and judges may need to make a significant contribution to expanding their ambit after enactment, by determining the scope of the provisions and filling any "gaps" which exist. In order to do so, judges may adopt techniques of interpretation drawn primarily from the Continental legal tradition (see above, 4–006) and engage in practices adopted by judges in Continental systems, such as having regard to a body of case law and making use of general principles (both of which are further considered below). Through this process, which may involve judges acting in a "quasi-legislative" capacity and creating law, the ambit of legislative provisions will continue to evolve progressively over time.

Illustrative reference

4–014   See: Chapter 14: *"Equal pay"* (14–006), where in *Macarthys Ltd v Smith* (*Macarthys*) the ECJ determined the scope of the provision based on art.119 (now 157) of the EC Treaty by reference to earlier ECJ case law, *Defrenne v Sabena* (*Defrenne*); and (14–012), where in *Garland v British Rail Engineering Ltd* (*Garland*) the ECJ examined the same provision by reference to earlier ECJ case law, *Defrenne* and *Worringham v Lloyds Bank Ltd* (*Worringham*).

This judicial function contrasts with that of judges in the English legal system when interpreting English legislation, which traditionally contains detailed provisions which tend to be comprehensive in coverage, specific in nature and formulated with a degree of precision. English judges therefore are concerned primarily with establishing whether particular facts fall within the meaning of the words used and have limited opportunity to explore the general scope of the legislative provisions under consideration, which will largely have been pre-determined at the time of enactment.

These differences in legislative styles and judicial function have caused particular difficulties with regard to the requirement in the ECA 1972 that English law complies with EU law. As the ambit of EU law has developed through judicial decisions, apparent deficiencies in English law may be revealed. Where such deficiencies exist, there may be said to be a "compliance gap" in English law and English judges have frequently had to confront such "gaps". Sometimes the ensuing difficulties have been resolved by judges modifying their traditional approaches to interpretation of legislation, e.g. by "gap filling" or by according priority to EU law irrespective of the position under English law (see below, 14–032). On other occasions, they have been resolved through the introduction of new legislation drafted in order to ensure compliance with EU obligations, prompted either in recognition by Parliament of an acknowledged deficiency or in response to a CJ decision finding that there is a deficiency.

Illustrative reference

4–015

See: Chapter 14: *"Equal pay"* (14–002 and 14–003) for examples of the drafting style employed in EU legislation (Directive 75/117) and English legislation (s.1 of the EPA 1970); and (14–002) for an example of a "compliance gap" in English law in s.1 of the EPA 1970.

▶ 3. Judicial Techniques

▷ *(a) Interpreting legislation*

Focus on underlying aims of provisions rather than their wording has been an **4–016** approach adopted by the CJ from the outset, as can be seen from the early case of Case 26/62 *Van Gend en Loos v Nederlandse Administratie der Belastingen* [1963] E.C.R. 1 (*Van Gend en Loos*) where the ECJ remarked (at 12) that:

". . . to ascertain whether the provisions of an international treaty extend so far in their effects it is necessary to consider the spirit, the general scheme and the wording of those provisions."

The CJ has evolved an interpretative tradition centred around the three matters to which reference was made in the *Van Gend en Loos* case, namely the spirit of the legislation, or what may be described as the teleological or purposive approach (teleological approach); the general scheme within which the legislation is found, or what may be described as the schematic or contextual approach (schematic approach); and the wording of the legislation, or what may be described as a textual or literal approach (textual approach). These approaches have been applied by the CJ, not as distinct alternatives, but in unison, and in order to ensure that the interpretation given to a provision is one which gives maximum effect to achieving the aims and objectives of the EU.

The logical starting point, whether it is a Treaty provision or a provision in legislation which is under scrutiny, is the textual approach which involves examination of the wording of the text and the meaning, on the face of it, of the language used. In some instances, the CJ may conclude that the ordinary meaning of the words can be applied, e.g. in Case 152/84 *Marshall v Southampton and South West Hampshire Area Health Authority* [1986] E.C.R. 723 (*Marshall*); and in Case C-91/92 *Faccini Dori v Recreb Srl* [1994] E.C.R. I-3325, it was held that, where art.189 (now 288), which describes the legislative acts that the political institutions of the EU are empowered to adopt, provides that "a directive shall be binding . . . upon each Member State to which it is addressed", the directive is not binding on individuals. The textual approach, however, may fail to provide a satisfactory conclusion for a number of reasons. First, it may give rise to difficulties because of the multi-lingual character of EU law. With several different language versions of the TFEU and legislation, the (ordinary) meaning may differ according to the particular language version and some versions may give a clearer indication of meaning than others. Naturally, the approach of the CJ is to seek to interpret provisions in a way that is consistent with all (or nearly all) of the different versions, although in some instances examination of the different versions may prove inconclusive. Secondly, the broad, general language of the provision itself may make it difficult to ascertain meaning from a textual approach and may give rise to uncertainty. Thirdly, a textual approach may produce a conflict with what the CJ perceives to be a fundamental aim or objective of the EU.

Where a textual approach fails to produce a satisfactory conclusion, the court may adopt a schematic and/or teleological approach, under which reference may be made to other legislative provisions (including provisions in or preambles to the legislation containing the particular provision or other legislation including the TFEU itself); a body of case law developed by the CJ; general principles in EU legislation and/or formulated and developed by the CJ through its case law; and the underlying aims or objectives of the EU. The schematic and/or teleological approaches were described by Lord Denning, M.R. in *James Buchanan & Co Ltd v Babco Forwarding and Shipping (UK) Ltd* [1977] Q.B. 208 at 213–214 (*James Buchanan*) as follows:

"They [*the ECJ*] adopt a method which they call in English by strange words—at any rate they were strange to me—the 'schematic and teleological' method of interpretation. It is not really so alarming as it sounds. All it means is that the judges do not go by the literal meaning of the words or by the grammatical structure of the sentence. They go by the design or purpose which lies behind it. When they come upon a situation which is to their minds within the spirit—but not the letter—of the legislation, they solve the problem by looking at the design and purpose of the legislature—at the effect which it was sought to achieve. They then interpret the legislation so as to produce the desired effect. This means that they fill in gaps, quite unashamedly, without hesitation. They ask simply: what is the sensible way of dealing with this situation so as to give effect to the presumed purpose of the legislation? They lay down the law accordingly. If you study the decisions of the European Court, you will see that they do it every day. To our eyes—short-sighted by tradition—it is legislation pure and simple. But to their eyes, it is fulfilling the true role of the courts."

Illustrative reference

See: Chapter 14: *"Equal pay"* (14–006), where in *Macarthys* the ECJ interpreted art.119 (now 157) of the EC Treaty in order to give effect to the aims of the article and, in doing so, made use of the text of art.119 (now 157) (textual), the text of other legislative provisions, e.g. the preamble to the Treaty (schematic), the purpose and objectives of art.119 (now 157) (teleological) and the social objectives of the EU (teleological), as well as referring to ECJ case law (*Defrenne*).

4–017

These techniques of interpretation are employed by the CJ in cases heard before it, which are those involving direct actions by EU institutions or Member States and applications for preliminary rulings under art.267 (ex 234). The techniques are similarly employed in cases heard by the GC (previously the CFI), which are generally those involving direct actions brought by natural or legal persons, although in limited instances they also include direct actions by Member States (e.g. some actions brought against the Council of Ministers and nearly all acts of the European Commission). It is also likely that the same techniques will be used by judicial panels e.g. the European Union Civil Service Tribunals, created by the European Council in exercise of its powers under art.257.

▷ *(b) Using previous cases*

The CJ's use of previous cases is broadly in keeping with the approach of judges in Continental systems (see above, 4–007). There is no formal doctrine of precedent and stare decisis, and the court is not bound by its own previous decisions. This is due in part to the influence of the Continental legal tradition but also to the particular requirements of the EU legal order. The latter factor has been explained by Arnull ("Owning up to Fallibility: Precedent and the Court of Justice" (1993) 30 C.M.L.R. 247 at 248) as follows:

4–018

"A doctrine of binding precedent on common law lines would have been entirely inappropriate in what was originally a court of first and last resort, many of whose decisions could only be changed by amending the Treaties, a cumbersome process requiring the agreement of all the Member States and ratification by each of them in accordance with their respective constitutional requirements. It was therefore imperative that the Court should have the power to change the direction of its case law and to depart from its previous decisions, particularly in cases with important constitutional implications."

Such freedom from the constraints of precedent might be considered particularly important in the context of art.267 (ex 234), whereby Member State courts can request the CJ's ruling on the interpretation of EU law when a question of interpretation arises in a domestic court. In this respect, it is important that the Member State courts feel free to refer cases even if the CJ has considered a similar question of interpretation in a previous case, a freedom bolstered by the knowledge that the CJ can reconsider questions of interpretation at any time. The absence of any formal doctrine of precedent means that all pronouncements of the CJ in its judgments have the same persuasive force and there is no distinction to be drawn between the ratio of a decision and obiter dicta, as in common law jurisdictions where this distinction is important (because the ratio may form a binding precedent but obiter dicta cannot).

The CJ does, however, observe the less restrictive principle of *res judicata*, which, simply, means that the decision in a case is final and binding as between the parties to that case and will be binding in a future case only if there is an identity of parties, cause and subject matter. If any such circumstances are absent, the court can depart from the earlier decision. The importance of the principle of *res judicata* was explained by Advocate General Lagrange in Case 28–30/62 *Da Costa v Nederlandse Belastingadministratie* [1963] E.C.R. 31 at 42:

". . . *res judicata* . . . is a wise rule; rather than enabling the court to shelter formally behind a previous judgment, as one shelters behind a law or regulation, it obliges it unceasingly to retain awareness of its responsibility, that is, to confront the realities of the situation with the legal rule in each action, which can lead it in appropriate cases to recognise its errors in the light of new facts, of new arguments or even of a spontaneous rethinking, or more frequently to alter its point of view *subtly* without changing it fundamentally, thus being party in the light of experience and the evolution of legal theories and economic, social or other phenomena, to what is called the evolution of case law. The rule that *res judicata* binds only the particular case is the weapon which permits courts to do this. Of course, they should in their wisdom only use this weapon prudently, on pain of destroying legal certainty, but it is necessary for them and they should not abandon it."

In the interests of maintaining certainty, however, the CJ, in practice, operates with a high level of consistency, generally preferring to follow its own previous decisions and rarely departing from a previous ruling. By generally following previous decisions, the CJ can develop a body of law on a particular area, known sometimes as *jurisprudence constante*. Such a body of case law supplements codified law and is a source of guidance for courts in future cases in that it gives substance to general propositions of law and contributes to the formulation and development of principles of general application (see above, 4–005 and 4–008). (For the development of a body of essentially judge-made principles from CJ case law, see the following cases on (a) the principle of supremacy of EU law: *Van Gend en Loos*; Case 6/64 *Costa v ENEL* [1964] E.C.R. 585 (*Costa*); Case 106/7 *Amministrazione delle Finanze Dello Stato v Simmenthal* [1978] E.C.R. 629 (*Simmenthal*); Case 246/89R *EC Commission v UK* [1989] 3 C.M.L.R. 601; and Case 221/89 *R. v Secretary of State for Transport Ex p. Factortame Ltd (No. 3)* [1992] Q.B. 680; and (b) the principle of direct effect of EU law: *Van Gend en Loos*; Case 43/71 *Politi v Italian Ministry of Finance* [1971] E.C.R. 1039 (*Politi*); Case 41/74 *Van Duyn v Home Office* [1974] E.C.R. 1337 (*Van Duyn*); and *Marshall*. These principles are further considered below, at 4–023.)

Although generally following its previous decisions, the CJ has on occasions refused to do so and has expressly overruled them, e.g. in *Brown v Rentokil* [1998] E.C.R. I-4185, a case concerning protection under the Equal Treatment Directive for female employees falling ill on account of pregnancy, the ECJ overruled its previous decision in *Larsson v Fotex Supermarked* [1997] E.C.R. I-2757. Whilst the principle of departing explicitly from previous decisions has become well established, instances of its occurrence nevertheless remain infrequent.

The CJ's approach to using previous cases and treating them as only persuasive authorities inevitably influences the form of its judgments, which are similar to those delivered by courts in Continental legal systems (see above, 4–007). Only one judgment is delivered and traditionally judgments have in general been concise with little detailed explanation of the decision, although an exposition of the relevant law is often found in the opinion of the Advocate General, whose role includes preparing a solution to the case and relating the solution to existing case law. However, CJ judgments have become more expansive over the years, with greater attention paid to the effect of previous case law. Indeed, there has been an increasing recognition of the need to provide an explanation when departing from previous decisions and also when declining to do so, in the interests of maintaining consistency and certainty. Further, there has been less of a tendency for the CJ to pay no regard to earlier decisions which may be considered "inconvenient" and a greater inclination to address such decisions with a view to "distinguishing" them in instances where the CJ does not wish to follow them but is not minded to overrule them, e.g. in Case C-100/01 *Ministre de l'Interieur v Aitor Oteiza Olazabal* [2002] E.C.R. I-10981 the court gave a detailed account of why it considered the case before it to be distinguishable from its earlier decision in Case 36/75 *Rutili v Minister for the Interior* [1975] E.C.R. 1219.

Illustrative reference

4–019

See: Chapter 14: *"Equal pay"* (14–006 and 14–012), for examples, in *Macarthys* and *Garland*, of the nature of opinions of Advocates General; and (14–012) for an example in *Garland* of the form of judgment delivered by the court.

The approach of the GC to using previous cases has, since its establishment (as the CFI) in 1988, been similar to that of the CJ. The GC's previous decisions are regarded by it as being only of persuasive authority, although these are likely to be followed in the interests of certainty and consistency. Nor has the GC regarded itself as bound by the previous decisions of the CJ, although that court is hierarchically superior to it, except in limited and well-defined circumstances. Such circumstances include, for example, where there is an appeal from the GC to the CJ and the CJ has referred the case back to the GC for judgment, since the second paragraph of art.54 of the EC Statute of the Court of Justice provides that in this case the GC "shall be bound by the decision of the Court of Justice on points of law". CJ decisions may be regarded by the GC as highly persuasive, but they are not considered by it to be binding. As was stated (by the CFI) in *NMB France v EC Commission* [1996] E.C.R. II-427, at [36], when declaring a second action by the applicants admissible notwithstanding the dismissal by the ECJ of a previous action by them based on similar arguments (in *NMB v EC Commission* [1992] E.C.R. I-1689):

> "It must be borne in mind at the outset that the Court of First Instance is only bound by the judgments of the Court of Justice, first, in the circumstances laid down in the second paragraph of Article 54 of the Statute of the Court of Justice of the European Community, and, secondly, pursuant to the principle of *res judicata*."

The second action, although similar, was not, in the court's view, "a mere replication" at [39] of the first and it followed that:

> ". . . this action is entirely admissible and that the Court of First Instance must therefore examine its merits. In doing so, it should take account simultaneously of the judgment in *NMB and Others v EC Commission* [1992] E.C.R. I-1689 and of the new issues raised by these proceedings."

After examination of the merits and consideration of the new issues raised, the action was dismissed. Although reaching a similar decision to the ECJ in the earlier action, it is clear that, in keeping with the civil law tradition, the court did not regard the ECJ's decision in that action as having more than persuasive authority. As Arnull (*The European Union and its Court of Justice* (2nd ed., Oxford University Press, 2006), p.637) has observed, by regarding ECJ decisions as (highly) persuasive but not binding:

> "The CFI . . . has struck a nice balance between deference to the case law of the Court of Justice and a natural desire to do justice in the cases it is called upon to decide. The creative tension which results from the unwillingness of the CFI to follow without question the decisions of the Court may be regarded as conducive to the healthy development of Community law."

▷ *(c) Using general principles*

The CJ and the GC, like many courts in Continental systems, make extensive use of **4-020** general principles both as propositions of law and as aids to interpretation. The origins of these general principles are diverse and include the texts of national constitutions, national laws and jurisprudence of Member States, international conventions signed by Member States, such as the European Convention on Human Rights, and principles of application in legal systems generally.

A general principle adopted by the CJ from the national laws and jurisprudence of Member States, for example, is the principle of proportionality, which was abstracted from the German legal system (see above, 4-008). The CJ has, as was acknowledged in the Case C-331/88 *R. v Minister of Agriculture, Food and Fisheries and Secretary of State for Health Ex p. Fedesa* [1990] E.C.R. I-4023, [13]:

> "consistently held that the principle of proportionality is one of the general principles of Community law. By virtue of that principle, the lawfulness of the prohibition of an economic activity is subject to the condition that the prohibitory measures are appropriate and necessary in order to achieve the objectives legitimately pursued by the legislation in question; when there is a choice between several appropriate measures recourse must be had to the least onerous, and the disadvantages caused must not be disproportionate to the aims pursued."

Thus, for example, in Case 261/81 *Rau v De Smeldt* [1982] E.C.R. 3961, a prohibitory measure in national legislation (in Belgium) requiring packaging of margarine in cube-shaped blocks, in order to prevent it from being confused with butter, was not necessary to achieve the legitimate object of avoiding confusion in the mind of the consumer, since in the court's view "consumers may in fact be protected just as effectively by other measures, for example, by rules on labelling, which hinder the free movement of goods less" [13].

A general principle adopted from an international convention, and from principles of application in legal systems generally (including several Member States), is the principle of respect for fundamental human rights. This was taken, in part, from the European Convention on Human Rights, and in part from the codes and case law of various legal systems, notably Germany, e.g. art.1 of the *Grundgesetz* (see above, 4-003). From adoption of the principle, the Charter of Fundamental Rights of the European Union was subsequently drawn up in 2000 and given legally binding status in 2009 (see above, 4-010).

In addition to using general principles as indicated above, the CJ has also developed through its case law principles of general application, such as supremacy and direct effect (see above, 4-018 and below, 4-023).

PART 3: THE IMPACT OF THE EUROPEAN UNION LEGAL ORDER ON STATUTORY INTERPRETATION AND THE DOCTRINE OF PRECEDENT IN ENGLISH LAW

▶ 1. Introduction

4–021   Certain legal implications usually follow the signing of an international treaty by the UK Government. The treaty does not have legal force until an Act of Parliament is passed giving it such effect. Treaties can, however, influence how English law is interpreted because of the presumption that English statutes are intended by Parliament to comply with international treaty obligations. Accordingly, in the event of any ambiguity in a statute, it might be interpreted to accord with such obligations. When the UK Government signed the EC Treaty, however, this was different from signing a normal international treaty in that the EC Treaty was intended not merely to create international obligations, but to require acceptance into a country's legal systems of an external legal order, which affects both substantive legal rights and judicial techniques.

The introduction of the EC legal order (as it then was) into the English legal system was effected by the ECA 1972, primarily ss.2 and 3. These sections (unusually for English legislation!) are expressed in broad, general terms which (perhaps intentionally) leave it unclear how penetration of the legal order into the English legal system is to be effected and to what extent it should take place. Not surprisingly, there have been differing judicial opinions on this matter. Equally, there have been differing judicial opinions on the implications for statutory interpretation and precedent, and the extent to which adaptations may need to be made to traditional English practices in these areas. Some judges have embraced penetration of the legal order into the English legal system with enthusiasm. Thus Lord Denning, M.R. in *Bulmer* stated (at [1974] Ch. 401 at 418–419):

"When we come to matters with a European element, the Treaty is like an incoming tide. It flows into the estuaries and up the rivers. It cannot be held back, Parliament has decreed that the Treaty is henceforward to be part of our law. It is equal in force to any statute . . .

The statute [*the ECA 1972*] is expressed in forthright terms which are absolute and all-embracing. Any rights or obligations created by the Treaty are to be given legal effect in England without more ado. Any remedies or procedures provided by the Treaty are to be made available here without being open to question. In future, in transactions which cross the frontiers, we must no longer speak or think of English law as something on its own. We must speak and think of community law, of community rights and obligations, and we must give effect to them. This means a great effort for the lawyers. We have to learn a new system. The Treaty, with the regulations and directives, covers many volumes. The case law is contained in hundreds of reported cases both in the European Court of Justice and in the national courts of the nine [*Member States*]. Many must be studied before the right result can be reached. We must get down to it."

Other judges, however, have been less enthusiastic. Thus in *Duke v GEC Reliance Ltd* [1988] A.C. 618, 639 (*Duke*) Lord Templeman (with whose speech all other members of the House of Lords agreed) appeared not to acknowledge the existence of the principle established by the ECJ in *Marleasing SA v La Comercial Internacional de Alimentation SA* [1990] E.C.R. I-4135 (*Marleasing*) that Member States' courts must interpret national legislation so as to comply with EU law in cases where EU law does not have direct effect (see below, 4–023):

"Section 2(4) of the European Communities Act 1972 does not in my opinion enable or constrain a British Court to distort the meaning of a British statute in order to enforce against an individual a Community directive which has no direct effect between individuals. Section 2(4) applies and only applies where Community provisions are directly applicable."

The application of this principle was, however, later acknowledged by a subsequent House of Lords in *Litster v Forth Dry Dock and Engineering Co Ltd* [1990] 1 A.C. 546 (*Litster*).

Differing views as to the penetration of the legal order into the English legal system, which have been influenced by judicial perceptions of the constitutional relationship between the EU and the UK, have perhaps inevitably resulted in differing judicial approaches with regard to the impact of the EU legal order on statutory interpretation and precedent. The following two sections below set out the constitutional relationship between the EU and the UK (see 4–022—4–024), examined from an EU and from a UK perspective, and the differing judicial approaches that have been taken to statutory interpretation (see 4–025—4–037) and precedent (see 4–038—4–040).

▶ 2. The Relationship Between the European Union and the United Kingdom

This relationship is considered from two perspectives, that of the EU, as articulated by the CJ in its judgments, and that of the UK, indicated initially in ss.2 and 3 of the ECA 1972 and subsequently in the way in which these sections have been interpreted by English courts.

4–022

▷ *(a) The European Union perspective*

4–023 From the outset, the European Communities had supra-national characteristics which it was envisaged would affect both the sovereignty of Member States and the legal rights of their citizens. This view is, in part, based on Treaty articles, including those stating objectives, e.g. art.3 of the TFEU (see above, 4–010) and those articles of the TFEU which define the powers of EU institutions such as art.288 (ex 249), which describes the legislation they can adopt, and art.267 (ex 234), which gives review and interpretative powers to the CJ (see above, 4–010). As early as 1962 in *Van Gend en Loos*, the court stated (at [1963] E.C.R. 1 at 12):

> ". . . the Community constitutes a new legal order of international law for the benefit of which the states have limited their sovereign rights, albeit within limited fields, and the subjects of which comprise not only Member States but also their nationals. Independently of the legislation of Member States, Community law therefore not only imposes obligations on individuals but is also intended to confer upon them rights which become part of their legal heritage. These rights arise not only where they are expressly granted by the Treaty, but also by reason of obligations which the Treaty imposes in a clearly defined way upon individuals as well as upon the Member States and upon the institutions of the Community."

Particular manifestations of this perception of the EU as a supra-national legal order are made by the twin principles of supremacy of EU law and direct effect, and the principle of indirect effect. These principles, whilst perhaps broadly based on the TFEU generally, have been developed by the CJ through a body of case law. Under the first principle, national courts may be required to accord priority to EU law when a conflict arises between national law and EU law. The foundation of this principle was laid in *Van Gend en Loos* and consolidated in *Costa*, in which the court (at [1964] E.C.R. 585 at 594) justified supremacy in the following terms:

> ". . . the law stemming from the treaty, an independent source of law . . . [*cannot*] because of its special and original nature, be overridden by domestic legal provisions, however framed, without being deprived of its character as Community law and without the legal basis of the Community itself being called into question.
>
> The transfer by the States from their domestic legal system to the Community legal system of rights and obligations arising under the Treaty carries with it a permanent limitation of their several rights, against which a subsequent uni-lateral act incompatible with the concept of the Community cannot prevail."

The CJ, as it developed this principle in later cases, subsequently confirmed in *Simmenthal* (at [1978] E.C.R. 629 at 644) that it applied to *all* provisions of national law, whatever their status, which conflict with EU law, whether introduced before or after the provision of EU law, and in Case 213/89 *R. v Secretary of State for*

Transport Ex p. Factortame (No. 2) [1991] 1 A.C. 603 held that the principle might require suspension of national legislation not only following a conflicting ruling from the CJ but also during the interim period between referral and ruling. This was because the point of EU law might, when determined, be decided in the claimant's favour and his putative rights under EU law were regarded as taking precedence over his rights (or, rather, lack of them) under the national legislation.

The second principle of direct effect clarifies the application of the principle of supremacy in that it defines which aspects of EU law are covered by the principle of supremacy and must be given priority. Those aspects of EU law, which can be invoked by individuals directly in national courts, are determined by various criteria, including whether the relevant provisions are clear, unambiguous and unconditional. The CJ has developed this principle incrementally through a body of case law and has decided that direct effect can apply in respect of provisions of the (TFEU) Treaty (see *Van Gend en Loos*), regulations (see *Politi*) and, to a certain extent, directives (see, e.g. *Van Duyn* and *Marshall*).

The combined effect of these twin principles is that all directly effective EU law takes precedence over any provisions of national law, whether introduced before or after entry into the EU or before or after the provision of EU law in question. On this view, Member States have surrendered their sovereign rights to legislate as they wish and national legislation contradicting directly effective EU law cannot have application. In addition, the Court has subsequently developed a principle of indirect effect, under which Member States' courts, in the case of EU law which does not have direct effect, are nevertheless required to interpret national legislation in accordance with such law. Initially the court in Case 14/83 *Von Colson v Land Nordrhein-Westfalen* [1984] E.C.R. 1891 appeared to confine its application to cases where national legislation was introduced to comply with an EC directive, but in Case 106/89 *Marleasing SA v La Comercial Internacional de Alimentation SA* [1990] E.C.R. I-4135 (*Marleasing*), the CJ stated that it should apply to all national legislation, whether or not adopted to comply with an EC directive. Thus under the *Marleasing* principle, or the principle of conforming interpretation as it is sometimes known, there is a general requirement for Member States' courts to interpret their national legislation as far as possible so as to achieve the purposes of EU directives. This principle is an extensive one and requires courts to interpret *any* provisions in national law which might have application in the particular case so as to ensure compliance with a directive. As the ECJ in *Pfeiffer v Deutsches Rotes Kreuz, Kreisverband Waldshut eV* [2005] I.C.R. 1307 observed (at [119]):

"when hearing a case between individuals, a national court is required, when applying the provisions of domestic law adopted for the purpose of transposing obligations laid down by a Directive, to consider the whole body of rules of national law and to interpret them, so far as possible, in the light of the wording and purpose of the directive in order to achieve an outcome consistent with the objective pursued by the Directive".

The CJ has subsequently extended this principle in Case C-105/03 *Criminal proceedings against Maria Pupino* [2005] E.C.R. I-5285 (*Pupino*) so that there is a similar requirement for Member States' courts to interpret their national legislation as far as possible so as to achieve the result which "Framework Decisions" made by the European Council are seeking to secure (in the case itself, EU criminal co-operation under the Framework Decision on Police and Judicial Cooperation in Criminal Matters), although "Framework Decisions" do not fall within the scope of the TFEU. These principles are further considered below at 4–035—4–037.

▷ (b) The United Kingdom perspective

4–024 The foundation for the relationship between the EU and the UK from the UK perspective is laid by the ECA 1972. Its provisions attempt to define the status of EU law, govern its relationship with national law and give directions to the English courts on the inter-relationship between the EU and English legal orders. Such provisions also seek to ensure penetration of the EU legal order into the English legal system and to determine the degree of precedence to be accorded to certain aspects of EU law that were required as a result of the UK's entry into the EC.

Section 2(1) recognises that certain aspects of EU law are intended to have immediate legal effect in the national system and provides that such EU law forms part of the law to which effect is to be given in national courts. It provides:

> "All such rights, powers, liabilities, obligations and restrictions from time to time created or arising by or under the Treaties, and all such remedies and procedures from time to time provided for by or under the Treaties, as in accordance with the Treaties are without further enactment to be given legal effect or used in the United Kingdom shall be recognised and available in law, and be enforced, allowed and followed accordingly; and the expression "enforceable EU right" and similar expressions shall be read as referring to one to which this subsection applies."

The supremacy of EC law is addressed by s.2(4), which provides that ". . . any enactment passed or to be passed . . . shall be construed and have effect subject to the foregoing provisions of this section", i.e. subject, inter alia, to the recognition of any "enforcable Community right" under s.2(1). As regards the meaning and effect of EU law, the judiciary is directed, albeit not expressly, to recognise the referral procedure to the CJ (under art.267 (ex 234)) and, in the absence of referral, to interpret EU law in accordance with the principles laid down by and decisions of the CJ. Section 3(1) provides:

> "For the purposes of all legal proceedings any question as to the meaning or effect of any of the Treaties, or as to the validity, meaning or effect of any EU instrument, shall be treated as a question of law (and, if not referred to the European Court, be for determination as such in accordance with the principles laid down by and any relevant decision of the European Court)."

Sections 2 and 3 of the ECA 1972 are expressed in broad, general terms, appearing to be drafted in a style perhaps more reminiscent of codified law in Continental systems, and they leave a number of important matters unclear. One such matter is the way in which precedence should be accorded to EU law under these sections in the light of the doctrine of Parliamentary sovereignty. This is considered immediately below. A further matter (and one of crucial importance to the matters considered in the book) is the impact of these sections on statutory interpretation and precedent, and the extent, if any, to which adaptations need to be made to traditional English practices in these areas. This is considered in the following section. In the light of the general wording in ss.2 and 3, judges may adopt different approaches in respect of both of these matters.

When ss.2 and 3 were introduced, inter alia, to ensure precedence for certain aspects of EU law, it was uncertain whether it was constitutionally possible for this to be achieved in the light of the doctrine of Parliamentary sovereignty. Under this doctrine, Parliament cannot bind its successors, so that no future Parliament can ever be bound by legislation passed by an earlier Parliament. A later Parliament can pass legislation which repeals any earlier legislation, either expressly or impliedly (in that its provisions conflict with or contradict provisions in the earlier legislation). Where this occurs, the doctrine requires courts to give effect to the later legislative provisions as representing the intention of Parliament. On this view, no legislation is entrenched in the UK, all legislation has equal status (cf. the position in Continental systems—see above, 4–003—where a written constitution contained in "constitutional legislation" may have superior status to "ordinary legislation") and the ECA 1972 has no superior status to other legislation passed subsequently. If such legislation contains provisions which conflict with EU law, effect may be given by courts to those provisions, notwithstanding the provisions in the ECA 1972 which require precedence to be accorded to EU law. However, where a conflict has arisen, courts have not given effect to the later provisions and have not regarded the provisions in the ECA 1972 as being impliedly repealed. Provisions in later statutes which might be contrary to EU law, such as the (discriminatory) requirements of Pt II of the Merchant Shipping Act 1988 in *R. v Secretary of State for Transport Ex p. Factortame Ltd* [1990] 2 A.C. 85 (see below, 4–037), have been regarded as taking effect subject to the provisions of the ECA 1972. As Lord Bridge remarked (at 140) in that case:

> "By virtue of section 2(4) of the Act of 1972 Part II of the Act of 1988 is to be construed and take effect subject to directly enforceable Community rights and those rights are, by section 2(1) of the Act of 1972, to be "recognised and available in law, and . . . enforced, allowed and followed accordingly; . . ." This has precisely the same effect as if a section were incorporated in Part II of the Act of 1988 which in terms enacted that the provisions with respect to registration of British fishing vessels were to be without prejudice to the directly enforceable Community rights of nationals of any member state of the E.E.C."

These remarks seem to envisage later statutes being read with an "implied proviso" that they take effect subject to directly enforceable Community rights, thus rendering the provisions of the ECA 1972 immune from implied repeal, and the High Court in *Thoburn v Sunderland City Council* [2003] Q.B. 151 (*Thoburn*) has gone on to hold that the ECA 1972 is a "constitutional" statute which can be repealed only by express words in a later statute or by words so specific that repeal is an irresistible inference. Laws L.J. stated (at [62]–[63]):

"[62] We should recognise a hierarchy of Acts of Parliament: as it were "ordinary" statutes and "constitutional" statutes. The two categories must be distinguished on a principled basis. In my opinion a constitutional statute is one which (a) conditions the legal relationship between citizen and state in some general, overarching manner, or (b) enlarges or diminishes the scope of what we would now regard as fundamental constitutional rights. (a) and (b) are of necessity closely related: it is difficult to think of an instance of (a) that is not also an instance of (b). The special status of constitutional statutes follows the special status of constitutional rights. Examples are Magna Carta 1297 (25 Edw 1), the Bill of Rights 1689 (1 Will & Mary sess 2 c 2), the Union with Scotland Act 1706 (6 Anne c 11), the Reform Acts which distributed and enlarged the franchise (Representation of the People Acts 1832 (2 & 3 Will 4 c 45), 1867 (30 & 31 Vict c 102) and 1884 (48 & 49 Vict c 3), the Human Rights Act 1998, the Scotland Act 1998 and the Government of Wales Act 1998. The 1972 [*European Communities*] Act clearly belongs in this family. It incorporated the whole corpus of substantive Community rights and obligations, and gave overriding domestic effect to the judicial and administrative machinery of Community law. It may be there has never been a statute having such profound effects on so many dimensions of our daily lives. The 1972 Act is, by force of the common law, a constitutional statute.

[63] Ordinary statutes may be impliedly repealed. Constitutional statutes may not. For the repeal of a constitutional Act or the abrogation of a fundamental right to be effected by statute, the court would apply this test: is it shown that the legislature's actual—not imputed, constructive or presumed—intention was to effect the repeal or abrogation? I think the test could only be met by express words in the later statute, or by words so specific that the inference of an actual determination to effect the result contended was irresistible. The ordinary rule of implied repeal does not satisfy this test. Accordingly, it has no application to constitutional statutes."

The ECA 1972 is thus not regarded as impliedly repealed in cases where provisions in later statutes conflict with EU law and his Lordship went onto set out (at [69]–[70]) his understanding of the proper relationship between EU and domestic law:

"[69] In my judgment . . . the correct analysis of that relationship involves and requires these following four propositions. (1) All the specific rights and obligations which EU law creates are by the 1972 Act incorporated into our domestic law and rank supreme: that is, anything in our substantive law inconsistent with any of these rights and obligations is abrogated or must be modified to avoid the inconsistency. This is true even where the inconsistent municipal provision is contained in primary legislation. (2) The 1972 Act is a constitutional statute: that is, it cannot be impliedly repealed. (3) The truth of (2) is derived, not from EU law, but purely from the law of England: the common law recognises a category of constitutional statutes. (4) The fundamental legal basis of the United Kingdom's relationship with the EU rests with the domestic, not the European, legal powers. In the event, which no doubt would never happen in the real world, that a European measure was seen to be repugnant to a fundamental or constitutional right guaranteed by the law of England, a question would arise whether the general words of the 1972 Act were sufficient to incorporate the measure and give it overriding effect in domestic law. But that is very far from this case.

[70] I consider that the balance struck by these four propositions gives full weight both to the proper supremacy of Community law and to the proper supremacy of the United Kingdom Parliament."

The general wording in ss.2 and 3, however, gives little indication of the way in which precedence should be accorded to EU law and experience has shown that judges have adopted different approaches to this matter. One approach has been to regard these sections as creating a rule of statutory construction which requires that English legislation be interpreted by the courts in accordance with EU law. Under this approach, effect would always be given to later legislation and it would be a matter of interpreting such legislation in a way which accords with EU law, although problems may arise, as will be seen, where there are difficulties in interpreting legislation so as to accord with EU law. An alternative approach has been to regard these sections as modifying the doctrine of Parliamentary sovereignty by requiring that, where later legislation does not accord with EU law, the courts should give effect to EU law, thereby rendering the English legislation ineffective. On this approach, the requirement to accord precedence to EU law under ss.2 and 3 might be regarded as having been "entrenched" and as introducing a form of review of the effectiveness of legislation by reference to a superior source of law, namely EU law. In this respect, the position may be said to be broadly similar to that in Continental systems (see above, 14–003) where the validity and effectiveness of ordinary legislation can be reviewed by reference to the written constitution.

Whichever of these approaches is adopted, the doctrine of Parliamentary sovereignty essentially remains fundamentally intact and, if an express statement were made by Parliament in later legislation either that ss.2 and 3 did not have application in respect of this legislation or that this legislation was not intended to accord with EU law, it is apparent that the courts would give effect to such a statement. This can be seen from the remarks of Laws L.J. in *Thoburn* at [63], mentioned above, and also from earlier remarks of Lord Denning, M.R. in *Macarthys*, where his Lordship stated (at [1979] 3 All E.R. 325 at 329):

> "If the time should come when our Parliament deliberately passes an Act with the intention of repudiating the Treaty or any provision in it or intentionally of acting inconsistently with it and says so in express terms—then I should have thought that it would be the duty of our courts to follow the statute of our Parliament."

If such action were taken by Parliament, the requirements to either interpret the legislation to accord with EU law or to treat the legislation as being invalid would, at least in respect of this particular legislation, (presumably) be suspended. Thus, in the ultimate analysis, the intention of Parliament as expressed in later legislation would (presumably) prevail, although it might be doubted whether, in practice, a court would be willing to find an express provision to be sufficiently clear to achieve this result.

▶ ## 3. Differing Judicial Approaches to the Implications of the ECA 1972 for Statutory Interpretation and Precedent

▷ ### (a) Introduction

4–025 It will be recalled that one matter left unclear by the ECA 1972, from the wording of ss.2 and 3, was the implications for statutory interpretation and precedent, and the extent to which adaptations might need to be made to traditional English practices in these areas (see above, 4–024). Two instances of the lack of clarity may be provided. First, s.3(1) provides that the meaning and effect of EU law should "if not referred to the European Court, be for determination as such in accordance with the principles laid down by and any relevant decision of the European Court". These words constitute the only express reference to the European Court (i.e. the CJ), apart from provisions in s.3(2) and (3) which provide respectively for judicial notice to be taken of its decisions or expressions of opinion and for the reception of evidence of its judgments or orders. The section appears to envisage cases being "referred" to the CJ, which presumably would be under the reference procedure contained in art.267 (ex 234) of the TFEU. No indication is given of when and in what circumstances a referral should be made and ultimately this will be a matter of the interpretation of art.267. Whether or not a case will be referred will depend on how an English court interprets art.267 and some judges may be more willing to refer than others. The extent to which referral is made will depend on the extent to which there is a significant role in the English legal system for the CJ as a higher interpretative body. If no referral is made, an English court will, under s.3(1), need to determine the meaning and effect of EU law in accordance with the "principles" laid down by the CJ. What might such "principles" encompass? Principles of substantive EU law laid down by the CJ in (relevant) case law decisions may be "principles"; techniques of interpretation employed by the CJ, such as teleological and schematic interpretation, may be "principles"; principles of general application such as supremacy and direct effect may be "principles"; and general principles such as proportionality and respect for human rights may be "principles". The extent to which recourse is had to "principles" in any or all of these senses by English courts will determine the extent to which they penetrate the English legal system and some judges might have greater recourse to them than others. Further, no guidance is given by the section as to the precedential effect(s), if any, in future cases, of rulings received from the CJ following referral of a case, or, in cases not referred, the precedential effect(s), if any, of relevant decisions of the CJ. The extent to which CJ rulings and decisions are regarded as (binding or persuasive) precedents will, again, determine the extent to which they penetrate the English legal system.

Secondly, s.2(4) provides that ". . . any enactment passed or to be passed . . . shall be construed and have effect subject to the foregoing provisions of this section". This means that English statutes must be construed and have effect subject, inter alia, to the recognition of any enforceable EU right under s.2(1). According to s.2(1), it would appear that "enforceable EU right" must be defined by reference to aspects of EU law which "in accordance with the Treaties are without further enactment to be given legal effect or used in the United Kingdom". What are enforceable EU rights will thus be a matter of EU law and will be determined in accordance with the principle of direct effect (see above, 4–023). These rights will thus, under s.3(1), need to be determined in accordance with the principles and decisions of the CJ. How should English statutory provisions be construed and have effect subject to enforceable EU rights? Statutory provisions might, when construed using traditional English techniques, have only one meaning which is in accordance with EU law or there may be ambiguity and an interpretation can be adopted which accords with EU law. However, the statutory provision may not accord with EU law using such techniques. If this is the case, it might, if CJ techniques of interpretation are employed, be construed to accord with EU law. Alternatively, if such techniques are not employed, the statutory provision will be in conflict with EU law and, if it is to be given effect subject to EU law, will mean that it does *not* have effect and EU law will prevail. It is not apparent from s.2(4) which of these approaches should be adopted and, perhaps inevitably, judges have differed in the approach taken. The extent to which one or other of these approaches has been adopted will determine the extent to which changes or modifications to the existing rules relating to statutory interpretation have taken place and new techniques of interpretation have permeated the English legal system.

The uncertainty as to the nature and scope of ss.2 and 3 enables judges to adopt a number of different approaches with respect to the significance of these sections for statutory interpretation and precedent. These approaches exhibit a wide spectrum of opinion about this matter:

— some envisage a more significant role in the English legal system for the CJ as a higher interpretative body than others;

- some envisage a more widespread application of principles laid down by the CJ, when determining the meaning and effect of EU law than others;
- some envisage more significant changes or modifications to the existing rules relating to statutory interpretation of English legislation, when construing it and giving it effect subject to EU law, than others; and
- some confine more narrowly the impact of CJ case law on the English precedent system than others.

No single approach has universal acceptance and, consequently, the remainder of this section of the chapter (4–026–4–041) is devoted to a more detailed examination of each of the stances outlined above.

▷ ## (b) Role of the ECJ as a higher interpretative body

4–026 Section 3(1) of the ECA 1972 envisages penetration of the English legal system by EU law as developed by the CJ and thereby countenances the existence of a new higher interpretative body in the system. One way in which such penetration may occur is via the art.267 (ex 234) reference procedure, under which a case can be referred to the CJ for a ruling on the interpretation of EU law (see above, 4–011). On return of the case to the national court, the national court is required to follow the ruling since this is binding on it (by virtue of CJ case law—see below, 4–038— which English courts must follow under s.3(1)). A reference under art.267 (ex 234), however, allows the CJ not only to interpret an issue of EU law but also, indirectly, to question the adequacy and, indeed, applicability of national law (see above, 4– 011). Regular referral of cases will therefore enable the CJ to play a significant role in the interpretation of law in the Member State court system.

Whilst some members of the judiciary have been prepared to refer cases to the CJ and to recognise it as the supreme interpreter in matters of EU law on the basis that it is in a better position to develop EU law, to employ Continental judicial techniques and to appreciate the policy needs of the EU—see, e.g. the remarks of Bingham J. in *Customs & Excise Commissioners v ApS Samex* [1983] 1 All E.R. 1042 at 1055–1056—other English judges have been more circumspect about involving the CJ via art.267 (ex 234) references. There was an initial reluctance to refer cases to the CJ, which can perhaps be traced back to the Court of Appeal's decision in *Bulmer*, where guidelines to assist English courts in the use of the reference procedure were laid down. Under these guidelines, a reference was seen essentially as an option of last resort, with Lord Denning, M.R. emphasising (at [1974] Ch. 401 at 424) "the importance of not overwhelming the European court by references to it" and stating (at 425) that ". . . in very many cases the English courts will interpret the Treaty themselves. They will not refer the question to the European court at Luxembourg".

As English courts have become more accustomed to the EU legal order and more familiar with its law and techniques, there has been a greater willingness to make use of the reference procedure. References have been made in many areas of law on a diverse range of topics, including employment law (*Marshall*), sex discrimination (*Webb v EMO Air Cargo (UK) Ltd* [1992] 4 All E.R. 929—see below, 4–036) and equal pay (*Macarthys* and *Garland*).

Indeed, English judges are now encouraged to refer questions concerning the interpretation of EU law to the CJ unless they are able, "with complete confidence" (per Sir Thomas Bingham, M.R. in *R. v International Stock Exchange of the United Kingdom and the Republic of Ireland Ex p. Else* [1993] Q.B. 534 at 545), to determine such questions themselves. Nevertheless, courts have also continued to follow the alternative to referral provided in s.3(1), namely, to determine EU law themselves "in accordance with the principles laid down by and any relevant decision of the European Court".

Illustrative reference

4-027

See: Chapter 14: "*Equal pay*" (14–005 and 14–011) where an art.177 (now 267) reference was made by the Court of Appeal in *Macarthys* and by the House of Lords in *Garland*; and (14–018) where the Court of Appeal in *Pickstone v Freemans Plc* (*Pickstone*) made no reference but itself interpreted EC law.

▷ *(c) Application of principles laid down by the CJ when determining the meaning and effect of EU law*

When determining the meaning and effect of EU law, courts will be required to **4-028** interpret articles in Treaties and EU legislative provisions, which are expressed in broad, general language and which contain propositions of law formulated as abstract statements of principle (see above, 4–010). Courts will have to have regard to any relevant CJ case law on these articles and provisions, since s.3 of the ECA 1972 requires them to determine the meaning and effect of EU law "in accordance with the principles laid down by and any relevant decision of the European Court". Thus, for example, when determining the meaning and effect of the principle of equal pay in EU law, regard will need to be had to the abstract statement of principle contained in art.157(1) and (2) (ex 141) of the TFEU, EU legislation in the form of Directive 2006/54 (which consolidates and amends a number of earlier directives relating to equal opportunities and equal treatment, including Directive 75/117 on equal pay—see 14–002) and CJ case law, such as *Defrenne* and *Jenkins*, through which that principle has been developed.

One view of the requirement in s.3 of the ECA 1972 to determine the meaning and effect of EU law "in accordance with the principles laid down by and any relevant decision of the European Court" might be that courts should have regard to CJ decisions on substantive EU law, i.e. to the propositions of law that have been formulated as principles in (relevant) CJ decisions. Some judges appear to have regarded the direction in s.3(1) as requiring them only to observe the case law of the CJ and any general principles contained therein as a source of propositions of substantive EU law to be considered when determining the outcome of cases before them. Use of CJ case law as a source of propositions of law may occur where an English court gives effect to a proposition of EU law contained (at least in part) in CJ case law by according it priority over English legislation or English common law, in accordance with the CJ principle of supremacy of EU law (see Priority Approach below, 4–032).

Another view of the requirement might be that courts should have regard to CJ techniques of interpretation, employing the same techniques as the CJ would do when interpreting EU law. Some judges appear to have regarded the direction in s.3(1) as requiring them to adopt CJ interpretative techniques, either alternatively or in addition to observing CJ case law containing propositions of substantive EU law. Thus some judges have concentrated on giving effect to the underlying aims of EU legislative provisions, rather than focusing on the particular words used in them, and, in doing so, have adopted schematic and/or teleological approaches to interpretation, used general principles, had recourse to a body of case law (*jurisprudence constante*), and engaged in "gap filling". Such techniques of interpretation, may well need to be adopted (quite apart from whether or not they are required by s.3), given the broad, general style in which EU law is drafted, if the meaning and effect of EU law are to be properly determined.

Whilst some judges have recognised the need to adopt, and have adopted, CJ techniques of interpretation when determining the meaning and effect of EU law, others have not done so, but have adhered to traditional English techniques. Thus in *Pickstone* the Industrial Tribunal followed the traditional English approach of focusing on the words used not only when interpreting an English legislative provision, s.1(2)(c) of the EPA 1970, but also an EC law provision, art.119 of the EC Treaty (now art.157 of the TFEU) (see Chapter 14, 14–015). Similarly, when the case of *R. v Henn, R. v Darby* [1978] 1 W.L.R. 1031 was heard in the Court of Appeal, the court interpreted both a provision of national law, s.42 of the Customs Consolidation Act 1876, which absolutely prohibited the importation into the UK of obscene goods, and an article of the EC Treaty, art.30 (now 34), which prohibited quantitative restrictions on imports by Member States, by focusing on the words used. On this basis, the Court of Appeal expressed the view (at 1036) that "Article 30 [*now 34*] did not apply to this case because the restriction [*in s.42, being an absolute prohibition*] was not related to a quantitative measure". Since, in the Court of Appeal's view, the law was clear, the court determined the meaning and effect of EC law itself and no art.177 (now 267) reference to the CJ was made.

On appeal, however, the House of Lords (*Henn and Darby v Director of Public Prosecutions* [1981] A.C. 850 (*Henn*)), counselled against the dangers of using a traditional English approach to interpretation when interpreting EC law. This might lead a court to an erroneous conclusion as to the meaning of EC law or lead to the conclusion that such meaning was clear and obvious and that, accordingly, there was no need to refer the case to the CJ under art.177 (now 267). As a result, the CJ would be denied the opportunity to correctly interpret EC law. The House of Lords felt that, had EC law been interpreted by reference to the CJ techniques of focusing on the underlying aims of art.30 (now 34) and by having recourse to a well-established body of CJ case law on that article, it would, contrary to the view taken by the Court of Appeal, have been regarded as encompassing not just quantitative restrictions but also absolute prohibitions. However, as the Court of Appeal had reached a contrary conclusion, albeit by adopting what the House of Lords felt was an inappropriate approach to interpretation of EC law, the House took the view that there was sufficient doubt to justify an art.177 (now 267) reference. As a result, the CJ, as a higher interpretative body, could interpret the point of EC law. Lord Diplock, with whose speech all other members of the House concurred, stated (at pp.904–906):

"In the Court of Appeal considerable doubt was expressed by that court whether an absolute prohibition on the import of a particular description of goods could amount to a quantitative restriction or a measure having equivalent effect, so as to fall within the ambit of Article 30 [*now 34*] at all. That such doubt should be expressed shows the danger of an English court applying English canons of statutory construction to the interpretation of the Treaty or, for that matter, of Regulations and Directives. What is meant by quantitative restrictions and measures having equivalent effect in Article 30 of the Treaty has been the subject of a whole series of decisions of the European Court to which the attention of the Court of Appeal ought to have been drawn. Section 3(1) of the European Communities Act 1972 expressly provides that the meaning and effect of any of the treaties "shall be treated as a question of law (and, if not referred to the European Court, be for determination as such in accordance with the principles laid down by and any relevant decisions of the European Court)."

. . . There is in fact a well-established body of case law of the European Court as to what amounts to a quantitative restriction or a measure having equivalent effect, within the meaning of article 30. So far from supporting the doubts expressed by the Court of Appeal whether an absolute prohibition of import of goods of a particular description could amount to a measure having equivalent effect to a quantitative restriction falling within article 30, these decisions of the European Court make it clear beyond peradventure that it does. . .

. . . in the light of this established case law of the European Court, it appeared to me to be so free from any doubt that an absolute prohibition of importation of goods of a particular description from other member states fell within article 30 that I should not have been disposed to regard the instant case as involving any matter of interpretation of that article that was open to question. But the strong inclination expressed by the Court of Appeal to adopt the contrary view shows that there is involved a question of interpretation on which judicial minds can differ . . . It was for this reason that your Lordships thought it proper to submit to the European Court for a preliminary ruling . . . as to the interpretation of article 30 . . ."

Where courts have adopted CJ interpretative techniques when determining the meaning and effect of EU law, rather than just having regard to principles laid down as propositions of law in CJ decisions, there has been a more widespread application, in the English legal system, of CJ principles and this has, over the years, become increasingly common as judges have become more familiar with and had greater exposure to these techniques.

Illustrative reference

4–029 See: Chapter 14: *"Equal pay"* (14–018) where in *Pickstone*, when interpreting art.119 of the EC Treaty (now art.157 of the TFEU), Nicholls L.J. in the Court of Appeal considered the aims of the article and adopted CJ interpretative techniques including teleological and schematic approaches to interpretation, used general principles and had recourse to previous ECJ case law; and Purchas L.J. in the Court of Appeal, although making no reference to the aims of art.119 of the EC Treaty (now art.157), adopted a schematic approach by having regard to Directive 75/117 on equal pay (now consolidated in Directive 2006/54) and considered previous CJ case law.

▷ *(d) Construing English legislation subject to EU law: changes or modifications to the traditional rules relating to statutory interpretation of English legislation*

4–030 In some cases, it may be possible to construe English legislation so that it accords with EU law without the need to depart from the traditional rules relating to statutory interpretation. If a statutory provision is interpreted, applying traditional English techniques of statutory interpretation, it may be found to have only one meaning and this meaning may accord with EU law. If it is found to have more than one meaning, and one of the meanings accords with EU law, then the ambiguity in a statutory provision can be resolved in favour of the meaning which accords with EU law. In this instance, EU law is used as an interpretative aid to resolve the ambiguity when construing the provision (Ambiguity Interpretation Approach). Where this approach is adopted by judges, it will not involve any change to the traditional rules of statutory interpretation. It will simply be an application of the normal rule of statutory interpretation that applies in respect of international treaty obligations, namely there is a presumption that Parliament intended the statute to conform with international treaty obligations (see Chapter 1, 1–088).

Illustrative references

See: Chapter 14: "*Equal pay*" (14–007 and 14–013) where examples of EU law being used to resolve an ambiguity can be seen in the judgment of Cumming-Bruce L.J. (obiter) in the Court of Appeal in *Macarthys* and in the judgments of the House of Lords in *Garland*.

4–031

In many cases, however, there may be no ambiguity. Here other approaches are needed and these approaches, to a greater or lesser extent, may involve departure from the traditional rules relating to statutory interpretation. Two alternative approaches have been adopted. One has been for judges to recognise that the English statutory provision, when interpreted using traditional English techniques, conflicts with EU law and to accord priority to EU law (Priority Approach). In this instance, there is no departure from traditional English techniques when interpreting the English statutory provision but simply an according of priority to EU law to resolve the conflict. The other has been to interpret the English statutory provision in a way so that it *does* accord with EU law, by departing from traditional English techniques and using more general techniques as employed by the CJ (General Interpretation Approach). Here there is a departure from the traditional English techniques and a recognition that, only if changes or modifications are made to the traditional rules, will it be possible in some cases to adopt a meaning that accords with EU law. Judges to varying degrees have adopted one or other of these approaches and, historically, seem to have simply opted to follow one approach or the other. There has been no hierarchical application in respect of the two, although it may be that the position has now been reached where courts are expected in the first instance to interpret English statutory provisions, using whatever techniques are possible, to secure compliance with EU law (i.e. attempt to secure a conforming interpretation of the English statutory provision with EU law) and, only if this proves impossible, to then go on to accord priority to EU law through disapplication of the English statutory provision. This would give a hierarchical application of the General Interpretation Approach taking precedence over the Priority Approach, with the latter coming into play only in the event that the former cannot deliver compliance with EU law. That this is how courts should proceed may perhaps be implicit in the following observations of Lord Walker in *Fleming (t/a Bodycraft) v Customs and Revenue Commissioners* [2008] 1 W.L.R. 195 (at [24]–[25]):

"[24] My Lords, it is a fundamental principle of the law of the European Union, recognised in section 2(1) of the European Communities Act 1972, that if national legislation infringes directly enforceable Community rights, the national court is obliged to disapply the offending provision. The provision is not made void but it must be treated as being (as Lord Bridge of Harwich put it in *R v Secretary of State for Transport, Ex p Factortame Ltd* [1990] 2 AC 85, 140) "without prejudice to the directly enforceable Community rights of

> nationals of any member state of the EEC". The principle has often been recognised [*in*] your Lordships' House . . .
>
> [25] Disapplication is called for only if there is an inconsistency between national law and EU law. In an attempt to avoid an inconsistency the national court will, if at all possible, interpret the national legislation so as to make it conform to the superior order of EU law: *Pickstone v Freemans plc* [1989] AC 66; *Litster v Forth Dry Dock & Engineering Co Ltd* [1990] 1 AC 546. Sometimes, however, a conforming construction is not possible, and disapplication cannot be avoided."

Whether or not this analysis is correct, both the Priority Approach and the General Interpretation Approach remain important as alternative ways of securing compliance with EU law and each is considered below.

(i) Priority approach

4-032 Where priority is accorded to EU law in the event of a conflict with English legislation, the English legislation is effectively ignored and EU law prevails. Legislative justification for this approach can be found in ss.2 and 3 of the ECA 1972. Under s.2(4), statutory provisions have to be construed and have effect subject to EU law and, when determining (under s.3(1)) the meaning and effect of EU law in accordance with principles laid down by the CJ, one (CJ) principle is the supremacy of EU law. The effect of this principle, which applies to those aspects of EU law which are of direct effect in Member States, is that national courts are required to accord priority to EU law when a conflict arises between national law and EU law (see above, 4–023). It might in fact be said this interpretation of the sections is broadly comparable to an interpretation adopted by courts in Continental legal systems and by the CJ. It would appear that the principle of supremacy (together with the principle of direct effect) is being used as an aid to interpretation of the sections in order to determine their scope or (perhaps) by filling a "gap" which might be felt to exist in those sections. It could thus be said that, where the Priority Approach is applied, the ECA 1972 itself has effectively been interpreted in accordance with such CJ principles. It may be that Lawton L.J. had this in mind in *Macarthys* (at [1979] 3 All E.R. 325 at 334) when he adopted the Priority Approach and regarded himself as being under an obligation to give effect to EC law "arising both from the decisions of the European Court of Justice in the two cases to which I have referred [*Defrenne, which expanded the principle of direct effect and Simmenthal, which expanded the principle of supremacy*] and s2 of the European Communities Act 1972".

Under this approach, there may be a change to the traditional rules of statutory interpretation with the recognition of a further rule of statutory interpretation. The further rule would be that, contrary to the usual position, interpretation of English legislation alone will not necessarily determine what the law is on a particular matter. Rather, in the event that such interpretation produces a conflict with EU law, it will be EU law that will determine what the law is on the particular matter.

Certainly this approach can be said to accord the necessary degree of penetration by the EU legal order into the English legal system. This is because, under this approach, EU law is treated as a statement of the law in England on the particular matter in question, rather than the English legislation constituting a statement of the law in England, and EU law is thus regarded as having superior status to the English legislation. Whilst this approach may accord the necessary degree of penetration as regards substantive law, it may afford little in the way of penetration of CJ techniques of interpretation in respect of English legislation, at least in cases where the tendency of judges has been to apply traditional English techniques of statutory interpretation when construing the English legislation.

Illustrative reference

See: Chapter 14: *"Equal pay"* (14–005 and 14–007) for examples of this approach in the judgments of Lawton and Cumming-Bruce L.JJ., and (on receipt of a ruling from the ECJ under art.177 (now 267)) the judgment of Lord Denning, M.R. in the Court of Appeal in *Macarthys*; and (14–020) the judgments of Nicholls L.J. and Sir Roualeyn Cumming-Bruce in the Court of Appeal in *Pickstone*.

4–033

(ii) General interpretation approach

Where this approach is adopted, English legislation is interpreted, using whatever **4–034** general techniques of interpretation are necessary, so that it accords with EU law. Legislative justification for this approach can be found in both ss.2 and 3 of the ECA 1972. Section 2(4) requires English statutory provisions to be construed and have effect subject to EU law and it may be that such provisions can only be interpreted to conform with EU law by employing CJ techniques of interpretation. The section may thus be seen as endorsing the use of such techniques. Section 3(1) refers to English courts determining the "effect" of EU law and the "effect" of EU law may depend on the approach adopted towards English legislation. If EU law is regarded as having "effect" as an aid to interpretation of English legislation, rather than having "effect" as a proposition of law with superior status (Priority Approach), then interpreting English legislation may be part of the process of determining the "effect" of EU law. As such, it may, under s.3(1), need to be done by reference to the principles and decisions of the CJ. These principles could include CJ techniques of interpretation, since these may be described as "principles laid down by . . . the European Court" under s.3(1). Thus application of these techniques when interpreting English legislation may be one way of determining the "effect" of EU law under s.3(1).

Under this approach, there may be a change to the traditional rules of statutory interpretation with the recognition of a further rule of statutory interpretation. The further rule would appear to be that, in cases where legislation is to be construed and to have effect subject to EU law in accordance with s.2(4), there is a presumption that Parliament intended the statute to conform with EU law. This rule would, in respect of the TFEU and EU law, apply instead of the rule that international treaties can act as an aid to interpreting a statute in order to resolve any ambiguity that might exist. In addition, the further rule may be seen as endorsing the introduction of different techniques of statutory interpretation. In order to give effect to this presumption, judges may need to eschew traditional English techniques and adopt interpretative techniques such as those favoured by the CJ. Such techniques will involve focusing on giving effect to the underlying aims of legislative provisions, rather than focusing on the particular words used, and, in doing so, adopting schematic and/or teleological approaches to interpretation, using general principles, having recourse to a body of case law and engaging in "gap filling". This approach can also be said to accord a high degree of penetration by the EU legal order into the English legal system, since the use of EU law as an interpretative aid and adoption of CJ techniques of interpretation, irrespective of ambiguity, may extend to a potentially wide range of English legislation.

4–035

Illustrative reference

See: Chapter 14: "*Equal pay*" (14–004), where Phillips J. in the Employment Appeal Tribunal in *Macarthys* appeared to focus on giving effect to the underlying aims of the EPA 1970, rather than focusing on the particular words in s.1(2) and (4) of that Act, and, in doing so, seemed to adopt schematic and teleological approaches to interpretation, and to have recourse to a body of case law on art.119 of the EC Treaty (now art.157); (14–005) where a schematic interpretation and "gap filling" approach to the EPA 1970 was adopted by Lord Denning, M.R. in the Court of Appeal in *Macarthys*; (14–020) where Purchas L.J. in the Court of Appeal in *Pickstone* interpreted s.1(2)(c) of the EPA 1970 by "gap filling"; and (14–021), where the House of Lords in *Pickstone* appeared to focus on the aims of the EPA 1970, rather than the particular words in s.1(2)(c), with Lords Templeman and Oliver engaging in "gap filling".

cf.

Chapter 14: "*Equal pay*" (14–005), where Cumming-Bruce L.J. in the Court of Appeal in *Macarthys* rejected a General Interpretation Approach of the EPA 1970 and (with Lawton L.J.) did not adopt a schematic approach or fill a "gap"; and (14–017), where the Court of Appeal in *Pickstone* followed the traditional English approach of focusing on the words used when interpreting s.1(2)(c) of the EPA 1970, with (14–020) Nicholls L.J. and Sir Roualeyn Cumming-Bruce (but not Purchas L.J.) according priority to EC law (Priority Approach) over s.1(2)(c), which was found to conflict with EC law.

The requirement to secure compliance with EU law under one or other of the above approaches (Priority Approach or General Interpretation Approach) applies in respect of EU law having direct effect. (Section 2(4) of the ECA 1972, which contains the requirement, directs courts to construe legislation "subject to the foregoing provisions of this section" and those provisions include, under s.2(1), "enforceable EU rights," which are those having direct effect—see above, 4–025.) However, since the passage of the ECA 1972, the CJ has widened the requirement to secure compliance with EU law beyond cases where EU law has direct effect. It has done so by developing the principle of indirect effect (see *Marleasing*, above, 4–023), which requires Member States' courts to interpret national legis- lation, in cases where EU law is relevant but not directly effective, and has extended this principle to include securing compliance with "Framework Decisions" (see *Pupino*, above, 4–023). This has seen an extension of the General Inter- pretation Approach to cases where EU law has only indirect effect (see below, 4– 036). Further, as will be seen, courts in some cases have also extended this approach to cases where EU law is *not* relevant (see below, 4–037). In both these instances, it can be said that there has been a change or modification in respect of the traditional rules of statutory interpretation, by the more widespread intro- duction of new techniques of interpretation. Extensions of the General Inter- pretation Approach to these two classes of case are considered in the following two sections.

(iii) Extension of the General Interpretation Approach by virtue of the principle of indirect effect

Requiring Member States' courts to interpret national legislation as far as possible **4–036** so as to comply with EU law, where EU law is not directly effective, may well extend the scope of the General Interpretation Approach because compliance may only be possible by adopting interpretative techniques favoured by the CJ (see above, 4– 016). English courts responded initially to this requirement with a lack of enthu- siasm, as can be seen from the decision of the House of Lords in *Duke v GEC Reliance Ltd* [1988] A.C. 618 (see above, 4-021), but, in *Litster v Forth Dry Dock and Engineering Co Ltd* [1990] 1 A.C. 546 (*Litster*), the House indicated that courts could depart from their traditional approach where English legislation had been speci- fically enacted in order to implement an EC directive which did not have direct effect. The legislation in question in the *Litster* case, the Transfer of Undertakings (Protection of Employment) Regulations 1981 (SI 1981/1794) had been introduced by Parliament to give effect to the UK's obligations under EC Directive 77/187 which provided for the safeguarding of employees' rights in the event of transfers of undertakings, businesses or parts of businesses. Lord Oliver stated (at 559):

"If the legislation can reasonably be construed so as to conform with those obligations, obligations which are to be ascertained not only from the wording of the relevant directive but from the interpretation placed on it by the Court of Justice of the European Communities, such a purposive construction will be applied even though, perhaps, it may involve some departure from the strict and literal application of the words which the legislature has elected to use."

The House of Lords held that "gap-filling" in respect of these Regulations, by implying words into them, was permissible and Lord Keith stated (at 554):

". . . it is the duty of the court to give to regulation 5 a construction which accords with the decisions of the European Court on the corresponding provisions of the Directive to which the regulation was intended by Parliament to give effect. The precedent established by *Pickstone v Freemans Plc.* indicates that this is to be done by implying the words necessary to achieve that result."

The House in *Litster* did not need to consider whether courts could depart from their traditional approach where national legislation was *not* intended to implement an EC directive, but this matter was subsequently considered by the House in *Webb v EMO Air Cargo (UK) Ltd* [1992] 4 All E.R. 929 (*Webb*) where the relevant legislation was passed *before* the relevant EC directive. In *Webb* the House of Lords, interpreting provisions of the Sex Discrimination Act 1975, held that there had been no unlawful sex discrimination where the appellant, an employee engaged initially to provide cover for a female employee who was on maternity leave but whose engagement was expected to continue thereafter, had been dismissed when she discovered that she herself was pregnant. In the House's view, there was no discrimination under the Act when comparing the appellant's case (of temporary unavailability through pregnancy) with that of a man who might be temporarily unavailable for medical reasons. The relevant circumstances in the one case were not materially different from the other, since there was unavailability in both cases and (per Lord Keith at [1992] 4 All E.R. 929 at 939) "the precise reason for the unavailability is not a relevant circumstance". Nevertheless, the House was less certain whether the appellant's dismissal might constitute a breach of EC Directive 76/207 and referred the case to the CJ under art.177 (now 267) for a ruling. The CJ (Case C-32/93 [1994] E.C.R. I-3567) gave a ruling that it would constitute a breach and, when the case returned to the House, the House ([1995] 4 All E.R. 577) concluded that the only way of reconciling the CJ ruling with the Act's provisions was to interpret the Act so that the temporary unavailability through pregnancy *was* a relevant circumstance. Lord Keith stated (at 939–940):

". . . it is for a United Kingdom court to construe domestic legislation in any field covered by a Community Directive so as to accord with the interpretation of the directive as laid down by the European Court, if that can be done without distorting the meaning of the domestic legislation . . . As the European Court said [*in Marleasing*] a national court must construe a domestic law to accord with the terms of a directive in the same field only if it is possible to do so. That means that the domestic law must be open to an interpretation consistent with the directive whether or not it is also open to an interpretation inconsistent with it."

The House felt that the Act was open to an interpretation consistent with EC Directive 76/207 and duly interpreted it as such, thereby confirming that the *Litster* approach of departing from traditional English interpretative techniques had more general application.

How far there is an extension in the General Interpretation Approach is governed by the extent to which a conforming interpretation is regarded as "possible" This matter has been addressed by the House of Lords in *Ghaidan v Godin-Mendoza* [2004] 3 All E.R. 411 (*Ghaidan*) where the House regarded the obligation established in *Marleasing* to interpret domestic law so far as it is possible to do so to make it compliant with EU law as "a significant signpost" (per Lord Steyn at 426) as to the meaning of the similar requirement in s.3(1) of the Human Rights Act 1998 to interpret domestic law so far as it is possible to do so to make it compliant with rights under the European Convention on Human Rights. The principles set out in *Ghaidan* have subsequently been applied by the courts to interpret domestic law in conformity with EU law—see, e.g., *Commissioners for HM Revenue and Customs v IDT Card Services Ireland Ltd* [2006] EWCA Civ 29 (*IDT Card Services*), *EBR Attridge Law LLP v Coleman* [2010] 1 C.M.L.R. 28 and *Vodafone 2 v The Commissioners for Her Majesty's Revenue & Customs* [2009] EWCA Civ 446 (*Vodafone 2*)—and it seems that a common approach is to be taken to conforming interpretation in these two areas. As to the principles to be applied, Lord Nicholls, delivering one of the judgments in *Ghaidan*, stated (at 423–424):

> ". . . the mere fact the language under consideration [*in the domestic legislation*] is inconsistent with a convention-compliant meaning does not of itself make a convention-compliant interpretation under s 3 impossible. Section 3 enables language to be interpreted restrictively or expansively. But s 3 goes further than this. It is also apt to require a court to read in words which change the meaning of the enacted legislation, so as to make it convention-compliant. In other words, the intention of Parliament in enacting s 3 was that, to an extent bounded only by what is "possible", a court can modify the meaning, and hence the effect, of primary and secondary legislation.
>
> Parliament, however, cannot have intended that in the discharge of this extended interpretative function the courts should adopt a meaning inconsistent with a fundamental feature of legislation. That would be to cross the constitutional boundary s 3 seeks to demarcate and preserve. Parliament has retained the right to enact legislation in terms which are not convention-compliant. The meaning imported by application of s 3 must be compatible with the underlying thrust of the legislation being construed. Words implied must, in the phrase of my noble and learned friend, Lord Rodger of Earlsferry, 'go with the grain of the legislation'. Nor can Parliament have intended that s 3 should require courts to make decisions for which they are not equipped. There may be several ways of making a provision convention-compliant, and the choice may involve issues calling for legislative deliberation."

In accordance with these principles, a conforming interpretation with EU law should therefore be given except in two instances. One is where the meaning given would be fundamentally inconsistent with some aspect of the domestic legislation and the other is where it would involve courts in decisions "for which they are not equipped". The latter may arise if the meaning given would have "exceedingly wide ramifications" (per Lord Steyn in *Ghaidan* (at 424)) or would "involve reading into the statute powers or duties with far-reaching practical repercussion . . . [*which*] would be beyond the scope of the legislation enacted by Parliament" (per Lord Rodger in *Ghaidan* (at 452)). It may similarly arise if the legislation concerns "issues of social policy which ought to be left to Parliament and not decided by judges" (per Lord Millett in *Ghaidan* (at 439)).

It is evident that CJ techniques of interpretation of English legislation under the General Interpretation Approach have been readily adopted by courts to secure compliance with EU law, whether it has direct or only indirect effect. There has over the years been an increasing willingness on the part of the courts to secure a conforming interpretation with EU law where at all possible and, following *Ghaidan*, to decline to follow this approach only in the limited instances to which reference is made above.

(iv) Extension of the General Interpretation Approach by adoption in cases where EU law is not relevant

4–037   Not only have new techniques been adopted by some judges when interpreting English legislation where EU law (whether directly effective or not) is relevant, but they have also been employed when interpreting English legislation which has no connection with EU law. Some (but not all) judges have shown a willingness to employ new techniques in such cases, perhaps being influenced in this respect by the penetration of the EU legal order into the English legal system. The case of *James Buchanan*, concerning the interpretation of English legislation passed specifically to implement an international treaty, provides a good example of the differing judicial approaches.

In this case, s.1 of the Carriage of Goods by Road Act 1965 gave the force of law to and incorporated the provisions (which were reproduced in a schedule to the Act) of an international treaty, the Convention on the Contract for the International Carriage of Goods by Road, which had been signed by the UK Government. The Court of Appeal took the view that it was permissible to depart from the traditional English approach to interpretation and to use interpretative techniques akin to those employed by the CJ to fill a "gap" which, in its view, existed in the provisions. Lord Denning, M.R. stated (at [1977] Q.B. 208 at 214):

> "In interpreting the Treaty of Rome (which is part of our law) we must certainly adopt the new ["*gap filling*"] approach. Just as in Rome, you should do as Rome does. So in the European Community, you should do as the European Court does. So also in interpreting an international convention (such as we have here) we should do likewise. We should interpret it in the same spirit and

by the same methods as the judges of other countries do. So as to obtain a uniform result. Even in interpreting our own legislation, we should do well to throw aside our traditional approach and adopt a more liberal attitude. We should adopt such a construction as will "promote the general legislative purpose" underlying the provision."

Both Roskill and Lawton L.JJ. (at 220 and 221–222 respectively) supported Lord Denning, M.R.'s view that such a construction should be adopted where English legislation sought to implement an international treaty, although neither endorsed the broader view put forward (obiter) by his Lordship for the adoption generally of such a construction when "interpreting our own legislation".

A markedly different approach, however, was taken when the case went on appeal to the House of Lords ([1978] A.C. 141). Although rejecting the Court of Appeal's view that a "gap" existed in the provisions, some members of the House went on to express the view (obiter) that, if a "gap" had existed, "gap filling" was not permissible and the traditional English approach to interpretation should be adhered to when interpreting provisions based on international treaties. Thus Viscount Dilhorne, for example, stated emphatically (at 156):

"I know of no authority for the proposition that one consequence of this country joining the European Economic Community is that the courts of this country should now abandon principles as to construction long established in our law. The courts have rightly refused to encroach on the province of Parliament and have refused to engage in legislation. To fill the gap which in his opinion existed, Lord Denning M.R. [*in the Court of Appeal*] rightly said would, in our eyes be 'legislation pure and simple.'"

Adoption of new techniques to interpret English legislation having no connection with EU law has not been confined to cases of legislation passed specifically to implement an international treaty, as in the *James Buchanan* case. A further example is provided by the House of Lords' case of *M v Home Office* [1994] 1 A.C. 377, which considered whether interim injunctive relief was available against Ministers of the Crown in judicial review proceedings. It had been decided by the House of Lords in an earlier case, *R. v Secretary of State for Transport Ex p. Factortame Ltd* [1990] 2 A.C. 85, that such relief was not available under the relevant legislative provision in s.31(2) of the Supreme Court Act 1981, which provided that ". . . an injunction [*may be*] granted under this subsection in any case where an application for judicial review, seeking that relief, has been made . . .". Although the wording might be broad enough to encompass the granting of interim relief, the House, employing traditional English techniques of interpretation, decided that Parliament had not intended such relief to be available. The case itself concerned the allegedly discriminatory effect of the requirement of British ownership and the other requirements of Pt II of the Merchant Shipping Act 1988, which prevented fishing vessels owned by Spanish nationals or managed in Spain from being registered under the legislation, and a reference was made to the CJ to determine whether this legislation was compatible with EC law. Before answering that question, the CJ ruled, in separate reference proceedings, that the rule of national law preventing interim injunctive relief had to be set aside. The House duly gave effect to this ruling (in *R. v Secretary of State for Transport Ex p. Factortame Ltd (No. 2)* [1991] 1 A.C. 603) and granted the relief sought. In *M v Home Office*, however, there was no connection with EU law and the ruling in *Factortame Ltd (No. 2)*, that national law preventing interim injunctive relief had to be set aside where legislation was incompatible with EC law, had no application. Nevertheless, the House declined to follow the previous interpretation of s.31(2), which, using traditional English techniques, had been adopted in *R. v Secretary of State for Transport Ex p. Factortame Ltd* [1990] 2 A.C. 85. A broad construction of the relevant provision was employed and the House in *M v Home Office* decided that interim injunctive relief *was* available against Ministers of the Crown in judicial review proceedings. In adopting this construction, the House was clearly influenced by the undesirability of interim injunctive relief being available in cases with an EU law dimension but not in other cases. As Lord Woolf (with whose judgment other members of the House agreed) observed (at 422), "It would be most regrettable if an approach which is inconsistent with that which exists in Community law should be allowed to persist if this is not strictly necessary".

Since English courts have shown themselves willing to use techniques employed by the CJ, when interpreting English legislation both in cases where EU law is relevant and in cases where it is not, it could be said that a high level of penetration by the EU legal order into the English legal system has been achieved. However, some judges adopt them with a much greater willingness and across a much broader spectrum than others, and developments in this area have been far from uniform. Nevertheless, decisions of the House of Lords in cases such as *Webb* and *M v Home Office* have shown a greater willingness to employ CJ techniques and, in cases where EU law is relevant, a determination to achieve a result which is consistent with the requirements of EU law.

▷ (e) The impact of ECJ case law on the English precedent system

4–038 It is unclear from ss.2 and 3 of the ECA 1972 what status should be given to CJ cases by an English court. It is uncertain whether a court, when determining the meaning and effect of EU law under s.3(1), should treat CJ cases differently from the way in which it would treat English cases. In addition, it is uncertain whether the same approach should be adopted whether an English court makes a reference to and receives a ruling from CJ under art.267 (ex 234) or whether it interprets EU law itself. Further, when construing English legislation subject to EU law under s.2(4), where different approaches have been adopted (see Ambiguity Interpretation Approach, General Interpretation Approach and the Priority Approach, above, 4–030—4–035), it is unclear whether the status to be accorded to CJ cases and the way in which they should be treated is the same for each of these approaches.

Although ss.2 and 3 leave a number of matters unclear, the CJ has nevertheless provided some indication of its views, where a case has been referred to it under art.267 (ex 234), of how its ruling in that case should be regarded on return of the case to the national court which referred it. The court stated in Case 29/68 *Milchkontor v Hauptzollamt Saarbrucken* [1969] E.C.R. 165 (*Milchkontor*) that a ruling given by it is binding on the court receiving it. To this extent, the notion of one court binding another court is introduced into the EU legal order. This is not, however, a departure from the principle of res judicata, i.e. that the decision in a case is generally final and binding only as between the parties to that case, since the ruling given by the CJ on an art.267 (ex 234) reference is confined to the particular case in question. This ruling consists of an interpretation or exposition of EU law, formulated in the abstract as a proposition of law rather than one which is dependent upon the material facts of the case, although the proposition will be formulated by reference to those facts. Although binding only on the parties to the case, the ruling is, however, one which the CJ (presumably) expects English courts in future cases to follow. Not only might the CJ expect English courts to follow rulings under art.267 (ex 234) following references from English courts, but it may also expect any of its other decisions (including rulings under art.267 (ex 234) following references from courts in other Member States) to be followed. However, it is clear that, as a matter of EU law, it would be open to an English court in any future case to refer the case before it to the CJ under art.267 (ex 234) for a ruling, notwithstanding the existence of a previous ruling or any other CJ decision on the particular point.

On receipt of a ruling under art.267 (ex 234) from the CJ, it will be for the English court to apply the ruling to the facts of the case before it. When a ruling is so applied, it may, from a traditional English perspective, become part of the ratio of that case and thus become part of a proposition of law based on the material facts of that case. As such, the ruling, as part of the ratio of the case, would therefore (presumably) be capable of forming a binding precedent, in the English sense, for application in future cases, although, of course, it would be open to a subsequent court to limit the scope of such ratio (and thus ruling) by distinguishing it on the ground that the case before it had materially different facts.

Whilst a ruling by the CJ returned to an English court may become part of the ratio of a case in the manner indicated above, it is less clear how any ruling returned to a national court of another Member State or any other decision of the CJ may do so. In any event, to the extent that any CJ ruling or decision has become part of the ratio of a case, the binding nature of the ratio may be called into question. If it is open to a court in any future case to make a reference to the CJ under art.267 (ex 234), as it is, the ratio of the previous case, even if of a superior court, may be no more than persuasive. A future court, whatever its status in the court hierarchy, will not be bound to follow the ratio, for it can refer the case to the CJ for a ruling. The otherwise binding nature of the ratio does not preclude the court from making such a reference. As the CJ stated in Case 166/73 *Rheinmühlen-Düsseldorf v Einfuhr-und Vorratsstelle für Getreide und Futtermittel* [1974] E.C.R. 33, 38–39, "a rule of national law whereby a court is bound on points of law by the rulings of a superior court cannot deprive the inferior courts of their power to refer to the [*European*] Court questions of interpretation of Community law involving such rulings". Further, if a reference is made and a ruling given by the CJ, the court receiving the ruling will then be required to give effect to it, following *Milchkontor*, notwithstanding the (otherwise binding nature of the) ratio of the previous precedent. As the Employment Appeal Tribunal stated in *B.J. Coote v Granada Hospitality Ltd* [1999] 3 C.M.L.R. 534 at 542, "we accept . . . [*the*] argument that the supremacy of the ECJ's decisions would be undermined were a lower court to feel obliged to follow a higher court's decision in preference to giving effect to what the European Court of Justice has determined". There would thus appear to have been a modification to the normal rule of precedent that the ratio of a higher court decision binds a lower court, in cases where EU law is relevant, since it will always be open to the lower to court to make an art.267 (ex 234) reference.

It is clear from the above that CJ cases may have a number of implications for the English doctrine of precedent. The extent of such implications, as will be seen below, may vary depending upon whether a court, when considering a point of EU law, decides to refer the case to the CJ under art.267 (ex 234) or decides itself to interpret that point.

(i) Implications of a decision to refer to the ECJ under art.267 (ex 234)

4–039 When cases have been referred to the CJ and rulings on points of EU law have been received by the courts which referred the cases, those courts invariably seem to have accepted the rulings as binding on them (in accordance with the CJ stated view in *Milchkontor* (see above, 4–038)). On receipt of such rulings, it is necessary for English courts to decide how the interpretations or expositions of EU law contained therein should be applied to the facts of the case. This may involve a consideration of the impact of the ruling on the provision in question in the English legislation and, as seen (see above, 4–030—4–035), different approaches have been adopted on this matter. In some cases, courts have regarded rulings as setting out a proposition of EU law which should be applied in preference to a provision in English legislation deemed to be inconsistent with that proposition (Priority Approach), an approach adopted, for instance, by the Court of Appeal in *Macarthys*, in which Lord Denning, M.R. stated (at [1981] 1 All E.R. 111 at 120):

> "We have now been provided with the decision of that court [*the ECJ*]. It is important now to declare, and it must be made plain, that the provisions of art 119 of the EEC Treaty [*now Art.157*] [*as interpreted by the ECJ on an Art.177 (now 267) reference from the present case*] take priority over anything in our English statute on equal pay which is inconsistent with art 119."

In other cases, courts have regarded the rulings as an aid to interpretation of a provision in English legislation. Thus courts have, on some occasions, used the ruling as an aid to resolving an ambiguity (Ambiguity Interpretation Approach) and, on other occasions, to interpret a provision in English legislation (not regarded as containing any ambiguity) in whatever manner is necessary to secure compliance with EU law (General Interpretation Approach). An instance of a court using a ruling as an aid to interpretation can be seen in *Garland*, where the House of Lords used a ruling to resolve an ambiguity in s.6(4) of the Sex Discrimination Act 1975 and where Lord Diplock stated (at [1982] 2 All E.R. 402 at 416) that it was necessary to obtain a ruling from the CJ "so as to provide the House with material necessary to aid it in construing s 6(4) of the Sex Discrimination Act 1975".

On occasions, courts receiving rulings have also expressed views (obiter) as to the status that such rulings will have in future cases. Thus, when the Court of Appeal in *Macarthys* received a ruling from the CJ that art.119 of the EC Treaty (now art.157) required equal pay for men and women even where they were not employed at the same time, Lord Denning, M.R. stated (at [1981] 1 All E.R. 111 at 120): "That interpretation must now be given by all the courts in England. It will apply in this case and in any such case hereafter". Similarly, Lord Diplock in the House of Lords in *Garland*, reflecting on the decision in that case to make a reference to the ECJ under art.177 (now 267), stated (at [1982] 2 All E.R. 402 at 415) that "it was desirable to obtain a ruling of the European Court that would be binding on all courts in England, including this House".

Such statements indicate that rulings containing an interpretation or exposition of EU law will be of general application, i.e. not limited in scope to future cases in which the ratio of the particular case in question might be considered applicable in view of the materially similar facts, and will apply irrespective of the position in the court hierarchy of either the court receiving the ruling or of any later court applying it. By regarding rulings returned to English courts as generally binding in this way (subject to exercise of the right to refer under art.267 (ex 234), the above statements appear to regard these rulings in much the same way as any other decisions of the CJ (including rulings under art.267 (ex 234) following references from courts in other Member States), a matter which is considered immediately below.

(ii) Implications of a decision by an English court to interpret EU law

An English court may interpret EU law itself and, once it has done so, it must **4–040** decide how its interpretation can be applied to the facts of the case before it. This may involve consideration of its impact on a pertinent provision in English legislation and, as seen (see above, 4–030—4–035), the adoption of the Ambiguity Interpretation Approach, the General Interpretation Approach or the Priority Approach.

In both interpreting EU law and adopting one or other of these approaches, English courts may have regard to CJ cases. These cases may include previous rulings under art.267 (ex 234) following references from English courts or from courts in other Member States, as well as any other decisions of the CJ. English courts appear to regard CJ cases in each instance as being binding generally. As a consequence, interpretations of EU law contained in such CJ cases may be binding on an English court in a particular case, irrespective of the presence or absence of similar material facts between the CJ case(s) and the case in question and irrespective of the position of the English court in the court hierarchy.

Instances of where English courts have had regard to CJ case law when interpreting EU law have included the decision of the Court of Appeal in *Pickstone* and the decision of the House of Lords in *Henn*. The Court of Appeal in *Pickstone* (see Chapter 14, 14–016—14–020) was concerned with interpreting two points of EC law, determining the scope of the principle of equal pay based on art.119 (now 157) and determining whether that principle had direct effect as regards work of equal value. On the first point, two of the three members of the Court of Appeal, Nicholls and Purchas L.JJ. found guidance on the interpretation of art.119 (now 157) in different decisions of the CJ, notwithstanding material differences in the facts of those cases from the case in question. Nicholls L.J. referred to the case of *Macarthys*, an earlier ECJ case in which a ruling had been given under art.177 (now 267) following a reference from the English Court of Appeal, whilst Purchas L.J. found guidance on the interpretation of art.119 (now 157) in *Defrenne*, an earlier case in which a ruling had been given under art.177 (now 267) following a reference from a Belgian court. On the second point, Nicholls and Purchas L.JJ. referred to two ECJ decisions, Case 96/80 *Jenkins v Kingsgate (Clothing Productions) Ltd* [1981] 1 E.C.R. 911 (*Jenkins*) and *Worringham*, in which rulings had been given under art.177 (now 267) following references from English courts. These cases provided interpretations on the direct effect[iveness] of the principle of equal pay based on art.119 (now 157) and were considered to have application in preference to an earlier Court of Appeal decision on direct effect[iveness], *O'Brien v Sim-Chem Ltd* [1980] 2 All E.R. 307. In *Henn* (see above, 4–028), the House of Lords had regard to "a well-established body of case law of the European court" (per Lord Diplock at [1981] A.C. 850 at 905), that provided guidance on the interpretation of art.30 (now 34), under which quantitative restrictions on importation of goods as between Member States were prohibited, when determining the scope of that article.

Once EU law has been interpreted having regard to CJ cases as indicated above, the English court must decide how such interpretation can be applied to the facts of the case. It may regard this interpretation as a proposition of EU law to be applied in preference to an inconsistent provision in English legislation (Priority Approach) or as an aid to interpretation of a provision in English legislation (Ambiguity Interpretation Approach or General Interpretation Approach). Whilst a court may unanimously adopt any of these approaches, equally it may not do so. Different approaches, for instance, were adopted by members of the Court of Appeal in *Pickstone* (see Chapter 14, 14–016—14–020) when deciding how the (directly effective) principle of equal pay based on art.119 (now 157), interpreted in accordance with CJ cases, should be applied. Nicholls L.J. and Sir Roualeyn Cumming-Bruce applied the court's interpretation of EC law in preference to the inconsistent provision in s.1(2)(c) of the EPA 1970 (Priority Approach), whilst Purchas L.J. used the court's interpretation of EC law as an aid to interpretation of s.1(2)(c) so that it accorded with EC law (General Interpretation Approach). This latter approach was the one subsequently taken by the House of Lords. Indeed, it may not always be easy to ascertain which of these two approaches has been applied, as can be seen from *A v National Blood Authority* [2001] 3 All E.R. 289. In this case, the High Court considered an action for damages under the Consumer Protection Act 1987 (CPA 1987), which implemented EEC Product Liability Directive 85/374, following the claimant's infection with hepatitis C after undergoing a blood transfusion. The ECJ in Case C-300/95 *EC Commission v United Kingdom* [1997] All E.R. (EC) 481, although it had not upheld the Commission's complaint that the UK Government had failed in the CPA 1987 to fulfil its obligations under the Directive, had nevertheless emphasised that the CPA 1987 would be implemented and construed as consistent with the wording and purpose of the Directive. In the case before the High Court, Burton J. stated (at [2]) that both parties:

> ". . . almost exclusively concentrated on the terms of the directive, on the basis that, in so far as the wording of the CPA, in relation to matters which have been the subject matter of particular issue in this case, differs from the equivalent articles in the directive, it should not be construed differently from the directive; and consequently the practical course was to go straight to the fount, the directive itself. As will be seen, the arguments were directed mainly to the true and proper construction of art 6 of the directive (the equivalent being s 3 of the CPA) and art 7(e) (the equivalent being s 4(1)(e)), and consequently it is with those articles, and not the relevant sections, with which this judgment will be primarily, if not exclusively, concerned."

Whilst on the face of it this might appear to be an instance of the General Interpretation Approach, in that there is reference to construing the CPA 1987 so that it accords with the EU law directive, in substance it seems to be more akin to the Priority Approach in that the focus is on the directive and not the English legislation.

CONCLUSION

This chapter has shown that, as a result of the UK's membership of the EU, the **4–041** English legal system has been subjected to pervasive and unfamiliar influences. Courts, in order to adapt to the EU legal order, have had to reappraise their approach in a number of ways. They have had to come to terms with interpreting Treaty articles and legislation drafted in a markedly different format to English legislation, adopting new techniques of interpretation and making use, to a greater or lesser extent, of various unfamiliar principles (notably supremacy, direct effect and proportionality). They have also had to make changes and modifications in their approach to and interpretation of English statutory provisions. Indeed, much of the material in this chapter has been concerned with how the courts have sought, with varying degrees of success, to come to terms with the prescriptive legal norms of the EU and to forge a marriage between the notions of tradition and established practice and the novel and intrusive demands of a supranational legal order. In some cases, markedly different approaches have been adopted, particularly when interpreting legislative provisions. On occasions, a traditional literal meaning has been employed, but courts seem to have come, with increasing frequency, to adopt a more purposive approach. No doubt this has been assisted by the passage of the Human Rights Act 1998 and the interpretative obligation under s.3(1) for courts to "read and give effect" to legislation in a way which is compatible with rights under the European Convention on Human Rights (see Chapter 5). Courts here similarly have had to adapt to the novel and intrusive demands of a supranational legal order. Additional techniques of interpretation have had to be adopted to comply with the obligation in s.3(1), as they have to secure compliance of legislation with EU law, and following *Ghaidan* there may be some assimilation of the techniques employed in these two areas and a measure of alignment and interchange of interpretative techniques as the courts seek to accommodate the requirements of these two legal orders (see above, 4–036).

How the courts have sought to come to terms with the EU legal order in relation to the topic of equal pay is considered in some detail in Chapter 14, which provides an informative cameo of the nature of the difficulties with which courts may be confronted. These difficulties are addressed through an examination of three decisions, to which reference has been made in this chapter, *Macarthys, Garland* and *Pickstone*. Notwithstanding the difficulties encountered, a number of established principles have nevertheless been developed through a series of cases, following on from the House of Lords' decision in *Pickstone*, on techniques of interpreting legislation to comply with EU law (and with Convention rights, on which see below, 5–014—5–015). Many of these have been set out above in this chapter but they have been conveniently set out in summary form by Sir Andrew Morritt, the Chancellor of the High Court, in *Vodafone 2* at [37]–[38] and are reproduced below:

> "[37] In summary, the obligation on the English courts to construe domestic legislation consistently with Community law obligations is both broad and far-reaching. In particular: (a) it is not constrained by conventional rules of construction (per Lord Oliver of Aylmerton in the *Pickstone* case, at p 126 B); (b) it does not require ambiguity in the legislative language (per Lord Oliver in the *Pickstone* case, at p 126 B and per Lord Nicholls of Birkenhead in *Ghaidan's* case, at para 32); (c) it is not an exercise in semantics or linguistics (per Lord Nicholls in *Ghaidan's* case, at paras 31 and 35; per Lord Steyn, at paras 48–49; per Lord Rodger of Earlsferry, at paras 110–115); (d) it permits departure from the strict and literal application of the words which the legislature has elected to use (per Lord Oliver in the *Litster* case, at p 577 A; per Lord Nicholls in *Ghaidan's* case, at para 31); (e) it permits the implication of words necessary to comply with Community law obligations (per Lord Templeman in the *Pickstone* case, at pp 120 H -121 A; per Lord Oliver in the *Litster* case, at p 577 A); and (f) the precise form of the words to be implied does not matter (per Lord Keith of Kinkel in the *Pickstone* case, at p 112 D; per Lord Rodger in *Ghaidan's* case, at para 122; per Arden LJ in the *IDT Card Services* case, at para 114).

[38] . . . The only constraints on the broad and far-reaching nature of the interpretative obligation are that: (a) the meaning should 'go with the grain of the legislation' and be 'compatible with the underlying thrust of the legislation being construed': see per Lord Nicholls in *Ghaidan v Godin-Mendoza* [2004] 2 AC 557, para 33; Dyson LJ in *Revenue and Customs Comrs v EB Central Services Ltd* [2008] STC 2209, para 81. An interpretation should not be adopted which is inconsistent with a fundamental or cardinal feature of the legislation since this would cross the boundary between interpretation and amendment (see per Lord Nicholls, at para 33, Lord Rodger, at paras 110–113 in *Ghaidan's* case; per Arden LJ in *R (IDT Card Services Ireland Ltd) v Customs and Excise Comrs* [2006] STC 1252, paras 82 and 113); and (b) the exercise of the interpretative obligation cannot require the courts to make decisions for which they are not equipped or give rise to important practical repercussions which the court is not equipped to evaluate: see the *Ghaidan* case, per Lord Nicholls, at para 33; per Lord Rodger, at para 115; per Arden LJ in the *IDT Card Services* case, at para 113."

5 THE EUROPEAN CONVENTION ON HUMAN RIGHTS AND THE HUMAN RIGHTS ACT 1998: INFLUENCE ON STATUTORY INTERPRETATION AND THE DOCTRINE OF PRECEDENT

5–001 This chapter is divided into three parts. Part 1 examines, first, the key features of the European Convention on Human Rights or, more particularly, the European Convention for the Protection of Human Rights and Fundamental Freedoms (Convention) regime, and, secondly, judicial techniques of the European Court of Human Rights (Strasbourg Court) in respect of legislation and case law. Part 2 examines the protection of Convention rights, with particular reference to the giving of "further effect" to such rights under various sections of the Human Rights Act 1998 (HRA 1998). Part 3 contains an assessment of the impact of the Convention regime and the HRA 1998 on statutory interpretation and the doctrine of precedent in English law. Where references are made to sections in the chapter, they are to sections in the HRA 1998 unless otherwise stated, and a list of abbreviations used throughout this chapter can be found at the end of Chapter 3 at 3–002 (as well as in the **Glossary of Abbreviations** on page xxv).

With renumbering of some of the articles of the Convention (although not those affecting substantive rights) in 1998 by the Eleventh Protocol to the Convention, the following method of citation has been adopted. When referring to current Convention provisions, the new number of the relevant article has been used, with a reference thereafter in brackets to the old number, preceded by the word "ex", e.g. art.32 (ex 45). When referring to previous cases, however, the old number of the relevant article, current at the time of the particular case, has been used, with a reference thereafter in brackets to the new number, preceded by the word "now", e.g. art.45 (now 32). In the case of quotations from previous cases, square brackets containing italicised text have been used (as they have throughout the book in order to denote an insertion), e.g. art.45 [*now 32*].

PART 1: THE CONVENTION REGIME

▶ # 1. Introduction

The Convention has been one of the most significant contributions to the **5–002** restructuring of post-Second World War Europe. The Council of Europe, a body established in 1949 in Strasbourg, was particularly concerned to ensure the future protection of fundamental human rights in Europe and with preventing violations such as those that had occurred in Nazi Germany. A European Convention on Human Rights and Fundamental Freedoms (Convention) was accordingly drawn up and signed in Rome by 14 States, including the United Kingdom (UK) and Ireland, in 1950.

The Convention, which has been ratified by 47 countries, including the 27 EU Member States, does not, however, protect all human rights. It protects only the "core" of basic human rights which, by consensus, were recognised as necessary to underpin the foundations of a Western democracy. The protection of these rights was accorded priority over economic and social rights, which were more likely to prove a source of controversy and were accordingly omitted. The majority of the rights protected are listed in the Convention itself, although some are contained in Protocols which have amended and extended the Convention's original scope. It is possible for States to give unqualified acceptance to these rights or to qualify the extent of their acceptance through "reservations" and/or "derogations".

The legislative scheme of the Convention regime, comprising the Convention and Protocols, is simpler than that of the EU and the institutional framework is also far less complex. It consists, principally, of two bodies, the Strasbourg Court and the Committee of Ministers. The Strasbourg Court hears applications by individuals claiming to be a victim of a violation of Convention rights—under art.34 (ex 25) applications may be received from any person, non-governmental organisation or group of individuals and various criteria for admissibility are set out in art.35 (ex 26 and 27)—and it gives judgments in respect of those applications. The Committee of Ministers exercises no judicial or quasi-judicial functions but has responsibility for ensuring that court judgments are adhered to and implemented. In addition, the Parliamentary Assembly has a consultative role in relation to the execution of the court's judgments which may lead to the placing of written questions relating to issues arising from those judgments before the Committee of Ministers.

The status of the Convention regime and its effect on parties to the Convention also differs from that of the EU. Although the Convention, like the EU, has the character of an international treaty, it is not a legal order infiltrating the laws and court hierarchy of parties to the Convention. The Convention simply requires that the rights declared in it must be secured within State jurisdictions and violations of those rights are given a remedy. Virtually all parties to the Convention seek to secure rights under the Convention by directly incorporating it into domestic law.

However, although the UK has not done this specifically, it has sought to give effect to certain of those rights through the HRA 1998 (see below, 5–010—5–018).

The Convention regime bears many of the hallmarks of the Continental legal tradition, as will be seen below when examining the key features of the regime and judicial techniques used, but this is not so indelibly associated with that tradition as the EU. The involvement of States with common law systems at the inception of the Convention regime, together with the character of the Convention as an international treaty, has meant that it incorporates features of common law and international legal traditions. The Convention regime has had an impact both on substantive English law (which is beyond the purview of this chapter) and on judicial techniques.

▶ 2. Key Features of the Convention Regime

▷ *(a) "Constitution"*

5–003 Consistent with the usual pattern in international law, the fundamental principles upon which the Convention regime is founded and the institutional framework designed to realise those principles are set out in written documents which constitute the basis of the "constitution" of the Convention legal order. In this respect, the position is in keeping with the Continental legal tradition and similar to the EU legal order (see Chapter 4). These written documents consist of the text of the Convention, together with further texts and documents, including Articles of the Statute of the Council of Europe and various Protocols (in particular Protocol 11) which have supplemented and amended the Convention. The Strasbourg Court is given a similar role to that of the CJ (previously the ECJ—see above, 4–001) in that it is required to act as guardian of the Convention by art.32 (ex 45), which provides that "the jurisdiction of the Court shall extend to all matters concerning the interpretation and application of the Convention".

▷ *(b) The Convention*

5–004 The drafting style adopted in the Convention has similarities both with the drafting style of legislation in the common law (English) tradition and with the style employed in codes in the Continental legal tradition, EU legislation and other international treaties and conventions. In some cases, articles contain detailed and precise provisions, e.g. art.6 (right to a fair trial) but in other instances broad, general language is used, e.g. art.8 (right to respect for private and family life), which provides:

> "(1) Everyone has the right to respect for his private and family life, his home and correspondence.

> (2) There shall be no interference by a public authority with the exercise of this right except such as is in accordance with the law and is necessary in a democratic society in the interests of national security, public safety or the economic well-being of the country, for the prevention of disorder or crime, for the protection of health or morals, or for the protection of the rights and freedoms of others."

Article 8, as can be seen, does not provide absolute protection for the right to respect for private and family life. It provides only qualified protection, by permitting interference in circumstances where certain criteria can be met (as set out in art.8(2)) and other articles make similar provision, e.g. art.9, which provides a right to freedom of thought, conscience and religion. Further, derogation (departure) from these rights might be justified in circumstances of public emergency under art.15. However, in some instances, Convention rights provide absolute protection and it is not possible, therefore, to derogate from them. This is the case, for instance, with the prohibition of torture under art.3 and the prohibition of slavery and forced labour under art.4.

▷ *(c) Judicial function*

The function of judges in the Strasbourg Court is broadly comparable with that of judges in the CJ/ECJ (see above, 4–005). Judges are concerned with interpreting codified law, may act in a "quasi-legislative" capacity and engage in various practices adopted by judges in Continental systems, such as "gap filling". **5–005**

Since 1998, with the introduction of a revised institutional framework by Protocol 11, the Strasbourg Court has been the only institution exercising judicial or quasi-judicial functions. Previously such functions were exercised by the European Commission on Human Rights (Commission), which could investigate alleged breaches of the Convention and give a decision on its findings as to the admissibility of the case for consideration by the Strasbourg Court. It could also submit reports on cases to the Committee of Ministers, giving an opinion as to whether there had been a violation of Convention rights, in cases decided by the Committee rather than the Strasbourg Court (e.g. cases not involving any new issue which were not referred to the Court). Although no judicial or quasi-judicial functions were exercised by the Committee of Ministers nor any reasoned judgments given in its decisions, opinions of the Commission, like Strasbourg Court judgments, were sophisticated, generally well-reasoned and contributed to the general jurisprudence surrounding the Convention. Although judicial or quasi-judicial functions are now exercised only by the (full-time) Strasbourg Court, decisions, reports and opinion of the Commission will nevertheless continue to be an important source of Convention law (as recognised by s.2(1) of the HRA 1998, which directs UK courts to have regard to these, as well as Strasbourg Court rulings, when determining questions which have arisen under the Act in connection with Convention rights—see below, 5–010).

▶ ## 3. Judicial Techniques

▷ ### (a) Interpreting the Convention

5-006 Since the Convention does not constitute "legislation" in the usual sense, it may perhaps be inappropriate to talk of (legislative) interpretation in this context. Nevertheless, all treaties require interpretation and the Strasbourg Court has inevitably been required to interpret the Convention in cases heard before it. This has led to a considerable body of case-law emerging on the interpretation of particular provisions. The approach adopted by the Strasbourg Court, in accordance with the requirements of international law under the Vienna Convention on the Law of Treaties 1969, has been a teleological one, comparable to that favoured in some Continental systems and employed by the CJ/ECJ (see above, 4–006 and 4–013—4–015). As the Strasbourg Court stated in *Soering v UK* (1989) 11 E.H.R.R 439 at 467 [87]:

> "In interpreting the Convention regard must be had to its special character as a treaty for the collective enforcement of human rights and fundamental freedoms (see IRELAND V. UNITED KINGDOM 2 E.H.R.R. 25, para.239). Thus, the object and purpose of the Convention as an instrument for the protection of individual human beings require that its provisions be interpreted and applied so as to make its safeguards practical and effective (see, *inter alia*, ARTICO V. ITALY 3 E.H.R.R. 1, para.33). In addition, any interpretation of rights and freedoms guaranteed has to be consistent with 'the general spirit of the Convention, an instrument designed to maintain and promote the ideals and values of a democratic society.' (see KJELDSEN, BUSK, MADSEN and PEDERSEN V. DENMARK 1 E.H.R.R. 711, para.53)."

Thus, for example, the right to a fair trial under Art.6 extends not only to court proceedings but also to cases where obstacles are placed in the way of proceedings. Accordingly, in *Golder v UK* (1975) 1 E.H.R.R. 524 the Strasbourg Court held that there had been a violation of the art.6 rights of the applicant, a serving prisoner, when he had been refused permission to correspond with a solicitor about instituting a defamation action against a prison officer, since he had been denied the right of access (through his solicitor) to a court.

The Strasbourg Court has also demonstrated a commitment to what may be described as an evolutive or dynamic approach to interpretation, i.e. that the Convention must be interpreted in the light of current social mores, thereby acknowledging that the meaning of provisions may change over time. Such an approach is broadly comparable to the objective approach to interpretation, of ascertaining legislative intention in the light of contemporary social conditions, favoured in some Continental legal systems (see Chapter 4, 4–006).

This is also similar to the ambulatory approach adopted by UK courts, when interpreting domestic legislative provisions (see Chapter 1, 1–072). Thus in *Tyrer v*

UK (1978) 2 E.H.R.R. 1, where it was held that the practice of birching (i.e. corporal punishment by beating) as a criminal punishment in the Isle of Man was a breach of the prohibition under art.3 of the Convention against "degrading treatment or punishment", the Strasbourg Court stated (at 26) that "the Convention is a living instrument which, as the Commission rightly stressed, must be interpreted in the light of present-day conditions" and indicated that judges, when interpreting the Convention, should be influenced by "the developments and commonly accepted standards in the penal policy of the member States and of the Council of Europe in this field" (at [31]). Similarly, in *Selmouni v France* (2000) 29 E.H.R.R. 403, a case involving ill-treatment in police custody, the Strasbourg Court stated (at 442) that it:

". . . considers that certain acts which were classified [*under Art.3*] in the past as "inhuman and degrading treatment" as opposed to "torture" could be classified differently in future. It takes the view that the increasingly high standard being required in the area of the protection of human rights and fundamental liberties correspondingly and inevitably requires greater firmness in assessing breaches of the fundamental values of democratic societies (para. 101)."

A consequence of this may be that older decisions afford less guidance than more recent ones when a contemporary construction of Convention rights is sought (in this respect, see, for example, the jurisprudence of the Strasbourg Court relating to the rights of transsexuals under art.8, culminating in *Goodwin v UK* (2002) 35 E.H.R.R. 447), which, of course, may have implications for the precedential value of the earlier decisions.

▷ *(b) Using previous cases*

The Strasbourg Court's approach to previous cases represents an unusual com- **5-007** bination of approaches in Continental and common law systems. The court is not bound by its previous decisions in the stare decisis sense and, to this extent, its use of previous cases may be said to be broadly comparable to the use of cases in Continental systems (see Chapter 4, 4–007). This is perhaps not surprising since the 14 States which signed the Convention at its inception all had systems based on the Continental legal tradition, apart from the UK and Ireland which had common law systems. Further, stare decisis would have been inappropriate in the Convention regime since the Strasbourg Court has to apply the Convention to a potentially limitless variety of facts occurring in a wide range of cultures and societies. Hence the Strasbourg Court, although not regarding itself as bound by its previous decisions in the stare decisis sense, has tended to concentrate on providing a particular answer on a specific set of facts (which is more akin to a common law approach). Thus the judgments contain far less articulation of statements capable of general application than CJ/ECJ judgments and often define the Convention provision specifically in the context of the facts of the case, rather than in a general, authoritative way intended to contribute to a body of case law on the point or to the evolution of a principle.

The Strasbourg Court has, nevertheless, over the years built up a consistent body of case law in certain areas, which may provide guidance for judges in future cases. This practice of contributing to and having regard to a body of case law has in fact become increasingly evident as the quantity of judgments produced by the Strasbourg Court has grown and might be considered broadly comparable to the practice in Continental legal systems and in the CJ/ECJ (see Chapter 4, 4–006 and 4–018).

This body of previous case law decisions is in most instances likely to be followed and applied in the interests of certainty and the consistent development of the jurisprudence of the Strasbourg Court. However, the Court may depart from earlier decisions where there exist "cogent reasons" for doing so, and these might include where it is necessary to "ensure that the interpretation of the Convention reflects societal changes and remains in line with present day conditions" (in this latter respect, see, for example, the accommodation of changing societal attitudes towards the rights of transsexuals evident in the Strasbourg Court's decision in *Goodwin v UK* (2002) 35 E.H.R.R. 447; and compare its earlier decisions in *Cossey v UK* (1990) 13 E.H.R.R. 622; and *Sheffield and Horsham v UK* (1998) 27 E.H.R.R. 163). Further, in *Borgers v Belgium* (1993) 15 E.H.R.R. 92, the Strasbourg Court declined to follow its earlier decision, *Delcourt v Belgium* (1979–80) 1 E.H.R.R. 355, when considering whether there had been a violation of the applicant's right under art.6 to a fair hearing before an independent tribunal on account of having no opportunity to reply to submissions made by the *avocat général* and the *avocat général*'s participation in the deliberations of the court which took place immediately after the hearing. In reaching its decision, the Court stated (at 107–109):

"The Court notes in the first place that the findings in the DELCOURT judgment on the question of the independence and impartiality of the Court of Cassation . . . remain entirely valid . . . It is, however, necessary to consider whether the proceedings before the Court of Cassation also respected the rights of the defence and the principle of the equality of arms [*i.e. equal treatment*], which are features of the wider concept of a fair trial (see, among other authorities, EKBATANI V. SWEDEN (1991) 13 E.H.R.R. 504, para. 30). This has undergone a considerable evolution in the Court's case law, notably in respect of the importance attached to appearances and to the increased sensitivity of the public to the fair administration of justice . . . (para.24)

Once the *avocat général* had made submissions unfavourable to the applicant, the latter had a clear interest in being able to submit his observations on them before argument was closed . . . (para.27)

Further and above all, the inequality was increased even more by the *avocat général*'s participation, in an advisory capacity, in the Court's deliberations . . . it could reasonably be thought that the deliberations afforded the *avocat général* an additional opportunity to promote, without fear of contradiction by

> the applicant, his submissions to the effect that the appeal should be dismissed (para.28)."

The Strasbourg Court accordingly found a violation of the applicants' rights, although judicial practices and procedure in the Court of Cassation had remained largely unchanged since the *Delcourt* case.

▷ (c) Using general principles

The Strasbourg Court has made use of general principles in interpreting the **5-008** Convention and in reaching decisions, in particular the principle of proportionality. The essence of this principle (see Chapter 4, 4–008) is that measures taken or penalties imposed should bear a reasonable relationship to their objectives and this has been consistently used by the court to assess the propriety of restrictions on human rights and fundamental freedoms which may exist in the legal systems of parties to the Convention. Since many of the rights guaranteed under the Convention, including the rights to respect for private and family life (art.8), freedom of expression (art.10) and freedom of assembly and association (art.11) may be restricted in the interests of other objectives, e.g. national security, public safety, the protection of health or morals or the rights of others, the court has used the principle of proportionality to interpret these articles to decide whether in particular cases a restriction imposed by a party to the Convention is justified.

In doing so, the Strasbourg Court has sought to balance adherence to the Convention with the plethora of prevailing national practices under the doctrine (or principle) of the margin of appreciation. This doctrine has developed in response to the multi-national character of the cases with which the Court is concerned. Conscious of the diversity of legal, social, ideological and cultural systems of the various parties to the Convention, the Court has looked for overall adherence to the fundamental principles of the Convention within a broad range of acceptable practice, rather than seeking to achieve uniformity of law and practice. Thus, although a party to the Convention must observe its principles, a broad range of discretion is left to it as to the methods, practices and procedures it adopts within its own system. This leeway or deference to national practices is referred to as the "margin of appreciation". Thus, in *R. v DPP Ex p. Kebilene* [1999] 3 W.L.R. 972, Lord Hope (at 993–994) described the doctrine of the margin of appreciation, in this context, as follows:

> "This doctrine is an integral part of the supervisory jurisdiction which is exercised over state conduct by the international court [*Strasbourg Court*]. By conceding a margin of appreciation to each national system, the court has recognised that the Convention, as a living system, does not need to be applied uniformly by all states but may vary in its application according to local needs and conditions. This technique is not available to the national courts when they are considering Convention issues arising within their own

> countries. But in the hands of the national courts also the Convention should be seen as an expression of fundamental principles rather than as a set of mere rules. The questions which the courts will have to decide in the application of these principles will involve questions of balance between competing interests and issues of proportionality."

Difficulties that may be encountered in seeking to achieve the proper balance between adherence to the Convention and the national practices of parties to the Convention are evident in *Dudgeon v United Kingdom* (1981) 4 E.H.R.R. 149, where the Strasbourg Court found that legislation in Northern Ireland criminalising homosexuality constituted a violation of the applicant's right to respect for private life under art.8. The Court held that compliance required that homosexual relations were permissible in certain circumstances and it was a matter for the UK Parliament to determine how the legislation should be amended so as to secure compliance with those rights. It was not necessary for any particular method to be adopted.

The course adopted by Parliament, through the Homosexual Offences (N.I.) Order 1982, was to make the position in Northern Ireland comparable to that which had existed in England and Wales since the passing of the Sexual Offences Act 1967. As a result, homosexual relations between consenting (civilian) male adults over the age of 21 in private were no longer a criminal offence. The 1967 Act was subsequently amended by s.143 of the Criminal Justice and Public Order Act 1994, as a result of which the age of consent was lowered to 18. In *Sutherland v UK* [1998] E.H.R.L.R. 117, however, the Commission held that fixing the minimum age for homosexual activities at 18, rather than 16 (the minimum age for heterosexual activities), was itself a violation of the right under art.8 and was discriminatory under art.14, and referred the matter to the Court. Following the reference of the matter by the Commission to the Court, the Sexual Offences (Amendment) Act 2000, which provided for a further lowering of the age of consent for homosexual acts between men from 18 to 16 (thereby equalising the age of consent for heterosexual and homosexual activities), was enacted. As a consequence, a subsequent application was made to strike out the proceedings pending in the Court and this was duly granted.

PART 2: SECURING CONVENTION RIGHTS: THE HRA 1998 AND GIVING "FURTHER EFFECT" TO CONVENTION RIGHTS

▶ 1. Introduction and Historical Background

5–009 Parties to the Convention are required to secure within their jurisdictions the rights declared in the Convention and to provide a remedy for violations of those rights. For many countries, the act of ratification of the Convention, as an international treaty, automatically incorporates it into their domestic law by virtue of their constitution. But for other countries, notably the UK, Ireland and the Nordic countries (Denmark, Finland, Norway and Sweden), legislation has to be introduced in order for international treaties to become part of domestic law.

The UK Government, on ratifying the Convention, did not, however, enact legislation to incorporate the Convention. It was assumed to be unnecessary, the view being taken that the rights and freedoms set out in the Convention were already protected adequately under UK law. The consequence of this was that the Convention did not have any legally binding effect under UK law and an individual could not directly invoke it before a UK court (cf. the ability of an individual in the UK to invoke aspects of EU law, e.g. the principle of equal pay, on which see Chapter 14). If an individual in the UK wished to allege contravention of human rights, it was necessary to do so by way of a private law claim, e.g. in tort, or for breach of contract, or for infringement of property rights in order to obtain a remedy, or by an application for judicial review.

If, however, a claim so framed did not result in a satisfactory remedy in respect of the contravention of the individual's human rights, then, provided domestic rights of appeal had been exhausted, an individual could apply for the case to be heard at Strasbourg on the ground that a Convention right had been denied. If the case was so heard, the Strasbourg Court might rule that UK law was failing to meet the standards required by the Convention. Whilst such a ruling had no legal effect in UK law, it could be effective in practice since the usual response (due to a combination of public embarrassment and political pressure) was for the UK Parliament to enact prospectively legislation or to alter administrative practices to remedy the defect. This occurred in a number of instances, e.g. *Sunday Times v UK* (1979) 2 E.H.R.R. 245, which led to the enactment of the Contempt of Court Act 1981; and *Dudgeon v UK* (1981) 4 E.H.R.R. 149 (see above, 5–008).

The high number of applications for cases to be heard at Strasbourg, and the attendant long delays and high costs led to increasing support for domestic courts to be given jurisdiction to give effect to the Convention. Following several unsuccessful attempts by MPs to introduce legislation in Parliament to incorporate the Convention into UK law, a commitment to incorporate it was contained in the Labour Party's manifesto for the 1997 General Election. Following its election, a White Paper, *Rights Brought Home: The Human Rights Bill* (Cm. 3782 (1997)), was issued and legislation based on the White Paper was subsequently enacted. This legislation, which became the HRA 1998, did not, however, directly incorporate the Convention in its entirety into UK law, but rather sought to give "further effect" to certain Convention rights which, thereby, became rights enforceable in the domestic courts (see *In re McKerr* [2004] 1 W.L.R. 807).

▶ 2. Giving "Further Effect" to Convention Rights

5–010 The rights to which the HRA 1998 seeks to give further effect are identified in s.1(1), which provides:

> "In this Act, 'the Convention rights' means the rights and fundamental freedoms set out in—
>
> (a) Articles 2 to 12 and 14 of the Convention,
> (b) Articles 1 to 3 of the First Protocol, and
> (c) Articles 1 and 2 of the Sixth Protocol,
>
> as read with Articles 16 to 18."

By s.1(2), these Articles are to have effect for the purposes of the Act subject to any "designated" derogation or reservation made under ss.14 and 15 respectively. Over the years, the UK has made a number of "designated" derogations from the Convention in connection with anti-terrorism policies in Northern Ireland, and, more recently, in response to the perceived threats from Al-Qaeda and "home-grown" terrorists. In some instances, the legality of such "designated" derogations has been challenged; see, for example, *Brannigan and McBride v UK* (1994) 17 EHRR 539.

The Articles are set out in Sch.1 to the Act (s.1(3)) and are:

(a) Articles 2 to 12 and 14 of the Convention

- the right to life (Art.2);
- prohibition of torture (Art.3);
- prohibition of slavery and forced labour (Art.4);
- right to liberty and security (Art.5);
- right to a fair trial (Art.6);
- no punishment without law (Art.7);
- right to respect for private and family life (Art.8);
- freedom of thought, conscience and religion (Art.9);
- freedom of expression (Art.10);
- freedom of assembly and association (Art.11);
- right to marry (Art.12);
- prohibition of discrimination (Art.14).

(b) Articles 1 to 3 of the First Protocol

- the protection of property;
- right to education;
- right to free elections.

(c) Articles 1 and 2 of the Sixth Protocol

- the abolition of the death penalty;
- death penalty in time of war.

These articles are, as indicated in s.1(1) above, to be read with arts 16–18. Articles 16–18 are not concerned with making provision for particular rights and freedoms but with interpretation of other Convention provisions.

Article 16 enables parties to the Convention to impose restrictions on the political activity of aliens, notwithstanding the provisions in arts 10, 11 and 14. Article 17 provides that nothing in the Convention may be interpreted as implying for any State, group or individual a right of action aimed at destroying or restricting any right or freedom set out in the Convention to a greater extent than is provided for in the Convention. Article 18 is concerned with preventing restrictions of rights permitted under the Convention being applied for purposes other than those for which they have been prescribed. This is to prevent legitimate restrictions being used for ulterior purposes, i.e. being subverted and used as a pretext for measures which have other, improper purposes.

Articles 1 and 13, although ratified by and binding on the UK Government, are excluded from "the Convention rights". Article 1 requires parties to the Convention to "secure to everyone within their jurisdiction" the rights and freedoms under the Convention and this is complemented by art.13 which provides that everyone shall have "an effective remedy before a national authority" for violation of their Convention rights. In the Government's view, the HRA 1998 itself secures to everyone within the UK the Convention rights and freedoms, and meets the requirement under art.13 through the remedial provisions contained in the Act, particularly s.8, under which a court can, in relation to acts of public authorities, grant "such relief or remedy, or make such order, within its powers as it considers just and appropriate" (see *Hansard*, HL Vol.583, col.475 (November 18, 1997)). "To incorporate expressly Article 13," Lord Irvine L.C. stated, "may lead to the courts fashioning remedies about which we know nothing other than the [*section*] 8 remedies which we regard as sufficient and clear" (see ibid., col.477).

Reluctance to incorporate expressly art.13 attracted some criticism but the Government, apparently apprehensive about possible judicial expansion of remedies, excluded it from the definition of "the Convention rights" in s.1(1). Other Convention rights also excluded, obviously, were those not ratified by the UK Government and not binding on it, e.g. rights under the Fourth Protocol, such as the right (under art.1) not to be imprisoned for debt. These rights do not fall within the scope of the HRA 1998.

The Act gives further effect to Convention rights (hereafter meaning Convention rights as defined in s.1(1)) in two ways. First, existing and future legislation has to be interpreted in conformity with Convention rights, although where a compatible interpretation is not possible the courts cannot disapply the legislation (as they may do in the case of domestic legislation that is found to be inconsistent with EU law—see Lord Walker in *Fleming (trading as Bodycraft) v Customs and Revenue Commissioners* [2008] 1 W.L.R. 195 (at [24]) and above, 4–031), and it will continue to have effect despite its incompatibility. Section 3(1) and (2) provide:

"(1) So far as it is possible to do so, primary legislation and subordinate legislation must be read and given effect in a way which is compatible with the Convention rights.

(2) This section—

(a) applies to primary and subordinate legislation whenever enacted;
(b) does not affect the validity, continuing operation or enforcement of any incompatible primary legislation; and
(c) does not affect the validity, continuing operation or enforcement of any incompatible subordinate legislation if (disregarding any possibility of revocation) primary legislation prevents removal of the incompatibility."

Certain courts, when satisfied that primary legislation is incompatible, or that subordinate legislation is incompatible and primary legislation prevents removal of the incompatibility, may make a "declaration of incompatibility" under s.4. These are the higher courts within the court hierarchy and include, under s.4(5), the Supreme Court, the Judicial Committee of the Privy Council, the Court of Appeal and the High Court (but not the Crown Court). A declaration of incompatibility has no immediate legal effect as regards the legislation or the case itself, since s.4(6) provides that it "(a) does not affect the validity, continuing operation or enforcement of the legislation in respect of which it is given; and (b) is not binding on the parties to the proceedings in respect of which it is made". Rather it is a mechanism for putting pressure on Parliament to take action to remove the incompatibility. However, as seen above (1–074), it would appear that there is an onus on the court to identify the incompatibility in sufficient detail to enable a Government Minister/ Secretary of State to determine what amending legislation is necessary to achieve compatibility (*R. (on the application of Wright) v Secretary of State for Health* [2007] EWCA Civ 999 [at 9] per May L.J.).

The HRA 1998 itself makes provision for "remedial action" by Parliament to remove such incompatibility. Section 10 provides for the use of Ministerial orders to amend legislation and render it compatible with Convention rights. These orders can be issued in certain circumstances, one of which is where a declaration of incompatibility has been made (s.10(1)(a)), provided that the Minister considers that there are "compelling reasons" for proceeding to issue an order (s.10(2)).

Secondly, s.6(1) provides: "It is unlawful for any public authority to act in a way which is incompatible with a Convention right". A "public authority" under s.6(3) is broadly defined. It includes a court or tribunal and (subject to limited exceptions) any person whose functions are of a public nature. The latter will most obviously include bodies such as government departments, local authorities and the police whose raison d'être is to carry out acts of a public nature, although it might also include other organisations whose activities encompass both public and private functions (for the distinction between "core" public authorities and "hybrid" public authorities, see *Aston Cantlow and Wilmcote with Billesley Parochial Church Council v Wallbank* [2003] UKHL 37). Where there is a dispute between private persons, s.6(1) will have no application and no right of action will be available under the section. Nevertheless, since a court or tribunal is a "public authority", it will be required to act in a way compatible with any relevant Convention rights when hearing a dispute between private persons, so effectively the obligation on the court or tribunal to act compatibly *will* extend to disputes between private persons (see below, 5–018).

The duty imposed by s.6(1) upon public authorities to act in a manner that is compatible with Convention rights is, however, subject to the defences set out in s.6(2). Thus, s.6(2) provides that s.6(1) will not apply if (a) as the result of primary legislation the authority could not have acted differently, or (b) the authority was acting so as to give effect to or enforce provisions of, or made under, primary legislation which cannot be read or given effect in a way that is compatible with Convention rights (for consideration of s.6(2)(b), see, for example, *Birmingham City Council v Doherty* [2008] UKHL 57).

Section 7 provides a specific remedy for cases where a person is affected by a public authority acting unlawfully contrary to s.6, which will be in addition to any other remedies that such a person may have, e.g. judicial review. Section 7(1) provides that a person who claims that a public authority has acted (or proposes to act) in a way which is made unlawful by s.6(1) may bring proceedings against the authority or rely on the Convention right or rights concerned in any legal proceedings, provided he is (or would be) a victim of the unlawful act. A person will, under s.7(7), be a "victim" for the purposes of s.7 only if he would be a victim for the purpose of art.34 (ex 25) of the Convention if proceedings were brought in the Strasbourg Court in respect of that act (see above, 5–002). Thus, a person will be able to make a claim under s.7 only if entitled to bring proceedings before the Court for violation of Convention rights. Whether a person would be so entitled will be determined in accordance with a considerable body of Strasbourg case law which has developed on this issue, concerned with assessing whether an applicant is affected to a sufficient degree by the violation in question. Where a court finds the act (or proposed act) of a public authority is (or would be) unlawful, it may, under s.8, grant to the victim such relief or remedy or make such order as it considers just and appropriate. This may include an award of damages. However, an award of damages is not made as a matter of course. An award will only be made in order to give "just satisfaction". In determining whether there is a case for "just satisfaction", a court must take into account any other relief or remedy that has been granted and the consequences of any decisions that have been made (see s.8(3) and *Dobson v Thames Water Utilities* [2009] 3 All E.R. 319, below, 8–007).

When seeking to give further effect to Convention rights in accordance with s.3 (interpreting legislation compatibly) and s.6 (unlawful for a public authority to act incompatibly), s.2(1) requires that rulings of various Strasbourg institutions be considered. It provides that a court or tribunal, when determining a question which has arisen under the Act in connection with a Convention right, must take into account such rulings, whenever made or given, so far as they are relevant to the proceedings in which that question has arisen. (This might include rulings in respect of art.13, notwithstanding that this article is excluded from "the Convention rights" (see above), a point acknowledged by the Government during the course of the legislation's passage.)

The rulings which must be taken into account include any judgment, decision, declaration or advisory opinion of the Strasbourg Court (s.2(1)(a)) together with opinions and decisions from other bodies which, prior to reorganisation of the Convention's institutional framework in 1998 (see above, 5–005), exercised judicial or quasi-judicial functions. The latter include opinions of the (now defunct) Commission given in a report (to the Committee of Ministers) adopted under art.31, namely, whether there has been a violation of Convention rights (s.2(1)(b)); decisions of the Commission in connection with arts 26 or 27(2), namely, the admissibility of petitions claiming a violation of Convention rights (s.2(1)(c)); and decisions of the Committee of Ministers taken under art.46, namely, whether there has been compliance with a judgment of the Strasbourg Court (s.2(1)(d)).

The provisions of the Act requiring further effect to be given to Convention rights did not, however, come into force in England and Wales on the passing of the Act. The Act received the Royal Assent on November 9, 1998, but, by s.22(3), the provisions were to come into force on a day to be appointed. This was October 2, 2000.

PART 3: THE IMPACT OF THE CONVENTION REGIME AND THE HUMAN RIGHTS ACT 1998 ON STATUTORY INTERPRETATION AND THE DOCTRINE OF PRECEDENT IN ENGLISH LAW

▶ 1. Introduction

5–011 As the Convention has not been incorporated into UK law, either on ratification or by the HRA 1998 (see above, 5–009), it might have been expected that it would have a lesser influence on the English legal system than EU law. Thus, unlike in the case of the EU legal order, there has been no obligation on courts to give effect to Convention provisions and case law or to adopt interpretation techniques or principles laid down by the Strasbourg Court. Nor has any provision been made for reference of cases to the Strasbourg Court comparable to the procedure for reference to the CJ/ECJ under art.267 of the TFEU (ex 234 of the EC Treaty). However, as will be seen in the following section, the Convention was not without some influence *prior* to the enactment of the HRA 1998.

Moreover, the HRA 1998, which, as seen above, was enacted to give "further effect" to certain Convention rights, has proved to be a growing source of litigation in diverse fields, the impact of which for present purposes is, perhaps, most apparent in the exploration by senior members of the judiciary of the nature and extent of the interpretative obligation imposed by s.3(1) (see below, 5–013). Indeed, there seems little reason to doubt that the HRA 1998 will continue to be a constant source of litigation, and that matters of interpretation are likely to be critical in many subsequent cases such as those concerned with ss.12 and 13 by virtue of which courts and tribunals are enjoined specifically to have particular regard to the importance of the rights of freedom of expression and freedom of thought, conscience and religion. Thus, under s.12, where a court or tribunal is considering whether to grant any relief which, if granted, might affect the exercise of the Convention right of freedom of expression, it must, under subs.(4):

". . . have particular regard to the importance of the Convention right of freedom of expression and, where the proceedings relate to material which the respondent [*the person against whom the application for relief is made*] claims, or which appears to the court, to be journalistic, literary or artistic material (or to conduct connected with such material), to—

(a) the extent to which—

   (i) the material has, or is about to, become available to the public; or
   (ii) it is, or would be, in the public interest for the material to be published;

(b) any privacy code."

Whilst under s.13(1), if a court or tribunal's "determination of any question arising under the Act might affect the exercise by a religious organisation (itself or its members collectively) of the Convention right of freedom of thought, conscience and religion, it must have particular regard to the importance of that right".

▶ ## 2. English Judicial Approaches to the Implications of the Convention for Statutory Interpretation and Precedent prior to the Human Rights Act 1998

Traditionally, international treaties, conventions or agreements (treaties) ratified by **5–012** the UK Government but not incorporated into domestic law have acted as an aid to statutory interpretation where legislative provisions are ambiguous and may assist in resolving the ambiguity in favour of an interpretation consistent with the UK's treaty obligations. In considering such treaties as aids, courts may take into account both the treaty and any relevant case law appertaining thereto, which in the case of the Convention includes the case law of the Strasbourg Court. When taken into account, such case law has only *persuasive* authority as a precedent. This continues to be the case under the HRA 1998, although courts are, under s.2(1), under a duty to take the case law into account (see above, 5–010). Prior to the Act, they had a discretion, but not a duty, to do so.

Prior to the enactment of the HRA 1998, English courts did not, however, seek to confine the Convention and its case law to instances where there was ambiguity in statutory provisions and showed a willingness to have recourse to them in other cases. Perhaps the most obvious instance of this was where courts had regard to the Convention when considering legislation that had been enacted to comply with it, in which case particular weight could be attached to the Convention (see, for example, *R. v Secretary of State for the Home Department Ex p. Norney* (1995) 7 Admin.L.R. 861). Other cases were identified by Balcombe L.J. in the Court of Appeal in *Derbyshire County Council v Times Newspapers Ltd* [1992] 3 All E.R. 65 (*Derbyshire*) where his Lordship stated (at 77):

> "Article 10 [*under which there is a right to freedom of expression*] . . . may be used when considering the principles upon which the court should act in exercising a discretion, eg whether or not to grant an interlocutory injunction . . . [*and*] may be used when the common law (by which I include the doctrines of equity) is uncertain."

Having decided that the common law was uncertain in respect of whether a local authority might sue for defamation, the Court of Appeal had regard to art.10 and took the view that it could not. When the case went on appeal to the House of Lords, the House took the view that the common law was *not* uncertain and reached its decision that the authority could not sue without reference to the Convention. However, reference was made to the Convention by way of reinforcing the decision which had been reached. As Lord Keith stated (at [1993] 1 All E.R. 1011 at 1021):

> "My Lords, I have reached my conclusion upon the common law of England without finding any need to rely upon the European convention . . . [*but*] I find it satisfactory to be able to conclude that the common law of England is consistent with the obligations assumed by the Crown under the treaty in this particular field."

Whilst the Convention might reinforce a decision where there was no ambiguity or uncertainty, it was equally apparent that before the enactment of the HRA 1998 the courts could reach a decision which conflicted with the Convention. As Ralph Gibson L.J. said in the Court of Appeal in *Derbyshire* (at 83):

> "If by established principles of English law it is clear that Derbyshire County Council has the right to sue . . . then this court must say so and let the action proceed. It would not matter that the consequence of so holding might be that the defendants, if they should lose the action, would satisfy the European Court of Human Rights that any verdict against them would constitute a breach of art 10 of the Convention . . . Article 10, as with any other provision of

> the convention, is not a rule of the law of this country: see *Brind v Secretary of State for the Home Dept* [1991] 1 All ER 720, [1991] AC 696."

The provisions of HRA 1998 make it clear that this approach is no longer possible. It *will* matter if the consequence of established principles of English law is a breach of a Convention right. If statutory provisions are found to conflict with the Convention, and cannot be read and given effect in a way which is compatible with Convention rights, the court will have to acknowledge the conflict and issue a declaration of incompatibility under s.4 (see above, 5–010). Similarly, if principles of common law are found to conflict with the Convention, it would appear to be unlawful for courts to give effect to them. Courts are, under s.6(3)(a), public authorities and, under s.6(1), "it is unlawful for any public authority to act in a way which is incompatible with a Convention right" (see below, 5–018). A court, if it were to give effect to principles of common law which are incompatible, would thus (presumably) be acting unlawfully and (presumably) would not do so.

▶ 3. Judicial Approaches to the Implications of the Human Rights Act 1998 for Statutory Interpretation and Precedent

▷ (a) Changes or modifications to the existing rules relating to statutory interpretation

(i) The interpretative obligation: legislative framework

It is conceivable that section 3(1), by requiring that all legislation must, so far as **5–013** possible, be read and given further effect in a way which is compatible with Convention rights, introduces a new rule of statutory interpretation (it has been so regarded by Zander, *The Law-Making Process* (6th ed., 2004), "The Human Rights Act 1998—a new rule of statutory interpretation", pp.184–189). However, this requirement is, itself, compatible with the broadly similar approach taken towards ss.2 and 3 ECA 1972 by some judges who appear to have understood these sections to require that domestic legislation should be interpreted using such means as are necessary to ensure that it complies with EU law (see, in particular, Chapter 4, 4–034—4–037)), and is consistent with the judicial acknowledgement that the interpretative obligations imposed by s.3(1) HRA 1998 and s.2(4) ECA 1972 are not dissimilar (see below, 5–014).

Under s.3(1), courts must not only seek to ascertain the legal meaning of a provision but are under a duty to attribute a legal meaning which is compatible with Convention rights. This is unless it is impossible to attribute a compatible legal meaning, in which case a declaration of incompatibility might be issued (see above, 5–010), as in *R. (on the application of Black) v Secretary of State for the Home Department* [2008] EWCA Civ 359. This duty extends to *all* cases, since s.3(2)(a) provides that the section applies to primary and subordinate legislation whenever enacted, i.e. to both existing and future legislation and thus sets a standard of general application. As Lord Cooke, a former President of the New Zealand Court of Appeal and latterly a law lord in the House of Lords, observed during the course of the legislation's passage (at *Hansard*, HL Vol.583, col.533 (November 18, 1997)), this provision:

> ". . . definitely goes further than the existing common law rules of statutory interpretation, because it enjoins a search for possible meanings as distinct from the true meaning—which has been the traditional approach in the matter of statutory interpretation in the courts."

Failure to comply, however, does not invalidate any primary legislation, for s.3(2)(b) goes on to provide that the section "does not affect the validity, continuing operation or enforcement of any incompatible primary legislation", thereby preserving the legislative supremacy of Parliament. As Lord Nicholls observed in *S (minors) (care order: implementation of care plan), Re* [2002] 2 W.L.R. 720 (*Re S*) (at [39]):

> "The Human Rights Act reserves the amendment of primary legislation to Parliament. By this means the Act seeks to preserve parliamentary sovereignty. The Act maintains the constitutional boundary. Interpretation of statutes is a matter for the courts; the enactment of statutes, and the amendment of statutes, are matters for Parliament."

Section 3(2)(c) provides similarly for the "validity, continuing operation or enforcement of 'any incompatible subordinate legislation, if (disregarding any possibility of revocation) primary legislation prevents removal of the incompatibility'". It appears that primary legislation will prevent the removal of the incompatibility where subordinate legislation is "inevitably incompatible because of the terms of the parent statute" (Lord Irvine L.C. at *Hansard*, HL Vol.583, col.1232, (November 3, 1997) or where the "nature of the primary legislation under which an order is made may be such that any subordinate legislation will necessarily be in conflict with convention rights" (Mr Geoffrey Hoon, Under-Secretary at the Lord Chancellor's Department, at *Hansard*, HC Vol.313, col.433, (June 3, 1998)). This might be the case, for instance, if some procedure in respect of a matter contained in primary legislation is to be prescribed in subordinate legislation; if the matter itself is incompatible with Convention rights, any procedure specified in subordinate legislation will of necessity be incompatible and the effect of s.3(2)(c) is that this will continue to have effect.

(ii) The interpretative obligation: expectation and practice

5–014 During the passage of the Human Rights Bill through Parliament, leading members of the government alluded to the manner in which it was expected the courts would approach the exercise of the interpretative obligation imposed by what was to become s.3(1) of the HRA 1998. Thus Lord Irvine L.C. stated (at

Hansard, HL Vol.583, col.535, (November 18, 1997)) that "we want the courts to construe statutes so that they bear a meaning that is consistent with the Convention whenever that is possible according to the language of the statute but not when it is impossible to achieve that".

The Home Secretary, Mr Jack Straw, also signalled that there should be a point beyond which courts should not be expected to go in the search for compatibility when he observed (at *Hansard*, HC Vol.313, col.422, (June 3, 1998)) "it is not our intention that the courts, in applying [*s.3*] should contort the meaning of words to produce implausible or incredible meanings." It was also anticipated, however, that a compatible interpretation should be achievable in many cases, and that, therefore, recourse by the courts to declarations of incompatibility would not often be necessary. As Lord Irvine L.C. remarked in this respect "in 99% of the cases that will arise, there will be no need for judicial declarations of incompatibility" (*Hansard*, HL Vol.585, col.840, (February 5, 1998)).

Since the HRA 1998 came into force in October 2000, the courts have been, to use the words of Lady Justice Arden writing extra-judicially ("The Interpretation of UK Domestic Legislation in the Light of European Convention on Human Rights Jurisprudence" (2004) Stat. L.R. 165 at 179), "feeling their way towards a set of rules and canons of construction that will apply where section 3(1) is in point". The judiciary in the course of "feeling their way" have acknowledged, broadly, that the interpretative obligation under s.3 is "a strong one" (per Lord Steyn in *R. v A (No. 2)* [2001] 2 W.L.R. 1546 at 1562) (*R. v A*), and is "of an unusual and far-reaching character" (per Lord Nicholls in *Ghaidan v Godin-Mendoza* [2004] 3 All E.R. 411 at 423 (*Ghaidan*)). This is not to say, however, that the interpretative duty of the courts under s.3(1) is without parallel. Indeed, in *Ghaidan* [at 426], Lord Steyn drew attention to the fact that in the course of drafting s.3(1) "the draftsman had resort to the analogy of the obligation under the EEC Treaty on national courts, as far as possible, to interpret national legislation in the light of the wording and purpose of directives". Moreover, in the recent case of *Vodafone 2 v The Commissioners for Her Majesty's Revenue & Customs* [2009] EWCA Civ 446 (*Vodafone 2*), Lord Morritt, the Chancellor of the High Court, stated (at [41]) that "the terms of that section [s.3(1)] are in substance the same as the terms of s.2(4) ECA 1972", whilst Longmore L.J. opined (at [68]) that the interpretative obligation under s.2(4) ECA 1972 "is not dissimilar to the obligation laid on the courts under section 3 of the Human Rights Act 1998". Further, as seen in Chapter 4 (above, 4–036), cases such as *Vodafone 2* and *IDT Card Services* also show that there appears to be a growing congruence in relation to the principles associated with the interpretative duties in respect of Convention rights under s.3(1) HRA 1998 and EU law under s.2(4) ECA 1972 (and the principle in *Marleasing*).

The exploration of the interpretative duty under s.3(1) HRA 1998 has provided, in particular, some clarification of the meaning to be attributed to the following (italised) operative words of s.3(1), i.e. "*so far as it is possible to do so*, primary legislation and subordinate legislation must be *read and given effect* in a way which is *compatible* with Convention rights". It has also identified the interpretative techniques that may be used by the courts to seek out a compatible interpretation, interpretative techniques that, as will be seen, resemble the techniques that may be employed by the courts under s.2(4) ECA 1972 and (in accordance with the principle in *Marleasing*) to secure an interpretation that makes a provision consistent with EU law. Such techniques are considered in the next section of this chapter (see below, 5–015).

The phrase *"so far as it is possible to do so"* gives the courts, as Lord Irvine L.C. intended (see above), the opportunity to find, wherever possible, a compatible interpretation, but it also anticipates the prospect that, in some instances, such an interpretation may not be achievable. In any event, it is clear, as the following observations of Lord Nicholls in *Ghaidan* (at 422–423) reveal, that the interpretative obligation under s.3 is not restricted to cases in which the words in question are capable of more than one *possible* meaning, i.e. where the courts are required to resolve an ambiguity, but applies equally in cases where the traditional "rules" of interpretation support one literal (and incompatible) meaning:

> "Section 3(1), read in conjunction with s 3(2) and s 4, makes one matter clear. Parliament expressly envisaged that not all legislation would be capable of being made convention-compliant by application of s 3. Sometimes it would be possible, sometimes not. What is not clear is the test to be applied in separating the sheep from the goats. What is the standard, or the criterion, by which 'possibility' is to be judged? A comprehensive answer to this question is proving elusive . . .
>
> One tenable interpretation of the word 'possible' would be that s 3 is confined to requiring courts to resolve ambiguities. Where the words under consideration fairly admit of more than one meaning the convention-compliant meaning is to prevail. Words should be given the meaning which best accords with the convention rights.
>
> This interpretation of s 3 would give the section a comparatively narrow scope. This is not the view which has prevailed. It is now generally accepted that the application of s 3 does not depend upon the presence of ambiguity in the legislation being interpreted. Even if, construed according to the ordinary principles of interpretation, the meaning of the legislation admits of no doubt, s 3 may none the less require the legislation to be given a different meaning."

The judicial treatment accorded to the second highlighted phrase, *"read and given effect"*, has shown that the word *"read"* and the expression *"given effect"* are to be regarded as creating two distinct, but related, imperatives. As Lord Rodger stated in *Ghaidan* (at 448–449):

> "The use of the two expressions, 'read' and 'give effect', is not to be glossed over as an example of the kind of cautious tautologous drafting that used to be typical of much of the statute book. That would be to ignore the lean elegance which characterises the style of the draftsman of the 1998 Act. Rather, s 3(1) contains, not one, but two, obligations: legislation is to be read in

a way which is compatible with convention rights, but it is also to be given effect in a way which is compatible with those rights. Although the obligations are complementary, they are distinct. So there may be a breach of one but not of the other . . . So, even though the heading of s 3 is 'interpretation of legislation', the content of the section actually goes beyond interpretation to cover the way that legislation is given effect."

The essence of the meaning of the final highlighted word, namely "*compatible*", was captured by Lady Justice Arden when she wrote, extra-judicially, in "The Interpretation of UK Domestic Legislation in the Light of European Convention on Human Rights Jurisprudence" (as above, at 170):

"It is sufficient if the statute passes the test of compatibility with no room to spare. The interpretative obligation does not require the courts to give the fullest expression to Convention rights or to find a meaning which would promote them to the fullest extent."

Thus, a meaning attributed to a statutory provision that can co-exist with a Convention right will suffice even though it may not totally reflect that right, or as Baroness Hale put it, pithily, in *Secretary of State for the Home Department v MB (FC); Secretary of State for the Home Department v AF (FC)* [2007] UKHL 46 (at [73]): "In interpreting the Act compatibly we [the judiciary] are trying to make it work."

However, notwithstanding the presence of s.3(1) as "strong adjuration" (per Lord Cooke in *R. v Director of Public Prosecutions Ex p. Kebilene*) [2000] 2 A.C. 326 at 373) by Parliament to read and give effect to legislation compatibly with Convention rights, the HRA 1998, as already seen, maintains the constitutional boundary between the courts and Parliament (see Lord Nicholls in *Re S* (at [39]), above, 5–013). Consequently, the interpretative obligation imposed by s.3(1) does not entitle the judiciary to legislate, and, moreover, where there are instances of incompatibility, which cannot be resolved by interpretation under s.3(1), the judiciary do not have the right to set aside offending legislation (see above, 5–010). In such cases, as we have seen, it may be possible to issue a declaration of incompatibility under s.4, which then gives rise to the ministerial power to make a remedial order under s.10 (for examples of cases in which declarations of incompatibility have been issued, see *R. (Anderson) v Secretary of State for the Home Department* [2003] 1 A.C. 837; *R. (on the application of Black) v Secretary of State for the Home Department* [2008] EWCA Civ 359 and the Appendix to the Opinion of Lord Steyn in *Ghaidan*). In *R. v A*, however, Lord Steyn opined (at [1563]) that a declaration of incompatibility should be regarded as "a measure of last resort", and expressed misgivings in his subsequent opinion in *Ghaidan* (at 425 and 428–429) about the manner in which the remedial scheme in the HRA 1998 under which "interpretation under section 3(1) is the prime remedial remedy and . . . resort to s 4 must always be an exceptional course" has been approached in some cases. This is not, however, to decry the use of declarations of incompatibility, where appropriate, for, as Baroness Hale said in *R. (on the application of the Countryside Alliance and others) v Her Majesty's Attorney General and another* [2007] UKHL 52 (at [113]) "such declarations [*of incompatibility*] have proved powerful incentives to Government and Parliament to put the matter right for if the court is right the United Kingdom is in breach of its international obligations in maintaining such a law on the statute book."

In many cases, therefore, a critical finding will relate to the question of whether a perceived incompatibility can be avoided by interpretation under s.3(1); if not, the issue of a declaration of incompatibility may be contemplated. Some guidance has been provided by the judges with regard to the circumstances in which it is likely that a case of incompatibility *cannot* be avoided by interpretation under s.3(1). Thus, a declaration of incompatibility probably cannot be avoided where such an interpretation would:

— lead to a meaning which contradicts, expressly or by necessary implication, the meaning given to the particular provision by the legislation (see Lord Hope in *R. v Lambert* [2001] 3 W.L.R. 206 at 234) (*Lambert*); or

— "radically alter" the effect of legislation and so defeat Parliament's original objective (see Lord Woolf in *Poplar Housing and Regeneration Community Association Limited v Secretary of State for the Environment, Transport and the Regions* [2002] Q.B. 48 (at [77]); or

— depart substantially from a fundamental feature of the legislation, e.g. where such departure has important practical repercussions which the court is not equipped to evaluate (see Lord Nicholls in *S, Re* (at [40]); or

— change the substance of a provision completely, e.g. to change a provision from one where Parliament says that *x* is to happen to one saying that *x* is not to happen (see Lord Rodger in *Ghaidan* (at 449)).

Conversely, it would appear that a meaning derived from the exercise of the interpretative obligation under s.3(1) will be acceptable where it goes "with the grain of the legislation" and is "compatible with the underlying thrust of the legislation being construed" (per Lord Nicholls in *Ghaidan* (at 424)).

(iii) The interpretative obligation: techniques of statutory interpretation

5–015 An exposition of the techniques of statutory interpretation that may be used by the courts in the exercise of the interpretative obligation under s.3(1) was given by Lord Hope in *Lambert*. His Lordship stated (at [81]):

> "As to the techniques that may be used, it is clear that the courts are not bound by previous authority as to what the statute means. It has been suggested that a strained or non-literal construction may be adopted, that words may be read in by way of addition to those used by the legislator and that the words may be 'read down' to give them a narrower construction than their ordinary meaning would bear: *Clayton & Tomlinson, The Law of Human Rights* (2000), vol. 1, p. 168, para. 4.28. It may be enough simply to say what the

effect of the provision is without altering the ordinary meaning of the words used: see *Brown v Stott* JC 328, 355B–C, per Lord Justice General Rodger. In other cases, as in *Vasquez v The Queen* [1994] 1 WLR 1304, the words used will require to be expressed in different language in order to explain how they are to be read in a way that is compatible. The exercise in these cases is one of translation into compatible language from language that is incompatible. In other cases, as in *R v A (No. 2)* [2002] 1 AC 45, it may be necessary for words to be read in to explain the meaning that must be given to the provision if it is to be compatible. But the interpretation of a statute by reading words in to give effect to the presumed intention must always be distinguished from amendment. Amendment is a legislative act. It is an exercise which must be reserved to Parliament."

However, notwithstanding the wide range of techniques which this extract shows may be employed under s.3(1) (for other observations upon these techniques, see, for example, Lord Steyn in *R. v A* (at 1563) and Lord Nicholls in *Ghaidan* (at 423–424)), the fundamental importance, as Lord Hope intimated, of judges not straying beyond the realms of interpretation when exercising the interpretative obligation has been emphasised in many of the cases e.g. *AS (Somalia) v Secretary of State for the Home Department* [2009] UKHL 32.

This has been especially so in those cases in which the question of whether words should be read into a statutory provision has arisen and in relation to which Lord Hope's cautionary words about maintaining a divide between interpretation and amendment are particularly apt. In this latter regard, the difference between interpretation of legislation and amendment, in the context of s.3(1), was explained by Lord Rodger in *Ghaidan*. His Lordship stated (at 454–455):

". . . it is possible for the courts to supply by implication words that are appropriate to ensure that legislation is read in a way which is compatible with convention rights. When the court spells out the words that are to be implied, it may look as if it is 'amending' the legislation, but that is not the case. If the court implies words that are consistent with the scheme of the legislation but necessary to make it compatible with convention rights, it is simply performing the duty which Parliament has imposed on it and on others. It is reading the legislation in a way that draws out the full implications of its terms and of the convention rights. And, by its very nature, an implication will go with the grain of the legislation. By contrast, using a convention right to read in words that are inconsistent with the scheme of the legislation or with its essential principles as disclosed by its provisions does not involve any form of interpretation, by implication or otherwise. It falls on the wrong side of the boundary between interpretation and amendment of the statute . . .

. . . the key to what it is possible for the courts to imply into legislation without crossing the border from interpretation to amendment does not lie in the number of words that have to be read in. The key lies in a careful consideration of the essential principles and scope of the legislation being interpreted. If the insertion of one word contradicts those principles or goes beyond the scope of the legislation, it amounts to impermissible amendment. On the other hand, if the implication of a dozen words leaves the essential principles and scope of the legislation intact but allows it to be read in a way which is compatible with convention rights, the implication is a legitimate exercise of the powers conferred by s 3(1). Of course, the greater the extent of the proposed implication, the greater the need to make sure that the court is not going beyond the scheme of the legislation and embarking upon amendment. Nevertheless, what matters is not the number of words but their effect . . .

. . . Attaching decisive importance to the precise adjustments required to the language of any particular provision would reduce the exercise envisaged by s 3(1) to a game where the outcome would depend in part on the particular turn of phrase chosen by the draftsman and in part on the skill of the court in devising brief formulae to make the provision compatible with convention rights . . . What matters is not so much the particular phraseology chosen by the draftsman as the substance of the measure which Parliament has enacted in those words . . . Parliament was not out to devise an entertaining parlour game for lawyers, but, so far as possible, to make legislation operate compatibly with convention rights. This means concentrating on matters of substance, rather than on matters of mere language."

The judicial practice of reading words into legislation is also, of course, used by the courts in fulfilment of their interpretative duty under s.2(4) ECA 1972. For example, in each of the cases of *Pickstone* and *Litster* (see Chapter 4, 4–035 and 4–036 respectively) the House of Lords read additional words into the relevant domestic legislation in order to ensure its compliance with EU law (directives). In fact in *Ghaidan*, both cases were referred to by Lord Steyn (at 427–428) and Lord Rodger (at 454) in order to "reinforce" the stance adopted under s.3(1) that a court may supply by implication words that are appropriate to ensure that domestic legislation is compatible with Convention rights.

However, notwithstanding the guidance proffered by Lord Rodger in *Ghaidan* and the judicial experience of reading words into domestic legislation in order to effect compliance with EU law, it may be difficult in any given case to determine when considering whether words should be read into a statutory provision where the dividing line between interpretation and amendment lies. Thus it is possible, for example, for judges in different courts in the same case to disagree about this dividing line, e.g. in *Re S* the House of Lords felt that the Court of Appeal had engaged in "judicial innovation" that went well beyond the boundary of interpretation. Equally, it is possible for judges in the same court to disagree on this matter, e.g. the House of Lords in *Ghaidan* (see Chapter 13) by a majority of 4–1, Lord Millett dissenting, decided that para.2 of Sch.1 to the Rent Act 1977, which allowed the spouse of a protected tenant to succeed to the tenancy on the tenant's death, was to be read so that "spouse" included the survivor of a same-sex partnership thereby ensuring that there was no violation of the survivor's right under art.14 (to non-discrimination) in relation to art.8(1) (his right to respect for his private and family life, *his home* and his correspondence). It is also conceivable, if a broader perspective is taken, that judges in a case may disagree about which of the techniques available to them should be used in order to ensure that an inter-pretation which is compatible with Convention rights is achieved, and, irrefutable, that the "spectrum of ways of construing a provision which is incompatible in order to make it compatible introduces considerable uncertainty into the statute book" (per Lady Justice Arden in "The Interpretation of UK Domestic Legislation in the light of European Convention on Human Rights Jurisprudence" (as above, at 179)).

▷ *(b) The impact of the HRA 1998 on the English precedent system*

(i) Provisions having an impact

There are various provisions in the HRA 1998 which may have an impact on the English precedent system. These include:

5–016

- section 2, under which there is a requirement for courts or tribunals, when determining questions arising under the Act in connection with a Convention right, to take into account Strasbourg Court decisions and other sources of Convention law;
- section 3(1), under which there is a requirement to interpret legislation, so far as possible, compatibly with Convention rights;
- section 4(2), under which a declaration of incompatibility where compatible interpretation is not possible can be issued;
- section 6(1), under which it is unlawful for a public authority (which, by s.6(3)(a), includes a court or tribunal) to act in a way which is incompatible with a Convention right; and
- section 7(1), under which a person who claims that a public authority has acted (or proposes to act) in a way made unlawful by s.6(1) may (a) bring pro-ceedings against the authority, or (b) rely on the Convention right(s) concerned in any legal proceedings, if he is (or would be) a victim of the unlawful act.

The impact of each of these provisions will be dependent upon how, over time, they are interpreted and applied. In ascertaining the meaning that Parliament intended the words to have in these particular provisions, courts will be guided, undoubtedly, by the overriding purpose of the HRA 1998, which was to give individuals the right to bring proceedings against the state or organs of the state where they have acted incompatibly with Convention rights and to provide a remedy for those individuals, without the need to have recourse to the Strasbourg Court. However, this right is restricted to such proceedings by s.7(1)(a) (see above) and so does not extend to bringing proceedings against other individuals where those individuals have acted incompatibly with Convention rights. As Lord Irvine L.C. explained during the legislation's passage (at *Hansard*, HC Vol.585, col.850, (February 5, 1998)):

> "We have sought to protect the rights of individuals against abuse of power by the state, broadly defined, rather than to protect them against each other. That is the only practical difference between full incorporation of Convention rights into our domestic law and the actual effect of the [*HRA 1998*]."

(ii) Impact in proceedings against a public authority

5-017 Where proceedings are brought by an individual against the state or a body of the state, as a public authority, it will be a matter for the court or tribunal (court) to decide whether the public authority has acted unlawfully under s.6(1). In determining that question, the court must interpret legislation (which will include any legislation under which a public authority might have been acting as well as the provisions in ss.6 and 7 themselves which confer the right to bring the proceedings) in accordance with s.3(1) and with the assistance of s.2 as relevant. Hence a court will be acting unlawfully if it delivers a decision which is incompatible with Convention rights.

The requirement to interpret legislation in accordance with s.3(1) in a way which, so far as possible, is compatible with Convention rights applies both to existing and future legislative provisions. This may have an impact in certain cases on the authority of precedents relating to the interpretation of existing legislative provisions. Thus, as stated (extra-judicially) by Lady Justice Arden in "The Interpretation of UK Domestic Legislation in the Light of European Convention on Human Rights Jurisprudence" (as above, at 178):

> "If a statute was interpreted before the commencement of the Human Rights Act 1998, that interpretation will not be binding on a court after the commencement of the Act if it is shown to result in violation of a Convention right."

Accordingly, such *binding precedents* on the (inconsistent) interpretation of the legislation will cease to be binding and a court seeking an interpretation consistent with Convention rights will not be bound by any previous (inconsistent) interpretation. This will be so irrespective of how authoritative that previous interpretation might otherwise have been. However, it has been suggested by Zander (*The Law-Making* Process, (6th ed., 2004) at p.255) that the opportunity for courts to escape *binding precedents* in this way is subject to the following limitation:

> "[T]his freedom to ignore binding precedent does not apply to decisions of higher courts given *after* the 1998 Act came into effect in October 2000. So, the Court of Appeal would be free to hold in 2004 that a 1980 House of Lords decision was inconsistent with the Convention and should therefore not be followed. But if the House of Lords in 2005 were to affirm its 1980 decision (regardless of whether it held it to be consistent with the ECHR or incompatible), the Court of Appeal would thereafter be obliged to follow the 2005 decision."

Further, when determining the question of compatibility under s.3(1), a court or tribunal (court) must, under s.2(1), take into account Strasbourg case law and other sources of Convention law (including general principles expressed either as propositions of law within the Convention or developed by the Strasbourg Court as aids to interpretation), in so far as they are considered relevant to the proceedings (see above, 5–010). Since the requirement is only to take into account the above sources in so far as courts consider them relevant, they will *not* constitute *binding precedents* for courts. Courts are free to decide the extent to which they are relevant on particular issues and the extent to which they shall be taken into account. Even if Strasbourg case law or other sources are considered relevant, s.2 does not require that they be applied but only that they be taken into account.

Technically, therefore, Strasbourg case law and other sources have only *persuasive* authority as precedents and courts can depart from them, as the House of Lords did in *Horncastle* (see above 1–023). Nevertheless, it is probable that in many cases Strasbourg case law will be regarded as *highly persuasive* and be followed. Indeed, an indicator of the weight that may be attached to Strasbourg case law was provided in *R. (RJM) v Secretary of State for Work and Pensions (Equality and Human Rights Commission intervening)* [2008] UKHL 63 in which it was intimated by the House of Lords that where the Court of Appeal considers that one of its decisions is inconsistent with a later decision of the Strasbourg Court it may, but is not obliged to, depart from that decision (see above, 1–021). In *Kay*, however, the House of Lords indicated that the lower courts are bound by and may not, therefore, depart from a House of Lords decision (and now, presumably, a Supreme Court decision) that they may regard as inconsistent with a later decision of the Strasbourg Court (see above, 1–023).

If courts take Strasbourg case law into account but do not apply it they should give reasons for doing so. Article 6(1) provides that "everyone is entitled to a fair and public hearing . . . by an independent and impartial tribunal" and this right to a fair hearing requires courts to give reasons for their judgments, which have to be sufficient so that a party can effectively exercise any right of appeal: *Hadjianastassiou v Greece* (1992) 16 E.H.R.R. 219. Whilst this does not mean that detailed explanations have to be given to all points raised by the case, it does mean that important and crucial aspects must be addressed: *Hiro Balani v Spain* (1995) E.H.R.R. 566. A court which does not apply Convention case law on such an aspect will be in breach of art.6(1).

When a decision is made by a court on the extent to which Strasbourg case law and other sources of Convention law are to be taken into account, or when a decision is made by a court interpreting (or reinterpreting) legislation so that it is compatible with Convention rights, this may form part of the ratio of the case. If it does and it is a decision of a higher court, it would seem that this might form a binding precedent for lower courts. This will similarly be the case where a court decides that legislation cannot be interpreted compatibly and issues a declaration of incompatibility (although any such decision may not operate as a precedent for long if, as anticipated, remedial action under s.10 to remedy the incompatibility (see above, 5–010) is taken promptly by the Government). However, even if a previous decision, in either of these instances, were to be regarded as binding by a subsequent court, that court might (as in any other case) choose not to follow the previous decision by regarding it as *distinguishable*.

(iii) Impact in other proceedings

5–018 The provision in s.6(1), under which it is unlawful for a public authority to act in a way which is incompatible with a Convention right, has a wider significance than simply enabling proceedings to be brought under s.7 against that authority by a person who is a victim of its unlawful act. First, a victim of an authority's unlawful act can, under s.7(1)(b), rely on the Convention right(s) concerned in *any* legal proceedings. Thus what has been said in (ii) above as regards precedent may have equal application where proceedings are *not* brought by a victim. This will most obviously cover cases where a public authority itself brings proceedings against a person who might be a victim of its actions (e.g. where proceedings are instituted for failing to comply with applicable legislative provisions). However, it would also seem to include cases involving proceedings between individuals where an individual is able to show, as an aspect of those proceedings, that he is a victim of a public authority acting incompatibly with a Convention right.

Secondly, and perhaps more wide-ranging in scope, the definition of "public authority" expressly includes a court or tribunal (s.6(3)(a)) and therefore it is incumbent on a court or tribunal (court) in *any* case before it to comply with s.6(1) and act compatibly with Convention rights. This means that a court must *generally* apply and develop the law compatibly with Convention rights, whether the law is statutory or common law and irrespective of who are the parties to the dispute before it. The onus is upon them to do so just as much in cases involving private individuals as in cases involving bodies carrying out acts of a public nature. As Lord Irvine L.C. remarked during the course of the passage of the HRA 1998 (*Hansard*, HL Vol.583, col.783, (November 24, 1997)):

> "We also believe that it is right as a matter of principle for the courts to have the duty of acting compatibly with the Convention not only in cases involving other public authorities but also in developing the common law in deciding cases between individuals. Why should they not? In preparing this Bill, we have taken the view that it is the other course, that of excluding Convention considerations altogether from cases between individuals which would have to be justified. The courts already bring Convention considerations to bear and I have no doubt that they will continue to do so in developing the common law . . . [*section*] 3 requires the courts to interpret legislation compatibly with the Convention rights and to the fullest extent possible in all cases coming before them."

Thus courts will be required to interpret the common law compatibly with Convention rights in cases concerning individuals and, indeed, it appears that they were seeking to do so prior to the Act's provisions coming into force. For example, in *Reynolds v Times Newspapers Ltd* [1999] 3 W.L.R. 1010, the House of Lords held, in furtherance of the existing common law position, that the common law should not recognise a category of qualified privilege, as a defence to defamation proceedings, under which all political information was privileged irrespective of the circumstances, because this would be to develop the common law in a way which was incompatible with the pertinent Convention right, namely art.10 (freedom of expression). In subsequent cases, other aspects of the law of defamation have been the subject of litigation in which the question of their compatibility has arisen, but in most of these cases, e.g. *Loutchansky v Times Newspapers Ltd* [2001] EWCA Civ 1805, the existing law, as in *Reynolds*, was found to be compatible with art.10 and applied accordingly.

Individuals in cases involving the common law can thus expect that the law appertaining to their dispute will be applied and developed under the HRA 1998 compatibly with Convention rights. Courts in disputes concerning them must not apply the common law incompatibly (since s.6 precludes courts, as public authorities, from doing so) nor must statutory provisions be interpreted incompatibly (since s.3(1) requires a compatible interpretation). Although individuals cannot institute proceedings against other individuals for acting in contravention of any Convention right and actions between individuals cannot lead to the grant of any remedy under the HRA 1998, the law will nevertheless be applied and developed compatibly in cases concerning individuals. Hence English law and the Convention should march in tandem, both as regards the common law and statute, and irrespective of the parties to the dispute. This effectively ensures that the law generally will be interpreted and applied compatibly in all cases. As Howell has cogently observed in "The Human Rights Act 1998: Land, Private Citizens, and the Common Law" (2007) 123 L.Q.R. 618 at 627:

> "It must also follow that if the court is itself a public authority sufficient under s.3, there is a strong argument that the courts must equally interpret the common law in a way compatible with the Convention. Although s.3 refers only to statute law not to common law, under its obligation as a public body under s.6 the court has to act in a way which is compatible with the Convention. The fact that the HRA does not refer to the common law is understandable if it is the actions of public authorities as emanations of the State (as in *Qazi* and *Kay*) which are being scrutinised. Public bodies owe their existence and obtain their legitimacy solely through legislation, although they are, of course, also bound by any relevant common law principles. But once the HRA is applied to actions between private parties, then not only is all legislation potentially open to scrutiny under s.3 but also by the same reasoning all common law. Not to apply the Convention to the common law would itself lead to arbitrary distinctions."

However, where incompatibility does arise, the position as regards statute and common law will be different. Section 3(2) expressly provides that the requirement for compatible interpretation in s.3(1) does not affect the validity, continuing operation or enforcement of primary legislation or subordinate legislation if primary legislation prevents the removal of the incompatibility. Thus the legislation continues to have effect, although it is open to (certain) courts to issue a declaration of incompatibility (see above, 5–010). In the case of the common law, however, there is no provision for its continuing validity. So if the common law is incompatible, the court must seek to develop and apply it in a way that is compatible with Convention rights. This will also ensure that the court, as a public authority, does not act unlawfully under s.6(1) by acting in a way (through applying incompatible common law) that is inconsistent with Convention rights.

The combined effect of ss.7(1)(b) and 6(3)(a) thus seems to be to require English law in *all* cases to be interpreted compatibly with Convention rights, again with the assistance of s.2 as relevant. If this is correct, the impact on precedent in other proceedings by virtue of these provisions would seem to be similar to the position that prevails where a victim brings proceedings against a public authority (see (ii) above).

▶ ## 4. Conclusion

5–019   It is clear that during the time the HRA 1998 has been in force, the judiciary have identified and, where appropriate, applied, interpretative techniques, which facilitate the exercise of the interpretative obligation under s.3(1), i.e. to interpret domestic legislation, as far as possible, in a manner compatible with Convention rights. However, it is equally apparent that, perhaps, the most radical of these techniques, namely the implication of words into statutory provisions ("reading-in") to achieve compatibility is, first, not an exercise with which judges are totally unfamiliar (see the cases of *Pickstone* and *Litster* (referred to above, at 5–015) in which the House of Lords read words into domestic legislation in order to ensure compliance with EU law), and, secondly, it is one which will be called upon only as a means of fostering interpretation not amendment of legislation. However, as has been seen, it is not always easy to demarcate the boundary between interpretation and amendment, and, in any given case, differing judicial views may be expressed as to where that boundary should be located. In any event, the veracity of the words of Lord Cooke during the legislation's passage through Parliament (at *Hansard*, HL Vol.583, col.1273, (November 3, 1997)) that "the common law approach to statutory interpretation will never be the same again" is now readily apparent.

It is also true that the HRA 1998 has transformed the operation of the doctrine of precedent to the extent that, as Lady Justice Arden observed, extra-judicially, (in "The Interpretation of UK Domestic Legislation in the Light of European Convention on Human Rights Jurisprudence" (as above, at [178]), it "does not apply in the same way". Perhaps, the most obvious departure from the norm lies in those cases where a judge (sitting in a court at any level) may adopt an interpretation of a statutory provision which is compatible with Convention rights in preference to an otherwise binding (but incompatible) precedent (see above, 5–017). It will be fascinating to see, over the course of time, how such authoritative interpretations fare when they are subjected to the test of compatibility.

Other matters include the degree of persuasiveness that will be or should be accorded to Strasbourg jurisprudence by the judiciary, and, consequentially, the influence it may have on the prospective moulding and development of domestic law (for a recent departure by the House of Lords from Strasbourg case law, see *Horncastle*, above, 1–023 and 5–017). Indeed, the weight to be attached to Strasbourg jurisprudence when juxtaposed with the doctrine of precedent will also be critical to the resolution of following dilemma identified, extra-judicially, by Lady Justice Arden in "The Interpretation of UK Domestic Legislation in the Light of European Convention on Human Rights Jurisprudence" (as above, at 178):

> "Where the position is that the courts have construed legislation on a previous occasion in accordance with the Convention but Convention jurisprudence has since then itself moved on in accordance with the evolutive approach adopted by the Strasbourg court, it is an open question whether the doctrine of precedent applies so that only a higher court may depart from a previously Convention compliant interpretation."

Finally, now that the Charter of Fundamental Rights of the European Union has been given the same legally binding status as Treaties of the European Union (see above, 4–010), it will be interesting to see to what extent, in the coming years, there is a convergence of the evolving human rights jurisprudence in the CJ and in the Strasbourg Court and, in turn, the impact that this may have on the domestic law of EU Member States.

PART 2

SELECTED CASE STUDIES

6 CONTRACTUAL OBLIGATIONS ARISING OUT OF AN INVITATION TO TENDER

▶ ## 1. Introduction

In order for actions to be brought for breach of contract by one party against **6-001** another, it is generally necessary for contractual obligations to have arisen between the parties. This will most usually occur where parties have expressly entered into a contract, although contractual obligations may arise by implication. The question of whether contractual obligations may arise by implication in the case of an invitation to tender was considered by the Court of Appeal in *Blackpool and Fylde Aero Club Ltd v Blackpool BC* [1990] 3 All E.R. 25. In this case, Blackpool Borough Council (the council) owned and managed an airport, for which some revenue was raised by granting a concession to an air operator to operate pleasure flights from the airport. The concession, due to expire in 1983, was held (and had been held for several years) by the Blackpool and Fylde Aero Club Ltd (the club). Shortly before expiry of the concession, invitations to tender for the concession were sent to the club and six other parties, all of whom were connected with the airport. The invitations required tenders to be enclosed in the envelope provided, without any name or mark to identify the sender, and submitted to the council by a specified date and time (12 noon on March 17, 1983) otherwise they would not be considered. The club's tender was placed in the council's letter box at the Town Hall an hour before the submission deadline, but the letter box was not emptied at 12 noon, as it should have been, by council staff. In consequence, the club's tender was regarded as having been submitted late and was not considered. The council subsequently notified one of the other parties that had tendered, Red Rose Helicopters, that its tender was accepted.

On making inquiries, the council discovered that the club had in fact submitted its tender before the deadline and decided to issue a second invitation to submit tenders. Tenders in response to this second invitation were duly submitted, including one from the club, but, following a threat of legal action by Red Rose Helicopters for breach of contract (on the basis that the council had accepted its tender and was contractually obliged to proceed with it), the council decided to disregard the tenders received in response to its second invitation and honour the contract made with Red Rose Helicopters. The council, in doing so, avoided legal action against it by Red Rose Helicopters, only to find that a claim was brought against it by the club. The club claimed damages for breach of contract, contending that the council had "warranted that if a tender was returned to the Town Hall, Blackpool before noon on Thursday the 17th March 1983 the same would be considered along with other tenders duly returned when the decision to grant the concession was made", and the council had acted in breach of that warranty. The club further claimed damages in the tort of negligence for breach of a duty to take reasonable care to see that, if a tender was submitted by the deadline, it would be considered along with other tenders.

This case study illustrates a number of points in relation to precedent and judicial approaches to determining cases:

- considering the scope of a well-established common law principle formulated during the 19th century, albeit in cases which were not binding on the Court of Appeal;

- the application of the maxim *expressio unius exclusio alterius* (the mention of one is the exclusion of the other) or, as it is incorrectly described in the report, *exclusio unius expressio alterius*!;

- whether precedents establishing the standard for implying a term into an existing contract and for finding a collateral contract (i.e. a contract subsidiary to a main contract) should apply and be adopted in respect of implying a contract;

- a reluctance to reach a decision which would be contrary to expectations and assumptions of parties in commercial transactions;

- a consideration obiter of whether the claim may succeed on one ground (breach of duty of care in the tort of negligence) when it has been determined that it may succeed on another ground (breach of contractual obligation); and

- a reluctance to consider matters (breach of duty of care in the tort of negligence) in respect of which the position was complicated and on which no decision needed to be reached to dispose of the appeal.

When the case was heard in the High Court, the trial judge found in favour of the club on both the claim for breach of contract and the claim for breach of duty in the tort of negligence. As Bingham L.J., delivering the main judgment in the Court of Appeal, stated (at 29 and 31):

"The judge resolved the contractual issue in favour of the club, holding that an express request for a tender might in appropriate circumstances give rise to an implied obligation to perform the service of considering that tender. Here, the council's stipulation that tenders received after the deadline would not be admitted for consideration gave rise to a contractual obligation (on acceptance by submission of a timely tender) that such tenders would be admitted for consideration.

. . . the judge also accepted, that if there was no contract at all between the parties the council none the less owed the club a duty to take reasonable care to see to it that if the club submitted a tender by the deadline it would be

> considered along with other tenders duly returned when the decision to grant the concession was made."

The council appealed to the Court of Appeal (and, since the council was the appellant, the decision ought to have been reported as *Blackpool Borough Council v Blackpool and Fylde Aero Club Ltd* and not as *Blackpool and Fylde Aero Club Ltd v Blackpool Borough Council* as it appears in the report), contending that the judge was wrong on each point.

▶ 2. The Contract Claim: the Council's Contentions

▷ *(a) Invitations to tender as invitations to treat not giving rise to contractual obligations*

(i) Supporting authority

A first contention advanced by the council was that there was a general principle of **6-002** law that invitations to tender amounted only to invitations to treat, i.e. invitations to receive offers and that no contractual obligation arose on the part of the person inviting tenders. In support of this general principle, reliance was placed on two 19th century cases, *Spencer v Harding* (1870) L.R. 5 C.P. 561 (*Spencer*) and *Harris v Nickerson* (1873) L.R. 8 Q.B. 286 (*Harris*). In *Spencer* the Court of Common Pleas (see above, 2–016) held that a circular offering to the wholesale trade for sale by tender the stock-in-trade of a business did not constitute an offer to sell to the person who submitted the highest tender. Subsequently, this decision was referred to by the Court of Queen's Bench (see above, 2–015) in *Harris* where Quain J., delivering one of the judgments, stated (at 288) that it was "direct authority" against the proposition that contractual obligations arose in the instant case, the court going on to hold that an advertisement indicating items would be sold by auction did not constitute a contract by the advertiser with anyone who attended the auction that the items would be included in the auction and there would be an opportunity to bid for them.

The council sought to rely on this general principle in support of its contention that no contractual obligations arose as a result of it inviting tenders to be submitted. As Bingham L.J. remarked (at 29):

> ". . . it was submitted that an invitation to tender in this form was well established to be no more than a proclamation of willingness to receive offers. Even without the first sentence of the council's invitation to tender in this case [*which provided that "The council do not bind themselves to accept all or any part of any tender"*], the council would not have been bound to accept the highest or any tender. An invitation to tender in this form was an invitation to

> treat, and no contract of any kind would come into existence unless or until, if ever, the council chose to accept any tender or other offer. For these propositions reliance was placed on *Spencer v Harding* (1870) LR 5 CP 561 and *Harris v Nickerson* (1987) LR 8 QB 286."

This general principle was recognised and accepted by the club. The principle was well established and, although the authorities on which it was based were not precedents binding on the Court of Appeal (being decisions of courts which, although no longer existing, are comparable in status to the High Court), there was no suggestion that the principle was wrong and the authorities ought not to have been followed. The club, however, sought to maintain that the principle was only a general one, not of universal application, and that there may be circumstances in which contractual obligations *could* arise. In this respect, the club could be said to be restricting the scope of the principle and to be distinguishing the cases which supported the principle by establishing material differences with the present case (although no mention is made of distinguishing in the report, either in the judgments or in the headnote). The essence of the club's contention was outlined in the judgment of Bingham L.J. (at 29–30):

> ". . . counsel for the club accepted that an invitation to tender was normally no more than an offer to receive tenders. But it could, he submitted, in certain circumstances give rise to binding contractual obligations on the part of the invitor, either from the express words of the tender or from the circumstances surrounding the sending out of the invitation to tender or (as here) from both. The circumstances relied on here were that the council approached the club and the other invitees, all of them connected with the airport, that the club had held the concession for eight years, having successfully tendered on three previous occasions, that the council as a local authority was obliged to comply with its standing orders and owed a fiduciary duty to ratepayers to act with reasonable prudence in managing its financial affairs and that there was a clear intention on the part of both parties that all timely tenders would be considered. If in these circumstances one asked of this invitation to tender the question posed by Bowen LJ in *Carlill v Carbolic Smoke Ball Co* [1893] 1 QB 256 at 266 [1891–4] All ER Rep 127 at 132, 'How would an ordinary person reading this document construe it?', the answer in the submission of counsel for the club was clear; the council might or might not accept any particular tender; it might accept no tender; it might decide not to award the concession at all; it would not consider any tender received after the advertised deadline; but if it did consider any tender received before the deadline and conforming with the advertised conditions it would consider all such tenders."

(ii) The view of the Court of Appeal

6-003 Although finding the council's submissions persuasive, Bingham L.J. was, along with other members of the court, prepared to accept that a contractual obligation could arise. His Lordship stated (at 30):

> "I found great force in the submissions made on behalf of the council and agree with much of what was said. Indeed, for much of the hearing I was of opinion that the judge's decision . . . could not be sustained in principle. But I am in the end persuaded that the argument proves too much. During the hearing the following questions were raised: what if, in a situation such as the present, the council had opened and thereupon accepted the first tender received, even though the deadline had not expired and other invitees had not yet responded? or if the council had considered and accepted a tender admittedly received well after the deadline? Counsel answered that although by so acting the council might breach its own standing orders, and might fairly be accused of discreditable conduct, it would not be in breach of any legal obligation because at that stage there would be none to breach. This is a conclusion I cannot accept, and if it were accepted there would in my view be an unacceptable discrepancy between the law of contract and the confident assumptions of commercial parties, both tenderers (as reflected in the evidence of Mr Bateson [*a club director*]) and invitors (as reflected in the immediate reaction of the council when the mishap came to light)."

(iii) Differing judicial approaches

As to contractual obligations arising, however, there was some difference of **6-004** approach on the part of Bingham L.J., who delivered the main judgment of the court, and Stocker L.J. who, although expressing agreement with Bingham L.J., also delivered a short judgment. Although the club's contention was that an invitation to tender could "in certain circumstances give rise to binding contractual obligations on the part of the invitor, either from the express words of the tender or from the circumstances surrounding the sending out of the invitation to tender or (as here) from both", Bingham L.J.'s recognition of a contractual obligation seemed to be based only on the circumstances surrounding the sending out of the invitation to tender. His Lordship made no reference to whether express words of the tender *could* give rise to a contractual obligation nor whether the express words of this particular tender *did* give rise to a contractual obligation. Bingham L.J. stated (at 30-31):

> ". . . where, as here, tenders are solicited from selected parties all of them known to the invitor, and where a local authority's invitation prescribes a clear, orderly and familiar procedure (draft contract conditions available for inspection and plainly not open to negotiation, a prescribed common form of tender, the supply of envelopes designed to preserve the absolute anonymity of tenderers and clearly to identify the tender in question and an absolute deadline) the invitee is in my judgment protected at least to this extent: if he submits a conforming tender before the deadline he is entitled, not as a matter of mere expectation but of contractual right, to be sure that his tender will after the deadline be opened and considered in conjunction with all other conforming tenders or at least that his tender will be considered if others are. Had the club, before tendering, inquired of the council whether it could rely on

> any timely and conforming tender being considered along with others, I feel
> quite sure that the answer would have been 'of course'. The law would, I think
> be defective if it did not give effect to that."

Since Bingham L.J. focused only on contractual obligations arising from the circumstances surrounding the sending out of the invitation to tender, this would
seem to comprise the ratio of his judgment. The ratio would not include, since no
reference was made to it, contractual obligations arising from the express words of
the tender.

Stocker L.J., in a brief judgment, expressed himself to be in agreement with
Bingham L.J., stating (at 32) at the commencement of his judgment:

> "I agree. I have had the advantage of reading in draft the judgment of
> Bingham LJ and add short observations of my own solely in deference to the
> lucid and interesting arguments of counsel put before the court."

Further, he remarked (at 32) at its conclusion: "I agree with the conclusions
reached by Bingham LJ, and with the detailed reasoning contained in his
judgment."

The "short observations" added by Stocker L.J. (at 32) included expression of the
view that the express words of the tender did give rise to contractual obligations,
as well as acknowledgement that such obligations arose from the circumstances
surrounding the sending out of the invitation to tender:

> "The format of the invitation to tender document itself suggests, in my view,
> that a legal obligation to consider to [*sic*] tender submitted before any award
> of a concession was made to any other operator was to be implied in the case
> of any operator of aircraft to whom the invitation was directed who complied
> with its terms and conditions. The fact that the invitation to tender was limited
> to a very small class of operators is itself of significance. The circumstances
> surrounding the issue of the invitation to tender and the formal requirements
> imposed by it support the conclusion. Of particular significance, in my view,
> was the requirement that tenders be submitted in the official envelope sup-
> plied and indorsed, as described by Bingham LJ, by the council. The purpose of
> this requirement must surely have been to preserve the anonymity of the
> tenderer and, in conjunction with the council's standing orders, to prevent any
> premature leak of the nature and amount of such tender to other interested or
> potentially interested parties. Such a requirement, as a condition of the validity
> of the tender submitted, seems pointless unless all tenders submitted in time
> and in accordance with the requirements are to be considered before any
> award of the concession is made. There can be no doubt that this was the
> intention of both parties, as exemplified by the council's actions when its error
> with regard to the time of receipt of the club's tender was appreciated. Such a
> common intention can, of course, exist without giving rise to any contractual
> obligations, but the circumstances of this case indicate to me that this is one of

the fairly rare exceptions to the general rule expounded in the leading cases of *Spencer v Harding* (1870) LR 5 CP 561 and *Harris v Nickerson* (1873) LR 8 QB 286. I therefore agree that in all the circumstances of this case there was an intention to create binding legal obligations if and when a tender was submitted in accordance with the terms of the invitation to tender, and that a binding contractual obligation arose that the club's tender would be before the officer or committee by whom the decision was to be taken for consideration before a decision was made or any tender accepted. This would not preclude or inhibit the council from deciding not to accept any tender or to award the concession, provided the decision was bona fide and honest, to any tenderer. The obligation was that the club's tender would be before the deciding body for consideration before any award was made."

Whilst Stocker L.J., unlike Bingham L.J., regarded contractual obligations as arising from both the express words of the tender and from the circumstances surrounding the sending out of the invitation to tender, the extent to which these views form part of the ratio of his judgment is less clear.

(iv) The ratio of the judgments and of the case

By expressing agreement with the conclusions reached by Bingham L.J. and the detailed reasoning contained in his judgment, Stocker L.J. may be taken to have endorsed, as part of the ratio of his judgment, the ratio of Bingham L.J.'s judgment that contractual obligations could and did arise from the circumstances surrounding the sending out of the invitation to tender. Further, Stocker L.J.'s statement that the express words of the tender gave rise to contractual obligations may also form part of the ratio of his judgment in that contractual obligations arose no less from the express words of the tender than from the circumstances surrounding the sending out of the invitation to tender. In other words, there were *two* factors, express words *and* circumstances, as a result of which contractual obligations arose. If this view is correct, then there would be a "dual" ratio (or perhaps a single ratio with two aspects) of Stocker L.J.'s judgment, namely, contractual obligations arising from both express words and circumstances. **6–005**

On the other hand, it is possible that there may only be a "single" ratio of Stocker L.J.'s judgment, which could be *either* contractual obligations arising from circumstances (with express words obiter) *or* from express words (with circumstances obiter). The ratio may be contractual obligations arising simply from circumstances. This was the ratio of Bingham L.J.'s judgment, which Stocker L.J. endorsed, and the observations added by Stocker L.J. that contractual obligations arose from express words may be seen as something which his Lordship did not have to decide, something which was not necessary to the decision which he reached, and something which was therefore only obiter in his judgment. But, conversely, the ratio may be that contractual obligations arose simply from express words. When adding his observations, Stocker L.J. stated (at 32) that the:

> "format of the . . . document itself suggests . . . a [*contractual*] obligation . . . [*and*] the circumstances surrounding the issue of the invitation to tender and the formal requirements imposed by it support the conclusion [*of there being a contractual obligation*]."

Thus, express words may be seen as *the* reason for contractual obligations arising (ratio), with the circumstances merely *supporting* the conclusion and, playing only a supporting role, *not* being necessary to the decision reached (obiter).

Thus it is possible that the judgments of Bingham and Stocker L.JJ. may both have the same ratio but equally it is possible that each may have a different ratio. This will depend on what is taken to be the ratio of Stocker L.J.'s judgment which, as stated above, is uncertain. In the light of this, it might be asked what the third member of the Court of Appeal, Farquharson L.J., who delivered no judgment, meant when he remarked "I agree" at the end of the case! With what was his Lordship agreeing?

Because it is not certain what is the ratio of Stocker L.J.'s judgment and with what Farquharson L.J. can be said to be expressing agreement, it is difficult to ascertain the ratio of the case. There would seem to be a number of possibilities:

(1) There may be a "dual" ratio of the case, of contractual obligations arising from the circumstances surrounding the sending out of the invitation to tender (ratio of judgments of Bingham, Stocker and Farquharson L.JJ.) and of contractual obligations arising from the express words of the tender (ratio of judgments of Stocker and Farquharson L.JJ.).
(2) There may be a "single" ratio of the case, of contractual obligations arising from the circumstances surrounding the sending out of the invitation to tender (ratio of judgments of Bingham, Stocker and Farquharson L.JJ.), if Stocker L.J.'s view of contractual obligations arising from the express words of the tender is obiter.
(3) There may be a "single" or a "dual" ratio of the case, if Stocker L.J.'s view of contractual obligations arising from the circumstances surrounding the sending out of the invitation to tender is obiter. The "dual" ratio would be contractual obligations arising from the express words of the tender (ratio of judgments of Stocker and Farquharson L.JJ.) and from the circumstances surrounding the sending out of the invitation to tender (ratio of judgments of Bingham and Farquharson L.JJ.). This is on the basis that Farquharson L.J. is taken to have agreed with Bingham L.J.'s view of contractual obligations arising from circumstances as ratio. If this is *not* the case, and Farquharson L.J. is taken to have agreed with Stocker L.J.'s view of contractual obligations arising from circumstances as obiter, then contractual obligations arising from circumstances will not be part of the ratio of the case. This is because it will be the ratio of only *one* judgment, that of Bingham L.J., and this will mean that it is not part of the ratio of the case. In this instance, there will be a "single" ratio of the case, of contractual obligations arising only from express words (ratio of judgments of Stocker and Farquharson L.JJ.).

▷ *(b) The application of the maxim* expressio unius exclusio alterius

A second contention advanced by the council was that, since it had specifically **6–006** stated that late tenders would not be considered but not that timely tenders would be considered, there was no contractual obligation to consider timely tenders submitted. As Bingham L.J. observed (at 29):

> "counsel [*for the council*] submitted that on a reasonable reading of this invitation to tender the council could not be understood to be undertaking to consider all timely tenders submitted. The statement that late tenders would not be considered did not mean that timely tenders would. If the council had meant that it could have said it. There was, although counsel did not put it in these words, no maxim exclusio unius expressio alterius."

The maxim *expressio unius exclusio alterius* is more commonly encountered in the context of statute law, as a principle of statutory interpretation, whereby the expression of one or more things of a particular class in a statute may be regarded as silently excluding all other members of the class (see above, 1–089). The maxim, whilst perhaps apt to describe the Council's contention, was nevertheless not one which the court was prepared to accept as having application in the present case. Bingham L.J. dealt with the matter briefly, stating (at 31):

> "It is of course true that the invitation to tender does not explicitly state that the council will consider timely and conforming tenders. That is why one is concerned with implication. But the council does not either say that it does not bind itself to do so, and in the context a reasonable invitee would understand the invitation to be saying, quite clearly, that if he submitted a timely and conforming tender it would be considered, at least if any other such tender were considered."

▷ *(c) Implying the existence of a contract*

A third contention advanced by the council was that, when considering whether a **6–007** contract should be implied, precedents establishing the standard for implying a term into an existing contract and for finding a collateral contract should apply and, when applied, would not be satisfied in the instant case. This contention was referred to by Bingham L.J. in the course of his judgment (at 29) as follows:

> ". . . the court should be no less rigorous when asked to imply a contract than when asked to imply a term in an existing contract or to find a collateral contract. A term would not be implied simply because it was reasonable to do so: *Liverpool City Council v Irwin* [1976] 2 All ER 39 at 43, [1977] AC 239 at 253. In order to establish collateral contracts, "Not only the terms of such contracts

> but the existence of an animus contrahendi on the part of all the parties to
> them must be clearly shewn": see *Heilbut Symons & Co v Buckleton* [1913] AC
> 30 at 47, [1911–13] All ER Rep 83 at 91. No lower standard was applicable here
> and the standard was not satisfied."

Whilst referring to the contention in these terms, Bingham L.J. did not, however,
address the question of whether the precedents (both of which were decisions of
the House of Lords) did have application. Rather, his Lordship (who was the only
member of the court to examine this contention, with Stocker L.J. making no
comment upon it) confined himself to a general statement that contractual
obligations could be inferred in the present instance. Bingham L.J. stated (at 31):

> "I readily accept that contracts are not to be lightly implied. Having examined
> what the parties said and did, the court must be able to conclude with con-
> fidence both that the parties intended to create contractual relations and that
> the agreement was to the effect contended for. It must also, in most cases, be
> able to answer the question posed by Mustill LJ in *Hispanica de Petroleos SA v
> Vencedora Oceanica Navegacion SA, The Kapetan Markos NL (No 2)* [1987] 2
> Lloyd's Rep 321 at 331: 'What was the mechanism for offer and acceptance?' In
> all the circumstances of this case (and I say nothing about any other) I have no
> doubt that the parties did intend to create contractual relations to the limited
> extent contended for. Since it has never been the law that a person is only
> entitled to enforce his contractual rights in a reasonable way (*White & Carter
> (Councils) Ltd v McGregor* [1961] 3 All ER 1178 at 1182, [1962] AC 413 at 430 per
> Lord Reid) counsel for the club was in my view right to contend for no more
> than a contractual duty to consider. I think it plain that the council's invitation
> to tender was, to this limited extent, an offer, and the club's submission of a
> timely and conforming tender an acceptance."

▷ (d) Distinguishing between reasonable expectations and contractual obligations

6-008 A fourth contention advanced by the council was that, since there was a reasonable expectation that the club's tender would be considered, there was no need for
the Council and the club to contract and therefore for contractual obligations to
arise between them. The substance of this contention was outlined by Bingham
L.J. (at 29):

> "Counsel submitted that the warranty contended for by the club was simply a
> proposition 'tailor-made to produce the desired result' (to quote Lord Tem-
> pleman in *CBS Songs Ltd v Amstrad Consumer Electronics plc* [1988] 2 All ER
> 484 at 497, [1988] AC 1013 at 1059) on the facts of this particular case. There
> was a vital distinction between expectations, however reasonable, and con-
> tractual obligations: see *Lavarack v Woods of Colchester Ltd* [1966] 3 All ER

683 at 690, [1967] 1 QB 278 at 294 per Diplock LJ. The club here expected its tender to be considered. The council fully intended that it should be. It was in both parties' interests that the club's tender should be considered. There was thus no need for them to contract. The court should not subvert well-understood contractual principles by adopting a woolly pragmatic solution designed to remedy a perceived injustice on the unique facts of this particular case."

This contention was summarily dispatched by Bingham L.J. (at 31) in the following terms:

"Counsel's fourth submission on behalf of the council is a salutary warning, but it is not a free-standing argument: if, as I hold, his first three submissions are to be rejected, no subversion of principle is involved. I am, however, pleased that what seems to me the right legal answer also accords with the merits as I see them."

▶ 3. The Tort Claim

The basis of the tort claim was that the council owed a duty of care to the club to **6-009** take reasonable care to ensure that, if the club submitted a tender by the deadline, it would be considered along with other tenders submitted by the deadline when the decision to grant a concession was made. The difficulty from the club's point of view, in seeking to establish the existence of such a duty of care, was that the only loss sustained by it was economic loss, i.e. the loss of profits caused by not obtaining (renewal of) the concession to operate pleasure flights. Courts are generally reluctant to recognise a duty of care to avoid causing pure economic loss which is unrelated to physical injury or damage to property, although the trial judge had held that, in the circumstances, the council did owe a duty of care to the club. The respective contentions in the Court of Appeal for the club, which sought to justify the trial judge's decision, and for the council, which sought to challenge it, were set out by Bingham L.J. in the course of his judgment (at 31) as follows:

"Counsel for the club sought to sustain this argument in particular by reliance on *Ministry of Housing and Local Government v Sharp* [1970] 1 All ER 1009, [1970] 2 QB 223, *Ross v Caunters (a firm)* [1979] 3 All ER 580, [1980] Ch 297 and *American Express International Banking Corp v Hurley* [1985] 3 All ER 564, none of which, he submitted, was inconsistent with the principles laid down in the recent decision of the House of Lords in *Caparo Industries plc v Dickman* [1990] 1 All ER 568, [1990] 2 WLR 358.

On behalf of the council it was urged that the court should not introduce a common law duty into an area of pre-contractual negotiations where the parties could, if they wished, have introduced such a duty by agreement but had not done so: see *Tai Hing Cotton Mill Ltd v Liu Chong Hing Bank Ltd* [1985]

> 2 All ER 947, [1986] AC 80. Although a duty to take reasonable care not to cause pure economic loss could be held to exist, such cases were rare and confined to limited classes of case which did not include the present case and with which the present case had no analogy. The plaintiff's task was even harder where, as counsel argued was the case here, his complaint was of a mere omission. Counsel argued, if it was necessary to do so, that *Ross v Caunters* was wrongly decided."

In *Ross v Caunters* a person named as a beneficiary in a will lost her bequest, thereby suffering economic loss, because solicitors acting for the testator had failed to warn him about the provisions of s.15 of the Wills Act 1837. These provide that attestation (witnessing) of a will by a beneficiary's spouse (which had been done in this case) invalidates the bequest or gift in the will to the beneficiary. The beneficiary succeeded in her claim against the solicitors in the High Court. Being a decision of the High Court, however, the Court of Appeal in *Blackpool*, had it been minded to do so, could have overruled this case.

The question of whether a duty was owed not to cause economic loss was (and is) a complex one, with the correctness of the decision in *Ross v Caunters* open to question in the light of the House of Lords' decision in *Caparo Industries plc v Dickman* [1990] 2 A.C. 605 (which as a matter of precedent was binding on the Court of Appeal) and it was not one which the Court of Appeal chose to consider. Bingham L.J. was prepared to express no more than a tentative view on the matter, a view which was only obiter since, having resolved the appeal on the contract claim, it was unnecessary to decide whether a claim might also succeed in tort. His Lordship stated (at 31):

> "This conclusion [*that the council was in breach of its contractual obligation to consider the club's tender*] makes it unnecessary to consider at length the club's alternative argument, which the judge also accepted, that if there was no contract at all between the parties the council none the less owed the club a duty to take reasonable care to see to it that if the club submitted a tender by the deadline it would be considered along with other tenders duly returned when the decision to grant the concession was made.
>
> . . . I am reluctant to venture into this somewhat unvirginal territory when it is unnecessary to do so for the purpose of deciding this case. Having heard the argument, I am tentatively of opinion that the objections on behalf of the council are correct and that the club cannot succeed on this point if they fail on the other. But I do not think it necessary or desirable to express a final conclusion."

Stocker L.J. likewise was of the view (at 32) that "no useful purpose can be served by consideration of the difficult questions which arise on the claim formulated in tort" and gave no consideration to this matter.

▶ 4. Conclusion

Perhaps unusually in this case, the court was concerned not with implying a term **6–010** into an existing contract but implying the existence of a contract itself in which there was a term that an invitee submitting a tender before the deadline was contractually entitled to have the tender opened and considered along with any other tenders that were considered. Whilst the contract contained a term to this effect, it might be questioned whether the contract in scope extended beyond this. As one commentator on the case remarked (Davenport, "Obligation to Consider Tenders" (1991) 107 L.Q.R. 201 at 202):

> "It is not easy to see what other term the contract contained. No term could be implied that the lowest tender would be accepted or even any tender would be accepted. It almost seems that the reasoning process of the court was that the implied term was necessary to give business efficacy to the relationship between the parties: the term needed a contract into which it could be implied: therefore the contract must exist. This reasoning process in effect uses the implied term test to find the contract which contains the term. This is, perhaps, unusual and may give a lead for later cases. It led to the just result, even if the contract was unusual in that it contained only one term and that was to be implied."

Whilst it may give a lead for later cases, it should be recognised that the court treated the case as rather exceptional. Thus Stocker L.J. remarked that it constituted "one of the fairly rare exceptions to the general rule expounded in the leading cases of *Spencer v Harding* (1870) L.R. 5 C.P. 561 and *Harris v Nickerson* (1873) L.R. 8 Q.B. 286" and the court seemed to place considerable emphasis on the particular features of the tendering arrangements in the case. Accordingly, as has been observed in another commentary on the decision (Adams and Brownsword, "More in Expectation than Hope: The Blackpool Airport Case" (1991) 54 M.L.R. 281 at 283), "since it would not otherwise be self-evident that these features had any special significance, by underlining their materiality the court made it very easy for future judges to distinguish the case".

This view has been reflected in later cases. Thus, in *Harmon CFEM Facades (UK) Ltd v The Corporate Officer of the House of Commons* (1999) 67 Con.L.R.1 (*Harmon*), *Blackpool* was distinguished by the High Court when considering whether requests for the submission of tenders for construction of the New Parliament Building providing additional office space for MPs and their staff created an implied contract, inter alia, to consider the tender alongside others submitted in compliance with the provisions of the Public Works Contracts Regulations 1991. His Honour Judge Humphrey Lloyd QC, sitting as a Deputy High Court judge, stated (at [209]–[210]):

> "[209] Mr White submitted that no contract should be implied since the statutory scheme of the Public Works [*Contracts*] Regulations provided not

only a remedy but an adequate remedy for dissatisfied contractors and thus made it not only unnecessary to infer a contract but its very existence precluded any contract arising. *Blackpool* was distinguishable since there was no other remedy available to the tenderer and there were special circumstances including the tenderer's prior history of having successfully tendered for the contract which was the subject of the procedure. Even in the special circumstances of *Blackpool* the implied contract was limited to one in which a tenderer was entitled, as a matter of contractual right, "to be sure that his tender w[ould] after the deadline [for submitting tenders] be opened and considered in conjunction with all other conforming tenders . . ." (see Bingham L.J. at page 1202C–D) . . .

[210] In my judgment Mr White's submissions are correct as regards the original tender. In *Blackpool* the plaintiff had delivered its tender before the expiry of the deadline but it was never considered since the Town Clerk's staff failed to put it before the committee. In fact the successful tender was lower than that submitted by the plaintiff but the council had made it clear that they would not be bound to accept the lowest tender. Accordingly, the plaintiff commenced proceedings maintaining that the express request for tenders gave rise to an implied obligation on the part of the council to consider all tenders duly received. It was on that basis that the Court of Appeal dismissed the defendant's appeal against the trial judge's decision to accede to the plaintiff's contentions. The case is perhaps no more than authority for the proposition that a contracting authority undertakes to consider all tenders received . . ."

Further, it may be that the case is confined in scope to tendering procedures by public authorities and does not have application to tendering procedures generally, for His Honour went onto to state (at [216]):

"I consider that it is now clear in English law that *in the public sector* where competitive tenders are sought and responded to, a contract comes into existence whereby the prospective employer impliedly agrees to consider all tenderers fairly: see *Blackpool* . . . [emphasis supplied]."

In addition, it may be confined to cases where only those specifically invited are permitted to submit tenders, as was the case in *Blackpool* and *Harmon*. Equally, however, it may apply to cases where any interested party is permitted to bid in response to a general advertisement, since in neither case did the court expressly consider whether an implied contract might arise in respect of any tendering procedures.

Although perhaps easily capable of being distinguished, *Blackpool* nevertheless provides what one commentator has described as "a flexible tool to give effect to the commercial expectations of the parties", albeit on a questionable legal basis (Arrowsmith, "The "Blackpool" implied contract governing public sector tenders: a review in the light of Pratt and other recent case law" [2004] P.P.L.R 125 at 131):

"... in the tendering situation there is no element of bargain—an exchange based on consideration from both sides—which is normally required for a binding contract; nor is there any intention to create legal relations ... The use of a contractual approach to protect bidders is thus questionable. Although Bingham L.J. [*in Blackpool*] expressly denied this, the court appears to be manipulating contractual principles simply to provide a remedy where it felt one ought to be given by some means."

Further Reading

Adams and Brownsword, "More in Expectation than Hope: The Blackpool Airport Case" (1991) 54 M.L.R. 281

Arrowsmith, "The "Blackpool" implied contract governing public sector tenders: a review in the light of Pratt and other recent case law" [2004] P.P.L.R. 125

Davenport, "Obligation to Consider Tenders" (1991) 107 L.Q.R. 201

7 EXISTING OBLIGATIONS AS CONSIDERATION IN CONTRACT

▶ ## 1. Introduction

7-001 It is a long established principle of the law of contract that the performance by one contracting party, or the promise to perform, of an existing obligation already owed to the other contracting party is no consideration for a promise made by the other contracting party. Since performance of the existing obligation does not constitute consideration, the promise by the other contracting party cannot as a general rule be enforced. This principle is traditionally based on the decision in *Stilk v Myrick* (1809) 2 Camp. 317 (*Stilk*), where a promise by a ship's captain, following the desertion of two members of the ship's crew, to divide the pay which would have been due to the two deserters amongst the remaining members of the crew, if the remaining members worked the ship back to London without the two deserters being replaced, was held not to be enforceable on the ground that (per Lord Ellenborough) "those who remain are bound by the terms of their original contract to exert themselves to the utmost to bring the ship in safety to her destined port". How far this principle still continues to have application is a matter of some doubt as a result of the Court of Appeal's decision in *Williams v Roffey Bros & Nicholls (Contractors) Ltd* [1990] 1 All E.R. 512 (*Williams*) and later cases in which *Williams* has been considered such as *Anangel Atlas Compania Naviera S.A. v Ishikawajima-Harima Heavy Industries Co Ltd (No. 2)* [1990] 2 Lloyd's Rep. 526 (*Anangel*); and *Selectmove Ltd Re* [1995] 1 W.L.R. 474 (*Selectmove*).

 This case study, which focuses primarily on the Court of Appeal's decision in *Williams*, illustrates a number of points in relation to precedent and judicial approaches to determining cases:

> ▶ the delivering of judgments by each member of a court, all of which contain a broad measure of agreement;
>
> ▶ following the ratio of a decision of a lower court in the court hierarchy;
>
> ▶ the unwillingness of a court to overrule decisions which, although not binding upon it, were of long standing and in which judgments were delivered by judges of particular eminence;
>
> ▶ the following by the Court of Appeal of an obiter statement in an earlier House of Lords' case;
>
> ▶ later cases determining whether facts in an earlier case were material facts forming part of the ratio of that (earlier) case and whether, accordingly, the earlier case was distinguishable;

- distinguishing an earlier case which was a binding precedent that the court was reluctant to follow;

- citation with approval of a passage contained in a textbook and reference to a journal article suggesting that a case might need reconsideration; and

- a recognition by the Court of Appeal that any modifications to a principle laid down by the House of Lords could be effected only by either the House itself or by Parliament.

▶ 2. The Decision in *Williams v Roffey Bros & Nicholls (Contractors) Ltd*

The defendants in this case had contracted to refurbish a block of flats and had **7-002** sub-contracted the carpentry work to the plaintiffs for what was acknowledged to be an unrealistic price of £20,000. The plaintiff got into financial difficulties as a result of the low price and was offered an additional £10,300 by the defendants to complete the work on time (so as to prevent the defendants being liable to a penalty for late completion under the refurbishment contract). The plaintiffs then substantially completed the work, but the defendants declined to pay the additional sum and the plaintiffs sued to recover. At issue was whether the defendants' promise to pay the additional sum of £10,300 was supported by consideration since the plaintiffs were already contractually bound to carry out the work for the contract price of £20,000. The decision in *Stilk*, to which reference has been made above, suggested that the defendants were not obliged to pay the additional sum of £10,300, but a bold submission was advanced by counsel for the plaintiff that *Stilk* and an earlier case which it approved, *Harris v Watson* (1791) Peake 102, should be overruled.

These two cases were first instance decisions of the Court of King's Bench (see above, 2–016) heard at nisi prius (which, in short, were civil actions heard by Royal Justices at sittings of the court, not in London, but at various locations throughout the country). As first instance decisions, they are equivalent in precedential strength to cases now heard in the High Court and were therefore not binding on the Court of Appeal. Counsel for the plaintiff's bold submission that these decisions should be overruled, however, did not find favour with the Court of Appeal in *Williams*. Although not adverted to in the leading judgment of Glidewell L.J. or in the judgment of Russell L.J., this point was addressed by Purchas L.J. who stated (at 525):

"Counsel for the plaintiff was bold enough to submit that *Harris v Watson*, albeit a decision of Lord Kenyon CJ, was a case tried at the Guildhall at nisi prius in the Court of King's Bench and that *Stilk v Myrick* was a decision also at nisi prius albeit a judgment of no less a judge than Lord Ellenborough CJ and that, therefore, this court was bound by neither authority. I feel I must say at once that, for my part, I would not be prepared to overrule two cases of such veneration involving judgments of judges of such distinction except on the strongest possible grounds since they form a corner-stone of the law of contract which has been observed over the years and is still recognised in principle in recent authority: see the reference to *Stilk v Myrick* to be found in *North Ocean Shipping Co Ltd v Hyundai Construction Co Ltd, The Atlantic Baron* [1978] 3 All ER 1170 at 1177, [1979] QB 705 at 712, *per* Mocatta J."

It is in fact less than clear whether the Court of Appeal could have overruled the principle in *Stilk* had it been minded to do so. Certainly the decision itself, as a first instance one, could have been overruled, but the principle also underlies the so-called rule in *Pinnel's Case* (1602) 5 Co. Rep. 117a ("that payment of a lesser sum on the day [*that it is due*] cannot be any satisfaction for the whole because it appears to the judges that by no possibility a lesser sum can be satisfaction to the plaintiff for a greater sum") and this rule was subsequently confirmed by the House of Lords in *Foakes v Beer* (1884) 9 App.Cas. 605. Since the principle in *Stilk* underlies the House of Lords' decision in *Foakes v Beer*—a decision to which no reference was made in *Williams*—the case of *Stilk* might be considered to have been impliedly approved by the House of Lords. As a principle approved by the House of Lords would be binding on the Court of Appeal, it might be questioned whether it would be open to the Court of Appeal to overrule *Stilk*.

The Court of Appeal, however, with all three members of the court delivering judgments, unanimously indicated acceptance of the principle in *Stilk*. The leading judgment was that of Glidewell L.J., with whose judgment Purchas L.J. and (perhaps) Russell L.J. appeared to express agreement.

▷ *(a) The judgment of Glidewell L.J.*

7–003 Glidewell L.J., after outlining the benefits accruing to the defendants from the agreement to pay the additional £10,300, went on to consider *Stilk* and the subsequent case law, before setting out what he conceived to be the present state of the law:

"In his address to us, counsel for the defendants outlined the benefits to the defendants which arose from their agreement to pay the additional £10,300 as (i) seeking to ensure that the plaintiff continued work and did not stop in breach of the sub-contract, (ii) avoiding the penalty for delay and (iii) avoiding the trouble and expense of engaging other people to complete the carpentry work. However, counsel submits that, though the defendants may have derived, or hope to derive, practical benefits from their agreement to pay the 'bonus', they derived no benefit in law, since the plaintiff was promising to do no more than he was already bound to do by his sub-contract, ie continue with the carpentry work and complete it on time. Thus there was no consideration for the agreement.

Counsel for the defendants relies on the principle of law which, traditionally, is based on the decision in *Stilk v Myrick* . . .

In *North Ocean Shipping Co Ltd v Hyundai Construction Co Ltd, The Atlantic Baron* [1978] 3 All ER 1170, [1979] QB 705 Mocatta J regarded the general principle of the decision in *Stilk v Myrick* as still being good law. He referred to two earlier decisions of this court [*Ward v Byham [1956] 2 All E.R. 318 and Williams v Williams [1957] 1 All E.R. 305*], dealing with wholly different subjects, in which Denning LJ sought to escape from the confines of the rule, but was not accompanied in this attempt by the other members of the court. [*at 518*]

. . . There is, however, another legal concept of relatively recent development which is relevant, namely that of economic duress. Clearly, if a sub-contractor has agreed to undertake work at a fixed price, and before he has completed the work declines to continue with it unless the contractor agrees to pay an increased price, the sub-contractor may be held guilty of securing the contractor's promise by taking unfair advantage of the difficulties he will cause if he does not complete the work. In such a case an agreement to pay an increased price may well be voidable because it was entered into under duress. Thus this concept may provide another answer in law to the question of policy which has troubled the courts since before *Stilk v Myrick* (1809) 2 Camp 317, 170 ER 1168, and no doubt led at the date of that decision to a rigid adherence to the doctrine of consideration.

This possible application of the concept of economic duress was referred to by Lord Scarman, delivering the judgment of the Judicial Committee of the Privy Council in *Pao On v Lau Yiu* [1979] 3 All ER 65 at 76. [*at 520*]

. . . It is true that *Pao On v Lau Yiu* is a case of a tripartite relationship, ie a promise by A to perform a pre-existing contractual obligation owed to B, in return for a promise of payment by C. But Lord Scarman's words seem to me to be of general application, equally applicable to a promise made by one of the original two parties to a contract.

Accordingly, following the view of the majority in *Ward v Byham* and of the whole court in *Williams v Williams* and that of the Privy Council in *Pao On v Lau* the present state of law on this subject can be expressed in the following proposition: (i) if A has entered into a contract with B to do work for, or to supply goods or services to, B in return for payment by B and (ii) at some stage before A has completely performed his obligations under the contract B has reason to doubt whether A will, or will be able to, complete his side of the bargain and (iii) B thereupon promises A an additional payment in return for A's promise to perform his contractual obligations on time and (iv) as a result of giving his promise B obtains in practice a benefit, or obviates a disbenefit, and (v) B's promise is not given as a result of economic duress or fraud on the part of A, then (vi) the benefit to B is capable of being consideration for B's promise, so that the promise will be legally binding.

> As I have said, counsel for the defendants accepts that in the present case by promising to pay the extra £10,300 the defendants secured benefits. There is no finding, and no suggestion, that in this case the promise was given as a result of fraud or duress.
>
> If it be objected that the propositions above contravene the principle in *Stilk v Myrick*, I answer that in my view they do not: they refine and limit the application of that principle, but they leave the principle unscathed, eg where B secures no benefit by his promise. It is not in my view surprising that a principle enunciated in relation to the rigours of seafaring life during the Napoleonic wars should be subjected during the succeeding 180 years to a process of refinement and limitation in its application in the present day.
>
> It is therefore my opinion that on his findings of fact in the present case, the judge was entitled to hold, as he did, that the defendant's promise to pay the extra £10,300 was supported by valuable consideration, and thus constituted an enforceable agreement. [*at 521–522*]"

It might be questioned, however, whether Glidewell L.J.'s view that the propositions formulated do not contravene the principle in *Stilk* and leave it unscathed is correct. Will there not in virtually all cases, including *Stilk* itself, be in practice a benefit to a contracting party to have performance rather than default by the other party? Indeed, as Smith, *The Law of Contract* (4th ed., 2002), p.79 has commented:

> "All three judges [*in Williams*] asserted that their decision was compatible with *Stilk v Myrick* but it is hard to see that this is so. Surely it was a great benefit (and the avoidance of a "disbenefit") to the master in that case to have the crew sail the ship home rather than abandon him and it in a foreign port. Indeed, there must be few cases in which it will not be a benefit to a contracting party to have the other party perform rather than default; and in any case where he has agreed to pay more to secure performance, it is self-evident that he regarded performance as a significant benefit."

▷ **(b) The judgment of Purchas L.J.**

7–004 The views of Purchas L.J. appear to accord with those of Glidewell L.J. since, although Purchas L.J. in the course of his judgment gave his own reasons why the promise to pay £10,300 was enforceable, his Lordship concluded his judgment by stating (at 527): "For these reasons and for the reasons which have already been given by Glidewell L.J., I would dismiss this appeal". Purchas L.J.'s own reasons for dismissing the appeal may perhaps be based on a greater willingness in modern times to find the existence of consideration in cases where a contracting party is performing an existing duty in return for a promise made by the other contracting party. Purchas L.J. stated (at 526–527):

"Although the passage cited below from the speech of Lord Hailsham LC in *Woodhouse AC Israel Cocoa Ltd SA v Nigerian Produce Marketing Co Ltd* [1972] 2 All ER 271 at 282, [1972] AC 741 at 757–758 was strictly obiter dicta I respectfully adopt it as an indication of the approach to be made in modern times. The case involved an agreement to vary the currency in which the buyer's obligation should be met, which was subsequently affected by a depreciation in the currency involved. The case was decided on an issue of estoppel but Lord Hailsham LC commented on the other issue, namely the variation of the original contract in the following terms:

'If the exchange letter was not variation, I believe it was nothing. The [buyers] asked for a variation in the mode of discharge of a contract of sale. If the proposal meant what they claimed, and was accepted and acted on, I venture to think that the [vendors] would have been bound by their acceptance at least until they gave reasonable notice to terminate, and I imagine that a modern court would have found no difficulty in discovering consideration for such a promise. Businessmen know their own business best even when they appear to grant an indulgence, and in the present case I do not think that there would have been insuperable difficulty in spelling out consideration from the earlier correspondence.'

In the light of those authorities the question now must be addressed: was there evidence on which the judge was entitled to find that there was sufficient consideration to support the agreement of April 9 [*to pay the additional £10,300*] . . .

. . . there was clearly a commercial advantage to both sides from a pragmatic point of view in reaching the agreement of 9 April. The defendants were on risk that as a result of the bargain they had struck the plaintiff would not or indeed possibly could not comply with his existing obligations without further finance. As a result of the agreement the defendants secured their position commercially. There was, however, no obligation added to the contractual duties imposed on the plaintiff under the original contract. Prima facie this would appear to be a classic *Stilk v Myrick* case . . . [*but*] comforted by the passage from the speech of Lord Hailsham LC, to which I have referred, I consider that the modern approach to the question of consideration would be that where there were benefits derived by each party to a contract of variation even though one party did not suffer a detriment this would not be fatal to the establishing of sufficient consideration to support the agreement. If both parties benefit from an agreement it is not necessary that each also suffers a detriment. In my judgment, on the facts as found by the judge, he was entitled to reach the conclusion that consideration existed and in those circumstances I would not disturb that finding. This is sufficient to determine the appeal."

It might be that Purchas L.J., like Glidewell L.J., was of the view that consideration could take the form of a practical benefit to a contracting party of having the other contracting party perform his contractual obligation rather than default.

Nevertheless, this point was not specifically addressed by Purchas L.J., although his Lordship did refer to "the commercial advantage to both sides from a pragmatic point of view" in reaching the agreement for the additional payment, indicating that it would suffice if there were "benefits derived by each party to a contract of variation even though one party did not suffer a detriment".

▷ ## (c) The judgment of Russell L.J.

7–005 It is less clear whether the views of Russell L.J. accorded with those of Glidewell L.J. Although Russell L.J. began his judgment (at 522) by expressing agreement with Glidewell L.J., it is not clear whether such agreement extended to the whole of Glidewell L.J.'s judgment or was confined to one particular aspect of it which was not related to the principle in *Stilk*:

> "I agree with and have nothing to add to the judgment of Glidewell LJ in so far as it relates to the defendant's submission that the plaintiff was not entitled to any part of the £10,300 because none of the eight flats had been completed. The judge found that there had been substantial completion and made a small deduction for defective and incomplete items. He did not identify those items nor define the extent of his deductions but no complaint is made about that. For the reasons appearing in the judgment of Glidewell LJ, supported as they are by *Hoenig v Issacs* [1952] 2 All ER 176, I have no doubt that the judge was right on what counsel for the defendants referred to as his secondary point.
>
> I find his primary argument relating to consideration much more difficult . . ."

If "agree with" and "have nothing to add to" in his Lordship's opening sentence are read conjunctively, this would mean that Russell L.J.'s agreement with Glidewell L.J.'s judgment extended only to the particular point mentioned, i.e. whether the plaintiff had performed his side of the contract in completing the flats. If, on the other hand, the words were read disjunctively, "have nothing to add" alone might relate to the particular point mentioned and "agree with" may indicate a general agreement with Glidewell L.J.'s judgment, which might, therefore, include Glidewell L.J.'s views on and his application of the principle in *Stilk*.

Even if Russell L.J. is regarded as agreeing with Glidewell L.J.'s view on *Stilk*, his Lordship nevertheless went on to give reasons of his own as to why the promise to pay £10,300 was enforceable. Like Purchas L.J., these may perhaps have been based on a greater willingness in modern times to find the existence of consideration. Russell L.J. stated (at 524):

> ". . . while consideration remains a fundamental requirement before a contract not under seal can be enforced, the policy of the law in its search to do justice between the parties has developed considerably since the early nineteenth century when *Stilk v Myrick* (1809) 2 Camp 317, 170 ER 1168 was decided by

Lord Ellenborough CJ. In the late twentieth century I do not believe that the rigid approach to the concept of consideration to be found in *Stilk v Myrick* is either necessary or desirable. Consideration there must still be but in my judgment the courts nowadays should be more ready to find its existence . . .

There was [*in the present case*] a desire on Mr Cottrell's [*the defendant's surveyor's*] part to retain the services of the plaintiff so that the work could be completed without the need to employ another sub-contractor. There was further a need to replace what had hitherto been a haphazard method of payment by a more formalised scheme involving the payment of a specified sum on the completion of each flat. These were all advantages accruing to the defendants which can fairly be said to have been in consideration of their undertaking to pay the additional £10,300. True it was that the plaintiff did not undertake to do any work additional to that which he had originally under-taken to do but the terms on which he was to carry out the work were varied and, in my judgment, that variation was supported by consideration which a pragmatic approach to the true relationship between the parties readily demonstrates.

For my part I wish to make it plain that I do not base my judgment on any reservation as to the correctness of the law long ago enunciated in *Stilk v Myrick*. A gratuitous promise, pure and simple, remains unenforceable unless given under seal. But where, as in this case, a party undertakes to make a payment because by doing so it will gain an advantage arising out of the continuing relationship with the promisee the new bargain will not fail for want of consideration."

Russell L.J. seemed to identify two advantages accruing to the defendants which might constitute consideration, namely, retention of the plaintiff's services so that the work could be completed without the need to employ another sub-contractor, and the replacement of a haphazard method of payment with a more formalised scheme involving payment of a specified sum on completion of each flat.

The former was in essence the approach which appeared to be adopted by Pur-chas and Glidewell L.JJ. of finding consideration in the benefit to a contracting party of performance, as against default, by the other contracting party. The latter, however, which was not mentioned by either Purchas or Gildewell L.JJ., went beyond this. With payment for completion of each flat, there was, unlike in the case of retention of the plaintiff's services, a variation of the terms on which the contract was carried out. Stage payments on completion of each of the flats might be seen as beneficial to the defendant in that money would be paid out by them only once work was completed and not in respect of work which was still to be done. This would avoid the situation which had arisen under the original terms of the contract where the defendant had advanced over 80 per cent of the money due in interim payments, although much less than 80 per cent of the work had been done. By the same token, there could be said to be a detriment to the plaintiffs in that money would now be advanced only on completion of work, whereas under the original terms of the contract interim payments might be made in respect of work still to be done. It should, however, be noted that in none of the judgments was any reference made to detriment being suffered by the plaintiff and it was accepted that it was sufficient if it could be shown that the defendant had received a benefit even if there was no detriment to the plaintiff. Glidewell L.J. (at 522) quoted with approval the following passage in *Chitty on Contracts* (25th ed., 1983), para.173:

> "The requirement that consideration must move from the promisee is most generally satisfied where some detriment is suffered by him: *e.g.* where he parts with money or goods, or renders services, in exchange for the promise. But the requirement may equally well be satisfied where the promisee confers a benefit on the promisor without *in fact* suffering any detriment."

The defendants could be said to be doing more than performing their existing duty, since they were now obliged to carry out the work on each flat before receiving any payment whereas under the original terms of the contract they might receive interim payments prior to work being done.

It may be queried whether the existence of consideration for the promise to pay an additional sum might be justified more easily on the ground that there was contractual performance with a variation of contract terms than on the ground that there was contractual performance and not default. If this is the case, it might be asked why neither Purchas nor Glidewell L.JJ. made reference to this.

▶ 3. The application of *Williams v Roffey Bros & Nicholls (Contractors) Ltd* in subsequent High Court and Court of Appeal decisions

7–006 As indicated in Chapter 1, the ratio of a particular decision is the proposition(s) of law based upon the material facts of that case and it may be subsequent courts which clarify and establish the ratio of a case. This occurred in respect of the decision in *Williams* which was subsequently considered by the High Court in *Anangel* and by the Court of Appeal in *Selectmove*.

In *Anangel*, counsel for the plaintiffs sought to distinguish *Williams* and argued for a restrictive interpretation of the case, but this argument did not find favour with Hirst J., who stated (at 545):

> "Mr Hunt [*counsel for the plaintiffs*] submitted that, because the Court of Appeal expressly refrained from overruling *Stilk*'s case, *Williams*' case should be read as having only a very narrow ambit, and was distinguishable on the grounds that in the present case, unlike *Stilk*'s case, it was the defendants and not the plaintiffs who were providing the services.

> I do not think that such a very narrow and artificial distinction can properly be drawn, and consider that the ratio of *Williams'* case is that, whoever provides the services, where there is a practical conferment of benefit or a practical avoidance of disbenefit for the promisee, there is good consideration, and it is no answer to say that the promisor was already bound; where, on the other hand, there is a wholly gratuitous promise, *Stilk*'s case still remains good law."

The court thus did not see the fact that it was the plaintiffs who had been providing the services in *Williams* as having been a material fact of the decision in that case. Accordingly, *Williams* was not distinguishable and consideration could be provided by the conferment of a benefit or avoidance of disbenefit, irrespective of who provided the service. As there was such a conferment on the defendants in *Anangel*, there was consideration to support their promise to reimburse the plaintiffs following an agreement for a substantial price reduction under a ship-building contract and such promise was enforceable.

In *Selectmove*, the appellants, a company, sought to enforce an agreement made with the Inland Revenue for payment by instalments of substantial amounts of tax owed, following the Inland Revenue's subsequent demand for payment to be made forthwith and its commencement of legal action to have the company compulsorily wound up. The appellants contended, inter alia, that the agreement to pay by instalments was legally enforceable because, although it was for the performance of the company's existing obligation to pay the tax owed, it was supported by consideration. The consideration alleged was the practical benefits to the Inland Revenue of payment under the agreement. As Peter Gibson L.J., delivering the judgment of the Court of Appeal, observed (at 480):

> "Mr Nugee [*counsel for the appellants*] . . . submitted that an additional benefit to the revenue was conferred by the agreement in that the revenue stood to derive practical benefits therefrom: it was likely to recover more from not enforcing its debt against the company, which was known to be in financial difficulties, than from putting the company into liquidation. He pointed to the fact that the company did in fact pay its further . . . [*tax*] liabilities and £7,000 of its arrears. He relied on the decision of this court in *Williams v Roffey Bros. & Nicholls (Contractors) Ltd* [1991] 1 Q.B. 1 for the proposition that a promise to perform an existing obligation can amount to good consideration provided that there are practical benefits to the promisee."

The Court of Appeal, however, held that *Williams* did not support this proposition. That case was considered to have established that a practical benefit could con-stitute good consideration in cases where the obligation under the agreement was to do work for or supply goods or services to the promisee. It did not establish, the Court of Appeal felt, that a practical benefit could constitute good consideration in cases where the obligation was to pay money, for that would be contrary to the House of Lords' decision in *Foakes v Beer* (1884) 9 App.Cas. 605. Whilst recog-nising the desirability of holding the agreement in the case in question to be legally enforceable, the court nevertheless was of the view that, as a matter of precedent, it was unable to do so in the light of the House's decision in that case. Peter Gibson L.J. stated (at 479–481):

"The [*trial*] judge held that the case fell within the principle in *Foakes v Beer* (1884) 9 App.Cas. 605. In that case a judgment debtor and creditor agreed that in consideration of the debtor paying part of the judgment debt and costs immediately and the remainder by instalments the creditor would not take any proceedings on the judgment. The House of Lords held that the agreement was nudum pactum, being without consideration, and did not prevent the creditor, after payment of the whole debt and costs, from proceeding to enforce payment of the interest on the judgment. Although their Lordships were unanimous in the result, that case is notable for the powerful speech of Lord Blackburn, who made plain his disagreement with the course the law had taken in and since *Pinnel's Case* (1602) 5 Co.Rep. 117a and which the House of Lords in *Foakes v Beer*, 9 App.Cas. 605, decided should not be reversed. Lord Blackburn expressed his conviction, at p.622, that

'all men of business, whether merchants or tradesmen, do every day recognise and act on the ground that prompt payment of a part of their demand may be more beneficial to them than it would be to insist on their rights and enforce payment of the whole.'

Yet it is clear that the House of Lords decided that a practical benefit of that nature is not good consideration in law. . .

Mr Nugee . . . referred to an article by Adams and Brownsword, "Contract, Consideration and the Critical Path" (1990) 53 M.L.R. 536, 539–540 which suggests that *Foakes v Beer*, 9 App.Cas. 605 might need reconsideration . . . [*but*] if the principle of *Williams v Roffey Bros. & Nicholls (Contractors) Ltd* [1991] 1 Q.B. 1 is to be extended to an obligation to make payment, it would in effect leave the principle in *Foakes v Beer*, 9 App.Cas. 605 without any application. When a creditor and debtor who are at arm's length reach agreement on the payment of a debt by instalments to accommodate the debtor, the creditor will no doubt always see a practical benefit to himself in so doing. In the absence of authority there would be much to be said for the enforceability of such a contract. But that was a matter expressly considered in *Foakes v Beer* yet held not to constitute good consideration. *Foakes v Beer* was not even referred to in *Williams v Roffey Bros. & Nicholls (Contractors) Ltd* [1991] 1 Q.B. 1, and it is in my judgment impossible, consistently with the doctrine of precedent, for this court to extend the principle in *Williams's* case to any circumstances governed by the principle of *Foakes v Beer*, 9 App.Cas. 605. If that extension is to be made, it must be by the House of Lords or, perhaps even more appropriately, by Parliament after consideration by the Law Commission."

The case of *Williams* was thus considered to be distinguishable. The agreement in that case involved work done for and goods and services supplied to the promisee, whereas in the present case the agreement was for the payment of money owed to the promisee. It might therefore be seen as a material fact, and to be part of the ratio of *Williams*, that, for a practical benefit to constitute good consideration, the agreement should be for work done and for goods and services supplied to the promisee. The ratio included such agreements but did not extend to agreements for money owing to the promisee. Accordingly, the trial judge was held to have been correct in his view that, following *Foakes v Beer*, the agreement between the company and the Inland Revenue was unenforceable due to the absence of consideration. In consequence, the Court of Appeal affirmed the trial judge's decision that the Inland Revenue could demand payment of the money owing to be made forthwith and could commence legal action to have the company compulsorily wound up.

Attempts to distinguish *Williams* and to restrict its application have continued in later cases, as can be seen from the High Court case of *South Caribbean Trading Ltd v Trafigura Beheer BV* [2005] 1 Lloyd's Rep. 128, where Colman J. stated (at [108]):

"But for the fact that *Williams v Roffey Bros.* was a decision of the Court of Appeal, I would not have followed it. That decision is inconsistent with the long-standing rule that consideration, being the price of the promise sued upon, must move from the promise . . . However, seeing that *Williams v Roffey Bros.* has not yet been held by the House of Lords to have been wrongly decided, and approaching the validity of consideration on the basis of mutuality of benefit, I would hold that SCT's threat of non-compliance with its delivery obligation under contract . . . precluded its reliance on the benefit that its performance by effecting delivery would confer on Trafigura. This threat was analogous to economic duress as contemplated in *Williams v Roffey Bros.*, supra. . ."

Whilst recognising that he was bound by the decision in *Williams* as a matter of precedent, his Lordship was nevertheless able to distinguish *Williams* on the ground that one material fact in that decision, the absence of economic duress, was not present in the case before the court. The threat of non-compliance with a delivery requirement under the contract was regarded as analogous to economic duress and, as had been recognised by Glidewell L.J. in *Williams*, one of the conditions for the application of *Williams* was that a "promise is not given as a result of economic duress" (see above, 7–003).

In contrast, however, the High Court in *Adam Opel GmbH, Renault S.A. v Mitras Automotive (UK) Limited* [2007] EWHC 3481 (QB) felt obliged to follow the decision in *Williams*, notwithstanding a finding of economic duress in the case before it, and made no attempt to distinguish it. Although holding an agreement under which car manufacturers made payments to a car components' supplier (which they were already contractually obliged to make) was voidable for economic duress, the court applied *Williams* and held that the claimants could not rely on an absence of consideration to avoid the agreement. Deputy Judge David Donaldson QC stated (at [41]–[43]):

> "[41] . . .Though all three judges [*in Williams*] claimed to accept the rule in *Stilk v Myrik*, it is wholly unclear how the decision in *Williams v Roffey* can be reconciled with it. On analysis, the benefit or advantage lay in an act or promise wholly coincident with the plaintiff's existing contractual obligation.
>
> [42] In terms of its result and the reasons advanced by the judges, however, *Williams v Roffey* would seem to permit any variation of a contract, even if the benefits and burdens of the variation move solely in one direction, and I am bound to apply the decision accordingly, whatever view I might take of its logical coherence. The law of consideration is no longer to be used to protect a participant in such a variation. That role has passed to the law of economic duress, which provides a more refined control mechanism, and renders the contract voidable rather than void.
>
> [43] Accordingly, GMR [*General Motors/Renault, the claimants*] cannot rely on absence of consideration, whether as a supplement or an alternative to economic duress."

The decision in *Williams*, on the basis of its application here, as expressed "to permit any variation of a contract, even if the benefits and burdens of the variation move solely in one direction", would seem to remain very much intact.

Further Reading

Austen-Baker, Richard, "A strange sort of survival of Pinnel's case: Collier v P & MJ Wright (Holdings) Ltd: Case Comment" (2008) 71 M.L.R. 611-620

Hird, Norma J, "Minding your own business—Williams v Roffey revisited: consideration re-considered" [1996] J.B.L. 254–265

Trukhtanov, Alexander, "Foakes v Beer: reform of common law at the expense of equity" (2008) 124 L.Q.R. 364–368

8 THE RIGHT TO SUE IN THE TORT OF PRIVATE NUISANCE

▶ 1. Introduction

The essence of the tort of private nuisance is the unreasonable interference with a person's (the claimant's) use or enjoyment of land, or some right over it, or in connection with it. Such interference usually emanates from the land of another (the defendant) and may comprise either an encroachment on the claimant's land, or direct physical injury to the claimant's land or property on it, or interference with the claimant's quiet enjoyment of land. **8-001**

In *Hunter v Canary Wharf Ltd; Hunter v London Docklands Development Corp* [1997] A.C. 655 (*Hunter*) one of the important questions that the House of Lords had to consider was who may bring an action in the tort of private nuisance. In cases where there is an encroachment upon or direct physical injury to a claimant's land the need for such a claimant to establish an interest in the land (a proprietary interest), e.g. as an owner or a tenant in order to found an action, is well established and self-evident for in these cases there is tangible damage to the land itself. This was not in issue in *Hunter*. However, in *Hunter* it was argued that, in cases where the nuisance constituted an interference with a person's quiet enjoyment of land, i.e. broadly speaking, its amenity value, the right to sue should not be so confined. Rather it should also extend to a person whose occupation of land for residential purposes was impaired by the nuisance, notwithstanding that such occupation was not founded on any proprietary interest in that land.

This was not a novel argument as it had been mooted in earlier cases. It was, however, a matter upon which different and arguably irreconcilable pronouncements had been made, notably in the two conflicting decisions of the Court of Appeal in *Khorasandjian v Bush* [1993] 3 All E.R. 669 (*Khorasandjian*) and *Malone v Laskey* [1907] 2 K.B. 141 (*Malone*). In *Khorasandjian*, a majority of the Court of Appeal (Dillon and Rose L.JJ.) accepted that the plaintiff, who lived at her parents' house but had no proprietary interest or right of occupation in that property (i.e. lived there as a licensee), could maintain an action in private nuisance. In making that determination, Dillon and Rose L.JJ. declined to follow the earlier decision in *Malone*, in which a licensee (i.e. the wife of an employee of a company which was the tenant of premises in which the couple lived) had been denied such a right, and purported to do so on the basis that the stance they had adopted was legitimate in the light of changed social conditions. Moreover, such departure in *Khorasandjian* from the principle established in *Malone* occurred in circumstances which did not appear to accord with any of the recognised exceptions to the rule that the Court of Appeal is bound by its previous decisions (see Chapter 1, 1–021).

The issues raised by this dichotomy in the context of case law and precedent are examined in the first edition of this book (see Chapter 6, pp.151–159). As will be seen, however, some of those issues remain pertinent to this case study.

This case study, which focuses on the right to sue in private nuisance, illustrates a number of points primarily, though not exclusively, in relation to precedent and judicial approaches to determining cases:

- ▶ the necessity for the House of Lords to decide which of two conflicting decisions of the Court of Appeal to follow, where a later decision of the Court of Appeal did not follow an earlier decision even though none of the recognised exceptions to the rule that the Court of Appeal is bound by its previous decisions was apparent;
- ▶ the authority accorded by a higher court to a precedent of a lower court;
- ▶ overruling or not following a precedent;
- ▶ the following of a dissenting judgment;
- ▶ the influence of policy considerations in determining propositions of law;
- ▶ the distinguishing of a previous decision;
- ▶ consideration of the views expressed by authors in articles and textbooks;
- ▶ consideration of decisions from other jurisdictions;
- ▶ the influence of international standards in the development of the law;
- ▶ assistance derived from a dictionary meaning of a word; and
- ▶ legislative intervention to fill a gap in the common law.

▶ 2. The Decision of the House of Lords in *Hunter v Canary Wharf Ltd; Hunter v London Docklands Development Corporation*

8–002 The litigation in this case arose out of the construction of the Canary Wharf Tower and the Limehouse Link Road in East London, and the serious disturbance and inconvenience which such construction caused to local residents. A substantial number of those residents initiated legal proceedings in which they sought to recover damages for negligence and nuisance, first, in respect of interference with the reception of television in their homes allegedly caused by the presence of the Canary Wharf Tower erected by Canary Wharf Ltd, and, secondly, in respect of the deposit on their properties of dust caused by the construction of the link road by London Docklands Development Corporation. Some of those residents were the owners or tenants of the houses in which they resided, i.e. they had a proprietary interest and a right to exclusive possession; others, without any such interest and right, comprised wives living in houses owned or let by their husbands, children living with their parents, relations of the owner or tenant, or lodgers.

These actions gave rise to certain preliminary issues, two of which (both concerning matters pertaining to the claims for damages for nuisance) were the subject of appeals to the House of Lords in *Hunter*. The two salient issues were, first, whether the alleged interruption of television reception in this case was capable of constituting an actionable nuisance (in respect of which the House of Lords gave a unanimous and negative response, and to which no further reference will be made in this case study), and, secondly, who may bring an action in the tort of private nuisance, which, of course, is the subject-matter of this case study.

These preliminary issues had been considered at first instance by Judge Richard Havery QC, sitting on official referees' business. (Circuit judges can be nominated as official referees to take difficult or technical issues of fact, on a reference from the High Court in any civil proceeding before it, after an application made by either party.) On the issue of who may bring an action in the tort of private nuisance, his Lordship held that a plaintiff must have a right to exclusive possession of the property to which the nuisance is alleged to have been caused. The Court of Appeal, where the only substantive judgment was delivered by Pill L.J. (with which Neill and Waite L.JJ. agreed), allowed an appeal by the plaintiffs and held that this was not necessary. The Court of Appeal held that, where the nuisance affected the amenity value of a property, occupation of that property as a home provided a sufficient link with that property to enable the occupier to sue in private nuisance, and that this proposition was in keeping with a trend in the law which had seen additional protection given to occupiers in some circumstances. On appeal, the House of Lords, by a 4–1 majority (Lord Cooke dissenting), reversed the decision of the Court of Appeal in this respect.

The remainder of this case study explores this divergence of judicial opinion within the House in *Hunter*, and also the consequences of the decision of the House of Lords in that case for the conflicting Court of Appeal decisions in *Khorasandjian* and *Malone*.

▷ (a) The approach of the majority

(i) The decision and its rationale

The majority judgments were delivered by Lords Goff, Lloyd, Hoffmann and Hope. **8–003**
These judgments show that their Lordships adopted a broadly similar approach to the question before them. However, it is possible to detect a slight difference of emphasis when the judgments of Lords Goff and Hope, and those of Lords Hoffmann and Lloyd are compared. This difference, although not immediately material in *Hunter*, because, as will be seen, the inevitable consequence of all the judgments is that licensees are not able to maintain an action in private nuisance, may conceivably be seen not merely as a matter of semantics but as pertinent to the manner in which the *ratio* of *Hunter* is expressed in subsequent cases. Thus, Lords Goff and Hope took the view that in order to bring an action in private nuisance a plaintiff must generally show that he has an interest in the land

affected by the nuisance, although, exceptionally, such an action might be maintained by a plaintiff who is in actual occupation of the land with exclusive possession of the land even though he cannot prove his right to be there. On the other hand, Lords Hoffmann and Lloyd, whilst neither questioning nor departing from the stance adopted by Lords Goff and Hope, tended to focus on the need for a plaintiff to establish a claim to exclusive possession, which is founded either in law, i.e. derived from an interest in the land or in fact, i.e. through actual occupation of the land, in order to found such an action. These nuances are exhibited in the following extracts.

In determining the question of who can sue in private nuisance, Lord Goff alluded to the historical origins of the tort of private nuisance, and placed reliance upon the opinions expressed by Professor Newark on the matter. His Lordship stated (at 687–688):

> "The basic position is, in my opinion, most clearly expressed in Professor Newark's classic article on "The Boundaries of Nuisance" (1949) 65 L.Q.R. 480 when he stated, at p.482, that the essence of nuisance was that "it was a tort directed against the plaintiff's enjoyment of rights over land . . ." The historical origin of the tort lay in the fact that:
>
> > "Disseisina, transgressio and nocumentum [nuisance] covered the three ways in which a man might be interfered with in his rights over land. Wholly to deprive a man of the opportunity of exercising his rights over land was to disseise [*dispossess*] him, for which he might have recourse to the assize of novel disseisin [*for a legal remedy*]. But to trouble a man in the exercise of his rights over land without going so far as to dispossess him was a trespass or a nuisance according to whether the act was done on or off the plaintiff's land:" p.481.
>
> Later, when distinguishing cases of personal injury, he stated, at pp.488–489:
>
> > "In true cases of nuisance the interest of the plaintiff which is invaded is not the interest of bodily security but the interest of liberty to exercise rights over land in the amplest manner. A sulphurous chimney in a residential area is not a nuisance because it makes householders cough and splutter but because it prevents them taking their ease in their gardens. It is for this reason that the plaintiff in an action for nuisance must show some title to the realty [*land*]."
>
> Finally, he proclaimed four theses which should be nailed to the doors of the Law Courts and defended against all comers. The first was that: "The term 'nuisance' is properly applied only to such actionable user of land as interferes with the enjoyment by the plaintiff of rights in land." There are many authoritative statements which bear out this thesis of Professor Newark. I refer in particular to *Sedleigh-Denfield v O'Callaghan* [1947] A.C. 880, 902–903, *per* Lord Wright; *Read v J. Lyons & Co. Ltd.* [1947] A.C. 156, 183, *per* Lord Simonds; *Tate & Lyle Food & Distribution Ltd. v Greater London Council* [1983] 2 A.C. 509,

> 536–537, *per* Lord Templeman; *Fleming, The Law of Torts*, 8th ed. (1992), p. 416."

Lord Goff then proceeded to give some guidance as to the categories of person who may sue in private nuisance, e.g. the freeholder or tenant of the relevant land, and indicated that, exceptionally, a person in exclusive possession of land might be entitled to sue in circumstances where that person is unable to prove his interest in or rights to the land. This "exception" (which did not arise in *Hunter*) did not detract, however, from his Lordship's conclusion (at 689) that "it has for many years been regarded as settled law that a person who has no right in the land cannot sue in private nuisance".

Lord Hope, who delivered a short judgment, approached the question in a similar vein. At the outset of his judgment, his Lordship opined (at 723) that the issues to be determined in the case were "best examined from the standpoint of principle", and that, in relation to the right to sue in private nuisance, once the principles underlying the tort of nuisance were appreciated it should be "relatively easy to identify those who have a right to sue for a remedy in private nuisance and those who have not". Lord Hope then identified those principles. His Lordship stated (at 723):

> "The tort of nuisance is an invasion of the plaintiff's interest in the possession and enjoyment of land. It is closely linked to the law of property and is often regarded as part of the law of neighbourhood. English law and Scots law differ as to the scope of nuisance as a legal category: see *Stair Memorial Encyclopaedia*, vol. 14 (1988), "Nuisance," p.792, para. 2019. In Scots law, for example, the law relating to servitudes [*easements, profits a prendre and natural rights*]— such as the servitude rights of air, light and prospect—are regarded as falling outside the scope of nuisance, whereas in English law—as the present case demonstrates—the law relating to easements is usually treated as a branch of the same legal category. In my opinion the English approach as disclosed by the authorities serves to emphasise the point that we are concerned here essentially with the law of property. The function of the tort, in the context of private nuisance, is to control the activities of the owner or occupier of property within the boundaries of his own land which may harm the interests of the owner or occupier of other land."

In the light of this exposition, and after differentiating between actions in nuisance and negligence, Lord Hope continued as follows (at 724):

> "So where it is the tort of nuisance which is being relied upon to provide the remedy—and I believe that the same rules should apply whether the remedy sought is that of an injunction or in damages—the plaintiff must show that he has an interest in the land that has been affected by the nuisance of which he complains. Mere presence on the land will not do. He must have a right to the land, for example as owner or reversioner [*a person entitled to a reversionary interest which gives a right to future enjoyment of land presently in the*

possession or occupation of another], or be in exclusive possession or occupation of it as tenant or under a licence to occupy. It may then be said that there is an unlawful interference with his use or enjoyment of the land or of his right over or in connection with it: see *Newcastle-under-Lyme Corporation v Wolstanton Ltd.* [1947] Ch. 92, 107, *per* Evershed J. Exceptionally, as in *Foster v Warblington Urban Council* [1906] 1 K.B. 648, his actual occupation of the land will be enough to demonstrate that he has a sufficient interest for a right of action in nuisance to exist. For the purposes of the present case however the important point to notice is that which Lord Wright made in *Sedleigh-Denfield v O'Callaghan* [1940] A.C. 880, 902–903: "With possibly certain anomalous exceptions, not here material, possession or occupation is still the test." "

In Lord Hoffmann's opinion, it was necessary in order to resolve the pertinent question of who can sue in the tort of private nuisance to ascertain what exactly the plaintiff was suing for—was it for causing discomfort to the person or for causing injury (damage) to the land? Both questions were regarded by Lord Hoffmann as fundamental to the scope of the tort of nuisance. In this context, his Lordship then undertook an examination of the juridical "roots" of the tort of nuisance, and considered in whom, as a matter of principle, the right to sue in respect of such a nuisance might be vested. On these matters, his Lordship stated (at 702–703):

"Up to about 20 years ago, no one would have had the slightest doubt about who could sue. Nuisance is a tort against land, including interests in land such as easements and profits. A plaintiff must therefore have an interest in the land affected by the nuisance. In *Sedleigh-Denfield v O'Callaghan* [1940] A.C. 880, 902–903, Lord Wright said:

"I do not attempt any exhaustive definition of that cause of action. But it has never lost its essential character which was derived from its prototype, the assize of nuisance and was maintained under the form of action on the case for nuisance. The assize of nuisance was a real action [*an action for the recovery of land*] supplementary to the assize of novel disseisin [*an action brought by a person who had recently been dispossessed of his land*]. The latter was devised to protect the plaintiff's seisin of his land [*right to possession of his land*], and the former aimed at vindicating the plaintiff's right to the use and enjoyment of his land. The assize became early superseded by the less formal procedure of an action on the case for nuisance, which lay for damages. This action was less limited in its scope, because whereas the assize was by a freeholder, the action lay also between possessors or occupiers of land. With possibly certain anomalous exceptions, not here material, possession or occupation is still the test."

In speaking of "possession or occupation" Lord Wright was in my view intending to refer both to a right to possession based upon (or derived through) title and de facto occupation. In each case the person in possession is entitled to sue in trespass and in nuisance. An example of an action for nuisance by a de facto possessor is *Foster v Warblington Urban District Council* [1906] 1 K.B. 648 in which the plaintiff sued the council for discharging sewage so as to pollute his oyster ponds on the foreshore. He had some difficulty in proving any title to the soil but Vaughan Williams L.J. said, at 659–660:

> "But, even if title could not be proved, in my judgment there has been such an occupation of these beds for such a length of time—not that the length of time is really material for this purpose—as would entitle the plaintiff as against the defendants, who have no interest in the foreshore, to sustain this action for the injury which is alleged has been done by the sewage to his oysters so kept in those beds."

Thus even a possession which is wrongful against the true owner can found an action for trespass or nuisance against someone else: *Asher v Whitlock* (1865) L.R. 1 Q.B. 1. In each case, however, the plaintiff (or joint plaintiffs) must be enjoying or asserting exclusive possession of the land: see *per* Blackburn J. in *Allan v Liverpool Overseers* (1874) L.R. 9 Q.B. 180. Exclusive possession distinguishes an occupier who may in due course acquire title under the Limitation Act 1980 from a mere trespasser. It distinguishes a tenant holding a leasehold estate from a mere licensee. Exclusive possession de jure or de facto, now or in the future, is the bedrock of English land law."

This concept of nuisance as a tort against land meant that a plaintiff's action in private nuisance, whatever the nature of that nuisance, must be in respect of the injury (damage) caused to the land. In this regard, Lord Hoffmann said (at 705–706):

> "*St. Helen's Smelting Co. v Tipping* was a landmark case. It drew the line beyond which rural and landed England did not have to accept external costs imposed upon it by industrial pollution. But there has been, I think, some inclination to treat it as having divided nuisance into two torts, one of causing "material injury to the property," such as flooding or depositing poisonous substances on crops, and the other of causing "sensible personal discomfort" such as excessive noise or smells. In cases in the first category, there has never been any doubt that the remedy, whether by way of injunction or damages, is for causing damage to the land. It is plain that in such a case only a person with an interest in the land can sue. But there has been a tendency to regard cases in the second category as actions in respect of the discomfort or even personal injury which the plaintiff has suffered or is likely to suffer. On this view, the plaintiff's interest in the land becomes no more than a qualifying condition or springboard which entitles him to sue for injury to himself.

> If this were the case, the need for the plaintiff to have an interest in land would indeed be hard to justify . . . In the case of nuisances "productive of sensible discomfort," [*however*], the action is not for causing discomfort to the person but, as in the case of the first category, for causing injury to the land. True it is that the land has not suffered 'sensible injury,' but its utility has been

diminished by the existence of the nuisance. It is for an unlawful threat to the utility of his land that the possessor or occupier is entitled to an injunction and it is for the diminution in such utility that he is entitled to compensation . . .

There may of course be cases in which, in addition to damages for injury to his land, the owner or occupier is able to recover damages for consequential loss. He will, for example, be entitled to loss of profits which are the result of inability to use the land for the purposes of his business. Or if the land is flooded, he may also be able to recover damages for chattels or livestock lost as a result. But inconvenience, annoyance or even illness suffered by persons on land as a result of smells or dust are not damage consequential upon the injury to the land. It is rather the other way about: the injury to the amenity of the land consists in the fact that the persons upon it are liable to suffer inconvenience, annoyance or illness."

Lord Lloyd, in the course of a succinct judgment, considered the issue before him in a manner apparently not dissimilar to that adopted by Lord Hoffmann. In so doing, his Lordship examined the question of the right to sue in respect of a private nuisance affecting the amenity value of land in the context of the right to sue in cases involving the other species of private nuisance. His Lordship said (at 696):

". . . the essence of private nuisance is easy enough to identify, and it is the same in all three classes of private nuisance, namely, interference with land or the enjoyment of land. In the case of nuisances within class (1) [*encroachment*] or (2) [*direct damage to land*] the measure of damages is . . . the diminution in the value of the land. Exactly the same should be true of nuisances within class (3) [*interference with quiet enjoyment*]. There is no difference of principle. The effect of smoke from a neighbouring factory is to reduce the value of the land. There may be no diminution in the market value. But there will certainly be loss of amenity value so long as the nuisance lasts . . .

If the occupier of land suffers personal injury as a result of inhaling the smoke, he may have a cause of action in negligence. But he does not have a cause of action in nuisance for his *personal* injury, nor for interference with his *personal* enjoyment . . . It . . . follows that the only persons entitled to sue for loss in amenity value of the land are the owner or the occupier with the right to exclusive possession."

Further, his Lordship concluded his consideration of this aspect of the appeal (at 699) by answering "the question in the same manner as Judge Havery", i.e. that a plaintiff in an action for private nuisance must have a right to exclusive possession of the property to which the nuisance is alleged to have been caused.

(ii) The impact of the decision on the authority of Malone and Khorasandjian

8–004 In view of the reasoning contained in the above extracts, it is not surprising that the majority called into question the authority, as a precedent, of the decision in

Khorasandjian. However, the statements made by their Lordships in this respect are not homogeneous, and in order to fully appreciate the significance of those statements it is apposite to consider them against the backdrop of a fuller exposition of the decisions in *Malone* and *Khorasandjian* than has been possible thus far. Such an exposition can be found in the following extracts from the judgment of Lord Goff. His Lordship stated (at 689–691):

"In that case [*Malone*], the manager of a company resided in a house as a licensee of the company which employed him. The plaintiff was the manager's wife who lived with her husband in the house. She was injured when a bracket fell from a wall in the house. She claimed damages from the defendants in nuisance and negligence, her claim in nuisance being founded upon an allegation . . . that the fall of the bracket had been caused by vibrations from an engine operating on the defendant's adjoining premises. The Court of Appeal held that she was unable to succeed in her claim in nuisance. Sir Gorell Barnes P. said, at p. 151:

"Many cases were cited in the course of the argument in which it had been held that actions for nuisance could be maintained where a person's rights of property had been affected by the nuisance, but no authority was cited, nor in my opinion can any principle of law be formulated, to the effect that a person who has no interest in property, no right of occupation in the proper sense of the term, can maintain an action for a nuisance arising from the vibration caused by the working of an engine in an adjoining house. On that point, therefore, I think that the plaintiff fails, and that she has no cause of action in respect of the alleged nuisance."

. . . The decision in *Malone v Laskey* on nuisance has since been followed in many cases . . . Recently, however, the Court of Appeal departed from the line of this authority in *Khorasandjian v Bush* [1993] Q.B. 727, a case which I must examine with some care . . .

The question before the Court of Appeal was whether the judge had jurisdiction to grant . . . an injunction, in relation to [*unwanted and harassing*] telephone calls made to the plaintiff at her parents' home. The home was the property of the plaintiff's mother, and it was recognised that her mother could complain of persistent and unwanted telephone calls made to her; but it was submitted that the plaintiff, as a mere licensee in her mother's house, could not invoke the tort of private nuisance to complain of unwanted and harassing telephone calls made to her in her mother's home. The majority of the Court of Appeal (Peter Gibson J. dissenting) rejected this submission, relying on the decision of the Appellate Division of the Alberta Supreme Court in *Motherwell v Motherwell* (1976) 73 D.L.R. (3d) 62. In that case, the Appellate Division not only recognised that the legal owner of property could obtain an injunction, on the ground of private nuisance, to restrain persistent harassment by unwanted telephone calls to his home, but also that the same remedy was open to his wife who had no interest in the property. In the Court of Appeal Peter Gibson J.

dissented on the ground that it was wrong in principle that a mere licensee or someone without any interest in, or right to occupy, the relevant land should be able to sue in private nuisance.

It is necessary therefore to consider the basis of the decision in *Motherwell v Motherwell* that a wife, who has no interest in the matrimonial home where she lives, is nevertheless able to sue in private nuisance in respect of interference with her enjoyment of that home. The case was concerned with a claim for an injunction against the defendant, who was the daughter of one of the plaintiffs, the other two plaintiffs being her brother and sister-in-law. The main ground of the complaint against the defendant was that, as a result of a paranoid condition from which she suffered which produced in her the conviction that her sister-in-law and her father's housekeeper were inflaming her brother and her father against her, she persistently made a very large number of telephone calls to her brother's and her father's homes, in which she abused her sister-in-law and the housekeeper. The Appellate Division of the Alberta Supreme Court, in a judgment delivered by Clement J.A., held that not only could her father and brother, as householders, obtain an injunction against the defendant to restrain the activity as a private nuisance, but so also could her sister-in-law although she had no interest in her husband's property."

Lord Goff then considered, in the light of the above, the issue which is central to this section of the case study, namely, the degree of authority which the decision in *Khorasandjian* should be endowed with as a precedent. In this respect, his Lordship began by explaining that, in his opinion, the decision in *Motherwell v Motherwell* (*Motherwell*) was founded on a misunderstanding of the decision in *Foster v Warblington Urban District Council* [1906] 1 K.B. 648 (*Foster*) upon which the Appellate Division of the Alberta Supreme Court in *Motherwell* had "very largely based" its decision. That misunderstanding was to wrongly assume that *Foster* was authority for the proposition that, in certain circumstances, a person in the position of a mere licensee, e.g. a wife in her spouse's house, is entitled to sue in private nuisance. His Lordship then opined that this misunderstanding undermined not only the authority of *Motherwell*, but also the authority of *Khorasandjian* to the extent that it was based on *Motherwell*. Thereafter, Lord Goff indicated that the decision in *Khorasandjian* was also flawed in other ways, and, in drawing attention to those flaws, criticised the Court of Appeal for seeking to develop the law relating to private nuisance in an unsatisfactory manner which was inconsistent with the earlier Court of Appeal decision in *Malone* by which it was bound. His Lordship stated (at 691–692):

"If a plaintiff, such as the daughter of the householder in *Khorasandjian v Bush*, is harassed by abusive telephone calls, the gravamen of the complaint lies in the harassment which is just as much an abuse, or indeed an invasion of her privacy, whether she is pestered in this way in her mother's or her husband's house, or she is staying with a friend, or is at her place of work, or even in her car with a mobile phone. In truth, what the Court of Appeal appears to have been doing was to exploit the law of private nuisance in order to create by the back door a tort of harassment which was only partially effective in that it was artificially limited to harassment which takes place in her home. I myself do not consider that this is a satisfactory manner in which to develop the law, especially when, as in the case in question, the step so taken was inconsistent with another decision of the Court of Appeal, viz. *Malone v Laskey* [1907] 1 K.B. 141, by which the court was bound. In any event, a tort of harassment has now received statutory recognition: see the Protection from Harassment Act 1997. We are therefore no longer troubled with the question whether the common law should be developed to provide for such a remedy. For these reasons, I do not consider that any assistance can be derived from *Khorasandjian v Bush*. . ."

Lord Goff concluded (at 694) that *Khorasandjian* "must be overruled in so far as it holds that a mere licensee can sue in private nuisance".

Lord Lloyd was similarly robust in his approach to the question of the degree of precedential authority to be given to *Khorasandjian*. Thus, his Lordship explored the juxtaposition of what he described as the "two irreconcilable decisions" of the Court of Appeal in *Malone* and *Khorasandjian*, stated that *Khorasandjian* was wrongly decided and should be overruled, and indicated that, accordingly, the Court of Appeal in *Hunter* had been incorrect to accord precedence to *Khorasandjian*. In the words of his Lordship (at 697–698):

"If *Malone v Laskey* was correctly decided, the decision below [*in the Court of Appeal*] cannot stand.

But the Court of Appeal [1996] 2 W.L.R. 348 evidently felt free to depart from *Malone v Laskey* in the light of the intervening decision of the Court of Appeal in *Khorasandjian v Bush* [1993] Q.B. 727. In the latter case, the daughter of the house was being pestered and threatened by unwanted telephone calls. Dillon L.J., giving the majority judgment, held that she had a cause of action in private nuisance. He regarded it as:

"ridiculous if in this present age the law is that the making of deliberately harassing and pestering telephone calls to a person is only actionable in the civil courts if the recipient of the calls happens to have the freehold or a leasehold proprietary interest in the premises in which he or she has received the calls."

As for *Malone v Laskey*, Dillon L.J. added, at p. 735: "The court has at times to reconsider earlier decisions in the light of changed social conditions; . . ." Dillon L.J. was influenced by a decision of the Appellate Division of the Supreme Court of Alberta in *Motherwell v Motherwell*, (1976) 73 D.L.R. (3d) 62 . . . [*Lord Lloyd then expressed misgivings about the decision in Motherwell similar to those which had been specified by Lord Goff (see above). His Lordship continued*]

> Judge Havery found himself in the awkward position of having to reconcile two irreconcilable decisions of the Court of Appeal in *Malone v Laskey* and *Khorasandjian v Bush*. He did so by suggesting that *Khorasandjian v Bush* had extended the law of private nuisance to cover cases of harassment. Your Lordships are free to express a preference.
>
> I can well understand Dillon L.J.'s concern to find a remedy for the wife or daughter who suffers from harassment on the telephone, whether at home or elsewhere. But to allow them a remedy in private nuisance would not just be to extend the existing law. It would not just be to get rid of an unnecessary technicality. It would be to change the whole basis of the cause of action. For the reasons given by Peter Gibson L.J. [*sic*] in his dissenting judgment in *Khorasandjian v Bush*, with which I agree, I would hold that that case was wrongly decided, and should be overruled. This removes an essential plank on which the reasoning of the Court of Appeal in the present case, ante, [*[1997] A.C.*] pp. 662G et seq., is based."

Lord Hope, unlike Lords Goff and Lloyd, did not explicitly state that *Khorasandjian* should be overruled. Nevertheless, his Lordship's choice of words in relation to *Khorasandjian* is indicative of a viewpoint which is substantially the same as that adopted by Lords Goff and Lloyd. Lord Hope said (at 725):

> "In my opinion the decision in *Khorasandjian v Bush* [1993] Q.B. 727 is open to criticism because the majority who adopted the same approach as that taken in *Motherwell v Motherwell*, 73 D.L.R (3d) 62—a decision which I think, with respect, is equally flawed on this ground—failed to apply the general rule of law, noted by Peter Gibson LJ [sic] at p.745A, that only an owner or occupier of the property affected can maintain an action for private nuisance. The interlocutory order which was made in that case and was held on appeal to have been worded appropriately was in the widest terms. It restrained the defendant from "using violence to, harassing, pestering or communicating with" the plaintiff. It was so widely drawn that it covered the defendant's conduct wherever he happened to be when making the unwanted telephone calls and wherever the plaintiff happened to be when she received them. Its use of language demonstrates that the case was concerned with the invasion of the privacy of the plaintiff's person, not the invasion of any interest which she might have had in any land. I would be uneasy if it were not possible by some other means to provide such a plaintiff with a remedy. But the solution to her case ought not to have been found in the tort of nuisance, as her complaint of the effects on her privacy of the defendant's conduct was of a kind which fell outside the scope of the tort."

In Lord Hoffmann's opinion, the difficulties associated with *Khorasandjian* arose as a result of a gap in the common law, i.e. the absence of a tort of intentional harassment, and because of an unwarranted attempt in that case to fill that gap by distorting the principles of law pertaining to private nuisance. However, on the basis that *Khorasandjian* should be seen as a case involving intentional harassment rather than nuisance, his Lordship adopted a more charitable assessment of *Khorasandjian* than the other members of the majority. Lord Hoffmann stated (at 707):

> "The perceived gap in *Khorasandjian v Bush* was the absence of a tort of intentional harassment causing distress without actual bodily or psychiatric illness . . . The law of harassment has now been put on a statutory basis (see the Protection from Harassment Act 1997) and it is unnecessary to consider how the common law might have developed. But . . . I see no reason why a tort of intention [*al harassment*] should be subject to the rule which excludes compensation for mere distress, inconvenience or discomfort in actions based on negligence . . . I do not therefore say that *Khorasandjian v Bush* was wrongly decided. But it must be seen as a case on intentional harassment, not nuisance."

It might be added, of course, that, as claims such as those made by the licensee in *Khorasandjian* will now fall to be determined in accordance with the Protection from Harassment Act 1997, *Khorasandjian* is, to that extent, redundant.

To conclude, it is clear that *Khorasandjian* was overruled, explicitly or implicitly, by three law lords and explained by the fourth in a manner which renders it largely superfluous. The concomitant re-assertion of the authority of *Malone* is also apparent. Further, the inevitable consequence of the majority expressing its preference (to adapt Lord Lloyd's words) in this way is that, as intimated above, a licensee cannot bring an action in private nuisance.

(iii) Resistance to calls for "modernisation" of the law

As has been seen, the majority, in reaching their decision and in applying *Malone* rather than *Khorasandjian*, affirmed that the question of who should have the right to sue in private nuisance should be determined in accordance with long-standing and established principles of law. In so doing, their Lordships rejected the general proposition, which had commended itself to the Court of Appeal in *Hunter*, namely, that the case should be determined by adapting those principles to meet present-day conditions (a course of action which, as indicated above, was also followed by the Court of Appeal in *Khorasandjian*). That is not to say, however, that their Lordships were oblivious to the "attractiveness" of such an approach. In this respect, Lord Lloyd stated (at 695):

8–005

> "He [*counsel for the plaintiffs*] submits that here the right to bring an action for nuisance is not confined to those with a proprietary interest, but extends to those who occupy the property as their home. This would include not only the wife and children of the owner, as has been held in the Court of Appeal, but also . . . a lodger with a contractual right to remain in the house as licensee, or a living-in servant or an au pair girl.

One can see the attraction in this approach. The wife, at least, if not the children, should surely be regarded nowadays as sharing the exclusive possession of the home which she occupies, so as to give her an independent right of action. There is also a superficial logic in the approach. Suppose there are two adjoining properties, affected by smoke from a neighbouring factory. One of the properties is occupied by a bachelor, the other by a married man with two children. If they are all equally affected by the smoke, it would seem to follow that the damages recoverable by the married man and his family should be four times the damages recovered by the bachelor. Many of the textbooks favour this approach. In the current edition of *Clerk & Lindsell on Torts*, 17th ed. (1995), pp. 910–911, para.18–39 it is said that such a conclusion would affect 'a degree of modernisation' in the law, "while freeing it from undue reliance upon the technicalities of land law.""

However, this approach had its limits. Lord Lloyd continued (at 696):

"Like, I imagine, all your Lordships, I would be in favour of modernising the law wherever this can be done. But it is one thing to modernise the law by ridding it of unnecessary technicalities; it is another thing to bring about a fundamental change in the nature and scope of a cause of action."

These words were echoed by Lords Hoffmann and Hope. Lord Hoffmann opined (at 707):

"There is a good deal in this case and other writings about the need for the law to adapt to modern social conditions. But the development of the common law should be rational and coherent."

Similarly, Lord Hope said (at 723):

"It is tempting to depart from principle out of sympathy for the plaintiffs or in search of a remedy for some objectionable activity, but in this area of the law it is important to resist the temptation and to rely instead on the guidance of principle. To do otherwise would risk confusion and be likely to lead to uncertainty in the development of the law, as the point would ultimately be reached when each case would have to be determined entirely on its own facts."

Moreover, as indicated above, all their Lordships were agreed that it was not appropriate in this instance to depart from established principle. In support of that position, Lord Goff gave an in-depth and incisive refutation of the "modernising" approach. His Lordship stated (at 692–693):

"The question therefore arises whether your Lordships should be persuaded to depart from established principle, and recognise such a right [*to sue in private nuisance*] in others who are no more than mere licensees on the land. At the heart of this question lies a more fundamental question, which relates to the scope of the law of private nuisance . . .

. . . it is right for present purposes to regard the typical cases of private nuisance as being those concerned with interference with the enjoyment of land and, as such, generally actionable only by a person with a right in the land. Characteristic examples of cases of this kind are those concerned with noise, vibrations, noxious smells and the like . . .

For private nuisances of this kind, the primary remedy is in most cases an injunction, which is sought to bring the nuisance to an end, and in most cases should swiftly achieve that objective. The right to bring such proceedings is, as the law stands, ordinarily vested in the person who has exclusive possession of the land. He or she is the person who will sue, if it is necessary to do so. Moreover, he or she can, if thought appropriate, reach an agreement with the person creating the nuisance, either that it may continue for a certain period of time, possibly on the payment of a sum of money, or that it shall cease, again perhaps on certain terms including the time within which the cessation will take place . . . But the efficacy of arrangements such as these depends upon the existence of an identifiable person with whom the creator of the nuisance can deal for this purpose. If anybody who lived in the relevant property as a home had the right to sue, sensible arrangements such as these might in some cases no longer be practicable.

Moreover, any such departure from the established law on this subject, such as that adopted by the Court of Appeal in the present case, faces the problem of defining the category of persons who would have the right to sue. The Court of Appeal adopted the not easily definable category of those who have a "substantial link" with the land, regarding a person who occupied the premises "as a home" as having a sufficient link for this purpose. But who is to be included in this category? It was plainly intended to include husbands and wives, or partners, and their children, and even other relatives living with them. But is the category also to include the lodger upstairs, or the au pair girl or resident nurse caring for an invalid who makes her home in the house while she works there? If the latter, it seems strange that the category should not extend to include places where people work as well as places where they live, where nuisances such as noise can be just as unpleasant or distracting. In any event, the extension of the tort in this way would transform it from a tort to land into a tort to the person, in which damages could be recovered in respect of something less serious than personal injury and the criteria for liability were founded not upon negligence but upon striking a balance between the interests of neighbours in the use of their land. This is, in my opinion, not an acceptable way in which to develop the law."

His Lordship then considered (at 693–694), first, whether as a matter of policy a special case could be made for a spouse of a husband or wife who had exclusive possession of the matrimonial home to be entitled to sue in private nuisance (a point also considered by Lord Hoffmann at 708), and, secondly, if not, whether this would cause any disadvantage to that spouse:

"For the purpose of this submission, your Lordships were referred to the relevant legislation, notably the Matrimonial Homes Act 1983 and the Family Law Act 1996. I do not however consider it necessary to go through the statutory provisions. As I understand the position, it is as follows. If under the relevant legislation the spouse becomes entitled to possession of the matrimonial home or part of it, there is no reason why he or she should not be able to sue in private nuisance in the ordinary way. But I do not see how a spouse who has no interest in the matrimonial home has, simply by virtue of his or her cohabiting in the matrimonial home with his or her wife or husband whose freehold or leasehold property it is, a right to sue. No distinction can sensibly be drawn between such spouses and other cohabitees in the home, such as children, or grandparents. Nor do I see any great disadvantage flowing from this state of affairs. If a nuisance should occur, then the spouse who has an interest in the property can bring the necessary proceedings to bring the nuisance to an end, and can recover any damages in respect of the discomfort or inconvenience caused by the nuisance. Even if he or she is away from home, nowadays the necessary authority to commence proceedings for an injunction can usually be obtained by telephone. Moreover, if the other spouse suffers personal injury, including injury to health, he or she may, like anybody else, be able to recover damages in negligence. The only disadvantage is that the other spouse cannot bring an independent action in private nuisance for damages for discomfort or inconvenience."

Lord Goff concluded his examination of these matters by referring to two sources from which he indicated he had derived no assistance in his deliberations. First, his Lordship cited what he described as a "slender and inconclusive line of authority" in certain American cases referred to in the supplement (1988) to *Prosser & Keeton on Torts* (5th ed., 1984), pp.621–622. Secondly, his Lordship referred to various academic works used by Lord Cooke in his dissenting judgment to support the view that the right to sue in private nuisance in respect of interference with amenities should no longer be restricted to those who have an interest in land. In this latter regard, Lord Goff observed (at 694):

"I feel driven to say that I found in the academic works which I consulted [*and which were cited by Lord Cooke, see below 8–006*] little more than an assertion of the desirability of extending the right of recovery in the manner favoured by the Court of Appeal in the present case. I have to say (though I say it in no spirit of criticism, because I know full well the limits within which writers of textbooks on major subjects must work) that I have found no analysis of the problem; and, in circumstances such as this, a crumb of analysis is worth a loaf of opinion."

▷ (b) The approach in the minority judgment

At the commencement of his dissenting judgment, Lord Cooke outlined his reason **8–006**
for departing, albeit with due diffidence, from the approach which had been
adopted by the other members of the House. His Lordship stated (at 711):

> "I begin my own contribution by respectfully acknowledging that they [*the draft judgments of the other members of the House which Lord Cooke had seen*] achieve a major advance in the symmetry of the law of nuisance. Being less persuaded that they strengthen the utility or the justice of this branch of the common law, I am constrained to offer an approach which, although derived from concepts found in those opinions, would lead to principles different in some respects . . . such assistance as I may be able to give . . . could not consist in mere conformity and deference; and, if the common law of England is to be directed into the restricted path which in this instance the majority prefer, there may be some advantage in bringing out that the choice is in the end a policy one between competing principles."

The alternative to the majority decision, which was subsequently proffered by Lord
Cooke, was based on an important initial premise, namely, that a distinction can be
drawn between the conditions of liability attaching to nuisances which cause injury
or damage to the land and those pertaining to "amenity" nuisances (a premise
which, of course, was not accepted by the majority). In this respect, his Lordship
said (at 711–712):

> "In so far as a nuisance consists in material damage to property, it is no doubt generally true, as stated by Cotton L.J. in *Rust v Graving Dock Co.*, 36 Ch.D. 113, 129–130, that damages must not be increased by any subdivision of interests. That was a case of flood damage where as to some of the land affected the plaintiff was only a reversioner [*a person entitled to a reversionary interest which gives a right to future enjoyment of land presently in the possession or occupation of another*]. But at least since the speech of Lord Westbury L.C. in *St. Helen's Smelting Co. v Tipping*, 11 H.L. Cas. 642, 650 it has been seen that a different category of nuisance is in issue when, as the Lord Chancellor put it, the action is brought on the ground of sensible personal discomfort, the personal inconvenience and interference with one's enjoyment, one's quiet, one's personal freedom, anything that injuriously affects the senses or the nerves. The Lord Chancellor was emphasising that in that category much must depend on the circumstances of the place, as has become familiar doctrine."

Thereafter, Lord Cooke continued (at 712–713):

> "But just as a distinction has been drawn, as to the conditions of liability, between material physical damage on the one hand and personal discomfort and the like on the other, so a distinction could perfectly logically be drawn between them as to the right to sue . . .

In tort the question "who may recover for disturbance of enjoyment of the amenity?" is, as I see it, a question to which no one answer, wide or narrow, is inevitably compelled.

Private nuisance is commonly said to be an interference with enjoyment of land and to be actionable by an occupier. But "occupier" is an expression of varying meanings . . . Your Lordship's House does not appear to have been called on hitherto to lay down precisely the meaning to be given to the expression in relation to interference with the amenities of land. There is a dictum by Lord Simonds in *Read v Lyons & Co. Ltd.* [1947] A.C. 156, 183, restricting a lawful claim in nuisance to one who has suffered an invasion of some proprietary or other interest in land; but it was obiter and not focused on interference with amenities. Where interference with an amenity of a home is in issue there is no a priori reason why the expression should not include, and it appears natural that it should include, anyone living there who has been exercising a continuing right to enjoyment of that amenity . . . A temporary visitor, however, someone who is "merely present in the house" (a phrase used by Fletcher Moulton L.J. in *Malone v Laskey* [1907] 2 K.B. 141, 154), would not enjoy occupancy of sufficiently substantial nature."

This acceptance, in principle, by Lord Cooke that occupation of a property as a home (as his Lordship referred to it later in his judgment) may act as an acceptable basis for establishing a right to sue in respect of an amenity nuisance made manifest the fundamental difference between his Lordship and the majority. It also enabled Lord Cooke to countenance the entitlement of spouses and/or children to sue in nuisance for unlawful interference with the amenities of their home, and, in so doing, to purport to distinguish *Malone*, and to comment favourably about the decisions in *Motherwell* and *Khorasandjian*. As to the position of a spouse in this type of case, his Lordship opined (at 713):

"*Malone v Laskey*, a case of personal injury from a falling bracket rather than an interference with amenities, is not directly in point, but it is to be noted that the wife of the subtenant's manager, who had been permitted by the sub-tenant to live in the premises with her husband, was dismissed by Sir Gorell Barnes P., at p. 151, as a person who had "no right of occupation in the proper sense of the term" and by Fletcher Moulton L.J. as being "merely present". My Lords, whatever the acceptability of those descriptions 90 years ago, I can only agree with the Appellate Division of the Alberta Supreme Court in *Motherwell v Motherwell*, at p. 77, that they are "rather light treatment of a wife, at least in today's society where she is no longer considered subservient to her husband." Current statutes give effect to current perceptions by according spouses a special status in respect of the matrimonial home, as by enabling the court to make orders regarding occupation (see in England the Family Law Act 1996, sections 30 and 31). Although such provisions and orders thereunder do not of themselves confer proprietary rights, they support in relation to amenities the force and common sense of the words of Clement J.A. in *Motherwell*, at p. 78:

> "Here we have a wife harassed in the matrimonial home. She has a status, a right to live there with her husband and children. I find it absurd to say that her occupancy of the matrimonial home is insufficient to found an action in nuisance." "

With regard to the status of children in such cases, Lord Cooke was initially more circumspect, but, after consideration of a number of sources including international standards pertaining to the rights of children, was ultimately supportive of their entitlement to sue in private nuisance. His Lordship stated (at 713–714):

> "The status of children living at home is different [*from that of a spouse*] and perhaps more problematical but, on consideration, I am persuaded by the majority of the Court of Appeal in *Khorasandjian v Bush* [1993] Q.B. 727 and the weight of North American jurisprudence to the view that they, too, should be entitled to relief for substantial and unlawful interference with the amenities of their home. Internationally the distinct interests of children are increasingly recognised. The United Nations Convention on the Rights of the Child, ratified by the United Kingdom in 1991 and the most widely ratified human rights treaty in history, acknowledges children as fully-fledged beneficiaries of human rights. Article 16 declares, inter alia, that no child shall be subjected to unlawful interference with his or her home and that the child has the right to the protection of law against such interference. International standards such as this may be taken into account in shaping the common law.
>
> The point just mentioned can be taken further. Article 16 of the Convention on the Rights of the Child adopts some of the language of article 12 of the Universal Declaration of Human Rights and Fundamental Freedoms (1953) (Cmd. 8969). These provisions are aimed, in part, at protecting the home and are construed to give protection against nuisances: see *Arrondelle v United Kingdom*, Application No. 7889/77 (1982) 26 D. & R. 5 (aircraft noise) and *Lopez Ostra v Spain* (1994) 20 E.H.R.R. 277 (fumes and smells from a waste treatment plant). The protection is regarded as going beyond possession or property rights: see *Harris, O'Boyle and Warbrick, Law of the European Convention on Human Rights* (1995), p.319. Again I think this is a legitimate consideration in support of treating residence as an acceptable basis of standing at common law in the present class of case."

The persuasive influence of North American jurisprudence, which was referred to by Lord Cooke in the above extract, was a matter which his Lordship revisited later in his judgment (see at 714–717) by examining a number of decisions in this area of the law by courts in Canada and the United States, and which were supportive of the stance that he had taken. In respect of decisions from the United States, however, Lord Cooke indicated (at 715) that his survey was not exhaustive as "there is a vast sea of United States case law into which a judgment cannot conveniently do more than dip". Consequently, his Lordship acknowledged (at 715):

"It will have to be enough to rely on the summary in the American Law Institute's Restatement which echoes *Prosser and Keeton on Torts*, 5th ed., pp. 621–622, and to give two illustrative cases [*Hosmer v Republic Iron & Steel Co (1913) 60 South. 801; and Bowers v Westvaco Corporation (1992) 419 S.E. (2d) 661*]."

Lord Cooke also found support in the realms of academic opinion. His Lordship stated (at 717):

"The preponderance of academic opinion seems also to be against confining the right to sue in private nuisance for interference with amenities to plaintiffs with proprietary interests in land. Professor John G. Fleming's condemnation of a "senseless discrimination"—see now his [*The Law of Torts*] 8th ed., p. 426—has already been mentioned [*at p.714*]. His view is that the wife and family residing with a tenant should be protected by the law of nuisance against forms of discomfort and also personal injuries, "by recognising that they have a 'right of occupation' just like the official tenant." *Clerk & Lindsell on Torts*, 17th ed., pp. 910–911, para.18–39, is to the same effect, as is *Linden, Canadian Tort Law*, 5th ed. (1993), pp. 521–522; while *Winfield & Jolowicz on Tort*, 14th ed. (1994), pp. 419–420 and *Markesinis & Deakin, Tort Law*, 3rd ed. (1994), pp. 434–435 would extend the right to long-term lodgers. *Salmond & Heuston on the Law of Torts*, 21st ed. (1996), p. 63, n. 96 and the New Zealand work *Todd, The Law of Torts in New Zealand*, 2nd ed. (1997), p. 537 suggest that the status of spouses under modern legislation should at least be enough; and the preface to the same edition of *Salmond & Heuston* goes further, by welcoming the decision in *Khorasandjian v Bush* [1993] Q.B. 727 as relieving plaintiffs in private nuisance cases of the need to show that they enjoyed a legal interest in the land affected."

However, in concluding his deliberations on this aspect of the appeal, Lord Cooke accepted that, irrespective of the assistance gleaned from the above sources, whether the approach advocated by the majority or that favoured by himself should be preferred was a question of the policy of the law. In this regard, his Lordship expressed, with clarity, the affinity which his approach bore to those values and matters that, in his opinion, should inform the policy of the law, and hence why that approach should be adopted. His Lordship opined (at 717–718):

"Although hitherto the law of England on the point has not been settled by your Lordship's House, it is agreed on all hands that some link with the land is necessary for standing to sue in private nuisance. The precise nature of that link remains to be defined, partly because of the ambiguity of 'occupy' and its derivatives. In ordinary usage the verb can certainly include 'reside in,' which is indeed the first meaning given in the *Concise Oxford Dictionary*.

In logic more than one answer can be given. Logically it is possible to say that the right to sue for interference with the amenities of a home should be confined to those with proprietary interests and licensees with exclusive possession. No less logically the right can be accorded to all who live in the home. Which test should be adopted, that is to say which should be the governing principle, is a question of the policy of the law. It is a question not capable of being answered by analysis alone. All that analysis can do is expose the alternatives. Decisions such as *Malone v Laskey* [1907] 2 K.B. 141 do not attempt that kind of analysis, and in refraining from recognising that value judgments are involved they compare less favourably with the approach of the present-day Court of Appeal in *Khorasandjian* and this case. The reason why I prefer the alternative advocated with unwonted vigour of expression by the doyen of living tort writers is that it gives better effect to widespread conceptions concerning the home and family.

Of course in this field as in most others there will be borderline cases and anomalies wherever the lines are drawn. Thus there are, for instance, the lodger and, as some of your Lordships note, the au pair girl (although she may not figure among the present plaintiffs). It would seem weak, though, to refrain from laying down a just rule for spouses and children on the ground that it is not easy to know where to draw the lines regarding other persons. Without being wedded to this solution, I am not persuaded that there is sufficient justification for disturbing the conclusion adopted by Pill L.J. with the concurrence of Neill and Waite L.JJ. *[in the Court of Appeal in the present case]*. Occupation of the property as a home is, to me, an acceptable criterion, consistent with the traditional concern for the sanctity of family life and the Englishman's home—which need not in this context include his workplace. As already mentioned, it is consistent also with international standards."

Thus, in short, Lord Cooke, as a matter of policy, took a broader view as to who might constitute an "occupier" than the majority, feeling that this was more in keeping with prevailing opinions and perceptions concerning the home and the family.

▶ 3. Conclusion

Within the realms of the law of torts, the immediate and obvious conclusion to be **8-007** drawn from the House of Lords' decision in *Hunter* is that the tort of private nuisance has been confirmed as fundamentally concerned with the protection of proprietary rights. This is an outcome which accords with its historical roots. It also reasserts the orthodoxy which had been challenged by the Court of Appeal both in *Khorasandjian* and *Hunter*; an orthodoxy which was adhered to subsequently, in a commercial context, by Judge Bowsher QC in the Technology and Construction Court (in the Queen's Bench Division of the High Court) in *Butcher Robinson & Staples Ltd v London Regional Transport* [1999] 36 E.G. 165.

However, in the context of this book, the House of Lords' decision in *Hunter* exhibits two particularly fascinating features—first, the markedly divergent views expressed by Lords Goff and Cooke about the assistance to be derived from certain court decisions in the United States and a collective of academic works to which they both referred, and, secondly, the willingness of Lord Cooke to recognise the influence which international standards embodied in the United Nations Convention on the Rights of the Child and the European Convention on Human Rights (Convention) may have on the shaping of the common law. In the latter respect, Lord Cooke acknowledged, as seen above (at 8–006), that the protection afforded to an individual may transcend possession or property rights, and that in cases such as *Hunter* this was "a legitimate consideration in support of treating residence as an acceptable basis of standing [i.e. *the right to sue*] at common law".

The question of the basis upon which the right to sue in nuisance should be determined was revisited, albeit obliquely, in the subsequent case of *McKenna v British Aluminium Ltd* [2002] Env. L.R. 30 (*McKenna*). In that case, which was heard after the HRA 1998 came into force, a number of individuals, who were resident proximate to the defendant's factory, instituted proceedings, inter alia, in private nuisance against the defendant. It was contended that, as a result of emissions and noise pollution from the defendant's factory and the consequent invasion of the claimants' privacy, the claimants had suffered mental distress and physical harm.

The defendant made an application to strike out the claims of those claimants, all children, who did not have a proprietary interest in their respective homes, and, in doing so, relied upon *Hunter*. It was argued for the "child" claimants that, in view of the undoubted interference with the claimants' enjoyment of their respective homes, the denial of a right to sue in nuisance in respect of that interference by the striking out of their claims would mean that effect was not given to art.8 of the Convention, which provides that "everyone has the right to respect for his private and family life, his home and his correspondence". It was suggested, therefore, that there was "at least an arguable case" that the court should, in accordance with its duty under s.6 of the HRA 1998 (see above, 5–010), develop the law to change this position and, thereby, to make the common law of private nuisance compatible with art.8. In his judgment, Neuberger J. acknowledged that it was the court's duty to develop the common law in a way that accommodated the principles enshrined in art.8, but he was unconvinced that it was appropriate to do this by extending a "property-based" claim such as private nuisance to cover claims such as those before the court in this case, i.e. for personal injury or personal damage. Nevertheless, Neuberger J.'s misgivings about the unsatisfactory position of the "child" claimants (whose claims, incidentally, he refused to strike out) are evident in the following extract (at 37):

"There is obviously a powerful case for saying that effect has not been properly given to Article 8.1 if a person with no interest in the home, but who has lived in the home for some time and had his enjoyment of the home interfered with, is at the mercy of the person who can bring the proceedings."

Further evidence of a human rights dimension is apparent in *Dobson v Thames Water Utilities* [2009] EWCA Civ 28. In this case, a group action for damages for negligence and nuisance and for damages under the HRA 1998 was instituted against Thames Water Utilities (Thames), a public authority. The claimants, who resided in the vicinity of a sewage treatment works for which Thames was responsible, complained that they had been affected by odours and mosquitoes coming from those works. Some claimants occupied properties as owners or lessees, whilst others occupied properties without any legal interest therein.

The significance of this case lies not in the Court of Appeal's endorsement of *Hunter* or in its award of damages in private nuisance to those claimants with a proprietary or possessory interest in affected land, but in its consideration of the possibility that the HRA 1998 may provide an alternative, limited, remedy for those without such an interest. Thus, if a public authority is responsible for interfering with a person's right to private and family life under art. 8 (as may be the case where there is an interference with amenity for the purpose of an action in private nuisance), an action will lie for breach of the public authority's obligations under s.6 HRA 1998 (see above, 5–010). However, as the Court of Appeal made clear, damages will only be awarded in such actions if this is necessary to afford just satisfaction to the claimant (see s.8 HRA 1998, above, 5–010). In the words of Waller L.J. [at 41]:

> ". . . where a public authority has been found to have acted 'unlawfully' the court 'may grant such relief or remedy. . .as it considers *just and appropriate*'. No award of *damages* is to be made unless, taking account of *all the circumstances* including any relief or remedy granted *in relation to the same act*, the court is satisfied that *the award is necessary* to afford *just satisfaction*."

One factor to be considered, therefore, in determining whether such an award of damages is necessary is whether those with a proprietary or possessory interest in the affected land have recovered damages for the interference in an action for private nuisance. In this respect, the pertinent question in *Dobson v Thames Water Utilities* was whether an award of damages in an action for private nuisance to the parents of a child thereby prevented the child in an action under s.6 of the HRA 1998 from recovering damages for breach of his rights under art.8. The Court of Appeal did not give a definitive answer to this particular question. Rather, it simply indicated that each case must be determined on its own facts, but also intimated that, where appropriate, an award of damages to those with a proprietary interest may well afford just satisfaction to other claimants. So it would seem that even if an action under s.6 of the HRA 1998 for the breach of rights under art.8 is sustainable, an award of damages is certainly not the inevitable outcome of that action, with the result that such an action is less appealing than one brought in private nuisance.

Further Reading

Cane, "What a nuisance!" (1997) 113 L.Q.R. 515

Howell, "The Human Rights Act 1998: Land, private citizens and the common law" (2007) 123 L.Q.R. 618

O'Sullivan, "Nuisance in the House of Lords—normal service resumed" [1997] C.L.J. 483

Tofaris, "Damages for sewage smells in nuisance and under the Human Rights Act 1998" [2009] C.L.J. 273

9 FALSE IMPRISONMENT, "DETENTION" AND THE MENTAL HEALTH ACT 1983

▶ 1. Introduction

The right not to be unlawfully detained, whether by another individual or by **9-001** organisations such as the police, the prison service or hospital authorities, is generally regarded as being one of the principal components of freedom within the law in a democratic society. The lawfulness or otherwise of detention, however, may not always be easy to ascertain, as can be seen in *R. v Bournewood Community and Mental Health NHS Trust Ex p. L* [1999] 1 A.C. 458 (*Bournewood*). In this case, L, aged 48, unable to speak, and with a severely limited level of understanding, had for over 30 years been a resident at Bournewood Hospital. He was incapable of expressing either consent or dissent to detention or to medical treatment. In 1994, although the hospital remained responsible for his care and treatment, he went to live with paid carers. In 1997, during one of his regular weekly attendances at a day centre, he became agitated. In the absence of his carers, who could not be immediately contacted, the day centre called out a local doctor who administered a sedative. L's social worker went to the day centre and, on her advice, L was taken by ambulance to Bournewood Hospital. Here he became increasingly agitated and was assessed by a psychiatrist who was "firmly of the view that he required in-patient treatment". Since L showed no desire to leave, the psychiatrist felt that it was unnecessary to compulsorily detain L under s.3 of the Mental Health Act 1983 (MHA 1983) and decided to admit him informally under s.131 of the MHA 1983. L was kept in an unlocked room, although the hospital would have compulsorily detained him had he made an attempt to leave.

Following a breakdown in relations with the hospital, L's carers, being of the view that he had been wrongfully detained, took legal action on L's behalf by instituting proceedings to secure his release and to obtain damages for the torts of false imprisonment (for his detention) and assault (for his medical treatment). The focus of the case was on the action for false imprisonment, rather than assault, and, for the action for false imprisonment to succeed, it was necessary to determine whether L had been detained and, if so, whether the detention was unlawful. The arguments on behalf of L and the Trust were essentially as follows:

It was argued on behalf of L that:

(a) he had been detained without his consent, because detention was a question of objective fact and there was evidence of detention, as L had not consented to his (informal) admission and was not free to leave; and

(b) his detention was unlawful, as: (i) the MHA 1983 contained a comprehensive statutory scheme, with formal compulsory admission criteria, for the admission, detention and treatment of mentally disordered patients who refuse their consent or who, like L, are incapable of giving their consent; and (ii) although s.131 of the MHA 1983 preserved the common law right for patients to be informally admitted, this preserved only the right to admit informally patients who consented. It did not preserve the right to admit patients incapable of giving their consent and to detain them under the common law doctrine or principle of necessity (under which action, considered necessary because it was impracticable to communicate with a person, could be justified if it was in his best interests).

It was argued on behalf of the Bournewood Community and Mental Health NHS Trust (the Trust) that:

(a) L had not been detained without his consent, as he had been informally admitted to the hospital without dissenting to admission, had remained there without restraint and had simply not chosen to leave; and
(b) (alternatively) if L had been detained, his detention was not unlawful, as: (i) L had been informally admitted and the statutory scheme under the MHA 1983 applied only to patients formally admitted and compulsorily detained because they refuse their consent; and (ii) s.131 of the MHA 1983 preserved the right to admit not only patients who consented to informal admission, but also patients who were incapable of giving their consent and the latter could be detained under the common law doctrine of necessity if such action was in their best interests.

In the High Court, Owen J. dismissed L's claims, taking the view that L had not been detained and that any detention (and treatment) would not have been unlawful as it could be justified under the common law doctrine of necessity. The Court of Appeal allowed L's appeal and took a contrary view. Not only had L been detained, but also the detention was unlawful: detention could be lawful only under the MHA 1983 and could not be justified under the common law doctrine of necessity. On appeal by the Trust to the House of Lords, the Court of Appeal's decision was reversed and the House held that L had not been unlawfully detained. On the question of whether L had been detained, members of the House differed in their view—a three to two majority held that L had not been detained—but, on the question of whether the Trust had acted unlawfully, were unanimous in their view that it had not. For the majority, L's treatment whilst in hospital could be justified under the common law doctrine of necessity and, for the minority, both detention and treatment could similarly be justified.

 This case study illustrates several points in relation to precedent and statutory interpretation:

> ▶ how courts may seek assistance from a dictionary definition of a word, and the potential problems of this approach;

- how courts may seek assistance from apparently analogous areas of the law when considering the meaning of a word or concept;

- reference to a case from another jurisdiction as an aid to statutory interpretation;

- consideration of the views expressed by authors in textbooks;

- use of marginal notes (or sidenotes) to a section as an aid to statutory construction;

- reference to one subsection of an Act in order to assist the interpretation of another subsection;

- reference to an earlier legislative provision containing identical language when interpreting a provision and whether there should be a departure from the meaning given to the earlier provision;

- policy considerations concerning a decision and its potential social, political and economic impact, evidenced by submissions received, with leave of the court, from interested bodies who were not parties to the proceedings;

- reference to the report of a Royal Commission to indicate the mischief at which subsequent legislation, based on the report, was aimed;

- reference to Government White Papers and ministerial statements as indicators of the intention of Parliament in enacting legislation;

- distinguishing a case;

- the broad or narrow view of the ratio of a case; and

- a consideration by the European Court of Human Rights as to whether rights under an Article of the European Convention on Human Rights had been violated.

▶ 2. The Decision of the High Court

In the High Court, Owen J. (whose judgment is not reported, but extracts from which are contained in judgments in the Court of Appeal and House of Lords) held that there had been no detention of L, who had been free to leave, and that the decision to "detain" and treat him was not unlawful. **9–002**

▷ *(a) Detention*

In deciding that L had not been detained, his Lordship considered the meaning of "detention" by making reference to a dictionary definition of the term and by drawing an analogy with the position of a person in a different area of the law, that of a suspect attending a police station: **9–003**

> "Detention is defined (*Oxford English Dictionary*) as kept in confinement or custody. I agree that if in fact [L] has been detained it matters not whether he

knows it or not but there must be some restraint within defined bounds. In some ways the position may be likened to that when a suspect attends a police station to 'help with police inquiries.' At that stage he is not detained although detention might follow on very quickly after an indication by the suspect that he was leaving. Likewise, only more strongly, here it can be said that [*L*] has at all times been free to leave because that is a consequence of an informal admission, and he will continue to be free to leave until Dr. Manjubhashini [*the psychiatrist who admitted L*] or somebody else takes steps to section him [*i.e. detain him compulsorily under the MHA 1983*] or otherwise prevent him leaving. In other words there will be no restraint of [*L*] until he has attempted to leave and [*the trust*], by its agent, has done something to prevent this."

Two points may be made concerning Owen J.'s approach to determining the meaning of "detention". First, in the absence of a clearly applicable and accepted legal meaning for the word, reference to a dictionary definition may appear an appropriate course. However, this may give rise to difficulties or uncertainty. Whilst his Lordship adopted the first-mentioned meaning of "detention" given in the *Oxford English Dictionary* (OED) of "keeping in custody or confinement", he went on to qualify this, as can be seen above, by adding a requirement that "there must be some restraint within defined bounds". (No mention was made by his Lordship on this point of *Meering v Grahame-White Aviation Co Ltd* (1919) 122 L.T. 44 (*Meering*), which contains a reference to such restraint and which was considered by the Court of Appeal—see below, 9–006.) He did not refer to further meanings given in the OED of "keeping in a place; holding in one's possession or control; retention". These meanings might perhaps be thought to have particular application to the meaning of "detention" in law, since they are described in the dictionary as "obsolete *except in Law*" (emphasis supplied). Had the meaning "holding in one's possession or control" been adopted, rather than "keeping in custody or confinement", no qualification of "restraint within defined bounds" may have been required. Such qualification suggests the need for some ascertainable physical boundaries, but it may be that a "holding in one's possession or control" of a person is possible without any such boundaries. Adoption of an alternative meaning contained in the OED (or, indeed, adoption of a definition contained in a different dictionary) might therefore have led Owen J. to a different conclusion. Reliance on a dictionary definition will thus not necessarily prove conclusive when seeking to ascertain the meaning of a word in a particular context.

Secondly, it may be questioned whether Owen J.'s analogy with the questioning of suspects by the police provides support for his view that L had not been detained. The phrase "help with police inquiries" used by Owen J. referred to a practice developed historically by the police to avoid restrictions on the questioning of suspects following arrest. It was based on the premise that a suspect had not been arrested, but was voluntarily answering questions in the police station. However, since the Police and Criminal Evidence Act 1984, to which Owen J. did not refer, the position of the "volunteer" member of the public has been clearly set out in s.29. This provides that such a person "shall be entitled to leave at will unless he is placed under arrest" and "he shall be informed at once that he is under arrest if a decision is taken by a constable to prevent him from leaving at will". A person is thus not to be regarded as voluntarily at the police station from the moment at which a decision is made that he would be prevented from leaving if he were to attempt to do so. He is regarded as arrested (detained) from the moment of that decision, even though the suspect has not attempted to leave and nothing has been done to implement the decision to prevent him. If the position of L is considered analogous, this might suggest that L *was* detained and should have been so regarded. Yet this was not the conclusion reached by Owen J., since his Lordship stated that "there will be no restraint [*and therefore no detention*] of L. until he has attempted to leave and [the trust], by its agent, has done something to prevent this".

▷ *(b) Unlawful detention (and treatment)*

Owen J. held that L had not been unlawfully "detained" and treated because he **9–004** had been admitted as an informal patient under s.131(1) of the MHA 1983: this section preserved the common law jurisdiction in respect of informal patients, and admission, detention and treatment could be justified under the common law doctrine of necessity. Section 131(1) provides:

> "Nothing in this Act shall be construed as preventing a patient who requires treatment for mental disorder from being admitted to any hospital or registered establishment in pursuance of arrangements made in that behalf and without any application, order or direction rendering him liable to be detained under this Act, or from remaining in any hospital or registered establishment in pursuance of such arrangements after he has ceased to be so liable to be detained."

Although the section itself makes no reference to informal admission, it is clear from the marginal note (or sidenote) to the section, which states "Informal admission of patients", that it is this with which the section is concerned. The section essentially provides that the MHA 1983 does not prevent a patient from being informally admitted ("Nothing in this Act shall be construed as preventing a patient . . . from being admitted . . .") to a hospital or registered establishment, even though there is no formal application for compulsory detention (". . . without any application, order or direction rendering him liable to be detained . . .") made under the provisions of the Act. In his Lordship's view, if the Act did not prevent informal admission and informal admission might take place outside the Act, admission, detention and treatment might be justified under the common law doctrine of necessity. The Act provided a comprehensive statutory regime only for patients formally admitted (and compulsorily detained). It did not apply to those informally admitted, such as L, and L's detention and treatment could be, and were, justified on the basis of necessity. Accordingly, Owen J. concluded that his detention and treatment were not unlawful.

Whilst what has been set out above gives some indication of his Lordship's approach, it gives no more than a general indication. The High Court's decision is unreported and this leaves a number of matters unclear. These include: (i) which (if any) aids to statutory interpretation were taken into account when construing the provision in s.131; (ii) which (if any) of the various case law authorities, as mentioned in the judgments of the Court of Appeal and House of Lords (see below, 9–005– 9–010), were considered; or (iii) which (if any) policy considerations (see below, 9–011) were taken into account.

▶ ## 3. The Decision of the Court of Appeal

9–005 The Court of Appeal, allowing L's appeal, held that L had been detained, his detention was unlawful and could not be justified under the common law doctrine of necessity.

▷ ## *(a) Detention*

9–006 Certainly, in the view of the Court of Appeal, L had been detained in fact and the following description of "the *de facto* detained", contained in Hoggett, *Mental Health Law*, 4th edn (1996), p.9 was considered by Lord Woolf, M.R. (at 464), delivering the judgment of the Court of Appeal, to be a description that "aptly fits L":

> ". . . those elderly or severely disabled patients, who are unable to exercise any genuine choice, but who do not exhibit active dissent which provokes professionals to invoke the compulsory procedures."

Whether L had been detained as a matter of law, however, was, as his Lordship acknowledged (at 465), "no easy question". Although citing the section in Owen J.'s judgment referring to a dictionary definition of "detention" and the analogy with a suspect giving "help with police enquiries" (see above, 9–003), this was referred to by Lord Woolf, M.R. only as a prelude to stating (at 466) that the court "did not consider that the judge was correct to conclude that L was 'free to leave'". Lord Woolf, M.R. gave no consideration to either a dictionary definition or the analogy referred to by Owen J. Rather, his Lordship focused attention on a lengthy passage from the judgment of Atkin L.J. in the Court of Appeal in *Meering v Grahame-White Aviation Co Ltd* (1919) 122 L.T. 44 at 53–54, which had been approved by Lord Griffiths in the House of Lords in *Murray v Ministry of Defence* [1988] 1 W.L.R. 692 at 701–702, of which the following is a truncated version:

> "It appears to me that a person could be imprisoned without his knowing it . . . So a man might in fact, to my mind, be imprisoned by having the key of a door turned against him so that he is imprisoned in a room in fact although he does not know that the key has been turned . . . If a man can be imprisoned by

having the key turned upon him without his knowledge, so he can be imprisoned if, instead of a lock and key or bolts and bars, he is prevented from, in fact, exercising his liberty by guards and warders or policemen. They serve the same purpose. Therefore it appears to me to be a question of fact. It is true that in all cases of imprisonment so far as the law of civil liability is concerned that 'stone walls do not a prison make,' in the sense that they are not the only form of imprisonment, but any restraint within defined bounds which is a restraint in fact may be an imprisonment."

It is clear from this passage that whether a person is detained is a matter of objective fact which does not depend on the presence or absence of consent or knowledge on his part. The passage, in this respect, formed part of the ratio of *Meering* (a point not referred to by Lord Woolf, M.R.), since that case was concerned with a person who was persuaded by works personnel at his place of employment to remain in an office until he was called to be seen, unaware that he was there pending the arrival of the police and unaware that he would have been prevented from leaving had he tried to do so. However, it is less clear that Atkin L.J.'s concluding statement in the passage, that "any restraint within defined bounds which is a restraint in fact may be an imprisonment" is part of the ratio. Whilst it was necessary to determine that there had (as a matter of objective fact) been a detention, whether a restraint needed to be "within defined bounds" to constitute detention was not a point which the court in *Meering* had to determine. Detention within the office clearly would have been within defined bounds and the statement may therefore be only obiter. Nevertheless, Lord Woolf, M.R. appeared to treat the passage not only as establishing that detention was a question of objective fact, but also as indicative of what might constitute detention.

No consideration was given by Lord Woolf, M.R. to the meaning of "restraint within defined bounds" and "restraint in fact" and his Lordship (at 465) moved on immediately to give his own understanding of the meaning of detention:

"In our judgment a person is detained in law if those who have control over the premises in which he is have the intention that he shall not be permitted to leave those premises and have the ability to prevent him from leaving".

As to how this legal meaning of "detention" applied to the facts of L's stay in hospital, Lord Woolf, M.R. thought it evident that those at the hospital with responsibility for L had no intention of allowing him to leave and could, and would, have prevented him from doing so. The consultant psychiatrist responsible for L's care, when dealing with L's admission, had stated in her affidavit (referred to by Lord Woolf, M.R. at 466): "If [L.] had resisted admission I would certainly have detained him under the Act as I was firmly of the view that he required in-patient treatment". Further, various letters written to L's carers by the psychiatrist indicated an unwillingness to permit L to return to his carers and these led his Lordship to conclude (at 467):

> "It is clear that the hospital was not prepared to countenance this. If they were not prepared to release L. into the custody of his carers they were not prepared to let him leave the hospital at all. He was and is detained there".

▷ *(b) Unlawful detention*

9–007 When considering whether detention might lawfully take place only under the MHA 1983 or whether, in the case of persons informally admitted, it might lawfully take place under the common law doctrine of necessity, Lord Woolf, M.R. examined both judicial statements concerning the MHA 1983 and the provision in s.131 itself. The judicial statements were contained in four cases, three English decisions and a Scottish decision concerning the Mental Health Act (Scotland) 1984, the Scottish equivalent of the MHA 1983. When examining and interpreting s.131(1) itself, his Lordship had regard to the provision in s.131(2) and to a White Paper reviewing previous mental health legislation.

In none of the three English cases was it necessary to decide whether a patient suffering from mental disorder, informally admitted to hospital for treatment of the disorder, could be detained under the common law doctrine of necessity. The cases were not therefore directly in point. Consequently, all were distinguishable and each could have been distinguished. Any statements in the cases concerning the circumstances which could give rise to lawful detention need not therefore have been followed, even if part of the ratio of the case. The ratio of a case is not binding on *any* court if the decision is distinguishable. Nor, indeed, is it clear that the statements regarding detention in the cases did form part of the ratio of the decisions and they may well have been only obiter. Further, there were in fact no *express* statements in the cases that detention could only be justified under the MHA 1983 and not, where there was an informal admission (without consent), under the common law doctrine of necessity. Rather, the cases contained statements from which Lord Woolf, M.R. *inferred* that this was the position. It will be seen from what has been said above that the three cases to which Lord Woolf, M.R. referred were not particularly persuasive as authorities.

The first case was *Re S-C (Mental Patient: Habeas Corpus)* [1996] Q.B. 599 (*S-C, Re*) and reference was made by Lord Woolf, M.R. (at 470) to the following statement of Sir Thomas Bingham, M.R. in the Court of Appeal in that case:

> "no adult citizen of the United Kingdom is liable to be confined in any institution against his will, save by the authority of law. That is a fundamental constitutional principle, traceable back to chapter 29 of Magna Carta 1297 (25 Edw. 1, c. 1), and before that to chapter 39 of Magna Carta 1215 (9 Hen. 3). There are, of course, situations in which the law sanctions detention. The most obvious is in the case of those suspected or convicted of crime. Powers then exist to arrest and detain. But the conditions in which those powers may be exercised are very closely prescribed by statute and the common law . . .

mental patients present a special problem since they may be liable, as a result of mental illness, to cause injury either to themselves or others. . . . Powers therefore exist to ensure that those who suffer from mental illness may, in appropriate circumstances, be involuntarily admitted to mental hospitals and detained. But, and it is a very important but, the circumstances in which the mentally ill may be detained are very carefully prescribed by statute. Action may only be taken if there is clear evidence that the medical condition of the patient justifies such action, and there are detailed rules prescribing the classes of person who may apply to a hospital to admit and detain a mentally disordered person."

The case of *S-C, Re*, as Lord Woolf, M.R. acknowledged (at 470), concerned the lawfulness of the *compulsory* detention of a patient in a mental hospital—the patient in this instance had been formally admitted and detained under the MHA 1983, unlike in the case of L, who had been admitted as an informal patient—and "no contention was advanced that this was justified at common law under the principle of necessity". "None the less, we think it clear", his Lordship stated (at 470), "that Sir Thomas Bingham M.R. considered that it was statute and statute alone that provided authority for a hospital to detain a mental patient".

It might be felt that the statement provides little in the way of persuasive authority for detention being justified only under statute and not under the common law doctrine of necessity. Certainly, had Lord Woolf, M.R. been minded to take a contrary view, it would not have been difficult to be dismissive of the statement. First, as mentioned above, the case was distinguishable. Secondly, the statement would not appear to be part of the ratio of the case. The case was concerned with whether a person might be compulsorily detained where one of the (procedural) requirements under the MHA 1983 had not been complied with and it was not therefore necessary to determine whether or not the statute provided the sole authority for detention. The statement could have been regarded as containing merely general observations in respect of the detention of mentally disordered persons (cf. the view taken by Lord Steyn in the nervous shock case of *White* in respect of remarks by Lord Oliver in *Alcock* concerning "participants" as primary victims—see Chapter 15, 15–018). The observations of Sir Thomas Bingham, M.R., made in the context of a person being detained against his will, refer only to mentally disordered persons as an instance of the law sanctioning such detention. Although referring to the circumstances in which the mentally ill may be detained being carefully prescribed by statute in this instance, the statement does not (expressly) indicate that detention can *only* be prescribed by statute. This is the inference drawn by Lord Woolf, M.R., but it is not the only inference that might be drawn. Where detention does take place by statute, the circumstances may be carefully prescribed, but this does not necessarily mean that detention might not be justified in other circumstances, e.g. outside the scope of the statutory provisions under the common law doctrine of necessity. Either inference might be drawn from what can only be described as a very general statement by Sir Thomas Bingham, M.R., which makes no reference to the legislation's provisions (or even its title), the position of informally admitted patients or the common law doctrine of necessity. Indeed, it is perhaps indicative of the statement's lack of persuasive weight that, when the case was heard in the House of Lords (which reached a contrary conclusion to the Court of Appeal), none of their Lordships made any reference to it (see below, 9–010).

The second case was *Re F (Mental Patient: Sterilisation), Re* [1990] 2 A.C. 1 (*Re F*), which was concerned with the lawfulness of an operation of sterilisation carried out on a mentally disordered patient residing in a mental hospital, and reference was made by Lord Woolf, M.R. to observations of Lord Brandon in the House of Lords. It was implicit in these observations, in the view of Lord Woolf, M.R., that the MHA 1983 alone provided authority for the detention of a patient for treatment for mental disorder. The observations to which reference was made included a statement by Lord Brandon that, whilst the MHA 1983 makes provision for the treatment of patients for conditions relating to their mental disorder:

> "The Act, however, does not contain any provisions relating to the giving of treatment to patients for any conditions other than their mental disorder [*e.g. a sterilisation operation, as in the case itself*]. The result is that the lawfulness of giving any treatment of the latter kind depends not on statute but the common law."

Lord Brandon went on to say that treatment could lawfully be given where patients were incapable of giving consent and where the medical treatment was in the best interests of such patients. It would be because such treatment could be justified in these circumstances under the common law doctrine of necessity that it would be lawful (although no mention was made of this by Lord Brandon). Whilst this does recognise the application of the doctrine in respect of patients suffering from mental disorder, it does so only with regard to treatment given to them for a condition *not relating to* their mental disorder. In L's case, the treatment given *did* relate to mental disorder and Lord Woolf (at 471) went on to refer to the following observations made by Lord Brandon in respect of such treatment:

> "In the case of adult patients suffering from mental disability, they will normally, in accordance with the scheme of the Mental Health Act 1983, be either in the care of guardians, who will refer them to doctors for medical treatment, or of doctors at mental hospitals in which the patients either reside voluntarily or are detained compulsorily. It will then again be the duty of the doctors concerned to use their best endeavours to do, by way of either an operation or other treatment, that which is in the best interests of such patients."

Lord Woolf, M.R. went on to remark (at 471):

> "It appears that Lord Brandon was only contemplating two situations in which normally a person would be an in-patient in a mental hospital: one where there was consent and the second where the statute had been invoked."

The inference drawn here from Lord Brandon's remarks is that patients either "reside voluntarily" in mental hospitals or they are "detained compulsorily" under the MHA 1983 (and cannot be detained under the common law doctrine of necessity). These remarks of Lord Brandon, however, would appear not to be part of the ratio of the case. There is nothing to indicate that the basis upon which the patient in *Re F* was residing in the hospital, that is, whether the patient was there as a result of an informal admission or a compulsory detention, was a material fact in the decision. The observations, from which the inference was drawn, would thus seem to be only obiter.

The third case to which Lord Woolf, M.R. referred was *R. v Kirklees MBC Ex p. C* [1993] 2 F.L.R. 187 (*Kirklees*), a case in which the applicant sought, inter alia, damages for false imprisonment following the decision of the local authority, into whose care she had been taken, to give consent for her admission to hospital for assessment of her mental condition. (Consent had been given by the local authority because the applicant, a girl aged 12, was incapable of giving consent herself.) The Court of Appeal, where judgments were delivered by Lloyd and Stuart-Smith L.JJ. (with which Farquharson L.J. agreed), held that there had been no false imprisonment, since a person might at common law be informally admitted, with consent, for assessment and the authority was entitled to give the consent. Although s.131 of the MHA 1983 referred only to the informal admission of patients for treatment, and preserved the common law in this respect, admission for assessment nevertheless continued to be lawful at common law. In reaching this decision, in the view of Lord Woolf, M.R. (at 471):

> "Lloyd and Stuart-Smith L.JJ. both presupposed that either a patient would be admitted for treatment under section 3 [*of the MHA 1983, which provides for compulsory admission*] or he would be a voluntary patient, that is a patient who had himself consented or in respect of whom, if he lacked the ability to consent, someone else had given consent on his behalf".

Again, the inference drawn here by Lord Woolf, M.R. is that patients are either detained when compulsorily admitted under the MHA 1983 or are admitted with consent, i.e. there can be lawful detention only under the MHA 1983 and not under the common law doctrine of necessity. Since it was not necessary in *Kirklees* to determine whether this was the case, any statements or inferences to this effect would not appear to be part of the ratio of the case and would only be obiter.

The final case to which Lord Woolf, M.R. referred (at 472), *B v Forsey* [1988] S.L.T. 572, was, in his Lordship's view, "the most relevant". This was a decision of the House of Lords, but from another jurisdiction, Scotland, which meant that it was only of persuasive authority for the Court of Appeal, albeit highly persuasive. The case, involving a consideration of the Mental Health (Scotland) Act 1984, the Scottish equivalent of the MHA 1983, was regarded as directly in point. It was concerned with whether the continued detention in hospital of a patient for treatment for mental disorder, beyond the expiry of a period of compulsory detention under the 1984 Act (whilst an application was made for a further period of compulsory detention), could be justified under the common law doctrine of necessity. The House of Lords held that it could not be so justified. Referring to this case, Lord Woolf, M.R. stated (at 472):

> "Lord Keith of Kinkel accepted that at common law an individual had power to detain a mentally disordered person in the case of necessity but he rejected the contention that the doctors were in the same position. He said, at p.576:
>
> > 'I am of opinion that it is impossible to reach any other conclusion than that the powers of detention conferred upon hospital authorities by the [*statutory*] scheme were intended to be exhaustive . . .'
>
> The Scottish legislation has an equivalent provision to section 131 of the Act of 1983 but Lord Keith regarded the provisions of the Scottish legislation comparable to those dealing with statutory provisions under the Act of 1983 as being 'absolutely inconsistent with a possible view that the legislature intended that a hospital authority should have a common law power to detain a patient otherwise than in accordance with the statutory scheme:' see p.576. He added:
>
> > 'That scheme contains a number of safeguards designed to protect the liberty of the individual. It is not conceivable that the legislature, in prohibiting any successive period of detention under provisions containing such safeguards, should have intended to leave open the possibility of successive periods of detention not subject to such safeguards. I would therefore hold that any common law power of detention which a hospital authority might otherwise have possessed has been impliedly removed.'"

Whilst this statement seems to have been regarded as part of the ratio of the decision, it was not, as a case from another jurisdiction, binding on the court. It was, however, highly persuasive and Lord Woolf, M.R., although recognising that the common law powers in Scotland are not necessarily the same as those in England, concluded (at 472) that "there appears to be no justification for not applying the logic of Lord Keith's reasoning to the position in England". Accordingly:

> ". . . the right of a hospital to detain a patient for treatment for mental disorder is to be found in, and only in, the Act of 1983, whose provisions apply to the exclusion of the common law principle of necessity".

Having reviewed the cases which he felt supported this view, Lord Woolf, M.R. (at 473) proceeded to consider the provision in s.131 of the MHA 1983 (which is set out above at 9–004):

> "Section 131, which preserves the right to admit a patient informally, addresses the position of a patient who is admitted and treated with consent. This seems implicit from the wording of section 131(2)."

By considering another provision in the Act, s.131(2), his Lordship adopted one of the principal aids to statutory interpretation, that of having regard to intrinsic material within a statute, by examining as a whole a section of the Act when considering the meaning of a particular provision within the section. Section 131(1) was interpreted having regard to s.131(2) (cited by Lord Woolf, M.R. earlier in his judgment and set out below as it was then worded), which is concerned with the admission to hospital of children who are capable of giving their consent:

> "In the case of a minor who has attained the age of 16 years and is capable of expressing his own wishes, any such arrangements as are mentioned in sub-section (1) above may be made, carried out and determined even though there are one or more persons who have parental responsibility for him (within the meaning of the Children Act 1989)."

That s.131(2) provides for the informal admission of a minor competent to give consent, even where those with parental responsibility may prefer him not to be admitted, suggested to Lord Woolf, M.R. that s.131(1) should similarly be interpreted to include only informal admissions of adult patients with their consent. This would accordingly exclude the case of a patient such as L, who, although informally admitted, was not admitted with consent and who was incapable of dissenting from his detention.

His Lordship found further support for his conclusion, that s.131 permitted only informal admission with consent, in a Government White Paper, *Review of the Mental Health Act 1959* (Cmnd. 7320), published in 1978. Although this was reviewing an earlier legislative enactment than the MHA 1983, the relevant provision in the 1959 Act (s.5(1)) had been re-enacted in s.131 without any change in wording and, Lord Woolf, M.R. stated (at 473), "the position was accurately stated" in the following paragraphs of the document:

> "1.5 It may be helpful to set out the position of informal patients as the government sees it. An informal patient enters hospital on his doctor's advice to receive the care and treatment he is advised is necessary or desirable and he will normally stay in hospital until discharged by the consultant. These are voluntary acts on his part. He can insist on leaving hospital if he wishes and can decline to accept a particular form or course of treatment. If he does so the consultant may, of course, refuse to continue to accept responsibility for treating him but that does not affect the patient's right to insist on leaving or to refuse treatment.
>
> 1.6 There is nothing in the Act which authorises or implies that an informal patient may be compelled without his consent to enter hospital or to receive treatment."

In Lord Woolf, M.R.'s view, this indicated that an informal patient was one who consented to admission and treatment, and s.131 did not authorise or imply that a patient who did not consent could (under compulsion) be admitted, detained and treated.

By taking into account the above document when interpreting the provision in s.131(1), his Lordship thus had regard to material extrinsic to the MHA 1983 (in addition, through reference to s.131(2), to intrinsic material—see above). Government White Papers, which often precede the introduction of legislation, are one of a wide range of pre-Parliamentary publications to which courts may refer, as extrinsic material, when seeking to ascertain Parliamentary intention, although, as mentioned in Chapter 1, 1–086, there have been differing views as to their place in the process of statutory interpretation. Although indicating Parliamentary intention in respect of an earlier legislative provision, s.5(1) of the MHA 1959, the White Paper might also be taken to indicate Parliamentary intention in relation to s.131 of the MHA 1983: in enacting an identically worded provision Parliament could be taken to intend that its meaning should remain unchanged.

In concluding his reference to the White Paper, Lord Woolf, M.R. remarked (at 473):

> "The trust has admitted L. and is detaining him for treatment for mental disorder without his consent and without the formalities required by the Act of 1983. It follows that they have acted and are acting unlawfully."

Before concluding his judgment, Lord Woolf M.R. (at 474) went on to express disapproval of the views expressed in "authoritative textbooks", which supported an interpretation of the Act (advocated by the Trust) which enabled patients informally admitted without their consent to be (lawfully) detained:

> "A troubling feature of this appeal is that the trust is not alone in mis-interpreting the affect [sic] of the Act. Apparently there could be many patients, especially those suffering from dementia, who are in the same position as L. This is no doubt partly a consequence of opinions expressed in the authoritative textbooks which support what has happened in this case: *Hoggett, Mental Health Law* [4th edn (1996)], p. 9 and *Jones, Mental Health Act Manual*, 5th ed., (1996), p. 340. We have differed from those opinions. The current practice cannot justify a disregard of the Act. This is especially true because of the undesirable consequences which can follow a practice which bypasses the safeguards which the Act provides for patients who are statutorily detained."

Although works of academic authors might be cited by judges with approval as persuasive authority analogous to persuasive precedents (see Chapter 1, 1–034), equally they might, as here, be disapproved. This may be so notwithstanding the particular eminence of the academic commentator, as where authors might themselves be members of the judiciary and their views constitute extra-judicial statements. Such was the case in this instance as regards the author of one of the texts to which Lord Woolf, M.R. referred. Professor Brenda Hoggett, after a distinguished academic career had, in 1994, as Mrs Justice Hale, become the first High Court judge to be appointed from a non-practising background.

▶ 4. The House of Lords

9–008 The House of Lords decided by a 3–2 majority that L had not been detained, but was unanimously of the view that the Trust had not acted unlawfully. For the majority, L's treatment whilst in hospital could be justified under the common law doctrine of necessity and, for the minority, both detention and treatment could similarly be justified.

▷ (a) Detention

9–009 When considering the meaning of "detention" for the purposes of the tort of false imprisonment, Lord Goff, with whose judgment Lords Lloyd and Hope agreed, emphasised (at 486) that "there must *in fact* be a complete deprivation of, or restraint upon, the plaintiff's liberty". This was a necessary requirement of the tort which, in his Lordship's view, was missing from the Court of Appeal's statement that "a person is detained in law if those who have control over the premises in which he is have the intention that he shall not be permitted to leave those premises and have the ability to prevent him from leaving" (see above, 9–006). In respect of this requirement, Lord Goff stated (at 486):

> ". . . the law is clear. As Atkin L.J. said in *Meering v Grahame-White Aviation Co. Ltd* (1919) 122 L.T. 44, 54, "any restraint within defined bounds which is a restraint in fact may be an imprisonment." Furthermore, it is well settled that the deprivation of liberty must be actual, rather than potential. Thus in *Syed Mahamad Yusuf-ud-Din v Secretary of State for India* (1903) 19 T.L.R. 496, 497 Lord Macnaughten said that: "Nothing short of actual detention and complete loss of freedom would support an action for false imprisonment." And in the *Meering* case, 122 L.T. 44, 54–55 Atkin L.J. was careful to draw a distinction between restraint upon the plaintiff's liberty which is conditional upon his seeking to exercise his freedom (which would not amount to false imprisonment), and an actual restraint upon his liberty, as where the defendant decided to restrain the plaintiff within a room and placed a policeman outside the door to stop him leaving (which would amount to false imprisonment)."

That the Court of Appeal had adopted a meaning of "detention" which failed to have regard to the need for an actual restraint (established by case law) seemed to bring a mild rebuke from Lord Goff, who stated (at 486):

> "In cases such as the present it is, I consider, important that the courts should have regard to the ingredients of the tort as laid down in the decided cases,

> and consider whether those ingredients are in fact found to exist on the particular facts of the case in question."

Lord Goff's approach was in contrast to that taken by Lords Nolan and Steyn, who expressed agreement with the view of the Court of Appeal that there had been a detention. When considering the question of "detention", Lord Nolan made reference neither to a dictionary definition nor to any decided cases. After quoting from a letter from the hospital psychiatrist to L's carers, and the Court of Appeal's reference to other letters, together with its conclusion that L "was and is detained there", his Lordship confined himself to remarking (at 492) that "with that conclusion too I agree". Lord Steyn, referring (at 495) only briefly to *Meering* in his concluding remarks on the question of "detention", similarly gave no detailed consideration to what might constitute "detention", stating (at 494–495):

> "It is unnecessary to attempt a comprehensive definition of detention. In my view, this case falls on the wrong side of any reasonable line that can be drawn between what is or what is not imprisonment or detention . . . Counsel for the trust . . . argued that L. was in truth always free not to go to the hospital and subsequently to leave the hospital. This argument stretches credulity to breaking point. The truth is that for entirely bona fide reasons, conceived in the best interests of L., any possible resistance by him was overcome by sedation, by taking him to hospital, and by close supervision of him in hospital. And, if L. had shown any sign of wanting to leave, he would have been firmly discouraged by staff and, if necessary, physically prevented from doing so. The suggestion that L. was free to go is a fairy tale . . . In my view L. was detained because the health care professionals intentionally assumed control over him to such a degree as to amount to complete deprivation of liberty."

In reaching the conclusion that L had been detained, Lord Steyn (at 495) alluded to various actions taken by the health care professionals in relation to L. These included L being "regularly sedated" by hospital staff to ensure that he "remained tractable" and nurses "were instructed to keep him under continuous observation and did so". In contrast, Lord Goff, in deciding that L had not been detained, made no reference to any such actions.

▷ *(b) Unlawful detention*

9–010 Although the House of Lords had been divided on the question of whether or not L had been detained, it was unanimous in its view that the Trust had not acted unlawfully (per the majority) in treating L whilst in hospital and (per the minority) in detaining and treating him. It was held that s.131 of the MHA 1983 permitted the informal admission to hospital and treatment of patients incapable of giving consent, where this was justified by the common law doctrine of necessity. This aspect of the case was considered only by Lords Goff and Steyn, for Lord Nolan expressed agreement in this respect with the judgment of Lord Goff.

Lord Goff, rather illogically, considered this aspect of the case before the issue of L's detention, an approach which appeared to attract some judicial criticism from Lord Steyn, who stated (at 494):

> "If instead one turns straight away to the lawfulness of the conduct of a defendant, one is not concentrating on the right question, namely *whether conduct which as a matter of fact amounts to detention or imprisonment is justified in law.* . .. To start with an inquiry into the lawfulness of conduct, or to conflate the two issues, is contrary to legal principle and authority. And such an approach tends to erode legal principles fashioned for the protection of the liberty of the individual."

When considering the meaning of s.131 and how it should be interpreted, both Lords Goff and Steyn made reference to its statutory history, since the provision was expressed in identical terms to an earlier statutory provision, s.5(1) of the Mental Health Act 1959 (MHA 1959). Consideration was given, first, to the meaning of that provision and, secondly, to whether, in the light of substantial amendments made to the MHA 1959 by the Mental Health (Amendment) Act 1982, a different meaning should be given to s.131. When considering the meaning of s.5(1), reference was made both by Lords Goff and Steyn to the Report of the *Royal Commission on the Law Relating to Mental Illness and Mental Deficiency* (the Percy Commission) which preceded the MHA 1959 and (in the case of Lord Goff) to ministerial statements during the passage of that legislation. In their Lordships' view, these indicated Parliament's intention that patients should, where possible, be informally admitted, rather than compulsorily detained under the Act, and informal admission could take place and be justified where a person was incapable of consenting under the common law doctrine of necessity. Thus, Lord Goff stated (at 483–484):

> ". . . the Percy Commission . . . recommended that compulsory detention should only be employed in cases where it was necessary to do so. The Percy Commission's views, and recommendations, on this point are to be found at pp.100–101, paras. 289–291 of their Report, which read:
>
> > ". . . 291. We therefore recommend that the law and its administration should be altered, in relation to all forms of mental disorder, by abandoning the assumption that compulsory powers must be used unless the patient can express a positive desire for treatment, and replacing this by the offer of care, without deprivation of liberty, to all who need it and are not unwilling to receive it. All hospitals providing psychiatric treatment should be free to admit patients for any length of time without any legal formality and without power to detain."
>
> Here we find a central recommendation of the Percy Commission and the mischief which it was designed to cure. This recommendation was implemented, in particular, by section 5(1) of the Act of 1959. That the Bill was introduced with that recommendation in mind is confirmed by ministerial

statements made in Parliament at the time: see Hansard (H.L.Debates, 4 June 1959, cols. 668–669).

Following the enactment of the Act of 1959, section 5(1) was duly implemented in the manner foreshadowed by the Percy Commission, a practice which . . . has been continued under section 131 of the Act of 1983, which is in identical terms."

Similarly, Lord Steyn stated (at 496):

". . . the Percy Report recommended a shift from the "legalism" whereby hospital patients were "certified" by special procedures to a situation in which most patients would be "informally" received in hospital, the term "informally" signifying "without any legal formality." This was to be achieved by replacing the existing system "by the offer of care, without deprivation of liberty, to all who need it and are not unwilling to receive it:" see the Report of the Royal Commission on the Law Relating to Mental Illness and Mental Deficiency 1954–1957 (1957) (Cmnd. 169), p.101, para. 291. The desired objective was to avoid stigmatising patients and to avoid where possible the adverse effects of "sectioning" [*i.e. compulsorily detaining*] patients. Where admission to hospital was required compulsion was to be regarded as a measure of last resort. The Mental Health Act 1959 introduced the recommended changes. Section 5(1) was the critical provision. The marginal note reads "Informal admission of patients."

. . . By section 131(1) of the Act of 1983 the provisions of section 5(1) of the Act of 1959 were re-enacted verbatim. And the same marginal note appears next to section 131. Prima facie section 131(1) must be given the same meaning as section 5(1). On this basis, section 131(1) also preserved the common law principle of necessity as a means of admitting compliant incapacitated individuals."

Whilst it was accepted on behalf of L that s.5(1) had preserved the common law principle of necessity, it was, as Lord Goff stated (at 484), "boldly suggested that section 131 should be given a different meaning, and be restricted to voluntary patients". The basis of this suggestion seems to have been that the MHA 1959 had been substantially amended by the Mental Health (Amendment) Act 1982, by the introduction of improved safeguards for detained patients, and that, following consolidation of these safeguards in the MHA 1983, compliant incapacitated persons should not be deprived of them. Accordingly, s.131 of the MHA 1983 should be more narrowly construed than s.5(1), so as to exclude compliant incapacitated persons. Such persons would then be subject to the improved statutory safeguards and not be deprived of them, as they would be if they were detained under the common law principle of necessity.

In rejecting this suggestion, Lord Goff (at 484–485) made reference to a 1981 White Paper, *Reform of Mental Health Legislation* (Cmnd. 8405), which preceded the introduction of the 1982 Act:

> ". . . it [*the suggestion*] is, in my opinion, wholly untenable, bearing in mind not only that section 131(1) is in identical terms to section 5(1) of the Act of 1959, but that I have been able to discover no trace, either in the 1982 Act or in the White Paper of November 1981 which preceded it (Reform of the Mental Health Legislation (Cmnd. 8405)), of any intention to depart from, or modify, the recommendations of the Percy Commission upon which section 5(1) was founded or to amend section 5(1) itself. On the contrary, it was expressly stated that the Act of 1959 had worked well. The main objects of the [*1982*] Bill, as summarised in paragraph 5 of the [*White Paper's*] introduction, were that the Bill improved safeguards for detained patients, clarified the position of staff looking after them and removed uncertainties in the law. The main improvements, summarised in paragraph 6, had no bearing on the position of informal patients admitted under section 5(1) of the Act of 1959, as was borne out by the succeeding paragraphs or indeed by the Act of 1982 itself."

A similar view was reached by Lord Steyn on the basis of "orthodox principles of statutory interpretation", although no reference was made to the White Paper. His Lordship stated (at 496–497):

> ". . . counsel for L. submitted that section 131(1), unlike its predecessor, only applies to consenting capacitated patients. He argued that contextual differences between the statutes of 1959 and 1983 required the court to intepret the language of section 131(1) of the Act of 1983 in a narrower sense than section 5(1) of the Act of 1959. He relied on the provisions of Part IV of the [*1983*] Act which are set out under the heading "Consent to Treatment." Part IV undoubtedly contains safeguards going beyond those in the Act of 1959, and also expressly made some of its provisions only applicable to those "liable to be detained under this Act," and others applicable also to "patients not liable to be detained under this Act." These provisions are not inconsistent with the interpretation that the meaning of section 131(1) of the 1983 Act is the same as the meaning of section 5(1) of the Act of 1959. Making due allowance for the improved safeguards for detained patients in the Act of 1983, the differences relied on do not in truth touch on the issue before the House and do not warrant a radical reinterpretation of identical statutory wording. On orthodox principles of statutory interpretation the conclusion cannot be avoided that section 131(1) permits the admission of compliant incapacitated patients where the requirements of the principle of necessity are satisfied."

It will be recalled that the Court of Appeal, when interpreting s.131(1), had focused its attention on an earlier White Paper than that referred to by Lord Goff, *Review of the Mental Health Act 1959*, to support its view that the section permitted the admission only of informal patients who consented to admission and not

243

compliant incapacitated patients (see above, 9–007). The interpretation adopted may thus be influenced by the particular material on which reliance is placed. Reference had also been made by the Court of Appeal to s.131(2) to support this view, but this was considered only briefly by Lord Goff and not at all by Lord Steyn. Lord Goff stated (at 485):

> "I should refer briefly to section 131(2) of the Act of 1983, which was relied upon by the Court of Appeal in support of their construction of section 131(1) . . . It is plain, in my opinion, that subsection (2) can have no impact upon the admission of informal patients under subsection (1) which is concerned with patients who consent as well as those who do not object. It is the former category that subsection (2) addresses, with special reference to minors."

Similarly, little attention was paid by the House of Lords to the four decisions on which the Court of Appeal had placed reliance in support of its view that detention could only take place under the MHA 1983. The Scottish decision on *B v Forsey* [1988] S.L.T. 572, considered by the Court of Appeal to be the "most relevant" of the four decisions (see above, 9–007), was not referred to at all by Lord Steyn and was considered by Lord Goff only as one of two "subsidiary points" at the conclusion of his judgment. In Lord Goff's view, the decision was distinguishable from the present case on the ground that it was concerned with whether the common law doctrine of necessity could be invoked to extend temporarily a statutory period of detention, whereas L's case was concerned with informal admission, and no reference had been made to the equivalent provision to s.131 in the Scottish legislation. His Lordship stated (at 489–490):

> "That case was concerned with the invocation of the common law to supplement the statutory power of compulsory detention to fill a lacuna which had appeared in the Scottish Act. This House held that the common law could not be invoked for that purpose, because the powers of detention conferred upon hospital authorities under the Mental Health (Scotland) Act 1984 were intended to be exhaustive. In my opinion, that decision has no relevance in the present case which is concerned with informal admission under the Act of 1983, and bringing a patient to hospital to enable him to have the benefit of such admission if he does not object to it. In this connection I observe that section 17(2) of the Scottish Act, which is the equivalent to section 131(1) of the Act of 1983, was not referred to in *B. v Forsey*."

His Lordship thus took a narrower view of the ratio of the case than had Lord Woolf, M.R. in the Court of Appeal. For Lord Goff, the ratio was that once a hospital had invoked the statutory power to detain, it could not thereafter resort to the common law doctrine of necessity, whereas for Lord Woolf, M.R. the ratio was that a hospital could not resort to the common law doctrine of necessity in *any* case, whether involving the exercise of statutory power or informal admission, as this had been impliedly removed by the statutory powers of detention (see above, 9–007).

The only other decision referred to, both by Lords Goff and Steyn, was *Re F*, although neither mentioned this when considering the meaning and interpretation of s.131. Lord Goff's first reference to the case was only *after* he had considered s.131 and concluded that the section permitted the informal admission of persons incapable of consenting. The case was thus not used as an aid to ascertaining the meaning and interpretation of the section and his Lordship (at 485) mentioned the decision only when considering how the common law doctrine of necessity might be *applied* to the treatment and care of such patients:

> "I turn briefly to the basis on which a hospital is entitled to treat, and to care for, patients who are admitted as informal patients under section 131(1) but lack the capacity to consent to such treatment or care. It was plainly the statutory intention that such patients would indeed be cared for, and receive such treatment for their condition as might be prescribed for them in their best interests . . . Such treatment and care can, in my opinion, be justified on the basis of the common law doctrine of necessity, as to which see the decision of your Lordships' House in *In re F. (Mental Patient: Sterilisation)* [1990] 2 A.C. 1."

Lord Goff's second reference to the case, as the second of his two "subsidiary points" at the conclusion of his judgment, was when considering the importance and scope of the common law doctrine of necessity. He stated (at 490):

> "The second point relates to the function of the common law doctrine of necessity in justifying actions which might otherwise be tortious and so has the effect of providing a defence to actions in tort. The importance of this was, I believe, first revealed in the judgments in *In re F. (Mental Patient: Sterilisation)* [1990] 2 A.C. 1 . . . The concept of necessity has its role to play in all branches of our law of obligations—in contract (see the cases on agency of necessity), in tort (see *In re F.*), and in restitution (see the sections on necessity in the standard books on the subject) and in our criminal law. It is therefore a concept of great importance. It is perhaps surprising, however, that the significant role it has to play in the law of torts has come to be recognised at so late a stage in the development of our law."

Lord Steyn's only reference to *Re F* was when mentioning the importance of approaching the mental health legislation against the context of the principles of the common law, which was *before* the meaning and interpretation of s.131 was considered. His Lordship stated (at 495–496):

> "The starting point of the common law is that when a person lacks capacity, for whatever reason, to take decisions about medical treatment, it is necessary for other persons, with appropriate qualifications, to take decisions for him: *In re F. (Mental Patient: Sterilisation)* [1990] 2 A.C. 1, 55H, *per* Lord Brandon of Oakbrook. The principle of necessity may apply. For the purposes of the present case it has been assumed by all counsel that the requirements of the principle are simply that (1) there must be "a necessity to act when it is not

practicable to communicate with the assisted person" and (2) "that the action taken must be such as a reasonable person would in the circumstances take, acting in the best interests of the assisted person:" *In re F.* [1990] 2 A.C. 1, 75H, *per* Lord Goff of Chieveley. There was not unanimity on this point in *In re F.* But I am content to approach the matter in the same way as counsel did . . ."

▶ 5. Policy Considerations

9-011   It is not clear whether any policy considerations were taken into account by Owen J. in the High Court when deciding the case, since the decision is unreported (see above, 9–004). When the case was before the Court of Appeal, policy considerations and the possible impact of the case on the practice of detaining patients outside the statutory powers of compulsory detention contained in the MHA 1983 seemed to receive no more than a passing reference. Lord Woolf, M.R. referred only briefly to the matter, stating (at 474):

"Apparently there could be many patients, especially those suffering from dementia, who are in the same position as L . . . The current practice cannot justify disregard of the Act. This is especially true because of the undesirable consequences which can follow a practice which bypasses the safeguards which the Act provides for patients who are statutorily detained."

The House of Lords, in contrast, devoted considerable attention to the possible implications of its decision. The House recognised that the decision of the Court of Appeal had caused, in the words of Lord Goff (at 481), "grave concern among those involved in the care and treatment of mentally disordered persons". This was because, as his Lordship went on to say:

"First and foremost, the effect of the judgment is that large numbers of mental patients who would formerly not have to be compulsorily detained under the Act of 1983 will now have to be so detained. Inquiries by the [*Mental Health Act*] Commission suggest that "there will be an additional 22,000 detained patients resident on any one day as a consequence of the Court of Appeal judgment plus an additional 48,000 admissions per year under the Act." This estimate should be set against the background that the average number of detained patients resident on any one day in England and Wales is approximately 13,000. (Andrea Humphrey, a civil servant of the Department of Health, gave a figure of 11,000 for those detained under the Act at any time prior to the judgment.) The Commission considered it to be very likely that the majority of patients to whom the Court of Appeal judgment applied would be patients in need of long term care; and further considered that, if the judgment is held to apply to patients receiving medical treatment for mental disorder in mental nursing homes not registered to receive detained patients, the above estimates were likely to be very much higher. It is obvious that there would in the result be a substantial impact on the available resources; the Commission recorded that the resource implications were likely to be considerable, not only for the mental health services and professionals who have to implement the Act, but also for Mental Health Review Tribunals and for the Commission itself. These concerns were also reflected in the affidavit sworn by Andrea Humphrey of the Department of Health, following widespread consultation. Deep concern about the effect of the judgment was expressed, in particular, by the President of the Royal Society of Psychiatrists, and the Chairman of the Faculty for Psychiatry and Old Age of that Society; and also by the Executive Director of the Alzheimer's Disease Society. The various responses referred not only to the impact on the patients themselves, but also to the resource implications and to the effect on relatives and carers.

The Commission also stated that the Court of Appeal's judgment had given rise to a number of legal uncertainties. Two particular questions described by the Commission as being 'of enormous practical importance,' arose with regard to mental nursing homes, viz. whether such homes were required to be registered to receive patients detained under the Act of 1983 before receiving patients like L., and whether homes not so registered are now obliged to register or to discharge such patients from their care."

The significance of this grave concern about the Court of Appeal's judgment had been acknowledged at the outset of the case when, rather unusually, three bodies who were recognised as having a particular interest applied for and were granted permission to intervene in the House of Lords. The Secretary of State for Health and the Registered Nursing Home Association were represented by counsel, and the Mental Health Act Commission intervened by way of written submissions. In allowing them to be represented the House of Lords was exercising its inherent power to control proceedings, for these bodies were not parties to the case nor were they expert witnesses giving evidence. This is relatively unusual within the English jurisdiction, but has similarities with procedures in European and US courts.

Whilst the social and economic implications of the Court of Appeal's decision might suggest that, as a matter of policy, it would be desirable if that decision were reversed, there were competing policy considerations that might suggest this would *not* be desirable. As Lord Goff stated (at 482):

"On the other hand, as the [*Mental Health Act*] Commission stressed, another result of the Court of Appeal's judgment was that, if patients such as L. had to be compulsorily detained under the Act of 1983 in order to be admitted to hospital, they would reap the benefit of the safeguards written into the Act for patients compulsorily detained. It appears from the Commission's written submission that the lack of statutory safeguards for patients informally admitted to hospital has been a matter of concern for the Commission, and that this concern has been expressed not only by the Commission itself but also by the authors of authoritative textbooks on the subject."

It is not clear to what extent these competing policy considerations influenced the House of Lords in reaching its conclusion that the Court of Appeal's decision should be reversed. Lord Goff, having set out these considerations, expressed no opinion on the matter. Having referred to an assurance by counsel for the Secretary of State that the question of safeguards for informal patients was "under consideration" and having remarked that "it is plain that he has to have regard to the resource implications of extension of the statutory safeguards to the very much larger number of patients who are informally admitted", Lord Goff (at 482) simply concluded that "this is a matter which is entirely for the Secretary of State, and not for your Lordships' House, whose task is to construe, and to apply, the Act as it stands".

Lord Steyn, in contrast, was clearly of the view that, as a matter of policy, it was desirable that the statutory safeguards contained in the Act for patients compulsorily detained should be extended to informally admitted patients. "If considerations of financial resources are put to one side", his Lordship stated (at 492), "there can be no justification for not giving to compliant incapacitated patients the same quality and degree of protection as is given to patients admitted under the Act of 1983". Decisions as to a person's incapacity and his detention may prove to be both controversial and complex, and protection was necessary to guard against professional failings and errors of judgment. In emphasising the importance of having such protection, Lord Steyn referred to a range of scholarly works in the field of psychiatry, stating (at 493–494):

". . . Parliament devised the protective scheme of the Act of 1983 as being necessary in order to guard amongst other things against misjudgment and lapses by the professionals involved in health care. This point requires some explanation. A hospital psychiatrist who decides that a patient ought to be admitted to hospital and treated makes a judgment which may be controversial. The clinical question may arise whether the patient is in truth incapacitated. The importance of this issue is described by *Grisso and Appelbaum, Assessing Competence to Consent to Treatment: A Guide to Physicians and Other Health Officials* (1998), p.1:

"Competence is a pivotal concept in decision-making about medical treatment. Competent patients' decisions about accepting or rejecting proposed treatment are respected. Incompetent patients' choices, on the other hand, are put to one side, and alternative mechanisms for deciding about their care are sought. Thus, enjoyment of one of the most fundamental rights in a free society—the right to determine what shall be done to one's body—turns on the possession of those characteristics that we view as constituting decision-making competent."

And the same authors have demonstrated how complex such an issue of competence may be: see also *Appelbaum, Almost a Revolution, Mental Health Law and The Limits of Change* (1994), ch. 4. Yet on the issue of competence depends a patient's right of autonomy: compare, however, the psychiatric argument for "trade off" between competence and the consequences of treating or not treating: Eastman and Hope, "The Ethics of Enforced Medical Treatment: The Balance Model", Journal of Applied Philosophy (1998) [*sic: sc. 1988*], vol. 5, no. 1, p. 49. Moreover, the broad question of what is an incompetent patient's best interests may involve a weighing of conflicting medical and social considerations. And, in regard to treatment, the moral right of a patient to be treated with dignity may pose acute problems. These are no doubt some of the reasons why Parliament thought it necessary to create a system of safeguards for those admitted under the Act of 1983. Parliament was not content in this complex and sensitive area to proceed on the paternalistic basis that the doctor is always right. If the decision of the Court of Appeal is reversed almost all the basic protections under the Act of 1983 will be inapplicable to compliant incapacitated patients . . . The result would be an indefensible gap in our mental health law . . . the law would be defective if it failed to afford adequate protective remedies to a vulnerable group of incapacitated mental patients."

His Lordship accordingly "would have wished to uphold the judgment of the Court of Appeal if that were possible" (494), but ultimately came to the conclusion that it was not, going on to remark (at 494):

"But as the issues were extensively probed in oral argument it became clear to me that, on a contextual interpretation of the Act of 1983, this course was not open to the House".

Lord Steyn's sentiments about the undesirability of reversing the Court of Appeal's decision were subsequently reiterated by his Lordship (at 497) at the end of his judgment:

"The general effect of the decision of the House is to leave compliant incapacitated patients without the safeguards enshrined in the Act of 1983. This is an unfortunate result. The Mental Health Act Commission has expressed concern about such informal patients in successive reports. And in a helpful written submission the Commission has again voiced those concerns and explained in detail the beneficial effects of the ruling of the Court of Appeal. The common law principle of necessity is a useful concept, but it contains none of the safeguards of the Act of 1983. It places effective and unqualified control in the hands of the hospital psychiatrist and other health care professionals. It is, of course, true that such professionals owe a duty of care to patients and that they will almost invariably act in what they consider to be the best interests of the patient. But neither habeas corpus nor judicial review are sufficient safeguards against misjudgments and professional lapses in the case of compliant incapacitated patients. Given that such patients are diagnostically indistinguishable from compulsory patients, there is no reason to withhold the specific and effective protection of the Act of 1983 from a large class of vulnerable mentally incapacitated individuals. Their moral right to be

> treated with dignity requires nothing less. The only comfort is that counsel for the Secretary of State has assured the House that reform of the law is under active consideration."

Lord Steyn was thus clearly of the view that, as a matter of policy, compliant incapacitated patients such as L should benefit from the same statutory safeguards as compulsorily detained patients. On occasions, as indicated in Chapter 1 (see 1–057), judges may well feel able to determine cases by reference to what is regarded as the best policy for the law to adopt, but in some instances, such as the present case, this may not be considered possible in the light of the relevant statutory provisions and/or case law authorities.

▶ 6. To the European Court and Legislative Reform

9–012 The ultimate outcome of the case was that L's claim for false imprisonment failed, since the conduct of the hospital was held to be justified under the common law doctrine of necessity. Whilst considerable attention in the case had been devoted to whether L had been detained and whether that detention was unlawful (on which there was a considerable difference in judicial opinion), one matter not addressed was whether the common law doctrine of necessity was compatible with Art.5(1)(e) of the European Convention on Human Rights (Convention), which permits "lawful detention of . . . persons of unsound mind" under national law, provided it is sufficiently certain and ascertainable to prevent arbitrary detention. It was contended (at 477) by counsel on behalf of the Secretary of State that it was, since the doctrine required objective evidence to support the doctor's decision to admit informally an incapacitated patient for treatment as being in the patient's best interests and in accordance with a responsible body of medical opinion. It did not therefore enable such a patient to be arbitrarily detained contrary to the Convention. Although 10 cases decided by the European Court of Human Rights (ECtHR) (see below, 2–023) were cited by counsel in argument before the House, none was referred to in any of the judgments. The contention that there was compliance with Art.5(1)(e), however, as will be seen, was ultimately to be rejected by the EctHR, to which an appeal was made on behalf of L against the House of Lords' decision.

Following the assurance given by counsel for the Secretary of State that the question of safeguards for informal patients was "under consideration" (see above, 9–011), the Government in September 1998 announced that a review of the MHA 1983 would be undertaken by a small committee of experts, led by Professor Genevra Richardson, whose task it would be "to kick-start a root and branch review of the 1983 Mental Health Act". A report, *Review of the Mental Health Act 1983*, was published by the Department of Health in November 1999 and it contained a short section emphasising the urgency of remedying what was described as "the legislative gap revealed in the *Bournewood* case". One of the reasons for urgency was, as the committee observed in its report (at p.113), that:

". . . the absence of adequate safeguards renders the government vulnerable under the provisions of the ECHR [*European Convention on Human Rights*] and thus the Human Rights Act".

Although no firm proposals for action on this issue were produced, the committee recommended that, under the scheme being put forward for new mental health legislation, the same safeguards for compulsorily admitted patients should extend to other patients and a mechanism should be provided for reviewing the detention of patients.

At the same time as it published the committee's report, the Department of Health produced a Green Paper, *Reform of the Mental Health Act 1983: Proposals for Consultation* (1999) (Cm. 4480), in which the view was expressed that the use of compulsory powers of detention for long-term patients with mental incapacity was often inappropriate. Acknowledging that a similar view had been expressed by the House of Lords in *Bournewood*, it was stated in the Green Paper (at p.72) that:

"such patients should be provided with statutory safeguards to ensure that care and treatment for mental disorder, particularly where restrictions of liberty are concerned, is in their best interests".

In a White Paper published the following year, *Reforming the Mental Health Act* (2000) (Cm. 5016-I), Pt 1 of which contained proposals for a New Legal Framework, the Government acknowledged that the area of adults with long-term mental incapacity was one "where the human rights of a very vulnerable group of people have never been given sufficient consideration in mental health statute" (para.2.39). It went on to state (at para.2.40) that ensuring that the best interests of these patients are properly considered and protected:

". . . can only be achieved through independent scrutiny. New legislation will place a duty on the clinical supervisor responsible for the care and treatment of a patient with long term mental incapacity to refer the care plan to a member of the expert panel for a second opinion when the care and treatment for a mental disorder continues for longer than 28 days. These cases will come within the remit of the Commission for Mental Health and there will be a right to apply to the [*Mental Health*] Tribunal to challenge detention and for a review where there are concerns about the quality and nature of the patient's care and treatment."

The Government subsequently published for consultation a draft Mental Health Bill in 2002, which provided a degree of statutory protection for the informal treatment of patients not capable of consenting to treatment, including a right to advocacy, the appointment of a nominated person and access to a tribunal. This was followed by a revised draft Mental Health Bill 2004, Cm. 6305–1, but it became clear that the Government's proposals would not be sufficient to meet the Art.5 requirements when the ECtHR (see above, 2–023) delivered its judgment on the appeal made on behalf of L in *HL v UK* (2004) App No.45508/99. The ECtHR found that L's detention in hospital amounted to a deprivation of liberty under the Convention and that the common law lacked the essential safeguards to permit detention in compliance with Art.5. This was because there were no formalised admission procedures indicating who could propose admission, for what reasons and on the basis of what kind of medical and other assessments and conclusions; no requirement to specify the exact purpose of admission (e.g. for assessment or for treatment); no limits on time, treatment or care attached to admission; no specific provision requiring continuing clinical assessment of the persistence of a disorder warranting detention; and no requirement for nomination of a representative of a patient to make certain objections on his behalf.

The Government's proposals did not meet these requirements, as the Minister of State at the Department of Health, Ms Rosie Winterton, (*Hansard*, HC Standing Committee A, col.251 (October 28, 2004)), acknowledged:

> ". . . there is no doubt that we still lack sufficient procedural safeguards to prevent further breaches of Article 5.1 in cases where patients are, in effect, deprived of their liberty in their best interests."

The draft Mental Health Bill 2004 was subsequently considered by a Joint Committee of the House of Commons and House of Lords, which reported in March 2005 ((HC Paper 95–I, HL Paper 79–I, Session 2004–05) and urged the Government to "bring forward a comprehensive and universal set of proposals to deal with hospitalisation and treatment of patients affected by the Bournewood judgment . . . as soon as possible" (Recommendation 29). In July 2005 the Government published its Response to the Committee's Report (Cm.6624), in which it committed itself to bringing forward proposals for new safeguards for those incapacitated patients who require treatment in their best interests in a way that involves deprivation of liberty, and procedural safeguards were subsequently introduced in the Mental Capacity Act 2005.

Section 5 of the 2005 Act provides that where acts are done in connection with the care or treatment of another, and the person doing them reasonably believes that the other lacks capacity in relation to the matter in question and that it will be in the other's best interests for the act to be done, he incurs no liability in relation to the act. This includes both civil and criminal liability. In the case where an act is done intending to restrain another, two further conditions in s.6 need to be satisfied: (a) the person doing the act must reasonably believe that it is necessary to do the act in order to prevent harm to the other; and (b) the act must be a proportionate response to the likelihood of the other suffering harm and the seriousness of that harm. A person will restrain another for these purposes if he uses or threatens to use force to secure the doing of an act which the other resists or if he restricts the other's liberty of movement, whether or not the other resists (which will cover patients in cases like *Bournewood*). However, s.4A, introduced by s.50 of the Mental Health Act 2007, specifically provides that the 2005 Act "does not authorise any person ('D') to deprive any other person ('P') of his liberty", except as provided by ss.4A and 4B. The former makes deprivation of liberty lawful in two instances, where a person is giving effect to a court decision in relation to another's personal welfare and where deprivation is authorised in accordance with the (very detailed) requirements contained in Sch.A1, whilst the latter authorises deprivation of liberty where it is necessary for life-sustaining treatment. The introduction of these provisions thus remedies the Art.5 deficiencies identified in *HL v UK* and brings the law into compliance with Convention rights under the ECHR.

Further reading

Dawson, "Necessitous detention and the informal patient" (1999) 115 L.Q.R. 40

Jones, "Detaining adults who lack capacity" [2007] P.N. 238

Keywood, "Detaining mentally disordered patients lacking capacity: the arbitrariness of informal detention and the common law doctrine of necessity" [2005] Med. L.R. 108

Scott-Moncrieff, "Making sense of Bournewood" [2005] J.M.H.L. 17

10 VIDEO CASSETTES AS OBSCENE ARTICLES

▶ ## 1. Introduction

10–001 Under s.2 of the Obscene Publications Acts 1959 (OPA 1959), it is an offence to publish an obscene article and, for the purposes of this offence, s.1(2) provides:

> "In this Act 'article' means any description of article containing or embodying matter to be read or looked at or both, any sound record, and any film or other record of a picture or pictures."

In *Att Gen's Reference (No. 5 of 1980)* [1981] 1 W.L.R. 88, the Court of Appeal was concerned with construing this statutory provision to decide whether a video cassette fell within the definition. The point had arisen in connection with a prosecution of persons who operated two cinema clubs in Soho at which obscene video cassettes were shown to paying customers. At their trial in the Crown Court, the judge had directed the jury to acquit on the ground that a video tape did not fall within the definition of "article" in s.1(2) of the OPA 1959 and the Attorney General, under s.36 of the Criminal Justice Act 1972, referred the following point of law for the opinion of the Court of Appeal:

> "Does a person who provides an obscene display of images on a screen to persons who are likely to be depraved and corrupted by that display publish an obscene article contrary to section 2 of the Obscene Publications Act 1959 in a case where the images are derived from video tape?"

This case study illustrates a number of points primarily, though not exclusively, in relation to statutory interpretation:

- ▶ the need to construe words in their ordinary meaning as they would have been understood by persons at the time the Act was passed;
- ▶ whether the ordinary meaning of words could encompass matters not envisaged by Parliament at the time the Act was passed;
- ▶ the mischief at which the statute was aimed, the construction of words in the context of the statute as a whole and the application of an ejusdem generis construction;
- ▶ a failure by the court at first instance, the Crown Court, to consider a relevant Divisional Court authority with the result that the Crown Court's decision could be said to have been reached per incuriam;

- whether the Crown Court would have been bound as a matter of precedent by that Divisional Court authority and whether, having failed to consider it, the Crown Court had wrongly decided the case;

- whether certain pronouncements of the Court of Appeal form part of the ratio of the case or are merely obiter; and

- the willingness of Parliament to introduce legislative amendments to statutory provisions to resolve doubts as to whether those provisions can be interpreted so as to encompass particular circumstances.

▶ 2. The Decision of the Crown Court

At the trial of the case in the Crown Court (see above, 2–007), the trial judge, **10–002** having satisfied himself that a video cassette was not an article "containing or embodying matter to be read or looked at" nor "a sound record" under s.1(2), had decided that it could not, alternatively, be described as a "film or other record of a picture or pictures" (see [1980] Crim. L.R. 723). This was on the basis of a defence submission that these words should be construed ejusdem generis and that a video cassette was not of the same genus or nature as a film. Ejusdem generis is a principle of statutory construction where, in the case of particular words followed by general words, the meaning of the general words is confined to a meaning of the same kind (ejusdem generis) as the particular words. It is not a separate, independent principle but a particular aspect of the wider principle that words must be read in their statutory context and the statute read as a whole. In the trial judge's view (referred to at [1981] 1 W.L.R. 88 at 92), the general words "other record of a picture or pictures" in s.1(2) should be restricted in meaning under this principle:

> "Does a video cassette fall within the words 'or other record of a picture or pictures'? Let me start this consideration by saying that I accept the submission that these words form part of one phrase or division, starting with the words 'any film.' Therefore the other record of a picture has to have some kinship with film."

This, the trial judge felt, was not the case since a video cassette was not a celluloid artefact with images imprinted on it (like a film), but a piece of plastic storing electrical impulses capable of being converted into audio-visual signals, these signals being transmitted, when the video tape was shown, via a cable to a television screen which converted them into images on the screen.

▶ 3. The Decision of the Court of Appeal

When the case was referred for the consideration of the Court of Appeal, the **10–003** Attorney General sought to maintain that the provision in s.1(2) was intended to include any article which could be used to show images. This could be seen as in keeping with the mischief at which the statute was aimed, namely the publication of obscene material, although no specific reference to this was made by the Attorney General. (Nor did the Court of Appeal make specific reference to the mischief at which the statute was aimed, although, as will be seen, the court did accept that this was the object of the statutory provisions, which is essentially the same thing—see below, p.259.) That the intention was to include any article which could be used to show images was demonstrated, the Attorney General contended, by the wide wording of the subsection and by the wording of subs.(3)(b) of s.1, under which a person publishes an article where "in the case of an article containing or embodying matter to be looked at or a record, [*he*] shows, plays or projects it". The essence of the contention, in respect of the reference to subs.(3)(b), was that subs.(2) should be read in its statutory context, although again no specific reference was made to this point. These contentions put forward by the Attorney General were outlined as follows in the only judgment delivered in the case, by Lawton L.J. (at 91–92):

> "Mr. Tudor Price [*counsel for the Attorney-General*] submitted that the wide words of subsection (2) indicate that any article which brought about the reproduction of an obscene image was within the contemplation of the Act and that the only kinds of reproduction of obscene images which were outside the Act were the two exemptions set out in the provisos. He went on to point out that in subsection (3) publication embraces a person who, in the case of an article containing or embodying matter to be looked at, or a record, shows, plays or projects it. He went on to remind the court that in subsection (2) the word 'record' occurs twice. On one occasion it has the adjective 'sound' in front of it and in the other case the adjectival phrase 'any film or other' comes before the word 'record'. It followed, so submitted Mr. Tudor Price, that an accused publishes an obscene article if it is in the form of a record and he shows, plays or projects it. The record may be either of sound or of pictures. A video tape does in fact constitute a record of pictures, albeit that it is a record which is made up of electrical impulses recorded on a video tape. As neither of the exemptions apply, so says Mr. Tudor Price, it follows that a video cassette, being a record of pictures, does constitute an 'article' within the meaning of section 1(2). As in this case there was clearly a publication of the video cassette, it follows that the judge ought not to have ruled as he did."

To counter the Attorney General's contention that it was the intention of Parliament that "article" should include anything which could be used to show images, counsel for the respondents sought to maintain that video cassettes could not have been within Parliament's contemplation when passing the Act since such items were not then generally available. As Lawton L.J. stated (at 92) in the course of his judgment:

> "To that submission [*by counsel for the Attorney-General*], Mr. Shields [*counsel for the first respondent*], whose argument has been adopted by Mr. Robertson,

on behalf of the other respondents, has made the following answer. He has reminded the court that in 1959, when the Obscene Publications Act was passed, video tapes had not got much beyond the experimental stage. They were probably used by broadcasting bodies (such as the British Broadcasting Corporation) but they were not on sale to the public as they are now. It follows, says Mr. Shields, that it is inconceivable that Parliament had video tapes in mind when it was deciding what articles should come within the description 'obscene articles' for the purposes of the Obscene Publications Act 1959. He says that this court should be slow to apply the words to a piece of electronic equipment which probably had not been within the contemplation of Parliament."

This argument was not accepted by the court, which felt that items of this nature may well have been within Parliament's contemplation. If this was the case, video cassettes could be said (although the court did not make reference to this) to fall within the mischief at which the statute was aimed when the legislation was introduced, namely, to use the words of Lawton L.J. (at 95), "to bring all articles which produced words or pictures or sounds within the embrace of the Act". Whether or not video cassettes did fall within Parliament's contemplation at the time the legislation was introduced, however, in the court's view it had to be determined whether video cassettes fell within the ordinary meaning of the words used. The primary focus was therefore on the literal interpretation of the statutory provision and whether this was capable of encompassing video cassettes. Lawton L.J. stated (at 92):

"We have kept in mind that particular admonition made by Mr. Shields, but if the clear words of the statute are sufficiently wide to cover the kind of electronic device with which we are concerned in this case, the fact that that particular form of electronic device was not in the contemplation of Parliament in 1959 is an immaterial consideration. In any event in 1959 Parliament would almost certainly have in mind the fact that electronic equipment for reproducing words and pictures was something likely to come about in the near future. In those circumstances it is not all that improbable that words were chosen which were wide enough to embrace any developments in the electronic field. But speculation as to what Parliament had in mind and what it probably had not got in mind is neither here nor there. It is the duty of this court to consider the wording of the Act and to construe the words in it (if they are words of ordinary English usage) in the ways in which they would have been understood by ordinary literate persons at the material time, namely in 1959."

With a view to establishing the ordinary meaning of the words in their statutory context, counsel for the respondents, unlike in the Crown Court, did not seek to advocate an ejusdem generis construction of the words "other record of a picture or pictures" in s.1(2). Nevertheless, the Court of Appeal expressed the view that the trial judge had been wrong to adopt an ejusdem generis construction and to require an "other record of a picture" to have some kinship with the preceding words "any film". Lawton L.J. (at 92–93) stated:

> "He [*the trial judge*] was wrong in that approach because what he had to do was to construe the words 'film or any other record' in the context of sub-section (2). It is clear that subsection (2) embraced a number of articles, starting with those which contained or embodied obscene matter, those which were in the form of a soundtrack and those which were a film or other record of pictures. The judge did not have the advantage of having cited to him the decision of the Divisional Court in *Derrick v Customs and Excise Commissioners* [1972] 2 Q.B. 28. Had he had the benefit of having that decision referred to him, he would have appreciated that he had to look at the subsection as a whole and not to pick out any particular group of words in the subsection."

The view expressed here by Lawton L.J. was obiter, since, as counsel had not advocated a ejusdem generis construction before the Court of Appeal, this was not a matter which the court had to decide. This was in contrast to the position at trial where adoption of the ejusdem generis principle formed part of the ratio of the case.

In the view of Lawton L.J., the trial judge had erred because the relevant authority of *Derrick v Customs and Excise Commissioners* (*Derrick*) had not been cited to him. It could be said that the trial judge's decision had been reached per incuriam because of the failure to consider this relevant authority. If the relevant authority which the court had failed to consider was a binding precedent on the court, the case would certainly be regarded as wrongly decided. However, the position is less clear where the authority is only persuasive, as seems to be the position here. Such authority as there is (*R. v Colyer* [1974] Crim. L.R. 243) suggests that Divisional Court decisions are not binding precedents on the Crown Court (see above, 1–021) and, if this is correct, it would have been open to the Crown Court in the present case to have refused to follow the Divisional Court's decision in *Derrick*. If the Crown Court could have refused to follow *Derrick*, it might be questioned whether its decision should be regarded as wrong on account of its failure to consider that case. It seems to have been assumed by Lawton L.J. that, had the decision in *Derrick* been cited to the trial judge in the present case, the trial judge would have followed that decision.

Rather than advocating a ejusdem generis construction, counsel for the respondents in the Court of Appeal sought to maintain that a video cassette would not fall within the ordinary meaning of the words "other record of a picture or pictures" in s.1(2), because the ordinary meaning of those words could extend only to those articles which were capable of being published under the Act and a video cassette was not capable of being published. The essence of the respondents' contention in this respect was set out in the judgment of Lawton L.J. (at 92–93):

> "Mr. Shields has submitted that even when that test [*of how the words would have been understood by ordinary literate persons in 1959 when the Act was*

passed] is applied, the words are not apt to cover what happens when a video cassette is played. He points out that subsection (2) embraces three different situations. The first is 'an article containing or embodying matter to be read or looked at or both'; secondly, a 'sound record' and thirdly, 'any film or other record of a picture or pictures.' . . . There being three types of article, each of them was dealt with, so he submits, specifically in section 1(3)(b) of the Act. That, he says, is shown by the way in which that paragraph is worded, because under it 'a person publishes an article who—in the case of an article containing or embodying matter to be looked at'—that is the first category of obscene article—'or a record'—which could cover both the second and third categories—'shows, plays or projects it'.

Mr. Shields submitted that a video cassette shows nothing. Anyone looking at it merely sees a piece of magnetised tape. There is nothing on that tape to indicate the presence of electrical impulses and certainly nothing on the tape to show pictures. So, so he submits, the word 'shows' is inapplicable. He went on to submit that the word 'plays,' bearing in mind the year in which this statute was passed, namely, 1959, clearly applied to a sound record mentioned in section 1(2). A video tape is not played in any sort of way that a sound record would have been played in 1959. For myself I am not all that certain of that because in 1959 there were many tape recorders and, in ordinary English, those who use tape recorders, play them. But be that as it may, assuming for the moment that the word 'plays' is inappropriate to a video cassette, Mr. Shields went on to submit that the word 'projects' is inapplicable to a video cassette. He submitted, again bearing in mind that the statute was passed in 1959, that the word 'projects' envisaged the kind of projection which there is for films, namely by projecting light behind the film and producing an image on a screen. That, he submitted, was not a concept which could be applicable to a video cassette."

Considering this contention, Lawton L.J. went on to state (at 95):

"The basic question is whether there is any substance in Mr. Shield's submission that the words in subsection (2) and subsection (3) are not apt to cover a video cassette. In our judgment they are. As Mr. Tudor Price [*counsel for the Attorney-General*] rightly submitted, the object of subsection (2) was to bring all articles which produced words or pictures or sounds within the embrace of the Act. There were only to be two exceptions [*contained in the proviso to subs.(3)(b), i.e. cinematograph exhibitions and television or sound broadcasts*].

In our judgment the words 'shows, plays or projects' in section 1(3)(b) are sufficiently wide to cover what happens when pictures are produced by way of a video cassette. It may be that Mr Shields was right in his submission that the word 'show', in the context of subsection (3)(b), implies looking at, but the words 'play or project' cover, in our judgment, what happens when a video tape is used in such a way as to produce pictures. As I have already indicated in ordinary parlance (this would have been the same in 1959 as it is today) when

> a tape recorder is used it is talked about as being played. We see no reason why the same sort of language should not apply to a video cassette which produces not sounds but pictures. Even if that is not right (and we think it is right) the word 'project' would be apt to cover what happens when a video cassette is brought into use, because what is happening is that electrical impulses recorded on the video tape are thrown onto the television screen by means of the use of an electric current. In ordinary parlance, they are projected onto the television screen."

The Court of Appeal accordingly went on to answer in the affirmative the question posed by the Attorney General in his reference (see above, 10–001), namely, that the provision of an obscene display of images on a screen constituted publication of an obscene article under the OPA 1959. However, in view of Lawton L.J.'s remarks in the passage cited immediately above, some element of doubt remains as to the ratio of the case.

Certainly, it would seem to be part of the ratio that a video cassette falls within the ordinary meaning of the words "other record of a picture or pictures" in s.1(2), for it is capable of being published under the Act in that a person can "play" it under s.1(3). But it is less clear whether it is part of the ratio in that it falls within the ordinary meaning of those words and is capable of being published because a person can "project" it under s.1(3). This might be considered to be merely obiter, since Lawton L.J., having decided that a person can "play" a video cassette, went on to state that "even if that is not right (and we think it is right) the word 'project' would be apt to cover what happens when a video cassette is brought into use". The view might be taken that it was not necessary to decide whether a person could "project" a video cassette, since the court had already decided that a person could "play" it. On this basis, the statement that a person can "project" a video cassette would be obiter.

On the other hand, immediately prior to deciding that a person can "play" a video cassette, Lawton L.J. had stated that "the words 'play or project' cover, in our judgment, what happens when a video tape is used is such a way as to produce pictures". The view might be taken therefore that the court has had equal regard to both words when deciding that a video cassette could be published. On this basis, the statement that a person can "project" a video cassette will be just as much a part of the ratio as the statement that a person can "play" it, it simply being the case that the court had considered the question of whether a person could "play" it first, in point of time, before it considered whether a person could "project" it. Whether or not it is part of the ratio that a person can "project" a video cassette, it is clearly not part of the ratio that a person can "show" a video cassette under s.1(3). Lawton L.J. seemed to be of the opinion that this would not be apt to describe what happens when pictures are produced by way of video cassette, in view of his remark that "it may be that Mr. Shields was right in his submission that the word 'show', in the context of subsection 3(b), implies looking at [*the article*]". A video cassette is not looked at, for, as Lawton L.J. had earlier remarked (at 93) when considering Mr Shields' submission, "a video cassette shows nothing. Anyone looking at it merely sees a piece of magnetised tape. There is nothing on that tape to indicate the presence of electrical impulses and certainly nothing on the tape to show pictures".

▶ 4. Conclusion

The outcome of this case was one which would clearly have considerable practical **10–004** implications for law enforcement in the field of obscenity control. If the Court of Appeal had decided, as the Crown Court had done, that video cassettes did not fall within the definition of "article" in s.1(2), it would not have been possible for prosecutions to be instituted under the OPA 1959 in respect of the showing of obscene video cassettes. Whilst video cassettes were not a major method of dis-seminating obscene publications at the time the case was heard in 1980, over the course of the 1980s they became the dominant medium for this type of material until subsequently superseded by computer disks such as CDs and DVDs. In order for effective enforcement action to have been taken, it would have been necessary for Parliament to have introduced legislation amending the definition of "article" in s.1(2) so as to include within it video cassettes. The Court of Appeal's interpretation of the words "other record of a picture or pictures" in s.1(2) to include video cassettes, however, precluded the need for any such amendment of the definition and meant that the policy of the legislation of seeking to regulate all forms of obscene material would not be frustrated.

Whilst the Court of Appeal's interpretation in this case enabled "article" in s.1(2) to encompass the technological development of the video cassette, difficulties have continued to arise with other technological developments, notably computer disks. Uncertainty has arisen as to whether a computer disk, or information contained on a computer disk, can constitute an "article" under s.1(2), and whether this is capable of being published under s.1(3) of the OPA 1959, particularly where information is transmitted electronically between computers. (These issues have been considered by the Court of Appeal in *R. v Fellows and Arnold* [1997] 2 All E.R. 548 and details of doubts and difficulties that arise in relation to obscene matter contained on computer disk can be found in Manchester, "Computer Pornography" [1995] Crim. L.R. 546 and "More About Computer Pornography" [1996] Crim. L.R. 645; and the Home Affairs Committee, *Computer Pornography*, First Report (1994) HC 126.) In the light of the prevailing uncertainty, the Home Affairs Committee recommended that the definition of "article" in s.1(2) be amended to include the words "any items which store data for immediate or future retrieval" and that "publication" under s.1(3) should be extended to such items where a person "transfers some or all of the information held on it to another article which stores data for immediate or future retrieval". This recommendation was adopted in part and a provision incorporated into para.3 of Sch.9 to the Criminal Justice and Public Order Act 1994. This provision made no amendment to the definition of "article" in s.1(2), the view of the Home Office being that the definition clearly covered a computer disk, but amended s.1(3) by providing that there is publication in the case where a person, "where the matter is data stored electronically, transmits that data".

Further Reading

Home Affairs Committee, *Computer Pornography*, First Report (1994) HC 126

Manchester, "Computer Pornography" [1995] Crim. L.R. 546

Manchester, "More About Computer Pornography" [1996] Crim. L.R. 645

11 THE REGULATION OF ABORTION

▶ ## 1. Introduction

The question of whether to permit abortion and, if so, the conditions under which it **11-001** should be lawful, has produced much controversy. For many, the deliberate destruction of an embryo or foetus is akin to murder, although others feel that a right to abortion is an important part of a woman's rights over her own body. The present legal position represents a compromise between these views in that abortion is a criminal offence under s.58 of the Offences Against the Person Act 1861 (OAPA 1861), although it is lawful if performed within the terms of the Abortion Act 1967. Section 58 of the OAPA 1861 provides:

> "Every woman, being with child, who, with intent to procure her own miscarriage, shall unlawfully administer to herself any poison or other noxious thing, or shall unlawfully use any instrument or other means whatsoever with the like intent, and whosoever, with intent to procure the miscarriage of any woman, whether she be or be not with child, shall unlawfully administer to her or cause to be taken by her any poison or other noxious thing, or shall unlawfully use any instrument or other means whatsoever with the like intent, shall be guilty of [*an offence*] . . ."

Section 1(1) of the Abortion Act 1967 provides:

> "Subject to the provisions of this section, a person shall not be guilty of an offence under the law relating to abortion when a pregnancy is terminated by a registered medical practitioner if two registered medical practitioners are of the opinion, formed in good faith—
>
> (a) that the pregnancy has not exceeded its twenty-fourth week and that the continuance of the pregnancy would involve risk, greater than if the pregnancy were terminated, of injury to the physical or mental health of the pregnant woman or any existing children of her family; or
> (b) that the termination is necessary to prevent grave permanent injury to the physical or mental health of the pregnant woman; or
> (c) that the continuance of the pregnancy would involve risk to the life of the pregnant woman, greater than if the pregnancy were terminated; or
> (d) that there is a substantial risk that if the child were born it would suffer from such physical or mental abnormalities as to be seriously handicapped . . ."

If, however, a registered medical practitioner (RMP) is of the opinion that the termination is immediately necessary to save the life of the pregnant woman or to prevent grave permanent injury to her physical or mental health, the opinion of two RMPs is not required (s.1(4)). Nor is it necessary in such a situation for the abortion to be carried out in hospital, as is otherwise required (s.1(3)).

In two important decisions, courts have been concerned with interpreting these statutory provisions to ascertain the lawfulness of abortions carried out. The first decision, *R. v Bourne* [1939] 1 K.B. 687, decided before the Abortion Act 1967, prescribed the circumstances in which abortions might lawfully be carried out, and involved an abortion performed by an obstetric surgeon on a 14-year-old girl who had become pregnant as a result of a brutal rape and the court had to determine whether the surgeon had "unlawfully" used an instrument with intent to procure a miscarriage contrary to s.58 of the OAPA 1861. The second decision, *Royal College of Nursing of the United Kingdom v Department of Health and Social Security* [1981] A.C. 800, was concerned with whether, following an advance in medical technique, a pregnancy could be said to be "terminated by a registered medical practitioner" under s.1(1) of the Abortion Act 1967 when the only steps taken in the process which could be considered to lead directly to the abortion were those taken by nurses rather than by doctors.

This case study illustrates a number of points primarily in relation to statutory interpretation:

- the construction of a statutory provision by reference to the wording of provisions in other statutes;
- reference to established and relevant common law principles when attributing a meaning to words used in a statutory provision;
- a declaration of the legal position in the absence of any applicable precedent;
- giving words their ordinary and natural meaning;
- construing words in their statutory context;
- reading words into statutory provisions;
- the literal and mischief rules of statutory interpretation and the "purposive" approach to interpreting statutes;
- the use of the long title and preamble to a statute, and marginal notes (or sidenotes) to a section, as aids to statutory construction;
- regard to considerations of policy when interpreting statutory provisions; and
- whether the interpretation of a statutory provision accorded with a statement of the legal position contained in a ministerial circular.

▶ 2. *R. v Bourne*

The abortion performed in *R. v Bourne* [1939] 1 K.B. 687 (*Bourne*) was carried out at **11–002**
St Mary's Hospital, London, by Mr Aleck Bourne, a well-known obstetric surgeon,
with the consent of the girl's parents, on the ground that, in his view, the continuance of the pregnancy would probably cause serious injury to the girl. He
invited prosecution for having done so and was duly charged under s.58 of the
OAPA 1861. Although it was accepted at his trial at the Central Criminal Court (see
above, 2–019) that he performed the operation "as an act of charity, without fee or
reward, and unquestionably believing that he was doing the right thing", if he had
"unlawfully" used an instrument with intent to procure a miscarriage, he would
nevertheless be liable under the statutory provision. Section 58 gives no indication
of any circumstances in which an abortion might lawfully be carried out, although a
later enactment, the Infant Life (Preservation) Act 1929, which created the offence
of child destruction, did provide that this offence would not be committed if the act
of destruction was done in good faith for the purpose only of preserving the
mother's life. This enactment had been passed because of doubts as to whether
any offence would be committed where a child was killed during the actual process
of birth. Such a killing would not amount to murder, for the child would not have
an existence fully independent of its mother and so there would be no killing of a
"life in being" as required under the definition of murder. Further, there was some
doubt as to whether this would amount to abortion, since s.58 required that the
woman be "with child". Accordingly, to fill this gap in the law, the 1929 Act was
passed. The Act did not amend the prohibition on abortion contained in s.58, but
created a separate offence, child destruction, which was committed where a
person, with the intention of destroying the life of a child capable of being born
alive before it had an existence independent of its mother, caused the child to die.
Nevertheless, the proviso to the 1929 Act, that no offence would be committed if
the act of destruction was done in good faith for the purpose only of preserving the
mother's life, was to play a significant part in the way in which in *Bourne* the court
interpreted the offence in s.58.

The two reports of the case, in the All England Reports and the King's Bench
Reports, give slightly different versions of Macnaghten J.'s summing up on the
interpretation of s.58. In both reports, his Lordship is reported as making reference
to the word "unlawfully" in s.58 and to the wording of a later statutory provision in
the 1929 Act with a view to assisting in the interpretation of this word in s.58, but
the King's Bench Report contains a fuller exposition of his reasoning. Further, it
also contains an additional line of argument not explicitly mentioned in the All
England Reports, i.e. the drawing of a comparison between the offence of abortion
and other offences of homicide in that, if there can be justification in limited
circumstances for other forms of killing, there may similarly be justification for
abortion. The King's Bench Report states (at 690–691):

"The defendant is charged with an offence against s.58 of the Offences
Against the Person Act, 1861. That section is a re-enactment of earlier statutes,

the first of which was passed at the beginning of the last century in the reign of George III (43 Geo. 3, c. 58, s.1). But long before then, before even Parliament came into existence, the killing of an unborn child was by the common law of England a grave crime: see Bracton, Book III. (De Corona), fol. 121. The protection which the common law afforded to human life extended to the unborn child in the womb of its mother. But, as in the case of homicide, so also in the case where an unborn child is killed, there may be justification for the act.

Nine years ago Parliament passed an Act called the Infant Life (Preservation) Act, 1929. [*Macnaghten J. then referred to s.1(1) of the Act, including the proviso that the section does not apply if the act is done in good faith and for the purpose only of preserving the life of the mother.*] It is true, as Mr. Oliver [*counsel for the defendant*] has said, that this enactment provides for the case where a child is killed by a wilful act at the time when it is being delivered in the ordinary course of nature; but in my view the proviso that it is necessary for the Crown to prove that the act was not done in good faith for the purpose only of preserving the life of the mother is in accordance with what has always been the common law of England with regard to the killing of an unborn child. No such proviso is in fact set out in s.58 of the Offences Against the Person Act, 1861; but the words of that section are that any person who "unlawfully" uses an instrument with intent to procure miscarriage shall be guilty of felony [*i.e. an offence*]. In my opinion the word "unlawfully" is not, in that section, a meaningless word. I think it imports the meaning expressed by the proviso in s.1, sub.s.1, of the Infant Life (Preservation) Act, 1929, and that s.58 of the Offences Against the Person Act, 1861, must be read as if the words making it an offence to use an instrument with intent to procure a miscarriage were qualified by a similar proviso."

Whilst *Bourne* illustrates how law reports may differ in their record of a case, both reports do support one particular point, namely, that in reaching his conclusion about "what has always been the common law of England with regard to the killing of an unborn child", Macnaghten J. made no reference to any earlier case. Indeed, his Lordship observed (at 690):

"It is, I think, a case of first instance, first impression. The matter has never, so far as I know, arisen before for a jury to determine in circumstances such as these, and there was, even amongst learned counsel, some doubt as to the proper direction to the jury in such a case as this."

The case is thus an illustration of the power of courts to declare (some might say "create") the law where there appears to be no precedent.

However, the case could also be taken as an example of where there is a declaration by a judge of the legal position without full consideration of the competing arguments. Macnaghten J.'s declaration of the law was that: the common law had always recognised that the act must be done not in good faith for the purpose of preserving the mother's life; the 1929 Act had expressly stated the common law in this respect; and the 1858 Act, although not expressly stating it, had imported it by use of the word "unlawfully". This is not, however, the only possible interpretation. It may be that, even if Macnaghten J. was correct in his declaration of the common law, s.58 might not have been intended to maintain the common law position. If it had been intended to do so, express provision to this effect could have been made, as was done in the 1929 Act. Failure to do so could indicate that the common law position was not in fact preserved by the word "unlawfully".

Further, it is possible that Macnaghten J. was incorrect in his declaration of the common law. It could be that the common law did not recognise that the act must be done not in good faith for the purpose of preserving the mother's life, that there was no common law position in this regard to be preserved by the word "unlawfully" in s.58 and that the 1929 Act contained an express provision on good faith which had not hitherto had any application. Since there had been no case in which the question of good faith had been judicially considered, it could not be stated with certainty what the common law position was in this respect. It is possible, therefore, that Macnaghten J.'s view of the common law may have been incorrect and that, prior to the provision in the 1929 Act, the law did not recognise that it would be lawful where acts were done in good faith for the purpose of preserving the mother's life. It has to be said, however, that, despite the absence of such authority, the prevailing opinion prior to 1929 did seem to accord with Macnaghten J.'s view that such acts were lawful. Thus, for example, it was stated in a leading contemporary textbook, *Russell on Crimes and Misdemeanours*, 7th edn (1909), Vol.1, p.830 that: "The word 'unlawfully' excludes from the section acts done in the course of proper treatment in the interests of the life or health of the mother". The only authority cited (in a footnote) in support of this proposition is a reference to a medical work, Taylor's *Medical Jurisprudence*. Reference to this work (6th edn, 1910, Vol. II, pp.144–146) reveals that this view rested solely on counsel's opinion:

"In the year 1895 the following case for the opinion of counsel was stated by the Royal College of Physicians . . .

. . . It not infrequently happens that a medical practitioner who is in attendance on a woman during her pregnancy, or at her confinement, becomes convinced that she will almost certainly die unless the child is in some way got rid of. He sees that unless something of the sort is done both mother and child may perish, but the former can be saved at the expense of the destruction of the latter. In such a case the question arises as to whether he is legally justified in destroying the child to save the mother. In practice such action is not uncommon, but that does not seem to affect its legality.

'Counsel will please advise the College:

. . .

3. Does the law forbid the procurement of abortion during pregnancy for the purpose of saving the mother's life?
4. Does it forbid the destruction of the child during labour where such destruction is necessary to save the mother's life?
5. In the event of questions 3 and 4 being answered in the affirmative, is a medical practitioner blameless if, in order to escape the risk of prosecution, he refrains from rendering assistance, and thus deliberately sacrifices the life of the patient when he could save it either (*a*) by inducing abortion, or (*b*) by destroying the child during labour?

. . .

The answers were as follows:—

. . .

3, 4 and 5. We are of opinion that the law does not forbid the procurement of abortion during pregnancy, or the destruction of the child during labour, where such procurement or destruction is necessary to save the mother's life.'"

It thus seems that Macnaghten J.'s view of the common law did represent the accepted view at the time. If "unlawfully" in s.58 were to be interpreted in accordance with Macnaghten J.'s view of preserving the common law, this would mean that the term "unlawfully" could be given a clear and sensible meaning under s.58: acts would be unlawful when not done in good faith and, if done in good faith, would be lawful. If s.58 was to be interpreted as not preserving the common law rule on good faith (or if there was no such rule to preserve), this would mean that all acts, whether done in good faith or not and whatever the circumstances, would be unlawful. In other words, there would be no circumstances where abortion was lawful and the word "unlawfully" in s.58 would be meaningless.

Macnaghten J.'s summing up led to an acquittal by the jury. There was no appeal and so the correctness or otherwise of his Lordship's view of the law was not tested in a higher court. Nevertheless, the summing up had an impact perhaps greater than the place of the trial court in the hierarchy of the courts might suggest, for it closely affected medical practice for almost 30 years, although lack of clarity in the summing up (which was to attract criticism in *Royal College*) left uncertainty as to the scope of the defence of acting in good faith for the purpose of preserving the mother's life. As Brazier and Cave (*Medicine, Patients and the Law*, 4th edn (2007), 14.2) has indicated:

"Some doctors interpreted this defence liberally to include the mother's mental health and even happiness. Others would intervene only to prevent a life-threatening complication of pregnancy endangering the woman."

▶ # 3. Royal College of Nursing of the United Kingdom v Department of Health & Social Security

The courts in *Royal College of Nursing of the United Kingdom v Department of Health and Social Security* [1981] A.C. 800 (*Royal College*) were concerned with determining whether, following an advance in medical technique, a pregnancy could be said to be "terminated by a registered medical practitioner" under s.1(1) of the Abortion Act 1967 when the only steps in the process which could be considered to lead directly to the abortion were those taken by nurses rather than by doctors (or "registered medical practitioners" to use the terminology of the Act).

11–003

▷ ## (a) The requirement in section 1(1) of the Abortion Act 1967 that a pregnancy be "terminated by a registered medical practitioner"

A major change to the law on abortion came with the Abortion Act 1967, which prescribed the circumstances in which abortion might lawfully be carried out (see above, 11–001). A central aim of the Act was to ensure that, although doctors would, in specified circumstances, be permitted to carry out abortions, so-called back-street abortionists would remain guilty of an offence. Section 1(1) accordingly provided that:

11–004

> ". . . a person shall not be guilty of an offence under the law relating to abortion when a pregnancy is terminated by a registered medical practitioner".

At the time the Act was passed, surgical methods, involving the use of a knife by doctors to remove the unborn child, were used to carry out abortions, but, in the early 1970s, a new procedure was developed. Under this procedure, the effecting of an abortion was done, in the words of Lord Denning, M.R. (at 803) in the Court of Appeal:

> ". . . by pumping a chemical fluid into the mother's womb. It is called prostaglandin. This fluid so affects the muscles and shape of the mother's inside that it forces her into labour prematurely—so that the unborn child is expelled from the body—usually dead, but sometimes at the point of death."

Nurses were directly involved in this new procedure, whereas all actions effecting the abortion by the traditional surgical method were performed by doctors. In *Royal College*, courts were concerned with the issue of whether a pregnancy was "terminated by a registered medical practitioner" under this new procedure, in which, although the abortion was carried out under the direction of a doctor, nurses assisting in the process performed the actual tasks which led directly to the foetus being aborted. These tasks are outlined below in a statement agreed between the parties in *Royal College*, as set out in the judgment of Lord Wilberforce (at 821) in the House of Lords, in which his Lordship marked with an asterisk those tasks, all of which were carried out by a nurse (or midwife), which could be considered to have a direct effect leading to abortion:

"1. The first step is for a thin catheter to be inserted via the cervix into the womb so as to arrive at, or create, a space between the wall of the womb and the amniotic sac containing the foetus. This is necessarily done by a doctor. It may, sometimes, of itself bring on an abortion, in which case no problem arises: the pregnancy will have been terminated by the doctor. If it does not, all subsequent steps except number four may be carried out by a nurse or midwife. The significant steps are as follows . . .:

2. The catheter (i.e. the end emerging from the vagina) is attached, probably via another tube, to a pump or to a gravity feed apparatus. The function of the pump or apparatus is to propel or feed the prostaglandin through the catheter to the womb. The necessary prostaglandin infusion is provided and put into the apparatus.

*3. The pump is switched on, or the drip valve is turned, thus causing the prostaglandin to enter the womb.

4. The doctor inserts a cannula into a vein.

*5. An oxytocin drip feed is linked up with the cannula. The necessary oxytocin (a drug designed to help the contractions) is supplied for the feed.

6. The patient's vital signs are monitored, so is the rate of drip or flow.

*7. The flow rates of both infusions are, as necessary, adjusted.

*8. Fresh supplies of both infusions are added as necessary.

9. The treatment is discontinued after discharge of the foetus, or expiry of a fixed period (normally 30 hours) after which the operation is considered to have failed.

The only steps in this process which can be considered to have a direct effect leading to abortion (abortifacient steps) are those asterisked. They are all carried out by the nurse or midwife. As the agreed statement records "the causative factor in inducing . . . the termination of pregnancy is the effect of the administration of prostaglandin and/or oxytocin and not any mechanical effect from the insertion of the catheter or cannula." All the above steps 2–9 are carried out in accordance with the doctor's instructions—which should, as regards important matters, be in writing. The doctor will moreover be on call, but may in fact never be called."

A concern in relation to this new procedure was whether nurses, rather than doctors, might be said to "terminate" the pregnancy under the Act. If that was the case, the abortion would not be a lawful abortion under the 1967 Act and nurses could be liable to prosecution under the OAPA 1861. The view of the Department of Health and Social Security (DHSS), however, contained in a letter and various annexes sent in February 1980 to all Regional and Area Health Authorities, was that abortions effected under the new procedure were carried out by doctors and not nurses and were therefore lawful under the 1967 Act:

> ". . . the Secretary of State is advised that the termination can properly be said to have been termination by the registered medical practitioner provided that it is decided upon by him, initiated by him, and that he remains throughout responsible for its overall conduct and control in the sense that any actions needed to bring it to conclusion are done by appropriately skilled staff acting on his specific instructions but not necessarily in his presence."

Nevertheless, a letter from a Government Department is only that Department's view of the law, and nurses were anxious that if a court took a different view of the effect of the 1967 Act they might be criminally liable, notwithstanding that they were acting as instructed by their employers who in turn were acting in accordance with the letter. In the light of this uncertainty, the Royal College of Nursing (RCN) sought a declaration from the High Court that the statement in the DHSS's letter about the legality of the role of nurses was wrong in law and that the duties they were expected to carry out (as described in the extract above from Lord Wilberforce's speech) involved contravention of s.58 of the OAPA 1861.

▷ *(b) The possible interpretations of "terminated by a registered medical practitioner"*

The RCN's entitlement to a declaration depended upon how the provision in s.1 of **11–005** the 1967 Act, that no offence was committed "when a pregnancy is terminated by a registered medical practitioner", was interpreted. The RCN contended that the provision should be given a strict, literal interpretation, so that a pregnancy was "terminated by" a RMP only where the actual acts of termination of a pregnancy were carried out by a RMP, and that under the new procedure pregnancy was not "terminated by" a RMP since actual acts of termination were done by nurses. Conversely, the DHSS contended that the provision should be given a broader construction, so that a pregnancy was "terminated by" a RMP where there was treatment for the termination of a pregnancy initiated by and carried out under the supervision of a doctor in accordance with recognised medical practice, and that under the new procedure pregnancy was "terminated by" a RMP since the treatment was so initiated and carried out. The arguments put forward before the High Court and the Court of Appeal in support of these contentions are not reported, but those advanced before the House of Lords are contained in the Appeal Cases Reports and these form the basis for the possible interpretations of "terminated by a registered medical practitioner" outlined in this section.

The RCN and DHSS maintained that their respective contentions fell within the ordinary meaning of the words "terminated by a registered medical practitioner". Thus, counsel for the RCN argued (at 817):

> "In section 1(1) of the Act the relevant words are "when a pregnancy is terminated by a registered medical practitioner", which mean exactly what they say and require that the actual acts of termination should be carried out by a doctor."

Counsel for the DHSS argued (at 815):

> "The process of termination of pregnancy by this [*new procedure*] method is initiated and supervised by a doctor. He does not have to be at the bedside to supervise every step, but he must be available. In the ordinary use of language that comes within the meaning of the relevant words in section 1(1) "terminated by a registered medical practitioner.""

Similarly, both maintained that their interpretation was in accordance with the intention of Parliament when passing the legislation. To substantiate its contention that a strict, narrow construction was in accordance with Parliament's intention, the RCN maintained (at 816) that:

> "The Act was meant to protect doctors who carried out abortions in the conditions laid down by way of exception to an otherwise unchanged criminal law. In 1967 the only methods of abortion known required acts to be done by the doctor or surgeon with his own hands. The Act dealt with things as they were. It is the duty of the court to give effect to Parliament's intention as it was expressed . . . The process of abortion has been confined to doctors by the Act of 1967 and there it should remain until Parliament decides otherwise."

If Parliament had intended the Act to be read so as to include actions carried out under the supervision of a doctor, it could have said so expressly, as it had done in other statutory provisions (see below, 11–007), and, if the Act was to be read so as to include such actions, this would involve reading words into the statute which were not there:

> "For the [*DHSS's*] letter of February 21, 1980 to be correct in law . . . it would be necessary to read into the relevant words of the Act, after "by a registered medical practitioner," the words "or by a suitably qualified person acting under his direction." 'Had Parliament intended the Act to be read in that way it would have said so . . . It is not right that words should be read into this Act since they are not there'" (at 819).

Although Parliament had used the term "treatment for the termination of pregnancy" in other provisions in the 1967 Act, such as ss.1(3) and 3(1), this did not mean (as the DHSS maintained) that treatment initiated and supervised by a doctor for "treatment" in those sections was equated with the actual act terminating the pregnancy. Accordingly, the provision in s.1(1) that "a pregnancy is terminated by a registered medical practitioner" did not mean "treatment for the termination of pregnancy" in the sense of treatment initiated and supervised by a doctor.

In support of its contention that a broad construction of s.1(1) was in accordance with the intention of Parliament, the DHSS maintained (at 815) that Parliament was not concerned solely with the actions of doctors:

> "Parliament was concerned with medical control of the treatment and wished to ensure that all persons concerned should have a defence. A narrow or restrictive meaning should not be put on the words of the Act".

Further, it was contended (at 819) that account should be taken of medical advances when interpreting the Act:

> "There is no reason for thinking that Parliament when it passed the Act of 1967 did not have in mind medical progress . . . The respondents' contention [*that the Act should be interpreted in accordance with Parliament's intention at the time of passing the Act, when the new technique had not been developed*], shutting the door to this treatment, cannot be within the scheme of the Act. The Act must be read in accordance with technical progress. The treatment is carried out on the specific instructions of a registered medical practitioner. The doctor who provides the means and makes the actual decision actually terminates the pregnancy; the nurse participates. What is done constitutes termination of pregnancy by a registered medical practitioner."

It was not necessary, the DHSS maintained (at 819), to read words into s.1(1) in order for the words "terminated by a registered medical practitioner" to encompass treatment carried out under the direction or supervision of a doctor:

> "If the words of an Act are capable of more than one meaning the court can choose between potential meanings which throw light on what the draftsman meant: *Stock*'s case [*Stock v Frank Jones (Tipton) Ltd*] [1978] 1 W.L.R. 231, 236. This case turns on what is meant by "carried out by." It is not necessary for the appellant's [*i.e. DHSS's*] purpose to read in the words suggested by the respondents."

In the view of the DHSS, if the words "terminated by a registered medical practitioner" in s.1(1) were to be construed in their statutory context, their meaning would be treatment for termination and not actual termination. There were references in other sections of the 1967 Act to "treatment for the termination of pregnancy" and the words in s.1(1) must be read in the light of this: "It all indicates that Parliament had treatment in mind and was referring to it in the Act" (at 815). The difference in wording between the sections was insignificant and did not indicate a difference in meaning (at 816):

> "Any imperfection in the wording of the Act is attributable to the fact that this was a private member's bill and Parliament did not have the advantage of the full procedure [*as*] in the case of other bills. But the words used [*in s.1(1)*] clearly mean that a termination of pregnancy should be within the Act if it is carried out in accordance with the procedure normally adopted in National Health Service hospitals [*i.e. in accordance with the DHSS's letter*]."

Perhaps not surprisingly, however, since it was difficult to refute, the DHSS did not address the RCN's point that Parliament, had it intended abortions to be carried out under the supervision of RMPs, could have expressly said so.

▷ *(c) The decision of the High Court*

11–006 Woolf J. refused the RCN's application for a declaration and granted the DHSS a declaration that its advice did not involve the performance of any unlawful acts by RCN members. His Lordship, whose judgment was not reported, accepted the DHSS's interpretation of s.1, "pronouncing 'without any doubt at all'", as Lord Edmund-Davies remarked in the House of Lords (at 830), "that the prostaglandin procedure is permissible within the terms of section 1 of the Act of 1967". The RCN did not think that there was no doubt at all about the matter and appealed to the Court of Appeal, which promptly reversed Woolf J.'s decision.

▷ *(d) The decision of the Court of Appeal*

11–007 The Court of Appeal unanimously allowed the RCN's appeal, but their Lordships were not unanimous in their approach to the question of how the words "terminated by a registered medical practitioner" in s.1(1) should be construed. Lord Denning, M.R. (at 805) emphasised the importance of confining attention to the statutory wording and the way in which that would be understood by those persons to whom the Act was directed:

> "Abortion is a subject on which many people feel strongly. In both directions. Many are for it. Many against it. Some object to it as the destruction of life. Others favour it as the right of the woman. Emotions run so high on both sides that I feel that we as judges must go by the very words of the statute—without stretching it one way or the other—and writing nothing in which is not there. Another thing to remember is that the statute is directed to the medical profession—to the doctors and nurses who have to implement it. It is they who have to read it and act upon it. They will read it—not as lawyers—but as laymen. So we should interpret it as they would."

Lord Denning, M.R.'s insistence on the importance of interpreting words as they would be understood by a specific class of persons might, however, be inconsistent with the general duty of the courts to interpret legislation in accordance with the intention of Parliament. It cannot necessarily be assumed that Parliament, when using particular words, would have intended that they should be interpreted in the sense in which such words are understood by the specialised groups most affected by the legislation. Lord Denning, M.R. continued (at 805):

> "If there should ever be a case in the courts, the decision would ultimately be that of a jury. Suppose that during the process the mother died or became seriously ill—owing to the nurse's negligence in administering the wrong chemical fluid—and the nurse was prosecuted under the Offences against the Person Act 1861 for unlawfully administering her a noxious thing or using other means with intent to procure her miscarriage. The nurse would have no defence unless the pregnancy was "terminated by a registered medical practitioner." Those are simple English words which should be left to a jury to apply—without the judge attempting to put his own gloss upon them: see *Cozens v Brutus* [1973] A.C. 861. I should expect the jury to say that the pregnancy was not terminated by a registered medical practitioner, but by a nurse."

The intimation that these are "simple English words which should be left to a jury to apply" might be inconsistent with Lord Denning, M.R.'s earlier assertion that the words should be interpreted as understood by doctors and nurses. Within the space of two paragraphs his Lordship suggested three groups of people whose understanding of the phrase "terminated by a registered medical practitioner" should be considered: doctors, nurses and jury members. It is possible that these groups would in fact share Lord Denning, M.R.'s understanding of these "simple English words", although it does not necessarily follow that a common understanding of their meaning would exist.

Lord Denning, M.R. subsequently looked at the meaning of the words in their statutory context. With no reference in s.1(1) to persons acting under the direction of a RMP, Parliament had, in his view (at 806), deliberately restricted its scope to actions personally undertaken by a RMP:

> "Statutes can be divided into two categories. In the first category Parliament has expressly said "by a registered medical practitioner or by a person acting in accordance with the directions of any such practitioner", or words to that effect: see the Radioactive Substances Act 1948, section 3(1)(a); Therapeutic Substances Act 1956, section 9(1)(a); Drugs (Prevention of Misuse) Act 1964, section 1(2)(g); Medicines Act 1968, section 58(2)(b); Tattooing of Minors Act 1969, section 1. In the second category Parliament has deliberately confined it, "by a fully registered medical practitioner," omitting any such words as "or by his direction": see the Human Tissues Act 1961, section 1(4). This statute is in the second category."

As his Lordship went on to say (at 806–807):

"If the Department of Health want the nurses to terminate a pregnancy, the Minister should go to Parliament and get the statute altered. He should ask them to amend it by adding the words "or by a suitably qualified person in accordance with the written instructions of a registered medical practitioner." I doubt whether Parliament would accept the amendment. It is too controversial. At any rate, that is the way to amend the law: and not by means of a departmental circular."

Nor did his Lordship think that the use of the words "treatment for the termination of pregnancy" in other provisions in the 1967 Act meant that the words "terminated by a registered medical practitioner" in s.1(1) in their statutory context meant treatment initiated and supervised by a RMP:

"The Solicitor-General [*for the DHSS*] emphasised the word "treatment" in sections 1(3), 3(1)(a) and (c) and 4(1). He suggested that section 1(1) should be read as if it said that a person should not be guilty of an offence "when the treatment (for termination of pregnancy) is by a registered medical practitioner." He submitted that whenever the registered medical practitioner did what the Department of Health advised it satisfied the statute, because the treatment, being initiated by him and done under his instructions, was "by" him.

I cannot accept this interpretation. I think the word "treatment" in those sections means "the actual act of terminating the pregnancy." When the medical induction method is used, this means the continuous act of administering prostaglandin from the moment it is started until the unborn child is expelled from the mother's body. This continuous act must be done by the doctor personally. It is not sufficient that it is done by a nurse when he is not present."

Whilst this made it clear that an abortion would be unlawful where the continuous act was done by a nurse in the absence of a doctor, it left unresolved the question of whether it would be unlawful where the doctor was present but the continuous act was done in part by a nurse assisting the doctor. Whether this was unlawful would seem to depend on whether in these circumstances it could be said that the actual act of terminating the pregnancy was being performed by the doctor, since Lord Denning, M.R. confined his interpretation of "terminated by a registered medical practitioner" in s.1(1) to actual termination by a doctor.

A similar interpretation was adopted by another member of the court, Sir George Baker. He alone made reference (at 811) to the long title of the Act and the marginal note (or sidenote) to s.1 as aids to interpretation:

"It is of primary importance to have clearly in mind what the Act says. Its long title is: "An Act to amend and clarify the law relating to termination of pregnancy by registered medical practitioners," and the marginal note to section 1 is "Medical termination of pregnancy.""

Further, unlike Lord Denning, M.R., Sir George made no reference to the words being interpreted in the sense in which they would be understood by nurses, doctors and jury members, but felt that the words were "clear and unambiguous" (at 811). Accordingly, he rejected the DHSS's contention that the words "terminated by a registered medical practitioner" in s.1(1) were capable of more than one meaning, and could include the meaning which the DHSS alleged the words bore (see above 11–005). Although he did not say so expressly, the clear implication seemed to be that the DHSS's contention did not fall within the ordinary meaning of the words and would involve reading words into the Act. He stated (at 811–813):

"The words "terminated by a registered medical practitioner" are by them-selves clear and unambiguous. The operative act or acts which have or are intended to have an abortifacient effect must be done by or performed or carried out by a registered medical practitioner . . .

The department's [*DHSS's*] case necessitates section 1(1) being read as meaning:

"If two registered medical practitioners are of opinion, formed in good faith etc., then provided that the treatment for termination of the pregnancy is carried out in a hospital vested in the Minister . . . or in a place approved for the time being etc., a person *participating or assisting in that treatment* and who would otherwise be guilty of an offence under the law relating to abortion as defined in this Act shall not be guilty of such an offence when *the treatment* is by a registered medical practitioner."

. . . it is not for judges "to read words into an Act of Parliament unless clear reason for it is to be found within the four corners of the Act itself," *per* Lord Loreburn L.C. in *Vickers, Sons & Maxim Ltd v Evans* [1910] A.C. 444, 445, cited by Viscount Dilhorne in *Stock v Frank Jones (Tipton) Ltd* [1978] 1 W.L.R. 231, 235A. Nor is a judge entitled to read an Act differently from what it says simply because he thinks Parliament would have so provided had the situation been envisaged at that time."

With regard to references to "treatment for termination of the pregnancy" in other sections of the 1967 Act and construction of the provision in s.1(1) that a pregnancy be "terminated by a registered medical practitioner" in accordance with these references, Sir George seemed not to share the view of Lord Denning, M.R. (see above) that "treatment" in these sections meant the actual act of terminating the pregnancy. Rather, Sir George appeared (at 812–813) to take the view that this term was used in direct contrast to "termination" and that consequently references to "treatment" provided no guidance as to the meaning of "termination":

"The word "treatment" appears in three other subsections of the Abortion Act, viz. section 1(3): "Except as provided by subsection (4) of this section,"—the emergency subsection—"any treatment for the termination of pregnancy must be carried out in a hospital . . ." This provision seems to me to be much wider than and in direct contrast to the words "terminated by." In my opinion treatment includes all that happens before the abortifacient is administered (or an instrument used), the nursing as distinct from acts of administration during the administration or use and care after the termination, and cannot be a guide to the interpretation of section 1(1).

In the "Application of Act to visiting forces etc.," section 3(1) reads:

"In relation to the termination of a pregnancy in a case where the following conditions are satisfied, that is to say—(a) the treatment for termination of the pregnancy was carried out in a hospital controlled by [visiting forces]; and (b) the pregnant woman had at the time of the treatment a relevant association with [visiting forces]; and (c) the treatment was carried out by a registered medical practitioner or a person who at the time of the treatment was a member of [the visiting force] appointed as a medical practitioner for that [visiting force] by the proper authorities of that [visiting force] . . ."

In (a) and (b) "treatment" is in direct contrast to the opening words "in relation to the termination of a pregnancy." Termination takes place during and is a part of treatment. At first sight (c) "treatment . . . carried out by a registered medical practitioner" gives some support to the liberal construction of section 1(1), but it also is governed by the words "in relation to the termination of a pregnancy;" it is for the application of the Act to a visiting force; and the provision is to give the visiting force the utmost freedom to arrange its own medical affairs within the ambit of our law.

Finally in the "conscience section," section 4: ". . . no person shall be under any duty . . . to participate in any treatment authorised by this Act to which he has a conscientious objection: . . ." This does not assist for if administration of an abortifacient or use of an instrument by a nurse on doctor's orders has not been authorised by the Act, she cannot be under a duty to participate.

Under the Abortion Regulations 1968 (S.I. 1968 No. 390), which the Minister of Health is required to make by section 2 of the Act, a certificate of the opinion of two registered medical practitioners must be given "before the commencement of the treatment for the termination of the pregnancy to which it relates": regulation 3(2). So too must the opinion that termination is immediately necessary to save life, under section 1(4), but if impracticable it may be given after the termination: regulation 3(3).

Under regulation 4 notices have to be given by the operating practitioner, that is "any practitioner who terminates a pregnancy," within seven days of the termination—not, be it noted, within seven days of the treatment after termination.

In my opinion there is nothing in the Act or Regulations to indicate that the intention of Parliament was other than that clearly expressed in the simple words "when a pregnancy is terminated by a registered medical practitioner." "

In Sir George's view (at 813–814), if Parliament had intended persons other than doctors to terminate pregnancies, it could have said so expressly, and in this respect his view accorded with that of Lord Denning, M.R.:

> ". . . the provision is clear and understandable. If the intention had been to make lawful the acts of persons participating in or carrying out the termination of a pregnancy on doctors' orders that could have been expressly stated either as the department suggest the section should be read, or by some other appropriate words; see the Radioactive Substances Act 1948, section 3(1)(a): ". . . a person acting in accordance with the directions of" a duly qualified general medical practitioner, or the Tattooing of Minors Act 1969, section 1: ". . . performed for medical reasons by a duly qualified medical practitioner or by a person working under his direction . . ."
>
> The Abortion Act 1967 requires the termination to be by the operative acts of the registered medical practitioner himself; his orders are not enough."

Brightman L.J., however, contrary to the views of Lord Denning, M.R. and Sir George Baker, felt that "terminated by a registered medical practitioner" in s.1(1) should be construed in accordance with references to "treatment for the termination of pregnancy" in other provisions in the Act. His Lordship stated (at 809):

> ". . . although the opening words of section 1 use the formula "a pregnancy is terminated," subsection (3), as also section 3(1)(a), refer to "*the treatment*" for termination of the pregnancy, and section 4(1) refers to "*treatment* authorised by this Act." It was submitted that where section 1(1) refers to a "pregnancy [being] terminated" by a doctor, it is in reality referring to "the treatment" for termination of a pregnancy being "carried out by" a doctor.
>
> I am disposed to accept this last submission and to read section 1(1) as meaning that a person shall not be guilty of an offence under the law relating to abortion "when *treatment* for termination of a pregnancy *is carried out by*" a registered medical practitioner. Such a construction does not in my opinion involve adding any words at all to the statute. I think it is what the section means on its true construction in the context in which the words are found."

Nevertheless, his Lordship took the view (at 810) that, under the new procedure, treatment for the termination of pregnancy was *not* carried out by doctors:

> ". . . it would be a misuse of language to describe such a termination of a pregnancy as done "by" a registered medical practitioner; or to describe such a treatment for termination of a pregnancy as "carried out by" a registered medical practitioner—however detailed and precise the written instructions given by the registered medical practitioner to the nurse. It would not be far removed from the nurse carrying out the operation from detailed instructions in a text book. The true analysis is that the doctor has provided the nurse with

> the means to terminate the pregnancy, not that the doctor has terminated the pregnancy.
>
> I decline to express a view as to precisely what does or does not need to be done by, or to be personally and immediately supervised by, the doctor in order to satisfy the stringent requirements of section 1."

Unlike Lord Denning, M.R. and Sir George Baker, Brightman L.J. made no reference to provisions in other statutes where specific mention was made of acting under the direction of a RMP, nor to the ordinary meaning of the words in s.1(1).

It can thus be seen that all three judges in the Court of Appeal came to the same conclusion, that the RCN should have the declaration that the advice from the DHSS was wrong in law, although not for the same reasons. The advice was wrong, according to Lord Denning, M.R. and Sir George Baker, because the words "terminated by" a registered medical practitioner in s.1(1) meant the carrying out of the actual acts of termination of pregnancy (as the RCN had contended) and this was not done by doctors under the new procedure. The advice was wrong, according to Brightman L.J., however, because these words meant the carrying out of treatment for the termination of pregnancy (as the DHSS had contended), but (rejecting the view of the DHSS) this treatment was not carried out by doctors under the new procedure but by nurses.

▷   (e) The decision of the House of Lords

11–008   The DHSS appealed to the House of Lords, where there was also a difference of opinion as to how s.1(1) should be interpreted. A majority of the House (Lords Diplock, Keith and Roskill) interpreted the words to mean the carrying out of treatment for the termination of pregnancy, as Brightman L.J. had done in the Court of Appeal but, unlike Brightman L.J., took the view that treatment was carried out by doctors under the new procedure. A minority (Lords Edmund-Davies and Wilberforce), however, interpreted the words in the way in which a majority of the Court of Appeal had interpreted them, namely as meaning the carrying out of the actual acts of termination of pregnancy. Accordingly, by a 3–2 majority, the appeal was allowed. The decision of the Court of Appeal was reversed and the declaration by Woolf J., that the DHSS's advice set out in its letter (see above, 11–004) did not involve the performance of any unlawful acts by members of the RCN, was restored.

Little reference was made by members of the House to the ordinary meaning of words and no comment was made on Lord Denning, M.R.'s remarks in the Court of Appeal that the words in s.1(1) should be interpreted in the sense in which they would be understood by doctors, nurses and jury members. However, Lord Keith, when considering the words in their statutory context, having regard to other provisions in the Act—as to which, see below, 11–011—did remark (at 834):

> "The sidenote to section 1 is "Medical termination of pregnancy." "Termination of pregnancy" is an expression commonly used, perhaps rather more by medical people than by laymen, to describe in neutral and unemotive terms the bringing about of an abortion. So used, it is capable of covering the whole process designed to lead to that result . . ."

Lord Keith thus seemed to regard the expression "termination", in its common usage, as including treatment leading to an abortion, thereby suggesting that the DHSS's contention fell within the ordinary meaning of the words in s.1(1). In contrast, Lord Edmund-Davies (at 831), dissenting, who made specific reference to the ordinary meaning of the words in s.1(1), took the view that that the DHSS's contention did not fall within them:

> ". . . the opening words of section 1(1) are clear and simple, clear to under-stand and simple to apply to the only abortive methods professionally accepted in 1967 when the Act was passed. Save in grave emergency, only a qualified doctor or surgeon could then lawfully perform the orthodox surgical acts, and the statute could have had no other person in mind. Then should section 1 be interpreted differently now that abortive methods undreamt of in 1967 have since been discovered and become widely applied? The answer must be that its simple words must not be distorted in order to bring under the statutory umbrella medical procedures to which they cannot properly be applied, however desirable such an extension may be thought to be. The extra-amniotic procedure first reported in 1971 has already been described by my noble and learned friend, Lord Wilberforce . . . [and] in my judgment, it is impossible to regard an abortion resulting from such procedure as one "ter-minated by a registered medical practitioner," for the acts indispensable to termination are in many cases performed not by the doctor but by the nurses over a long period of hours after the doctor last saw the pregnant woman. And, despite the claims of the Solicitor-General that he sought simply to give the statutory words "their plain and ordinary meaning," he substantially departed from that approach by submitting that they should be read as meaning "terminated by treatment for the termination of pregnancy carried out by a registered medical practitioner in accordance with recognised medical practice." "

Greater attention, however, was paid to examining the words in their statutory context and various approaches were adopted with regard to ascertaining the intention of Parliament and construing the words so as to give effect to this intention.

(i) The approach of the majority

Essentially, the majority sought to ascertain Parliamentary intent by reference to the policy behind the 1967 Act and to the words "treatment for the termination of pregnancy" in other sections of the Act, which were considered to be an important

11–009

part of the statutory context for the construction of the words "terminated by a registered medical practitioner" in s.1(1).

(1) Policy behind the 1967 Act

11–010 This was most fully considered by Lord Diplock (at 825–826), who, after referring to the description of the Act in its long title as "An Act to amend and clarify the law relating to termination of pregnancy by registered medical practitioners", sought to establish the mischief at which the statute was aimed with a view to ascertaining its purpose:

> ". . . its purpose in my view becomes clear if one starts by considering what was the state of the law relating to abortion before the passing of the Act, what was the mischief that required amendment, and in what respect was the existing law unclear. . .
>
> It had long been generally accepted that abortion was lawful where it was necessary to save the pregnant woman's life; but what circumstances, if any, short of this legitimised termination of a pregnancy does not appear to have attracted judicial notice until, in 1938, the matter was put to a sagaciously selected test by Mr Aleck Bourne, a well-known obstetrical surgeon . . .
>
> The summing up by Macnaghten J. in *Rex v Bourne* [1939] 1 K.B. 687 resulted in an acquittal. So the correctness of his statement of the law did not undergo examination by any higher authority. It still remained in 1967 the only judicial pronouncement on the subject. No disrespect is intended to that eminent judge and former head of my old chambers, if I say that his reputation is founded more upon his sturdy common sense than upon his lucidity of legal exposition. Certainly his summing up, directed as it was to the highly exceptional facts of the particular case, left plenty of loose ends and ample scope for clarification. For instance, his primary ruling was that the onus lay upon the Crown to satisfy the jury that the defendant did not procure the miscarriage of the woman in good faith for the purpose only of "preserving her life" but this requirement he suggested to the jury they were entitled to regard as satisfied if the probable consequence of the continuance of the pregnancy would be to "make the woman a physical or mental wreck"—a vivid phrase borrowed from one of the witnesses but unfortunately lacking in precision. The learned judge would appear to have regarded the defence as confined to registered medical practitioners, and there is a passage in his summing up which suggests that it is available only where the doctor's opinion as to the probable dire consequences of the continuation of the pregnancy was not only held bona fide but was also based on reasonable grounds and adequate knowledge—an objective test which it would be for the jury to determine whether, upon the evidence adduced before them, it was satisfied or not."

These critical comments were designed to demonstrate the lack of certainty in the earlier law as regards the scope of lawful abortions and to indicate that it was this lack of certainty which the 1967 Act was intended to resolve. Thus, Lord Diplock (at 826–827) continued:

> "Such then was the unsatisfactory and uncertain state of the law that the Abortion Act 1967 was intended to amend and clarify. What the Act sets out to do is to provide an exhaustive statement of the circumstances in which treatment for the termination of pregnancy may be carried out lawfully . . .
>
> . . . the policy of the Act, it seems to me, is clear. There are two aspects to it: the first is to broaden the grounds upon which abortions may be lawfully obtained; the second is to ensure that the abortion is carried out with all proper skill and in hygienic conditions . . ."

The policy behind the 1967 Act was considered to a much lesser extent by Lords Keith and Roskill. Lord Keith concentrated on construing s.1(1) by reference to other sections of the Act where the words "treatment for termination of the pregnancy" appeared (see below, 11–011) and mentioned policy (at 835) only at the end of his judgment after reaching his conclusion on how s.1(1) should be interpreted:

> "I therefore conclude that termination of pregnancy by means of the procedures under consideration is authorised by the terms of section 1(1). This conclusion is the more satisfactory as it appears to me to be fully in accordance with that part of the policy and purpose of the Act which was directed to securing that socially acceptable abortions should be carried out under the safest conditions attainable. One may also feel some relief that it is unnecessary to reach a decision involving that the very large numbers of medical practitioners and others who have participated in the relevant procedures over several years past should now be revealed as guilty of criminal offences."

Lord Roskill, who like Lord Diplock took into consideration (at 835) the long title of the 1967 Act, did not address the matter of policy directly, although his Lordship referred to the social purpose of the legislation:

> ". . . the long title of the Abortion Act 1967 is "An Act to amend and clarify the law relating to the termination of pregnancy by registered medical practitioners." The respondents accepted before your Lordships' House that the Act of 1967 had a social purpose, namely the making of abortions available more freely and without infringement of the criminal law but subject always to the conditions of that Act being satisfied. But Parliament sought to achieve that admitted social purpose not as in the case of some social reforms by expressly creating some positive entitlement on the part of members of the public to that which the statute sought to achieve but by enacting in section 1(1) that "a person" (not, be it noted, simply "a registered medical practitioner") should "not be guilty of an offence under the law relating to abortion" provided that certain other conditions were satisfied. "The law relating to abortion" was defined in section 6 as meaning "sections 58 and 59 of the Offences against the Person Act 1861, and any rule of law relating to the procurement of

abortion . . ." Thus the scheme of the Act of 1967 was to exempt from the sanctions of the criminal law imposed principally by the Offences against the Person Act 1861 upon those who carried out or attempted to carry out abortions those, but only those, who carried them out in a manner which satisfied all the requirements of the Act of 1967."

(2) "Treatment for termination of the pregnancy" in other sections of the 1967 Act as context for the interpretation of "terminated by a registered medical practitioner" in s.1(1)

11–011   The majority were unanimously of the view that references in other sections of the 1967 Act to the words "treatment for termination of the pregnancy" formed an important part of the statutory context for construing the words in s.1(1) and indicated that Parliament's intention was for s.1(1) to have application where treatment was initiated and supervised by doctors. Thus, Lord Diplock, having referred to references in the Act to "treatment for the termination of pregnancy" on the one hand and references to "terminated" or "termination" on the other, stated (at 827–828):

". . . the draftsman appears to use the longer and the shorter expressions indiscriminately, as is shown by a comparison between subsections (1) and (3) of section 1 . . . Furthermore, if "termination" or "terminated" meant only the event of miscarriage and not the whole treatment undertaken with that object in mind, lack of success, which apparently occurs in one to two per cent of cases, would make all who had taken part in the unsuccessful treatment guilty of an offence under section 58 or 59 of the Offences against the Person Act 1861. This cannot have been the intention of Parliament.

The requirement of the Act as to the way in which treatment is to be carried out, which in my view throws most light upon the second aspect of its policy [*that abortion is carried out with all proper skill and in hygienic conditions*] and the true construction of the phrase in subsection (1) of section 1 which lies at the root of the dispute between the parties to this appeal, is the requirement in subsection (3) that, except in cases of dire emergency, the treatment must be carried out in a National Health Service hospital (or private clinic specially approved for that purpose by the minister). It is in my view evident that in providing that treatment for termination of pregnancies should take place in ordinary hospitals, Parliament contemplated that (conscientious objections apart) like other hospital treatment, it would be undertaken as a team effort in which, acting on the instructions of the doctor in charge of the treatment, junior doctors, nurses, para-medical and other members of the hospital staff would each do those things forming part of the whole treatment, which it would be in accordance with accepted medical practice to entrust to a member of the staff possessed of their respective qualifications and experience.

Subsection (1) although it is expressed to apply only "when a pregnancy is terminated by a registered medical practitioner" . . . also appears to contemplate treatment that is in the nature of a team effort and to extend its protection to all those who play a part in it. The exoneration from guilt is not confined to the registered medical practitioner by whom a pregnancy is terminated, it extends to any person who takes part in the treatment for its termination."

Lord Keith (at 834) was also convinced that the words "when a pregnancy is terminated" in s.1(1), when considered in the context of other provisions in the 1967 Act, did not refer to the mere physical occurrence of termination, but envisaged termination of pregnancy as being a process of treatment. In reaching this conclusion, his Lordship made reference, inter alia, to ss.1(3), 3 and 4, as did Lord Roskill, who stated (at 837–838):

". . . I have read and re-read the Act of 1967 to see if I can discern in its provisions any consistent pattern in the use of the phrase "a pregnancy is terminated" or "termination of a pregnancy" on the one hand and "treatment for the termination of a pregnancy" on the other hand. One finds the former phrase in section 1(1) and (1)(a), the latter in section 1(3), the former in section 1(4), the latter in section 2(1)(b), and again in section 3(1)(a) and (c). Most important to my mind is section 4 which is the conscientious objection section. This section in two places refers to "participate in treatment" in the context of conscientious objection. If one construes section 4 in conjunction with section 1(1), as surely one should do in order to determine to what it is that conscientious objection is permitted, it seems to me that section 4 strongly supports the wider construction of section 1(1). It was suggested that the acceptance of the appellants' [DHSS] submission involved re-writing that subsection so as to add words which are not to be found in the language of the subsection. My Lords, with great respect to that submission, I do not agree. If one construes the words "when a pregnancy is terminated by a registered medical practitioner" in section 1(1) as embracing the case where the "treatment for the termination of pregnancy is carried out under the control of a doctor in accordance with ordinary current medical practice" I think one is reading "termination of pregnancy" and "treatment for termination of pregnancy" as virtually synonymous and as I think Parliament must have intended they should be read . . . This is, I think, the view which appealed to Woolf J. and to Brightman L.J. and I find myself in respectful agreement with that view."

However, Lord Roskill (at 838) rejected Brightman L.J.'s view that treatment under the new procedure was carried out not by doctors but by nurses and accordingly abortions did not fall within the protection conferred by s.1(1):

"But with respect I am unable to share the learned Lord Justice's view on the facts. I think that the successive steps taken by a nurse in carrying out the

> extra-amniotic process are fully protected provided that the entirety of the treatment for the termination of the pregnancy and her participation in it is at all times under the control of the doctor even though the doctor is not present throughout the entirety of the treatment."

His Lordship's view was shared both by Lord Diplock (at 828–829) and by Lord Keith, although the latter also addressed the novel point of whether termination might be effected by more than one person. Lord Keith stated (at 835):

> "Given that the termination of pregnancy under contemplation in section 1(1) includes the whole process of treatment involved therein, it remains to consider whether, on the facts of this case, the termination can properly be regarded as being "by a registered medical practitioner." In my opinion this question is to be answered affirmatively. The doctor has responsibility for the whole process and is in charge of it throughout. It is he who decides that it is to be carried out. He personally performs essential parts of it which are such as to necessitate the application of his particular skill. The nurse's actions are done under his direct written instructions. In the circumstances I find it impossible to hold that the doctor's role is other than that of a principal, and I think he would be very surprised to hear that the nurse was the principal and he himself only an accessory. It is true that it is the nurse's action which leads directly to the introduction of the abortifacient drugs into the system of the patient, but that action is done in a ministerial capacity and on the doctor's orders. Even if it were right to regard the nurse as a principal, it seems to me inevitable that the doctor should also be so regarded. If both the doctor and the nurse were principals, the provisions of the subsection would be still satisfied, because the pregnancy would have been terminated by the doctor notwithstanding that it had also been terminated by the nurse."

(ii) The approach of the minority

11–012 The minority took a different view from the majority with respect to the policy behind the legislation and little regard was paid to the references to "treatment for termination of the pregnancy" in other sections of the 1967 Act. Attention instead was focused on interpreting the words used by Parliament in s.1(1) and not engaging in what, in their view, would amount to reading words into the statute, with (brief) reference being made in addition to the absence in the 1967 Act of express words providing for actions to be undertaken under the supervision or direction of a RMP.

(1) Policy behind the 1967 Act

11–013 Whilst the majority saw the policy as being primarily to extend the scope of lawful abortion, Lord Edmund-Davies felt that this was not so and that the policy of the Act was both to extend and to restrict the law. Making reference to the preamble to the Act, His Lordship stated (at 829–31):

"In its preamble it is described as an Act "to amend and clarify the law relating to termination of pregnancy by registered medical practitioners," and, far from simply enlarging the existing abortion facilities, in the true spirit of compromise it both relaxed and restricted the existing law. . .

[I]t would be quite wrong to regard the Act of 1967 as wholly permissive in character, for it both restricted and amplified the existing abortion law. It amplified "the law relating to abortion" as declared in *Rex v Bourne* [1939] 1 K.B. 687 by extending it in section 1(1)(a) to cases where "the continuance of the pregnancy would involve risk to the . . . physical or mental health of . . . any existing children of [the pregnant woman's] family, greater than if the pregnancy were terminated"; and in section 1(1)(b) by including the case of "substantial risk that if the *child* were born it would suffer from such physical or mental abnormalities as to be seriously handicapped."

On the other hand, the Act also restricted the *Bourne* law in several ways. The pregnancy must now be terminated "by a registered medical practitioner," and this even if, in the words of section 1(4), "the termination is immediately necessary to save the life or to prevent grave permanent injury to the physical or mental health of the pregnant woman," whereas *Rex v Bourne* imposed no such restriction in the cases predicated, and a qualified doctor who was not a registered medical practitioner could have invoked the decision in that case. And, save in those circumstances of urgency, abortive treatment is required under the Act to be carried out in such premises as are designated in section 1(3) and section 3. Again, in the forefront is the requirement in section 1(1) of the opinion of two doctors that the risks indicated in (a) or (b) are involved if pregnancy were allowed to go full term. And a further practical (though not legal) restriction was imposed by the requirement under section 2(1)(b) that the "registered medical practitioner who terminated a pregnancy [must] give notice of the termination and such other information relating to the termination as may be . . . prescribed." "

Although Lord Edmund-Davies did not say so expressly, the implication of his remarks is that the Act should not necessarily be interpreted in a way which would extend the scope of lawful abortion (as would be the case if effect was given to the DHSS's contention as to the meaning of the words in s.1(1)).

Lord Wilberforce, on the other hand, seemed to take the view (at 821–822) that the policy of Parliament was to confine the carrying out of abortions to doctors and to prevent abortions being carried out by unqualified persons:

". . . I start from the point that in 1967—the date of the Act—the only methods used to produce abortions were surgical methods; of these there were several varieties . . . Parliament must have been aware of these methods and cannot have had in mind a process where abortifacient agents were administered by nurses. They did not exist. Parliament's concern must have been to prevent existing methods being carried out by unqualified persons and to insist they should be carried out by doctors. For these reasons Parliament no doubt used the words, in section 1(1) ". . . pregnancy . . . terminated by a registered medical practitioner . . ."

In interpreting an Act of Parliament it is proper, and indeed necessary, to have regard to the state of affairs existing, and known by Parliament to be existing, at the time. It is a fair presumption that Parliament's policy or intention is directed to that state of affairs . . . when a new state of affairs, or a fresh set of facts bearing on policy, comes into existence, the courts have to consider whether they fall within the Parliamentary intention. They may be held to do so, if they fall within the same genus of facts as those to which the expressed policy has been formulated. They may also be held to do so if there can be detected a clear purpose in the legislation which can only be fulfilled if the extension is made. How liberally these principles may be applied must depend upon the nature of the enactment, and the strictness or otherwise of the words in which it has been expressed. The courts should be less willing to extend expressed meanings if it is clear that the Act in question was designed to be restrictive or circumscribed in its operation rather than liberal or permissive. They will be much less willing to do so where the subject matter is different in kind or dimension from that for which the legislation was passed. In any event there is one course which the courts cannot take, under the law of this country; they cannot fill gaps; they cannot by asking the question 'What would Parliament have done in this current case—not being one in contemplation—if the facts had been before it?' attempt themselves to supply the answer, if the answer is not to be found in the terms of Act itself.

In my opinion this Act should be construed with caution. It is dealing with a controversial subject involving moral and social judgments on which opinions strongly differ. It is, if ever an Act was, one for interpreting in the spirit that only that which Parliament has authorised on a fair reading of the relevant sections should be held to be within it. The new (post-1967) method of medical induction is clearly not just a fresh species or example of something already authorised. The Act is not for "purposive" or "liberal" or "equitable" construction. This is a case where the courts must hold that anything beyond the legislature's fairly expressed authority should be left for Parliament's fresh consideration.

Having regard particularly to the Act's antecedents and the state of affairs existing in 1967, which involved surgical action requiring to be confined to termination by doctors alone, I am unable to read the words "pregnancy terminated by a registered medical practitioner" as extended or extensible to cover cases where other persons, whether nurses, or midwives, or even lay persons, play a significant part in the process of termination."

(2) Not reading words into the statute

Although Lords Wilberforce and Edmund-Davies appeared to take different views **11–014** of the policy behind the legislation, they were nevertheless in agreement that, in order to give effect to the intention of Parliament, s.1(1) should be interpreted restrictively so that actual termination of pregnancy needed to be by a RMP for abortions to be lawful. Both were of the view that the DHSS's contention would amount to reading words into the statute and both went on to state (obiter) that, even if the section was to be interpreted as the DHSS contended, the treatment would not in any event be treatment by a RMP. Thus Lord Wilberforce (at 823) observed:

> "[*The DHSS's*] contention . . . was that the words "pregnancy is terminated by a registered medical practitioner" mean "pregnancy is terminated by treatment of a registered medical practitioner in accordance with recognised medical practice." But, with all respect, this is not construction: it is rewriting. And, moreover, it does not achieve its objective. I could perhaps agree that a reference to treatment could fairly be held to be implied: no doubt treatment is necessary. But I do not see that this alone carries the matter any further: it must still be treatment by the registered medical practitioner. The additional words, on the other hand, greatly extend the enactment, and it is they which are supposed to introduce nurse participation. But I cannot see that they do this."

Similarly, Lord Edmund-Davies (at 831–832), alluding to the DHSS's contention, remarked:

> ". . . this is redrafting with a vengeance. And even were it permissible, it would still remain to consider what *part* the doctor played in the treatment, in order to ensure that it was not so remote from the termination as to make it impossible to say in any realistic sense that it was he who terminated the pregnancy. I am in respectful agreement with Brightman L.J., who said of the extra-amniotic procedure:
>
> > ". . . it would be a misuse of language . . . to describe such a treatment for termination of a pregnancy as 'carried out by' a registered medical practitioner. . ."

(3) References to "treatment for the termination of pregnancy" in other sections of the 1967 Act

Little regard was paid to such references by the minority. No mention was made of **11–015** this by Lord Wilberforce. Lord Edmund-Davies (at 832) did not go beyond contrasting the language used in these provisions with that used in s.1(1):

> "It is true that the word "treatment" is to be found in several places in the Act, and that the phrase "treatment for the termination of pregnancy" appears

both in section 1(3) and in section 3(1), but both are significantly different from the language of section 1(1)."

(4) Absence of express provision for actions to be undertaken under the supervision or direction of a RMP

11–016 This matter (to which no reference was made by the majority), although addressed only briefly by Lords Wilberforce and Edmund-Davies, was nevertheless considered by their Lordships to provide a significant indication that actions carried out under the supervision or direction of a RMP were not within the contemplation of Parliament when passing the legislation. Lord Wilberforce (at 823–824) stated:

"It is significant, as Lord Denning M.R. [*in the Court of Appeal*] has pointed out, that recognised language exists and has been used, when it is desired that something shall be done by doctors with nurse participation. This takes the form "by a registered medical practitioner or by a person acting in accordance with the directions of any such practitioner." This language has been used in four Acts of Parliament (listed by Lord Denning M.R.), three of them prior to the Act of 1967, all concerned with the administration of substances, drugs or medicines which may have an impact upon the human body. It has not been used, surely deliberately, in the present Act. We ought to assume that Parliament knew what it was doing when it omitted to use them."

Similar sentiments were expressed by Lord Edmund-Davies (at 832):

". . . had Parliament been minded to legislate on the lines which the appellants [*DHSS*] submit was its aim, Lord Denning M.R. demonstrated by reference to several earlier statutes in the medical field that the legislature had already to hand suitable words which would have rendered unnecessary any such expansive interpretation as that favoured in the present instance by the Solicitor-General."

It can be seen that interpretation of the provision in s.1(1) that "a pregnancy is terminated by a registered medical practitioner" gave rise to a considerable divergence of judicial opinion. At the conclusion of the case, of the nine judges who had considered the case, four (Lord Denning, M.R. and Sir George Baker in the Court of Appeal; and Lords Wilberforce and Edmund-Davies in the House of Lords) were of the view that the provision meant actual acts performed by a RMP to terminate pregnancy; and five (Woolf J. at first instance; Brightman L.J. in the Court of Appeal; and Lords Diplock, Keith and Roskill in the House of Lords) were of the view that the provision meant treatment supervised and directed by a RMP to terminate pregnancy. Of these five, all except Brightman L.J. were of the view that, under the new procedure, treatment was supervised and directed by a RMP to terminate pregnancy. Accordingly, five judges supported the RCN's view of the law that nurses were acting unlawfully under the new procedure and four supported the DHSS's view that they were not.

The arguments in *Royal College* are finely balanced and there is no obviously "correct" solution to the question of statutory interpretation in issue. The case provides a clear illustration of the fact that in litigation there may be compelling arguments that can be advanced by each party and that what turns out to be the "correct" solution may depend upon how far a litigant is able to pursue his case and possibly also upon which judges happen to be involved.

▶ 4. Further Difficulties?

The *Royal College* case, however, has almost certainly not solved all potential **11–017** difficulties with s.1(1) of the Abortion Act. Just as that case resulted from the development of a new form of termination, so other treatments, more recently, have been developed which might give rise to legal difficulty, e.g. the drug Mifepristone, a synthetic steroid compound marketed under the brand name Mifegyne in the United Kingom and given official approval for use as an abortifacient in 1991. Three 200mg doses of the drug are taken by the pregnant woman, normally within the first seven weeks of pregnancy, and the woman is then allowed home after a minimum period of two hours' observation. She returns 36–48 hours later for the insertion of a prostaglandin vaginal pessary which should ensure a successful termination. Kennedy and Grubb, *Medical Law*, 3rd edn (2000), p.1478, however, point out that in some cases the effects of the Mifepristone occur before the woman returns to the hospital for the prostaglandin vaginal pessary:

> "In 55% of cases bleeding (and, therefore, the potential for a 'miscarriage') occur within 48 hours of administering Mifepristone. In a proportion of cases (about 3%) termination will occur before readmission".

Where termination occurs before readmission, it might be questioned whether there has been an abortion lawfully carried out under the Abortion Act 1967. It could be argued that in this 3 per cent of cases the woman, by taking the doses of the drug, has brought about the abortion and that the pregnancy has not been "terminated by a registered medical practitioner". However, the *Royal College* case, which gave a broad interpretation to that phrase, may indicate that the abortion in these circumstances would be lawful because the treatment, requiring three 200mg doses of the drug, is prescribed by a doctor and carried out under his directions. Kennedy and Grubb (at pp.1478–1479) take the former view and consider *Royal College* to be distinguishable:

> "Legally, the situation is analogous to a case where a doctor provides the means (eg pills) for a patient to kill himself. It is the patient who commits suicide. The doctor is guilty of assisting suicide, if anything. It cannot be said that he is guilty of murder since the law regards the patient's actions as the cause of death. *Mutatis mutandis*, here the woman causes her own termination. The provisions of the Abortion Act 1967 would not be complied with . . .

In one sense, a doctor does have responsibility for the patient throughout the treatment. However, it is a different kind of responsibility from that contemplated in the *Royal College of Nursing* case. In that case the responsibility denoted the right to control those who acted on his behalf in a professional capacity. In the case of Mifepristone, the responsibility relates to the doctor's ethical and legal duty to his patient. The relationship is neither one of control nor one where the patient (in administering the drug to herself) can be said to act on the doctor's behalf or be in his charge. It is unlikely that a future court would further expand the meaning of the 1967 Act to cover the use of Mifepristone."

It remains to be seen whether this view is correct.

Further reading

Argent and Pavey, "Can nurses legally perform surgical induced abortion?" (2007) 33 *Journal of Family Planning and Reproductive Health Care* 79

Royal College of Nursing of the United Kingdom v Department of Health and Social Security [1981] Crim. L.R. 322

12 WIVES AS PROSECUTION WITNESSES

▶ 1. Introduction

In *Hoskyn v Metropolitan Police Commissioner* [1978] 2 All E.R. 136 (*Hoskyn*), the **12–001** House of Lords was faced with the question of deciding whether a wife who was a competent witness (permitted to give evidence) was compellable and thus could be required to do so against her husband on a charge of personal violence on her by him. The competency of the wife to give evidence on a charge of personal violence had been established in *R. v Lord Audley* (1631) 3 State Tr. 401 and it had been decided in *R. v Lapworth* [1931] 1 K.B. 117 (*Lapworth*) by the Court of Criminal Appeal (see above, 2–013) that, on the basis that competent witnesses were generally compellable, the wife was also a compellable witness in such a case. There was thus established Court of Appeal authority directly in point on the very issue which the House of Lords had to decide, authority which had been followed both by the trial judge and by the Court of Appeal in the present case. The Court of Appeal had, however, certified that a point of law of general public importance was involved and leave to appeal to the House of Lords was given. The House, by a 4–1 majority (Lord Edmund-Davies dissenting), decided that the wife was not a compellable witness and overruled *Lapworth*. There were separate judgments by three of the four members of the majority, Viscount Dilhorne and Lords Wilberforce and Salmon, with the fourth member, Lord Keith, expressing himself to be in agreement with Lord Wilberforce.

This case study illustrates several points in relation to precedent:

- ▶ the differing interpretations of previous authorities by their Lordships;
- ▶ the overruling of an established Court of Appeal authority, directly in point, of some years standing;
- ▶ the according of particular weight to statements by certain judges of repute;
- ▶ judicial pronouncements in decisions which are extempore where judgment has not been reserved;
- ▶ a consideration of persuasive authorities from other jurisdictions;
- ▶ the citation of views expressed in textbooks;
- ▶ the influence of policy considerations on judicial decision-making and on statutory interpretation;
- ▶ obiter statements made in cases; and
- ▶ a dissenting judgment which ultimately came to represent the present law following a statutory reversal of the principle established by the House of Lords in the case under consideration.

▶ 2. The Differing Interpretations of Previous Authorities

12-002 Although there were 19 cases referred to in total in the various judgments, there were three main authorities on which reliance was placed: *R. v Inhabitants of All Saints, Worcester* (1817) 6 M. & S. 194 (*All Saints, Worcester*); *Leach v R* [1912] A.C. 305 (*Leach*); and *Lapworth*.

▷ *(a) R. v Inhabitants of All Saints, Worcester*

12-003 In this case, in order to determine whether under the Poor Laws a female pauper should be removed to the parish of All Saints, Worcester from the parish of Cheltenham, it was relevant to determine whether the pauper was married to one George Willis. One of the parties sought to prove that this was not the case on the ground that, although the pauper had gone through a ceremony of marriage with George Willis, George Willis was already married to another person, Ann Willis, at that time. Ann Willis was called to give evidence of the marriage and objection was taken to her competency. The Court of King's Bench (see below, 2–015) held that she was a competent witness and in the course of his judgment Bayley J. remarked (at 200):

> ". . . it appears to me that Ann Willis was a competent witness . . . It does not appear that she objected to be examined or demurred to any question. If she had thrown herself on the protection of the Court on the ground that her answer to the question put to her might criminate her husband, in that case I am not prepared to say that the Court would have compelled her to answer; on the contrary, I think she would have been entitled to the protection of the Court."

The statement by Bayley J. appeared to support the view that the wife was not compellable, although clearly this was not a matter which the court had to decide. The wife had not objected to being examined in that case and so it was not necessary to decide whether she could be compelled to give evidence. As such, Bayley J.'s remarks were not part of the ratio of the case, but merely obiter and therefore only of persuasive authority in any court. Even if the remarks had been ratio, however, they would not have been binding on the House of Lords, as they were made in the Court of King's Bench whose decisions have the same precedential status as decisions of the High Court (see above, 2–015).

These remarks of Bayley J. were regarded as particularly persuasive by Lord Salmon in *Hoskyn* (at 149–150):

> "That pronouncement [*of Bayley J.*] was, no doubt, obiter, but coming from such a master of the common law it deserves to be treated with the greatest respect: I regard it as being of the highest persuasive authority."

This approach of Lord Salmon of expressing high regard for a previous judicial statement which accorded with his view of the present case might be compared with that of Lord Edmund-Davies who, when expressing support for *Lapworth* in his dissenting judgment, stated (at 158) that "the reputation of few criminal judges of this century stands as high as Avory J., who gave the judgment of the court" (see below, 12–005).

No other members of the majority expressed such high regard for Bayley J.'s remarks, although reliance was placed upon them. Viscount Dilhorne, recognising the case to have been the first one in which the compellability of a wife appeared to have come under consideration, felt (at 145) that an inference of non-compellability could be drawn from the case. In his Lordship's opinion, had the wife been a compellable witness by virtue of the fact that she was competent to give evidence, there would have been some reference by members of the court to this:

"If in 1817 it was held in some quarters that a wife who was competent was ipso facto compellable, I cannot but think that Lord Ellenborough CJ and Bayley J would have referred to it".

That no such reference was made suggested the wife was not compellable, although his Lordship did not go so far as to state that the case supported that view, confining himself instead to stating that it lent no support to the view that she was compellable.

The remaining member of the majority who delivered judgment, Lord Wilberforce (at 140), confined himself to quoting without comment the remarks of Bayley J. and their subsequent citation in a prominent textbook as indicating that the wife was not compellable:

"As to this passage [*of Bayley J.'s*] the authoritative textbook Taylor on Evidence, 10th Edn (1906) para 1368 says:

'But although by the common law rule of incompetency, the wife may be *permitted* to give evidence which may indirectly criminate her husband, it by no means follows that she can be *compelled* to do so; and the better opinion is that under it she may throw herself on the protection of the Court, and decline to answer any question which would tend to expose her husband to a criminal charge.'"

A similar view to that expressed in *Taylor on Evidence*, to which Viscount Dilhorne also referred (at 145), is contained in *Phillips and Anderson on Evidence*, 10th edn (1852), p.73 and *Roscoe's Digest*, 11th edn (1890), p.143. After referring to these works, Lord Wilberforce concluded by recognising that "other views are expressed in other textbooks", although no reference was made to any by his Lordship.

Courts do not as a general rule make reference to the views of authors of textbooks or other works, since what an author says is not the law, but the author's view of what the law is. It is cases and statutes which contain the law. However, courts do on occasions refer to the views of authors, particularly where there is no authority in point or where the authorities are in a state of conflict or uncertainty.

The *All Saints, Worcester* case, relied upon in varying degrees by all members of the majority, was not regarded by Lord Edmund-Davies dissenting as supportive of the proposition that the wife was not a compellable witness. First, his Lordship (at 154) appeared to regard the case as distinguishable in that there were material differences between it and the present case:

> "The facts were widely different from those of the present case: it had nothing to do with personal violence, and no spouse was accused. But the differences by no means stop there. In proceedings of a quasi-criminal character for the removal of a female pauper, it was material to ascertain whether C had gone through a ceremony of marriage with her. As it was in the interests of one of the parties to establish that he had not, they called A to prove that she had some years earlier married C and that the marriage was still subsisting. It was beyond doubt that A was a competent witness in the removal proceedings . . ."

Secondly, his Lordship (at 154–155) did not regard the dicta of Bayley J. as a clear pointer against compellability, since:

> ". . . in the course of his judgment Bayley J said:
>
>> 'It does not appear that she objected to be examined, or demurred to any question. If she had thrown herself on the protection of the Court on the ground that her answer to the question put to her might criminate her husband, in that case I am not prepared to say that the Court would have compelled her to answer; on the contrary, I think she would have been entitled to the protection of the Court . . .'
>
> These words of a judge of outstanding quality are heavily relied on by your Lordships as a powerful indication that it is a mistake to equate competence at common law with compellability, as they have been by Taylor and by some other (but by no means all) textbook writers who rely on them as their sole authority for that proposition. But in fact the case had nothing to do with competence or compellability to testify, but solely with privilege, and confusion between the three concepts is commonplace (Cowen and Carter, Essays on the Law of Evidence (1956), p 220):
>
>> 'There are certain questions which a witness may refuse to answer if he so wishes. He is said to be privileged in respect of those questions. It should be clear, therefore, that competence without compellability (or bare competence) is not the same as privilege. Compellability is concerned with whether a witness can be forced by a party to give evidence at all. Privilege is concerned with whether a witness who is already in the box is obliged to answer a particular question . . .'

> I have to say, with respect, that a similar confusion has arisen in relation to *R v Inhabitants of All Saints, Worcester* . . ."

His Lordship accordingly concluded (at 156) that:

> ". . . the *All Saints, Worcester* case, in my judgment, has accordingly nothing to do with the compellability of a witness competent at common law; it merely deals with the entitlement of a witness, competent for some purposes but not for others, to be privileged not to answer certain questions put to her".

Since the *All Saints, Worcester* case was not concerned with compellability, this could be seen as a further ground for distinguishing it, in addition to the material differences identified between it and the present case, namely that it was not concerned with personal violence; no spouse was accused; and the proceedings were only of a quasi-criminal character (see above).

▷ *(b) Leach v R*

In this case, the House of Lords decided that a wife was not a compellable witness **12-004** under s.4(1) of the Criminal Evidence Act 1898 (CEA 1898). Section 4(1) made a wife a competent witness, but made no reference to compellability. It provided that the spouse of a person charged with one of the offences specified in the Schedule to the Act could be called as a witness for the prosecution or defence without the consent of the person charged, whilst s.4(2) provided that nothing in the Act should affect the case where a husband or wife of a person charged with an offence may at common law be called as a witness without the consent of that person. The opinion of the House was expressed in three judgments, in which the following statements were made:

(a) Lord Loreburn L.C. referred (at 308) to "a fundamental and old principle to which the law has looked, that you ought not to compel a wife to give evidence against her husband in matters of a criminal kind".

(b) Lord Halsbury remarked (at 310–311) that: "I should have asked, when it was proposed to call the wife against the husband: 'Will you show me an Act of Parliament that definitely says you may compel her to give evidence?' because since the foundation of the common law it has been recognised that this is contrary to the course of the law".

(c) Lord Atkinson stated (at 311): "The principle that a wife is not to be compelled to give evidence against her husband is deep seated in the common law of this country, and I think if it is to be overturned it must be overturned by a clear, definite and positive enactment".

The view of Lord Wilberforce and Viscount Dilhorne in *Hoskyn* was that their Lordships in *Leach* were concerned with interpreting s.4(1) of the CEA 1898 and not with the position at common law where a charge of personal violence was involved.

Nevertheless, both felt the observations in *Leach* to have equal application to the common law. Lord Wilberforce stated (at 141–142):

> "My Lords, it is certain that their Lordships were dealing with a point of statutory construction (of s4 of the 1898 Act), that they were not called on to pronounce on the position at common law, and that anything they said, expressly or by implication, as to the latter would be outside what they were called on to decide. Nevertheless, I cannot believe that they would have used the strong and unqualified expressions which they did, if they had thought that there were special cases, outside the ambit of the statute, in which a wife was compellable. If they had so thought they would surely have thought it necessary to deal with the argument by analogy: '. . . it is true that the principle we are stating is not absolute: there are exceptions at common law, when the wife is competent and compellable, but that does not affect the position under statute', or at least qualify in some way their general statements. And if they had been asked: 'What about the case where a wife was competent at common law? Does not the ordinary rule make her compellable?' they would surely have answered: 'No, because the considerations which led the law to treat her as competent do not in any way weaken the force of the principle we have stated that a wife ought not to be forced into the witness box, a principle of general application and fundamental importance.'"

Viscount Dilhorne remarked (at 145–146):

> "In *R v Acaster and Leach* (1911) 7 Cr App R 84 the Court of Criminal Appeal held that a person who could be called by virtue of s.4(1) was compellable. On appeal to this House this decision was reversed (*Leach v R* [1912] AC 305). Although this decision was as to the construction of s4(1) of the Act, the report of the argument in this House in the Criminal Appeal Reports shows that the question was gone into very thoroughly and it is to my mind inconceivable that the six members of this House who sat ignored the position at common law."

On the above analysis that the House was dealing with a point of statutory construction, observations that a wife was not a compellable witness would form part of the ratio of the case only in relation to s.4(1) of the CEA 1898. In so far as these observations might have application to the common law where a charge of personal violence was involved, which both Lord Wilberforce and Viscount Dilhorne thought they would, they were only obiter since this fell outside the ambit of what the House was called on to decide.

This view that the observations were obiter in relation to the common law where a charge of personal violence was involved was not, however, shared by Lord Salmon, who (at 151) considered them to be part of the ratio of the case. He regarded the observations in *Leach* that the wife was not compellable under s.4(1) as based on her not being compellable at common law. It was because she was not compellable at common law that she was not compellable under s.4(1). Non-compellability at common law was, therefore, part of the reasoning behind the decision that she was not compellable under s.4(1) and so was an integral part of the ratio of the case:

"It seems to me that the finding that you could not infer into a statute a power to compel a wife to give evidence against her husband in a criminal matter was based on their Lordships' opinion that it was contrary to the common law to compel a wife to give such evidence and that such compulsion could be introduced into a statute only by plain and express words. Although their Lordships were only construing a statute, their ratio decidendi was based largely on their opinion as to the effect of the common law and therefore cannot in my view be regarded as merely obiter dicta. I regard *Leach's* case [1912] AC 305 as a binding authority for the proposition that a wife can never be a compellable witness against her husband unless expressly made so by statute."

Thus, Lord Salmon took a broader view of the ratio of *Leach* than Lord Wilberforce and Viscount Dilhorne. His view was that *Leach* decided that a wife was never compellable against her husband unless statute specifically so provided. The view of Lord Wilberforce and Viscount Dilhorne was narrower, that *Leach* decided that a wife was not a compellable witness only in those cases which were covered by s.4(1) of the CEA 1898.

Lord Edmund-Davies, dissenting, shared the view of Lord Wilberforce and Viscount Dilhorne that the observations in *Leach* in relation to the compellability of a wife at common law were obiter. The observations in *Leach* were expressed in unreserved judgments and, his Lordship felt, required "the closest scrutiny". Where judgments are delivered extempore immediately after the conclusion of the case, there is no opportunity for consideration or reflection or for taking account of possible implications. Subjecting the observations in *Leach* to close scrutiny, Lord Edmund-Davies explained (at 156–157) why they should not be relied upon to establish that the wife was not compellable in the present case:

"Strong reliance is placed on obiter dicta in [*Leach*] . . . but there are features of the undoubtedly extempore views . . . which require the closest scrutiny. In *Leach* [1912] AC 305 Lord Loreburn LC stressed at the outset that the only question for determination was as to the meaning of the Criminal Evidence Act 1898 . . . The reference of Lord Loreburn LC [1912] AC 305 at 309 to 'a fundamental and old principle to which the law has looked, that you ought not to compel a wife to give evidence against her husband in matters of a criminal kind' is, I suggest, one relating to the general *incompetence* of spouses as witnesses for the prosecution, for a little later the point is made that, but for s4(1)—

'the wife could not have been *allowed* to give evidence, and the result of what [*sic*] was that the wife could not have been compelled to do so, and was protected against compulsion.'

My Lords, the speech of Lord Halsbury clearly proceeds on the basis (which I have respectfully to submit was manifestly wrong) that a wife can never give evidence in criminal proceedings unless an Act of Parliament expressly makes her competent to do so . . .

. . . there remains the opinion expressed by Lord Atkinson [1912] AC 305 at 311: 'The principle that a wife is not to be compelled to give evidence against her husband is deep seated in the common law of this country . . .'. All that can be said about that pronouncement is that it is based on no cited authority and that it was unnecessary for the determination of the only issue in that case, which was whether the husband or wife of the defendant can, in cases governed by s4(1) of the 1898 Act, be compelled to give evidence against his or her will."

His Lordship accordingly thought (at 157) that it was wrong to regard the dicta in *Leach* as decisive of the point in issue in the present case:

"My Lords, it is not, I submit, right to regard these obiter dicta in *Leach* [1912] AC 305 as decisive of the point in issue in the present case. For what it is worth, they were certainly not so regarded by Mr Herman Cohen, a criminal lawyer who, within a few months of the delivery of those speeches, thanking his 'learned friends, Dr. Kenny, Downing Professor in the University of Cambridge, and Mr. S. Phipson, author of a well-known work on Evidence, for suggestions', published a pamphlet entitled 'Spouse-Witnesses in Criminal Cases'. After considering the speeches in *Leach* [1912] AC 305, the author wrote:

'The question, then is, when by the common law a spouse-witness is admissible for the Crown, is he or she compellable? There seems to be no binding authority at all upon the point . . . The complete silence of the great common law writers on the point seems to show that they took it for granted that a competent witness for the Crown was compellable . . . "At common law," said Mr. (now Mr. Justice) Rowlatt (1912) 7 Cr App Rep 157 at 168, "the wife was merely incompetent, the question of compellability could not arise; but once you get rid of incompetence, compellability follows. . . ."

'It is submitted that this reasoning, in the absence of other authorities, is correct and that, in the case of the common law exception, when a spouse-witness may be called, he or she is a compellable witness for the Crown.

'The language of Lord Atkinson in giving judgment in *Leach*'s case [1912] AC 305 seems, at first sight, opposed to this view . . . But, it is submitted, the noble and learned Lord is referring solely to the general rule applicable to the case under decision—a point in relation to a statutory offence on which statute law is silent and the common law must be invoked, *not* to the recognised common law exceptions, as to which the argument for the Crown was: Once you go back to the general common law and make the

> wife competent like anyone else, you make her an ordinary witness liable to a *subpoena* [*i.e. compellable*]."'

▷ *(c) R. v Lapworth*

In this case, the defendant was convicted of causing grievous bodily harm to his **12–005** wife, who was unwilling to give evidence against him, but who was compelled to do so following a ruling by the trial judge that the wife was a compellable witness. This ruling was upheld by the Court of Criminal Appeal (see above, 2–013), where Avory J. stated (at 121–123):

". . . we are satisfied that at common law the wife was always a competent witness for the prosecution when the charge against her husband was one of having assaulted her. Once it is established that she is a competent witness, it follows that she is a compellable witness; that is to say that she, having made her complaint of, or independent evidence having been given of, an assault on her by her husband, and she having been summoned, as she may be, she is, like all other witnesses, bound to answer any questions put to her . . .

It is said that there is no direct authority on this point. It does sometimes happen, where it has been recognised generally that a certain state of the law exists and where it has never been called into question, that there is no direct authority. I doubt whether this question has ever been raised before in this direct fashion so as to provide a decision. In every day practice it has been assumed that if a wife is so situated on coming into Court expresses a desire not to, or a reluctance to, give evidence for the Crown it is the duty of the Court, in order to ascertain the facts, to direct her to give evidence and, if necessary, compel her to do so.

It has been suggested that in the case of *Leach v Rex* . . . the speeches of the Law Lords contained expressions which are inconsistent with the view of the law that I take . . . [*but*] we are satisfied that . . . the Law Lords had not present to their minds the case, which is now before this Court, where personal violence was alleged to have been done by a wife to her husband or by a husband to his wife, and that they had no intention of including such a case in their observations."

It was the view of the majority in *Hoskyn* that *Lapworth* had been wrongly decided by the Court of Criminal Appeal because the court had wrongly interpreted and failed to apply the decision of the House of Lords in *Leach*. Viscount Dilhorne (at 147) stated:

"I must say that it appears to me improbable that this House in *Leach* [1912] AC 305 did not have regard to cases of violence between spouses. I see no reason for the conclusion that their observations as to the non-compellability of wives as witnesses were not intended to apply to wives asked to testify against their husbands on charges of violence.

I do not regard this decision [*in Lapworth*] as satisfactory. It is perhaps particularly unfortunate that the observations of Bayley J in *R v Inhabitants of All Saints, Worcester*, 6 M & S 194 at 200 and the passage from Taylor on Evidence, 9th Edn (1895), p 892 were not brought to the court's attention. . . . The conclusion to which I have come in the light of the authorities to which I have referred and to which the court in *R v Lapworth* [1931] 1 KB 117, [1930] All ER Rep 340 was not referred is that the decision in that case was wrong."

Similar sentiments were expressed by Lord Salmon (at 151) and Lord Wilberforce (at 142–143).

Lord Edmund-Davies, dissenting, was supportive of the decision in *Lapworth* and the judgment of Avory J., for whom he expressed (at 158) a high regard: "The reputation of few criminal judges this century stands as high as Avory J." Lord Edmund-Davies accepted (at 159) the propositions that the wife was competent to give evidence on a charge of personal violence and, once competency was established, compellability followed:

"Your Lordships, in effect, challenge that sequence of propositions which Avory J regarded as both self-evident and well-established. I must be allowed to say that your reluctance to accept his view derives seemingly from a harking-back to the strong opposition at common law to one spouse ever testifying against the other, an opposition based on a variety of reasons, such as the unity of person, the fear of consequent discord and dissension, and the natural repugnance created by such a prospect. But what, with respect, appears to me to be inadequately recognised is the magnitude of the decision in 1631 [*in R. v Lord Audley*] that in cases turning on violence by one spouse to the other none of the established arguments against testifying must be allowed to prevail. Once that conclusion was arrived at, I see no objection or difficulty in holding that in such cases as the present a spouse, being competent to testify, was also a compellable witness."

His Lordship concluded his judgment with the following remarks (at 160):

"*Lapworth* [1931] 1 KB 117, [1930] All ER Rep 340 is the only authority cited to your Lordships which bears directly on the facts of this case, and Avory J claimed to be doing no more than asserting what had long been the law. The decision itself must surely have since been applied in countless cases without any known expressions of outrage or resentment. It is, with respect, a decision which should find favour with this House today."

▶ 3. Persuasive Authorities from Other Jurisdictions

Decisions from other common law jurisdictions on the point in issue in a particular **12–006** case are of persuasive authority and may be followed by the court determining the issue. The extent to which decisions from other jurisdictions will be taken into account and how persuasive these will be considered to be varies considerably and is difficult to predict. Account is perhaps more likely to be taken of such decisions where there is an absence of English authority, but they may be referred to even where there is English authority directly in point, as in the present case. Both Viscount Dilhorne and Lord Wilberforce made reference to authorities from other jurisdictions, although no mention of any such authorities was made by Lords Salmon or Edmund-Davies. Viscount Dilhorne, when considering *Lapworth*, referred (at 147) to two Australian cases, *R. v Phillips* and *Riddle v R*:

> "In the course of the argument [*in Lapworth*] the only cases referred to were *Leach v R* [1912] AC 305, the *Lord Audley* case (1631) 3 State Tr 401 and *R v Phillips* [1922] SASR 276, decided in South Australia, where Angus Parsons J held that a husband was not a compellable witness against his wife on a charge of wounding. This case followed the decision of the High Court of Australia in *Riddle v R* (1911) 12 CLR 622 where Griffith CJ at 627 posed the question: 'Was a wife compellable at common law to give evidence against her husband?' and, after referring to *R v Inhabitants of All Saints, Worcester* (1817) 6 M. & S. 194 and Taylor on Evidence, 10th Edn (1906), he appears to have agreed with a view expressed in Taylor that the better opinion was that she was not.
>
> In *R v Lapworth* [1931] 1 KB 117, [1930] All ER Rep. 340 Avory J delivered the judgment of the court. He accepted that there was no direct authority on the point and said that that sometimes happened where it was recognised that a certain state of the law existed when it had never been called in question. It is perhaps unfortunate that *Riddle v R* (1911) 12 CLR 622 was not drawn to the court's attention."

A more comprehensive reference to other authorities was, however, made by Lord Wilberforce (at 143):

> "I will add that I have taken into account the position, so far as it has been made clear, in other jurisdictions. In Scotland the law has been clear since 1836 in favour of compellability: *HM Advocate v Commelin* (1836) 1 Swin 291. In Australia, the High Court, on a New South Wales appeal, obiter it is true, but after a careful analysis of the authorities by Griffith CJ, expressed a view, before the English case of *Leach v R* [1912] AC 305, against compellability (*Riddle v R* (1911) 12 CLR 622). The same view has been taken in South Australia (*R v Phillips* [1922] SASR 276). In Victoria, Gavan Duffy J following *Lapworth* and

not *Riddle* expressed the opposite opinion (*Sharp v Rodwell* [1947] VLR 82 at 85).

In Canada a learned article by Dean Weir [1931] Can BR 216 suggested that *R v Lapworth* should be followed, but since then judicial opinions have been expressed either way: *R v Lonsdale* (1973) 15 CCC (2d) 201 (compellable), *R v Carter* (1978) 28 CCC (2d) 219 (not compellable). In this state of authority it would be invidious to assert where the 'better opinion' is to be found."

▶ 4. The Influence of Policy Considerations

12–007 Courts, when reaching decisions on which there is no binding authority, may well be influenced by their views as to what the law should be. The outcome of the case may thus depend on the arguments and policy considerations in favour of a particular course and what is perceived to be the best policy for the law to adopt. This was recognised by Lord Edmund-Davies at the beginning of his judgment (at 152):

> "My Lords, when your Lordships' House is called on to determine a question of law regarding which there are no binding precedents and no authorities directly in point, and where it has accordingly to perform an act of law-making, I apprehend that the decision will largely turn on what is thought most likely to advance the public weal . . . however elaborate the language employed in rationalising the conclusion arrived at in such hitherto unchartered circumstances, a declaration of what, in the opinion of this House, the law is will largely be influenced by the individual views of your Lordships recording what *should* be the law."

There are arguments, essentially of policy, either way in the present case. There are two main arguments against making a wife compellable. One is that it would undermine the marital relationship and the other is that the public would regard with repugnance the idea of a wife testifying against her husband. These arguments form the basis for the common law rule that a wife is not generally competent to give evidence against her husband and they might have similar application as a justification for not compelling a wife to give evidence in those cases where she might be competent to do so. Thus, Lord Salmon remarked (at 148–149):

> "At common law, the wife of a defendant charged with a crime, however serious, was not, as a general rule, a competent witness for the Crown . . .
>
> This rule seems to me to underline the supreme importance attached by the common law to the special status of marriage and to the unity supposed to exist between husband and wife. It also no doubt recognised the natural repugnance of the public at the prospect of a wife giving evidence against her husband in such circumstances.

The only relevant exception to the common law rule that a wife was not a competent witness at her husband's trial was when he was charged with a crime of violence against her.

. . . The instant case turns solely on whether, at common law, the wife of a defendant charged with having committed a crime of violence against her is not only a competent but also a compellable witness against her husband.

The main argument on behalf of the Crown is that all persons who are competent witnesses normally are also compellable witnesses. And therefore, so the argument runs, in cases in which wives are competent witnesses it follows that they also must be compellable witnesses. This seems to me to be a complete non sequitur for it takes no account of the special importance which the common law attaches to the status of marriage. Clearly, it was for the wife's own protection that the common law made an exception to its general rule by making the wife a competent witness in respect of any charge against her husband for a crime of violence against her. But if she does not want to avail herself of this protection, there is, in my view, no ground for holding that the common law forces it on her.

In many such cases, the wife is not a reluctant or unwilling witness; she may indeed sometimes be an enthusiastic witness against her husband. On the other hand, there must also be many cases when a wife who loved her husband completely forgave him, had no fear of further violence, and wished the marriage to continue and the pending prosecution to fail. It seems to me altogether inconsistent with the common law's attitude towards marriage that it should compel such a wife to give evidence against her husband and thereby probably destroy the marriage."

Similar sentiments were expressed by Lord Wilberforce (at 142) when commenting upon the views of members of the Court of Criminal Appeal in *Lapworth* that a wife was a compellable witness. Viscount Dilhorne, both towards the beginning of his judgment (at 144) and at the end of it (at 148), also made reference to the unity between husband and wife and the importance of maintaining confidence between them, and the repugnance at compelling an unwilling wife to give evidence against her husband.

In favour of compellability is the argument that the court of trial is investigating a crime and evidence of that crime should be freely available. Thus, Lord Edmund-Davies, dissenting, remarked (at 153–154):

". . . some of your Lordships have described the idea that an affirmative answer is called for [*to the certified question of whether a wife is compellable*] as 'repugnant' to the married state and, as such, entirely unacceptable. This attitude may be contrasted with that adopted in the instant case by Geoffrey Lane LJ [*in the Court of Appeal*] who, after reviewing most of the legal authorities brought to light by the admirable researches of the appellant's counsel, said:

'It must be borne in mind that the court of trial in circumstances such as this, where personal violence is concerned (and this case is a good example where wounding with a knife is concerned) is not dealing merely with a domestic dispute between husband and wife, but it is investigating a crime. It is in the interests of the state and members of the public that, where that is the case, evidence of that crime should be freely available to the court which is trying the crime. It may very well be that the wife or the husband, as the case may be, is the only person who can give evidence of that offence. In those circumstances, it seems to us that there is no reason in this case for saying that we should in any way depart from the ruling . . . in *Lapworth* . . .'

. . . I readily confess to a complete absence of any feeling of 'repugnance' that, in the circumstances of the instant case, Mrs Hoskyn was compelled to testify against the man who had three days earlier become her husband. And, agreeing as I do with the attitude of Geoffrey Lane LJ, I am regretfully unable to accept the view expressed by my noble and learned friend, Lord Salmon, that, '. . . if she does not want to avail herself of [the law's] protection, there is, in my view, no ground for holding that the common law forces it on her'."

If the law was to adopt a policy of not making the wife compellable, the outcome may, his Lordship stated (at 159), be unjust acquittals in particularly horrific or serious cases:

"This House had only a few years ago to deal with a case arising from events as horrible as those which led to Lord Audley's conviction in 1631. Indeed, the facts in *Director of Public Prosecutions v Morgan* [1975] 2 All ER 347, [1976] AC 182 were startlingly similar, for there too a husband had procured other men to rape his wife. It surely creates a revulsion going far beyond 'repugnance' if the wronged wife at the last moment declined to testify against her husband and, in consequence, he and the four other accused were acquitted, so inextricably did her evidence involve all five accused . . .

Such cases are too grave to depend simply on whether the injured spouse is, or is not, willing to testify against the attacker. Reluctance may spring from a variety of reasons and does not by any means necessarily denote that domestic harmony has been restored. A wife who has once been subjected to a 'carve up' may well have more reasons than one for being an unwilling witness against her husband. In such circumstances, it may well prove a positive boon [*for*] her to be directed by the court that she has no alternative but to testify. But, be that as it may, such incidents ought not to be regarded as having no importance extending beyond the domestic hearth."

In essence, there are two legitimate interests, each worthy of the law's protection, which come into conflict in this case. As the Criminal Law Revision Committee observed in its Eleventh Report, Cmnd.4991 (1972), para.147:

"How far the wife of the accused should be competent and compellable for the prosecution . . . is in these days essentially a question of balancing the desirability that all available evidence which might conduce to the right verdict should be before the court against (i) the objection on social grounds of disturbing marital disharmony more than is absolutely necessary and (ii) what many regard as the harshness of compelling a wife to give evidence against her husband."

The Committee was in favour of maintaining the then existing rule in *Lapworth* that a wife was compellable against her husband on a charge of personal violence on her by him and, although the Committee's Report was not implemented by Parliament, effect was given to the Committee's view when Parliament introduced in the Police and Criminal Evidence Act 1984 a statutory reversal of the *Hoskyn* principle.

▶ 5. Statutory Reversal of *Hoskyn v Metropolitan Police Commissioner*

It is, of course, open to Parliament to reverse by statute the effect of any judicial decision with which it disagrees and this occurred in respect of the decision in *Hoskyn*. The ruling of the majority in that case was subsequently reversed by s.80 of the Police and Criminal Evidence Act 1984. This provision (as subsequently amended) now provides:

12–008

"(2) In any proceedings the spouse or civil partner of a person charged in the proceedings shall, subject to subsection (4) below, be compellable to give evidence on behalf of that person.

(2A) In any proceedings the spouse or civil partner of a person charged in the proceedings shall, subject to subsection (4) below, be compellable—

(a) to give evidence on behalf of any other person charged in the proceedings but only in respect of any specified offence with which that other person is charged; or
(b) to give evidence for the prosecution but only in respect of any specified offence with which any person is charged in the proceedings.

(3) In relation to the spouse or civil partner of a person charged in any proceedings, an offence is a specified offence for the purposes of subsection (2A) above if—

(a) it involves an assault on, or injury or a threat of injury to, the spouse or civil partner or a person who was at the material time under the age of 16;
(b) it is a sexual offence alleged to have been committed in respect of a person who was at the material time under that age; or

> (c) it consists of attempting or conspiring to commit, or of aiding, abetting, counselling, procuring or inciting the commission of, an offence falling within paragraph (a) or (b) above.
>
> (4) No person who is charged in any proceedings shall be compellable by virtue of subsection (2) or (2A) above to give evidence in the proceedings."

During the course of the legislation's passage, the Government resisted an amendment seeking to delete the provision in s.80, primarily on the grounds of the overriding importance of curtailing violent criminal conduct. The Home Office Minister, Mr David Mellor (*Hansard*, HC, Standing Committee E, col.1675, (March 13, 1984)), emphasised:

> ". . . the crucial importance to the community that any crime, but especially crimes of violence, should be cleared up. Violence in the home is a particular problem, whether against a spouse or against children. That factor determined the view of the CLRC [*Criminal Law Revision Committee*] that public interest requires a spouse to be compellable in cases of personal violence."

It can be seen that s.80 seeks to confine compellability, in relation to spouses or civil partners of a person who is charged, to cases where the charge is a "specified offence". Under subs.(3), this includes only offences involving assault, injury or threat of injury to the spouse or civil partner or any person under the age of 16, a sexual offence in respect of any person under the age of 16, or inchoate offences in relation to these offences. Compellability in the case of assaults etc and sexual offences on persons under the age of 16 "reflects, inter alia, the desirability of convicting fathers who have committed violent or sexual offences against their children; offences in relation to which a wife may well be both a cogent and a reluctant witness" (*per* Lord Phillips C.J. in *R v L* [2008] EWCA Crim 973 [at 29]).

Such a case arose in *R v L*, which involved several counts of indecent assault and rape by a father on his daughter. For most of the counts, the daughter was under the age of 16 at the material time, but, in respect of the count of rape on which the issue of the wife's compellability arose, the daughter was aged 19 at the time of the offence. On the ordinary wording of s.80, this would not make the wife a compellable witness against her husband, as there is no assault etc or sexual offence in relation to a person under the age of 16 and in *R v L* the trial judge duly ruled that the defendant's wife (who had made a short statement to the police and who declined to give evidence) was not a compellable witness against him.

The prosecution nevertheless applied to admit in evidence the wife's statement to the police, pursuant to s.114 of the Criminal Justice Act 2003, under which hearsay evidence is admissible in certain circumstances. The trial judge made a ruling that he had power to admit under s.114, rejecting the defendant's contentions that his wife should have been advised by the police that she could not be compelled to give evidence against her husband at trial; that the admission of the statement would be contrary to, or would wrongly circumvent s.80; and that it would be unfair or contrary to the interests of justice to admit it. On appeal against the defendant's conviction, the trial judge's ruling was upheld. Lord Phillips C.J. stated (at [31]), in respect of the contention that the defendant's wife should have been advised by the police that she could not be compelled to give evidence against her husband:

"We can see no basis for such a requirement. The need to caution a suspect arises from the fundamental principle that a person cannot be required to give evidence that may incriminate himself. The policy against compelling a wife to give evidence against her husband is not the same. To caution a wife before taking evidence from her could inhibit the investigation of crime. We do not think that the policy that prevents a wife from giving evidence against her husband requires such a limitation upon the powers of investigation of the police to be implied."

His Lordship nevertheless went onto observe, obiter (at [33]), that:

". . . it does not follow that there may not be circumstances in which the police will be well advised to make it plain to a wife that she need not make a statement that implicates her husband."

On the contention by the defendant that, if the wife's statement could be admitted under s.114, this was tantamount to compelling a wife to give evidence against her husband and offended against the spirit of s.80, Lord Phillips C.J. stated (at [35]):

"Compelling a wife to give evidence is not the same thing as permitting another witness to give evidence of a voluntary statement made by the wife in the past. Thus section 80 of PACE does not pose a legal bar to the admission of such evidence. Furthermore, if a wife has voluntarily made a statement to the police, the identity between husband and wife and the risk of marital discord will not be in play if that statement is subsequently placed in evidence to the same extent as if the wife is asked to give oral evidence to the jury that implicates her husband. Nevertheless, it could well be objectionable if the police take a witness statement from a wife, intending to call her to give evidence, and then seek to place it in evidence when the wife states that she does not wish to give evidence against her husband. There is an obvious paradox in excusing the wife from giving evidence, but then placing before the jury in the form of a hearsay statement the very evidence that she does not wish to give.

In any such case, whether or not it is just to admit the statement must depend upon the facts of the individual case. In the circumstances of the present case, we can see no injustice in admitting the statement. The law has made it clear that the interests of convicting a husband of child abuse take precedence over the demands of marital duty and harmony that would otherwise protect the wife from being compelled to give evidence. Here, as we have said, the appellant was charged with a lengthy course of sexual abuse of his daughter, much of it at a time when she was under 16. Whether or not in these circumstances the wife could have been compelled to give evidence, we consider that the public interest was served by the admission of her evidence, adding weight as this did to the overall case against her husband as well as to the case against him in respect of the non "specified offences."

It seems clear that the Court of Appeal was firmly of the view that it was in the interests of justice for the wife's evidence to be put before the court, but the decision calls into question the underlying policy and effect of s.80, under which the spouse or civil partner is a compellable witness only in specified and clearly defined instances falling within the section. As one commentator has observed (Ormerod, "Witnesses: compellability—spouse as witness for prosecution" [2008] Crim. L.R. 823, 824–825):

". . . the court's approach to s.114(1)(d) of the Criminal Justice Act 2003 and its obiter comments on compellability and cautioning are surprising and controversial. The lack of any need to caution a non-suspect spouse that she cannot be compelled to give evidence against her husband, coupled with the possibility for her statements to be admitted under s.114(1)(d) appears to undermine totally the policy and effect of s.80 of the Police and Criminal Evidence Act 1984 (PACE). That approach is, with respect, more than "a paradox" (at [35]): it is inconsistent with s.80.

Section 80 of PACE provides that W is a compellable witness for the Crown "in respect of" any "specified offences" with which her husband is charged (s.80(2A)(b)). "Specified offence" is defined in s.80(3) as meaning one involving "an assault on, or injury or threat of injury" to the spouse or someone under 16 or a sexual offence in respect of a person under 16 or inchoates of these forms of offence. In this case the alleged rape with which L is charged occurred when the daughter was 19 years old. On a natural interpretation of the section, W is therefore not compellable. Nevertheless, the Lord Chief Justice doubts whether s.80 does prevent W being compelled to give *any* evidence in the case. Section 80(2A) provides that W shall be compellable for the Crown "but only *in respect of* any specified offence with which any person is charged". L was charged with some indecent assaults on V when she was under 16. Could W's evidence in relation to the rape be compelled by being treated as also "in respect of" the indecent assaults? The court declines to decide this "nice point" (at [22]). Authority from the pre-1984 law is against adopting such an interpretation (see *Deacon* (1973) 57 Cr. App. R. 688) as is academic opinion (P. Creighton, "Spouse Competence and Compellability" [1990] Crim. L.R. 34 at 39–41).

Section 80 seeks to strike a balance between respecting matrimonial harmony and ensuring that evidence is available from the spouse or civil partner in the more serious categories of case in which independent evidence (from outside the home) is less likely to be available. It has long been recognised that in seeking to strike this balance s.80 produces arbitrary and unpalatable distinctions: e.g. W compellable when D kisses a 15-year-old, but not when he rapes a 16-year-old (see C. Tapper, *Cross and Tapper on Evidence,* 9th edn (1999), p.222). It may well be time for Parliament to readdress the policy behind s.80. It is doubtful whether s.80 really does help to preserve marriages, and even if it does, should the institution of marriage (or civil partnerships) be allowed to take precedence over the demands of the criminal justice system in convicting the guilty? If the court is correct in allowing s.114(1)(d) of the 2003 Act to circumvent s.80, then a spouse will only be non-compellable where she does not make any pre-trial statement incriminating her husband. If that is the case, there is very obvious need for a review of the policy behind s.80.

The court suggests that compelling a wife to give evidence in relation to a non-specified offence is "not the same thing" as permitting another witness to give evidence of her previous voluntary statement which incriminates her husband. But surely it has the same effect in terms of the potential to destroy matrimonial harmony, which is the very thing that s.80 was designed to protect in these cases."

It remains to be seen whether in the light of *R v L* any review of the policy behind s.80 takes place.

Further Reading

Creighton, "Spouse Competence and Compellability" [1990] Crim. L.R. 34

Manchester, "Wives as Crown Witnesses" [1978] C.L.J. 249

Ormerod, "Witnesses: compellability—spouse as witness for prosecution" [2008] Crim. L.R. 823.

13 SUCCESSION RIGHTS UNDER THE RENT ACT 1977

▶ ## 1. Introduction

13–001 Where a person (the tenant), who is entitled to a residential tenancy under the Rent Act 1977 (RA 1977), dies, the tenant's spouse or civil partner (terms which, respectively, include "a person who was living with the . . . tenant as his or her wife or husband" and "a person who was living with the original tenant as if they were civil partners") or certain other members of the tenant's family may be entitled to a tenancy by way of succession under the RA 1977. The relevant provisions of the RA 1977, namely paras 2 and 3 of Sch.1 (as amended by the Housing Act 1988 and the Civil Partnership Act 2004), provide as follows:

> "2.—(1) The surviving spouse, *or surviving civil partner*, (if any) of the original tenant, if residing in the dwelling-house immediately before the death of the original tenant, shall after the death be the statutory tenant if and so long as he or she occupies the dwelling-house as his or her residence.
>
> (2) For the purposes of this paragraph—
>
> (a) a person who was living with the original tenant as his or her wife or husband shall be treated as the spouse of the original tenant, and
> (b) *a person who was living with the original tenant as if they were civil partners shall be treated as the civil partner of the original tenant.*
>
> 3—(1) Where paragraph 2 above does not apply, but a person who was a member of the original tenant's family was residing with him in the dwelling-house at the time of and for the period of 2 years immediately before his death then, after his death, that person or if there is more than one such person such one of them as may be decided by agreement, or in default of agreement by the county court, shall be entitled to an assured tenancy of the dwelling-house by succession."
>
> [*Amendments introduced by the Civil Partnership Act 2004 are in italics.*]

The tenancy to which the tenant's surviving spouse or civil partner may be entitled under the above statutory scheme, i.e. a statutory Rent Act tenancy (under para.2(1)) is more advantageous than the tenancy to which the qualifying members of the tenant's family (who are usually, but not necessarily, linked to the tenant by virtue of a blood relationship, e.g. a parent, grandparent or child) may succeed, i.e. an assured tenancy (under para.3(1)). This is particularly so in two respects. First, the rent payable under an assured tenancy is the contractual rent or the market rent which in many cases may be markedly more than the rent payable under a statutory Rent Act tenancy. The latter is known as a fair rent. It is calculated by taking into account the factors set out in s.70 of the RA 1977. Secondly, an assured tenant may be evicted for non-payment of rent without the need to satisfy a court (as is required in the case of a statutory Rent Act tenancy) that it is reasonable to grant a possession order in favour of the landlord. In other words, the tenure of the surviving spouse or surviving civil partner in the property is accorded greater protection; a differential which may be rationalised on the basis that the survivor of the couple should be treated in much the same way as the original tenant, bearing in mind that the two of them set up their home together in the property and consequently, in such circumstances, their security of tenure in that property should not be dependent on which of them is the first to die.

In *Ghaidan v Godin-Mendoza* [2004] 3 All E.R. 411 (*Ghaidan*), the House of Lords was asked to consider whether para.2 of Sch.1 to the RA 1977 (prior to its amendment by the Civil Partnership Act 2004), which allowed the "spouse" of a tenant to succeed to a statutory Rent Act tenancy on the tenant's death, could be construed so that the word "spouse" in that paragraph included the survivor of a same-sex partnership.

Although the substantive law has changed since *Ghaidan* was decided, this case study illustrates several points in relation to statutory interpretation:

- ▶ the exercise of the interpretative obligation under s.3 of the Human Rights Act 1998 (HRA 1998) by reading in words to a statutory provision to ensure its compatibility with Convention rights;
- ▶ a dissenting judgment relating to the scope and application of s.3 of the HRA 1998;
- ▶ the influence of policy considerations in the interpretative process;
- ▶ the relevance of a recurrent theme in the history of legislative provisions in the context of the interpretation of those provisions; and
- ▶ the presumption that Parliament does not intend to legislate in breach of its international obligations.

▶ 2. The Decision of the House of Lords in *Ghaidan v Godin-Mendoza*

Mr Godin-Mendoza and Mr Wallwyn-James, who were homosexuals, began living together in 1972. In 1983, they moved into a flat in London owned by Mr Ghaidan. They lived together in the flat until Mr Wallwyn-James's death in 2001. The tenancy of the flat, which was governed by the RA 1977, had been in the deceased's name. Following Mr Wallwyn-James's death, Mr Ghaidan, the landlord, commenced proceedings in the county court for possession of the flat. Mr Godin-Mendoza claimed that, on the death of Mr Wallwyn-James, he succeeded to a statutory Rent Act tenancy of the flat (with the comparative advantages, outlined

13–002

above, which this type of tenancy bestowed), because he was the surviving spouse of Mr Wallwyn-James within the meaning of para.2(1) of Sch.1 to the RA 1977.

At first instance, Judge Cowell decided that on the death of Mr Wallwyn-James, Mr Godin-Mendoza did not succeed to the tenancy of the flat as the surviving spouse of Mr Wallwyn-James within the meaning of para.2(1), but that he was entitled to an assured tenancy of the flat by succession, because he could be regarded as a member of Mr Wallwyn-James's "family" under para.3(1) of Sch.1 to the RA 1977. In making this determination, the judge followed the decision of the House of Lords in *Fitzpatrick v Sterling Housing Association* [2001] 1 A.C. 27 (*Fitzpatrick*), which was based on similar facts and decided before the HRA 1998 came into force, that para.2(1) did not include the survivor of a same-sex partnership. Mr Godin-Mendoza appealed to the Court of Appeal. The Court of Appeal (Kennedy, Buxton and Keene L.JJ.) allowed his appeal. It held that Mr Godin-Mendoza was entitled to succeed to a statutory Rent Act tenancy of the flat under para.2(1). In reaching its decision, the Court of Appeal looked to the HRA 1998 and, in so doing, considered two fundamental questions: first, whether para.2 discriminated, without justification, on the ground of sexual orientation; and, secondly, if so, whether para.2 could be read and given effect, as required by s.3(1) of the HRA 1998 in a manner which was compatible with Convention rights (see Chapter 5, 5–013—5–015). The Court of Appeal answered the first question in the affirmative and, thereafter in addressing the second question, it interpreted the words "as his or her wife or husband" in para.2(2) to mean "*as if they were* his wife or husband" in order to ensure that the provision included homosexual as well as heterosexual couples (and, thereby, covered Mr Godin-Mendoza's position). The Court of Appeal's decision was also made in apparent disregard of the above-mentioned House of Lords decision in *Fitzpatrick*. Mr Ghaidan appealed to the House of Lords. The questions raised in the House of Lords were the same as those considered by the Court of Appeal. In this respect, Lord Nicholls outlined the position as follows ([2004] 3 All E.R. 411 at 417–418):

> "Mr Godin-Mendoza's claim is that this difference in treatment [*of a heterosexual couple living together in a house as husband and wife and a homosexual couple living together in a house (which would prevail if Mr Ghaidan's appeal were to succeed)*] infringes art 14 of the European Convention for the Protection of Human Rights and Fundamental Freedoms 1950 (as set out in Sch 1 to the 1998 Act) read in conjunction with art 8. Article 8 does not require the state to provide security of tenure for members of a deceased tenant's family. Article 8 does not in terms give a right to be provided with a home: see *Chapman v UK* (2001) 10 BHRC 48 at 72 (para 99). It does not 'guarantee the right to have one's housing problem solved by the authorities': see *Marzani v Italy* (1999) 28 EHRR CD 175 at 179. But if the state makes legislative provision it must not be discriminatory. The provision must not draw a distinction on grounds such as sex or sexual orientation without good reason. Unless justified, a distinction founded on such grounds infringes the convention right embodied in art 14, as read with art 8. Mr Godin-Mendoza submits that the distinction drawn by para

2 of Sch 1 to the 1977 Act is drawn on the grounds of sexual orientation and that this difference in treatment lacks justification.

That is the first step in Mr Godin-Mendoza's claim. That step would not, of itself, improve Mr Godin-Mendoza's status in his flat. The second step in his claim is to pray in aid the court's duty under s 3 of the 1998 Act to read and give effect to legislation in a way which is compliant with convention rights. Here, it is said, s 3 requires the court to read para 2 so that it embraces couples living together in a close and stable homosexual relationship as much as couples living together in a close and stable heterosexual relationship. So read, para 2 covers Mr Godin-Mendoza's position. Hence he is entitled to a declaration that on the death of Mr Wallwyn-James he succeeded to a statutory tenancy."

Lord Nicholls, Lord Steyn, Lord Rodger, Lord Millett and Baroness Hale, who heard the appeal, delivered full and reasoned judgments. In the event, a 4–1 majority (Lord Millett dissenting), admitted Mr Godin-Mendoza's claim, upheld the decision of the Court of Appeal and, accordingly, dismissed Mr Ghaidan's appeal. However, notwithstanding the agreement of the majority as to the outcome of the case, the nature and focus of their respective judgments differed. In the leading judgment, Lord Nicholls, with whose judgment Lord Steyn, Lord Rodger and Baroness Hale concurred, examined, fully, both of the questions which were germane to the resolution of the appeal, namely whether discrimination as alleged by Mr Godin-Mendoza was present, and, if so, whether the exercise of the interpretative obligation in s.3 of the HRA 1998 could lead to para.2 being read and given effect in a way that was compatible with Convention rights. By comparison, Lord Steyn, after expressing his agreement with the judgments of Lord Nicholls, Lord Rodger and Baroness Hale, stated, specifically, that he would not comment on the case generally, and proceeded to explore the parameters of s.3(1) of the HRA 1998 and how it had been applied by the courts since the HRA 1998 came into force. In a similar vein, Lord Rodger, after stating his agreement with the judgments of Lord Nicholls, Lord Steyn and Baroness Hale, chose to dedicate his judgment, predominantly, to the making of observations about s.3 of the HRA 1998 (for reference to the views of Lord Steyn and Lord Rodger on s.3 of the HRA 1998, see Chapter 5, 5–014—5–015). Baroness Hale, who endorsed the reasons given by Lord Nicholls for dismissing the appeal and agreed with the opinions of Lord Steyn and Lord Rodger on the scope and application of s.3 of the HRA 1998, adopted a discursive approach in a relatively brief judgment. Her Ladyship considered, inter alia, the lines of inquiry pursued in cases concerned with alleged discrimination under art.14 of the Convention, and, in this context, opined that homosexual couples may have exactly the same sort of interdependent relationship as heterosexual couples and, consequently, that such same-sex relationships might be regarded as "marriage-like" for the purpose of the RA 1977. In his dissenting judgment, Lord Millett, although agreeing with the views of the majority on the question of discrimination, i.e. that an ordinary reading of para.2 (as had occurred in *Fitzpatrick*) led to discriminatory treatment of homosexual couples which was incompatible with their

Convention rights, decided, nevertheless, that this paragraph could not, in accordance with the interpretative obligation under s.3 of the HRA 1998, be read and given effect in a manner that was compatible with Convention rights. In his Lordship's opinion, the perceived shortcomings of para.2 were matters for Parliament, not the courts.

The remainder of this case study focuses, principally, on the judicial deliberations in the House relating to the matters which were determinative of the appeal in this case. For consideration of judicial observations made in *Ghaidan* about the *general* scope and application of s.3 of the HRA 1998, see Chapter 5, 5–014—5–015.

▷ *(a) Discrimination*

13–003 As indicated above, the basis of Mr Godin-Mendoza's claim in this regard was that para.2, as interpreted in *Fitzpatrick*, infringed his Convention right under art.14 when read in conjunction with art.8 by drawing a distinction on the ground of sexual orientation which lacked justification. In this respect, the essence of art.14, namely its prohibition of discrimination in respect of Convention rights, was captured by Lord Nicholls, who stated (at 418):

> "Discrimination is an insidious practice. Discriminatory law undermines the rule of law because it is the antithesis of fairness. It brings the law into disrepute. It breeds resentment. It fosters an inequality of outlook which is demeaning alike to those unfairly benefited and those unfairly prejudiced. Of course all law, civil and criminal, has to draw distinctions. One type of conduct, or one factual situation, attracts one legal consequence, another type of conduct or situation attracts a different legal consequence. To be acceptable these distinctions should have a rational and fair basis. Like cases should be treated alike, unlike cases should not be treated alike. The circumstances which justify two cases being regarded as unlike, and therefore requiring or susceptible of different treatment, are infinite. In many circumstances opinions can differ on whether a suggested ground of distinction justifies a difference in legal treatment. But there are certain grounds of factual difference which by common accord are not acceptable, without more, as a basis for different legal treatment. Differences of race or sex or religion are obvious examples. Sexual orientation is another. This has been clearly recognised by the European Court of Human Rights: see, for instance, *Frette v France* [2003] 2 FCR 39 at 54 (para 32). Unless some good reason can be shown, differences such as these do not justify differences in treatment. Unless good reason exists, differences in legal treatment based on grounds such as these are properly stigmatised as discriminatory."

Before the House, it was common ground that para.2 was a legislative provision which fell within the scope of the right to respect for a person's home guaranteed by art.8, and that, in view of the distinction between heterosexual and same-sex partnerships emanating from this paragraph (as interpreted by *Fitzpatrick*), art.14 was "engaged in the present case". However, Counsel for Mr Ghaidan sought to justify this distinction on the basis that the aim of the legislation was to protect the traditional family; a phrase which did not encompass same-sex partnerships because same-sex partners are unable to have children with each other and children are less likely to be part of a same-sex household. Lord Nicholls saw little merit in this purported justification. His Lordship stated (at 420–421):

"Protection of the traditional family unit may well be an important and legitimate aim in certain contexts . . . But it is important to identify the element of the 'traditional family' which para 2, as it now stands, is seeking to protect. Marriage is not now a prerequisite to protection under para 2. The line drawn by Parliament is no longer drawn by reference to the status of marriage. Nor is parenthood, or the presence of children in the home, a precondition of security of tenure for the survivor of the original tenant. Nor is procreative potential a prerequisite. The survivor is protected even if, by reason of age or otherwise, there was never any prospect of either member of the couple having a natural child.

What remains, and it is all that remains, as the essential feature, under para 2 is the cohabitation of a heterosexual couple. Security of tenure for the survivor of such a couple in the house where they live is, doubtless, an important and legitimate social aim. Such a couple share their lives and make their home together. Parliament may readily take the view that the survivor of them has a special claim to security of tenure even though they are unmarried. But the reason underlying this social policy, whereby the survivor of a cohabiting heterosexual couple has particular protection, is equally applicable to the survivor of a homosexual couple. A homosexual couple, as much as a heterosexual couple, share each other's life and make their home together. They have an equivalent relationship . . .

This being so, one looks in vain to find justification for the difference in treatment of homosexual and heterosexual couples. Such a difference in treatment can be justified only if it pursues a legitimate aim and there is a reasonable relationship between the means employed and aim sought to be realised. Here, the difference in treatment falls at the first hurdle: the absence of a legitimate aim . . .

In the present case the only suggested ground for according different treatment to the survivor of same-sex couples and opposite sex couples [*the protection of the traditional family*] cannot withstand scrutiny. Rather, the present state of the law as set out in para 2 of Sch 1 to the 1977 Act may properly be described as continuing adherence to the traditional regard for the position of surviving spouses, adapted in 1988 [*by the Housing Act 1988*] to take account of the widespread contemporary trend for men and women to cohabit outside marriage but not adapted to recognise the comparable position of cohabiting same-sex couples. I appreciate that the primary object of introducing the regime of assured tenancies and assured shorthold tenancies in 1988 was to increase the number of properties available for renting in the private sector. But this policy objective of the Housing Act 1988 can afford no justification for amending para 2 so as to include cohabiting heterosexual partners but not cohabiting homosexual partners. This policy objective of the Act provides no reason for, on the one hand, extending to unmarried cohabiting heterosexual partners the right to succeed to a statutory tenancy but, on the other hand, withholding that right from cohabiting homosexual partners. Paragraph 2 fails to attach sufficient importance to the convention rights of cohabiting homosexual couples."

Baroness Hale was similarly dismissive of the submission that the difference in treatment between heterosexual and same-sex partnerships might be justified on the basis that it was intended to protect the traditional family. Her Ladyship stated (at 461):

". . . a homosexual couple whose relationship is marriage-like in the same ways that an unmarried heterosexual couple's relationship is marriage-like are indeed in an analogous situation. Any difference in treatment is based upon their sexual orientation. It requires an objective justification if it is to comply with art 14. Whatever the scope for a 'discretionary area of judgment' in these cases may be, there has to be a legitimate aim before a difference in treatment can be justified. But what could be the legitimate aim of singling out heterosexual couples for more favourable treatment than homosexual couples? It cannot be the *protection* of the traditional family. The traditional family is not protected by granting it a benefit which is denied to people who cannot or will not become a traditional family. What is really meant by the 'protection' of the traditional family is the *encouragement* of people to form traditional families and the *discouragement* of people from forming others. There are many reasons why it might be legitimate to encourage people to marry and to discourage them from living together without marrying. These reasons might have justified the Act in stopping short of marriage. Once it went beyond marriage to unmarried relationships, the aim would have to be encouraging one sort of unmarried relationship and discouraging another. The Act does distinguish between unmarried but marriage-like relationships and more transient liaisons. It is easy to see how that might pursue a legitimate aim and easier still to see how it might justify singling out the survivor for preferential succession rights. But, as Buxton LJ ([2002] 4 All ER 1162 at [21]) pointed out, it is difficult to see how heterosexuals will be encouraged to form and maintain such marriage-like relationships by the knowledge that the equivalent benefit is being denied to homosexuals. The distinction between heterosexual and homosexual couples might be aimed at discouraging homosexual relationships generally. But that cannot now be regarded as a legitimate aim. It is inconsistent with the right to respect for private life accorded to 'everyone', including homosexuals, by art 8 since *Dudgeon v UK* (1981) 4 EHRR 149. If it is not legitimate to discourage homosexual relationships, it cannot be legitimate

> to discourage stable, committed, marriage-like homosexual relationships of the sort which qualify the survivor to succeed to the home."

In the absence, therefore, of a justification for the difference in treatment accorded to heterosexual and same-sex relationships, the House concluded that para.2 when construed without regard to s.3 of the HRA 1998 infringed Mr Godin-Mendoza's Convention right under art.14 when read in conjunction with art.8.

▷ (b) The impact of s.3 of the HRA 1998

13-004

As indicated above (see 13–002), the judgments of Lord Steyn and Lord Rodger were concerned, principally, with examining the *general* scope and application of s.3 (although Lord Steyn also expressed his reservations about the manner in which s.3 had been approached in some cases which were decided before *Ghaidan* (see, in particular, at 428)). Consideration of such matters was also pivotal to the judgments of Lord Nicholls and Lord Millett. The broad import of these deliberations is explored in Chapter 5 (at 5–014–5–015), but, in the context of this case study, it is their Lordships' observations about the nature of the interpretative obligation under s.3, in particular, the circumstances in which words may be "read in" to a statutory provision in order to ensure its compatibility with Convention rights, which has particular relevance to the decision in *Ghaidan*. In this respect, their Lordships' views, in the abstract, were broadly convergent. Thus, Lord Nicholls opined (at 423–424):

> "Section 3 enables language to be interpreted restrictively or expansively. But s 3 goes further than this. It is also apt to require a court to read in words which change the meaning of enacted legislation, so as to make it convention-compliant. In other words, the intention of Parliament in enacting s 3 was that, to an extent bounded only by what is 'possible', a court can modify the meaning, and hence, the effect, of primary and secondary legislation.
>
> Parliament, however, cannot have intended that in the discharge of this extended interpretative function the courts should adopt a meaning inconsistent with a fundamental feature of legislation. That would be to cross the constitutional boundary s 3 seeks to demarcate and preserve. Parliament has retained the right to enact legislation in terms which are not convention-compliant. The meaning imported by application of s 3 must be compatible with the underlying thrust of the legislation being construed. Words implied must, in the phrase of my noble and learned friend Lord Rodger of Earlsferry, 'go with the grain of the legislation'. Nor can Parliament have intended that s 3 should require courts to make decisions for which they are not equipped. There may be several ways of making a provision convention-compliant, and the choice may involve issues calling for legislative deliberation."

Similarly, Lord Millett stated (at 438–440):

". . . the obligation [*under s.3*] arises (or at least has significance) only where the legislation in its natural and ordinary meaning, that is to say as construed in accordance with normal principles, is incompatible with the convention. Ordinary principles of statutory construction include a presumption that Parliament does not intend to legislate in a way that would put the United Kingdom in breach of its international obligations. This presumption will often be sufficient to enable the court to interpret the statute in a way which will make it compatible with the convention without recourse to s 3. It is only where this is not the case that s 3 comes into play. When it does, it obliges the court to give an abnormal construction to the statutory language and one which cannot be achieved by resort to standard principles and presumptions.

This is a difficult exercise, for it is one which the courts have not hitherto been accustomed to perform, and where they must accordingly establish their own ground rules for the first time. It is also dangerously seductive, for there is bound to be a temptation to apply the section beyond its proper scope and to trespass upon the prerogative of Parliament in what will almost invariably be a good cause . . .

. . . s 3 requires the court to read legislation in a way which is compatible with the convention only 'so far as it is possible to do so'. It must, therefore, be possible, *by a process of interpretation alone*, to read the offending statute in a way which is compatible with the convention . . .

. . . I respectfully agree with my noble and learned friend Lord Nicholls of Birkenhead that even if, construed in accordance with ordinary principles of construction, the meaning of the legislation admits of no doubt, s 3 may require it to be given a different meaning. It means only that the court must take the language of the statute as it finds and give it a meaning which, however, unnatural or unreasonable, is intellectually defensible. It can read in and read down; it can supply missing words, so long as they are consistent with the fundamental features of the legislative scheme; it can also do considerable violence to the language and stretch it almost (but not quite) to breaking point. The courts must 'strive to find *a possible* interpretation compatible with convention rights' see *R v A* at [44] per Lord Steyn (my emphasis). But it is not entitled to give it an impossible one, however much it would wish to do so.

In my view s 3 does not entitle the court to supply words which are inconsistent with a fundamental feature of the legislative scheme; nor to repeal, delete, or contradict the language of the offending statute."

However, it was the *application* of the notions identified in these statements *in Ghaidan* upon which the majority and Lord Millett disagreed. Put simply, the majority were satisfied that, in exercise of the interpretative obligation under s.3, it was possible and justifiable to "read in" words to para.2 and, thereby, give effect to it in a manner that was compatible with Convention rights; Lord Millett was not so inclined. The rationale for the majority's decision was evident in the following statement of Lord Nicholls (at 424):

> "Paragraph 2 of Sch 1 to the 1977 Act is unambiguous. But the social policy underlying the [*Housing Act*] 1988 extension of security of tenure under para 2 to the survivor of couples living together as husband and wife is equally applicable to the survivor of homosexual couples living together in a close and stable relationship. In this circumstance I see no reason to doubt that application of s 3 to para 2 has the effect that para 2 should be read and given effect to as though the survivor of such a homosexual couple were the surviving spouse of the original tenant. Reading para 2 in this way would have the result that cohabiting heterosexual couples and cohabiting homosexual couples would be treated alike for the purposes of succession as a statutory tenant. This would eliminate the discriminatory effect of para 2 and would do so consistently with the social policy underlying para 2. The precise form of words read in for this purpose is of no significance. It is their substantive effect which matters."

Lord Rodger, in furtherance of the stance adopted by the majority, indicated, towards the end of his judgment which had otherwise comprised general observations about the scope and application of s.3, that he could not discern any principle underlying the RA 1977 as a whole, or Sch.1 in particular, which required that only the survivor of a long-term heterosexual relationship should be treated as a statutory tenant. Moreover, his Lordship felt that to interpret para.2(2) to include the survivor of a long-term homosexual relationship would not contradict any cardinal principle of the RA 1977, and "would simply be a modest development of the extension of the concept of 'spouse' which Parliament itself made when it enacted para 2(2) in 1988". Lord Rodger (at 457) proffered the following interpretation of para.2(2) as a means of reading and giving effect to para.2 in a way which was compatible with Mr Godin-Mendoza's art.8 and art.14 Convention rights:

> "A person, whether of the same or of the opposite sex, who was living with the original tenant in a long-term relationship shall be treated as the spouse of the original tenant."

Lord Steyn stated merely that, with regard to the circumstances of the case, the Court of Appeal, in his opinion, came to the correct conclusion and endorsed its reasoning on the use of s.3.

Lord Millett, in his dissenting judgment, rejected the interpretation which the majority, using s.3, adopted in relation to para.2. His Lordship described such interpretation "as an interpretation of the existing legislation which it not only does not bear but which is manifestly inconsistent with it". In Lord Millett's opinion, the language of para.2 and its legislative history showed that the essential feature of the relationship which Parliament had in contemplation was an open relationship between persons of the *opposite* sex. The admitted discrimination to which this might give rise in relation to couples of the same sex was a matter for resolution by

Parliament and not the courts. In this respect, his Lordship alluded to Parliament's intent to alleviate such discrimination in the circumstances countenanced by the Civil Partnerships Bill (subsequently enacted as the Civil Partnership Act 2004), which was being debated at that time in the House of Lords (acting in its legislative capacity). Lord Millett concluded his judgment with a strong rebuttal of what he clearly regarded as a misconceived and inappropriate exercise by the majority of the interpretative obligation under s.3. His Lordship stated (at 446–447):

"By what is claimed [*by the majority*] to be a process of interpretation of an existing statute framed in gender-specific terms, and enacted at a time when homosexual relationships were not recognised by law, it is proposed to treat persons of the same sex living together as if they were living together as husband and wife and then to treat such persons as if they were lawfully married. It is to be left unclear as from what date this change in the law has taken place. If we were to decide this question we would be usurping the function of Parliament; and if we were to say that it was from the time when the European Court of Human Rights decided that such discrimination was unlawful we would be transferring the legislative power from Parliament to that court. It is, in my view, consonant with the convention for the contracting states to take time to consider its implications and to bring their laws into conformity with it. They do not demand retrospective legislation.

Worse still, in support of their conclusion that the existing discrimination is incompatible with the convention, there is a tendency in some of the speeches of the majority to refer to loving, stable and long-lasting homosexual relationships. It is left wholly unclear whether qualification for the successive tenancy is confined to couples enjoying such a relationship or, consistently with the legislative policy which Parliament has hitherto adopted, is dependent on status and not merit.

In my opinion all these questions are essentially questions of social policy which should be left to Parliament."

Notwithstanding the cogency of Lord Millett's dissent, Mr Ghaidan's appeal was dismissed, and Mr Godin-Mendoza duly succeeded to a statutory Rent Act tenancy.

▶ 3. Conclusion

13–005 In one respect, it can be argued that the impact of *Ghaidan*, as a precedent, may be diminished by the enactment of various statutory provisions, most notably those within the Civil Partnership Act 2004 (which came into force on December 5, 2005), which have conferred on same-sex couples, in defined circumstances, rights and responsibilities similar to those created by marriage. Nevertheless, in other respects (which are particularly pertinent to this book), it is and will continue to be significant. First, it provides authoritative expositions and guidance on the *general* scope and application of s.3 of the HRA 1998, in relation to which Lord Nicholls conceded the courts were "still cautiously feeling their way forward". Secondly, it exhibits the difficulties inherent in *applying* s.3 in any given case, and shows that what to several senior judicial minds may be regarded as a matter of interpretation to another is seen as trespassing upon the legislative function of Parliament. Thirdly and finally, it would appear to provide an example in the case of *Fitzpatrick* of where a decision of the House of Lords on the interpretation of a statutory provision prior to the HRA 1998 will not be treated as binding or persuasive after the coming into force of that Act where the interpretation is shown to be inconsistent with Convention rights.

Further Reading

Kavanagh, "The Role of Parliamentary Intention in Adjudication under the Human Rights Act 1998" (2006) 26 O.J.LS. 179

Kavanagh, "Constitutional Review under the UK Human Rights Act" (Cambridge University Press, 2009), ch.3

Van Zyl Smit, "The New Purposive Interpretation of Statutes: HRA section 3 after Ghaidan v Godin-Mendoza" (2007) 70 M.L.R. 294

14 EQUAL PAY

▶ ## 1. Introduction

14-001 The primary purpose of this case study on equal pay is to provide illustrations of the approach of the Court of Justice (CJ) to the interpretation of legislation and to case law, and of the impact of the European Union (EU) legal order on statutory interpretation and the doctrine of precedent in English law. It does, however, also provide examples of traditional English approaches to statutory interpretation and precedent. Equal pay is an area of EU law characteristic of the EU law-making process described in Chapter 4 in that a provision in the Treaty on the Functioning of the European Union (TFEU), expressed in general terms and in the language of abstract principle, has been given further elucidation and substance by EU leg- islation and by decisions of the CJ. From the legislation and case law, a new principle may be said to have emerged, based on and developed by determining the scope of the abstract statement of principle in the provision in the TFEU. The relevant TFEU provision in the case of equal pay is now art.157, although at the time of the cases featured in this study it was art.119 of the EC Treaty. (Following ratification in 2009 of the European Reform Treaty (Lisbon, 2004), the EC Treaty has been amended and renamed the "Treaty on the Functioning of the European Union" and there has been renumbering of articles in the Treaty—see Chapter 4, 4-001.) As the references are to art.119 in the cases in this study, it has seemed more appropriate to use the citation "art.119 (now 157)" when considering them, although when referring to the article generally, prior to consideration of the cases, the citation "art.157 (ex 119)" has been used.) Further elucidation and substance to art.157 (ex 119) is provided by Directive 75/117 and by the ECJ cases of *Defrenne v Sabena* (80/70) [1971] E.C.R. 445 (*Defrenne*); and *Jenkins v Kingsgate (Clothing Productions) Ltd* (96/80) [1981] 1 E.C.R. 911 (*Jenkins*). Thus, there may be said to be two principles relevant to the field of equal pay:

— the abstract statement of principle contained in art.157 (ex 119); and
— the more detailed and substantial principle based on art.157 (ex 119), but developed through secondary legislation and a body of case law.

In the case studies, the former principle is referred to as the principle of equal pay *articulated in* art.119 (now 157) and the latter is referred to as the principle of equal pay *based on* art.119 (now 157).

As indicated in Chapter 4, the EU legal order has provoked a range of approaches by English judges to a number of issues in relation to statutory interpretation and precedent. The selection of any single case would be insufficient to illustrate this range of approaches and, for this reason, three cases involving claims brought in English courts have been chosen from the body of litigation on equal pay. These three cases, for which relevant citations are provided in the text, are *Macarthys Ltd v Smith* (*Macarthys*); *Garland v British Rail Engineering Ltd* (*Garland*); and *Pickstone v Freemans Plc* (*Pickstone*).

This case study illustrates a number of points in relation to statutory interpretation and precedent:

▶ interpreting statutory provisions by focusing on their underlying aims, general spirit and objectives;

▶ textual, teleological and schematic interpretation of statutory provisions;

▶ "gap filling" in statutory provisions;

▶ broad and narrow interpretation of statutory provisions;

▶ interpreting English statutory provisions so as to secure compliance with EU law (Ambiguity Interpretation Approach and General Interpretation Approach);

▶ according priority to EU law over inconsistent English statutory provisions (Priority Approach);

▶ interpreting statutory provisions by focusing on the words used in those provisions and giving them their ordinary meaning;

▶ (not) interpreting a statutory provision to remedy the mischief at which the provision was aimed;

▶ having regard to legislation and a body of case law as a source of guidance when interpreting the scope of an EC Treaty provision;

▶ a refusal by the Court of Appeal to follow one of its previous decisions in the light of subsequent ECJ decisions;

▶ adoption of a purposive approach when interpreting a statutory provision; and

▶ reference to Parliamentary debates on draft regulations implementing a statutory provision when interpreting that provision.

The format of the chapter comprises an introductory section on the legislative framework surrounding the principle of equal pay based on art.157 (ex 119), followed by an examination of each case sub-divided by reference to the tribunals and courts in which the case was considered.

▶ 2. The Legislative Framework

Article 157(1) and (2) (ex 119), which is expressed in general terms, provides: **14–002**

"(1) Each Member State shall ensure that the principle of equal pay for male and female workers for equal pay or work of equal value is applied.

> (2) For the purpose of this Article, 'pay' means the ordinary basic or minimum wage or salary and any other consideration, whether in cash or in kind, which the worker receives, directly or indirectly, in respect of his employment, from his employer."

This provision is given further elucidation and substance, inter alia, by Directive 2006/54 on the implementation of the principle of equal opportunities and equal treatment of men and women in matters of employment and occupation. Article 4 of the Directive covers Prohibition of Discrimination and provides:

> "For the same work or for work to which equal value is attributed, direct and indirect discrimination on grounds of sex with regard to all aspects and conditions of remuneration shall be eliminated.
>
> In particular, where a job classification system is used for determining pay, it shall be based on the same criteria for both men and women and so drawn up as to exclude any discrimination on grounds of sex."

This Directive consolidates and amends a number of earlier directives relating to equal opportunities and equal treatment, including Directive 75/117, which concerned equal pay (equal pay directive). Article 1 of Directive 75/117 is essentially replicated in art.4 of Directive 2006/54.

Whilst Directive 2006/54 in some respects amplifies the scope of art.157 (ex 119), it does not do so in any detailed sense and its provisions are rather general and abstract in nature. Since both art.157 (ex 119) and the Directive give little indication as to scope, CJ judges must determine their general ambit. This may entail judges engaging in "gap filling" by reading in or implying words into art.157 (ex 119) or the Directive. Thus, for instance, art.157 (ex 119) provides that "pay", as well as covering ordinary basic or minimum wage or salary, includes "any other consideration . . . in kind", which has been held to include benefits received by employees which continue into retirement (see *Garland*, below 14–008—14–013).

At the time of the decisions in *Macarthys, Garland* and *Pickstone*, the English legislation on equal pay was contained in the Equal Pay Act 1970 (EPA 1970), as later amended by the Equal Pay (Amendments) Regulations 1983 and the Equal Pay Act 1970 (Amendment) Regulations 2003 and 2004. Two of these decisions, *Macarthys* and *Pickstone*, concerned claims under the EPA 1970, whilst the claim in *Garland*, which was concerned with benefits and different treatment on the ground of sex, proceeded under the Sex Discrimination Act 1975 (SDA 1975). The question of equal pay, however, arose in *Garland* since, under art.119(2) (now 157(2)), "pay" included not only ordinary basic or minimum wage or salary, but also "any other consideration . . . in kind" (see above). Both the EPA 1970 and the SDA 1975 have now been repealed by the Equality Act 2010, which consolidated the diverse and complex range of primary and secondary legislation on anti-discrimination law. The vast majority of the provisions of the Equality Act 2010 were brought into force on October 1, 2010 by the Equality Act 2010 (Commencement No.1) Order 2010 (SI

2010/1736). The length and complexity of the provisions of the EPA 1970 preclude their reproduction *in toto*, but examples are extracted, as appropriate, throughout this chapter, e.g. s.1(1), (2) and (4) of the EPA 1970 (see below, 14–003). This legislation, like the Equality Act 2010 which succeeds it, is drafted in traditional English style, with detailed provisions which tend to be comprehensive in coverage, specific in nature and formulated with a degree of precision.

As a result of these differences in legislative drafting styles, together with the traditional English approach to the interpretation of legislation of focusing on the words used in the statutory provision, deficiencies in English law in failing to meet the requirements of EU law may occur, leading to a "compliance gap" in English law (see Chapter 4, 4–014). This arose in the context of equal pay where the broad general principles of EC law were enacted in the EPA 1970 and the SDA 1975 as precise and detailed rules, which often received a literal interpretation by the courts. This resulted in action that is clearly discriminatory not falling within the specific wording of the Act and led to litigation in which provisions in UK legislation were challenged as failing to comply with EU law. In some instances, challenges took the form of claims brought by individuals in the English courts (as with the three cases examined in this chapter), some of which resulted in art.177 (now 267) references being made to the ECJ. In other instances, proceedings were instituted by the European Commission against the UK in the ECJ for failure to comply with EU law, e.g. *EC Commission v United Kingdom* (61/81) [1982] E.C.R. 2601; and *EC Commission v United Kingdom* (65/82) [1983] E.C.R. 3431. It was the finding of deficiencies in the UK legislation as a result of these two cases that led to the enactment of the Equal Pay (Amendments) Regulations 1983 (see below, 14–014 and 14–021).

▶ 3. *Macarthys Ltd v Smith*

Mrs Smith was appointed trainee stockroom manageress by Macarthys Ltd on **14–003** January 21, 1976 and was promoted to the post of stockroom manageress on March 1, 1976. Her predecessor, Mr McCullough, had left the post of stockroom manager on October 20, 1975. Mrs Smith claimed that, once promoted to the post of manageress, she was entitled to pay equal to that which Mr McCullough had been receiving at the time of his departure. The applicable English legislation was s.1 of the EPA 1970, the relevant subsections of which are set out below, with phrases particularly relevant for the purposes of the case underlined for ease of reference:

> "(1) If the terms of a contract under which a woman is employed at an establishment in Great Britain do not include (directly or by reference to a collective agreement or otherwise) an equality clause they shall be deemed to include one.

(2) An equality clause is a provision which relates to terms (whether concerned with pay or not) of a contract under which a woman is employed (the "woman's contract"), and has the effect that

(a) where the woman is employed on like work with a man in the same employment
   (i)   if (apart from the equality clause) any term of the woman's contract is or becomes less favourable to the woman than a term of a similar kind in the contract under which that man is employed, that term of the woman's contract shall be treated as so modified as not to be less favourable, and
   (ii) if (apart from the equality clause) at any time the woman's contract does not include a term corresponding to a term benefiting that man included in the contract under which he is employed, the woman's contract shall be treated as including such a term;
(b) where the woman is employed on work rated as equivalent with that of a man in the same employment
   (i)   if (apart from the equality clause) any term of the woman's contract determined by the rating of the work is or becomes less favourable to the woman than a term of a similar kind in the contract under which that man is employed, that term of the woman's contract shall be treated as so modified as not to be less favourable, and
   (ii) if (apart from the equality clause) at any time the woman's contract does not include a term corresponding to a term benefiting that man included in the contract under which he is employed and determined by the rating of the work, the woman's contact shall be treated as including such a term.

. . .

(4) A woman is to be regarded as employed on like work with men if, but only if, her work and theirs is of the same or a broadly similar nature, and the differences (if any) between the things she does and the things they do are not of practical importance in relation to terms and conditions of employment; and accordingly in comparing her work with theirs regard shall be had to the frequency or otherwise with which any such differences occur in practice as well as to the nature and extent of the differences."

▷ (a) Macarthys in the Industrial Tribunal and the Employment Appeal Tribunal

14–004 The Industrial Tribunal (see above, 2–010) accepted that the work of Mrs Smith and Mr McCullough was indeed "like work" under s.1(2)(a) of the EPA 1970 and that there was no justification for paying them different salaries on objective grounds, i.e. the sole reason for the difference was sex discrimination. In the light of this finding, the only issue in contention was whether Mrs Smith was entitled to compare her job with that of a predecessor or whether a comparison could be made only with a colleague employed contemporaneously with her. The Industrial Tribunal, the decision of which was not reported, found in Mrs Smith's favour, as did the Employment Appeal Tribunal (EAT) (see above, 2–010) ([1978] 2 All E.R. 746), in which judgment was given by Phillips J., who indicated that the outcome depended on the interpretation given to s.1(2) and (4) of the EPA 1970. Counsel for the employers argued that the use of the present tense in these sections (see phrases underlined above) meant that only contemporaneous employment qualified for comparison under the Act. The EAT agreed that an interpretation which focused on the words used in the statutory provision would produce that result and Phillips J. stated (at 748):

"Under the Act, equality of treatment is required where the woman is employed on 'like work' with a man in the same employment. Thus an essential feature of any claim . . . is a comparison of the woman's case with that of a man in the same employment, and this is so whether the claim is brought under s 1(2)(a) ('like work') or under s1(2)(b) ('evaluation study'). The claimant must show, in the first case, that she is employed on 'like work' with the man in the same employment, or in the second case that she is employed on work rated as 'equivalent' with that of a man in the same employment. So far there is nothing in the Act to indicate with certainty that it is not permissible for a woman for this purpose to compare her situation with that of a man formerly in the employment of the same employers, but who is no longer so employed. The language which strongly suggests that it is not permissible is that to be found in s1(2)(a)(i)(ii) and in s1(4). The use of the present tense in these provisions strongly suggests that what is in contemplation is contemporaneous employment. There is not much doubt, and so much was conceded in the argument on the hearing of the appeal, that this is the ordinary meaning of the language used."

If such a construction was adopted, however, this might, as Phillips J. acknowledged, lead to some strange results, such as no comparison being possible under the legislation where on day one a male employee left his employment and on day two was replaced by a female employee at half the salary. Such results could be avoided if s.1(2) and (4) was not given a narrow interpretation focusing on the words used, but a broad interpretation so as to accord with the principle of equal pay based on art.119 (now 157). The EAT favoured such a broad interpretation. Little attempt was made, however, to interpret the principle of equal pay based on art.119 (now 157) to determine whether it permitted a comparison with persons previously employed. Phillips J. in his judgment appeared to assume that it did, making reference only to art.119 (now 157) and the ECJ case of *Defrenne*. Although the former contained a statement of abstract principle relating to equal pay and the latter was part of the body of law which elucidated that principle, neither provided any specific guidance as to whether the principle of equal pay based on art.119 (now 157) extended to cases of non-contemporaneous employment. In adopting a broad interpretation, the EAT's approach would seem to be in keeping with the general approach to interpretation adopted by the CJ of focusing not so much on the words used in legislative provisions, but on their underlying aims, general spirit and objectives. Further, the EAT's approach would appear to be in keeping with the CJ's interpretative techniques of teleological interpretation and of having recourse to case law and general principles as sources of guidance when interpreting legislative provisions. In support of this approach, Phillips J. in his judgment referred (at 748), inter alia, to an earlier judgment delivered by the EAT in the case of *Snoxell v Vauxhall Motors Ltd* [1977] 3 All E.R. 770, where the EAT had stated (at 777–778):

"In *Defrenne v Sabena* [1976] ICR 547, it was decided that art 119 must be directly applied in the courts of member States . . . It seems to us that, speaking generally, the [*Sex Discrimination Act 1975*] and the [*Equal Pay Act 1970*] constitute a proper and sufficient fulfilment by this country of its treaty obligations in respect of art 119, and a sufficient statement of the principle of equal pay there enshrined. It is important to observe that art 119 establishes a principle, with little or no detail of the way in which it is to be applied. It appears to us that the 1975 Act, and the 1970 Act, must be construed and applied subject to, and so as to give effect to, the principle. As we have pointed out (*eg* in *Capper Pass Ltd v Lawton* [1977] 2 All ER 11 at 14, [1977] QB 852 at 856) a system of equal pay may take many forms, and it does not appear that art 119 requires the member states to apply the principle in identical ways provided that the principle is satisfied. Thus art 119 itself is not precise. The principle is that "men and women should receive equal pay for equal work." Article 119 does not condescend to particulars in the sense of prescribing whether "equal work" means the same work, or work of equal value, or some other variant. And, in fact, the member states have in force different systems of equal pay, based on different criteria. So, in general the 1970 Act seems to be in conformity with the requirements of the principle. It seems to us that as far as industrial tribunals and the appeal tribunal are concerned, the correct approach is to give effect to *Defrenne v Sabena* [1976] ICR 547 by construing and applying the 1970 Act in conformity with art 119. In this way it will be unnecessary for a claimant to make a separate claim specifically under art 119, and it will be understood that a claim under the 1970 Act will entitle a claimant to any remedy which he could claim under art 119, inasmuch as the 1970 Act is to be so construed and applied . . .

In the cases which have come for decision before the appeal tribunal we have not encountered any particular ambiguity or obscurity in the 1970 Act. However, it at once became obvious that it would be possible to construe its provisions, particularly s1(4), either narrowly or broadly. For the reasons which we have given in various decisions (in particular *Capper Pass Ltd v Lawton* [1977] 2 All ER 11, [1977] QB 852 and *Dugdale v Kraft Foods Ltd* [1977] 1 All ER 454, [1976] 1 WLR 1288) we have taken the view that it is right to construe the 1970 Act broadly having regard to its object. Any doubt as to the propriety of this method of construction and application of the 1970 Act seems to us to be

> set at rest by reflecting that, following the decision in *Defrenne v Sabena* [1976] ICR 547, there is an obligation to apply art.119 directly in the courts of the member states. As it seems to us, it is only by so construing and applying the Equal Pay Act 1970 that it is possible to honour this obligation."

Phillips J. went on to endorse the view which the EAT had taken in this case, stating (at 749):

> "We have found some assistance here in this approach. What has to be given effect to is the *principle* of art 119, and the principle is that men and women should achieve equal pay for equal work. An Act which permitted discrimination of the kind instanced in the example given above [*of a male employee on day one leaving his employment and being replaced by a female employee on day two at half the salary*] would not be a successful application of the principle."

Phillips J. also advanced a further justification for the EAT's preferred interpretation of s.1(2) and (4), namely, the legislative context surrounding those provisions. The legislative context was seen as not just the EPA 1970 itself, but the EPA 1970 and the SDA 1975 taken together, which "should be construed and applied in harmony, as together they constitute a single code" (at 749). Thus, if Mrs Smith's claim had concerned not unequal pay for like work but denial of another type of benefit, such as a difference in holiday entitlement, she would have been able to bring her claim under the SDA 1975 and under this statute comparison with the entitlements given to a male predecessor would have been allowed. However, s.6(6) of the SDA 1975 excluded claims relating to the payment of money under an employment contract, leaving Mrs Smith with no alternative but to bring a claim under the EPA 1970. If the EPA 1970 was to be interpreted to exclude comparisons with previous employment, this would produce the unsatisfactory result of Mrs Smith losing her claim simply because of the particular legislative provisions on which she had been forced to rely. Accordingly, the EAT was of the view that both Acts should be construed together as a single code. The approach here of construing both Acts together as a single code would seem to be in keeping with the (schematic) approach to interpretation adopted by the CJ.

Thus, the EAT effectively departed from the traditional English approach of focusing on the words used in the statutory provision in favour of focusing on the underlying aims, general spirit and objectives of the statutory provision and employing both teleological and schematic interpretation techniques. In doing so, the EAT did not seem to be adopting the Ambiguity Interpretation Approach, of seeking to use the principle of equal pay based on art.119 (now 157) to resolve an ambiguity in s.1(2) and (4), since at no point was any reference made by the EAT to ambiguity. Rather, the EAT appeared to be adopting the General Interpretation Approach, of interpreting these provisions in a way which ensured compliance with the principle of equal pay based on art.119 (now 157), even though this required a departure from the ordinary meaning of the words.

Accordingly, the EAT decided that Mrs Smith was entitled to make a comparison with an individual previously employed on "like work". Nevertheless, the EAT sought to confine comparisons to situations where the individual with whom the comparison was being drawn had left the employment only a short interval before the arrival of the new employee who was being paid at a lower rate. In the EAT's view, differences in pay following substantial intervals could be explained on many grounds and to permit such comparisons would be to introduce a new scheme based on the comparison of posts or jobs, not of individuals, and would thus go beyond the intended scheme of the EPA 1970. The EAT accepted that such "redrafting" was beyond its remit. As Phillips J. stated (at 750), "what we cannot do is to construe it in such a way as in effect to introduce a new scheme for which it does not provide".

It might be felt, however, that the EAT had, at least to a limited extent, construed s.1(2) and (4) so as to bring within them situations for which they did not provide. Construction so as to permit comparison with individuals employed a short time previously arguably did not fall within the wording of the provisions and was included only by adoption of a "gap-filling" technique of interpretation as traditionally employed by the CJ. This technique would essentially involve "reading in" words into s.1(2)(a) so that it effectively provided:

". . . where a woman is employed on like work with a man in the same employment at the same time or where a short interval exists between the employment of the man and the woman".

Two alternative approaches might have been adopted by the EAT. First, the EAT might have adhered to a traditional English approach to statutory interpretation and given the words their ordinary meaning, which would have precluded claimants from adopting comparisons with individuals previously employed. So interpreted, s.1(2) and (4) would have been inconsistent with the principle of equal pay based on art.119 (now 157) and might be considered invalid under ss.2 and 3 of the ECA 1972, under which EU law must prevail (Priority Approach). Secondly, the EAT might have ceded the interpretative function to the ECJ by making an art.177 (now 267) reference to enable the ECJ to decide whether the principle of equal pay based on art.119 (now 157) enabled comparisons to be made with individuals previously employed, a course which, as will be seen, was adopted by the Court of Appeal.

▷ (b) Macarthys in the Court of Appeal: reference to the ECJ

14–005 In the Court of Appeal ([1979] 3 All E.R. 325), Lord Denning, M.R. followed the approach of the EAT, but Lawton and Cumming-Bruce L.JJ. did not do so. On the appropriate approach to interpretation of the English statute, Lawton L.J. followed the traditional English approach of giving the words their ordinary meaning. His Lordship said (at 332–333):

> "In my judgment the grammatical construction of s1(2) is consistent only with a comparison between a woman and a man in the same employment at the same time. The words, by the tenses used, look to the present and the future but not to the past. They are inconsistent with a comparison between a woman and a man, no longer in the same employment, who was doing her job before she got it.
>
> . . . As the meaning of the words used in s 1(2) and (4) is clear and no ambiguity whether patent or latent, lurks within them, under our rules for the construction of Acts of Parliament the statutory intention must be found within those words. It is not permissible to read into the statute words which are not there or to look outside the Act, as counsel for Mrs Smith invited us to do and Phillips J did, to read the words used in a sense other than that of their ordinary meaning. Counsel for Mrs Smith submitted that the Act [*of 1970*] should be read in harmony with the Sex Discrimination Act 1975; but that Act, as s 6(6) expressly provides, 'does not apply to benefits consisting of the payment of money when the provision of those benefits is regulated by the woman's contract of employment'. It follows, so it seems to me, to be irrelevant that the Sex Discrimination Act 1975 does allow a comparison between the benefits, other than those consisting of money, which a man got when doing a job and which his successor, a woman, did not get when doing the same job, whereas under the Act [*of 1970*] relied upon by Mrs Smith in this case comparison in relation to pay is outside it."

It can be seen that reading words into the statute ("gap filling") and the schematic approach to interpretation (of regarding the EPA 1970 and the SDA 1975 as a single code to be construed harmoniously), both of which are techniques favoured by the CJ and which had been employed by the EAT, were emphatically rejected. Lawton L.J. (at 333) recognised, however, that "we cannot . . . ignore art 119 and apply what I consider to be the plain meaning of the Act", although in his view there was uncertainty as to whether or not the principle of equal pay based on art.119 (now 157) was confined to cases where men and women were doing like work contemporaneously. This uncertainty could not be resolved, his Lordship felt (at 333), using a traditional English approach to statutory interpretation, for he was not convinced that when art.119 (now 157) was construed:

> ". . . in accordance with the canons of construction as used in our court for finding out the meaning of statutes and deeds, its ambit was confined to men and women doing like or broadly similar work side by side at the same time. The part of the article which begins with the words 'Equal pay without discrimination based on sex' takes in para. (a) 'the same work' or 'the same job' after a man as well as alongside a man. In my opinion there is some doubt whether art 119 applies to the facts of this case."

Lawton L.J., when construing art.119 (now 157), thus confined himself to using the traditional English approach of focusing on the words used. The article is, however, expressed in broad, general language, and it is difficult when construing this provision (or similarly drafted EU legislation) to ascertain meaning from focusing on the words used. In view of the uncertainty, Lawton L.J. felt that a reference should be made under art.177 (now 267) for the CJ to give a ruling to resolve the uncertainty. This would then enable the Court of Appeal to fulfil its obligation to give effect to art.119 (now 157), which, in his Lordship's view, arose both by virtue of s.2 of the ECA 1972 and ECJ case law on direct effect and supremacy, namely, *Defrenne* and *Amministrazione Delle Finanze Dello Stato v Simmenthal SpA* (106/77) [1978] E.C.R. 629 (*Simmenthal*). Lawton L.J. thus appeared to regard himself as bound by principles, in this instance direct effect and supremacy, formulated and developed by the ECJ through a body of case law, stating (at 334):

> "Being in doubt as to the ambit of art 119 and being under an obligation arising both from the decisions of the European Court of Justice in the two cases to which I have referred [*Defrenne* and *Simmenthal*] and s2 of the European Communities Act 1972 to apply that article in our courts, it seems to me that this is a situation to which art 177 of the EEC Treaty applies. I consider that a decision is necessary as to the construction of art 119 and I would request the European Court of Justice to give a ruling on it.
>
> . . . as I am in doubt as to what is the right construction of art 119 when our canons of construction are applied and in ignorance as to how the European Court of Justice would construe that article when it applies its own rules of construction, I consider myself under a judicial duty not to guess how that court would construe it but to find out how it does."

Cumming-Bruce L.J. (at 335) endorsed Lawton L.J.'s approach:

> "I am left so far wholly unconvinced that there is any reason for giving s1(2)(a)(i) a meaning other than that which at first impression I thought was the ordinary and natural meaning of the words.
>
> This is what Phillips J thought too. But he thought that the effect of art 119 of the EEC Treaty was clear . . . and that it was permissible to use the article as an aid to construction of the English statute . . . I take a different view on each point. Like Lawton LJ I do not find it easy to discern the application of art 119 to the circumstances contemplated by s1(2)(a)(i) of the English statute having regard to my construction thereof. I take the view that art 119, which expresses a general principle, may be perfectly consistent with the English legislation as I construe it. But I am not sure about that, and therefore agree that the court at Luxembourg [*the CJ*] should give an authoritative answer to that question. Secondly, I do not think that it is permissible, as an aid to construction, to look at the terms of the Treaty. If the terms of the Treaty are adjudged in Luxembourg to be inconsistent with the provisions of the Equal Pay Act 1970,

> European law will prevail over that municipal legislation. But such a judgment in Luxembourg cannot affect the meaning of the English statute."

There was thus a rejection of the General Interpretation Approach adopted by the EAT—"I do not think it is permissible, as an aid to construction, to look at the terms of the Treaty"—and an adoption, evident in his Lordship's penultimate sentence, of the Priority Approach under which EU law prevails over English legislation in the event of conflict.

Lord Denning, M.R., however, dissenting, followed the approach of the EAT. There was no indication that such construction would be possible only where there was ambiguity, so it would appear that Lord Denning, M.R., like the EAT, adopted the General Interpretation Approach. However, in the event that harmony with EU law could not be achieved by adopting this approach, then, in his Lordship's view, EU law would prevail (Priority Approach). Lord Denning, M.R. stated (at 329):

> "Under s 2(1) and (4) of the European Communities Act 1972 the principles laid down in the Treaty are 'without further enactment' to be given legal effect in the United Kingdom: and have priority over 'any enactment passed or to be passed' by our Parliament. So we are entitled and I think bound to look at art 119 of the EEC Treaty because it is directly applicable here: and also any directive which is directly applicable here; see *Van Duyn v Home Office (No 2)* [1975] 3 All ER 190, [1975] Ch 358. We should, I think, look to see what those provisions require about equal pay for men and women. Then we should look at our own legislation on the point, giving it, of course, full faith and credit, assuming that it does fully comply with the obligations under the Treaty. In construing our statute, we are entitled to look to the Treaty as an aid to its construction; but not only as an aid but as an overriding force. If on close investigation it should appear that our legislation is deficient, or is inconsistent with Community law, by some oversight of our draftsmen, then it is our bounden duty to give priority to Community law."

In accordance with this approach his Lordship began by determining the meaning and effect of EU law by looking at art.119 (now 157) to see what its provisions required about equal pay for men and women, Lord Denning, M.R. stated (at 329):

> "Article 119 is framed in European fashion. It enunciates a broad general principle and leaves the judges to work out the details. In contrast the Equal Pay Act is framed in English fashion. It states no general principle but lays down detailed specific rules for the courts to apply (which, so some hold, the courts must interpret according to the actual language used) without resort to considerations of policy or principle.
>
> Now consider art 119 in the context of our present problem. Take the simple case envisaged by Phillips J. A man who is a skilled technician working single-handed for a firm receives £1.50 an hour for his work. He leaves the employment. On the very next day he is replaced by a woman who is equally

capable and who does exactly the same work as the man but, because she is a woman, she is only paid £1.25 an hour. That would be a clear case of discrimination on the ground of sex. It would, I think, be an infringement of the principle in art 119 which says 'that men and women should receive equal pay for equal work'. All the more so when you take into account the explanatory sentence in art 119 itself which says:

'. . . Equal pay without discrimination based on sex means . . . that pay for work at time rates shall be the same for the same job.'

If you go further and consider the Council directive of 10th February 1975, EEC Council Directive 75/117, art 1 it becomes plain beyond question:

'The principle of equal pay for men and women outlined in Article 119 of the Treaty, hereinafter called "principle of equal pay", means, for the same work or for work to which equal value is attributed, the elimination of all discrimination on grounds of sex with regard to all aspects and conditions of remuneration.'

That directive . . . is relevant as showing the scope of the principle contained in art 119. It shows that it applies to the case of the skilled technician (which I have put) and that the difference between the woman and the man should be eliminated by paying her £1.50 an hour just like the man.

In my opinion therefore art 119 is reasonably clear on the point; it applies not only to cases where the woman is employed on like work *at the same time* with a man in the same employment, but also when she is employed on like work in succession to a man, that is, in such close succession that it is just and reasonable to make a comparison between them."

Thus, his Lordship, in determining the scope of the principle of equal pay articulated in art.119 (now 157), adopted both a textual approach, by having regard to the language of the article itself, and a schematic approach, by having regard to art.1 of Directive 75/117 which provided that the principle of equal pay based on art.119 (now 157) required the elimination of sex discrimination in relation to remuneration (see above, 14–002). In doing so, however, the focus was not on giving a meaning to the words used in art.119 (now 157) to see whether they encompassed comparison with non-contemporaneous work, but on whether such comparison fell within the principle of equal pay articulated in art.119 (now 157) as prescribed by the article's aims and objectives. In his Lordship's view, it did, since, if the position were otherwise, then the article's aim and objective of eliminating sex discrimination in relation to remuneration would not be met. However, Lord Denning, M.R. did not regard *all* comparisons with non-contemporaneous work as falling within the principle of equal pay. For reasons which were not stated, comparisons, in his view, could be made only in cases where women were employed in close succession to men.

Lord Denning, M.R. then considered the provisions in the EPA 1970 which, in his view, should be interpreted so as to be consistent with art.119 (now 157). This could be achieved by adopting interpretative techniques traditionally employed by the CJ, namely a schematic interpretation of construing the EPA 1970 and the SDA 1975 as a single code and "gap filling" by reading the words "in succession" into s.1(2)(a)(i), thereby avoiding sex discrimination and ensuring that the section would accord with the aims and objectives of art.119 (now 157). His Lordship stated (at 330):

> "Section 1(2)(a)(i) of the Equal Pay Act 1970 introduces an 'equality clause' so as to put a woman on an equality with a man 'where the woman is employed on' like work with 'a man in the same employment'. The question is whether the words 'at the same time' are to be read into that subsection so that it is confined to cases where the woman and the man are employed at the same time in the same employment.
>
> Reading that subsection as it stands, it would appear that the draftsman had only in mind cases where the woman was employed *at the same time* as a man. The use of the present tense 'is' and of the phrase 'in the same employment' carry the connotation that the woman and the man are employed on like work *at the same time*.
>
> Section 1(2)(b)(i) does not however carry the same connotation. It introduces an equality clause: '. . . where the woman is employed on work rated as equivalent with that of a man in the same employment . . .' That subsection looks at the value of the work done in the job. If the job is rated as equivalent in value, the woman should get the rate for the job, no matter whether she is employed at the same time as the man or in succession to him.
>
> Some light is thrown on the problem by reference to the Sex Discrimination Act 1975. It applies to all cases of discrimination against a woman in the employment field: see ss1 and 6(1) and (2) except where she is paid less money than the man: see s6(6). Now take a case where a man leaves his job and the employer discriminates against an incoming woman by offering her (not less money) but less benefits than he would offer a man for the same job: for instance, less holidays or less travelling facilities or the like. And she accepts them. That would be discrimination against her on the ground of her sex. It would be unlawful under ss1 and 6(1) and (2). In such a case you would think that there should be an 'equality clause' introduced under s1(2) of the Equal Pay Act: so that, in regard to her holidays or her travel facilities, she would be put on equal terms with the man. But in order to achieve that just result, it is necessary to extend s1(2)(a) so that it extends not only to employment 'at the same time' as the man but also to employment in succession to a man.
>
> Now stand back and look at the statutes as a single code intended to eliminate discrimination against women. They should be a harmonious whole. To achieve this harmony s 1(2)(a)(i) of the Equal Pay Act should not be read as if it included the words 'at the same time'. It should be interpreted so as to apply to cases where a woman is employed at the same job doing the same work 'in succession' to a man."

Lord Denning, M.R. concluded (at 330) that:

> ". . . we reach this very desirable result: it means that there is no conflict between art 119 of the Treaty and s1(2) of the Act of 1970 and that this country will have fulfilled its obligations under the Treaty".

In the light of this statement, it might be assumed that under s.1(2) a comparison could be made only with individuals who were employed a short time previously, although Lord Denning, M.R. made no statement to this effect. However, his Lordship did make such a statement in respect of art.119 (now 157) (see above), observing that it applied to cases where a woman was employed "in such close succession [*to a man*] that it is just and reasonable to make a comparison between them" and, if s.1(2) is not to be in conflict with art.119, it is essential for such a limitation to apply to s.1(2). This would be in keeping with the view expressed by the EAT that a comparison could be made only with individuals employed a short time ago (see above, 14–004).

Lord Denning, M.R.'s approach, however, did not find favour with a majority of the court, Lawton and Cumming-Bruce L.JJ., taking the view that an art.177 (now 267) reference to the CJ was necessary. This left to the CJ the task of interpreting art.119 (now 157) to determine whether it applied where a woman was employed on like work in succession to a man.

▷ (c) Macarthys in the ECJ

14–006 The ECJ (Case 129/79 [1980] E.C.R. 1275) held that the principle of equal work based on art.119 (now 157) did not require simultaneous employment of the individuals whose employment was being compared. The court's judgment, which was typically succinct and lacking in reasoned explanation, simply stated (at 1288) that, when interpreting art.119 (now 157) as regards "equal work":

> "The scope of that concept, which is entirely qualitative in character in that it is exclusively concerned with the nature of the services in question, may not be restricted by the introduction of a requirement of contemporaneity".

Some insight into the ECJ's decision, however, can perhaps be gained from the opinion tendered to the ECJ by Advocate General Capotorti. Under ECJ procedure, an opinion is prepared for the court by an Advocate General, whose role is to act in the public interest as the "conscience of the court". The function of the Advocate General is to prepare a solution to the case and to relate the solution to existing case law. The relevant issues were examined in some depth by Capotorti A.G. in his opinion, as can be seen from the following extract (at 1292):

> "The Court of Appeal asks, first, whether the principle of equal pay for men and women for "equal work", referred to in Article 119 of the EEC Treaty and Article 1 of the Council directive . . . is confined to cases in which the men and

women concerned are contemporaneously engaged on equal work within the same undertaking.

A restriction on the application of the principle of Article 119 in the sense indicated by that question is not warranted by the wording of that provision which confines itself to laying down, as a condition for its application, similarity in the services rendered, without in fact mentioning any criterion of contemporaneity. In addition . . . the *Defrenne* case in holding Article 119 to be directly applicable, refers to the case "where men and women receive unequal pay for equal work carried out in the same establishment" (paragraph 22 of the Decision) without requiring contemporaneity in the work in question.

Nor is the restriction mentioned justified by the objectives of Article 119. As is clearly stated in the aforementioned *Defrenne* judgment . . .

> "Article 119 pursues a double aim. First, in the light of the different stages of the development of social legislation in the various member states, the aim of Article 119 is to avoid a situation in which undertakings established in States which have actually implemented the principal [*sic*] of equal pay suffer a competitive disadvantage in intra-Community competition as compared with undertakings established in States which have not yet eliminated discrimination against women workers as regards pay. Secondly, this provision forms part of the social objectives of the Community, which is not merely an economic union, but is at the same time intended, by common action, to ensure social progress and seek the constant improvement of the living and working conditions of their peoples, as is emphasised by the preamble to the Treaty." "

Capotorti A.G. in this opinion attempted to define the aims of art.119 (now 157) and, in doing so, used a number of interpretative techniques, including reference to the text of art.119 (textual), the text of other legislative provisions, e.g. the preamble to the Treaty (schematic), the purpose and objectives of art.119 (teleological) and the social objectives of the EU itself (teleological), as well as having recourse to ECJ case law (*Defrenne*).

Following the ECJ's ruling that art.119 (now 157) was not restricted by any requirement of contemporaneity, the case was referred back to the Court of Appeal.

▷ (d) Macarthys: Court of Appeal response to ECJ ruling

When the Court of Appeal reconsidered the case ([1981] 1 All E.R. 111), the court **14–007** unanimously dismissed the employers' appeal. The ECJ's ruling that art.119 (now 157) required equal pay for a woman employed on like work in succession to a man was, in the Court of Appeal's view, binding on all English courts and the ECA 1972 required the article to prevail over any inconsistent provisions in the EPA 1970 (Priority Approach). The court accordingly held that Mrs Smith was entitled to compare herself with Mr McCullough, the man previously employed by Macarthys Ltd. Lord Denning, M.R. stated (at 120):

> "We have now been provided with the decision of that court [*the ECJ*]. It is important now to declare, and it must be made plain, that the provisions of art 119 of the EEC Treaty take priority over anything in our English statute on equal pay which is inconsistent with art 119. That priority is given by our own law. It is given by the European Communities Act 1972. Community law is now part of our law; and, whenever there is any inconsistency, Community law has priority . . . I turn therefore to the decision given by the European Court. The answer they gave was that the man and the woman need not be employed at the same time. The woman is entitled to equal pay for equal work, even when the woman is employed after the man has left. That interpretation must now be given by all the courts in England. It will apply in this case and in any such case hereafter."

Lawton and Cumming-Bruce L.JJ. expressed their agreement with the judgment of Lord Denning, M.R., although Cumming-Bruce L.J. indicated that the view which he had expressed at the initial Court of Appeal hearing (see above, 14–005), that "a judgment [*by the ECJ*] in Luxembourg cannot affect the meaning of an English statute", was not intended to have application where there was ambiguity in the English statutory provisions. His Lordship reaffirmed his view that it was inappropriate, in the absence of ambiguity, to have recourse to art.119 (now 157) to interpret s.1(2) and (4) of the EPA 1970 (thereby reaffirming his rejection of the General Interpretation Approach), but indicated obiter (at 121) that he would have been prepared to have had recourse to art.119 (now 157) had there been any ambiguity (thereby endorsing the Ambiguity Interpretation Approach).

▶ 4. *Garland v British Rail Engineering Ltd*

14–008 British Rail Engineering Ltd (BREL) provided free travel for all employees, their spouses and dependent children, and continued to provide this benefit on retirement for all male employees, but not for female employees. Mrs Garland (and a number of her female colleagues) claimed that this constituted sex discrimination contrary to the SDA 1975 because she was denied a benefit which, in like circumstances, was afforded to a man. Since the case concerned benefits and different treatment on the ground of sex, the provisions of the SDA 1975, rather than those of the EPA 1970, were particularly appropriate for challenging the validity of the company's action. As the claim was made under the SDA 1975, the question of whether withdrawal of such a benefit might infringe either the provisions of the EPA 1970 or the principle of equal pay based on art.119 (now 157) was not one which, on the face of it, would appear to arise. However, as will be seen, whether such a benefit could constitute "pay" under art.119 (now 157), in that "pay" included not only ordinary basic or minimum wage or salary, but also "any other consideration . . . in kind" (see above, 14–002), was in due course considered by the House of Lords.

Mrs Garland's claim under the SDA 1975 was based on s.6(2), which provides:

"It is unlawful for a person, in the case of a woman employed by him at an establishment in Great Britain, to discriminate against her

(a) in the way he affords her access to opportunities for promotion, transfer or training, or to any other benefits, facilities or services, or by refusing or deliberately omitting to afford her access to them, or

(b) by dismissing her, or subjecting her to any other detriment."

BREL relied on s.6(4) to argue that the free travel benefit was excluded from s.6(2), as s.6(4) provided that "subsections (1)(b) and (2) do not apply to provision in relation to death or retirement". BREL contended that the words "provision in relation to . . . retirement" in s.6(4) should be broadly interpreted and extend to any arrangement or scheme, or anything undertaken, which manifested itself after retirement. Mrs Garland, however, contended that these words should be more narrowly interpreted and restricted to benefits, facilities or services provided only on retirement, thereby excluding ones available during employment which extended into retirement.

▷ *(a) Garland in the Industrial Tribunal and the EAT*

BREL's contention was upheld by the Industrial Tribunal, whose decision was not reported, but Mrs Garland appealed successfully to the EAT ([1978] 2 All E.R. 789). No compelling reasons appear to have been advanced by Phillips J., delivering the judgment of the EAT, for preferring the meaning advanced by Mrs Garland. However, his Lordship might have justified that meaning by reference to the underlying aims or purpose of the legislation, namely, the avoidance of sex discrimination. His Lordship, after referring to the competing arguments, continued (at 792): **14–009**

"The . . . conclusion we have reached is that the words cannot have the very wide meaning for which counsel for the employers contends. In other words we do not think that the mere fact that the effects of an arrangement or a scheme, or what is done, manifest themselves after retirement necessarily means that for that reason alone what is being done, or arranged, was a 'provision in relation to retirement' . . . What, as it seems to us, has to be looked for is to see whether what is being done is part and parcel of the employer's system of catering for retirement, or whether, as here, the case is merely one where a privilege has existed during employment and has been allowed to continue after retirement."

Accordingly, the EAT held that Mrs Garland was not precluded from basing her claim on s.6(2) of the SDA 1975 by s.6(4).

▷ (b) Garland in the Court of Appeal

14–010 The Court of Appeal ([1979] 2 All E.R. 1163) reversed the decision of the EAT, preferring the broader interpretation of s.6(4). Brief judgments were delivered by Lord Denning, M.R. and Lawton L.J., with Geoffrey Lane L.J. concurring. Lord Denning, M.R. rejected (at 1166) counsel for Mrs Garland's contention for a narrow interpretation:

> "Counsel for Mrs Garland [*in support of his contention*] . . . took, as an instance, a facility for belonging to a sports club. A man might be given a life membership. A woman might be given annual membership. That would be unlawful discrimination. It was a privilege which existed during employment, and was allowed to continue after employment. It was not, he said, a 'provision in relation to retirement'.
>
> I cannot subscribe to that argument. It limits unduly the words in sub-s(4) of s6. It seems to me that a provision whereby a man, or woman, is granted, on retirement, certain travel facilities is a 'provision in relation to retirement'."

Lawton L.J., also rejecting a narrow interpretation, remarked briefly (at 1167–1168):

> ". . . [*counsel for one of Mrs Garland's colleagues*] accepted that the construction of the subsection is largely a matter of first impression. My first impression was that the words 'provision in relation to death or retirement' meant 'provision about . . . retirement'. Nothing has been said in the arguments which has made me change that first impression."

The Court of Appeal, like the EAT, concentrated solely on the words used in the SDA 1975 when interpreting s.6(4), although attributing to the words a different meaning from the EAT. No compelling reasons were advanced for the different meaning preferred and no reference was made to the underlying aims or purpose of the legislation, although arguably the Court of Appeal attributed a meaning to the words which was inconsistent with the (presumed) underlying aims or purpose of the legislation, namely, the avoidance of sex discrimination.

Neither the EAT nor the Court of Appeal considered whether the principle of equal pay based on art.119 (now 157) had application and, if so, whether this would have provided guidance as to which meaning should be adopted. This failure to give consideration to art.119 (now 157) was due to counsel not raising the matter. If raised, it may have been considered applicable. If free travel was part of the package Mrs Garland received, and could expect to continue receiving during and after her employment, the free travel might constitute part of her "pay", in that it was "consideration . . . in kind" under art.119 (now 157) (see above, 14–002). If s.6(4) was interpreted to give effect to the principle of equal pay based on art.119 (now 157), this would mean adoption of the narrow meaning of the words "provision in relation to . . . retirement" in s.6(4). Consequently, the free travel provided during employment and extending into retirement would not be a "provision in relation to . . . retirement", but part of benefits relating to employment and, as such, should have been provided on an equal basis with male employees under s.6(2) of the SDA 1975.

▷ *(c) Garland in the House of Lords: reference to the ECJ*

On appeal to the House of Lords ([1982] 2 All E.R. 402), preliminary arguments **14–011** were presented relating to the relevance of art.119 (now 157), which were sufficient to persuade the House to seek a ruling under art.177 (now 267) from the ECJ in respect of the following questions (referred to at 411):

> "1. Where an employer provides (although not bound to do so by contract) special travel facilities for former employees to enjoy after retirement which discriminate against former female employees . . . is this contrary to:
>
> (a) Article 119 of the EEC Treaty?
> (b) Article 1 of Council Directive 75/117/EEC?
> (c) Article 1 of Council Directive 76/207/EEC?
>
> 2. If the answer to Questions 1(a), 1(b) or 1(c) is affirmative, is Article 119 or either of the said directives directly applicable in Member States so as to confer enforceable Community rights upon individuals in the above circumstances?"

This approach of referring the case to the ECJ might be contrasted with that of Lord Denning, M.R. in the Court of Appeal in *Macarthys* (see above, 14–005), in which his Lordship himself sought to interpret art.119 (now 157). That the House of Lords did not itself seek to interpret the article was explained by Lord Diplock when determining the appeal following a ruling from the ECJ on the above questions. The reason advanced (see below, 14–013), was that there was not, at the time of the reference, "so considerable and consistent a line of case law of the European court on the interpretation and direct applicability of art 119 as would make the answer [*to the certified questions*] too obvious and inevitable" ([1982] 2 All E.R. 413 at 415).

▷ *(d) Garland in the ECJ*

An opinion prepared for the court (see above, 14–006) by VerLoren van Themaat **14–012** A.G. (Case 12/81 [1982] E.C.R. 359) drew particular attention to previous ECJ case law when addressing the first question. He stated (at 373):

> ". . . I would remind the Court that besides applying to the ordinary basic or minimum wage or salary the principle of equal pay enunciated in Article 119 also applies to any other consideration, whether in cash or in kind, provided that two conditions are fulfilled:

(1)   It must be paid directly or indirectly by the employer to the employee;

(2)   The payment must be in respect of his employment.

In his opinion in the first *Defrenne* case (Case 80/70 [1971] ECR 445) Mr Advocate General Dutheillet de Lamothe explained in detail why in his opinion pensions (*inter alia*) paid directly by an employer to a former employee fall within the ambit of Article 119. I find his arguments convincing and believe that they also apply *mutatis mutandis* to facilities like those at issue here . . . The judgment in the first *Defrenne* case itself states at paragraph 6 that "the provision in the second paragraph of the article extends the concept of pay to any other consideration, whether in cash or in kind, whether immediate or future, provided that the worker receives it, albeit indirectly, in respect of his employment from his employer". Therefore the assumption in that judgment too is that Article 119 also encompasses future consideration fulfilling the other conditions of Article 119 to which I have referred. Mr Advocate General Warner in his opinion in the *Worringham* case (Case 69/80 [1981] ECR 796) so far as is here material came to similar conclusions to those of Mr Dutheillet de Lamothe.

It is therefore clear in any event from the Court's previous decisions that Article 119 also covers future consideration."

The provision of discriminatory travel facilities extending into retirement were duly considered to constitute "pay", as (future) "consideration . . . in kind", and accordingly to contravene art.119 (now 157).

The ECJ, following the Advocate General's opinion, and relying on the concept of pay in art.119 (now 157) as defined in *Defrenne* (see above), set out (at 369) its conclusions and the succinct reasoning which supported them:

". . . 6. According to the order making the reference for a preliminary ruling when male employees of the respondent undertaking [*British Rail Engineering Ltd*] retire from their employment on reaching retirement age they continue to be granted special travel facilities for themselves, their wives and their dependent children.

7. A feature of those facilities is that they are granted in kind by the employer to the retired male employee or his dependants directly or indirectly in respect of his employment.

8. Moreover, it appears from a letter sent by the British Railways Board to the trade unions on 4 December 1975 that the special travel facilities granted after retirement must be considered to be an extension of the facilities granted during the period of employment.

9. It follows from those considerations that rail travel facilities such as those referred to by the House of Lords fulfil the criteria enabling them to be treated as pay within the meaning of Article 119 of the EEC Treaty.

10. The argument that the facilities are not related to a contractual obligation is immaterial. The legal nature of the facilities is not important for the purposes of the application of Article 119 provided that they are granted in respect of the employment.

11. It follows that where an employer (although not bound to do so by contract) provides special travel facilities for former male employees to enjoy after their retirement this constitutes discrimination within the meaning of Article 119 against former female employees who do not receive the same facilities."

The ECJ accordingly answered the first question posed in the affirmative, without the need to consider whether there had been any contravention of the Directives, and went on to give an affirmative answer to the second question (see above, 14–011). The ECJ concluded (at 370–371) that art.119 (now 157) had direct effect and could confer enforceable Community rights on individuals in the circumstances of the present case.

▷ *(e) Garland in the House of Lords: response to ECJ ruling*

On receipt of the ECJ's ruling, the House of Lords ([1982] 2 All E.R. 413) had no **14–013** difficulty in deciding which of the two alternative interpretations of s.6(4) (see above, 14–008) should be adopted. A narrow interpretation should be given, meaning that travel facilities such as those in Mrs Garland's case were not a "provision in relation to . . . retirement" under s.6(4) of the SDA 1975 and therefore were not excluded from the anti-discrimination provisions of s.6(2). Accordingly, Mrs Garland's claim should succeed. Lord Diplock, delivering the only judgment, said (at 415–416):

"My Lords, even if the obligation to observe the provisions of art 119 were an obligation assumed by the United Kingdom under an ordinary international treaty or convention and there were no question of the treaty obligation being directly applicable as part of the law to be applied by the courts in this country without need for any further enactment, it is a principle of construction of United Kingdom statutes, now too well established to call for citation of authority, that the words of a statute passed after the treaty has been signed and dealing with the subject matter of the international obligation of the United Kingdom are to be construed, if they are reasonably capable of bearing such a meaning, as intended to carry out the obligation and not be to be inconsistent with it. A fortiori this is the case where the treaty obligation arises under one of the Community treaties to which s2 of the European Communities Act 1972 applies.

The instant appeal does not present an appropriate occasion to consider whether, having regard to the express direction as to the construction of enactments 'to be passed' which is contained in s2(4), anything short of an express positive statement in an Act of Parliament passed after 1 January 1973 that a particular provision is intended to be made in breach of an obligation assumed by the United Kingdom under a Community treaty would justify an English court in construing that provision in a manner inconsistent with a Community treaty obligation of the United Kingdom however wide a departure from the prima facie meaning of the language of the provision might be needed in order to achieve consistency. For, in the instant case the words of s6(4) of the Sex Discrimination Act 1975 that fall to be construed, 'provision in relation to . . . retirement', without any undue straining of the ordinary meaning of the language used, are capable of bearing either the narrow meaning accepted by the Employment Appeal Tribunal or the wider meaning preferred by the Court of Appeal but acknowledged by that court to be largely a matter of first impression. Had the attention of the court been drawn to art 119 of the EEC Treaty and the judgment of the European Court in *Defrenne v Sabena* Case 43/75 (1976) [1981] 1 All ER 122, I have no doubt that, consistently with statements made by Lord Denning MR in previous cases, they would have construed s6(4) so as not to make it inconsistent with art 119.

In order to decide whether the construction of s6(4) in fact adopted by the Court of Appeal was inconsistent with art 119, and whether that alternative construction adopted by the Employment Appeal Tribunal was consistent with it, it was desirable to obtain a ruling of the European Court that would be binding on all courts in England, including this House, on the question of the effect of art 119 on the kind of discrimination as respects concessionary travel facilities after retirement to which Mrs Garland was subjected by her employer simply because she was a woman and not a man.

Although I do not believe that any of your Lordships had any serious doubt what answer would be given to that question by the European Court, there was not in existence at 19 January 1981, the date when the order of reference under art 177 was made, so considerable and consistent a line of case law of the European Court on the interpretation and direct applicability of art 119 as would make the answer too obvious and inevitable to be capable of giving rise to what could properly be regarded as 'a question' within the meaning of art 177. It thus became mandatory on this House, as a court from whose decisions there is no possibility of appeal under internal law, to refer to the European Court the questions that were in fact referred . . . so as to provide the House with material necessary to aid it in construing s6(4) of the Sex Discrimination Act 1975."

The ECJ explicitly stated that art.119 (now 157) required provision on equal terms for men and women of special travel facilities during retirement (see above, 14–012). This interpretation of the article was treated as binding on the House. Thus, in deciding to adopt the meaning of s.6(4) which was consistent with the ECJ's interpretation of art.119 (now 157), the House of Lords effectively used the article to resolve the ambiguity in s.6(4) (Ambiguity Interpretation Approach). A more difficult question, to which Lord Diplock adverted, that the House did not have to face (since s.6(4) could be interpreted so as to comply with art.119 (now 157), without departing from an ordinary meaning of the words used in the section), would have been the approach to be taken if the words were not reasonably capable of bearing a meaning which would have ensured compliance with the article. In this case, it would have been necessary for the House to consider whether it should depart from a prima facie ordinary meaning of the language of the provision, and to interpret s.6(4) so as to ensure that it was consistent with art.119 (now 157). This course (General Interpretation Approach) was one which the House was subsequently to consider in *Pickstone* (see below, 14–021), albeit in relation to provisions under the EPA 1970.

▶ 4. *Pickstone v Freemans Plc*

Amongst the various jobs in the Freemans company were two different posts, **14–014** "warehouse operative" and "checker warehouse operative" (checker operative). Both men and women were employed as warehouse operatives at equal rates of pay, but these rates were less than those paid to a male checker operative, Mr Phillips. Mrs Pickstone (along with four female colleagues) contended that the work she was doing was of equal value to that of a checker operative and that, by being paid at a lower rate, Freemans Plc were in contravention of s.1(2)(c) of the EPA 1970 and the principle of equal pay based on art.119 (now 157). Section 1(2)(c) was added to the EPA 1970 by the Equal Pay (Amendments) Regulations 1983 (SI 1983/1794, reg.2), following a decision by the ECJ in *EC Commission v United Kingdom* (61/81) [1982] E.C.R. 2601 that the UK was failing in its obligations under EU law by providing no remedy in respect of work of "equal value" which did not fall within s.1(2)(a) or (b) of the EPA 1970 (see above, 14–003). The ECJ had ruled that a remedy in respect of work of "equal value" was required by the principle of equal pay based on art.119 (now 157) and s.1(2)(c) was enacted so as to comply with that requirement. It provides:

> "Where a woman is employed on work which, not being work in relation to which paragraph (a) or (b) above applies, is, in terms of the demands made on her (for instance under such headings as effort, skill and decision), of equal value to that of a man in the same employment
>
> (i) if (apart from the equality clause) any term of the woman's contract is or becomes less favourable to the woman than a term of a similar kind in the contract under which that man is employed, that term of the woman's contract shall be treated as so modified as not to be less favourable, and
> (ii) if (apart from the equality clause) at any time the woman's contract does not include a term corresponding to a term benefiting that man included in the contract under which he is employed, the woman's contract shall be treated as including such a term."

Whether Mrs Pickstone could base a claim for work of equal value on a comparison with male checker operatives depended on how the words "not being work in relation to which paragraph (a) or (b) above applies" in s.1(2)(c) were construed and whether they were capable of more than one meaning. Counsel for the employers contended that they were not and the words unambiguously meant that para.(c) applied only where a woman was employed on work which did not fall within para.(a) or (b). Since Mrs Pickstone was employed on like work with men as warehouse operatives, counsel maintained, her case fell within para.(a) and it was thus excluded from the scope of para.(c). Accordingly, no comparison could be made with male checker operatives for work of equal value. Counsel for Mrs Pickstone, however, maintained that the words were ambiguous and that one of the possible meanings was that there would only be "work in relation to which paragraph (a) . . . applies" if a woman *chose* to compare herself to a man with whom she was doing like work. If a woman elected *not* to compare herself with a man doing like work under para.(a), there would not be "work in relation to which paragraph (a) . . . applies" and it would therefore be open to the woman to proceed with a claim under para.(c).

▷ ## (a) Pickstone in the Industrial Tribunal and the EAT

14–015 The Industrial Tribunal accepted the argument that the words in s.1(2)(c) were not ambiguous and no claim was possible by Mrs Pickstone. Although the Industrial Tribunal's decision was not reported, it is stated in the report of the case in the EAT ([1986] I.R.L.R. 335) that the Industrial Tribunal took the view that the words "not being work in relation to which paragraph (a) or (b) above applies" meant that:

> "It is only if there is no man doing like work that a woman is entitled to ask a tribunal to consider work of equal value . . . If . . . there are men doing like work she can compare the terms and conditions of her employment with those of any of those men but in our view she cannot make use of [*para.*] (c). We do not agree . . . that a woman is entitled to compare her work with a man whether or not there are men doing like work with her. We say this because it seems to us that the Act provides, in terms, that she cannot do so. She must exhaust [*paras*] (a) or (b) before going on to [*para.*] (c)."

It is also stated in the report (at 336) that the Industrial Tribunal took the view that:

> "so far as Community law was relevant, it arrived at the same result. Directive 75/117 refers to 'the same work or work to which equal value is attributed': in the words of the Tribunal, 'it is only if there is no "same work" that one goes on to the alternative of work to which equal value is attributed'."

It can be seen that the Industrial Tribunal regarded the use of the word "or" in the Directive as indicating that comparisons in respect of "the same work" and "work to which equal value is attributed" were mutually exclusive, so that a person doing one type of work could not make a comparison with a person engaged on the other type of work. Accordingly, the Industrial Tribunal decided that a comparison with work of equal value was not permissible under art.119 (now 157). The position under the Directive was thus considered to be the same as under s.1(2)(c), with the Industrial Tribunal in both cases essentially focusing on the words used in the provisions.

It is not clear to what extent or in what respect EU law was considered by the Industrial Tribunal, since the report of the case in the EAT simply records that "so far as Community law was relevant" the position was the same as under s.1(2)(c) of the EPA 1970. No indication is given of the Industrial Tribunal's view of the implications of EU law for English law, namely whether the Industrial Tribunal regarded art.119 (now 157) and the Directive as having priority over s.1(2)(c) (Priority Approach) or as determining interpretation of s.1(2)(c) either in the event of ambiguity (Ambiguity Interpretation Approach) or in the absence of ambiguity (General Interpretation Approach) in that provision.

Mrs Pickstone appealed to the EAT, but it similarly took the view that her case fell outside s.1(2)(c). The wording of the provision was considered to admit of only one meaning and, as this was the case, no recourse was had to the principle of equal pay based on art.119 (now 157). As Garland J. stated (at 336), "since we do not consider the statute to be ambiguous, it is not necessary to rely on Community legislation as an aid to construction". By deciding that EU law was relevant only in the event of ambiguity in the statutory provision, the EAT apparently adopted the Ambiguity Interpretation Approach. However, the EAT did consider whether art.119 (now 157) and Directive 75/117 should prevail over s.1(2)(c) as interpreted (Priority Approach). For priority to be accorded, it was necessary, under s.2 of the ECA 1972, for the article and/or Directive to have direct effect as regards work of equal value (a point which appeared not to be addressed by the Industrial Tribunal, which seemed to interpret the Directive without any consideration of the implications for English law of that interpretation). The EAT took the view that the article and Directive were *not* of direct effect in this context, relying on a decision of the Court of Appeal, *O'Brien v Sim-Chem Ltd* [1980] 2 All E.R. 307 (*O'Brien*). It was *not* therefore necessary to accord priority to the article and Directive over s.1(2)(c) and the EAT considered itself free to apply what, in its view, was the clear, unambiguous meaning of the words in s.1(2)(c).

▷ *(b) Pickstone in the Court of Appeal*

(i) Introduction

The Court of Appeal ([1987] 3 All E.R. 756) also took the view that the wording of **14–016** s.1(2)(c) was unambiguous and precluded comparison with work of equal value where a person was engaged on like work with a man under s.1(2)(a). Nevertheless, there was a significantly different approach both to the requirements and to the implications of EU law. The Court of Appeal maintained that art.119 (now 157) enabled a woman to make a comparison with a man engaged on work of equal value, even where the woman was engaged on like work with a man, and that the article was directly effective in respect of work of equal value. Accordingly, in the court's view, art.119 (now 157) prevailed over the conflicting national legislation in s.1(2)(c) (Priority Approach). Therefore, Mrs Pickstone was able, by virtue of the article, to base a claim on a comparison with male checker operatives undertaking work of equal value, notwithstanding the fact that a comparison could have been made with a man engaged on like work.

(ii) Construction of section 1(2)(c)

14–017 The Court of Appeal considered that the words "not being work in relation to which paragraph (a) or (b) above applies" were not ambiguous and meant that there could be no comparison with a person engaged on work of equal value under s.1(2)(c) where comparison was possible under either s.1(2)(a) or (b). Although the court recognised that the mischief at which s.1(2)(c) was aimed was the failure of the EPA 1970, as originally drafted, to provide a remedy for unequal pay in cases of work of equal value, Nicholls L.J., delivering one of the two main judgments, felt unable to construe the provision in a way which enabled the mischief to be remedied. There was no ambiguity in the meaning of the words and consequently Nicholls L.J. felt unable to depart from the language used to remedy the mischief. His Lordship stated (at 764–765):

> ". . . the mischief which the introduction of para (c) into s1(2) of the Equal Pay Act 1970 was intended to cure . . . was the omission (save for the cases covered by para (b)) of any provision in the 1970 Act for equal pay in cases of work of equal value. The European Court expressed its conclusion in *EC Commission v UK* [1982] ECR 2601 at 2617 as follows:
>
>> '14. Accordingly, by failing to introduce into its national legal system in implementation of the provisions of [the equal pay directive] such measures as are necessary to enable all employees who consider themselves wronged by failure to apply the principle of equal pay for men and women for work to which equal value is attributed and for which no system of job classification exists to obtain recognition of such equivalence, the United Kingdom has failed to fulfil its obligation under the Treaty.'
>
> Paragraph (c) was added to s1(2) as Parliament's legislative response to that decision . . . if the employers' argument on the construction of s1(2)(c) is correct, two consequences would seem to follow inescapably. The first is that s1(2)(c) of the 1970 Act would, in part, have failed to remedy the mischief which it must be taken to have been intended to cure, in that the Act still would not provide a remedy in all cases of work of equal value: it would provide a remedy only in those cases where currently no man is engaged on the same work. The second consequence . . . would be that in this respect the United Kingdom would, apparently, have still not wholly fulfilled its obligations under the EEC Treaty and the equal pay directive.

> Needless to say, I am extremely reluctant to construe s1(2)(c) in a way that would have these consequences. None the less I have found the employers' arguments on the meaning of the exclusionary words in s1(2)(c) [*i.e. "not being work in relation to which paragraph (a) or (b) above applies"*] cogent to the extent that, indeed, I have found myself driven to the conclusion that those words are not ambiguous and are not fairly capable of the meaning submitted by counsel for the applicants."

Purchas L.J., who delivered the other main judgment, reached a similar conclusion (at 769) that "para (c) read in its ordinary sense, is plain and contains no ambiguity", whilst Sir Roualeyn Cumming-Bruce stated (at 776) that "on their ordinary meaning the words 'not being work in relation to which paragraph (a) or (b) above applies' are plain and unambiguous".

(iii) Construction of art.119 (now 157)

The Court of Appeal took the view that comparison with work of equal value was permissible under art.119 (now 157). The court, rather than referring the case to the ECJ, was prepared to examine and interpret the article to determine whether it enabled a woman to make a comparison with a man engaged on work of equal value, even where the woman was engaged on like work with a man. In doing so, Nicholls L.J., in keeping with the ECJ's approach of focusing on aims, spirit and objectives when interpreting legislation and adopting a teleological approach, began with a consideration of the underlying objectives of art.119 (now 157). His Lordship stated (at 760): **14–018**

> "This article had two objects: firstly, in the economic field, to avoid the situation in which undertakings established in states which had implemented the principle of equal pay would suffer a disadvantage in competition within the Community with undertakings established in states which had not then eliminated pay discrimination against women workers; secondly, in the social field, 'by common action, to ensure social progress and seek the constant improvement of the living and working conditions of [*the member states'*] peoples' (see *Defrenne v Sabena* Case 43/75 [1981] 1 All ER 122 at 133, [1976] ECR 455 at 472)."

His Lordship then adopted a schematic approach to interpretation of art.119 (now 157) by considering the legislative context surrounding the article and referred to Directive 75/117, in particular art.1, to elucidate the scope of the principle of equal pay based on art.119 (now 157). In examining the directive, Nicholls L.J. maintained that it encompassed work of equal value and that, since the purpose of the Directive was to amplify the scope of art.119 (now 157), the Article itself covered work of equal value. His Lordship stated (at 761–762):

> "Article 119 enshrines a broad, general principle: equal pay for equal work. The equal pay directive makes clear that in this context equal work embraces work of equal value as well as work which is the same. I can see no justification for

implying into this general principle, whereunder equal work includes both these categories, a rigid and inflexible limitation, to the effect that, although a woman is entitled to compare herself with a man doing work of equal value, she is only so entitled if and so long as no man is doing the same work as herself, and that whenever and for so long as there is a man doing the same work the woman cannot make that comparison, even if the difference in pay is attributable solely to grounds of sex. It makes the presence per se of one man doing the same work, which in some cases might be wholly fortuitous or even, possibly, a situation contrived by an unscrupulous employer, a decisive factor, regardless of all the other circumstances of the case."

Immediately thereafter, Nicholls L.J. considered what guidance, if any, might be obtained from ECJ case law on the principle of equal pay based on art.119 (now 157) and found guidance in the ECJ's decision in *Macarthys*. From an English perspective, *Macarthys* may not be considered to be a relevant authority (and therefore distinguishable), in that it was concerned with a non-contemporaneous comparison with a man engaged on like work, whereas this case was concerned with comparison with a man engaged on work of equal value. From a European perspective, however, the case of *Macarthys*, as part of the body of law assisting in determining the scope of the principle of equal pay based on art.119 (now 157), might be considered to be a relevant source of guidance on that principle. Thus, Nicholls L.J. stated (at 762):

"Although this precise point has not been considered by the European Court, support for the broad approach I have adopted to the interpretation of art 119 can be obtained from the decision of the European Court in *Macarthys Ltd v Smith* Case 129/79 [1981] 1 All ER 111, [1981] QB 180 . . . [*where*] the European Court held that the crucial question was whether there was a difference in treatment between a man and a woman performing 'equal work' within art 119. The court said ([1981] 1 All ER 111 at 118–119, [1981] QB 180 at 198):

'11. . . . The scope of that concept, which is entirely qualitative in character in that it is exclusively concerned with the nature of the services in question, may not be restricted by the introduction of a requirement of contemporaneity.

12. It must be acknowledged, however, that, as the Employment Appeal Tribunal properly recognised, it cannot be ruled out that a difference in pay between two workers occupying the same post but at different periods in time may be explained by the operation of factors which are unconnected with any discrimination on grounds of sex. That is a question of fact which it is for the court or tribunal to decide.'

Thus 'equal work' involves a comparison between the work (the nature of the services) performed by the woman and the work done by the man, and in making that comparison it is not essential that the man is still doing that work or that he was ever doing it at the same time as the woman. Absence of

Pickstone v Freemans Plc

> contemporaneity does not prevent the comparison being made, although such absence is material when considering, as a question of fact, whether the reason for the difference in pay is discrimination on grounds of sex. I do not see how this interpretation of art 119 permits of the conclusion that none the less contemporaneity is of the essence in relation to work of equal value, in that a woman is entitled to equality of pay with a man whose work is of equal value but only so long as contemporaneously there is no man doing the same work as herself."

Purchas L.J. adopted a similar, although not identical, approach, making no reference to the underlying aims, spirit and objectives of art.119 (now 157) nor to the ECJ's decision in *Macarthys*, but relying on Directive 75/117 and the ECJ's decision in *Defrenne* for guidance. His Lordship stated (at 771):

> "Applying the decision in *Defrenne v Sabena*, I would be prepared to construe art 119, as explained by the equal pay directive, as affording relief to a person who is receiving 'unequal pay', either for the same work or for work of equivalent value, and that the two concepts are not mutually exclusive but are integral parts of the same concept."

The third member of the court, Sir Roualeyn Cumming-Bruce, dealt with the matter briefly (at 776), making reference to Directive 75/117:

> "Article 119 of the EEC Treaty, as explained by EC Council Directive 75/117, gives an applicant the right to claim that he or she is entitled to equal pay when engaged under a contract of employment which imposes on the employee the obligation to do work of equal value to the work of any other employee of the opposite sex in the same establishment . . . Article 119 does not exclude such comparison on the ground that an employee of the opposite sex is engaged on the same or like work on the same remuneration as the applicant."

The court's approach, of interpreting the principle of equal pay based on art.119 (now 157), rather than referring the case to the ECJ for a ruling under art.177 (now 267), was in marked contrast to that of the House of Lords in *Garland*, where the House declined to interpret art.119 (now 157) because, in the words of Lord Diplock (at [1982] 2 All E.R. 402 at 415), of the absence of a "considerable and consistent . . . line of case law of the European Court on the interpretation and direct applicability of art 119" (see above, 14–011). Nicholls and Purchas L.JJ. decisively rejected an art.177 (now 267) reference approach in *Pickstone* (Sir Roualeyn Cumming-Bruce making no reference to this matter). Thus, Nicholls L.J. stated (at 766):

> ". . . counsel for the applicants submitted that if he was wrong on the con-struction of the 1970 Act, so that the appeal falls to be determined according to the meaning and effect of art 119 of the EEC Treaty, this court should seek

> rulings from the European Court on the relevant questions [*of whether a comparison with work of equal value was permissible under Art.119 where a person was engaged on like work with a man and of whether Art.119 was directly effective*]. In my view, in the exercise of its discretion this court should not accede to that submission. The position under Community law on both the material points is sufficiently clear for it to be appropriate for this court to deal with both these points (as it happens, in favour of the applicants) without any reference to the European Court."

Purchas L.J. stated (at 770):

> "As I read the position, it is this. If it is possible to detect a clear general approach to a particular question of construction from the judgments of the European Court, then a domestic court, not being 'a final court' within art 177 [*i.e. one from which, broadly speaking, no further appeal is possible*] should not exercise its discretion to refer to the European Court, but should attempt to construe the article in question . . ."

(iv) Direct effectiveness of art.119 (now 157)

14–019   The Court of Appeal rejected the EAT's view that, following the Court of Appeal's decision in *O'Brien*, art.119 (now 157) had no direct effect in respect of work of equal value and thus did not need to be accorded priority under the ECA 1972. Although a decision of the Court of Appeal in one case would as a general rule, from a traditional English viewpoint, be a binding precedent on the same court in a later case under the doctrine of stare decisis, the position is less than clear where there is an issue of EU law involved. The decision would not appear to be binding in the strict sense, since it would be open to the later court not to follow the earlier case, but to make a reference to the ECJ under art.267 (ex 177). If no reference was made, the question may arise as to whether the earlier Court of Appeal decision should be followed. It would appear (as will be seen from the extract below from the judgment of Nicholls L.J.) that, where there is ECJ case law subsequent to the earlier case, which might justify a different conclusion being reached, the court will not be bound by the decision in that earlier case. In such a situation, the case would seem to fall within the second exception to the general rule that the Court of Appeal is bound by its previous decisions, recognised in *Young v Bristol Aeroplane Co Ltd* [1944] K.B. 718, namely, a Court of Appeal decision which is inconsistent with a subsequent decision of (the House of Lords or) the CJ (see Chapter 1, 1–021). In the Court of Appeal's view in the present case, *O'Brien* was inconsistent with subsequent decisions of the ECJ and should not therefore be followed. These subsequent decisions were ones which should be followed and to which the court was obliged (under the ECA 1972) to give effect. Nicholls L.J. stated (at 763–764):

> "*O'Brien's* case came before the Court of Appeal in 1979. Since then Community jurisprudence has moved on. The European Court has authoritatively clarified the effect of art 1 of the equal pay directive, and also the position

regarding direct enforceability of rights under art 119, and I conceive that on these points of Community law it is the duty of this court to give effect to those later decisions of the European Court. In March 1981 . . . the European Court held that art 1 of the equal pay directive did not alter the content or scope of the principle of equal pay outlined in art 119 (see *Jenkins v Kingsgate (Clothing Productions) Ltd* [1981] 1 WLR 972 at 984, [1981] ECR 911 at 927). Earlier in the same month, in *Worringham v Lloyds Bank Ltd* Case 69/80 [1981] 2 All ER 434, [1981] 1 WLR 950, the European Court had to consider whether art 119 or art 1 of the equal pay directive conferred enforceable Community rights on individuals where contributions were made by an employer bank to two staff retirement benefit schemes, there being one scheme for men and another for women. The court held that the contributions paid by the employer in the name of the employee were 'pay' within the meaning of art 119 . . . On direct applicability the court said ([1981] 2 All ER 434 at 447, [1981] 1 WLR 950 at 969):

'23. As the court has stated in previous decisions (*Defrenne v Sabena* [1981] 1 All ER 122, [1976] ECR 455 and *Macarthys Ltd v Smith* [1981] 1 All ER 111, [1981] QB 180) art 119 of the Treaty applies directly to all forms of discrimination which may be identified solely with the aid of the criteria of equal work and equal pay referred to by the article in question, without national or Community measures being required to define them with greater precision in order to permit of their application. Among the forms of discrimination which may be thus judicially identified, the court mentioned in particular, cases where men and women receive unequal pay for equal work carried out in the same establishment or service, public or private. In such a situation the court is in a position to establish all the facts enabling it to decide whether a woman receives less pay then a man *engaged in the same work or work of equal value.*' (My emphasis.)

The court concluded ([1981] 2 All ER 434 at 447, [1981] 1 WLR 950 at 970):

'27. In this case the fact that contributions are paid by the employer solely in the name of men and not in the name of women *engaged in the same work or work of equal* value leads to unequal pay for men and women which the national court may directly establish with the aid of the pay components in question and the criteria laid down in art 119 of the Treaty.

28. For those reasons, the reply to the third question should be that art 119 of the Treaty may be relied on before the national courts and that these courts have a duty to ensure the protection of the rights which this provision vests in individuals . . .' (My emphasis.)

In my view that decision covers the present case. The five applicants and Mr Phillips [*the male checker operative employed by Freemans plc*] work in the same establishment, and I can see no relevant distinction between the banking employees in *Worringham*'s case and the applicants in the present case with regard to the ability of the court to determine, without further national or

Community measures, whether a woman was or was not engaged in work of equal value."

A similar view was expressed by Purchas L.J. (at 773):

"The judgments in *O'Brien v Sim-Chem Ltd* were, of course, delivered before the ruling of the European Court in *Jenkins v Kingsgate (Clothing Productions) Ltd*. In so far as the court's attention in *O'Brien's* case was paid to the direct enforceability of art 1 of the equal pay directive, the judgments have been overtaken by the subsequent decisions of the European Court in 1981 in *Jenkins's* case and *Worringham v Lloyds Bank Ltd* [1981] 2 All ER 434, [1981] 1 WLR 950."

Purchas L.J. continued (at 775):

". . . the decisions of the European Court demonstrate a clear pattern of development as regards the direct enforceability of art 119 of the EEC Treaty as follows.

(1) The expression 'equal pay for equal work' is to receive a broad interpretation. 'Pay' is given a very wide definition in art 119 itself. It would be inconsistent if work were not treated similarly.

(2) Article 1 of the equal pay directive merely confirms that the expression 'equal work' shall have an equally wide interpretation, that is not only 'same work' *but also* 'work to which equal value is attributed'.

(3) The sense of (1) and (2) cannot be said to support the contention that 'same work' must always exclude 'work to which equal value is attributed' in choosing the most appropriate route by which to arrive at 'equal work'.

(4) The expression in *Defrenne v Sabena* [1981] 1 All E.R. 122 at 134, [1976] E.C.R. 455 at 473 'direct and overt discrimination which may be identified solely with the aid of . . . criteria based on equal work and equal pay' has been followed through the cases and remains the touchstone of direct enforceability. Attempts to limit its range by equating 'equal work and equal pay' to 'same work and equal pay' have invariably been rejected and in any event ignore the effect of art 1 of the equal pay directive in defining 'equal work and equal pay'.

. . .

(6) That a discrimination which appears on the face of a direct comparison to demonstrate unequal pay for one type of work and another type of work to which equal value is attributed at the same place of employment must . . . be directly enforceable."

Sir Roualeyn Cumming-Bruce, in a concise statement of his views on this matter, remarked (at 777):

"The judgments of the European Court to which Purchas and Nicholls LJJ have referred point clearly enough to the conclusion that the equal pay rights established by art 119 as explained in the [*equal pay*] directive are directly enforceable in a national court in a case where the national legislation is such as to restrict the rights conferred on employees by art 119."

(v) The impact of art.119 (now 157)

Although the ordinary meaning of the language in s.1(2)(c) precluded comparison **14–020** with work of equal value in Mrs Pickstone's case, such comparison was permissible under art.119 (now 157) and the Court of Appeal unanimously decided that Mrs Pickstone's right under EU law to make such comparison should be upheld. There was, however, a difference of approach as to how this should be effected. Nicholls L.J. and Sir Roualeyn Cumming-Bruce took the view that the principle of equal pay based on art.119 (now 157) prevailed and took priority over the inconsistent provision in s.1(2)(c) (Priority Approach). Purchas L.J., on the other hand, appeared to interpret s.1(2)(c) in such a way so as to ensure that it was in accordance with the principle of equal pay based on art.119 (now 157) (General Interpretation Approach).

Nicholls L.J. simply accepted the inconsistency between s.1(2)(c) and art.119 (now 157) and allowed the latter to prevail. In his Lordship's view, having recourse to the Article to construe s.1(2)(c) was permissible only where there was ambiguity in the statutory provision, which could be resolved by adopting a meaning consistent with art.119 (now 157) (Ambiguity Interpretation Approach). Since there was no ambiguity, Nicholls L.J. declined to depart from the language used and interpret s.1(2)(c) in such a way so as to ensure conformity with art.119 (now 157), thus effectively rejecting the General Interpretation Approach. His Lordship stated (at 766):

"But, given that the exclusionary words [*"not being work in relation to which paragraph (a) or (b) above applies" in s.1(2)(c)*] are unambiguous and are not reasonably capable of the meaning which would carry out the United Kingdom's treaty obligations in this field, for my part, as at present advised, I have great difficulty in seeing how the effect of s2(4) of the European Communities Act 1972 in such case can be to require the English court, nevertheless, to ascribe some other, artificial meaning to those words."

The question of whether s.1(2)(c) could be construed in such a way as to ensure that it was consistent with art.119 (now 157) was not addressed by Sir Roualeyn Cumming-Bruce, who briefly observed (at 777) that "the European remedy is available to the applicant to the industrial tribunal even though there can be no remedy available under national legislation".

Purchas L.J., in contrast, indicated his willingness to interpret s.1(2)(c) so as to accord with the principle of equal pay based on art.119 (now 157) by reading words into s.1(2)(c), thereby "filling a gap" in the legislation. He stated (at 776):

"There is clear authority that in a case of conflict Community law must prevail. Two courses are open to the court: (1) to refer two questions to the European Court asking (a) does s1(2)(c) comply with art 119? (b) is art 119 directly enforceable in the United Kingdom courts in cases where the discrimination arises in cases of unequal pay for work to which an equivalent value is attributed? (2) to construe s1(2) of the 1970 Act so as to conform with the principles of art 119 by inserting the words necessary to achieve a result that is not inconsistent with Community law as I understand it . . . This could be achieved by amending the relevant part of s 1(2)(c) to read: '. . . not being work which can more fairly be compared under paragraphs (a) or (b) above . . .'

Since under art 177 of the EEC Treaty reference to the European Court is discretionary so far as this court is concerned, and in view of the firm con-clusion I have reached with regard to the state of Community law, I would favour the second of the two courses."

▷ (c) Pickstone in the House of Lords

14-021 The approach of the House of Lords ([1988] 2 All E.R. 803), in which substantive judgments were delivered by Lords Keith, Oliver and Templeman, with Lords Brandon and Jauncey indicating agreement with the views expressed therein, was in marked contrast to the Court of Appeal. Their Lordships did not confine themselves to focusing on the words used in s.1(2)(c), but, in keeping with the general approach to interpretation adopted by the ECJ, concentrated on the aims and purpose of s.1(2)(c), which, as its legislative background demonstrated, was to ensure that the provisions of the EPA 1970 complied with EU law. Their Lordships accordingly sought to construe s.1(2)(c) in a way which ensured that it complied with EU law (General Interpretation Approach), although each of their Lordships expressed his own view as to how s.1(2)(c) might be construed so as to secure compliance.

Lord Keith referred to the ECJ's decision in *EC Commission v United Kingdom* (61/81) [1982] E.C.R. 2601, which had identified the failure of the EPA 1970 to fulfil obligations under EU law, and to the draft regulations (incorporated unchanged in final form in a statutory instrument) which implemented s.1(2)(c) and which sought to remedy this failure. His Lordship, however, simply confined himself to construing s.1(2)(c) "purposively" without any precise indication of how that might be achieved in terms of the wording of the section. Lord Keith stated (at 806–807):

"The question is whether the exclusionary words in para (c) [*i.e. "not being work in relation to which paragraph (a) or (b) above applies"*] are intended to have effect whenever the employers are able to point to *some* [*emphasis supplied*] man who is employed by them on like work with the woman claimant within the meaning of para (a) or work rated as equivalent with hers within the meaning of para (b), or whether they are intended to have effect only where

the *particular* [*emphasis supplied*] man with whom she seeks comparison is employed on such work. In my opinion the latter is the correct answer. The opposite result would leave a large gap in the equal pay provision, enabling an employer to evade it by employing one token man on the same work as a group of potential women claimants who were deliberately paid less than a group of men employed on work of equal value with that of the women. This would mean that the United Kingdom had failed yet again fully to implement its obligations under art 119 of the Treaty and the equal pay directive, and had not given full effect to the decision of the European Court in *EC Commission v UK* Case 61/81 [1982] ECR 2601. It is plain that Parliament cannot possibly have intended such a failure. The draft regulations of 1983 were presented to Parliament as giving full effect to the decision in question. The draft regulations were not subject to the parliamentary process of consideration and amendment in committee, as a Bill would have been. In these circumstances and in the context of s2 of the European Communities Act 1972 I consider it to be entirely legitimate for the purpose of ascertaining the intention of Parliament to take into account the terms in which the draft was presented by the responsible Minister and which formed the basis of its acceptance . . . There was no suggestion that the exclusionary words in para (c) were intended to apply in any other situation than where the man selected by a woman complainant for comparison was one in relation to whose work para (a) or para (b) applied. It may be that, in order to confine the words in question to that situation, some necessary implication falls to be made into their literal meaning. The precise terms of that implication do not seem to me to matter. It is sufficient to say that words must be construed purposively in order to give effect to the manifest broad intention of the maker of the regulations and of Parliament."

Lord Templeman similarly made reference to the ECJ's decision in *EC Commission v United Kingdom* and to the draft regulations which implemented s.1(2)(c), although he did not confine himself to examining the regulations, but referred, in addition, to Parliamentary debates on the regulations. His Lordship stated (at 814):

"The 1983 regulations were intended to give full effect to Community law and to the ruling of the European Court [*in EC Commission v United Kingdom*] which directed the United Kingdom government to introduce legislation entitling any woman to equal pay with any man for work of equal value if the difference in pay is due to the difference in sex and is therefore discriminatory . . . The draft of the 1983 regulations was not subject to any process of amendment by Parliament. In these circumstances the explanations of the government and the criticisms voiced by members of Parliament in the debates which led to approval of the draft regulations provide some indications of the intentions of Parliament. The debate on the draft regulations in the House of Commons which led to their approval by resolution was initiated by the Under Secretary of State for Employment, who, in the reports of the

House of Commons for 20 July 1983 (46 HC Official Report (6th series) col 479), said:

'The Equal Pay Act allows a woman to claim equal pay with a man . . . if she is doing the same or broadly similar work, or if her job and his have been rated equal through job evaluation in effort, skill and decision. However, if a woman is doing different work from a comparable man, or if the jobs are not covered by a job evaluation study, the woman has at present no right to make a claim for equal pay. This is the gap, identified by the European Court, which we are closing.'"

With a view to giving effect to this purpose, Lord Templeman considered how the words in s.1(2)(c) might be construed so as to secure compliance with EU law. This could be achieved by reading certain words into the section, his Lordship stating (at 813) that "there must be implied in para (c) after the word 'applies' the words 'as between the woman and the man with whom she claims equality'".

Lord Oliver also referred to the ECJ's decision in *EC Commission v United Kingdom* and to the draft regulations which implemented s.1(2)(c). As regards the former, his Lordship stated (at 816):

". . . the amendment introduced in 1983, following the ruling of the Court of Justice of the European Communities in *EC Commission v UK* Case 61/81 [1982] ECR 2601, was intended to fill the gap to which that case had drawn attention and to complete what was quite obviously intended to be a comprehensive code for dealing with sex discrimination in the area of pay and conditions at work."

As regards the latter, he stated (at 818):

". . . it is perfectly plain that the amendments to the 1970 Act were inserted for the purpose of completing the compliance by the United Kingdom with its treaty obligations under art 119 and the equal pay directive . . . It is worth noting that the explanatory note (which is not, of course, part of the regulations but is of use in identifying the mischief which the regulations were attempting to remedy) states:

'Regulation 2 amends section 1 of the Equal Pay Act 1970 to enable a woman to take advantage of an equality clause where she is employed on work of equal value to that of a man in the same employment.'

Those regulations having been passed with the manifest and express purpose of producing a full compliance with the United Kingdom's obligation, they fall to be construed accordingly . . ."

With a view to giving effect to this purpose, Lord Oliver expressed himself to have been particularly influenced by the views of Lord Templeman, which had persuaded him to depart from the view which he had initially formed of how the section should be interpreted. His initial view had been that, on the wording of s.1(2)(c), Mrs Pickstone was not entitled to make the comparison sought, but, under the persuasive influence of Lord Templeman's views, Lord Oliver adopted a different interpretation of the section. This different interpretation, which involved reading certain words into the section to secure compliance with EU law, enabled her to make the comparison sought. Lord Oliver stated (at 816–817):

> "The critical question . . . is whether the Court of Appeal, in common with the industrial tribunal and the Employment Appeal Tribunal, was right in concluding that the applicants' claim was not one which could be made under the provisions of the 1970 Act. I have to confess to sympathising with that conclusion which coincided with the very definite opinion which I myself had formed at the conclusion of the hearing. Indeed, it is only the persuasive speech delivered by my noble and learned friend Lord Templeman which has enabled me to change the opinion which I had formed . . . I am now persuaded that it can and that para (c) is to be construed as if modified in the manner suggested by my noble and learned friend [*Lord Templeman*] or as if it included a parenthetic phrase and read '(c) where a woman is employed on work which, not being work in relation to which (in respect of the man hereinafter mentioned) paragraph (a) or (b) above applies, is . . . etc'. It must, I think, be recognised that so to construe a provision which, on its face, is unambiguous involves a departure from a number of well-established rules of construction. The intention of Parliament has, it is said, to be ascertained from the words which it has used and those words are to be construed according to their plain and ordinary meaning. The fact that a statute is passed to give effect to an international treaty does not, of itself, enable the treaty to be referred to in order to construe the words used in other than in their plain and unambiguous sense . . . I think, however, that it has also to be recognised that a statute which is passed in order to give effect to the United Kingdom's obligations under the EEC Treaty falls into a special category and it does so because, unlike other treaty obligations, those obligations have, in effect, been incorporated into English law by the European Communities Act 1972."

Thus, whilst Lord Oliver endorsed Lord Templeman's approach of implying into s.1(2)(c) after the word "applies" the words "as between the woman and the man with whom she claims equality", he nevertheless added his own alternative version of words which might be implied, as a parenthetic phrase, into the section, namely "(in respect of the man hereinafter mentioned)". This "gap filling" in legislation was recognised by his Lordship (at 817):

> "If . . . the section is to be read literally and in accordance with its terms, para (c) cannot apply to that work so long as para (a) applies to it. It can be made to apply in only one of two ways. Either there has to be given to the word 'applies' an artificial meaning which will enable it to be read in the sense of 'is applied by the claimant as part of her claim' or there has to be read into the Act some qualifying words which will restrict the word 'applies' to a particular

> comparator selected by the claimant. Either way, a construction which permits the section to operate as a proper fulfilment of the United Kingdom's obligation under the [EC] Treaty involves not so much doing violence to the language of the section as filling a gap by an implication which arises, not from the words used, but from the manifest purpose of the Act and the mischief it was intended to remedy."

The House of Lords' approach, of focusing on the aims and purpose of s.1(2)(c) and implying words into the section, was sufficient to resolve the case in Mrs Pickstone's favour. However, it was recognised that, although such a course could be adopted in this particular case, it might not be appropriate in all circumstances. As Lord Templeman observed (at 815):

> "In *Duke v Reliance Systems Ltd* [1988] 1 All ER 626, [1988] 2 WLR 359 this House declined to distort the construction of an Act of Parliament which was not drafted to give effect to a directive and which was not capable of complying with the directive as subsequently construed by the European Court. In the present case I can see no difficulty in construing the 1983 regulations in a way which gives effect to the declared intention of the government of the United Kingdom responsible for drafting the regulations and is consistent with the objects of the EEC Treaty, the provisions of the equal pay directive and the rulings of the European Court."

Nevertheless, subsequent to its decision in *Duke v Reliance Systems Ltd*, the House has shown a willingness to depart from a traditional approach to (or to "distort") the construction of an Act of Parliament where the Act was not drafted to give effect to a directive—see *Webb v EMO Air Cargo (UK) Ltd* [1992] 4 All E.R. 929 (considered in Chapter 4, 4–036).

Perhaps as a final comment it can be said that this case shows how differently constituted tribunals or courts can adopt fundamentally different approaches to what superficially should be a simple exercise in statutory interpretation, namely, ascertaining the meaning of the words "not being work in relation to which paragraph (a) or (b) above applies" in s.1(2)(c) of the EPA 1970.

Further Reading

Ellis, "Supremacy of Parliament and European Law" (1980) 96 L.Q.R. 511

Freeman, "Community Law and Work of Equal Value" [1987] C.L.J. 410

Hood Phillips, "A Garland for the Lords: Parliament and .Community Law Again" (1982) 98 L.Q.R. 524

Simpson, "Equal Pay in the Court of Appeal" (1980) 43 M.L.R. 209

PART 3

TRACING THE EVOLUTION OF LAW IN SELECTED FIELDS

15 NERVOUS SHOCK OR PSYCHIATRIC INJURY

▶ ## 1. Introduction

The law relating to the right of a person to recover damages where he has **15–001** sustained nervous shock or psychiatric injury (which has become the more favoured term in recent years) has developed considerably over the last 100 years or so. (Throughout this case study, the term "nervous shock" rather than "psychiatric injury" is generally used, since this is the term used in the majority of the cases considered. However, the two terms are regarded as interchangeable for the purposes of this study, notwithstanding that the latter may be broader in scope in that it may encompass conditions not arising as a result of the infliction of shock).

In its initial stages of development, the law was sceptical about allowing any right of recovery at all, a stance which was no doubt, in part, attributable to the fact that nervous shock was not a well-established and recognisable medical condition. However, a successful claim for damages for nervous shock was brought in *Wilkinson v Downton* [1897] 2 Q.B. 57 (*Wilkinson*), where a wife suffered shock when the defendant falsely represented to her that her husband had met with a serious accident and broken both his legs. In this instance, the defendant's conduct was intentional and malicious and the claim was considered analogous to torts (civil wrongs) of trespass to the person such as assault and battery. Whilst nervous shock might be sustained through intentional conduct, as here, a far more likely scenario is one of nervous shock sustained through the negligent conduct of another. This might arise, notably, as a result of road traffic accidents, either through fear of the person suffering nervous shock for his own safety or for the safety of a third party involved in an accident. Where a person sustains nervous shock due to another's negligent conduct, he must establish, in order to bring a successful claim in the tort of negligence, that that other owed him a duty of care, was in breach of that duty of care and that the damage suffered in consequence of the breach is not too remote.

At the time of *Wilkinson*, the first case where a successful claim was made for nervous shock, there were a number of established categories and situations where the courts had held a duty of care to exist and where liability would arise if negligence could be proved. New duty situations were from time to time recognised, usually by analogy with existing categories. The duty owed by a user of the highway to other highway users and to those on property adjoining the highway to take care not to inflict personal injury or physical damage was a well-established category and in *Dulieu v White & Sons* [1901] 2 K.B. 669 the Divisional Court extended this duty to take care not to inflict nervous shock and held that such shock sustained was not too remote a consequence of the breach of duty. In a series of decisions since this case the courts have sought to establish the parameters of liability and to delineate, in some measure at least, the criteria for determining liability. These decisions demonstrate how the ambit of liability has, over the years, been expanded, and in more recent years sustained some degree of contraction, and how the law has reached its present state. There are a number of important matters in relation to precedent which arise in these decisions and particular attention has been paid to these when considering the cases.

This case study illustrates a number of points in relation to case law and precedent:

- ▶ consideration of decisions from other jurisdictions;
- ▶ whether a statement forms part of the ratio of a judgment, and of a case, or is only obiter;
- ▶ the precedential status of a decision of the Privy Council;
- ▶ consideration of the views expressed by authors in textbooks and journals;
- ▶ the distinguishing of previous decisions;
- ▶ the expression obiter of tentative views on matters on which it was not necessary for a decision to be reached;
- ▶ a broad or narrow view of a ratio;
- ▶ the importance of policy considerations in determining propositions of law;
- ▶ differing views on policy considerations;
- ▶ the difficulty of determining the ratio of a case where several judgments are delivered which contain different reasoning;
- ▶ reference to the views of the Law Commission;
- ▶ judicial pronouncements in decisions which are extempore where judgment has not been reserved;
- ▶ disregard of an obiter statement; and
- ▶ adoption of an obiter statement which becomes part of the ratio of a judgment.

▶ 2. *Dulieu v White & Sons*

15-002 The question of whether liability might arise in tort where a person sustained nervous shock as a result of another's negligence appears to have first directly been raised in England in 1901, when the case of *Dulieu v White & Sons* [1901] 2 K.B. 669 (*Dulieu*) came before a Divisional Court consisting of Kennedy and Phillimore JJ. The case concerned a claim for damages for illness caused by the shock resulting to the plaintiff, who was serving behind the bar in a public house, when the defendants' servant (employee) negligently drove a horse-drawn van into the public house. It was contended by the defendants, first, that the plaintiff's statement of claim disclosed no cause of action, on the grounds that the duty of care to avoid causing physical injury did not extend to physical injury directly produced from fright without any accompanying impact, and secondly, that the damage sustained was too remote.

> ## (a) Duty of care not extending to physical injury directly produced from fright without any accompanying impact

Phillimore J. (at 682–683), in rejecting the first contention, placed reliance, inter **15–003**
alia, on an Irish decision, *Bell v Great Northern Railway Co of Ireland* (1890) 26 L.R.Ir. 428 (*Bell*):

> "I think there may be cases in which A. owes a duty to B. not to inflict a mental shock on him or her, and that in such a case, if A. does inflict such a shock upon B.—as by terrifying B.—and physical damage thereby ensues, B. may have an action for the physical damage, though the medium through which it has been inflicted is the mind.
>
> I think, for example, that it may well be, as the Exchequer Division in Ireland held in the case of Bell v Great Northern Railway Company of Ireland (1890) 26 L.R.Ir. 428, that a railway company has a duty to its passengers to use its best endeavours to convey them, not merely safely, but securely in the etymological sense of the word, and that when it fails, and physical damage accrues to a passenger through the fright which its failure occasions, the passenger may have an action."

Kennedy J. (at 673–675) followed a similar approach, although going into rather more detail as regards the authorities on which reliance was placed:

> "That fright—where physical injury is directly produced by it—cannot be a ground of action merely because of the absence of any accompanying impact appears to me to be a contention both unreasonable and contrary to the weight of the authority. Leaving out of sight, as perhaps involving special considerations, cases of wilful wrongdoing such as *Wilkinson v Downton* [1897] 2 Q.B. 57 . . . we have as reported decisions, which go far in my judgment to negative the correctness of any such contention, *Jones v Boyce* (1816) 1 Stark. 493; 18 R.R. 812, *Harris v Mobbs* (1878) 3 Ex.D. 268, and *Wilkins v Day* (1883) 12 Q.B.D. 110. All the three cases are cited by Wright J. in his judgment in *Wilkinson v Downton* [1897] 2 Q.B. at p.61 . . . Further, we have directly in point the decision given in December, 1882, by the Common Pleas Division in Ireland . . . in the unreported case of *Byrne v Great Southern and Western Railway Company of Ireland* and affirmed on appeal in a judgment delivered by the late Sir Edward Sullivan, and the approval of this decision in 1890 by the Exchequer Division in *Bell v Great Northern Railway of Ireland* (1890) 26 L.R.Ir. 428. In the course of his judgment in the last cited case Palles C.B. expressly points out

(26 L.R.Ir. at p.442) that in the circumstances in *Byrne v Great Southern and Western Railway Company of Ireland* there was nothing in the nature of impact and the portions of the evidence which he quotes clearly show that this was so. In *Victorian Railways Commissioners v Coultas*, 13 App.Cas. 222 . . . the Privy Council expressly declined to decide that impact was necessary."

At this juncture (at 675), Kennedy J. went on to introduce a limitation in respect of the duty:

"It is not, however, to be taken that in my view every nervous shock occasioned by negligence and producing physical injury to the sufferer gives a cause of action. There is, I am inclined to think, at least one limitation. The shock, where it operates through the mind, must be a shock which arises from a reasonable fear of immediate personal injury to oneself. A. has, I conceive, no legal duty not to shock B.'s nerves by the exhibition of negligence towards C., or towards the property of B. or C. The limitation was applied by Wright and Bruce JJ. in the unreported case of *Smith v Johnson & Co.*, referred to by Wright J. at the close of his judgment in *Wilkinson v Downton* [1897] 2 Q.B. 57, 61. In *Smith v Johnson & Co.* a man was killed by the defendant's negligence in the sight of the plaintiff, and the plaintiff became ill, not from the shock produced by the fear of harm to himself, but from the shock of seeing another person killed. The Court held that this harm was too remote a consequence of the negligence. I should myself, as I have already indicated, have been inclined to go a step further, and to hold upon the facts in *Smith v Johnson & Co.* that, as the defendant neither intended to affect the plaintiff injuriously nor did anything which could reasonably or naturally be expected to affect him injuriously, there was no evidence of any breach of legal duty towards the plaintiff . . ."

It is appropriate to consider at this point the status of the limitation introduced by Kennedy J. and whether it forms part of the ratio of his judgment or whether it is merely obiter. It could be said to be ratio in that reasonable fear for one's immediate personal safety is a material fact and an essential and integral part of the rule allowing the plaintiff to make a successful claim; it was because the plaintiff suffered shock through a reasonable fear of immediate personal injury to herself that she was able to recover. On the other hand, it could be said to be obiter since the plaintiff in this case had suffered shock through fear for her own safety and so it did not have to be decided whether a claim could be made only by someone who suffered shock through fear for his own safety. Any view expressed as to whether recovery was restricted to such a person might be seen as going beyond what needed to be decided and was accordingly obiter.

A further matter to be considered here, if the limitation did form part of the ratio of Kennedy J.'s judgment, is whether it formed part of the ratio of the case. In the section quoted earlier from Phillimore J.'s judgment (see above), no reference was made to any such limitation. His Lordship referred (at 682–683) to a duty by A not to inflict mental shock upon B and "if A. does inflict such a shock upon B.—as by terrifying B.—and physical damage thereby ensues, B. may have an action for the physical damage". The reference here to terrifying B, with use of the word "as", may suggest terrifying B is an instance of the way in which the fear may arise rather than an essential pre-requisite for the duty. Phillimore J.'s formulation of the duty thus may be expressed in broader terms than Kennedy J.'s. It appeared to admit the possibility of fear arising in other ways, which might include fear for another's safety. Since Phillimore J. did not endorse the limitation introduced by Kennedy J., the limitation would not appear to be part of the ratio of the case. Where more than one judgment is delivered in a case, a rule or proposition of law needs to be agreed upon by a majority of judges before it may be said to be part of the ratio and, with only two judges in *Dulieu*, this was not the case here.

▷ *(b) Damage sustained too remote*

The defendants' second contention, that the damage sustained was too remote, **15-004** although supported by a decision of the Judicial Committee of the Privy Council, *Victorian Railways Commissioners v Coultas* (1888) 13 App. Cas. 222 (*Coultas*), was also rejected. Privy Council decisions, whilst particularly persuasive as precedents since members sitting on the Committee are usually members of the Supreme Court (and, prior to 2009, were Law Lords), are not binding on any English court (see above, 1-030), and both Kennedy and Phillimore JJ. declined to follow the decision in this instance. Kennedy J., whilst recognising the precedential strength of the decision, indicated his willingness to depart from it on account of judicial reservations as to its correctness and criticism of the decision by prominent legal authors. His Lordship stated (at 676–677):

"It remains to consider the second and somewhat different form in which the defendants' counsel put his objection to the right of the plaintiff to maintain this action. He contended that the damages are too remote, and relied much upon the decision of the Privy Council in *Victorian Railways Commissioners v Coultas*, 13 App.Cas. at p.225. In that case the principal circumstances were that the appellants' gate-keeper negligently invited the male plaintiff and his wife, who were driving in a buggy, to enter the gate at a crossing when a train was approaching, and, though there was no actual collision with the train, the escape was so narrow and the danger so alarming that the lady fainted and suffered a severe nervous shock, which produced illness and a miscarriage. The Colonial Court had entered judgment for the plaintiff for the amount found by the jury at the trial of the action brought against the appellants for negligence. The Privy Council reversed this decision. The principal ground of their judgment is formulated in the following sentence: 'Damages arising from mere sudden terror unaccompanied by any actual physical injury but occasioning a nervous or mental shock cannot under such circumstances, their Lordships think, be considered a consequence which, in the ordinary course of things, would flow from the negligence of the gate-keeper', 13 App.Cas. at p.225. A judgment of the Privy Council ought of course to be treated by this Court as

> entitled to very great weight indeed; but it is not binding upon us, and, in venturing most respectfully not to follow it in the present case, I am fortified by the fact that its correctness was treated by Lord Esher M.R. in his judgment in *Pugh v London, Brighton & South Coast Ry. Co.* [1896] 2 Q.B. 248, at p.250 as open to question; that it was disapproved by the Exchequer Division in Ireland in *Bell v Great Northern Railway Company of Ireland*, 26 L.R.Ir. 428 where, in the course of his judgment, Palles C.B. gives a reasoned criticism of the Privy Council judgment, which, with all respect, I entirely adopt; and, lastly, by the fact that I find the judgment has been unfavourably reviewed by legal authors of recognised weight such as Mr. Sedgwick, On Damages, 8th ed. p.861, Sir Frederick Pollock, The Law of Torts, 6th ed. pp.50–52, and Mr. Beven, Negligence in Law, 2nd ed pp.76–83."

Phillimore J. likewise emphasised the persuasive nature only of the *Coultas* case as a precedent, remarking (at 683) that it "is an authority to be treated with the utmost respect, but no more binding on us even as to the res decisa than it was upon the Exchequer Division in Ireland [*in Bell*]" and going on (at 685) to dismiss the contention as to remoteness:

> "The difficulty in these cases is to my mind not one as to the remoteness of the damage, but as to the uncertainty of there being any duty. Once get the duty and the physical damage following on the breach of duty, and I hold that the fact of one link in the chain of causation being mental only makes no difference. The learned counsel for the plaintiff [*sic*] has put it that every link is physical in the narrow sense. That may be or may not be. For myself, it is unimportant."

The *Coultas* decision was not the only one relied upon by the defendants in support of their contention that the damage sustained was too remote, and reference was made to two American cases: a decision of the New York Court of Appeals in *Mitchell v Rochester Ry Co* (1896) 151 N.Y.107; and a decision of the Supreme Judicature Court of Massachusetts in *Spade v Lynn and Boston Rail Road* (1897) 60 Am.St.Rep. 393. These cases, as foreign court decisions, were, like *Coultas*, only of persuasive authority and, to the extent that they supported the defendants' contention, Kennedy J. (at 678–681) and Phillimore J. (at 685–686) declined to follow them.

▶ 3. *Hambrook v Stokes Bros*

15–005 The limitation in respect of the duty advanced by Kennedy J. in *Dulieu*, that the shock must be suffered through fear for one's own safety, was followed by Branson J. in *Hambrook v Stokes Bros* [1925] 1 K.B. 141 (*Hambrook*), when hearing an action brought under the Fatal Accidents Act 1846 by the plaintiff in respect of the (financial) loss sustained as a result of the death of his wife from nervous shock. The incident which gave rise to the shock was a runaway lorry moving at increasing speed down a steep and narrow street, as a result of the defendants' servant (employee) negligently leaving it unattended at the top of the street without taking proper precautions to secure it.

The plaintiff's wife had taken her three children across the street on their way to school and the children had gone a short way up the street and out of her sight past a bend, when the lorry, ricocheting from one side of the road to the other, hurtled round the bend and came to a stop when it crashed into a baker's shop some 15–20 feet from the plaintiff's wife. The plaintiff contended that the shock to his wife was due either to a reasonable fear of immediate personal injury to herself or of injury to her children, although, as Sargant L.J. observed (at 160):

". . . the evidence given did not indicate with absolute certainty whether the shock was due (1.) to apprehension of immediate injury to herself from the lorry, though her exclamations seem to negative this view, or (2.) from apprehension of injury having been caused by the lorry to one or other of her children. And, on the latter hypothesis, it is not quite clear whether the apprehension of this danger was solely due to the realization that the lorry had been charging down the street in which her children were, or was due to, or aggravated by, statements made to her that a little girl wearing spectacles (as her girl did) had been injured."

The case, unusually for a civil case, was heard before a jury and Branson J., following the view expressed by Kennedy J. in *Dulieu*, directed the jury that, if the shock which resulted in the wife's death was caused by fear for her children's safety as distinguished from fear for her own, the plaintiff could not maintain an action. The jury found for the defendants and the plaintiff appealed, inter alia, on the ground that Branson J.'s ruling was a misdirection to the jury as to the law.

A majority of the Court of Appeal, Bankes and Atkin L.JJ., allowed the plaintiff's appeal and directed that there must be a new trial. The Court of Appeal might have resolved the appeal by holding that the plaintiff could maintain an action on account of there having been an admission of negligence by the defendants in their pleading of the case, for Atkin L.J. stated (at 156):

". . . in the present case the plaintiff must show a breach of duty to her, but this she shows by the negligence of the defendants in the care of their lorry. I am clearly of opinion that the breach of duty to her is admitted in the pleadings. I do not appreciate the nature of the admission, unless it is an admission of negligence which, if supported by damage, would give the plaintiff a cause of action. This seems made plain by the fact that the only traverse in the defence [*i.e. point disputed by the defence*] is that the negligence caused damage, and by the, to me, conclusive fact that the same admission of negligence covers the cause of action of the infant plaintiff [*who had been struck by the lorry*] to whom the duty is not in dispute.

But apart from the admission in the pleadings, I think that the cause of action is complete . . ."

His Lordship then went on to examine the question of whether a duty might be owed and, in particular, whether the duty might be circumscribed by Kennedy J.'s limitation. Both Bankes and Sargant L.JJ., dissenting, however, made no reference to an admission of negligence in the pleadings and confined themselves to examination of whether a duty was owed. Since negligence had been admitted in the pleadings, it may be that any views expressed as to whether a duty was owed were not part of the ratio of the case and were only obiter. (This seems to have been the opinion of Lord Thankerton in *Bourhill v Young* [1943] A.C. 92, since his Lordship, when considering *Hambrook*, stated that "there are certain obiter dicta on the question of duty, which might be considered too wide, and I reserve my opinion on them"—see below, 15–006).

When considering whether the plaintiff could maintain an action, Bankes L.J. (at 152) held that he could do so if he could establish:

> ". . .that the death of his wife resulted from the shock occasioned by the running away of the lorry, that the shock resulted from what the plaintiff's wife either saw or realised through her own unaided senses, and not from something which some one told her, and that the shock was due to a reasonable fear of immediate personal injury to herself or her children."

The limitation specified by Kennedy J. in *Dulieu*, that shock caused through fear for another's safety was not actionable, was considered by Bankes L.J. to have only the status of an obiter dictum, although even if it had been regarded as ratio it would not, as a Divisional Court decision, have been binding on the Court of Appeal. Thus, his Lordship stated (at 151) that:

> "I think that the dictum of Kennedy J., laid down in quite general terms in that case, cannot be accepted as good law applicable in every case."

His Lordship (at 149–150) sought to distinguish the present case from that of *Smith v Johnson & Co* (*Smith*), on which Kennedy J. had relied in support of the limitation:

> "In introducing this limitation the learned judge [*Kennedy J.*] relies upon a reference by Wright J. in the case of *Wilkinson v Downton* [1897] 2 Q.B. 57, 61 to a previous decision in the unreported case of *Smith v Johnson & Co.*, in which a Divisional Court had held that where a man was killed in the sight of the plaintiff by the defendant's negligence, and the plaintiff became ill, not from the shock for fear of harm to himself, but from the shock of seeing another person killed, this harm was too remote a consequence of the negligence. It must be noticed that the facts in this last mentioned case . . . are very different from the facts of the present case. It may well be that the duty of a person to take care does not extend to a person in the position of the plaintiff in *Smith v Johnson & Co.* . . . and yet may extend to a person in the position of the plaintiff's wife."

Atkin L.J. (at 154) similarly regarded the statement of Kennedy. J. in *Dulieu* as obiter, although, in contrast to Bankes L.J., mentioned the decision in *Smith* only in passing when reviewing the authorities on nervous shock. No reference was made to the case when considering the correctness of the dictum of Kennedy J. in *Dulieu* and no attempt was made to distinguish *Smith*. Instead, reliance was placed on two decisions with which Kennedy J.'s limitation was considered to be inconsistent: *Pugh v London, Brighton and South Coast Ry Co* [1896] 2 Q.B. 248 (*Pugh*), a case not referred to by Bankes L.J.; and *Wilkinson*, a case mentioned by Bankes L.J. only for its reference to *Smith*. Atkin L.J. stated:

"The case [*Dulieu*] is important for the dictum of Kennedy J. which Branson J. followed in the present case, to the effect that the shock where it operates through the mind must be a shock which arises from reasonable fear of immediate personal injury to oneself. I will discuss the correctness of this dictum later. I do not see that Phillimore J. expressed any definite opinion upon this point . . . [*at 155*]

I can find no principle to support the self-imposed restriction stated in the judgment of Kennedy J. . . . It appears to me inconsistent with the decision in *Pugh v London, Brighton and South Coast Ry. Co.* [1896] 2 Q.B. 248 [*where a railway signalman suffered shock caused by the excitement and alarm of successfully averting a train accident*], and with the decision in *Wilkinson v Downton* [1897] 2 Q.B. 57 [*for the facts of which, see above, 15–001*], in neither of which cases was the shock the result of the apprehension of the injury to the plaintiff. It would result in a state of the law in which a mother, shocked by fright for herself, would recover, while a mother shocked by her child being killed before her eyes, could not, and in which a mother traversing the highway with a child in her arms could recover if shocked by fright for herself, while if she could be cross-examined into an admission that the fright was really for her child, she could not. In my opinion such distinctions would be discreditable to any system of jurisprudence in which they formed the part. Personally I see no reason for excluding the bystander in the highway who receives injury in the same way from apprehension of or the actual sight of injury to a third party. There may well be cases where the sight of suffering will directly and immediately physically shock the most indurate heart; and if the suffering of another be the result of an act wrongful to the spectator, I do not see why the wrongdoer should escape . . . [*at 157*]

It may be that to negative Kennedy J.'s restriction is to increase possible actions. I think this may be exaggerated. I find only about half-a-dozen cases of direct shock reported in about thirty years, and I do not expect that shocks to bystanders will outnumber them. But if they do, in the words of Kennedy J., 'I should be sorry to adopt a rule'—in this case the restriction—'which would bar all such claims on grounds of policy alone, and in order to prevent the possible success of unrighteous or groundless actions . . .' [*at 158*]"

Sargant L.J., dissenting, and adopting as the ratio of his judgment Kennedy J.'s limitation in *Dulieu*, considered the case of *Smith* not to be distinguishable from the present case. Considering the case of *Smith* to be "of the highest importance" (at 162) where shock was caused through the sight of apprehension of impact on a third party, his Lordship stated (at 163):

> "No doubt in the case of *Smith v Johnson & Co.* the person killed was a stranger to the plaintiff, while here the persons with regard to whom apprehension was entertained were the young children of Mrs. Hambrook herself. But I cannot think that this makes any real difference, if the question is regarded, as I think it ought to be regarded, from the point of view of the extent of the duty of the defendant towards the public in or near the highway. If he has no duty to avoid shocking them by killing or endangering strangers, can it be reasonably held that he has such a duty to avoid shocking them by killing or endangering their friends or relatives? And, if so, what degree of friendship or relationship is the defendant to expect as that which will reasonably or naturally result in harmful nervous shock? It seems to me that, when once the requirement is relaxed, that the shock is to be one caused by the plaintiff's apprehension of damage to himself, the defendant is exposed to liability for a consequence which is only reached by a new and quite unusual link in the chain of causation, and which cannot therefore properly be held to have been within his ordinary and reasonable expectation."

The case of *Wilkinson* relied upon by Atkin L.J. was considered to be distinguishable and "not really in point" (at 164), since it was "founded on intentional and malicious wrongdoing". A similar view was taken of *Pugh*, also relied upon by Atkin L.J., which was "merely a decision on what amounted to an accident within the meaning of a policy" (at 164).

Thus, each member of the court in *Hambrook*, when considering the correctness of Kennedy J.'s limitation in *Dulieu* and the authorities supporting or against the limitation, treated the authorities in different ways. Sargant L.J. treated *Smith* on which Kennedy J. had relied as directly in point, Bankes L.J. treated it as distinguishable and Atkin L.J. accorded it little attention. Atkin L.J. considered the cases of *Pugh* and *Wilkinson* to negate Kennedy J's limitation, Sargant L.J. regarded them as distinguishable and Bankes L.J. made no mention of the former and a mention of the latter only for its reference to *Smith*.

▶ 4. *Bourhill v Young*

15–006 The decisions in *Dulieu* and *Hambrook* were subsequently considered by the House of Lords in *Bourhill v Young* [1943] A.C. 92 (*Bourhill*), a case heard on appeal from the Court of Session in Scotland. Here the plaintiff sought damages for nervous shock sustained as a result of hearing the impact of a road traffic accident caused by the negligence of a motor cyclist and, apparently, later seeing a pool of blood on the road. The accident occurred some 45–50 feet away from where the plaintiff, who had just stepped off a tram, was standing and was not witnessed by her. Counsel for the plaintiff contended (at 96) that:

> "The question for the House is whether the view of Kennedy J. in *Dulieu v White & Sons* [1901] 2 K.B. 669, 675 that to give rise to a cause of action "the shock, where it operates through the mind, must be a shock which arises from a reasonable fear of immediate personal injury to oneself" is correct, or whether the opposite view expressed in *Hambrook v Stokes Brothers* [1925] 1 K.B. 141 . . . should prevail."

The House, however, avoided determination of this question by taking the view that no duty of care was owed to her by the motor cyclist. The motor cyclist was considered to owe a duty to drive with reasonable care to avoid the risk of injury, which included injury by shock although no direct impact occurred, to such persons as he could reasonably foresee might be injured by his failure to exercise that care, but it was held not to be foreseeable that the plaintiff would be affected. In reaching this decision, the House seemed to be particularly influenced by the fact that the plaintiff was not within the area of potential danger arising as a result of the motor cyclist's negligence—see, e.g. at 99, 102, 105, 111 and 117 of the report. Although the House of Lords in *Bourhill* did not make reference to the "neighbour principle" formulated by Lord Atkin in *Donoghue v Stevenson* [1932] A.C. 562, 580 (i.e. "You must take reasonable care to avoid acts or omissions which you can reasonably forsee would be likely to injure your neighbour. Who then, in law, is my neighbour? The answer seems to be persons who are so closely and directly affected by my act that I ought reasonably to have them in contemplation as being so affected when I am directing my mind to the acts or omissions which are called in question."), the House appeared effectively to apply it by holding that a duty would not be owed unless it was reasonably foreseeable that the plaintiff would suffer nervous shock.

By deciding that no duty was owed to the plaintiff, it was not necessary to determine the question which had divided the Court of Appeal in *Hambrook*, i.e. whether a duty might extend to cases where shock arose from a reasonable fear of immediate personal injury to persons other than oneself. Nevertheless, members of the House did go on to express, obiter, tentative views on this matter. Lord Wright (at 111–112) expressed provisional agreement with the majority decision in *Hambrook* that shock could include fear for another's safety:

> ". . . it may well be that some day this House will have to examine the exact meaning and effect of what Kennedy J. said in *Dulieu v White & Sons* [1901] 2 K.B. 669, 675. He was, he said, inclined to think that there was at least one limitation: "The shock, where it operates through the mind, must be a shock which arises from a reasonable fear of immediate personal injury to oneself." That statement, if meant to lay down a rigid rule of law, has been overruled by the Court of Appeal in *Hambrook v Stokes Brothers* [1925] 1 K.B. 141, which now lays down the English law, unless it is set aside by this House. As at present

> advised, I agree with that decision. Kennedy J.'s dictum, if intended to lay down a rigid limitation, is not, I think in accordance with principle or with cases like *Wilkinson v Downton* [1897] 2 Q.B. 57. It finds no support in the judgment of Phillimore J., who implicitly lays down a wider principle, but as I may some day have to decide the question in this House, I prefer to express here no final opinion."

Lord Porter (at 114–116) considered at some length the case of *Hambrook* without indicating any dissent from that decision and a later remark (at 120), made after a subsequent consideration of Scottish authorities and the Irish case of *Bell*, might suggest approval of that decision:

> "In all three countries, no doubt, shock occasioned by deliberate action affords a valid ground of claim (see *Wilkinson v Downton* [1897] 2 Q.B. 57 . . .), and so, I think, does shock occasioned by reasonable apprehension of injury to oneself or others, at any rate, if those others are closely connected with the claimant."

On the other hand, Lord Russell inclined to the view that shock, to be actionable, should arise from fear for one's own safety, stating (at 102–103):

> "My Lords, we heard a lengthy argument addressed to the questions whether *Hambrook v Stokes Brothers* [1925] 1 K.B. 141 was rightly decided, and, if so, whether the decision was in accordance with the law of Scotland as expounded in the numerous Scottish decisions cited to us. In the view which I have taken of the present case [*that no duty is owed*] it is unnecessary to express a final view upon these questions. I will only say that, as at present advised, I see no reason why the laws of the two countries should differ in this respect, and I prefer the dissenting judgment of Sargant L.J. to the decision of the majority in *Hambrook v Stokes Brothers* [1925] 1 K.B. 141."

The position of Lords Thankerton and Macmillan is less clear and both reserved their opinion, although to the extent that any indication was given there seemed to be a lack of support for *Hambrook*. Thus, Lord Thankerton, when considering *Hambrook*, stated (at 100) that "there are certain obiter dicta on the question of duty, which might be considered too wide, and I reserve my opinion on them", whilst Lord Macmillan remarked (at 105):

> "[*Finding no duty*] is sufficient for the disposal of the case and absolves me from considering the question whether injury through mental shock is actionable only when, in the words of Kennedy J., the shock arises from a reasonable fear of immediate personal injury to oneself (*Dulieu v White & Sons* [1901] 2 K.B. 669, 682), which was admittedly not the case in the present instance . . . I shall observe only that the view expressed by Kennedy J. has in Scotland the support of a substantial body of authority, although it was not accepted by the Court of Appeal in England in *Hambrook v Stokes Brothers* [1925] 1 K.B. 141, notwithstanding a powerful dissent by Sargant L.J. This

House has not yet been called upon to pronounce on the question either as a matter of Scots law or as a matter of English law, and I reserve my opinion on it."

Whilst tentative views were expressed on the correctness of *Hambrook*, matters such as the relationship between the person suffering shock and the victim of the accident and the closeness of the plaintiff to the scene of the accident, and the relationship between these factors and the reasonable foresight that the plaintiff would suffer shock, were not addressed. Nor, as will be seen, were these issues subsequently clarified by the Court of Appeal in *King v Phillips* and *Boardman v Sanderson*.

▶ ## 5. *King v Phillips*

The correctness of the decision in *Hambrook* and its subsequent status following **15–007** the House of Lords' decision in *Bourhill* was considered initially by Donovan J. in a first instance decision in *Dooley v Cammell Laird & Co Ltd and Mersey Insulation Co Ltd* [1951] 1 Lloyd's Rep. 271 and later by the Court of Appeal in *King v Phillips* [1953] 1 Q.B. 429 (*King*). In the former decision, an employee sustained nervous shock through his fear that colleagues might have been injured when the crane he was operating, due to provision of a weak rope for the sling, dropped a load into the hold of a ship. He sought damages, but the defendants denied the existence of a duty, relying on *Bourhill*. Donovan J. stated (at 276):

"Mr. Scholefield Allen, on behalf of Mersey Insulation, denies that any such duty was owed to the plaintiff; for, he says, the plaintiff suffered merely nervous shock, and the duty to take care to avoid inflicting nervous shock is owed only to a person who, in the circumstances obtaining, may suffer nervous shock through some physical impact upon himself, his wife or child, or through the reasonable fear of such impact. The plaintiff in this case was not such a person. The principle upon which this suggested limitation of duty rests is not easy to discern. It was first suggested by Mr. Justice Kennedy in *Dulieu v White & Sons*, [1901] 2 K.B. 669, but was expressly negatived by a majority of the Court of Appeal in *Hambrook v Stokes Brothers*, [1925] 1 K.B. 141. Mr. Scholefield Allen keeps open the argument that the latter case was wrongly decided. He goes further and says it is in conflict with the later decision of the House of Lords in *Hay* (or *Bourhill*) v. *Young* . . ."

His Lordship rejected this contention, taking the view that it was accepted in *Bourhill* that the ambit of persons affected by negligence may extend beyond those actually subject to physical impact. Apart from Lord Russell, "none of the other members of the House of Lords who heard *Hay's* case disapproved of *Hambrook v Stokes Brothers*" (at 227) and, in Donovan J.'s opinion, a duty was owed in the present case, since the defendants ought reasonably to have foreseen injury to the plaintiff as a consequence of providing a weak rope to the sling.

The correctness of *Hambrook*, following *Bourhill*, was further considered in *King*. In this case, a mother suffered nervous shock, after hearing her son scream, when she looked out of an upstairs window and saw the defendant's taxi backing onto his tricycle and the tricycle under the taxi, without being able to see her son. The mother (and her son, who was not seriously injured) sued the defendant in negligence, relying on *Hambrook*, but the defendant denied that any duty was owed to the mother because, following *Bourhill*, she was outside the range of reasonable anticipation of the taxi driver. McNair J. ([1952] 2 All E.R. 459 at 461–462) upheld the defendant's contention:

> "It seems to me to be contrary to common sense to say that a taxi-driver ought reasonably to have contemplated that, if he backed his taxi without looking where he was going, he might cause injury by shock, or any other injury, to a woman in a house some seventy or eighty yards away up a side street.
>
> It was urged by counsel on behalf of the plaintiff that so far as this court was concerned the matter was concluded against the view which I have adopted by the decision of the Court of Appeal in *Hambrook v Stokes Brothers* [1925] 1 K.B. 141. I am unable to accept this submission, as it is plain that in that case the breach of duty was admitted in the pleadings and in so far as there are any differences in the statement of legal principles in the judgments of Bankes L.J., and Atkin L.J., from the views expressed in *Bourhill*'s case [1943] A.C. 92 in the House of Lords, I am bound to follow the latter."

McNair J.'s reasons for not following *Hambrook* seemed to be twofold. First, in *Hambrook*, unlike in the present case, the breach of duty was admitted in the pleadings. As has been stated earlier (see above, 15–005), since this was so, it may be that views expressed in *Hambrook* as to whether a duty was owed were obiter, in which case the matter would not have been "concluded against the view" taken by McNair J. in the present case. Accordingly, McNair J. was not bound by the decision in *Hambrook* to find in favour of the plaintiff. Secondly, where there were any differences in the statement of legal principles between *Hambrook* and *Bourhill*, the latter as a matter of precedent had to be followed. One area of difference between *Hambrook* and *Bourhill* concerned whether a claim could be maintained where nervous shock was sustained through fear for another's safety. The majority view of Bankes and Atkin L.JJ. in *Hambrook* was that it could, but, as has been seen above, opinions expressed on this matter by members of the House of Lords in *Bourhill* differed. Some members of the House of Lords in *Bourhill* were apparently in agreement with the majority view in *Hambrook*, but others were not. Since differing opinions were expressed in *Bourhill*, it might be questioned why McNair J. felt obliged to follow the opinions in *Bourhill* which differed from those in *Hambrook* rather than those which accorded with it. Further, if these opinions in *Bourhill* as to the majority view in *Hambrook* were obiter (see above, 15–006), it might be questioned whether McNair J. was bound as a matter of precedent to follow the opinions anyway.

McNair J.'s decision was unanimously affirmed by the Court of Appeal. The court differed, however, in its approach to the *Hambrook* case. A majority of the court, distinguishing *Hambrook*, took the view that no duty was owed to the plaintiff. Hodson L.J. (at 443–444), whilst recognising it was difficult to draw any valid distinction on the facts between that case and the present one, felt that McNair J. had been justified in his refusal to regard himself as bound by *Hambrook* on the ground that a breach of duty had been admitted in that case:

"The appellant contends that . . . the case is on all fours with and, indeed, stronger than *Hambrook v Stokes Brothers*, in which the Court of Appeal, by a majority, found that a husband was entitled to recover in an action under the Fatal Accidents Acts where the death of his wife was caused by shock brought about by fear for her child's safety. That case, it is said, was not overruled by *Bourhill v Young*, and accordingly, McNair J. was wrong in directing himself by the speeches delivered in the House of Lords with regard to the earlier decision. This criticism is, I think, ill-founded. In *Bourhill v Young* their Lordships had to deal with a case in which no breach of duty was admitted, while in *Hambrook v Stokes Brothers* there was an admission of negligence, so that the question of breach of duty did not arise.

It seems to me that, in the absence of the admission, Lord Thankerton would not have approved the decision in *Hambrook v Stokes Brothers*. He quoted a passage from Atkin L.J.'s judgment: "I agree that in the present case the plaintiff must show a breach of duty to her, but this she shows by the negligence of the defendants in the care of their lorry. I am clearly of opinion that the breach of duty to her is admitted in the pleadings," and continued: "But there are certain obiter dicta on the question of duty, which might be considered too wide, and I reserve any opinion on them." Lord Russell of Killowen preferred the dissenting judgment of Sargant L.J.; Lord Macmillan reserved his opinion upon the case; Lord Wright said that, as at present advised, he agreed with the decision, and Lord Porter expressed no dissent, emphasising that all the Lords Justices were careful to point out that the vital problem was the extent of the duty and not the remoteness of the damage, a view with which he agreed.

In these circumstances, although I think that it is difficult to draw a valid distinction on the facts between this case and *Hambrook v Stokes Brothers*, I think that McNair J. was entitled to treat the decision of the majority of the Court of Appeal in the way in which he did, for the reasons which he gave and for those which can be extracted from the speeches to which I have referred in *Bourhill v Young*."

Singleton L.J., in contrast, although recognising the admission of breach of duty in *Hambrook*, did seem to be of the view that that case was distinguishable on its facts. The ground for distinguishing *Hambrook* appeared to be physical proximity to the scene of the accident. His Lordship stated (at 436–437).

"The decision of this court in *Hambrook v Stokes Brothers* was not directly overruled by the House of Lords in *Bourhill v Young*; indeed it could not be, for in *Hambrook v Stokes Brothers* there was an admission of negligence which presupposed the existence of a duty towards the plaintiff. Atkin L.J. however, considered that case apart from the question of pleading, and his judgment, if I may humbly say so, commends itself to me. He, however, was considering a case which on its facts is far removed from the present. In that case the mother who died from the shock some time later, was on the highway—a narrow road—not far from the scene of an accident to one of her children."

Denning L.J., unlike Hodson and Singleton L.JJ., took the view that a duty was owed to the plaintiff in accordance with *Hambrook*. However, his Lordship was of the view that the plaintiff could not recover because, unlike in *Hambrook*, the shock sustained was too remote. Denning L.J. felt that *Hambrook* was distinguishable on the ground that the taxi driver could not reasonably have foreseen, when backing his taxi, that a mother some distance away would suffer nervous shock, whereas the lorry driver ought to have foreseen that a runaway lorry might seriously shock the mother of children in the danger area. His Lordship stated (at 441–442):

". . . there can be no doubt since *Bourhill v Young* that the test of liability for shock is foreseeability of injury by shock . . .

. . . I think that we should follow *Hambrook v Stokes Brothers* so far as to hold that there was a duty of care owed by the taxi driver not only to the boy, but also to his mother. In that case the negligence took place 300 yards from the place where the mother was standing [*i.e. at the top of the street where the lorry was left unattended*] In this case it was only 70 or 80 yards. In that case the mother was not herself in any personal danger. Nor was she here. In that case she suffered shock by fear for the safety of her children from what she saw and heard. So did she here. In that case the mother was in the street, and in this case at the window of the house. I do not think that makes any difference. Nevertheless, I think that the shock in this case is too remote to be a head of damage. It seems to me that the slow backing of the taxicab was very different from the terrifying descent of the runaway lorry. The taxicab driver cannot reasonably be expected to have foreseen that his backing would terrify a mother 70 yards away, whereas the lorry driver ought to have foreseen that a runaway lorry might seriously shock the mother of children in the danger area."

The mother being some distance from the scene of the accident in this case and thus outside the area of potential (physical) danger seemed to have been a significant consideration in the court's decision that the plaintiff could not recover. In distinguishing *Hambrook*, both Singleton and Denning L.JJ. referred to the mother in that case, unlike in *King*, being "on the highway" (per Singleton L.J.) or "in the danger area" (per Denning L.J.).

▶ 6. *Boardman v Sanderson*

The case of *King* itself was subsequently distinguished in *Boardman v Sanderson*   **15–008**
[1964] 1 W.L.R. 1317 (*Boardman*) where the Court of Appeal held that a duty was
owed by the defendant, who had visited a garage with the plaintiff and the
plaintiff's son to collect his car, when he negligently reversed over the son's foot
whilst the plaintiff was within earshot in the office paying the defendant's garage
bill. Ormrod L.J. stated (at 1320):

> "I do not propose to deliver an elaborate judgment on the law applicable to
> this case, but it seems to me this case is distinguishable from *King v Phillips*.
> That was a case of a taxi driver negligently backing a taxicab and running into
> a child on a tricycle. It so happened that the child's mother lived 70 or 80
> yards away and heard screams, looked out of her window, and was extremely
> shocked. In that case, the majority of the court took the view that the claim
> was not maintainable because the driver could not reasonably foresee that if
> he drove negligently and injured the child the mother would be immediately
> on the scene of the accident; it was quite by chance and unknown to the driver
> that she happened to live 70 or 80 yards away. In this case the defendant did
> know that the father was only a few yards away and therefore the defendant
> could reasonably have foreseen, if he were negligent and as a result of that
> negligence he did injury to the infant, that the father would be immediately
> upon the scene and might be shocked as, indeed, he was shocked."

Thus, according to Ormrod L.J., there appeared to be two grounds for distinguishing *King*, namely, proximity to the scene of the accident and awareness of the
plaintiff's existence. In *King* it was "unknown to the driver that she [*the plaintiff*]
happened to live 70 or 80 yards away", whereas in the present case the defendant
"did know that the father was only a few yards away".

That the plaintiff in the present case had not witnessed the incident was seen as
irrelevant and the Court of Appeal rejected a contention that, for the plaintiff to
recover, it was necessary for him to have witnessed the accident. Ormrod L.J.
stated (at 1321):

> "Mr. Richardson, on behalf of the defendant submitted that this case must be
> considered on a similar basis with *Hay* (or *Bourhill*) *v Young*, one of the leading
> cases on this question of injury by shock. In that case the plaintiff, who was a
> fish wife loading fish from a tramcar into her basket, did not see the accident
> happen and only saw the results of it when she was moved by the noise to go
> and see what had happened. In the present case, too, the father did not see
> the accident but was only moved to see what had happened when he heard
> the infant scream. Mr. Richardson has endeavoured to submit that the line of
> distinction must be drawn somewhere and that must depend on whether the
> accident was witnessed by the plaintiff, and that if, in this case, the father did
> not witness the accident he cannot succeed. There has been no authority

> produced to the court to bear out that submission and, for my part, I must say I find it difficult to understand why the line should be drawn in that arbitrary fashion. It may be that, in some cases, that is a proper line to draw, as in *Hay* (or *Bourhill*) *v Young*, and it may be that in that case, as in many others, the proposed plaintiff does not come within the area of contemplated danger. On the other hand, clearly the facts of these cases are infinitely variable and it would be difficult, if not impossible, to draw any line of distinction and say in one case the plaintiff should succeed and in another case he should not."

A duty was owed by the defendant, his Lordship went on to state (at 1322), "not only to the infant but also to the near relatives of the infant who were, as he knew, on the premises, within earshot, and likely to come upon the scene if any injury or ill befell the infant". It might be questioned whether this statement about a duty being owed to "near relatives" (whoever they might be) was part of the ratio of the case or only obiter. This may depend on whether a broad or narrow view is taken on the ratio. If a narrow view is taken, the case may be said to establish, as a proposition of law, that a parent may recover for nervous shock sustained in these circumstances. Whether near relatives other than parents might recover would not be a matter which the court had to decide and may be considered to be obiter. However, if a broad view is taken and the plaintiff being a parent was not considered to be a material (essential) fact, the ratio of the case may be anyone who is a "near relative" may recover.

▶ *7. McLoughlin v O'Brian*

15-009 Prior to the case of *McLoughlin v O'Brian* (*McLoughlin*) coming before the Court of Appeal ([1981] Q.B. 599) and subsequently the House of Lords ([1983] A.C. 410), the only other appellate court decision after *Boardman* involving nervous shock appears to have been *Hinz v Berry* [1970] 2 Q.B. 40, in which the Court of Appeal was concerned with the question of assessment of damages in such cases (and not the question of liability). There were, however, a number of first instance decisions in which the question of liability for nervous shock was considered and in which the reasonable foresight principle was applied, e.g. *Chadwick v British Railways Board* [1967] 1 W.L.R. 912 (*Chadwick*), where the plaintiff recovered for nervous shock sustained when he went to assist in rescue work following a train accident.

In *McLoughlin*, the plaintiff was at home two miles away at the time of an accident involving members of her family and sustained nervous shock on being taken to see them in hospital two hours later, and application of the reasonable foresight principle by the trial judge led to dismissal of the plaintiff's claim. The possibility of her suffering injury by nervous shock was held not to be reasonably foreseeable. The plaintiff appealed to the Court of Appeal, which upheld the decision of the trial judge, but not on the same ground. The Court of Appeal took the view that shock was foreseeable but that on policy grounds, namely, the fear of indeterminate liability (sometimes termed "the floodgates argument"), a duty should be denied.

Although the Court of Appeal found for the defendant, leave to appeal to the House of Lords was granted and counsel for the defendant reserved the right to argue that recovery for nervous shock was limited to those suffering shock through fear for their own personal safety in accordance with the limitation propounded by Kennedy J. in *Dulieu*. This limitation—essentially one of policy—had not been followed by a majority of the Court of Appeal in *Hambrook*, but the difference of judicial opinion expressed in that case had not been resolved by the House of Lords in *Bourhill* (see above, 15–005 and 15–006). In the event, this line of argument was not pursued, although it seems likely that it would not have met with success if it had been. As Lord Wilberforce observed (at 418):

> "While damages cannot, at common law, be awarded for grief and sorrow, a claim for damages for "nervous shock" caused by negligence can be made without the necessity of showing direct impact or fear of immediate personal injuries for oneself. The reservation made by Kennedy J. in *Dulieu v White & Sons* [1901] 2 K.B. 669, though taken up by Sargant L.J. in *Hambrook v Stokes Brothers* [1925] 1 K.B. 141, has not gained acceptance, and although the respondents, in the courts below, reserved their right to revive it, they did not do so in argument. I think that it is now too late to do so."

The lines of argument pursued by the defence were that it was not reasonably foreseeable that a mother in the plaintiff's position would suffer nervous shock and that, even if it was foreseeable, no duty was owed in accordance with the existing established authorities, and there were no policy justifications for extending the duty to cases like the present which would result in a substantial widening of the classes of persons entitled to sue.

The defendant's first line of argument was unanimously and decisively rejected. As Lord Bridge remarked (at 433):

> "My Lords, in the instant case I cannot help thinking that the learned trial judge's conclusion that the appellant's illness was not the foreseeable consequence of the respondents' negligence was one to which, understandably, he felt himself driven by the authorities. Free of authority and applying the ordinary criterion of reasonable foreseeability to the facts, with an eye "enlightened by progressive awareness of mental illness" (the language of Stephenson L.J. [1981] Q.B. 599, 612), any judge must, I would think, share the view of all three members of the Court of Appeal, with which I understand all your Lordships agree, that in the words of Griffiths L.J. at p.617, it was
>
> > "readily foreseeable that a significant number of mothers exposed to such an experience might break down under the shock of the event and suffer illness".
>
> The question, then, for your Lordships' decision is whether the law, as a matter of policy, draws a line which exempts from liability a defendant whose negligent act or omission was actually and foreseeably the cause of the plaintiff's psychiatric illness and, if so, where that line is to be drawn.

> Before attempting to answer the question, it is instructive to consider the historical development of the subject as illustrated by the authorities, and to note, in particular, three features of that development. First, it will be seen that successive attempts have been made to draw the line beyond which liability should not extend, each of which has in due course had to be abandoned. Secondly, the ostensible justification for drawing the line has been related to the current criterion of a defendant's duty of care, which, however, expressed in earlier judgments, we should now describe as that of reasonable foreseeability. But, thirdly, in so far as policy considerations can be seen to have influenced any of the decisions, they appear to have sprung from the fear that to cross the chosen line would be to open the floodgates to claims without limit and largely without merit."

The policy argument of drawing a line exempting a defendant from liability and its relationship with the criterion of reasonable foresight was a matter on which there was a divergence of opinion in the House, although all members were in favour of allowing the plaintiff's appeal. Lord Bridge, after reviewing the authorities, went on to say (at 439–442):

> "My Lords, looking back I think it is possible to discern that there only ever were two clear lines of limitation of a defendant's liability for "nervous shock" for which any rational justification could be advanced in the light of both of the state of the law of negligence and the state of medical science as judicially understood at the time when those limitations were propounded. In 1888 it was, no doubt, perfectly sensible to say: "Damages arising from mere sudden terror unaccompanied by any actual physical injury, but occasioning a nervous or mental shock, cannot . . . be considered a consequence which, in the ordinary course of things, would flow from . . . negligence" (*Victorian Railway Commissioners v Coultas*, 13 App.Cas. 222, 225). Here the test, whether of duty or of remoteness, can be recognised as a relatively distant ancestor of the modern criterion of reasonable foreseeability. Again, in 1901 it was, I would suppose, equally sensible to limit a defendant's liability for "nervous shock" which could "reasonably or actually be expected" to be such as was suffered by a plaintiff who was himself physically endangered by the defendant's negligence (*Dulieu v White & Sons* [1901] 2 K.B. 669, 675). But once that line of limitation has been crossed, as it was by the majority in *Hambrook v Stokes Brothers* [1925] 1 K.B. 141, there can be no logical reason whatever for limiting the defendant's duty to persons in physical proximity to the place where the accident, caused by the defendant's negligence, occurred . . .

> In approaching the question whether the law should, as a matter of policy, define the criterion of liability in negligence for causing psychiatric illness by reference to some test other than that of reasonable foreseeability it is well to remember that we are concerned only with the question of liability of a defendant who is, ex hypothesi, guilty of fault in causing the death, injury or danger which has in turn triggered the psychiatric illness . . .

In the end I believe that the policy question depends on weighing against each other two conflicting considerations. On the one hand, if the criterion of liability is to be reasonable foreseeability simpliciter, this must, precisely because questions of causation in psychiatric medicine give rise to difficulty and uncertainty, introduce an element of uncertainty into the law and open the way to a number of arguable claims which a more precisely fixed criterion would exclude. I accept that the element of uncertainty is an important factor. I believe that the "floodgates" argument, however, is, as it always has been, greatly exaggerated. On the other hand, it seems to me inescapable that any attempt to define the limit of liability by requiring, in addition to reasonable foreseeability, that the plaintiff claiming damages for psychiatric illness should have witnessed the relevant accident, should have been present at or near the place where it happened, should have come upon its aftermath and thus have had some direct perception of it, as opposed to merely learning of it after the event, should be related to some particular degree to the accident victim—to draw a line by reference to any of these criteria must impose a largely arbitrary limit of liability."

His Lordship accordingly concluded (at 443) that "there are no policy considerations sufficient to justify limiting the liability of negligent tortfeasors by reference to some narrower criterion than that of reasonable foreseeability".

A similar view was taken by Lord Scarman (at 429–31), who expressed his agreement with Lord Bridge's judgment, although delivering a relatively short judgment himself:

"I accept his [*Lord Bridge's*] approach to the law and the conclusion he reaches . . .

Policy considerations will have to be weighed: but the objective of the judges is the formulation of principle. And, if principle inexorably requires a decision which entails a degree of policy risk, the court's function is to adjudicate according to the principle, leaving policy curtailment to the judgment of Parliament. Here lies the true role of the two law-making institutions in our constitution. By concentrating on principle the judges can keep the common law alive, flexible and consistent, and can keep the legal system clear of policy problems which neither they, nor the forensic process which it is their duty to operate, are equipped to resolve. If principle leads to results which are thought to be socially unacceptable, Parliament can legislate to draw a line or map out a new path.

The real risk to the common law is not its movement to cover new situations and new knowledge but lest it should stand still, halted by a conservative judicial approach . . .

The present case is a good illustration. Certainty could have been achieved by leaving the law as it was left by *Victorian Railways Commissioner v Coultas*, 13 App.Cas. 222, or again, by holding the line drawn in 1901 by *Dulieu v White &*

Sons [1901] 2 K.B. 669, or today by confining the law to what was regarded by Lord Denning M.R. in *Hinz v Berry* [1970] 2 Q.B. 40, 42, as "settled law," namely that ". . . damages can be given for nervous shock caused by the sight of an accident, at any rate to a close relative."

But at each landmark stage common law principle, when considered in the context of developing medical science, has beckoned the judges on. And now . . . common law principle requires the judges to follow the logic of the "reasonably foreseeable test" so as, in circumstances where it is appropriate, to apply it untrammelled by spatial, physical, or temporal limits. Space, time, distance, the nature of the injuries sustained, and the relationship of the plaintiff to the immediate victim of the accident, are factors to be weighed, but not legal limitations, when the test of reasonable foreseeability is to be applied . . .

Why then should not the courts draw the line, as the Court of Appeal manfully tried to do in this case? Simply because the policy issue as to where to draw the line is not justiciable."

Acceptance of reasonable foreseeability as the sole criterion and policy issues not being justiciable were, however, decisively rejected by Lord Edmund-Davies. His Lordship stated (at 426–428):

"My Lords, in the present case two totally different points arising from the speeches of two of your Lordships call for further attention. Both relate to the Court of Appeal's invoking public policy. Unless I have completely misunderstood my noble and learned friend, Lord Bridge of Harwich, he doubts that any regard should have been had to such a consideration and seemingly considers that the Court of Appeal went wrong in paying any attention to it. The sole test of liability, I read him as saying, is the reasonable foreseeability of injury to the plaintiff through nervous shock, resulting from the defendants' conceded default. And, such foreseeability having been established to their unanimous satisfaction, it followed that in law no other course was open to the Court of Appeal than to allow this appeal. I have respectfully to say that I cannot accept this approach. It is true that no decision was cited to your Lordships in which the contrary has been held, but that is not to say that reasonable foreseeability is the only test of the validity of a claim brought in negligence . . .

My understanding . . . is that . . . [*Lord Scarman*] shares (though for a different reason) the conclusion of my noble and learned friend, Lord Bridge of Harwich, that in adverting to public policy, the Court of Appeal here embarked upon a sleeveless errand, for public policy has no relevance to liability at law. In my judgment, the proposition [*of Lord Scarman*] that "the policy issue . . . is not justiciable" is as novel as it is startling. So novel is it in relation to this appeal that it was never mentioned during the hearing before your Lordships. And it is startling because in my respectful judgment it runs counter to well-established and wholly acceptable law.

I restrict myself to recent decisions of your Lordships' House. [*His Lordship then referred to Rondel v Worsley [1969] 1 A.C. 191; Dorset Yacht Co Ltd v Home Office [1970] A.C. 1004; and Herrington v British Railways Board [1972] A.C. 877*].

My Lords, in accordance with such a line of authorities, I hold that public policy issues are justiciable."

Whilst indicating that policy considerations could be taken into account, Lord Edmund-Davies nevertheless, as Lord Bridge critically pointed out at the end of his judgment (at 443):

". . . stops short of indicating his view as to where the limit of liability should be drawn or as to the nature of the policy considerations (other than the 'floodgates' argument, which I understand he rejects) which he would invoke to justify such a limit".

Lord Wilberforce, on the other hand, gave a clearer indication of where the bounds of liability should be drawn, stating (at 421–423):

". . . there remains, in my opinion, just because "shock" in its nature is capable of affecting so wide a range of people, a real need for the law to place some limitation upon the extent of admissible claims. It is necessary to consider three elements inherent in any claim: the class of persons whose claims should be recognised; the proximity of such persons to the accident; and the means by which the shock is caused. As regards the class of persons, the possible range is between the closest of family ties—of parent and child, or husband and wife—and the ordinary bystander. Existing law recognises the claims of the first: it denies that of the second, either on the basis that such persons must be assumed to be possessed of fortitude sufficient to enable them to endure the calamities of modern life, or that defendants cannot be expected to compensate the world at large. In my opinion these positions are justifiable, and since the present case falls within the first class, it is strictly unnecessary to say more. I think, however, that it should follow that other cases involving less close relationships must be very carefully scrutinised. I cannot say that they should never be admitted. The closer the tie (not merely the relationship, but in care) the greater the claim for consideration. The claim, in any case, has to be judged in the light of the other factors, such as proximity to the scene in time and place, and the nature of the accident.

As regards proximity to the accident it is obvious that this must be close in both time and space. It is, after all, the fact and consequences of the defendant's negligence that must be proved to have caused the "nervous shock." Experience has shown that to insist on direct and immediate sight or hearing would be impractical and unjust and that under what may be called the "aftermath" doctrine one who, from close proximity, comes very soon upon the scene should not be excluded. In my opinion, the result in *Benson v Lee* [1972] V.R. 879 [*an Australian case, where a mother recovered after rushing to the scene of an accident from her home which was 100 yards away*] was correct and indeed inescapable. It was based, soundly, upon:

> "direct perception of some of the events which go to make up the accident as an entire event, and this includes . . . the immediate aftermath . . ." (p.880.)

. . . Finally, and by way of reinforcement of "aftermath" cases, I would accept, by analogy with "rescue" situations, that a person of whom it could be said that one could expect nothing else than that he or she would come immediately to the scene—normally a parent or spouse—could be regarded as being within the scope of foresight and duty. Where there is not immediate presence, account must be taken of the possibility of alterations in the circumstances, for which the defendant should not be responsible.

Subject only to these qualifications, I think that a strict test of proximity by sight or hearing should be applied by the courts.

Lastly, as regards communication, there is no case in which the law has compensated shock brought about by communication by a third party. In *Hambrook v Stokes Brothers* [1925] 1 K.B. 141, indeed, it was said that liability would not arise in such a case and this is surely right. It was so decided [*by the Saskatchewan Court of Appeal*] in *Abramzik v Brenner* (1967) 65 D.L.R. (2d) 651. The shock must come through sight or hearing of the event or of its immediate aftermath. Whether some equivalent of sight or hearing, e.g. through simultaneous television, would suffice may have to be considered."

Since Lord Edmund-Davies gave no indication as to the nature of the policy considerations that should be taken into account nor any indication as to where the limits of liability should be drawn (see above), it cannot be ascertained whether his views accorded with those expressed above by Lord Wilberforce. Further, whilst Lord Wilberforce considered that policy considerations should limit or restrict the application of the reasonable foresight criterion, it may be that his views on this matter and on where the boundary of liability should be drawn were only obiter. This was certainly the view taken by Lord Oliver in *Alcock v Chief Constable of South Yorkshire* [1992] 1 A.C. 310 (*Alcock*) (see below, 15–010), since his Lordship stated (at 414) that Lord Wilberforce "found it, in the event, unnecessary to determine the boundary since the case then before the House concerned a claim within a category which had already been clearly established" and further stated (at 415) that Lord Wilberforce's remarks on the limits of liability "were, in any event, obiter since the question of fixing lines of demarcation by reference to public policy did not in fact arise".

At this point, it can be stated that two judges (Lords Bridge and Scarman) appeared to regard reasonable foresight unrestricted by policy considerations as the criterion to be applied and two judges (Lords Edmund-Davies and Wilberforce) considered that policy considerations should limit or restrict the application of the reasonable foresight criterion. The view of the one remaining judges, Lord Russell, was, therefore, critical in determining what might be considered to be the ratio of the case. Lord Russell's judgment, however, which is reproduced here in full, is a brief one. His Lordship recognised that policy considerations may have application in appropriate cases, but did not feel that policy considerations should limit or restrict the reasonable foresight criterion in the present case. He stated (at 429):

"My Lords, I make two comments at the outset. First: we are not concerned with any problems that might have been posed had the accident not been wholly attributable to the negligence of the respondents, but partly attributable to negligent driving by the injured son of the plaintiff.

Secondly: the plaintiff is to be regarded as of normal disposition or phlegm: we are therefore not concerned to investigate the applicability of the "thin skull" cases to this type of case.

The facts in this case, and the physical illness suffered by the plaintiff as a result of mental trauma caused to her by what she learned, heard and saw at the hospital, have been set out in the speech of my noble and learned friend, Lord Wilberforce, and I do not repeat them.

All members of the Court of Appeal concluded that that which happened to the plaintiff was reasonably foreseeable by the defendants as a consequence of their negligence on the road. (In some cases, and at all levels, a reasonable bystander seems to be introduced as a relevant mind: I do not understand why: reasonable foreseeability must surely be something to be attributed to the person guilty of negligence.)

But if the effect on this wife and mother of the results of negligence is considered to have been reasonably foreseeable, I do not see the justification for finding the defendants not liable for damages therefore. I would not shrink from regarding in an appropriate case policy as something which may feature in a judicial decision. But in this case what policy should inhibit a decision in favour of liability to the plaintiff? Negligent driving on the highway is only one form of negligence which may cause wounding or death and thus induce a relevant mental trauma in a person such as the plaintiff. There seems to be no policy requirement that the damage to the plaintiff be on or near the highway. In the last analysis any policy consideration seems to be rooted in a fear of floodgates opening—the tacit question "What next?" I am not impressed by that fear—certainly not sufficiently to deprive the plaintiff of just compensation for the reasonably foreseeable damage to her. I do not consider that such deprivation is justified by trying to answer in advance the question posed "What next?" by a consideration of relationships of plaintiff to the sufferers or deceased, or other circumstances: to attempt in advance solutions, or even guidelines, in hypothetical cases may well, it seems to me, in this field, do more harm than good.

I also would allow this appeal."

It might be questioned whether Lord Russell's views accorded more with those of Lords Bridge and Scarman or with those of Lords Edmund-Davies and Wilberforce. If they accorded more with the former, then the ratio of the case would appear to be that recovery for nervous shock is dependent on the criterion of reasonable foresight unrestricted by policy considerations. If they accorded more with the latter, the ratio of the case would appear to be that there are policy considerations which can and do limit the application of the reasonable foresight criterion, although only Lord Wilberforce gave any indication of what those limitations might be.

▶ 8. *Alcock v Chief Constable of South Yorkshire*

15–010 The case of *Alcock v Chief Constable of South Yorkshire* [1992] 1 A.C. 310 (*Alcock*) concerned an action by 16 plaintiffs who suffered nervous shock as a result of the Hillsborough football disaster, in which over 90 people were killed. The action was brought against the Chief Constable of South Yorkshire, who was responsible for policing arrangements at the football stadium. Virtually all of the plaintiffs were related in some way to persons killed or injured in the stadium, some being present in other parts of the ground, with others seeing television coverage of the incident.

At first instance, Hidden J., referring both to the judgments of Lord Wilberforce and Lord Bridge in *McLoughlin*, but without addressing the differences between them or what represented the ratio of the case, found in favour of 10 of the plaintiffs. Those entitled to recover were those who had a close relationship with the person killed or injured, that of parent and child, or of brother and sister, whether or not they had been present at the ground. Those with a less close relationship, such as grandparents and uncles, were not entitled to recover, even if present at the scene.

There was an appeal to the Court of Appeal by the six unsuccessful plaintiffs and by the defendants in respect of being held liable to 9 of the 10 plaintiffs. (The only case in respect of which the defendants did not appeal was that of William Pemberton, who had gone to the match with his son, who was one of those killed in the disaster, but had remained on the coach to watch the game on the coach's television.) The Court of Appeal, dismissing the appeals of the unsuccessful plaintiffs and allowing the defendants' appeals in respect of the nine successful plaintiffs, took the view that none of the plaintiffs was entitled to succeed. The court sought to confine the duty to cases both where there was a parent–child or husband–wife relationship and where there was close proximity in terms of time and space to the scene of the accident or its immediate aftermath. There was an appeal to the House of Lords by 10 of the 15 plaintiffs who had been unsuccessful in the Court of Appeal and the House affirmed the Court of Appeal's decision.

In reaching its decision to reject the plaintiffs' claims, the House did not make a clear pronouncement on the ratio of *McLoughlin* and did not decisively resolve the differences in approach which had been evident in that case. Indeed, as in *McLoughlin* itself, there were variations in approach in their Lordships' speeches in

Alcock. Neither Lord Ackner nor Lord Jauncey specifically addressed the issue of the ratio of *McLoughlin*, although both decisively rejected the reasonable foresight criterion simpliciter for establishing a duty of care (see 401–402 and 419 respectively) and the tenor of both judgments seemed to be in favour of Lord Wilberforce's approach. Indeed, Lord Jauncey in his judgment, when considering *McLoughlin*, referred only to the speech of Lord Wilberforce and not to any other member of the House in that case. Further, Lord Keith may perhaps have regarded the approach of Lord Wilberforce as representing the ratio, for he stated (at 395–396):

"The leading speech [*in McLoughlin*] was delivered by Lord Wilberforce . . . [*who*] expressed the opinion that foreseeability did not of itself and automatically give rise to a duty of care owed to a person or class of persons and that considerations of policy entered into the conclusion that such a duty existed.

. . . Lord Bridge of Harwich, with whom Lord Scarman agreed, at p.431D–E, appears to have rested his finding of liability simply on the test of reasonable foreseeability of psychiatric illness affecting the plaintiff as a result of the consequences of the road accident, at pp.439–443. Lord Edmund-Davies and Lord Russell of Killowen both considered the policy arguments which led the Court of Appeal to dismiss the plaintiff's claim to be unsound: pp. 428, 429. Neither speech contained anything inconsistent with that of Lord Wilberforce."

Lord Oliver, without expressing agreement with Lord Keith's judgment, appeared to hold a similar view, for he stated (at 413–414):

"The principal argument in the appeal has centred round the question whether, as the plaintiffs contend, the decision of this House in *McLoughlin v O'Brian* [1983] 1 A.C. 410 establishes as the criterion of a duty owed by the defendants to the plaintiff a simple test of the foreseeability of injury of the type in fact sustained or whether, as the defendant maintains, the case imports also a necessary requirement, either as a matter of public policy or as a measure of proximity, of the existence of some close blood or marital relationship between the appellants and the victims of the negligent conduct . . . In this House, although the members of the Committee were unanimous in allowing the appeal, the speeches displayed distinct differences of approach. All were agreed that actually witnessing or being present at or near the scene of an accident was not essential to ground liability in an appropriate case, but that the duty might equally be owed to one who comes upon the immediate aftermath of the event. Thus such a person, given always the reasonable foreseeability of the injury in fact sustained and of such persons witnessing it, may be within the area of proximity in which a duty of care may be found to exist.

The diversity of view arose at the next stage, that is to say that of ascertaining whether the relationship between the plaintiff and the primary victim was such as to support the existence of such a duty. That can be expressed in various ways. It may be asked whether, as a matter of the policy of the law, a relationship outside the categories of those in which liability has been established by past decisions can be considered sufficiently proximate to give rise to the duty, quite regardless of the question of foreseeability. Or it may be asked whether the injury of the type with which these appeals are concerned can ever be considered to be reasonably foreseeable where the relationship between the plaintiff and the primary victim is more remote than that of an established category. Or, again, it may be asked whether, even given proximity and foreseeability, nevertheless, the law must draw an arbitrary line at the boundary of the established category or some other wider or narrower category of relationship beyond which no duty will be deemed to exist. Lord Wilberforce, at p.422, appears to have favoured the last of these three approaches, but found it, in the event, unnecessary to determine the boundary since the case then before the House concerned a claim within a category which had already been clearly established . . . The approach of Lord Edmund-Davies and Lord Russell of Killowen, as I read their speeches, was similar to that of Lord Wilberforce. On the other hand, Lord Bridge of Harwich, with whom Lord Scarmen agreed, rejected an appeal to policy considerations as a justification for fixing arbitrary lines of demarcation of the duty in negligence."

Lord Lowry did not himself deliver a judgment—his Lordship contented himself with remarking that he had enjoyed the advantage of reading in draft the speeches of other members of the House and did not consider it would be helpful to add any further observations of his own—but concurred in the unanimous conclusion of the House that the appeals should be dismissed.

There thus seemed to be a large measure of support from members of the House in *Alcock* for the views of Lord Wilberforce in *McLoughlin* and certainly no dissent from the approach which Lord Wilberforce had adopted. The criterion of reasonable foresight simpliciter was rejected, which appeared to indicate a lack of support for the approach of Lord Bridge in *McLoughlin*, although Lord Oliver (at 415) did make some attempt to reconcile Lord Bridge's approach with that of Lord Wilberforce.

Whilst the House in *Alcock* generally followed the approach of Lord Wilberforce in *McLoughlin* that policy considerations should limit the application of the reasonable foresight criterion, no member of the House sought to establish particular policy limitations in respect of the class of persons entitled to make a claim. Thus, for example, Lord Keith stated (at 397):

"I would not seek to limit the class by reference to particular relationships such as husband and wife or parent and child. The kinds of relationship which may involve close ties of love and affection are numerous, and it is the existence of such ties which leads to mental disturbance when the loved one suffers a catastrophe. They may be present in family relationships or those of close friendship, and may be stronger in the case of engaged couples than in that of persons who have been married to each other for many years. It is common knowledge that such ties exist, and reasonably foreseeable that those bound by them may in certain circumstances be at real risk of psychiatric illness if the loved one is injured or put in peril. The closeness of the tie would, however, require to be proved by a plaintiff, though no doubt being capable of being presumed in appropriate cases. The case of a bystander unconnected with the victims of an accident is difficult. Psychiatric injury to him would not be ordinarily, in my view, within the range of reasonable foreseeability, but could not perhaps be entirely excluded from it if the circumstances of a catastrophe occurring very close to him were particularly horrific."

Similarly, Lord Oliver stated (at 415–416):

"I see no logic and no virtue in seeking to lay down as a matter of "policy" categories of relationship within which claims may succeed and without which they are doomed to failure in limine. So rigid an approach would, I think, work great injustice and cannot be rationally justified . . . That is not, of course, to say that the closeness of the relationship between plaintiff and primary victim is irrelevant, but the likelihood or unlikelihood of a person in that relationship suffering shock of the degree claimed from the event must be a most material factor to be taken into account in determining whether that consequence was reasonably foreseeable."

Again, Lord Jauncey stated (at 422):

"I would respectfully agree with Lord Wilberforce [*in McLoughlin*] that cases involving less close relatives should be very carefully scrutinised. That, however, is not to say that they should necessarily be excluded. The underlying logic of allowing claims of parents and spouses is that it can readily be foreseen by the tortfeasor that if they were involved in the immediate aftermath of a serious accident or disaster, they would, because of their close relationship of love and affection with the victim be likely to suffer from nervous shock. There may, however, be others whose ties of relationship are just as strong. I do not consider that it would be profitable to try and define who such others might be or to draw a dividing line between one degree of relationship and another. To draw such a line would necessarily be arbitrary and lacking in logic. In my view the proper approach is to examine each case on its own facts in order to see whether a claimant has established so close a relationship of love and affection to the victim as might be reasonably expected in the case of spouses, parents and children."

However, policy limitations were adopted in respect of the proximity of the plaintiff to the accident and the means by which the shock was caused. Liability was restricted to those in close proximity to the accident in terms of time and space, and to those who suffered nervous shock as a result of direct or immediate sight or hearing of the accident or of its immediate aftermath. The point was considered in some detail by Lord Oliver, who stated (at 416–417):

"The necessary element of proximity between plaintiff and defendant is furnished, at least in part, by both physical and temporal propinquity and also by the sudden and direct visual impression on the plaintiff's mind of actually witnessing the event or its immediate aftermath . . . In my opinion, the necessary proximity cannot be said to exist where the elements of immediacy, closeness of time and space, and direct visual or aural perception are absent. I would agree with the view expressed by Nolan L.J. [*in the Court of Appeal*] that there may well be circumstances where the element of visual perception may be provided by witnessing the actual injury to the primary victim on simultaneous television, but that is not the case in any of the instant appeals and . . . the televised images seen by the various plaintiffs cannot be equiparated [*sic*] with "sight or hearing of the event." Nor did they provide the degree of immediacy required to sustain a claim for damages for nervous shock . . . the shock in each case arose not from the original impact of the transmitted image, which did not . . . depict the suffering of recognisable individuals. These images provided no doubt the matrix for imagined consequences, giving rise to grave concern and worry, followed by a dawning consciousness over an extended period that the imagined consequence had occurred, finally confirmed by news of the death, and in some cases, subsequent visual identification of the victim. The trauma is created in part by such confirmation and in part by the linkage in the mind of the plaintiff of that confirmation to the previously absorbed image. To extend the notion of proximity in cases of immediately created nervous shock to this more elongated and, to some extent, retrospective process may seem a logical analogical [*sic*] development. But, as I shall endeavour to show, the law in this area is not wholly logical and whilst having every sympathy with the plaintiffs . . . I cannot for my part see any pressing reason of policy for taking this further step along a road which must ultimately lead to virtually limitless liability."

In conclusion, therefore, the ratio of *Alcock* would appear to be that, where a plaintiff suffers nervous shock through witnessing an incident involving other persons, a duty of care is owed to the plaintiff to avoid causing nervous shock where:

(a) it can reasonably be foreseen that the plaintiff will suffer nervous shock;
(b) there is a sufficiently proximate relationship between plaintiff and defendant based on ties of love and affection, proximity not being limited as a matter of policy by reference to particular relationships; and
(c) there is sufficient proximity to the accident in terms of time and space, proximity being limited as a matter of policy to those who suffer nervous shock through direct or immediate sight or hearing of the accident or of its immediate aftermath.

▶ 9. *Page v Smith*

In *Page v Smith* [1996] A.C. 155, the plaintiff, whilst driving his car, was involved in a **15–011** collision with the defendant's car due to the latter's negligent driving. The plaintiff was physically unhurt in the collision, but, as a direct result of the accident, suffered nervous shock. A condition from which the plaintiff suffered (myalgic encephalomyelitis, or post viral fatigue syndrome) became chronic and permanent, and he was unable to work again. Otton J., at first instance, took the view that the nervous shock cases had no relevance because the plaintiff was not a spectator of the accident who suffered shock from what he witnessed happening to another, but was directly involved and suffered shock directly from experiencing the accident. Since physical injury to the plaintiff was clearly foreseeable, although in the event it did not occur, the defendant was held liable on the "take your victim as you find him" principle. His Lordship accordingly did not consider the question of whether the defendant should have foreseen injury by nervous shock.

The defendant appealed to the Court of Appeal ([1994] 4 All E.R. 522), contending, inter alia, that Otton J., in deciding that the plaintiff's injury was foreseeable, had: (a) wrongly failed to consider whether a person of reasonable fortitude would have suffered nervous shock from the accident as it occurred; and (b) wrongly determined that foreseeability of injury from nervous shock was not necessary in the case of a plaintiff who had been directly involved in the accident and was not a mere spectator. It was contended that the "take your victim as you find him" principle did not apply when foreseeability was being considered, where the court was always judging matters on the basis of a person of reasonable fortitude, and applied only at a later stage when damages were being considered. It applied only where it could be shown that some damage was foreseeable and its effect was to make the defendant liable for all damage, whether or not its precise nature and extent were foreseeable. It was further contended that foreseeability of injury from nervous shock was necessary in all cases, there being no difference in this respect between the case of a spectator and a person directly involved in an event, except that the consequences were more likely to be foreseeable in the case of the latter than the former.

These contentions were accepted by the Court of Appeal. The court took the view that the question of whether injury by nervous shock was reasonably foreseeable needed to be considered in all cases and went on to hold that, in the circumstances, injury by nervous shock was not reasonably foreseeable in a person of ordinary fortitude as a result of what happened to the plaintiff. Accordingly, the defendant's appeal was allowed. Thereupon the plaintiff appealed to the House of Lords, where the point at issue was stated succinctly by Lord Keith (at [1996] A.C. 155, 167):

> "The question primarily at issue is whether in claims for damages due to nervous shock it is in all cases incumbent upon the plaintiff to prove that injury by nervous shock was reasonably foreseeable by the defendant, or whether it

suffices, where the plaintiff was himself involved in an accident, for him to prove that personal injury of some kind was reasonably foreseeable as a result of it. The trial judge took the latter view but the Court of Appeal unanimously took the former."

The House of Lords, by a 3–2 majority, allowed the appeal and held that, in the case of those involved in an accident, reasonable foresight of physical injury was sufficient to enable a plaintiff to recover damages for nervous shock. Although reasonable foresight of nervous shock was required in the case of persons who witnessed an accident or came upon its aftermath ("secondary victims"), it was not required in the case of participants who were directly involved in an accident ("primary victims"). The leading judgment of the majority was delivered by Lord Lloyd (with whose judgment Lords Ackner and Browne-Wilkinson expressed agreement). His Lordship referred to the three previous House of Lords' decisions in *Bourhill, McLoughlin* and *Alcock* and stated (at 184):

"In all these cases the plaintiff was the secondary victim of the defendant's negligence. He or she was in the position of a spectator or bystander. In the present case, by contrast, the plaintiff was a participant. He was himself directly involved in the accident, and well within the range of foreseeable physical injury. He was the primary victim. This is thus the first occasion on which your Lordships have had to decide whether, in such a case, the foreseeability of physical injury is enough to enable the plaintiff to recover damages for nervous shock.

The factual distinction between primary and secondary victims of an accident is obvious and of long standing. It was recognised by Lord Russell of Killowen in *Bourhill v Young* [1943] A.C. 92, when he pointed out that Mrs. Bourhill was not physically involved in the collision . . . In *Alcock*'s case [1992] 1 A.C. 310 . . . Lord Oliver of Aylmerton said, at p.407, of cases in which damages are claimed for nervous shock:

"Broadly they divide into two categories, that is to say, those cases in which the injured plaintiff was involved, either mediately, or immediately, as a participant, and those in which the plaintiff was no more than the passive and unwilling witness of injury caused to others."

Later in the same speech, at pp.410–411, he referred to those who are involved in an accident as the primary victims, and to those who are not directly involved, but who suffer from what they see or hear, as the secondary victims. This is, in my opinion, the most convenient and appropriate terminology.

Though the distinction between primary and secondary victims is a factual one, it has, as will be seen, important legal consequences. So the classification of all nervous shock cases under the same head may be misleading."

His Lordship went on to state (at 187):

"I must say at once that I prefer the simplicity of the judge's approach to what, with respect, seems to be an unnecessary complication introduced by the Court of Appeal. Foreseeability of psychiatric injury remains a crucial ingredient when the plaintiff is the secondary victim, for the very reason that the secondary victim is almost always outside the area of physical impact, and therefore outside the range of foreseeable physical injury. But where the plaintiff is the primary victim of the defendant's negligence, the nervous shock cases, by which I mean the cases following on from *Bourhill v Young*, are not in point. Since the defendant was admittedly under a duty not to cause the plaintiff foreseeable physical injury, it was unnecessary to ask whether he was under a separate duty of care not to cause foreseeable psychiatric injury."

The case of *Bourhill* and subsequent decisions, regarded as "not in point", were thus effectively distinguished (although the headnote to the case merely records that *Bourhill* and other cases, e.g. *McLoughlin*, were "considered"). A material fact in those cases was that the plaintiff was a secondary victim, a fact which was absent in the present case. Further, considerations of policy, relevant in those cases to limit the potential number of claimants, had no application where primary victims suffered nervous shock. Lord Lloyd continued (at 189):

"Are there any disadvantages in taking the simple approach adopted by Otton J.? It may be said that it would open the door too wide . . . a very important consideration in claims by secondary victims. It is for this reason that the courts have, as a matter of policy, rightly insisted on a number of control mechanisms. Otherwise, a negligent defendant might find himself being made liable to all the world. Thus in the case of secondary victims, forseeability of injury by shock is not enough. The law also requires a degree of proximity . . . This means not only proximity to the event in time and space, but also proximity of relationship between the primary victim and the secondary victim. A further control mechanism is that the secondary victim will only recover damages for nervous shock if the defendant should have foreseen injury by shock to a person of normal fortitude or "ordinary phlegm."

None of these mechanisms are required in the case of a primary victim. Since liability depends on forseeability of physical injury, there could be no question of the defendant finding himself liable to all the world. Proximity of relationship cannot arise and proximity in time and space goes without saying.

Nor in the case of the primary victim is it appropriate to ask whether he is a person of "ordinary phlegm". In the case of physical injury there is no such requirement. The negligent defendant, or more usually his insurer, takes his victim as he finds him. There is no difference in principle, as Geoffrey Lane J. pointed out in *Malcolm v Broadhurst* [1970] 3 All E.R. 508, between an eggshell skull and an eggshell personality. Since the number of potential claimants is limited by the nature of the case, there is no need to impose any further limit by reference to the person of ordinary phlegm. Nor can I see any justification for doing so."

Having reached the provisional conclusion that Otton J.'s approach was correct, Lord Lloyd proceeded to examine previous authorities "to see if there was anything which supports the contrary view taken by the Court of Appeal" (at 190). His Lordship (at 190) was of the view that:

"All the dicta which appear to support the contrary view are to be found in cases where the plaintiff was a secondary victim, and they almost all go back to an observation of Denning L.J. in *King v Phillips* [1953] 1 Q.B. 429, 441, an observation which has very frequently been repeated, but has often, I suspect, been misunderstood."

Lord Lloyd stated (at 193):

". . . Denning L.J.'s celebrated dictum at p.441 [*is*]:

"Howsoever that may be, whether the exemption for shock be based on want of duty or on remoteness, there can be no doubts [*sic*] that since *Bourhill v Young* that the test of liability for shock is foreseeability of injury by shock."

The danger of any good phrase is that it gets repeated so often and applied so uncritically that in the end it tends to distort the law. Denning L.J.'s dictum is wrong in two respects. It is both too wide and too narrow. It is too wide where the plaintiff is a secondary victim, as she was in *King v Phillips*. For subsequent cases have shown that foreseeability of injury by shock is not the sole test: see *Alcock*'s case [1992] 1 A.C. 310, 396, *per* Lord Keith . . . The test is also too narrow, where, as here, the plaintiff is the primary victim. There is nothing in *Bourhill v Young* to displace the ordinary rule that where the plaintiff is within the range of foreseeable physical injury the defendant must take his victim as he finds him. The whole point of *Bourhill v Young* was that the plaintiff was *not* within the range of foreseeable physical injury. She was not "involved" in the collision. There was, therefore, no way that she could recover damages unless she could show that the defendant ought to have foreseen injury by shock. It is only in that limited sense that it was ever true to say that liability for shock depends on foreseeability of injury by shock. The dictum has no application where the plaintiff is the primary victim of the defendant's negligence."

Decisions considered by Lord Lloyd, in which reference had been made to Denning L.J.'s dictum, included two Australian cases, *Mount Isa Mines Ltd v Pusey* (1970) 125 C.L.R. 383; and *Jaensch v Coffey* (1984) 155 C.L.R. 549; and a decision of the Privy Council, *Overseas Tankship (UK) Ltd v Morts Dock & Engineering Co Ltd (The Wagon Mound)* [1961] A.C. 388. The last-mentioned decision, which established that the essential factor in determining liability is whether the damage in question (in the case itself, damage by fire) is of such a kind as the reasonable man should have foreseen, was, like the Australian cases, not binding on the House. This would be so even if approval of Denning L.J.'s dictum formed part of the ratio of the case. It was, however, regarded as "perhaps the strongest authority supporting the view taken [*in the present case*] by the Court of Appeal" (at 195). Nevertheless, Lord Lloyd was of the view that the Privy Council's approval of Denning L.J.'s dictum should not be regarded as endorsing its general application. He stated (at 196):

"Viscount Simonds, in tendering the advice of the Privy Council . . . in the course of his judgment, at p.426, . . . cited . . . the dictum of Denning L.J. in *King v Phillips* [1953] 1 Q.B. 429, 441, and added: "Their Lordships substitute the word 'fire' for 'shock' and endorse this statement of the law."

Viscount Simonds did not attempt to define what he meant by "kind of damage" and the concept is apt to be elusive, as Mr. R.W.M. Dias and Professor Jolowicz have pointed out in their comments [1961] C.L.J. 23–30: see also *Clerk and Linsdell on Torts*, 16th ed. (1989), at pp. 587–588. It is clear that Viscount Simonds regarded shock as a "kind of damage." Otherwise, he would not have cited Denning L.J.'s dictum. But the case was not in any way concerned with liability for shock . . . I do not think that the Privy Council was intending to indicate that Denning L.J.'s dictum applied across the board in personal injury actions, or that psychiatric injury is a "different kind of damage" from physical injury, for the purposes of establishing the relevant duty of care. Although the Privy Council in *The Wagon Mound* has often been regarded as having approved the full width of Denning L.J.'s dictum, I consider this goes too far . . . I prefer to regard the reference to the dictum as being more by way of illustration. If so, then it does not stand in the way of a sensible and practical approach to cases where the plaintiff is the primary victim of the defendant's negligence, along the lines proposed by the judge."

His Lordship accordingly upheld the trial judge's approach that the defendant need only have reasonably foreseen that the plaintiff might suffer physical injury as a result of his negligence and it was not necessary that he should have reasonably foreseen injury by shock. In concluding his judgment, Lord Lloyd stated (at 197):

". . . the following propositions can be supported. 1. In cases involving nervous shock, it is essential to distinguish between the primary victim and secondary victims. 2. In claims by secondary victims the law insists on certain control mechanisms, in order as a matter of policy to limit the number of potential claimants. Thus the defendant will not be liable unless psychiatric injury is foreseeable in a person of normal fortitude. These control mechanisms have no place where the plaintiff is the primary victim. 3. In claims by secondary victims, it may be legitimate to use hindsight in order to be able to apply the test of reasonable foreseeability at all. Hindsight, however, has no part to play where the plaintiff is the primary victim. 4. Subject to the above qualifications, the approach in all cases should be the same, namely, whether the defendant can reasonably foresee that his conduct will expose the plaintiff to the risk of personal injury, whether physical or psychiatric. If the answer is yes, then the duty of care is established . . ."

Lords Keith and Jauncey, dissenting, referred to observations in several decided cases, which, in their opinion, supported the view that foresight of nervous shock was required in all cases. Particular reference was made to Denning L.J.'s dictum in *King* and its approval in *The Wagon Mound*, as well as two decisions of the Australian High Court–*Mount Isa Mines Ltd v Pusey* (1970) 125 C.L.R. 383; and *Jaensch v Coffey* (1984) 155 C.L.R. 549–to which Lord Lloyd had alluded. Referring to these Australian decisions, Lord Jauncey stated (at 173) that "as is often the case in the field of negligence valuable contributions to the discussion are to be found in judgments of the High Court of Australia" and also went on to make reference to a decision of the Supreme Court of California, *Dillon v Legg* (1968) 29 A.L.R. 3d 1316. The requirement of foresight of nervous shock, supported by these authorities, was regarded as being of general application and not confined to secondary victims such as bystanders. Lord Jauncey stated (at 175–176):

> "It was urged upon your Lordships that all these cases involved bystanders as opposed to participants and that they were therefore not relevant to the present appeal where the appellant was directly involved in the collision. I reject this submission for two reasons. In the first place, in none of the judgments was it suggested that the need to prove foreseeability of nervous shock was other than a general requirement applicable to all cases where damages therefor were claimed . . . In the second place, foreseeability of injury is necessary to determine whether a duty is owed to the victim. Unless such injury can be foreseen the victim is not a neighbour within the celebrated dictum of Lord Atkin in *Donoghue v Stevenson* [1932] A.C. 562 and cannot recover . . . I have no doubt that the Court of Appeal were correct to conclude that the appellant could only succeed if he could demonstrate that nervous shock giving rise to some form of psychiatric illness was a foreseeable consequence of the respondent's negligence."

Thus, Lords Keith and Jauncey did not regard these decisions as distinguishable and, like the Court of Appeal, were of the view that nervous shock was not reasonably foreseeable in the circumstances, so the plaintiff was not entitled to recover. The majority, however, held that, in the case of primary victims of an accident, proof of reasonable foresight of personal injury of some kind, whether physical or psychiatric, was sufficient. Since proof of physical injury was foreseeable, the plaintiff was entitled to recover. The difference between the majority and minority approaches essentially seems to be the view taken of the ratio of cases such as *Bourhill* and subsequent decisions. The majority appear to have taken a narrower view of the ratio, regarding the principles in those cases as applicable only where the plaintiff was a secondary victim, and the minority a broader view, considering that the principles applied irrespective of whether the plaintiff was a primary or secondary victim. As for the ratio of *Page v Smith* itself, this would appear to be that where a person is a primary victim of an accident and suffers nervous shock, it is sufficient if he is within the range of foreseeable physical injury and it need not be foreseeable that he will suffer nervous shock (since this and other control mechanisms apply only in respect of secondary victims).

▶ 10. *White v Chief Constable of South Yorkshire*

The case of *White v Chief Constable of South Yorkshire* [1998] 3 W.L.R. 1509 (*White*), **15-012**
sometimes referred to as *Frost v Chief Constable of South Yorkshire* (as, for
example, in *Grieves v F T Everard & Sons Ltd* [2008] 1 A.C. 281–see below, 15-020),
concerned an action by 39 plaintiffs, all of whom were serving police officers on
duty at the time of the Hillsborough football disaster and who suffered nervous
shock as a result of tending victims at the tragedy. The defendant in the action was
the Chief Constable of South Yorkshire, who was responsible for policing
arrangements at the football stadium. Five plaintiffs, four of whom had been on
duty at the stadium, with the fifth (Sgt Janet Smith) responsible for stripping
bodies and completing casualty forms at a hospital, were selected as representative of the various roles carried out by the remaining claimants.

At first instance, Waller J. dismissed the plaintiffs' claims. His Lordship rejected the
argument that the plaintiffs could recover damages as primary victims simply on
the basis that the defendant was in breach of the duty of care owed by him to the
police officers which was analogous to that owed by an employer to his employees.
(Police officers constitutionally hold an office rather than being employed under
contract by their Chief Constable, so the relationship is analogous to, rather than
one of, employer–employee.) He held that a relationship analogous to employer
and employee existed between plaintiffs and defendant, giving rise to a duty of
care embracing nervous shock, but that duty did not arise where the police officer
was a secondary victim, unless he could succeed as a rescuer (on which, see
Chadwick, above, 15–009) and such a duty could not place a police officer in a
better position than a bystander. He further held that, where police officers were
carrying out a rescue operation, they were to be regarded as professional rescuers
and a duty was owed only where they were intimately participating in the incident
or its immediate aftermath. Applying these principles, his Lordship held that all of
the plaintiffs' claims must fail. They could not establish that they were primary
victims on the basis of their employment relationship and (as secondary victims)
were owed no duty since, except in the case of one plaintiff (Inspector Henry
White), they were not carrying out a rescue operation. Inspector White, however,
who had joined the end of the line bringing victims out of the pens, although a
rescuer, was not intimately participating in the incident or its immediate aftermath
and so did not fall within the scope of the duty owed to professional rescuers.

The Court of Appeal ([1998] Q.B. 254), by a majority, allowed the appeals of the
four plaintiffs who had been on duty at the stadium, but dismissed the appeal of
Sgt Smith. The majority held that a duty of care embracing nervous shock was
owed to persons who were directly involved as participants as a result of their
employment relationship (which essentially made them primary victims.) This duty
was owed to all four plaintiffs who had been on duty at the stadium. Further,
rescuers (whether professional rescuers or not) were a special category and were
owed a duty since they were also directly involved as participants (and thus
essentially were primary victims). This duty was owed only to three of the four

plaintiffs on duty at the stadium, however, for one plaintiff (P.C. Glave) "was not a rescuer because he was not involved in the incident at the pens end of the ground or its immediate aftermath" (per Rose L.J. at 267). No duty at all, however, was owed to Sgt Smith as a result of the employment relationship, since this did not extend to those who were outside the area of risk where the incident occurred, nor (as was conceded) was she a rescuer to whom a duty was owed. Judge L.J. dissented, taking the view that, if a duty was to be owed to the plaintiffs as primary victims, then, in accordance with the view of Lord Lloyd in *Page v Smith*, they needed to be within the range of physical injury. None of the plaintiffs was at any time present in an area where they were exposed to the (actual or apprehended) risk of physical injury and this made them secondary victims to whom control mechanisms (or policy limitations) applied. As such, proximity (of relationship, time and space) needed to be established and this was lacking.

There was an appeal by the defendant to the House of Lords and the House, by a majority, allowed the appeal. As in the lower courts, arguments focused on whether the plaintiffs were primary or secondary victims in accordance with the classification adopted in *Page v Smith*, in the light of their employment relationship with the defendant and their actions as rescuers. In essence, whether or not the plaintiffs were primary victims, and thus not subject to the control mechanisms, depended on the scope of that category. The plaintiffs were not directly injured in an accident in the same way that the plaintiff had been in *Page v Smith* and were not within the range of foreseeable physical injury, but equally they were not merely secondary victims who were in the position of a spectator or bystander. Were primary victims only those who were within the range of foreseeable physical injury and all other victims (including the plaintiffs) were secondary victims, or could primary victims extend beyond this (to include the plaintiffs), with secondary victims restricted to spectators or bystanders? Whether the plaintiffs were to be included within the category of primary victims, to whom a duty was owed, would depend on whether they could so be regarded on the basis of their employment relationship with the defendant and/or their actions as rescuers. As will be seen, different views were expressed on these issues.

The judgments of their Lordships are not particularly conducive to easy analysis and the following structure of considering the employment argument and the rescue argument in favour of a duty, in each instance under the existing law and as a matter of policy, is advanced with a degree of caution. In particular, when making reference to a point made in a particular judgment, it has been felt necessary on occasions, in order to facilitate understanding, to make reference in parentheses to whether persons might be primary or secondary victims, although these terms may not have been used expressly in respect of that point in the judgment.

▷ *(a) The employment argument*

15–013 A 4–1 majority of the House (Lord Goff dissenting) held that the plaintiffs were not owed a duty (as primary victims) by virtue of their employment relationship. For the majority, the leading judgments were delivered by Lords Steyn and Hoffmann (with whose judgments Lord Browne-Wilkinson expressed agreement), and there was a relatively short judgment by Lord Griffiths. All three of the substantive majority judgments addressed the matter both from the point of view of whether a duty might be owed under the existing law and whether a duty should, as a matter of policy, be owed.

(i) A duty under the existing law

Lord Steyn was clearly of the view that no duty was owed to the plaintiffs as **15–014** primary victims, since such victims encompassed only those within the range of foreseeable physical injury, and the ordinary rules of the law of tort which contained restrictions (relating to secondary victims) applied in respect of the employment relationship. After referring (at 1543) to the House's decision in *Alcock* and the increasing influence of (restrictive) policy considerations ("since *McLoughlin's* case [1983] 1 A.C. 410 the pendulum has swung and the House of Lords have taken greater account of policy considerations both in regard to economic loss and psychiatric injury"), his Lordship stated (at 1544–1545):

> "The decision of the House of Lords in *Page v Smith* [1996] A.C. 155 was the next important development in this branch of the law. The plaintiff was directly involved in a motor car accident. He was within the range of potential physical injury. As a result of the accident he suffered from chronic fatigue syndrome. In this context Lord Lloyd of Berwick adopted a distinction between primary and secondary victims: Lord Ackner and Lord Browne-Wilkinson agreed. Lord Lloyd said that a plaintiff who had been within the range of foreseeable injury was a primary victim. Mr. Page fulfilled this requirement and could in principle recover compensation for psychiatric loss. In my view it follows that all other victims, who suffer pure psychiatric harm, are secondary victims and must satisfy the control mechanisms laid down in the *Alcock* case. There has been criticism of this classification: see H. Teff, "Liability for Negligently Inflicted Psychiatric Harm: Justifications and Boundaries" [1998] C.L.J. 91, 93. But, if the narrow formulation by Lord Lloyd of Berwick of who may be a primary victim is kept in mind, this classification ought not to produce inconsistent results. In any event, the decision of the House of Lords in *Page v Smith* [1996] A.C. 155 was plainly intended, in the context of pure psychiatric harm, to narrow the range of potential secondary victims. The reasoning of Lord Lloyd and the Law Lords who agreed with him was based on concerns about an ever widening circle of plaintiffs.
>
> . . . The argument was that the present case can be decided on conventional employer's liability principles . . . [*and*] the duty of an employer to care for the safety of his employees and to take reasonable steps to safeguard them from harm. When analysed this argument breaks down. It is a non sequitur to say that because an employer is under a duty to an employee not to cause him physical injury, the employer should as a necessary consequence of that duty (of which there is no breach) be under a duty not to cause the employee

psychiatric injury: see Chris Hilton, "Nervous Shock and the Categorisation of Victims" (1998) 6 Tort L.Rev. 37, 42. The rules to be applied when an employee brings an action against his employer for harm suffered at his workplace are the rules of tort. One is therefore thrown back to the ordinary rules of the law of tort, which contain restrictions on the recovery of compensation for psychiatric harm. This way of putting the case does not therefore advance the case of the police officers."

Lord Hoffmann, unlike Lord Steyn, appeared to leave open the question of whether primary victims were confined to those within the range of foreseeable physical injury. His Lordship recognised the equivocal nature of the remarks in *Page*, stating (at 1551):

"The plaintiffs say they were primary victims because they were not "spectators or bystanders." The defendants say the plaintiffs were secondary victims because they were not "within the range of foreseeable physical injury." Both arguments have some support from the speeches in *Page v Smith* [1996] A.C. 155 . . ."

There was, however, a similar acknowledgement of a more restrictive approach in recent years based on policy considerations (or control mechanisms). Lord Hoffmann stated (at 1548–1549):

"For a long time during this century, it remained unclear whether the basis of liability for causing a recognised psychiatric illness was simply a question of foreseeability of that type of injury in the same way as in the case of physical injury . . . [and] if the foreseeability test was to be taken literally and applied in the same way as the test for liability for physical injury, it would be hard to know where the limits of liability could be drawn . . .

There was a time when it seemed that English law might arrive at this position. It came within a hair's breadth of doing so in *McLoughlin v O'Brian* [1983] 1 A.C. 410, one of those cases in which one feels that a slight change in the composition of the Appellate Committee would have set the law on a different course. But the moment passed and when the question next came before your Lordships' House in *Alcock v Chief Constable of South Yorkshire Police* [1992] 1 A.C. 310, judicial attitudes had changed . . . The House decided that liability for psychiatric injury should be restricted by what Lord Lloyd of Berwick (in *Page v Smith* [1996] A.C. 155, 189) afterwards called "control mechanisms," that is to say more or less arbitrary conditions which a plaintiff had to satisfy and which were intended to keep liability within what was regarded as acceptable bounds."

This passage is instructive as a candid recognition that the outcome of a case may well depend on factors other than previous judicial authorities (or legislative provisions). The outcome may depend on "the composition of the Appellate Committee" (or equally the composition of any other court), i.e. the views of the judges hearing the case, and "more or less arbitrary conditions . . . which were intended to keep liability within . . . acceptable bounds". Having referred to these conditions, his Lordship went on to consider critical views expressed in respect of them by academic authors and by the Law Commission, as well as radical suggestions for reform, although acknowledging that these suggestions could not be adopted by the House in its judicial capacity. Lord Hoffmann stated (at 1550–1551):

> "The position which the law has reached as a result of *Alcock v Chief Constable of South Yorkshire Police* [1992] 1 A.C. 310 has not won universal approval. The control mechanisms have been criticised as drawing distinctions which the ordinary man would find hard to understand. Jane Stapleton has said that the mother who suffers psychiatric injury after finding her child's mangled body in a mortuary "might wonder why the law rules her child's blood too dry to found an action:" see "In Restraint of Tort" in *The Frontiers of Liability*, p.84. Equally, the spectacle of a plaintiff who has, ex hypothesi, suffered psychiatric illness in consequence of his brother's death or injury, being cross-examined on the closeness of their ties of love and affection and then perhaps contradicted by the evidence of a private investigator might not be to everyone's taste: see the Law Commission Report on Liability for Psychiatric Illness (Law Com. No. 249), para. 6.24.
>
> Academic writers have made contradictory but equally radical suggestions for reform. Mullany and Handford, in their excellent book *Tort Liability for Psychiatric Damage*, advocate getting rid of the control mechanisms and, in the light of advances in psychiatric knowledge, equating psychiatric injury to physical injury. Jane Stapleton, on the other hand, would abolish recovery for psychiatric injury altogether and revert to the law as stated in *Victorian Railway Commissioners v Coultas*, 13 App.Cas. 222: see the article to which I have already referred.
>
> . . . The Law Commission in its recent Report No. 249 inclines somewhat to the Mullany and Handford point of view by recommending that the condition of close ties of love and affection for secondary victims be retained in a modified form but that the other two [*presence at the accident or its immediate aftermath, and psychiatric injury being caused by direct perception of the accident or its immediate aftermath*] be abolished.
>
> . . . But . . . neither of the radical solutions, or indeed the Law Commission solution, is open to your Lordships. It is too late to go back on the control mechanisms as stated in the *Alcock* case [1992] 1 A.C. 310. Until there is legislative change, the courts must live with them and any judicial developments must take them into account."

As to the claim to primary status on the part of the plaintiffs based on the employment relationship, Lord Hoffmann (at 1553–1554), unlike Lord Steyn, examined existing case law on which reliance had been placed to support the existence of a duty:

"The plaintiffs rely upon four cases as establishing the right of an employee to recover for psychiatric injury caused by witnessing or apprehending injury which his employer's negligence has caused to others. Three are English and the other is a case in the High Court of Australia. Only one of the English cases (*Dooley v Cammel Laird & Co. Ltd.* [1951] 1 Lloyd's Rep. 271) is reported in full; the reasoning in *Galt v British Railways Board* (1983) 133 N.L.J. 870 has been condensed to a single sentence and that of *Wigg v British Railways Board*, The Times, 4 February 1986 is also abbreviated. All appear to have been extempore first instance judgments given on circuit. I think that, on a fair reading, they were each regarded by the judges who decided them as raising one question of fact, namely whether psychiatric injury to the plaintiff was a foreseeable consequence of the defendant's negligent conduct. This was in accordance with the law as it was thought to be at the time. There was no reference to the control mechanisms, which had not yet been invented. In *Wigg's* case, Tucker J. expressly said that the only question was that of foreseeability, referring to the speech of Lord Bridge of Harwich in *McLoughlin v O'Brian* [1983] 1 A.C. 410. This was a view which might well have prevailed, but the subsequent retreat from principle in *Alcock v Chief Constable of South Yorkshire Police* [1992] 1 A.C. 310 meant that it, and the other two cases, had either to be given up as wrongly decided or explained on other grounds. The same is true of the Australian case of *Mount Isa Mines Ltd. v Pusey*, 125 C.L.R. 383, whose interest resides entirely in the judgment of Windeyer J. Only one of the other judges found it necessary to discuss the principles of liability for psychiatric injury and he expressly refrained from considering whether it could be based upon the employee relationship. Windeyer J. thought that it could, but only as part of his wider thesis that foreseeable physical and foreseeable psychiatric injury should not be distinguished. He was at pains to say, at p. 404, that although the plaintiff was owed a duty of care as employee, his position was no different from that of anyone else to whom injury, whether physical or psychiatric, was reasonably foreseeable.

In the *Alcock* case itself, Lord Oliver of Aylmerton attempted an ex post facto rationalisation of the three English cases by saying that in each, the plaintiff had been put in a position in which he was, or thought he was about to be or had been, the immediate instrument of death or injury to another. In *Wigg's* case, for example, the plaintiff was the driver of a train which had caused the death of a passenger by moving off when he was trying to board. The driver had started because the guard, for whom the employer was vicariously liable, had negligently given the signal. This is an elegant, not to say ingenious, explanation, which owes nothing to the actual reasoning (so far as we have it) in any of the cases. And there may be grounds for treating such a rare category of case as exceptional and exempt from the *Alcock* control mechanisms. I do not need to express a view because none of the plaintiffs in this case come within it. In [*the Scottish case of*] *Robertson v Forth Road Bridge Joint Board*, 1995 S.C.L.R. 466 Lord Hope adopted Lord Oliver's explanation of the English cases and rejected a claim for psychiatric injury by employees who had

> witnessed the death of a fellow employee in the course of being engaged on the same work. I respectfully agree with the reasoning of my noble and learned friend [*Lord Steyn*], which I regard as a rejection of the employment relationship as in itself a sufficient basis for liability."

The four authorities on which reliance was placed were not, for a number of reasons, particularly persuasive authorities. First, the three English cases were all "extempore first instance judgments given on circuit" and so were not of strong persuasive authority. Secondly:

> ". . . each [*was*] regarded by the judges who decided them as raising one question of fact, namely whether psychiatric injury to the plaintiff was a reasonably foreseeable consequence of the defendant's negligent conduct".

As the cases were concerned only with this question, and not with whether a duty might arise by virtue of the employment relationship, they were effectively distinguished. Thirdly, reliance on the Australian case was not on the ratio of the decision (which itself would be only of persuasive authority), but on the view of only one of the (five) judges in the case. Fourthly, the view of that judge was not focused specifically on a duty not to cause psychiatric illness being owed by virtue of the employment relationship (and the circumstances in which that might be owed), but on the broader issue of comparable treatment of employees where reasonably foreseeable injury was sustained, whether that be physical or psychiatric injury. Against these decisions, Lord Hoffmann adopted the reasoning in a Scottish case, *Robertson v Forth Road Bridge Joint Board* 1995 S.C.L.R. 466, which in his view supported a rejection of the employment relationship as a basis for establishing liability.

The remaining member of the majority who delivered judgment, Lord Griffiths, summarily dismissed the plaintiffs' claim based on the employment relationship, stating (at 1514) that the control mechanisms established in *Alcock* "should apply to all those not directly imperilled or who reasonably believe themselves to be imperilled, irrespective of whether they are employees or not". In this respect, his Lordship's view appears to accord with that of Lord Steyn that primary victims encompass only those within the range of foreseeable physical injury. All others would be secondary victims to whom the control mechanisms applied.

(ii) A duty as a matter of policy

15–015

If the existing law did not give rise to a duty of care, a new duty might nevertheless be recognised by the House if there were compelling policy arguments in favour of doing so. Conversely, no new duty would be recognised if there were compelling policy arguments against doing so and this was the view taken by the majority, although their reasoning in this respect was not identical. All mentioned the unfairness of the police being able to claim when others exposed to the same horror were unable to do so. Lord Hoffmann stated (at 1553):

"Why should the policeman, simply by virtue of the employment analogy and irrespective of what they actually did, be treated differently from first aid workers or ambulancemen? . . .

. . . I do not think it would be fair to give police officers the right to a larger claim merely because the disaster was caused by the negligence of other policemen. In the circumstances in which the injury was caused, I do not think that this is a relevant distinction and if it were to be given effect, the law would not be treating like cases alike."

Lord Griffiths stated (at 1514):

". . . this . . . means that the police will be entitled to recover damages whereas spectators and others on duty in the ground who were exposed to the same horror and risk of psychiatric injury will not be able to do so. I can not believe that this would be a fair or acceptable state of the law."

Lord Steyn stated (at 1545):

"The claim of the police officers on our sympathy, and the justice of the case, is great but not as great as that of others to whom the law denies redress."

Although recognising the unfairness, Lord Steyn, however, appeared to be more concerned with the potentially wide scope for liability if a duty was to be recognised (the "floodgates" argument). Whilst acknowledging that there was a "weighty moral argument" in favour of allowing damages to be recovered, since "the police perform their duties for the benefit of us all", his Lordship stated (at 1545):

". . . the pragmatic rules governing the recovery of damages for pure psychiatric harm do not at present include police officers who sustain such injuries while on duty. If such a category were to be created by judicial decision, the new principle would be available in many different situations e.g. doctors and hospital workers who are exposed to the sight of grievous injuries and suffering."

An additional "difficulty" in respect of "where the justice lay" was also recognised by his Lordship, who stated (at 1545):

". . . police officers who are traumatised by something they encounter in their work have the benefit of statutory schemes which permit them to retire on pension. In this sense they are already better off than bereaved relatives who were not allowed to recover in the *Alcock* case."

Although Lord Hoffmann made no reference to this latter factor, it was taken into account by Lord Griffiths, who stated (at 1514):

"If anything one would expect the police to be at a disadvantage [*compared to others exposed to the same horror*]. The police are trained to deal with catastrophic incidents and are reasonably well compensated under the terms of their service if they do suffer injury in the course of their duties."

(iii) Lord Goff's dissent

Lord Goff was of the view that the duty owed to primary victims was not, under the existing law, confined to those who were within the range of foreseeable physical injury and that this had not been established as a necessary requirement in *Page*. His Lordship interpreted the remarks of Lord Lloyd in *Page*, that the plaintiff was "well within the range of foreseeable physical injury", as being merely descriptive of the position of the plaintiff in that particular case, as not intended to indicate a necessary attribute of a primary victim and, in any event, as being no more than an obiter dictum. A plaintiff involved in an event as a participant might be a primary victim, even if not within the range of foreseeable physical injury. Lord Goff stated (at 1526–1528):

15–016

". . . we owe the distinction between primary and secondary victims to the opinion of Lord Oliver in the *Alcock* case [1992] 1 A.C. 310, 407. Although he indicated a secondary victim as one who is "no more than the passive or unwilling witness of injury to other," he made no attempt to define a primary victim, describing him simply as one who is "involved, either mediately or immediately as a participant," and giving miscellaneous examples of such persons. In *Page v Smith* [1996] A.C. 155, 184A–B, however, Lord Lloyd said of the plaintiff in that case that he "was a participant. He was himself directly involved in the accident, *and well within the range of foreseeable physical injury. He was the primary victim.*" As the Law Commission have pointed out in their Report (see Law Com. 249 at paras. 2.52–2.60), the words which I have emphasised have led to considerable confusion . . . and have led many . . . to understand that case to have laid down that presence within the range of foreseeable physical injury is a necessary attribute of a primary victim . . .

I am however satisfied that . . . Lord Lloyd [*did not*] intend to reach any such conclusion (which would in any event have been no more than an obiter dictum) . . . Lord Lloyd accepted the distinction between primary and secondary victims drawn by Lord Oliver in the *Alcock* case [1992] 1 A.C. 310, 410–411, where, as Lord Lloyd said, Lord Oliver

"referred to those who are involved in an accident as primary victims, and to those who are not directly involved, but who suffer from what they see or hear, as the secondary victims."

Yet the effect of the proposition now under consideration would be that the category of secondary victims is no longer to be restricted to witnesses, or 'bystanders' as they are sometimes called, but is to be extended to include all victims other than those who were within the range of foreseeable physical injury. Furthermore, it appears from Lord Oliver's speech in *Alcock*'s case, which Lord Lloyd here invoked, that he did not regard presence within the range of foreseeable physical injury as a necessary attribute of a primary victim. This was made plain by the fact that he included among primary victims those coming to the aid of others injured or threatened (see p. 408E), citing *Chadwick v British Railways Board* [1967] 1 W.L.R. 912, and plaintiffs in cases such as *Dooley v Cammell Laird & Co. Ltd* [1951] 1 Lloyd's Rep. 271

> "where the negligent act of the defendant has put the plaintiff in the position of being, or thinking that he is about to be or has been, the involuntary cause of another's death or injury"

with the result that he has suffered psychiatric illness (see p.408E–G). In the latter group of cases there is ordinarily no question of the plaintiff having been within the range of foreseeable physical injury, and in the *Chadwick* case that factor was treated as irrelevant by the trial judge, Waller J. Indeed cases such as *Dooley*, and rescue cases such as *Chadwick* and the well known Australian case of *Mount Isa Mines Ltd. v Pusey*, 125 C.L.R. 383 (in which the successful plaintiff was never in any physical danger), are in direct conflict with the conclusion which has been attributed to Lord Lloyd in the passages now in question. In this connection it is significant that no reasons were given in *Page v Smith* why any such limitation should be placed on recovery by primary victims; the point was not even discussed. Had it been considered, Lord Lloyd would have had to face up to the well known decisions already referred to which are inconsistent with the proposition, and to consider whether he should follow them or whether he should distinguish or depart from them and, if the latter, why he should do so. The absence of any reference by Lord Lloyd to those decisions of itself renders it inconceivable that the passages in his judgment now in question should have been intended by him to have the effect attributed to them. The matter is, in my opinion, put beyond all doubt by the summary of his conclusions with which Lord Lloyd ended his opinion: see *Page v Smith* [1996] A.C. 155, 197E–H. After stating certain principles which he regarded as applicable in the case of secondary victims, he said:

> "Subject to the above qualifications, the approach in all cases should be the same, namely, whether the defendant can reasonably foresee that his conduct will expose the plaintiff to the risk of personal injury, whether physical or psychiatric."

This proposition, plainly designed to express Lord Lloyd's opinion that fore-seeability of physical injury to the plaintiff is a sufficient condition of liability for psychiatric injury, is inconsistent with the proposition that it is also a necessary condition of such liability.

. . . It is plain, in my opinion, that Lord Lloyd's strategy was to *expand* recovery by primary victims not only in the manner I have indicated [*i.e. by holding that foreseeability of physical injury justifies recovery in respect of unforeseeable psychiatric injury even though no physical injury is suffered*] but also by restricting the applicability of the "reasonable fortitude" and "hindsight" tests to secondary victims; but that he had no strategy to *restrict* recovery by primary victims, whether by restricting recovery to cases where physical injury was foreseeable or otherwise.

For all these reasons I am satisfied that the passages in Lord Lloyd's opinion, to which I have referred, should be read as merely descriptive of the position of the plaintiff in *Page v Smith* [1996] A.C. 155, and not as having the effect ascribed to them."

Having taken the view that primary victims could encompass participants, even if not within the range of foreseeable physical injury, his Lordship proceeded to consider whether employees might recover damages for nervous shock, as primary victims, from their employers. In making reference to the nature of an employer's duties, Lord Goff referred to a leading textbook on employer's liability, a Law Commission Consultation Paper and various case law authorities (including a Scottish case), which in his view supported a distinction between employees who merely witnessed an event while at work and those who were involved in an event in the course of their employment where physical injury or death occurred to another. He stated (at 1527–1529):

". . . all the employer's duties "are connected in some sense to what happens to the employee while at work" (see *Munkman on Employer's Liability*, p. 33); and it is with cases arising in this context that we are concerned. I put on one side those cases in which an employee is seeking damages from his employer in respect of stress at work, as to which see *Munkman on Employer's Liability*, pp. 128–130, and *Walker v Northumberland County Council* [1995] I.C.R. 702 (commented on by the Law Commission in its Consultation Paper No. 137, paras 2.49–2.50). But in the authorities relating to the recovery by an employee from his employer of damages for psychiatric injury, arising from the death or physical injury of another, we find a distinction being drawn between those cases in which the employee has in the course of his employment been involved in the event which resulted in the other's physical injury or death, to which I would add involvement in the aftermath of that event, and other cases in which he has, while at work, incidentally witnessed that event and its outcome.

As to the former, a useful example is to be found in *Young v Charles Church (Southern) Ltd.*, 24 April 1997 . . . [*where*], [*a*]s a result of *Page v Smith*, the Court of Appeal was concerned with the question whether the plaintiff was within the range of physical injury, and were able to hold on the facts of the case that he was. But for present purposes the important finding of the majority, Evans and Hutchinson L.JJ., was that the plaintiff was involved as a participant in the accident. Hutchinson L.J. put the matter very clearly:

"[*The plaintiff*] had just given the pole to Cook who was within six feet or so of the latter when Cook received the fatal shock [*from the pole coming into contact with an overhead power cable*]. Though he had turned away to get

411

> the shorter support poles to be used to maintain the long pole in the vertical position, he could in my view properly be regarded as still participating in the erection of that long pole at the moment it touched the electric cable. . ."

The circumstances of that case can be compared to those of the two Scottish cases of *Robertson v Forth Road Bridge Joint Board*, 1995 S.C.L.R. 466 . . . [*where*] [*t*]he argument for the pursuers [*the Scottish term for a plaintiff*] was essentially that they were so directly involved in the accident as to be within the ambit of their employers' duty of care to them. This argument was however rejected by the Lord President, who regarded the case not as one of active participation in the event, but as one where the pursuers were merely bystanders or witnesses, in which event . . . as the pursuers did not comply with the control mechanisms applicable in the case of claimants who were only witnesses, their claim must fail. The case therefore provides authority that, in a claim by an employee against his employer for damages for psychiatric injury arising from death or injury to another, his claim will fail if he is simply a bystander who witnesses the event, and is not an active participant in it (or I would add, its aftermath). It was perhaps open to the Lord President to take the view that the two pursuers were at the time actively involved . . . in which event the reclaiming motion would no doubt have been granted [*i.e. the claim that a duty was owed would have been allowed*]; but he took a different view of the facts of the case."

Having reached the view that the existing law could support a duty of care in cases where an employee was an active participant (and a primary victim), Lord Goff alluded briefly to whether a duty should be recognised as a matter of policy. Unfairness of the police being able to claim when others exposed to the same horror were unable to do so was, for the majority, a prominent policy consideration for denying a duty. For Lord Goff, however, the police were not being treated more favourably, for the basis for claiming and recovering damages was different. His Lordship stated (at 1531–1532):

". . . in the present case . . . a number of relatives of victims at Hillsborough failed in claims for damages in respect of psychiatric injury which they advanced in *Alcock*'s case [1992] 1 A.C. 310, and it has been suggested that it would be unacceptable if police officers were entitled to a wider basis of recovery as employees. However this is not, in my opinion, the position at law. The difference between the two categories arises not from the applicability of special rules in the case of secondary victims (which, in my opinion, apply to both categories) but from the fact that, whereas police officers who became involved on the ground in the aftermath of the disaster can claim against the Chief Constable as "employees," strangers who intervened will have to justify their intervention, for example by bringing themselves within the broad category of "rescuers," to which I will turn in a moment. In this connection I wish to record that the claims of the plaintiffs in the *Alcock* case were not

> advanced on the basis that they were rescuers, a fact which must be borne in
> mind when comparisons are drawn between those plaintiffs and the plaintiffs
> in the present case."

Lord Goff accordingly concluded that neither the existing law nor considerations of
policy precluded the plaintiffs from recovering damages and held that they were
entitled to do so on the basis of their employment relationship with their Chief
Constable.

▷ *(b) The rescue argument*

A majority of the House held that the plaintiffs were not owed a duty (as primary   **15–017**
victims) by virtue of being rescuers. Lords Steyn and Hoffmann (with whose
judgments Lord Browne-Wilkinson expressed agreement) held that a duty was
owed to a rescuer only where he exposed himself to danger or reasonably believed
himself to be so exposed (per Lord Steyn) or was within the range of foreseeable
physical injury (per Lord Hoffmann). Lord Griffiths dissented from this view, considering that a duty should be owed provided there was immediate help given at
the scene of the accident, but the position of Lord Goff, as will be seen, is less
clear. His Lordship's view appeared to be that persons involved in the aftermath of
an accident, whether or not they might be (or might be described as) rescuers,
might recover as primary victims on account of the nature and extent of their
involvement. This indicates that a duty is owed not by virtue of being a rescuer, but
by virtue of involvement, and it would seem to be on this basis that the headnote
to the case records only Lord Griffiths dissenting as regards a duty not being owed
to the plaintiffs as rescuers. This suggests a decision by a 4–1 majority in this
respect, but it is apparent that Lord Goff's view does not accord with the other
three members of the majority as regards the circumstances when a duty is owed
to persons who might be in the category of a rescuer. Thus, the case appears to
decide, but by a 3–2 majority, that a duty is owed to rescuers only where they
expose themselves to danger or reasonably believed themselves to be so exposed
or were within the range of foreseeable physical injury. It would seem to be not
only Lord Griffiths dissenting on this issue, but also Lord Goff, a point that is not
apparent from the headnote.

As in the case of the employment argument, the questions of whether a duty
might be owed under the existing law and whether a duty should, as a matter of
policy, be owed, were addressed.

(i) A duty under the existing law

Lord Steyn followed a similar approach to that which he had taken in respect of   **15–018**
the employment argument, taking the view that the duty owed to primary victims
encompassed only those within the range of foreseeable physical injury, or as he
expressed it, in respect of rescuers, those who were exposed to danger or thought
they were so exposed. The observations of Lord Oliver in Alcock about

"participants" as primary victims were regarded as general observations, to which no reference was made by other members of the House, and were effectively dismissed as obiter. Lord Steyn stated (at 1546):

> "Counsel for the appellant is invoking the concept of a rescuer as an exception to the limitations recognised by the House of Lords in the *Alcock* case [1992] 1 A.C. 310 and *Page v Smith* [1996] A.C. 155 . . . The specific difficulty counsel faces is that it is common ground that none of the four police officers were at any time exposed to personal danger and none thought that they were so exposed. Counsel submitted that this is not a requirement. He sought comfort in the general observations in the *Alcock* case of Lord Oliver about the category of "participants:" see p.407E. None of the other Law Lords in the *Alcock* case discussed this category. Moreover, the issue in respect of rescuers [*sic*] entitlement to recover for psychiatric harm was not before the House on that occasion and Lord Oliver was not considering the competing arguments presently before the House. The explanation of Lord Oliver's observations has been the subject of much debate. It was also vigorously contested at the bar. In my view counsel for the appellant has tried to extract too much from general observations not directed to the issue now before the House."

The decision in *Chadwick v British Railways Board* [1967] 1 W.L.R. 912, which had been relied upon by the appellants in support of their argument, in addition to the observations of Lord Oliver in *Alcock*, was in essence distinguished. It was regarded as a material fact in that case that the plaintiff had been in personal danger, although this had not been the cause of the nervous shock (which was due to the "horror of the whole experience"), whereas the plaintiffs had not been exposed to any personal danger in the present case. Lord Steyn stated (at 1546):

> "Counsel was only able to cite one English decision in support of his argument namely the first instance judgment in *Chadwick v British Railways Board* [1967] 1 W.L.R. 912. Mr Chadwick had entered a wrecked railway carriage to help and work among the injured. There was clearly a risk that the carriage might collapse. Waller J. said, at p. 918:
>
>> "although there was clearly an element of personal danger in what Mr Chadwick was doing, I think I must deal with this case on the basis that it was the horror of the whole experience which caused his reaction."

On the judge's findings the rescuer had passed the threshold of being in personal danger but his psychiatric injury was caused by "the full horror of his experience" when he was presumably not always in personal danger. This decision has been cited with approval: see *McLoughlin v O'Brian* [1983] 1 A.C. 410, *per* Lord Wilberforce, at p. 419, *per* Lord Edmund-Davies, at p. 424, and *per* Lord Bridge of Harwich, at pp. 437–438; and in the *Alcock* case [1992] 1 A.C. 310, *per* Lord Oliver, at p. 408. I too would accept that the *Chadwick* case was correctly decided. But it is not authority for the proposition that a person who never exposed himself to any personal danger and never thought that he was in personal danger can recover pure psychiatric injury as a rescuer. In order to recover compensation for pure psychiatric harm as rescuer it is not necessary to establish that his psychiatric condition was *caused* by the perception of personal danger. And Waller J. rightly so held."

Lord Hoffmann, like Lord Steyn, sought to dismiss observations in *Alcock* as obiter, expressly indicating them to be so, and regarded the plaintiff in *Chadwick* as having been within the range of foreseeable injury (and thus essentially in personal danger). His Lordship stated (at 1554–1556):

"The second way in which the plaintiffs put their case is that they were not "bystanders or spectators" but participants in the sense that they actually did things to help. They submit that there is an analogy between their position and that of a "rescuer," who, on the basis of the decision on Waller J. in *Chadwick v British Railways Board* [1967] 1 W.L.R. 912, is said to be treated as a primary victim, exempt from the control mechanisms.

In *Chadwick's* case, the plaintiff suffered psychiatric injury as a result of his experiences in assisting the victims of a railway accident. He spent 12 hours crawling in the wreckage, helping people to extricate themselves and giving pain killing injections to the injured. Waller J. said, at p. 921, that it was foreseeable that "somebody might try to rescue passengers and suffer injury in the process." The defendants therefore owed a duty of care to the plaintiff. He went on to say that it did not matter that the injury suffered was psychiatric rather than physical but in any event "shock was foreseeable and . . . rescue was foreseeable." Thus the judge's reasoning is based purely upon the foreseeability of psychiatric injury in the same way as in other cases of that time. And I think there can be no doubt that if foreseeability was the only question, the judge's conclusion was unexceptionable . . .

The cases on rescuers are . . . simple illustrations of the application of general principles of foreseeability and causation to particular facts. There is no authority which decides that a rescuer is in any special position in relation to liability for psychiatric injury . . .

There does not seem to me to be any logical reason why the normal treatment of rescuers on the issues of foreseeability and causation should lead to the conclusion that, for the purpose of liability for psychiatric injury, they should be given special treatment as primary victims when they were not within the range of foreseeable physical injury and their psychiatric injury was caused by witnessing or participating in the aftermath of accidents which caused death or injury to others. It would of course be possible to create such a rule by an ex post facto rationalisation of *Chadwick v British Railways Board* [1967] 1 W.L.R. 912. In both *McLoughlin v O'Brian* [1983] 1 A.C. 410 and in *Alcock v Chief Constable of South Yorkshire* [1992] 1 A.C. 310, members of the House referred to *Chadwick's* case [1967] 1 W.L.R. 912 with approval. But I do not think that too much should be read into these remarks. In neither case was it argued that

> the plaintiffs were entitled to succeed as rescuers and anything said about the duty to rescuers was therefore necessarily obiter. If one is looking for an ex post facto rationalisation of *Chadwick*'s case, I think that the most satisfactory is that offered in the Court of Appeal in *McLoughlin v O'Brian* [1981] Q.B. 599, 622 by my noble and learned friend, Lord Griffiths, who had been the successful counsel for Mr Chadwick. He said:
>
> > "Mr Chadwick might have been injured by a wrecked carriage collapsing on him as he worked among the injured. A duty of care is owed to a rescuer in such circumstances. . ."
>
> If Mr Chadwick was, as Lord Griffiths said, within the range of foreseeable physical injury, then the case is no more than an illustration of the principle applied by the House in *Page v Smith* [1996] A.C. 155, namely that such a person can recover even if the injury he actually suffers is not physical but psychiatric. And in addition (unlike *Page v Smith* [1996] A.C. 155) Waller J. made a finding that psychiatric injury was also foreseeable."

Lord Griffiths, in contrast, although making no reference to the observations in *Alcock* in the context of a duty owed to rescuers, did not regard *Chadwick* as restricted in scope to cases where the plaintiff had been in personal danger. His Lordship stated (at 1514):

> "If the rescuer is in no physical danger it will only be in exceptional cases that personal injury in the form of psychiatric injury will be foreseeable for the law must take us to be sufficiently robust to give help at accidents that are a daily occurrence without suffering a psychiatric breakdown. But where the accident is of a particularly horrifying kind and the rescuer is involved with the victims in the immediate aftermath it may be reasonably foreseeable that the rescuer will suffer psychiatric injury as Mr Chadwick did when trying to bring relief and comfort to the victims of the Lewisham train disaster. Mr Chadwick suffered his injury because of the terrible impact on his mind of the suffering he witnessed in his rescue attempt, and not because of any fear for his own safety: see *Chadwick v British Railways Board* [1967] 1 W.L.R. 912. What rescuer ever thinks of his own safety? It seems to me that it would be a very artificial and unnecessary control, to say a rescuer can only recover if he was in fact in physical danger. A danger to which he probably never gave any thought, and which in the event might not cause physical injury."

By stating that "Mr Chadwick suffered his injury because of the terrible impact on his mind of the suffering he witnessed in his rescue attempt, and not because of any fear for his own safety", Lord Griffiths appeared not to regard the plaintiff being exposed to personal danger as a material fact in the decision (and thus not part of the ratio of the case.) Lord Goff took a similar view of the case, stating (at 1532):

> "He [*Mr Chadwick*] was exposed to some physical danger, but the trial judge (Waller J.) treated that as irrelevant. It was, he held, the whole horror of the situation which affected Mr Chadwick, who as a result suffered psychiatric injury . . . When we contemplate the full horror of the disaster . . . it is scarcely surprising that the judge treated the physical danger as irrelevant; and it is scarcely surprising too that, in *McLoughlin v O'Brian* [1983] 1 A.C. 410, 438, Lord Bridge of Harwich stated that, as far as he knew, no one had ever doubted that the case was rightly decided. But it is also plain that the circumstances were wholly exceptional. It must be very rare that a person bringing aid and comfort to a victim or victims will be held to have suffered foreseeable psychiatric injury as a result."

(ii) A duty as a matter of policy

15–019 Differing views were expressed on the question of whether a duty should, as a matter of policy, be owed to a rescuer only where the rescuer was within the range of foreseeable physical injury. The primary policy consideration on which attention was focused was the acceptability (or fairness) of persons recovering damages when they had assisted in rescue operations or the aftermath of a disaster (as the plaintiffs had done in the present case), as compared to claims by the relatives of victims which could succeed only within narrow confines (and which in *Alcock* were held not to encompass the claims of relatives of victims in the same Hillsborough disaster in respect of which the plaintiffs were making their claims). There were, in addition, other factors to which reference was made. These included the potentially wide scope for liability if a duty was to be recognised (the "floodgates" argument) and, if a duty was to be owed to those rendering assistance, the difficulty of drawing a line between them and bystanders.

Acceptability and "floodgates" appear to have been the policy considerations which led Lord Steyn, who dealt with the matter only briefly, to reject the imposition of a duty. His Lordship stated (at 1547):

> ". . . in order to contain the concept of rescuer in reasonable bounds for the purposes of the recovery of compensation for pure psychiatric harm the plaintiff must at least satisfy the threshold requirement that he objectively exposed himself to danger or reasonably believed that he was doing so. Without such limitation one would have the unedifying spectacle that, while bereaved relatives are not allowed to recover as in the *Alcock* case, ghoulishly curious spectators, who assisted in some peripheral way in the aftermath of a disaster, might recover. For my part the limitation of actual or apprehended dangers is what proximity in this special situation means. In my judgment it would be an unwarranted extension of the law to uphold the claims of the police officers."

Lord Hoffmann, considering the matter more fully, acknowledged that recognition of a duty might encourage the offer of assistance, but nevertheless rejected the imposition of a duty. This was on the grounds of acceptability and the difficulty of drawing a line between those assisting and bystanders, but not on the basis of the "floodgates" argument. His Lordship stated (at 1556–1557):

> "Should then your Lordships take the incremental step of extending liability for psychiatric injury to "rescuers" (a class which would now require definition) who give assistance at or after some disaster without coming within the range of foreseeable physical injury? It may be said that this would encourage people to offer assistance. The category of secondary victims would be confined to "spectators and bystanders" who take no part in dealing with the incident or its aftermath. On the authorities, as it seems to me, your Lordships are free to take such a step.
>
> In my opinion there are two reasons why your Lordships should not do so. The less important reason is the definitional problem to which I have alluded. The concept of a rescuer as someone who puts himself in danger of physical injury is easy to understand. But once this notion is extended to include others who give assistance, the line between them and bystanders becomes difficult to draw with any precision. For example, one of the plaintiffs in the *Alcock* case [1992] 1 A.C. 310, a Mr O'Dell, went to look for his nephew. "He searched among the bodies . . . and assisted those who staggered out from the terraces:" p. 354. He did not contend that his case was different from those of the other relatives and it was also dismissed. Should he have put himself forward as a rescuer?
>
> But the more important reason for not extending the law is that in my opinion the result would be quite unacceptable. I have used this word on a number of occasions and the time has come to explain what I mean. I do not mean that the burden of claims would be too great for the insurance market or the public funds, the two main sources for the payment of damages in tort. The Law Commission may have had this in mind when they said that removal of all the control mechanism would lead to an "unacceptable" increase in claims, since they described it as a "floodgates" argument. These are questions on which it is difficult to offer any concrete evidence and I am simply not in a position to form a view one way or the other. I am therefore willing to accept that, viewed against the total sums paid as damages for personal injury, the increase resulting from an extension of liability to helpers would be modest. But I think that such an extension would be unacceptable to the ordinary person because (though he might not put it this way) it would offend against his notions of distributive justice. He would think it unfair between one class of claimants and another, at best not treating like cases alike and, at worst, favouring the less deserving against the more deserving. He would think it wrong that policemen, even as part of a general class of persons who rendered assistance, should have the right to compensation for psychiatric injury out of public funds while the bereaved relatives are sent away with nothing.

> . . . I have no doubt that most people would regard it as wrong to award compensation for psychiatric injury to the professionals and deny compensation for similar injury to the relatives."

This notion of distributive justice was regarded as overriding any search for and development of principle. His Lordship continued (at 1557):

> "It may be said that the common law should not pay attention to these feelings about the relative merits of different classes of claimants. It should stick to principle and not concern itself with distributive justice. An extension of liability to rescuers and helpers would be a modest incremental development in the common law tradition and, as between these plaintiffs and these defendants, produce a just result. My Lords, I disagree. It seems to me that in this area of the law, the search for principle was called off in *Alcock v Chief Constable of South Yorkshire Police* [1992] 1 A.C. 310. No one can pretend that the existing law, which your Lordships have to accept, is founded upon principle. I agree with Jane Stapleton's remark that "once the law has taken a wrong turning or otherwise fallen into an unsatisfactory internal state in relation to a particular cause of action, incrementalism cannot provide the answer:" see *The Frontiers of Liability*, vol. 2, p. 87. Consequently your Lordships are now engaged, not in the bold development of principle, but in a practical attempt, under adverse conditions to preserve the general perception of the law as [a] system of rules which is fair between one citizen and another . . .
>
> Naturally I feel great sympathy for the plaintiffs, as I do for all those whose lives were blighted on that day at Hillsborough. But I think that fairness demands that your Lordships should reject them."

Lord Griffiths, in contrast, did not accede to the view that it would be unacceptable and unfair to allow the plaintiffs to recover nor did he regard the "floodgates" argument as a basis for denying the existence of a duty. His Lordship stated (at 1514–1515):

> "If it is foreseeable that the rescuer may suffer personal injury in the form of psychiatric injury rather than physical injury, why should he not recover for that injury? The fear is expressed that if foreseeability of psychiatric injury is sufficient it will open the floodgates to claims, many of an unmeritorious kind, from those who give assistance at an accident. I believe that the courts are well capable of controlling any such flood of claims. Whether or not a person is to be regarded as a rescuer will be a question of fact to be decided on the particular facts of the case. Trivial or peripheral assistance will not be sufficient: see *McFarlane v E.E.Caledonian Ltd.* [1994] 2 All E.R. 1 . . .
>
> A line has to be drawn in rescue cases between rescue in the sense of immediate help at the scene of the disaster, and treatment of victims after

they are safe. I do not believe that this will be difficult to recognise on the facts of a particular case.

. . . I do not share the view that the public would find it in some way offensive that those who suffered disabling psychiatric illness as a result of their efforts to rescue the victims should receive compensation, but that those who suffered the grief of bereavement should not. Bereavement and grief are a part of the common condition of mankind which we will all endure at some time in our lives. It can be an appalling experience but it is different in kind from psychiatric illness and the law has never recognised it as a head of damage. We are human and we must accept as a part of the price of our humanity the suffering of bereavement for which no sum of money can provide solace or comfort. I think better of my fellow men than to believe that they would, although bereaved, look like dogs in the manger upon those who went to the rescue at Hillsborough."

Lord Goff, although making no reference to the "floodgates" argument, similarly did not consider that it would be unacceptable and unfair to allow the plaintiffs to recover. The suggestion that a duty should be denied to the plaintiffs as a matter of policy, by a control mechanism limiting recovery to primary victims who were within the range of foreseeable physical injury, could not, his Lordship felt, be accepted for a variety of reasons. Lord Goff stated (at 1534–1536):

"I am compelled to say that I am unable to accept this suggestion because in my opinion (1) the proposal is contrary to well established authority; (2) the proposed control mechanism would erect an artificial barrier against recovery in respect of foreseeable psychiatric injury and as such is undesirable; and (3) the underlying concern is misconceived. I will consider each of these objections in turn.

(1) *The proposal is contrary to well established authority*

I have here in mind the cases to which I have previously referred, concerned (a) with rescuers, and (b) with those who have, as a result of another's negligence, been put in the position of being, or of thinking that they are, the involuntary cause of another's death or injury. As I have already recorded, the most relevant cases concerned with the first category (rescuers) are *Chadwick v British Railways Board* [1967] 1 W.L.R. 912 (in which the trial judge treated the fact that there was some danger of physical injury as irrelevant), and (on one view) *Mount Isa Mines Ltd. v Pusey*, 125 C.L.R. 383 (in which the plaintiff was not in physical danger). In this connection it is important that the decision in *Chadwick's* case [1967] 1 W.L.R. 912 was approved, without qualification, in your Lordships' House in *McLoughlin v O'Brian* [1983] 1 A.C. 410, *per* Lord Wilberforce, at p. 419, *per* Lord Edmund-Davies, at p. 424, and *per* Lord Bridge of Harwich, at pp. 437–438, and again in *Alcock's* case [1992] 1 A.C. 310, 408, *per* Lord Oliver. As to the second category, the most relevant case is *Dooley v Cammell Laird & Co. Ltd.* [1951] 1 Lloyd's Rep. 271 in which, as in other cases of this kind, the plaintiff was never in any personal danger. Furthermore, both categories of case were stated by Lord Oliver in the *Alcock* case [1992] 1 A.C. 310, 408 to be examples of primary victims, in the case of which he plainly did not consider that there was any applicable control mechanism, for example any requirement that the plaintiff should have been within the range of foreseeable physical injury. Having regard in particular to the prominence now given to Lord Oliver's opinion in the *Alcock* case in segregating cases of secondary victims as those cases to which special control mechanisms apply, it would be a remarkable departure from existing authority now to create a new control mechanism, viz. that the plaintiff must have been exposed to the risk of physical injury, and to hold that this mechanism is applicable in the case of primary victims. What is here at issue therefore is not whether we should *extend* liability for psychiatric injury to primary victims who do not come within the range of foreseeable physical injury. The question is whether, having regard to existing authority, we should *restrict* liability for psychiatric injury to primary victims who are within the range of such injury.

(2) The proposed control mechanism would erect a new artificial barrier against recovery in respect of foreseeable psychiatric injury and as such is undesirable

The control mechanisms now in force are those established in *Alcock's* case to be applicable in the case of secondary victims, viz. (a) a close tie of love and affection to the immediate victim, (b) proximity in time and space to the incident or its aftermath, and (c) perception by sight or hearing, or its equivalent, of the event or its aftermath. These rules, being arbitrary in nature, are widely perceived to create unjust and unacceptable distinctions: see, in particular, the criticisms of Professor Jane Stapleton in "In Restraint of Tort," in *Frontiers of Liability* (1994) ed. Peter Birks, pp. 95–96. To introduce the control mechanism now proposed in the case of primary victims would in the same way create distinctions regarded as unjust and unacceptable.

To illustrate the point, let me take the always useful extreme example. Suppose that there was a terrible train crash and that there were two Chadwick brothers living nearby, both of them small and agile window cleaners distinguished by their courage and humanity. Mr A. Chadwick worked on the front half of the train, and Mr B. Chadwick on the rear half. It so happened that, although there was some physical danger present in the front half of the train, there was none in the rear. Both worked for 12 hours or so bringing aid and comfort to the victims. Both suffered P.T.S.D [*post-traumatic stress disorder*] in consequence of the general horror of the situation. On the new control mechanism now proposed, Mr A. would recover but Mr B. would not. To make things worse, the same conclusion must follow even if Mr A. was unaware of the existence of the physical danger present in his half of the train. This is surely unacceptable. May I stress that, although I have taken an extreme example, the contrast I have drawn could well arise in real life; and the new control mechanism now proposed could provoke criticisms of the same kind as those which have been made of the mechanisms recognised in the *Alcock* case [1992] A.C. 310.

(3) *The underlying concern is misconceived*

I sense that the underlying concern, which has prompted a desire to introduce this new control mechanism, is that it is thought that, without it, the policemen who are plaintiffs in the present case would be "better off" than the relatives in the *Alcock* case who failed in their claims, and that such a result would be undesirable. To this, there are at least three answers. First, the control mechanisms which excluded recovery by the relatives in the *Alcock* case would, in my opinion, have been equally applicable to the policemen in the present case if on the facts they had (like the relatives) been no more than witnesses of the consequences of the tragedy. Second, the question whether any of the relatives might be able to recover because he fell within the broad category of rescuer is still undecided; and, strangely, the control mechanism now proposed to exclude the claims of the policemen in the present case would likewise exclude the claims of relatives if advanced on the basis that they were rescuers. Third, however, it is in any event misleading to think in terms of one class of plaintiffs being "better off" than another. Tort liability is concerned not only with compensating plaintiffs, but with awarding such compensation against a defendant who is responsible in law for the plaintiff's injury. It may well be that one plaintiff will succeed on the basis that he can establish such responsibility, whereas another plaintiff who has suffered the same injury will not succeed because he is unable to do so. In such a case, the first plaintiff will be "better off" than the second, but it does not follow that the result is unjust or that an artificial barrier should be erected to prevent those in the position of the first plaintiff from succeeding in their claims. The true requirement is that the claim of each plaintiff should be judged by reference to the same legal principles.

For all these reasons I am unable to accept the need for, or indeed the desirability of, the new control mechanism now proposed."

There was thus a marked difference of view expressed by their Lordships in respect of the acceptability and fairness of recognising or denying the existence of a duty of care.

▶ 11. *Grieves v F T Everard & Sons Ltd*

15-020 In *Grieves v F T Everard & Sons Ltd* [2008] 1 A.C. 281 (*Grieves*), where several cases involving a number of claimants and different employers were heard simultaneously, actions were brought claiming damages in negligence for exposure to asbestos based on the appearance on X-ray of pleural plaques (a scarring of the lungs by asbestos fibres). Holland J., at first instance, took the view that, where X-rays of pleural plaques showed permanent penetration of the body by asbestos fibres, this in itself did not give rise to a cause of action, but that it did so when coupled with the risk that the asbestos fibres would give rise to disease and the anxiety generated about that risk.

The Court of Appeal allowed the defendants' appeals, taking the view that aggregating these matters, which individually could not establish a cause of action, was not sufficient to enable a claim for damages to succeed. The Court of Appeal, by a majority, also held that one claimant who had suffered a depressive illness as a result of worrying about the consequences of his exposure to asbestos could not claim for his psychiatric injury caused by the fear of contracting the disease. It was contended on behalf of this particular claimant that there was a freestanding claim for psychiatric injury on the basis that physical injury was a foreseeable consequence of the breach of duty and recovery could be made for psychiatric injury in accordance with the principle in *Page v Smith*, where it had been held that proof of reasonable foresight of personal injury of some kind, whether physical or psychiatric, was sufficient (see above, 15–011).

Considering the application of this principle in the case before it, the Court of Appeal sought to distinguish *Page* and, in doing so, made reference to two decisions of the US Supreme Court. Lord Phillips C.J. stated (at [2006] I.C.R. 1458 at [88]–[90]):

> "Lord Lloyd's formulation of principle in *Page v Smith* has not been without its critics, not least Lord Goff of Chievely in his dissent in *Frost v Chief Constable of South Yorkshire Police* [1992] AC 455. The decision is none the less binding on this court. The issue is whether Lord Lloyd's test of liability can be applied to the facts of this case. Lord Lloyd's test was applied in the context of a road traffic accident in which the plaintiff was a participant and which, for that reason, foreseeably exposed him to the risk of physical injury. The report of *Norfolk v Western Railway* suggests that the American Supreme Court has adopted a similar approach. At paragraph 146 Ginsburg J referred to the 'zone-of-danger' test:
>
>> "That test confines recovery for stand-alone emotional distress claims to plaintiffs who: (1) "sustain a physical impact as a result of a defendant's negligent conduct"; or (2) "are placed in immediate risk of physical harm by that conduct" that is, those who escaped instant physical harm, but were "within the zone of danger of physical impact"."
>
> Following *Metro North Commuter Rail Co. v Buckley* 521 US 424 138 L. Ed. 2d 560 (which involved exposure to asbestos but no physical manifestation of disease) the Supreme Court held that the zone-of-danger test could not properly be extended so as to render a defendant who negligently exposed a plaintiff to the risk of asbestos-induced cancer liable for emotional distress caused by the fear of developing cancer.
>
> By similar reasoning we do not consider that the test in *Page v Smith* can properly be extended so as to render a defendant who negligently exposes a

> claimant to the risk of contracting a disease liable for free-standing psychiatric injury caused by the fear of contacting the disease."

On appeal to the House of Lords, the House upheld the Court of Appeal's decision that a claim could not be based on aggregation of the pleural plaques with the risk of future asbestos-related disease and anxiety at such a prospect. It also upheld the Court of Appeal's decision that the claimant who had suffered a depressive illness could not claim for his psychiatric injury and, like the majority of the Court of Appeal, distinguished *Page*. Counsel for the defendants (at [2008] 1 A.C. 281, 286) sought to distinguish *Page* on the grounds that it was confined to cases where psychiatric injury resulted from a sudden, shocking event that had already happened, and, in the alternative, invited the House to depart from the principle in *Page* that foresight of personal injury of some kind, whether physical or psychiatric, was sufficient:

> "The claim for freestanding psychiatric injury relies on the *Page v Smith* doctrine. Too much has been read into *Page v Smith* [1996] AC 155 which is distinguishable from the present claimant's case. *Page v Smith* did not provide an alternative route to establishing liability, without the need to show reasonable foreseeability. *Page v Smith* was confined to cases where a sudden, shocking event gives rise to psychiatric injury without any later intervening step. In the present case exposure to asbestos cannot in itself cause psychiatric injury and the injury was caused over a long period. The advice of doctors many years later gave rise to a realisation of the risks undergone. There is no causal link and the injury could not be foreseen . . .
>
> In the alternative, the House of Lords should now depart from *Page v Smith* under the Practice Statement (Judicial Precedent) [1966] 1 WLR 1234 and hold that, in all cases of psychiatric injury not associated with physical injury, reasonable foreseeability of psychiatric injury must be proved."

The invitation to depart from *Page* was not accepted—three members, Lords Hoffmann (at [32]), Hope (at [52]) and Mance (at [104]), expressly stated that they would not depart from the decision—and the House preferred instead to distinguish *Page*.

The leading judgment was delivered by Lord Hoffmann, who considered *Page* not to have caused practical difficulties, and sought to confine its application to cases where an event had occurred which might result in psychiatric injury. No reference, however, was made to the event being a sudden and shocking one (as put forward by counsel), nor was any reference made to the two US Supreme Court decisions mentioned by Lord Phillips C.J. in the Court of Appeal. His Lordship stated (at [32]–[33]):

> "Counsel for the defendant invited the House to depart from the decision in *Page v Smith* on the ground that it was wrongly decided. It has certainly had no shortage of critics, chief of whom was Lord Goff of Chieveley in *Frost v Chief*

Constable of South Yorkshire Police [1999] 2 AC 455 , supported by a host of academic writers. But I do not think that it would be right to depart from *Page v Smith*. It does not appear to have caused any practical difficulties and is not, I think, likely to do so if confined to the kind of situation which the majority in that case had in mind. That was a foreseeable event (a collision) which, viewed in prospect, was such as might cause physical injury or psychiatric injury or both. Where such an event has in fact happened and caused psychiatric injury, the House decided that it is unnecessary to ask whether it was foreseeable that what actually happened would have that consequence. Either form of injury is recoverable.

In the present case, the foreseeable event was that the claimant would contract an asbestos-related disease. If that event occurred, it could no doubt cause psychiatric as well as physical injury. But the event has not occurred. The psychiatric illness has been caused by apprehension that the event may occur. The creation of such a risk is, as I have said, not in itself actionable. I think it would be an unwarranted extension of the principle in *Page v Smith* to apply it to psychiatric illness caused by apprehension of the possibility of an unfavourable event which had not actually happened."

Lord Rodger distinguished *Page* on the ground that the case was concerned with psychiatric injury developed in response to a past event and in this respect followed the same approach as Lord Hoffmann. A further ground of distinction, however, was also advanced, namely, that in *Page* the mechanism causing the onset of the psychiatric injury (the car crash) was the same as that liable to result in physical harm to the claimant, which was not so in the present case. His Lordship stated (at [95]–[96]):

"My Lords, in *Page v Smith* the plaintiff suffered psychiatric harm as a result of being exposed to the risk of, but escaping, instant physical harm. In other words, he developed his illness as an immediate response to a past event. Here, by contrast, Mr Grieves developed his illness on learning of a risk that he might possibly develop asbestosis or mesothelioma at some uncertain date in the future . . .

Mr Kent [*counsel for the claimant*] drew attention to a further, associated, point of distinction. In *Page v Smith* [1996] AC 155 the mechanism (the crash) which caused the onset of the plaintiff's psychiatric harm was the same mechanism as had been liable to result in physical harm to him. Here, by contrast, the mechanisms are different. The risk that Mr Grieves would develop asbestosis or mesothelioma was caused by the defendants' wrongdoing. On the other hand, his depression is due to his doctor intervening to tell him about the plaques and to the events following on that, including, possibly, some misinformation provided to him by other people. The distinction confirms that an award of damages for Mr Grieves's illness would go further than the award for the plaintiff's illness in *Page v Smith*."

Lord Hope also distinguished the case on two grounds. The first ground was similar, but not identical, to that of Lords Hoffmann and Rodger, with Lord Hope seeking to confine the application of *Page* to cases where psychiatric injury was caused by fear or distress resulting from involvement in an accident caused by the defendant's negligence or its immediate aftermath. Lord Hope's second ground, which is that the causal chain in the present case extended far beyond that in *Page*, as the apprehension of injury in the present case was cumulative and ongoing over a long period of time, whereas in *Page* it was immediate in response to a sudden and alarming accident, has some similarities with and seems to be a variant of Lord Rodger's second ground. His Lordship, who in formulating the second ground made reference to a journal case comment on the Court of Appeal's decision in the present case, stated (at [52]-[55]):

"On his first argument Mr Grieves [*the claimant*] seeks to bring his case within the ratio of *Page v Smith* [1996] AC 155 . He maintains that he was a primary victim of the defendants' negligence in exposing him to asbestos dust. So it was not necessary in his case to ask whether the defendants should have foreseen that he, as person of normally robust constitution, would suffer psychiatric injury. The defendants advanced various criticisms of that case which, as is well known, has given rise to much controversy. They invited the House to depart from that decision and to hold that, as in the case where damages are sought for physical injury, foreseeability of psychiatric injury should be the test for the recovery of damages by those who suffer psychiatric injury. The effect would be . . . that the essential factor in determining liability for the consequences of an act of negligence is foreseeability of the damage that is complained of. Attractive though that argument is, I would prefer to leave it for another day. On the facts of Mr Grieves's case, *Page v Smith* is distinguishable.

There are two reasons for taking this view. First, the factor that precipitated Mr Grieves's psychiatric illness was not a stressful event caused by the breach of duty, such as the accident which gave rise to Mr Page's nervous shock. As Dr Rajiv Menon, a consultant psychiatrist, records in his report, Mr Grieves had a long-standing, anticipatory fear of developing an asbestos-related disease. But he did not become ill until he was told that slight pleural thickening had been detected when his chest was x-rayed in August 2000, more than 20 years after the date when he was last exposed to asbestos dust.

In *Frost v Chief Constable of South Yorkshire Police* [1999] 2 AC 455, 500, Lord Steyn said that, in view of the difficulties that they gave rise to, the only prudent course was to treat the categories as reflected in authoritative decisions such as *Alcock v Chief Constable of South Yorkshire Police* [1992] 1 AC 310 and *Page v Smith* [1996] AC 155 as settled for the time being but to leave any expansion of this corner of the law to Parliament. . . . Although the issue in that case was whether they could be classified as secondary victims, I would apply Lord Steyn's cautionary advice to the present case too. The labels that were identified in *Page v Smith* should not be extended beyond what was in contemplation in that case. The category of primary victim should be confined to persons who suffer psychiatric injury caused by fear or distress resulting from involvement in an accident caused by the defendant's negligence or its immediate aftermath. A person like Mr Grieves who suffers psychiatric injury because of something that he may experience in the future as a result of the defendant's past negligence is in an entirely different category. The immediacy that is characteristic of the situation that applies to primary victims as contemplated in *Page v Smith* [1996] AC 155 is lacking in his case.

Secondly, the causal chain between his inhalation of the asbestos dust and the psychiatric injury is stretched far beyond that which was envisaged in *Page v Smith* [1996] AC 155. That case was concerned with an immediate response to a sudden and alarming accident, for the consequences of which the plaintiff had no opportunity to prepare himself. In this case Mr Grieves inhaled asbestos dust for about eight years. It was not until the end of that period that he became worried. This was because of the risk that he or his wife or daughter might contract a disease in the future. And his depression did not occur until he was told 20 years later about the results of his chest x-ray. He believed then that his worst fears were being realised. But this was because of the information that he had now been given by his doctor, not because of anything that happened or was done to him by his employers while he was inhaling the asbestos. His exposure at work was not to stress, but to risk: Sarah Green, "Risk Exposure and Negligence" (2006) 122 LQR 386, 389 [*commenting on the Court of Appeal decision in the present case, Grieves*)."

Lord Scott, although dealing concisely with the distinguishing of *Page*, essentially seemed to adopt a similar view to Lord Hope, stating (at [77]):

"Mr Kent [*counsel for the claimant*] . . . submitted . . . that *Page v Smith* was distinguishable from Mr Grieves's case. It was distinguishable, he submitted, because the psychiatric illness had directly resulted from the motorcar collision. There had been no intervening causative event. By contrast, in Mr Grieves's case, his psychiatric illness had not been directly caused by his exposure to asbestos dust but had resulted from his worry about his liability to future illness and his reaction to the x-rays and medical reports which had disclosed the presence of pleural plaques in his lungs. I am in agreement with Mr Kent that *Page v Smith* is distinguishable on that basis . . ."

Lord Mance, in a short judgment, expressed himself to be in agreement with the reasons given by all other members of the House for distinguishing *Page*, stating (at [104]):

"On the application of *Page v Smith* [1996] AC 155 in the appeal by Mr Grieves, assuming that case to have been correctly decided, I agree that it can and should be distinguished on its facts for reasons given by all of your Lordships. As interpreted by the majority of the House in *Frost v Chief Constable of South Yorkshire Police* [1999] 2 AC 455, it concerned psychiatric injury arising as an

> immediate consequence of an obvious accident, in which the claimant could foreseeably have been physically injured at the time."

It is apparent from the extracts above that the House essentially treated *Page* as confined to its particular facts and there was unwillingness to extend the scope of the principle in that case. The House's decision thus reflects the approach advocated by Lord Steyn in *Frost v Chief Constable of South Yorkshire Police* [1999] 2 A.C. 455, 500 that:

> ". . . the only sensible general strategy for the courts is to say thus far and no further. The only prudent course is to treat the pragmatic categories as reflected in authoritative decisions such as the *Alcock* case [1992] 1 A.C. 310 and *Page v. Smith* [1996] A.C. 155 as settled for the time being but by and large to leave any expansion or development in this corner of the law to Parliament."

It seems likely that these sentiments were in the minds of the Law Lords when reaching their decision and, indeed, in the course of their judgments both Lord Hope (at [54]) and Lord Rodger (at [95]) made explicit reference to Lord Steyn's remarks.

▶ 12. The Way Ahead?

15-021 It has been seen that the right to recover damages for nervous shock has developed and been expanded through a series of decisions since the beginning of the last century. The law has developed on an incremental basis, with cases building on earlier decisions, as the parameters of liability have unfolded. Alternative views as to the basis for liability have prevailed at different periods of time and judicial attitudes have fluctuated between an expansive and restrictive approach. In consequence, decisions need to be assessed in their historical context and may, if decided at a different period of time, result in a different outcome (e.g. *King v Phillips* [1953] 1 Q.B. 429 "can no longer be supported on its facts", per Lord Lloyd in *Page v Smith* [1996] A.C. 155 at 198). As Lord Hoffmann observed in *White* (at [1998] 3 W.L.R. 1509 at 1550):

> ". . . this story of the ebb and flow of tort liability for psychiatric injury has often been told and I have recounted it again at some length only because I think it must be borne in mind when we come to deal with the authorities. In order to give due weight to the earlier decisions, particularly at first instance, it is necessary to have regard to their historical context. They cannot simply be laid out flat and pieced together to form a timeless mosaic of legal rules. Some contained the embryonic forms of later developments; others are based on theories of liability which had respectable support at the time but have since been left stranded by the shifting tides."

The outcome has been, as Lord Steyn remarked in *White* (at [1998] 3 W.L.R. 1509 at 1547), that:

> ". . . the law on the recovery of compensation for pure psychiatric harm is a patchwork quilt of distinctions which are difficult to justify . . . [*and*] in reality there are no refined analytical tools which will enable the courts to draw lines by way of a compromise solution in a way which is coherent and morally defensible".

All of the cases given detailed consideration in this case study, apart from *Grieves*, have essentially been ones in which claims for nervous shock have been based, to some extent at least, on the occurrence of an accident or horrific incident with which the claimants have had some connection, but the parameters of recovery for nervous shock are not restricted to such cases. There have been further developments in the law in more recent years to allow for recovery for nervous shock in other instances.

Although the claim in *Grieves* was unsuccessful, it is now recognised that psychiatric illness arising from being made to undertake stressful work can give rise to liability, as established in the landmark High Court case of *Walker v Northumberland County Council* [1995] 1 All E.R. 737, to which the House of Lords in *White* referred (and which is mentioned in the extract from Lord Goff's judgment at 15–016 above). This case, "put on one side" by Lord Goff as a case "in which an employee is seeking damages from his employer in respect of stress at work" (and thus considered not to have application to the case before him), was subsequently cited with approval by the Court of Appeal in *Garrett v Camden London BC* [2001] EWCA Civ 395 and in *Hatton v Sutherland* [2002] 2 All E.R. 1 (*Hatton*). In cases where nervous shock results from stress at work it is recognised that the ordinary principles of employer's liability apply and that there are no special control mechanisms having application. It is apparent from *White* that the control mechanisms do not apply in all cases, for, as Lord Hoffmann observed (at [1998] 3 W.L.R. 1509 at 2551),

> "[t]he control mechanisms were plainly never intended to apply to all cases of psychiatric injury . . . [*and*] contemplate that the injury has been caused in consequence of death or injury suffered (or apprehended to have been suffered or as likely to be suffered) by someone else".

Indeed, in respect of stress at work, the Court of Appeal in *Hatton* has expressly held (at [22]) that:

> "There are . . . no special control mechanisms applying to claims for psychiatric (or physical) injury or illness arising from the stress of doing the work which the employee is required to do".

Legal rules delineating the right to recover damages in the field of nervous shock have been entirely the result of judicial development of the law through the above cases. There has been no statutory intervention by the legislature, as there has been in other jurisdictions such as in the Australian state of New South Wales. There the rights of persons sustaining injury from "nervous or mental shock" have been specified in and are regulated by legislation, a matter to which Lord Ackner referred in his judgment in *Alcock* (at [1992] 1 A.C. 310 at 404). In the opinion of Lord Oliver in *Alcock* (at 417), it would be preferable, if there were to be further extensions in the scope of liability in this country, for this to be effected by Parliament rather than by the courts:

> "I . . . believe that further pragmatic extensions of the accepted concepts of what constitutes proximity must be approached with the greatest caution. *McLoughlin v O'Brian* [1983] 1 A.C. 410 was a case which itself represented an extension not, as I think, wholly free from difficulty and any further widening of the area of potential liability to cater for the expanded and expanding range of the media of communication ought, in my view, to be undertaken rather by Parliament, with full opportunity for public debate and representation, than by the process of judicial extrapolation."

Indeed, his Lordship concluded his judgment by remarking (at 419) that:

> "Policy considerations . . . could, I cannot help but feeling, be much better accommodated if the rights of persons injured in this way were to be enshrined in and limited by legislation as they have been in the Australian statute law to which my noble and learned friend, Lord Ackner, has referred."

It remains to be seen if and when there will be any legislative intervention in this field.

Whilst this case study has examined an area in which propositions of law have been developed through a series of cases without any legislative intervention by Parliament, the next case study will examine an area where the law has developed through a series of cases, following which legislation has been introduced, and where the courts have subsequently had to consider how that legislation should be interpreted.

Further Reading

Green, "Risk Exposure and Negligence" (2006) 122 L.Q.R. 386

Law Commission, *Liability for Psychiatric Illness* Com.No.249, 1998

Mullaney and Handford, *Tort liability for Psychiatric Damage*, 2nd edn, (Lawbook Co, Australia, 2006)

Murphy, "Negligently Inflicted Psychiatric Harm: A Re-Appraisal" [1995] *Legal Studies* 415

Nolan, "Psychiatric injury at the crossroads" [2004] *Journal of Personal Injury Law* 1

Teff, *Causing Psychiatric and Emotional Harm* (Hart Publishing, 2009)

Teff, "Liability for negligently inflicted psychiatric harm: justifications and boundaries" [1997] C.L.J. 91

Teff, "Liability for psychiatric illness after Hillsborough" (1992) 12 O.J.L.S. 440

16 MARITAL RAPE

▶ 1. Introduction

16–001 It is an offence for a man to rape another person and the offence of rape, traditionally confined to vaginal sexual intercourse without the victim's consent, is presently defined as intentionally penetrating the vagina, anus or mouth of another person, where that other does not consent to penetration and there is no reasonable belief that the other consents: s.1(1) of the Sexual Offences Act 2003. However, until recently, no offence of rape was committed by a husband who had intercourse with his wife without her consent. The rule precluding marital rape, to which limited exceptions had over the years been recognised (e.g. where the wife had already obtained a court order of separation), had existed for centuries, but in *R v R* [1992] 1 A.C. 599 both the Court of Appeal and the House of Lords declared that, in the light of the degree of social change which had taken place over the course of time, it should no longer represent the law. The impact of this change in the law was potentially enormous: a survey reported by Barton and Painter ("Rights and wrongs of marital sex" (1991) 141 N.L.J. 394) had shown rape by one's husband to be the commonest form of rape, with one in every seven wives reporting being the victim of marital rape.

The abolition of the husband's immunity was subsequently given statutory force by the Criminal Justice and Public Order Act 1994, and in an application by R to the European Court of Human Rights the decision in *R v R* was held not to be in contravention of Art.7 of the European Convention on Human Rights through the imposition of retrospective criminality (*CR v United Kingdom* (1996) 21 E.H.R.R. 363). The history of the rule and of its reversal provides an insight into how law develops within a common law system.

 This case study illustrates a number of points in relation to precedent and statutory interpretation:

- ▶ the origins of a common law rule (that a husband cannot rape his wife) based on a statement contained in a textbook, albeit one written by a Chief Justice of England;
- ▶ the subsequent consideration of this statement and its acceptance in varying degrees by English courts;
- ▶ the development over a series of cases, through the ratio or by way of obiter dicta contained in them, of exceptions or qualifications to this common law rule;
- ▶ legislative intervention by Parliament and the impact of this on the common law rule;
- ▶ ascertaining the intention of Parliament when interpreting the legislation;

- the persuasive nature of a decision from another jurisdiction, Scotland, on this area of law;
- the relationship between judicial law-making and the legislative functions of Parliament;
- the rejection of the common law rule of grounds of social policy;
- the approach of the European Court of Human Rights to the issue of whether rights under an article of the European Convention on Human Rights had been violated;
- the difficulty of making a distinction between whether a court is distinguishing or merely considering a previous case; and
- a refusal to distinguish a case.

▶ 2. Extra-Judicial Lawmaking

The origins of the rule precluding marital rape lay not in a judicial decision or **16–002** statutory provision, but, unusually, in a statement in one of the oldest textbooks on English criminal law, *Pleas of the Crown*, written by Sir Matthew Hale, a Chief Justice of England in the 17th century. Statements in textbooks or other works are not generally considered to have the force of law, but there are exceptional instances where courts rely upon such statements as authority for a legal rule. The rule precluding marital rape is one such instance for, where this issue has arisen, courts have made it clear that the original source of the law was to be found in the writings of Hale. In his *Pleas of the Crown*, Hale in fact dealt with the matter briefly, stating (in Vol.1, p.629):

> "But the husband cannot be guilty of a rape committed by himself upon his lawful wife, for by their mutual matrimonial consent and contract the wife hath given herself up in this kind unto her husband, which she cannot retract".

No reference was made by Hale of any authority for this statement of the law. It was not that the custom of offering authority for points of law was undeveloped in the 17th century. Indeed, on the two pages containing the passage on marital rape there are seven references to cases or statutes as authority for statements of the law on other points related to rape. It may be that Hale's view represented the prevailing and established view at the time, notwithstanding that there was no case to which reference could be made in support, although this must remain a matter of doubt, for as counsel for the prosecution observed in *R v R* [1992] 1 A.C. 599 at 614:

> "There is nothing in the works of the early textbook writers, Glanvill, Bracton or Dalton, nor in the most respected authority, *Coke's Institutes*, which supports *Hale*. If Hale was merely recognising a well known principle of law it is surprising that no authority is cited in support of it."

Whether or not Hale's view did represent the prevailing and established view at the time, it was not in fact until the late 19th century, in *R. v Clarence* (1888) 22 Q.B.D. 23, that a court appears to have given consideration to Hale's pronouncement on marital rape. As will be seen, courts until *R v R* gave great weight to Hale's words on marital rape, although not always accepting them uncritically or without qualification.

▶ ## 3. *R. v Clarence*

16–003 In *R. v Clarence* (1888) 22 Q.B.D. 23 (*Clarence*), the defendant, knowing that he was suffering from venereal disease, had intercourse with his wife who was unaware he was suffering from the disease, and infected her. He was charged not with rape, but with offences of inflicting grievous bodily harm and assault occasioning actual bodily harm contrary to ss.20 and 47 of the Offences Against the Person Act 1861 (OAPA 1861) respectively. The defendant was convicted following a direction by the trial judge to the jury that the defendant could be found guilty notwithstanding that the victim was his wife. A case was stated by the judge for the opinion of the Court for Crown Cases Reserved (see above, 2–014) as to whether this was a correct direction. The court, which was composed of such of the judges of the High Court who were able to attend, usually sat with five members, although in *Clarence*, there was an unusually large number of judges in attendance, 13, and nine were of the opinion that the trial judge's direction was not correct. The defendant's conduct was held not to constitute an offence under either s.20 or s.47 and the convictions were quashed.

Some of the judges alluded to the question of whether the defendant's conduct might constitute rape, although since the defendant was not charged with this offence this was not a matter which the court had to decide. Comments on this matter were thus obiter, but give some indication of the extent to which Hale's views were accepted. One judge who alluded to the question, Stephen J., an eminent criminal lawyer, did so only at the end of his judgment, by way of correcting a comment from counsel in respect of a view expressed by his Lordship in his textbook *Digest of the Criminal Law*. Stephen J. stated (at 46):

> "I wish to observe on a matter personal to myself that I was quoted as having said in my Digest of the Criminal Law that I thought a husband might under certain circumstances be indicted for rape on his wife. I did say so in the first edition of that work, but on referring to the last edition . . . it will be found that that statement was withdrawn."

Whilst not expressly indicting support for Hale's view, of which no mention was made, his Lordship's revised opinion appeared to accord with it. Pollock B., on the other hand, endorsed Hale's view which was accepted without qualification (at 63–64):

"The husband's connection with his wife is not only lawful, but it is in accordance with the ordinary condition of married life. It is done in pursuance of the marital contract and of the status which was created by marriage, and the wife as to the connection itself is in a different position from any other woman, for she has no right or power to refuse her consent. As is said by Lord Hale in his Pleas of the Crown, vol. i p.629: 'By their mutual matrimonial consent and contract the wife hath given up herself in this kind unto her husband, which she cannot retract.'"

Hawkins J., with whose judgment Day J. concurred, observed (at 51) that there could be no rape by a husband of his wife because the wife had given her consent to intercourse by the marriage ceremony, which accorded with Hale's view (although no reference was made to this), but his Lordship added that the wife may be justified in retracting that consent:

". . . this marital privilege [*to have sexual intercourse with his wife*] does not justify a husband in endangering his wife's health and causing her grievous bodily harm, by exercising his marital privilege when he is suffering from venereal disorder of such a character that the natural consequence of such communication will be to communicate the disease to her. Lord Stowell in *Popkin v Popkin*, cited in *Durant v Durant*, 1 Hagg.Eccl.Rep. 767, said, "the husband has a right to the person of his wife, but not if her health is endangered." So to endanger her health and cause her to suffer from loathsome disease contracted through his own infidelity, cannot, by the most liberal construction of his matrimonial privilege, be said to fall within it; and although I can cite no direct authority upon the subject, I cannot conceive it possible seriously to doubt that a wife would be justified in resisting by all means in her power, nay, even to the death, if necessary, the sexual embraces of a husband suffering from such contagious disorder."

The case of *Popkin v Popkin*, to which Hawkins J. referred to substantiate his view that a wife may retract consent, was not directly in point, since it concerned not a criminal matter but a civil action for divorce on the grounds of adultery. This point was not explicitly mentioned by Hawkins J. who, if minded to do so, could have distinguished the case as being irrelevant to the criminal issue of the marital exception to rape.

In the view of Hawkins J. (at 51–52), if the wife was justified in retracting consent (as she would be where, as in *Clarence*, her husband had venereal disease), and her husband was to have intercourse with her without her consent, this would make the husband liable for assault, although not for rape:

". . . wilfully to place his diseased person in contact with hers without her express consent amounts to an assault. It has been argued that to hold this would be to hold that a man who suffering from gonorrhoea has communication with his wife might be guilty of the crime of rape. I do not think this would be so. Rape consists in a man having sexual intercourse with a woman

> without her consent, and the marital privilege being equivalent to consent given once for all at the time of the marriage, it follows that the *mere act of sexual communion is lawful*; but there is a wide difference between a simple act of communion which is *lawful*, and an act of communion *combined with infectious contagion* endangering health and causing harm, which is *unlawful*. It may said that assuming a man to be diseased, still as he cannot have communion with his wife without contact, the communication of the disease is the result of a lawful act, and, therefore, cannot be criminal. My reply to this argument is that if a person having a privilege of which he may avail himself or not at his will and pleasure, cannot exercise it without at the same time doing something not included in this privilege and which is unlawful and dangerous to another, he must either forego his privilege or take the consequences of his unlawful conduct."

However, his Lordship added (at 52) that, even if the husband was to be charged with rape in such a case, "no jury would be found to convict . . . except under very exceptional circumstances".

Thus, although the views of Hawkins J. in large measure accorded with those of Hale, as his Lordship's recognition of the *possibility* that a husband may be convicted of raping his wife, albeit only in very exceptional circumstances, meant that he did not give unqualified support to Hale's view. Willis J., in contrast, was of the opinion (at 33) that, if a husband was liable for assault where his wife was justified in retracting consent, he would also be guilty of rape:

> "If intercourse under the circumstances now in question constitute an assault on the part of the man, it must constitute rape, unless, indeed, as between married persons rape is impossible, a proposition to which I certainly am not prepared to assent, and for which there seems to me to be no sufficient authority."

Wills J. made no reference to Hale's statement of the law, but there was clearly a much more substantial departure from it on the part of his Lordship than on the part of Hawkins J.

There was also a substantial departure by Field J., who (at 57–58) made specific reference to the statement in Hale's *Pleas of the Crown*, but declined to accept it as authoritative:

> "Then, did the wife of the prisoner consent? The ground for holding that she did so, put forward in argument, was the consent to marital intercourse which is imposed upon every wife by the marriage contract, and a passage from Hale's Pleas of the Crown . . . was cited, in which it is said that a husband cannot be guilty of rape upon his wife . . . The authority of Hale, C.J., on such a matter is undoubtedly as high as any can be, but no other authority is cited by him for this proposition, and I should hesitate before I adopted it. There may, I think, be many cases in which a wife may lawfully refuse intercourse, and in

which, if the husband imposed it by violence, he might be held guilty of a crime. Suppose a wife for reasons of health refused to consent to intercourse, and the husband induced a third person to assist him while he forcibly perpetrated the act, would any one say that the matrimonial consent would render this no crime? And there is the great authority of Lord Stowell for saying that the husband has no right to the person of his wife if her health is endangered: *Popkin v Popkin*."

Whist Field J. recognised that a wife's consent may be retracted and she may lawfully refuse intercourse, it is not clear from his Lordship's judgment whether a husband who had intercourse with his wife against her will in such circumstances would be guilty of rape. His Lordship stated only that the husband "might be held guilty of a crime" in such a case and did not specify whether this would be rape, or simply assault, or both. Like Hawkins J., Field J. also referred to *Popkin v Popkin* to support his contention that a wife may retract her consent, although this was not directly in point on this issue of marital rape (see above).

Finally, A.L. Smith J., although making no reference to Hale, appeared to accept Hale's premise that a wife by marriage consented to intercourse with her husband, although not, it would seem, Hale's contention that the consent cannot be retracted. He stated (at 37):

"At marriage the wife consents to the husband exercising the marital right. The consent then given is not confined to a husband when sound in body, for I suppose that no one would assert that a husband was guilty of an offence because he exercised such right when afflicted with some complaint of which he was then ignorant. Until the consent given at marriage be revoked, how can it be said that the husband in exercising his marital right has assaulted his wife? In the present case at the time the incriminated act was committed, the consent given at marriage stood unrevoked."

Since no indication was given as to the circumstances in which consent might be revoked, it cannot be said with certainty whether his Lordship's view is contrary to or consistent with that of Hale. If, for instance, consent might be revoked within an existing marriage, A.L. Smith J.'s view would be contrary to that of Hale, but if consent might be revoked only through termination of the marriage (e.g. by divorce), it would be consistent with it. Further, no indication was given as to whether, if consent is revoked and the husband has intercourse with his wife without her consent, this would constitute rape by the husband. It is recognised that there could be an assault in such a case, but it does not necessarily follow that the husband would also be guilty of rape. Differing views were expressed on this point by Hawkins J. and Wills J. (see above) and it cannot be ascertained from A.L. Smith J.'s judgment what was his Lordship's view on this matter.

▶ ## 4. Qualification of Hale's Views by Subsequent Judicial Decisions

16-004 Although there had been some opposition to Hale's views in *Clarence* and some qualification of them, Hale's basic proposition seems not to have been seriously challenged in the following 60 years. It was not until the case of *R. v Clarke* [1949] 2 All E.R. 448 (*Clarke*) that a prosecution was instituted against a husband for raping his wife, the alleged rape having taken place after the wife had obtained a justices' court order that she was no longer bound to cohabit with her husband on the grounds of his persistent cruelty. At trial, Clarke's counsel moved to quash the indictment as not disclosing any offence known to the law. Byrne J., although quoting with approval Hale's view of the law, did not, however, regard Hale's proposition that the wife could not retract her consent to intercourse as an absolute one. In his Lordship's view (at 449), her consent to intercourse could be and was revoked in the present circumstances:

> "The position, therefore, was that the wife, by process of law, namely, by marriage, had given consent to the husband to exercise the marital right during such time as the ordinary relations created by the marriage contract subsisted between them, but by a further process of law, namely, the justices' order, her consent to marital intercourse was revoked. Thus, in my opinion, the husband was not entitled to have intercourse with her without her consent. For these reasons, this motion fails."

Although losing this preliminary argument, Clarke nevertheless pleaded not guilty to the charge of rape and was acquitted by the jury.

A narrow or broad view of the ratio of this case may be taken. A narrow view would be that consent can be revoked only by a court order. A broad view would be that consent given by virtue of the marriage ceremony continues only "during such time as the ordinary relations created by the marriage contract subsisted between them [*i.e. husband and wife*]" and that a court order would be one way, but not the only way, in which such ordinary relations might have ceased to exist. Such relations might also have ceased to exist if, for instance, the parties had agreed to live apart and steps had been taken with a view to ending the marriage. The scope of the ratio in *Clarke* was considered in *R. v Miller* [1954] 2 Q.B. 282 (*Miller*), where the alleged rape took place after the wife had filed a petition for divorce on the ground of her husband's adultery and after there had been a partial hearing of the petition. The wife had given evidence at this hearing, but the hearing had been adjourned for the attendance of her husband and no court order had been made. Counsel for the defendant (at 283), contending for a narrow view of the ratio of *Clarke*, moved to quash the indictment:

> "It is submitted that, apart from an order of the court, to which effect must be given, the proposition in Hale is still good law, and that consent cannot be

> validly retracted either bilaterally, by agreement between the spouses, or unilaterally—as is the case here—by the wife's refusal."

However, counsel for the prosecution (at 284) argued for a broader view of the ratio of *Clarke*:

> "Byrne J. in *Rex v Clarke* enunciated the principle to be applied in these terms: "No doubt on marriage the wife consents to the husband's exercise of the marital right of intercourse during such time as the ordinary relations created by the marriage contract subsist between them." In the present case divorce proceedings have been instituted and a petition is on the file, and so long as the parties were in fact living apart the ordinary relations of marriage cannot be said to exist, and the wife can be taken to have withdrawn her consent to intercourse otherwise to be implied from the marriage."

The ratio of *Clarke*, whatever view was taken of its scope, was not binding on the trial judge in *Miller*, Lynskey J. Both cases were heard at Assizes and in the case of such courts (which have, since 1971, ceased to exist and have been replaced by the Crown Court—see above, 2–019) the general rule that courts are not bound by their own previous decisions applies. Although not binding, the ratio of *Clarke* was, however, of persuasive authority. Lynskey J.'s view was that it was not so narrow as to be confined to cases where a court order had been made, but was not so broad as to encompass the facts of the case before him. His Lordship (at 289–290) accordingly took the view that the wife's consent had not been revoked:

> "There has been no separation order, no judicial separation and no agreement to separate. If there had been an agreement to separate, particularly if it had contained a non-molestation clause, I should have come to the conclusion that that revoked the wife's consent as well . . .
>
> Can I say that because the wife has left her husband and has brought a petition for divorce that one must infer a revocation of the wife's implied consent? I have considered the matter very carefully, and I cannot see that, because a petition for divorce has been presented, that has any effect in law upon the existing marriage. It is not until a decree nisi, or possibly a decree absolute, has been pronounced that the marriage and its obligations can be said to have been terminated. It is not as if there had been some interim order of a court. The petition might be rejected and in that event also the marriage would still be subsisting and consent to marital intercourse as given in the marriage contract still be unrevoked. The result is that I must apply the law as it stands, there being no evidence which enables me to say that here the wife's implied consent to marital intercourse has been revoked by an act of the parties or by an act of the courts."

The views expressed above by Lynskey J. in respect of consent being revoked where there was an agreement to separate and when a decree nisi, or possibly a decree absolute, had been pronounced were obiter. There had been no agreement to separate nor had any decree been pronounced. What his Lordship had to decide was whether a separation by the parties and a filing of a petition for divorce amounted to revocation of consent and his decision that it did not represents the ratio of the case. Lynskey J.'s obiter comments in respect of consent being revoked where a decree nisi had been granted were, however, subsequently applied in the Crown Court by Park J. in *R. v O'Brien* [1974] 3 All E.R. 663 at 665, where an alleged rape had taken place after the wife had obtained a decree nisi of divorce:

> "In my judgment a decree nisi effectively brings a marriage to an end. Between the pronouncement of a decree nisi and the obtaining of a decree absolute a marriage subsists as a mere technicality. There can be no question that by a decree nisi a wife's implied consent to marital intercourse is revoked. Accordingly, a husband commits the offence of rape if he has sexual inter- course with her thereafter without her consent."

Park J.'s ruling, that a wife's consent was revoked by a decree nisi, in this instance constitutes the ratio, since this was the issue which had to be decided in this case.

Whilst these decisions recognised that there may be occasions when a husband could be guilty of raping his wife, as first instance decisions they were of no more than persuasive authority for subsequent courts. It was not until *R. v Steele* (1976) 65 Cr.App.R. 22 (*Steele*) was heard by the Court of Appeal that the scope of the marital rape exemption was considered at appellate court level and a binding precedent established. In *Steele*, the defendant had sexual intercourse with his wife without her consent, after having given an undertaking to the county court (fol- lowing his wife's application to the court for an injunction to restrain him from approaching her) not to assault, molest or otherwise interfere with his wife. He was convicted at trial and appealed on the ground that her consent to intercourse was not revoked by the undertaking given. The principle laid down by Hale was accepted by the Court of Appeal without question. Geoffrey Lane L.J. stated (at 24):

> "As a general principle, there is no doubt that a husband cannot be guilty of rape upon his wife. The reason [*is stated*] in Sir Matthew Hale's *Pleas of the Crown*, Vol. 1 at p. 629 . . . No doubt in times gone by there were no cir- cumstances in which the wife could be held to have retracted the overall consent which, by the marriage ceremony, she gave to sexual intercourse with her husband. Researches have faied to reveal any exception to the general rule until 1949: that was the case of Clarke . . ."

His Lordship then went on to consider *Miller* and *R. v O'Brien* before he continued (at 25):

> "In this case, the circumstances are of course different from any of these in the three cases to which I have referred. Here there has been no decree of the Court, here there has been no direct order of the Court compelling the hus- band to stay away from his wife. There has been an undertaking by the

husband not to molest his wife. The question which the Court has to decide is this. Have the parties made it clear, by agreement between themselves, or has the Court made it clear by an order or something equivalent to an order, that the wife's consent to sexual intercourse with her husband implicit in the act of marriage, no longer exists? A separation agreement with a non-cohabitation clause, a decree of divorce, a decree of judicial separation, a separation order in the justices' court containing a non-cohabitation clause and an injunction restraining the husband from molesting the wife or having sexual intercourse with her are all obvious cases in which the wife's consent would be sucessfully revoked. On the other hand, the mere filing of a petition for divorce would clearly not be enough, the mere issue of proceedings as a preliminary to apply for an ex parte injunction to restrain the husband would not be enough but the granting of an injunction to restrain the husband would be enough because the Court is making an order wholly inconsistent with the wife's consent and an order, breach of which would or might result in the husband being punished by imprisonment.

What then of the undertaking in lieu of an injunction? It is, in the judgment of this Court, the equivalent of an injunction. It is given to avoid, amongst other things, the stigma of an injunction. Breach of it is enforceable by the Court and may result in imprisonment. It is, in effect equivalent to the granting of an injunction. Indeed, whether one considers this as equivalent to the order of the Court or the equivalent of an agreement between the parties, it does not matter. It may indeed have aspects of both. The effect is to eliminate the wife's matrimonial consent to intercourse."

The observations made by Geoffrey Lane L.J. in the first of the two paragraphs above as to the instances in which consent may or may not be revoked are obiter, since these were not matters which the Court of Appeal had to determine. It is his remarks in the second of the two paragraphs that consent was revoked by the undertaking given to the court, which represent the ratio of *Steele*. His reasoning why consent was revoked was that the undertaking was "equivalent to the order of the Court or the equivalent of an agreement between the parties", his Lordship taking the view that consent might be revoked by either of these means, as is evident from the question which his Lordship stated was for the court to decide:

"The question which the Court has to decide is this. Have the parties made it clear, by agreement between themselves, or has the Court made it clear by an order or something equivalent to an order, that the wife's consent to sexual intercourse with her husband implicit in the act of marriage, no longer exists?"

Since consent was revoked by the undertaking, inter alia, because the undertaking was equivalent to an agreement between the parties, revocation of consent by agreement would appear to form part of the ratio of the case. No reference was made, however, by Geoffrey Lane L.J. to any supporting authority for this proposition. Although Lynskey J. had expressed the view, obiter, in *Miller* that consent might be revoked by agreement, no mention was made of this by Geoffrey Lane L.J. in his judgment in *Steele* when considering the decision in that case.

In all of these cases, the courts were concerned with considering the extent to which consent might be revoked under the principle laid by Hale that a wife, by marriage, had consented to sexual intercourse with her husband. Hale's principle itself remained unchallenged and no consideration was given to whether and how the law should develop in the broader context of social policy. However, this position was soon to change.

▶ 5. Reform at the end of the 20th Century

16–005 In 1976 Parliament produced the first statutory definition of rape. Prior to this, although the offence of rape was contained in statute—s.1 of the Sexual Offences Act 1956 provided that "it is an offence for a man to rape a woman"—the offence was not defined by statute and its definition remained a matter for the common law. Section 1(1) of the Sexual Offences (Amendment) Act 1976 (SOAA 1976) provided:

> "For the purposes of section 1 of the Sexual Offences Act 1956 (which relates to rape) a man commits rape if—(a) he has unlawful sexual intercourse with a woman who at the time of the intercourse does not consent to it; and (b) at the time he knows that she does not consent to the intercourse or he is reckless as to whether she consents to it . . ."

The opportunity to make a clear statement of the position on the marital exception was not taken, although, as will be seen, the meaning of the word "unlawful" in this context was to become a central issue in the development of the law on this point (see below, 16–007 and 16–008).

The next case which was to have a dramatic impact on development of English law in this area was not, however, one concerned with the construction of s.1(1), but was a case heard in Scotland. This case was *S v H.M. Advocate* 1989 S.L.T. 469, where the High Court of Scotland was concerned with determining whether an indictment which charged a husband with the rape of his wife while they were cohabiting could be upheld. The court in this case was not concerned with the construction of s.1(1) because the SOAA 1976 did not extend to Scotland. When a statute is passed, there is a presumption that it applies to the whole of the UK (i.e. England, Wales, Scotland and Northern Ireland, but not the Channel Islands or the Isle of Man), but this presumption is displaced where a statute contains an "extent" section specifying its application. Such an extent section was contained in the SOAA 1976, s.7(6) of which provided that the Act did not apply to Scotland and Northern Ireland. In consequence, in Scotland, the statutory definition of rape in the SOAA 1976 did not have application and the offence of rape remained subject to the common law operating in that jurisdiction. Although the laws and legal systems of England and Scotland have very different origins and forms, courts have often stressed the desirability of uniformity in the two jurisdictions, especially where points of law common to both systems are involved, and, as will be seen, the case heard in Scotland was to assume a pivotal role in the development of the English law of rape.

In *S v H.M. Advocate*, it was recognised by Lord Emslie, the Lord Justice-General (at 471–472), delivering the judgment of the High Court, that the common law of Scotland on this matter could be traced back to the writings of Baron Hume, whose views as shown below were likely to have been based on those of Hale:

> "To discover what the law of Scotland is on the subject one begins with an unequivocal statement by Baron Hume which denies the relevancy of a charge of rape against a husband . . . [*which*] was subsequently echoed in the works of subsequent authoritative commentators on the criminal law of Scotland. The first edition of Hume on *Crimes* was published in 1797. Baron Hume himself was responsible for the second and third editions in 1819 and 1829 and important statement on the particular question appeared in all these editions . . .
>
> There is no doubt that if it was the law of Scotland that a husband is not amenable to a charge of raping his wife, the rule rests solely upon the sentence in Hume which was simply adopted and repeated in different language by the commentators and writers on the criminal law. Since, as Hume acknowledged, he made liberal use of English texts but did not regard them as providing authority for any view he expressed about the law of Scotland, it is we think likely that the view expressed by Hume . . . was taken from Hale . . ."

The rule had been justified by Baron Hume on the basis that the wife had "surrendered her person" to her husband "in that sort", but Lord Emslie (at 473) went on to reject this justification as having no application to contemporary society:

> "Whatever Hume meant to encompass in the concept of a wife's "surrender of her person" to her husband "in that sort" the concept is to be understood against the background of the status of women and the position of a woman at the time when he wrote. Then, no doubt, a married woman could be said to have subjected herself to her husband's dominion in all things. She was required to obey him in all things. Leaving out of account the absence of property, a wife's freedoms were virtually non-existent, and as she had in particular no right whatever to interfere in her husband's lives and upbringing of any children of the marriage.
>
> By the second half of the 20th century, however, the status of women, and the status of a married woman, in our law have changed quite dramatically. A husband and wife are now for all practical purposes equal partners in marriage and both husband and wife are tutors and curators of the children. A wife is not obliged to obey her husband in all things nor to suffer excessive sexual demands on the part of her husband. She may rely on such demands as evidence of unreasonable behaviour for the purposes of divorce. A live system

> of law will always have regard to changing circumstances to test the justification for any exception to the application of a general rule. Nowadays it cannot seriously be maintained that by marriage a wife submits herself irrevocably to sexual intercourse in all circumstances . . . Revocation of a consent which is revocable must depend on the circumstances. Where there is no separation this may be harder to prove but the critical question in any case must simply be whether or not consent has been withheld. The fiction of implied consent has no useful purpose to serve today in the law of rape in Scotland. The reason given by Hume for the husband's immunity from prosecution upon a charge of rape of his wife, if it ever was a good reason, no longer applies today. There is now, accordingly, no justification for the supposed immunity of a husband."

The High Court accordingly upheld the indictment and ruled that the charge against the husband should proceed to trial.

16-006 It was not long before the English courts were faced with a similar question, which would involve construing the offence of rape in the SOAA 1976 with its reference to the need for "unlawful" sexual intercourse. In the following year, in July 1990, the case of *R v R* [1991] 1 All E.R. 747 was heard at Leicester Crown Court. In this case, the couple had married in August 1984 and separated, without any court order, in October 1989. According to the wife, the separation came about because she had been advised on medical grounds against having intercourse and had thereafter declined to enter into sexual relations with her husband. Two days after the separation, the husband telephoned his wife at her mother's home where she had gone to live and said that he was going to see about a divorce. The wife saw her solicitors later the same month. In November, the husband went to the wife's home and broke into the house, tore her clothing and caused her injury, and, according to the wife, forced sexual intercourse upon her, or attempted to do so. He was charged with rape, and his counsel made a submission to the trial judge, Owen J., that the charge of rape was not known to the law where the defendant was the husband of the victim.

In considering this submission, Owen J. examined the history of the law since Hale. When referring to the Court of Appeal case of *Steele*, his Lordship noted (at 752) that it was "a strong court" which had heard this case and, from this decision, as regards the wife's implied consent, "it is apparent that it can be revoked by agreement between the parties". Whilst the agreement in *Steele* was of a formal nature, being an undertaking to the court which was regarded as the equivalent of an injunction (see above, 16-004), the facts of *R v R* did not disclose any formalised agreement or undertaking between the parties. In this case, the wife had left home, the husband had told her by telephone that he was going to see about a divorce and, some months later, the wife had consulted her solicitors. There had been no order from a court, nor had the wife started legal proceedings, as had happened in the earlier cases dealt with above. Nevertheless, Owen J. (at 754) felt that there was sufficient evidence to establish an agreement and, by recognising one to exist, continued the process of gradual extension of the law that had taken place through the earlier decisions:

> "I have been asked by Mr Milmo [*counsel for the prosecution*] to consider this question: what, in law, will suffice to revoke that consent which the wife gives to sexual intercourse upon marriage and which the law implies from the facts of the marriage? He submits that that consent may be brought to an end in a number of ways. Firstly, it may be brought to an end by a court order or, for that matter, that which appears to be the equivalent of a court order . . . Secondly, he says that it may be terminated and revoked by agreement of the parties. There is here some reason for saying that, on one reading of the facts, there may have been such an agreement of the parties. The agreement clearly could be an implicit agreement. I do not read any of the judgments, to which I have been referred, as requiring that a piece of paper should be signed or that an agreement should be drawn up in the presence of a solicitor or a notary public. It must be sufficient for there to be an agreement of the parties. Of course, an agreement of the parties means what it says. It does not mean something which is done unilaterally. As I have indicated, there is (certainly upon one reading of the facts and, as it seems to me, upon the normal reading of the facts) sufficient here to imply that the wife, by withdrawing from cohabitation as she did, and in the circumstances in which she did, clearly indicated to her husband that it was her intention not to have sexual intercourse with him again.
>
> As it seems to me, from his action in telephoning her and saying that he intended to see about a divorce and thereby to accede to what she was doing, there is sufficient here to indicate that there was an implied agreement to a separation and to a withdrawal of that consent to intercourse, which the law, I will assume and accept, implies."

His Lordship (at 754) then went on to consider whether there might be a third instance in which consent might be revoked, namely, where there was withdrawal from cohabitation by one of the parties. In Owen J.'s view, this would suffice, even though no agreement existed between the parties, and in reaching this view his Lordship regarded himself as doing no more than making a declaration of the common law:

> "The next question is whether a third set of circumstances may be sufficient to revoke that implied consent. Mr Milmo [*counsel for the prosecution*] argues that the withdrawal of either party from cohabitation is sufficient for that consent to be revoked. Mr Buchanan [*counsel for the defendant*] says: it is not for you, a humble puisne judge, to be making law. That is for Parliament, which should be considering the matter and not you.
>
> I accept that it is not for me to make the law. However, it is for me to state the common law as I believe it to be. If that requires me to indicate a set of circumstances which have not so far been considered as sufficient to negative

consent as in fact doing so, then I must do so. I cannot believe that it is part of the common law of this country that where there has been withdrawal of either party from cohabitation, accompanied by a clear indication that consent to sexual intercourse has been terminated, that that does not amount to a revocation of that implied consent. In those circumstances, it seems to me that there is ample here, both on the second exception and the third exception, which would enable the prosecution to prove a charge of rape or attempted rape against this husband."

In the light of the above, it might legitimately be asked (and the answer is not readily apparent) whether, as Owen J. decided that there was sufficient evidence for the second exception to apply, his statement in respect of the third exception and its application is obiter, or, whether, as he felt that both the second and third exceptions applied, both form part of the ratio of the case.

In reaching his decision, Owen J. had considered the existing case law as it had developed since the time of Hale, but had made no reference to the statutory definition of rape which had been enacted in the SOAA 1976 with its requirement for "unlawful" sexual intercourse to have taken place. His Lordship's reasons for making no reference are set out at the beginning of his judgment (at 748):

". . . Mr Milmo QC [*counsel for the prosecution*] has just told me, he does not argue that that [*the SOAA 1976*] affects the position that I am asked to consider. Mr Buchanan [*counsel for the defendant*] has not suggested that it affects the position, and I do not intend to consider it any further."

Following Owen J.'s rejection of the submission that there could be no offence committed, the defendant pleaded not guilty to rape, but guilty to attempted rape for which he was sentenced to three years' imprisonment. He appealed against his conviction for attempted rape on the basis that Owen J.'s rejection of the submission was wrong in law, but before the appeal was heard decisions were made in another two Crown Court cases involving marital rape. In one of these, *R v C (Rape: Marital Exemption)* [1991] 1 All E.R. 755, the principle laid down by Hale, accepted without question by Owen J. in *R v R*, was considered to no longer represent the law. Simon Brown J. stated (at 758):

"In my judgment, the position in law today is, as already declared in Scotland [*in S v H.M. Advocate 1989 S.L.T. 469*], that there is no marital exemption to the law of rape".

In view of the position taken by Simon Brown J., it is pertinent to consider whether the Court of Appeal's acceptance in *Steele* of Hale's proposition that there could be no marital rape was a binding precedent on Simon Brown J. which would preclude him from rejecting Hale's proposition. The answer to this question will depend on whether that proposition formed part of the ratio of *Steele* or was only obiter. In the view of Simon Brown J. (at 758), it was "technically, but an obiter dictum, a statement not necessary for the decision in that case, which, in any event, went against the husband". However, if it was necessary to decide whether a court undertaking could revoke the wife's marital consent to intercourse (as it was in *Steele*), it might be said that acceptance of the existence of that marital consent (on which rests Hale's proposition that there could be no marital rape) was necessary for the decision and thus part of the ratio of the case.

In the other Crown Court case, *R v J (Rape: Marital Exemption)* [1991] 1 All E.R. 759, the impact of the statutory definition of rape in the SOAA 1976 on the principle laid down by Hale, which had not been considered by Owen J. in *R v R* (or by Simon Brown J. in *R v C*), was examined. In this case, a submission was made to Rougier J. by counsel for the defendant that no offence was committed by a husband when raping his wife on account of the inclusion of the word "unlawful" in s.1(1)(a) of the SOAA 1976. This, it was contended, meant "outside marriage" and sexual intercourse within marriage therefore fell outside the statutory definition of rape in the SOAA 1976, thus preserving Hale's principle that there could be no marital rape. This contention was accepted by Rougier J., whose view (at 767) was that the scope of marital rape was now a matter of statutory interpretation:

> "Once Parliament has transferred the offence from the realm of common law to that of statute and, as I believe, has defined the common law position as it stood at the time of the passing of the [1976] Act, then I have very grave doubt whether it is open to judges to continue to discover exceptions to the general rule of marital immunity by purporting to extend the common law any further. The position is crystallised as at the making of the Act and only Parliament can alter it."

When the case of *R v R* went on appeal, the effect of the SOAA 1976, with its **16-007** requirement that rape involved "unlawful" sexual intercourse, was considered by a full Court of Appeal consisting of five judges, (Lord Lane C.J.; the President of the Family Division, Sir Stephen Brown; and three Lord Justices, Watkins, Neill and Russell, L.JJ.). Judgment was delivered by Lord Lane C.J., who, after referring to Owen J.'s decision at first instance in *R v R* and the decisions in *R v C* and *R v J*, summarised three possible solutions, and their drawbacks, which were exemplified by these decisions. In the course of this summary, his Lordship referred to such matters as: the literal approach to the meaning of "unlawful"; previous judicial decisions, including the Scottish case (as persuasive authority) of *S v H.M. Advocate*; the position adopted in other jurisdictions; the proper scope for judges as opposed to Parliament in developing the law; and the intention, when including the word "unlawful" in the SOAA 1976, of Parliament and (if theory allows there to be a difference) of the draftsman of the SOAA 1976. Lord Lane C.J.'s summary (at [1992] 1 A.C. 599 at 609–611) was as follows:

> "(1) *The literal solution.* The Act of 1976 by defining rape as it did and including the word "unlawful" made it clear that the husband's immunity is preserved, there being no other meaning for the word except "outside the bounds of matrimony". It is not legitimate to treat the word as surplusage when there is a proper meaning which can be ascribed to it.

(2) *The compromise solution*. The word "unlawful" is to be construed in such a way as to leave intact the exceptions to the husband's immunity which have been engrafted on to Hale's proposition from the decision in *Rex v Clarke* onwards and is also to be construed so as to allow further exceptions as the occasion may arise.

(3) *The radical solution*. Hale's proposition is based on a fiction and moreover a fiction which is inconsistent with the proper relationship between husband and wife today. For the reasons expressed by Lord Emslie in *S. v H.M. Advocate*, it is repugnant and illogical in that it permits a husband to be punished for treating his wife with violence in the course of rape but not for the rape itself which is an aggravated and vicious form of violence . . .

The drawbacks are these. The first solution requires the word "unlawful" to be given what is said to be its true effect. That would mean that the husband's immunity would remain unimpaired so long as the marriage subsisted. The effect would be to overrule the decisions in *Rex v Clarke* . . . and all the other cases which have engrafted exceptions on to Hale's proposition. It is hard to believe that Parliament intended that result. If it was intended to preserve the exceptions which existed at the time the Act of 1976 came into force, it would have been easy to say so.

The second or compromise solution adopts what is, so to speak, the open-ended interpretation of the Act of 1976 and would permit further exceptions to be engrafted on to Hale's proposition. In particular, an exception in circumstances such as those in the instant case where the wife has withdrawn from cohabitation so as to make it clear that she wishes to bring an end to matrimonial relationships. There would be formidable difficulties of definition and interpretation. How, one asks, would it be possible accurately to define "withdrawal from cohabitation?" It is not every wife who can, as the wife here could, go to live with her parents or indeed has anywhere else other than the matrimonial home in which to live. It may be thought that a total abolition of the immunity would be a preferable solution, as has been the experience in some other common law jurisdictions, Canada, Victoria, New South Wales, Western Australia, Queensland, Tasmania and notably in New Zealand, where the compromise solution was found to be unworkable.

The third or radical solution is said to disregard the statutory provisions of the Act of 1976 and, even if it does not do that, it is said that it goes beyond the legitimate bounds of judge-made law and trespasses on the province of Parliament. In other words the abolition of a rule of such long standing, despite its emasculation by later decisions, is a task for the legislature and not the courts. There are social considerations to be taken into account, the privacy of marriage to be preserved and questions of potential reconciliation to be weighed which make it an inappropriate area for judicial intervention. It can be seen that there are formidable objections, and others no doubt exist, to each of the possible solutions.

What should be the answer?

Ever since the decision of Byrne J. in *Rex v Clarke* courts have been paying lip service to the Hale proposition, whilst at the same time increasing the number of exceptions, the number of situations to which it does not apply. This is a legitimate use of the flexibility of the common law which can and should adapt itself to changing social attitudes.

There comes a time when the changes are so great that it is no longer enough to create further exceptions restricting the effect of the proposition, a time when the proposition itself requires examination to see whether its terms are in accord with what is generally regarded today as acceptable behaviour.

For the reasons already adumbrated, and in particular those advanced by the Lord Justice-General in *S. v H.M. Advocate* with which we respectfully agree, the idea that a wife by marriage consents in advance to her husband having sexual intercourse with her whatever her state of health or however proper her objections (if that is what Hale meant), is no longer acceptable. It can never have been other than a fiction, and fiction is a poor basis for the criminal law . . .

It seems to us that where the common law rule no longer even remotely represents what is the true position of a wife in present day society, the duty of the court is to take steps to alter the rule if it can legitimately do so in the light of any relevant Parliamentary enactment. That in the end comes down to a consideration of the word "unlawful" in the Act of 1976. It is at the best, perhaps a strange word to have used if the draftsman meant by it "outside marriage." However sexual intercourse outside marriage may be described, it is not "unlawful" if one gives to the word its ordinary meaning of "contrary to law". . .

The alternative . . . would be to interpret the word as including the various exceptions to the husband's immunity . . . If so, one asks whether the situation crystallises at the date the Act came into force. If that is the case, then all the decisions since the time when the Act of 1976 came into force which have narrowed the husband's immunity have been wrongly decided.

It may be on the other hand that the draftsman intended to leave it open to the common law to develop as it has done since 1976.

The only realistic explanations seem to us to be that the draftsman either intended to leave the matter open for the common law to develop in that way or, perhaps more likely, that no satisfactory meaning at all can be ascribed to the word and that it is indeed surplusage. In either event, we do not consider that we are inhibited by the Act of 1976 from declaring that the husband's immunity as expounded by Hale no longer exists. We take the view that the time has now arrived when the law should declare that a rapist remains a rapist subject to the criminal law, irrespective of his relationship with his victim.

> The remaining and no less difficult question is whether, despite that view, this is an area where the court should step aside to leave the matter to the parliamentary process. This is not the creation of a new offence, it is the removal of a common law fiction which has become anachronistic and offensive and we consider that it is our duty having reached that conclusion to act upon it."

It can be seen from the final paragraph of the extract above that Lord Lane C.J. was particularly concerned to demonstrate that the Court of Appeal was not straying into Parliament's territory of creating new offences. Such a view might not, however, commend itself to defendants in marital rape cases, to whom it might have seemed that the Court of Appeal had created an offence of marital rape which, as a matter of general application, had not previously existed.

16–008 Although the husband's conviction was upheld by the Court of Appeal in *R v R*, leave to appeal to the House of Lords was granted, the Court of Appeal certifying that a point of law of general public importance was involved in the decision, namely, "Is a husband criminally liable for raping his wife?". In the House of Lords, Lord Keith's speech, with which all other members of the House agreed, essentially considered the matter from three perspectives: the justifications for Hale's statement of the law, both at the time the statement was made and at the present time; the position developed and established through English case law; and the effect which the SOAA 1976 had had upon the law.

As regards justifications, Lord Keith (at 616) emphasised the importance of the common law developing to accord with changing social conditions:

> "The common law is . . . capable of evolving in the light of changing social, economic and cultural developments. Hale's proposition reflected the state of affairs in these respects at the time it was enunciated. Since then the status of women, and particularly of married women, has changed out of all recognition in various ways which are very familiar and upon which it is unnecessary to go into detail. Apart from property matters and the availability of matrimonial remedies, one of the most important changes is that marriage is in modern times regarded as a partnership of equals, and no longer one in which the wife must be the subservient chattel of the husband. Hale's proposition involves that by marriage a wife gives her irrevocable consent to sexual intercourse with her husband under all circumstances and irrespective of the state of her health or how she happens to be feeling at the time. In modern times any reasonable person must regard that conception as quite unacceptable."

In reaching this view, Lord Keith attached particular weight to the Scottish case of *S v H.M. Advocate* (see above, 16–005), from which he quoted approvingly and at length. Although only of persuasive authority, as a decision of the High Court of Justiciary in Scotland, Lord Keith concluded (at 618):

> "I consider the substance of that reasoning to be no less valid in England than in Scotland. On grounds of principle there is now no justification for the marital exception in rape".

His Lordship then considered the English cases from *Clarence* onwards, laying emphasis upon those where courts had held that there should be a variety of exceptions to the original position adopted by Hale and concluded (at 621) that this might justify a complete departure from the original position:

> "The position then is that that part of Hale's proposition which asserts that a wife cannot retract the consent to sexual intercourse which she gives on marriage has been departed from in a series of decided cases. On grounds of principle there is no good reason why the whole proposition should not be held inapplicable in modern times."

Lord Keith considered finally the statutory provision in the SOAA 1976 and whether this might inhibit rejection of the marital exception in rape. Rejection would not be possible if "unlawful" was to be interpreted as meaning "outside the bond of marriage", for intercourse within marriage would then fall outside the statutory definition of rape and the effect of this would be the preservation of the principle laid down by Hale that marital rape did not constitute an offence. Whether "unlawful" should be given this meaning depended on whether this interpretation represented the intention of Parliament. It was contended by counsel for the defendant (at 613) that it did:

> "The word "unlawful" got into the 1976 Act, not by accident, but by design. The draughtsman [*sic*] believed that the immunity propounded by Hale was still good law, subject to the exceptions recognised by the common law at the date of the passing of the Act."

This argument was not, however, accepted by Lord Keith, who was of the view that the word "unlawful" in the context of the SOAA 1976 did not bear the meaning of "outside the bond of marriage", a meaning which his Lordship felt was not the normal meaning to be attributed to this word. This was notwithstanding the decision of the Court of Criminal Appeal (see above, 2-013) in *R v Chapman* [1959] 1 Q.B. 100 that the word "unlawful" did bear this meaning for the purposes of the offence under s.19 of the Sexual Offences Act 1956 of taking a girl under the age of 18 out of the possession of her parents for the purposes of the girl having unlawful sexual intercourse with men or a particular man. Although Lord Keith recognised the appropriateness of construing the provision in the SOAA 1976 (which defined rape) along with the 1956 Act (which provided that it was an offence for a man to rape a woman), so that the provisions of the latter Act formed part of the context of the former, he attached greater importance, as will be seen, to construing the provision in the SOAA 1976 in the context of the exceptions to the marital exemption contained in the decided cases. Thus, Lord Keith stated (at 621–623):

"The argument is that "unlawful" in the subsection means outside the bond of marriage. That is not the most natural meaning of the word, which normally describes something which is contrary to some law or enactment or is done without lawful justification or excuse. Certainly in modern times sexual intercourse outside marriage would not ordinarily be described as unlawful. If the subsection proceeds on the basis that a woman on marriage gives a general consent to sexual intercourse, there can never be any question of intercourse with her by her husband being without her consent. There would thus be no point in enacting that only intercourse without consent outside marriage is to constitute rape.

Reg v Chapman [1959] 1 Q.B. 100 is founded on in support of the favoured construction. That was a case under section 19 of the Sexual Offences Act 1956, which provides:

"(1) It is an offence, subject to the exception mentioned in this section, for a person to take an unmarried girl under the age of 18 out of the possession of her parent or guardian against his will, if she is so taken with the intention that she shall have unlawful sexual intercourse with men or with a particular man.

(2) A person is not guilty of an offence under this section because he takes such a girl out of the possession of her parent or guardian as mentioned above, if he believes her to be of the age of 18 or over and has reasonable cause for the belief."

It was argued for the defendant that "unlawful" in that section connoted either intercourse contrary to some positive enactment or intercourse in a brothel or something of that kind. Donovan J., giving the judgment of the Court of Criminal Appeal, rejected both interpretations and continued, at p.105:

"If the two interpretations suggested for the appellant are rejected, as we think they must be, then the word 'unlawful' in section 19 is either sur-plusage or means 'illicit'. We do not think it is surplusage, because other-wise a man who took such a girl out of her parents' possession against their will with the honest and bona fide intention of marrying her might have no defence, even if he carried out that intention. In our view the word simply means 'illicit', i.e., outside the bond of marriage. In other words, we take the same view as the trial judge. We think this interpretation accords with the common sense of the matter, and with what we think was the obvious intention of Parliament. It is also reinforced by the alternatives specifically mentioned in sections 17 and 18 of the Act of 1956, that is, 'with the intention that she shall marry or have unlawful intercourse. . .'"

In that case there was a context to the word "unlawful" which by cogent reasoning led the court to the conclusion that it meant outside the bond of marriage. However, even though it is appropriate to read the Act of 1976 along with that of 1956, so that the provisions of the latter Act form part of the context of the former, there is another important context to section 1(1) of the

1976 Act, namely the existence of the exceptions to the marital exemption contained in the decided cases. Sexual intercourse in any of the cases covered by the exceptions still takes place within the bond of marriage. So if "unlawful" in the subsection means "outside the bond of marriage" it follows that sexual intercourse in a case which falls within the exceptions is not covered by the definition of rape, notwithstanding that it is not consented to by the wife. That involves that the exceptions have been impliedly abolished, If the intention of Parliament was to abolish the exceptions it would have been expected to do so expressly, and it is in fact inconceivable that Parliament should have had such an intention. In order that the exceptions might be preserved, it would be necessary to construe "unlawfully" as meaning "outside marriage or within marriage in a situation covered by one of the exceptions to the marital exemption." Some slight support for that construction is perhaps to be gathered from the presence of the words "who at the time of the intercourse does not consent to it," considering that a woman in a case covered by one of the exceptions is treated as having withdrawn the general consent to intercourse given on marriage but may nevertheless have given her consent to it on the particular occasion. However, the gloss which the suggested construction would place on the word "unlawfully" would give it a meaning unique to this particular subsection, and if the mind of the draftsman had been directed to the existence of the exceptions he would surely have dealt with them specifically and not in such an oblique fashion. In *Reg. v Chapman* Donovan L.J. *[sic]* accepted, at p.102, that the word "unlawfully" in relation to carnal knowledge had in many early statutes not been used with any degree of precision, and he referred to a number of enactments making it a felony unlawfully and carnally to know any woman-child under the age of 10. He said, at p.103 "one would think that all intercourse with a child under 10 would be unlawful; and on that footing the word would be mere surplusage." The fact is that it is clearly unlawful to have sexual intercourse with any woman without her consent, and that the use of the word in the subsection adds nothing. In my opinion there are no rational grounds for putting the suggested gloss on the word, and it should be treated as being mere surplusage in this enactment, as it clearly fell to be in those referred to by Donovan L.J. *[sic]* . . ."

It can be seen that at several points in his speech Lord Keith referred to the task of discovering the intention of Parliament in using the word "unlawful". His Lordship's conclusion that its use in this case was "mere surplusage", with no intention to continue the rule concerning the marital exception, provided him with a clear avenue towards his preferred solution of ending the hold which Hale's proposition still had on the English law. That this was his preferred solution can be seen from his reference (at 621) to the question of "whether section 1(1) of the Act of 1976 presents an insuperable obstacle to that sensible course [*of rejecting Hale's proposition*]".

The case of *R v R* was decided shortly before *Pepper v Hart* [1993] 1 All E.R. 42 (see above, 1–084) and at that time courts still held firmly to the principle that they **16–009** should not refer to the record of Parliamentary debates as an aid to interpretation. It is instructive to consider what Lord Keith might have discovered if he had been able to consult *Hansard*. During the course of the passage of the SOAA 1976, at the Committee Stage of the Bill, a backbencher, Mr George Cunningham, tabled an amendment which would have expressly made a husband liable for the rape of his wife. There was considerable support for the amendment. The Government, however, declined to support the amendment, although its stance had little to do with the substantive merits of the proposed change, as can be seen from the following exchange between Mr Alexander Lyon, the Minister of State at the Home Office, and Mr Cunningham (at *Hansard*, HC, Standing Committee F, March 24, 1976, col.25):

> "**Mr Alexander W. Lyon**: This, however, is an issue of principle which has not received the same wide public discussion as the other elements in the Bill . . . I know with what scepticism my Hon. Friend will accept the suggestion that I am about to make to him. I shall rely on a time-honoured Treasury device of saying that [*another*] Committee is considering this area [*The Criminal Law Revision Committee, which, after a further six years, reported in 1984 in favour of continuing the existing doctrine of the marital exception to rape: Criminal Law Revision Committee, Fifteenth Report, Sexual Offences, Cmnd. 9213*]—
>
> **Mr Cunningham**: Oh really!
>
> **Mr Lyon**: and I shall endeavour to see that the matter is brought to its attention in order that it can give a more considered judgment of the implications of the proposal."

The amendment was pressed to a vote, and the Committee voted seven to four in favour, only for the amendment to be reversed when the Bill was considered at the Report Stage. If Lord Keith had felt able to take into account the proceedings of Parliament in interpreting the words of the SOAA 1976, he would clearly have found that, in spite of strong support for making a husband liable for raping his wife, the intention was to leave in place the common law rule preserving the marital exemption.

Whether or not Lord Keith's impression of the intention of Parliament in passing the SOAA 1976 was correct, the decision in *R v R* was generally well received, even if there were some doubts about whether such crucial issues of policy should be determined by the courts rather than by Parliament. In the wake of the case, the Law Commission in a report entitled *"Rape within Marriage"* (Law Com. No.205 (1992) HC 167) recommended that the offence of rape be redefined by omitting from the statutory definition the word "unlawful", which had been interpreted to be mere surplusage. The Commission felt that it was "undesirable to leave on the statute book an enactment on a matter of this importance that contains words that have no effect" (para.1.13) and, further, that:

> ". . . if the word 'unlawful' is to remain . . . that perpetrates on the face of the statute an unnecessary element of uncertainty about the word's meaning, if

any, in those other sections of the 1956 Act that have not yet been the subject of specific judicial decision" (para.2.6).

Initially the Government took no action to implement this recommendation, although when Lord Lester, a Liberal Democrat peer, moved an amendment in the House of Lords during the Committee Stage of the Criminal Justice and Public Order Bill 1994 seeking to implement the Law Commission's recommendation that the word "unlawful" be omitted from the statutory definition, the Government gave its support to the amendment. Earl Ferrers, a Home Office Minister, whilst noting that the amendment "merely confirms in statute what is already in law", approvingly proclaimed it to be "an important declaration of Parliament's belief that a man who rapes his wife can expect no special treatment under the law" (*Hansard*, HL, Vol. 555, col.1630, (June 14, 1994)). Interestingly, his Lordship went on to remark that "it is open to question whether Hale's pronouncement that a man could not be guilty of raping his wife ever reflected the broad opinion of the general public" (ibid.), a view which might be contrasted with that of Hawkins J. in *Clarence* (see above, 16–003) that "no jury would be found to convict a husband of rape on his wife except under very exceptional circumstances".

The outcome of the Government's acceptance of Lord Lestor's amendment was that s.142 of the Criminal Justice and Public Order Act 1994 repealed the definition of rape contained in the SOAA 1976. Section 142 substituted a new provision for s.1 of the Sexual Offences Act 1956, which in its original form had simply stated that it was an offence for a man to rape a woman (see above, 16–005), and this new provision contained a definition of rape in which the word "unlawful" did not appear. Not only, however, did the new provision give statutory effect to the decision in *R v R* by removing the word "unlawful" and confirming that the marital exemption from the offence of rape no longer applied, but it also introduced two other important changes. One of these changes was effected by s.1(1) and the other by s.1(2). These can be readily identified by comparing the new provision, which is set out below, with those which it replaced (see above, 16–005). For ease of comparison, these two changes in the new provision (now itself replaced by s.1(1) of the Sexual Offences Act 2003—see above, 16–001) are italicised:

"1.—(1) It is an offence for a man to rape a woman *or another man*.

(2) A man commits rape if—

(a) he has sexual intercourse with a person (*whether vaginal or anal*) who at the time of the intercourse does not consent to it; and

(b) at the time he knows that the person does not consent to the intercourse or is reckless as to whether that person consents to it."

The Criminal Justice and Public Order Act 1994 marked the end of the chapter of developments that had eventually led to the major change in the legal status of wives as victims of rape by their husbands. However, the case of *R v R* continued to have some significance in two contexts: first, in subsequent litigation by the defendant R, and secondly in the reactions of later courts to the approach taken by the House of Lords in that case to the development of the law.

16–010 R, whose conviction and sentence to three years' imprisonment had been upheld by the House of Lords, subsequently applied to the European Commission on Human Rights, claiming that he had been convicted of rape even though at the time of the incident his conduct did not constitute a criminal offence. His complaint was that his conviction represented the retrospective application of what was effectively a new law criminalising marital rape which had been created by the English courts in the course of his own prosecution. This, he claimed, was contrary to art.7(1) of the European Convention on Human Rights, which provides that:

> "No one shall be held guilty of any criminal offence on account of any act or omission which did not constitute a criminal offence under national or international law at the time when it was committed".

The Commission concluded, by a majority of 14 votes to 3, that there had been no violation of art.7. Subsequently the European Court of Human Rights confirmed, in *SW v United Kingdom; CR v United Kingdom* (1996) 21 E.H.R.R. 363, that there had been no violation of the Convention in R's case.

Article 7 deals with the legitimacy of convictions under the criminal law, and both the Commission and the Court addressed the issue in R's application in the context of the concept of law in a common law system where courts regularly develop the rules which they then seek to apply. The approach of the Commission was set out in its opinion at 374–375, paras 44 and 47–48:

> "Article 7(1) reflects the principle, found also in other provisions of the Convention in the context of requirements that interferences with or restrictions in the exercise of fundamental rights must be "in accordance with law" or "prescribed by law", that individuals should be able to regulate their conduct with reference to the norms prevailing in the society in which they live. That generally entails that the law must be adequately accessible—an individual must have an indication of the legal rules applicable in a given case—and he must be able to foresee the consequences of his actions, in particular, to be able to avoid incurring the sanction of the criminal law.
>
> Where law is developed by application and interpretation of courts in a common law system, their law-making function must remain within reasonable limits. Article 7(1) excludes that any acts not previously punishable should be held by the courts to entail criminal liability or that existing offences should be extended to cover facts which previously did not clearly constitute a criminal offence.
>
> It is however compatible with the requirements of Article 7(1) for the existing elements of an offence to be clarified or adapted to new circumstances or developments in society in so far as this can reasonably be brought under the original concept of the offence. The constituent elements of an offence may

not however be essentially changed to the detriment of an accused and any progressive development by way of interpretation must be reasonably foreseeable to him with the assistance of appropriate legal advice if necessary."

The standard of foreseeability required for the law to meet the standards of art.7 was considered by the Commission to have been correctly stated by the Court in the earlier case of *The Sunday Times v United Kingdom* (1979) 2 E.H.R.R. 245 at para.49:

". . . a norm cannot be regarded as a 'law' unless it is formulated with sufficient precision to enable the citizen to regulate his conduct: he must be able— if need be with appropriate advice—to foresee, to a degree that is reasonable in the circumstances, the consequences which a given action may entail. Those consequences need not be foreseeable with absolute certainty: experience shows this to be unattainable. Again, whilst certainty is highly desirable, it may bring in its train excessive rigidity and the law must be able to keep pace with changing circumstances. Accordingly, many laws are inevitably couched in terms which, to a greater or lesser extent, are vague and whose interpretation and application are questions of practice."

The Commission applied this approach to the facts of R's case and concluded (at 393, para.60) that because there had been a de facto separation with an expressed intention of both parties to seek a divorce:

". . . there was a basis on which it could be anticipated that the courts could hold that the notional consent of the wife was no longer to be implied. In particular, given the recognition by contemporary society of women's equality of status with men in marriage and outside it and of their autonomy over their own bodies, the Commission considers that this adaptation in the application of the offence of rape was reasonably foreseeable to an applicant with appropriate legal advice."

However, two Commissioners, Mr L. Loucaides, with whom Mr M.A. Nowicki agreed, took a different view (at 396) of how likely it was that either laymen or lawyers could have foreseen the change brought about by the House of Lords:

"The fact that a change of the law so as to remove the [*husband*'s] immunity was necessary does not make any difference for the purposes of the principle safeguarded under Article 7(1) of the Convention. Such change could have been effected through legislation. A change through the case law of the courts could not have been reasonably foreseeable to the applicant even with the assistance of legal advice and consequently, in my view, there has been a breach of that Article in this case."

The history of the English law on the husband's immunity as it stood before R's prosecution, as considered in this chapter, may or may not have suggested to a competent lawyer that its abandonment by a court was imminent. What is surely inconceivable is that someone in R's position would have thought it appropriate or necessary to seek legal advice before engaging in the behaviour for which he was prosecuted. The apparent acceptance of such a fiction as part of the interpretation of article 7 seems particularly inapt in these circumstances.

When the case progressed from the Commission to the European Court of Human Rights, the general principles applicable to the alleged violation of the Convention were considered. The judgment illustrates the Court's approach to the interpretation of the Convention and contains (at 398–399) an interesting examination of the concept of law and the manner of its development through the courts:

"The guarantee enshrined in Article 7, which is an essential element of the rule of law, occupies a prominent place in the Convention system of protection, as is underlined by the fact that no derogation from it is permissible under Article 15 in time of war or other public emergency. It should be construed and applied, as follows from its object and purpose, in such a way as to provide effective safeguards against arbitrary prosecution, conviction and punishment.

Accordingly, as the Court held in its *Kokkinakis v Greece* judgment of 25 May 1993, Article 7 is not confined to prohibiting the retrospective application of the criminal law to an accused's disadvantage: it also embodies, more generally, the principle that only the law can define a crime and prescribe a penalty (*nullum crimen, nulla poena sine lege*) and the principle that the criminal law must not be extensively construed to an accused's detriment, for instance by analogy. From these principles it follows that an offence must be clearly defined in the law. In its aforementioned judgment the Court added that this requirement is satisfied where the individual can know from the wording of the relevant provision and, if need be, with the assistance of the courts' interpretation of it, what acts and omissions will make him criminally liable. The Court thus indicated that when speaking of "law" Article 7 alludes to the very same concept as that to which the Convention refers elsewhere when using that term, a concept which comprises written as well as unwritten law and implies qualitative requirements, notably those of accessibility and foreseeability.

However clearly drafted a legal provision may be, in any system of law, including criminal law, there is an inevitable element of judicial interpretation. There will always be a need for elucidation of doubtful points and for adaptation to changing circumstances. Indeed, in the United Kingdom, as in the other Convention States, the progressive development of the criminal law through judicial law-making is a well entrenched and necessary part of legal tradition. Article 7 of the Convention cannot be read as outlawing the gradual clarification of the rules of criminal liability through judicial interpretation from case to case, provided that the resultant development is consistent with the essence of the offence and could reasonably be foreseen."

The issue of the reasonable foreseeability, at the time of the offence, of the development brought about by the House of Lords was dealt with at two further points in the judgment of the Court (at 401–402):

> "This was an area where the law had been subject to progressive development and there were strong indications that still wider interpretation by the courts of the inroads on the immunity was probable. In particular, given the recognition of women's equality of status with men in marriage and outside it and of their autonomy over their own bodies, the adaptation of the ingredients of the offence of rape was reasonably foreseeable, with appropriate legal advice, to the applicant . . .
>
> The decisions of the Court of Appeal and then the House of Lords [*in R v R*] did no more than continue a perceptible line of case law development dismantling the immunity of a husband from prosecution for rape upon his wife. There was no doubt under the law as it stood on [*the date of the rape*] that a husband who forcibly had sexual intercourse with his wife could, in various circumstances, be found guilty of rape. Moreover, there was an evident evolution, which was consistent with the very essence of the offence, of the criminal law through judicial interpretation towards treating such conduct generally as within the scope of the offence of rape. This evolution had reached a stage where judicial recognition of the absence of immunity had become a reasonably foreseeable development of the law."

There is some ambiguity about the requirement that a development "could reasonably be foreseen". Does it mean that the change in the law must be reasonably foreseeable as being a *(highly) likely* or *probable* development, or merely as a *possible* development? Must it be foreseeable as being either likely or probable to happen in the immediate future (for example, in a prosecution brought against the person who should have foreseen the change at the time of the incident leading to his prosecution), or simply as being a possible development at some point in the perhaps distant future? These issues were not explored in the Court's judgment.

16–011 Although the approach of the House of Lords in *R v R* to the development of the law concerning marital rape was thus received favourably by the European Court of Human Rights, the House of Lords has twice in more recent cases dealing with different issues explicitly considered the approach adopted in *R v R* and then declined to pursue a similar line. The first case was *R v Clegg* [1995] 1 A.C. 482 (*Clegg*), in which a soldier had been convicted on a charge of murder for a killing while on duty with a patrol in Northern Ireland. Clegg had fired three shots at the windscreen of a stolen car which was approaching him at speed. He fired a fourth shot, after the car had passed, and this hit and killed a passenger in the car. At his trial, it was accepted that the first three shots had been fired in self-defence, but it was found that the fourth shot had been fired with the intention of causing death or serious bodily harm and could not have been fired in self-defence (or in defence of fellow soldiers) as the car had passed and there was no danger. The trial judge also ruled, in respect of the firing of the fourth shot, that there was insufficient evidence to raise the defence under s.3(1) of the Criminal Law Act (Northern Ireland) 1967 that he was using reasonable force to effect an arrest of the car driver. On appeal to the (Northern Ireland) Court of Appeal, the court, reviewing the evidence, held that the defence under s.3(1) ought to have been considered. It decided, however, that there had been no miscarriage of justice by failing to consider it, as the firing of the fourth shot was a grossly excessive and disproportionate use of force. The court nevertheless certified for the House of Lords, as a point of law of general public importance, the question of whether a soldier on duty, who killed a person with the intention necessary for murder, should be guilty of manslaughter rather than murder if the firing was in self-defence (or defence of another, or in the prevention of crime or the arrest of an offender) but where it constituted force that was excessive and unreasonable in the circumstances. Lord Lloyd, with whose decision and reasons Lords Keith, Browne-Wilkinson, Slynn and Nicholls agreed, concluded (at 498):

> "I regret that under existing law, on the facts found by the trial judge, he had no alternative but to convict of murder".

Lord Lloyd went on to consider whether the law should be changed. In reviewing the relationship between the courts and the legislature in the development of the law, Lord Lloyd referred to *R v R* and commented (at 500):

> "I am not averse to judges developing law, or indeed making new law, when they can see their way clearly, even where questions of social policy are involved. A good recent example would be the affirmation by this House of the decision of the Court of Appeal (Criminal Division) that a man can be guilty of raping his wife . . .".

The limiting expression "when they can see their way clearly" may seem somewhat imprecise. Lord Lloyd may have intended this to be a reference to the words italicised in the passage from Lord Simon's dissenting judgment in *DPP for Northern Ireland v Lynch* [1975] A.C. 653 at 695, which his Lordship had quoted in the previous paragraph of his judgment:

> "I am all for recognising frankly that judges do make law. And I am all for judges exercising this responsibility boldly at the proper time and place—that is, *where they can feel confident of having in mind, and correctly weighed, all the implications of their decision*, and where matters of social policy are not involved which the collective wisdom of Parliament is better suited to resolve. (*Emphasis added*.)"

Even when amplified as in the passage from Lord Simon, the "seeing clearly" criterion lacks precision, and may in practice simply mean that judges should only develop or make new law when they are sure that they wish to do so. In coming to the conclusion that the House of Lords in *Clegg* should not follow the lead given by *R v R* in creating new law, Lord Lloyd referred to the fact that, although self-defence and the use of force in the prevention of crime had been developed as part of the common law (as complete defences resulting in an acquittal), Parliament had relatively recently introduced legislation dealing with the issue in s.3 of the Criminal Law (Northern Ireland) Act 1967 without taking the opportunity to create a qualified defence reducing murder to manslaughter in cases where the defendant had used excessive force in preventing a crime. The unstated contrast with *R v R* is that the House of Lords in that case had been dealing with an area of the law where there had been no legislative activity. In addition, Lord Lloyd pointed out that the possibility of allowing the reduction of murder to manslaughter in the situation exemplified by Clegg was bound up with the wider issue of whether the mandatory life sentence for murder should be maintained. He felt that the wider issue, and therefore the specific issue involved in *Clegg*, should only be decided by Parliament.

The second case where the approach in *R v R* was considered was *C (A Minor) v DPP* [1996] 1 A.C. 1 (*C (A Minor)*). This case dealt with the issue of doli incapax—the rebuttable presumption that meant (until its eventual abolition by s.34 of the Crime and Disorder Act 1998) that between the minimum age of criminal responsibility (10 years) and the age of 14, a defendant was presumed not to know that his act was seriously wrong and, on that basis, to be held not guilty of any crime. In dismissing the appeal of C, aged 12, against his conviction of a charge of interfering with a motor cycle with the intent to commit theft, the Divisional Court had viewed the presumption as divisive, perverse, outdated and unprincipled, and held that it was no longer part of the law.

The decision in *R v R* was not used in argument before the Divisional Court. However, there was an appeal to the House of Lords in which the Crown, supporting the decision of the Divisional Court to abandon the presumption, invited their Lordships, in the words of Lord Lowry, to "take courage" from the decision in *R v R*. The House of Lords acknowledged serious problems with the presumption and its application by the courts, but concluded that it required legislation to effect a change. In rejecting the invitation to take a bold line with a long-established common law rule as happened in *R v R*, Lord Lowry (at 38) pointed to some of the differences between the two cases:

> "*Reg v R* dealt, in the first place, with a specific act and not with a general principle governing criminal liability. It was based on a very widely accepted modern view of marital rape and it derived support from a group of up-to-date decisions. The principle rejected in *Reg v R* stood on a dubious legal foundation. . . . Moreover, unlike the presumption here, Hale's doctrine had not been given the stamp of legislative, judicial, governmental and academic recognition."

A possible analogy with the approach to the development of the law taken in *R v R* was thus clearly rejected by both Lord Lloyd in *Clegg* and Lord Lowry in *C (A Minor)*. It is less clear, however, whether the case of *R v R* could be said to have been distinguished in these cases. In some law reports in which the case of *C (A Minor)* is reported, the headnote to the case states that *R v R* was distinguished (see [1996] 1 A.C. 1; [1995] 2 W.L.R. 383; [1995] 2 Cr. App. R. 166; and [1995] R.T.R. 261), whilst in others no mention is made of it being distinguished (see [1995] 2 All E.R. 43; [1995] 1 F.L.R. 933; and (1995) 159 J.P. 269). In the law reports in which the case of *Clegg* is reported, no reference is made in any of the headnotes to *R v R* being distinguished (see [1995] 1 A.C. 482; [1995] 2 W.L.R. 80; [1995] 1 All E.R. 334; and [1995] 1 Cr. App. R. 507). The divergent views reflected in the headnotes to these cases illustrate how it may be misleading to think in terms of straightforward, consistently applicable principles at work within the system of precedent.

It seems that the House of Lords clearly signalled in *Clegg* and *C (A Minor)* that any freedom that might have been suggested by *R v R* for judges to change established law should be used in only very limited circumstances. As to what those circumstances might be, Lord Lowry in *C (A Minor)* (at 28) gave some guidance as to relevant considerations that judges should take into account when contemplating changes to established law:

> "It is hard, when discussing the propriety of judicial law-making, to reason conclusively from one situation to another . . . I believe, however, that one can find in the authorities some aids to navigation across an uncertainly charted sea. (1) If the solution is doubtful, the judges should beware of imposing their own remedy. (2) Caution should prevail if Parliament has rejected opportunities of clearing up a known difficulty or has legislated, while leaving the difficulty untouched. (3) Disputed matters of social policy are less suitable areas for judicial intervention than purely legal problems. (4) Fundamental legal doctrines should not be lightly set aside. (5) Judges should not make a change unless they can achieve finality and certainty."

Lord Lowry's remarks on the place of judicial law-making set limits on the range of legitimate opportunities for judicial development of the law. On the other hand, the significance of his Lordship's comments may lie in their acknowledgement that, in appropriate circumstances (such as those surrounding the abolition of the husband's immunity from rape), it will be proper for judges to consider making changes even to fundamental legal doctrines.

Such judicial development of the law, however, is contentious and has attracted criticism. Indeed, submissions have been made to the Court of Appeal that the House of Lords in *R v R* acted ultra vires and exceeded its powers by deciding to change the law in its judicial capacity when Parliament in its legislative capacity had decided against doing so. In *R v Graham L* [2003] EWCA Crim 1512, Pill L.J. stated (at paras [10]–[12]):

> "[10] Sir Ivan [*Lawrence Q.C., counsel for the appellant*] criticises the decision of the House of Lords in *R v R*. He refers to academic comment on it and makes other submissions. His principal submission developed at the hearing has been that the House of Lords in *R v R* acted *ultra vires*. He submits that, in deciding as they did, the House of Lords in their judicial capacity put themselves above

Parliament. Reliance is placed on the fact that when the Sexual Offences (Amendment) Bill was before the House of Commons in 1976 it contained a clause which introduced the crime of marital rape. In a reasoned statement the Minister of State for the Home Office, Mr Brynmor John, announced that it was proposed to remove the relevant clause from the bill. After a three-hour debate in the House, the amendment for removing the clause was agreed to without a division. Sir Ivan submits that it is a manifest injustice, when the House of Commons had taken that view that the House of Lords in its judicial capacity should have reached the decision that they did in *R v R*. The Criminal Law Revision Committee had considered the question of marital rape in 1984 and had concluded that the defence of marriage should remain, albeit introducing a further exception to the very limited exceptions which were already in existence. Parliament had specifically decided not to change the law and it was not open to the House of Lords in its judicial capacity to decide as it did in *R v R*.

[11] The decision of the House was defective in two respects: first, that it legislated in the face of a Parliamentary decision in 1976 not to legislate; and second, that the decision in effect had a retrospective effect in that conduct which had occurred before the decision, as in *R v R* itself, was by the decision made unlawful. Sir Ivan submits that it is important that the House of Lords should revisit this question in the light of social and legal changes since 1992, including the enactment of the Human Rights Act 1998. They should do so out of a concern to ensure that justice is done, and having regard to the strong academic opinion against the 1992 decision. It is submitted that the House had insufficient regard to the Parliamentary decision in 1976 and, moreover, that the European Court of Human Rights, in upholding the principles stated in *R v R*, fell into the same error. It must be pointed out that both in the House of Lords and in the European Court of Human Rights reference was made to the withdrawal of the clause in 1976. In our judgment it cannot be said that either court was unaware of the Parliamentary history involved. In the European proceedings the history was considered in some detail.

[12] Thus it is submitted that the decision in *R v R* is wrong. Even if it is correct, it should now be revisited. This court should take such action as would enable the matter to be reargued in the House of Lords. The House of Lords now has power to reverse its own decisions. It should be given the opportunity, submits Sir Ivan, to re-affirm a fundamental constitutional principle that it is not for the courts to create new offences; it is for Parliament. The question has some practical importance for the appellant because if the number of life sentences were to be reduced, he would have a better opportunity of release on licence at an earlier stage. The European Court of Human Rights, it is submitted, has misunderstood English law and Parliamentary practice in stating the principles it has."

These submissions, which were made in respect of a rape which took place prior to *R v R*, were not, however, accepted by the court. Pill L.J. stated (at paras [17]–[18]):

"[17] We have considered the submissions of Sir Ivan, but . . . [i]n our judgment the principle established in the House of Lords is clear. The decision was reached following a full consideration of the issues and nothing has happened subsequently which renders it arguable that the House of Lords should reverse their decision either in relation to all the pre-1994 charges or in relation to those which took place during the period of years prior to the decision of the House of Lords in *R v R* . . .

[18] In relation to the submission that the will of Parliament has been perverted, we find nothing irregular or beyond its powers in the House of Lords reaching the decision it did, notwithstanding that about fifteen years earlier a conscious decision had been taken by a vote of the House of Commons not to introduce by way of statute what the House of Lords held in 1992. It in no way derogates from the principle of the sovereignty of Parliament that the House of Lords should act as it did, notwithstanding the decision of the House of Commons many years before (or even had it been more recent), not to take the action which the House of Lords took. We have referred to the speech of Lord Lowry in *R v DPP* [*sic*]. We can see nothing offensive to the powers of Parliament. The court refuses the application for leave to appeal . . ."

A subsequent Court of Appeal in *R v C (Barry)* [2004] EWHC Crim 292 reaffirmed the view taken in *R v Graham L* and declined to distinguish that case and other decisions on the ground that the rape had taken place at a much earlier time (1970) when (it was alleged) the accused could not have reasonably foreseen with legal advice that he was committing an offence. Judge L.J. stated (at para.[25]):

"[25] Consistently with the outcome in *R v R* [1992] 1 AC 599, it is now clearly established by the decision of this court in *R v L (Graham)* [2003] EWCA Crim 1512, that a man may properly be convicted of raping his wife when the incident occurred before the decision of *R v R*. The reasoning of the European Court of Human Rights, together with our analysis of the supposed immunity, and a true understanding of the limitations on its ambit before March 1991, lead us to conclude that the distinction Mr Marson [*counsel for the appellant*] sought to base on the dates when the different rapes occurred in *SW v United Kingdom*; *CR v United Kingdom*, and again in *R v L (Graham)*, and the present case is not sustained. The prosecution of this defendant for rape did not infringe his rights under the Convention."

In conclusion, therefore, it might be said that the courts have shown a strong determination to make fundamental changes to legal rules where they have undoubtedly thought these to be appropriate, as with the abolition of the husband's immunity from rape, although, as the decisions in *R v Clegg* and *C (A Minor) v DPP* show, the courts have shown a reluctance to do so except in the clearest of cases.

Further Reading

Barton, "The story of marital rape" (1992) 108 L.Q.R. 260

Giles, "Judicial law-making in the criminal courts: the case of marital rape" [1992] Crim. L.R. 407

Lawrence, "Punishment without law: how ends justify the means in marital rape" [2006] Denning L.J. 37

Osborne, "Does the end justify the means? Retrospectivity, Article 7, and the marital rape exemption" [1996] E.H.R.L.R. 406

Virgo, "Marital rape—the fast or slow track to law reform?" [1991] C.L.J. 19

17 APPROPRIATION IN THEFT

▶ 1. Introduction

17–001 In order for a person to be guilty of the offence of theft, s.1(1) of the Theft Act 1968 requires that "he dishonestly appropriates property belonging to another with the intention of permanently depriving the other of it". Section 3(1) of the Act provides that:

> ". . . any assumption by a person of the rights of an owner amounts to an appropriation, and this includes, where he has come by the property (innocently or not) without stealing it, any later assumption of a right to it by keeping or dealing with it as owner".

Whether, for an appropriation to occur, an absence of consent on the part of the person to whom the property belongs (the owner) is required, or whether appropriation can occur irrespective of whether or not there is consent, has been considered in a series of cases, which are examined in this case study. No reference to the owner's consent is made in either s.1(1) or s.3(1), so it was essentially a question of statutory construction whether a person could or could not appropriate property where there was consent on the part of the owner. Different views were expressed on this matter, both in the Court of Appeal and in the House of Lords, in a number of cases up to and including the House of Lords' decision in *Director of Public Prosecutions v Gomez* [1993] A.C. 442 (*Gomez*).

 This case study illustrates a number of points in relation to precedent and statutory interpretation:

- ▶ whether words can be read into a statutory provision;
- ▶ the difficulty of deciding whether statements in cases are part of the ratio or are only obiter;
- ▶ the distinguishing of cases;
- ▶ the Court of Appeal professing itself to be bound by views expressed in the House of Lords;
- ▶ inconsistent judicial decisions;
- ▶ when ascertaining the meaning of a word used in a statutory provision, having regard to a dictionary definition of the word, to other sections of the statute in question, to a committee report (including a draft Bill) preceding the legislation, and to a presumption that statutory provisions do not make changes in the existing law beyond those expressly stated or arising by necessary implication;
- ▶ the entertaining of submissions based on academic discussion or comment;

- the broad or narrow scope of a proposition of law;
- disapproving and overruling of decisions;
- conflicting decisions of the same court and the operation of stare decisis; and
- the importance of looking at a statute as a whole and having regard to other sections in it as an intrinsic aid to ascertaining meaning.

▶ 2. The House of Lords' Decision in *Lawrence v Metropolitan Police Commissioner*

The first case in which consideration was given to the question of whether there **17–002** could be theft with or without the owner's consent was *Lawrence v Metropolitan Police Commissioner* [1972] A.C. 626 (*Lawrence*). The facts of the case were set out in the judgment of Viscount Dilhorne in the only judgment delivered in the House of Lords (at 627–628):

". . . the appellant was convicted on December 2, 1969, of theft contrary to section 1(1) of the Theft Act 1968. On September 1, 1969, a Mr. Occhi, an Italian who spoke little English, arrived at Victoria Station on his first visit to this country. He went up to a taxi driver, the appellant, and showed him a piece of paper on which an address in Ladbroke Grove was written. The appellant said that it was very far and very expensive. Mr. Occhi got into the taxi, took £1 out of his wallet and gave it to the appellant who then, the wallet being still open, took a further £6 out of it. He then drove Mr. Occhi to Ladbroke Grove. The correct lawful fare was in the region of 10s 6d. The appellant was charged with and convicted of the theft of the £6."

The conviction was upheld both by the Court of Appeal and the House of Lords. The first of two questions certified for the House of Lords by the Court of Appeal as involving a point of law of general public importance was whether s.1(1) of the Act was to be construed as though it contained the words "without the consent of the owner" or words to that effect. Such words had been an express requirement of the offence of larceny in s.1(1) of the Larceny Act 1916, which had been repealed and replaced by the offence of theft in the Theft Act 1968, and the defence argument on appeal was primarily directed towards whether similar words could be implied into s.1(1) of the 1968 Act. There was, however, also a secondary argument (at [1972] A.C. 626 at 631) directed towards the meaning of "appropriates":

""Appropriates" is meant in a pejorative, rather than a neutral, sense in that appropriation is against the will of the owner. Parliament has not radically departed from the old concept of larceny in omitting the words "without the consent of the owner.""

This secondary argument was, however, given no consideration at all by the House when delivering judgment and the House was quite dismissive of the defence's primary argument. The Court of Appeal's certified question was answered by the House, quite emphatically, in the negative. Viscount Dilhome stated (at 631–632):

> "The main contention of the appellant in this House and in the Court of Appeal was that Mr. Occhi had consented to the taking of the £6 and that, consequently, his conviction could not stand. In my opinion, the facts of this case to which I have referred fall far short of establishing that Mr. Occhi had so consented.
>
> Prior to the passage of the Theft Act, which made radical changes in and greatly simplified the law relating to theft and some other offences, it was necessary to prove that the property alleged to have been stolen was taken "without the consent of the owner" (Larceny Act 1916, section 1(1)). These words are not included in section 1(1) of the Theft Act 1968, but the appellant contended that the subsection should be construed as if they were, as if they appeared after the word "appropriates." Section 1(1) reads as follows:
>
>> "A person is guilty of theft if he dishonestly appropriates property belonging to another with the intention of permanently depriving the other of it; and 'thief' and 'steal' shall be construed accordingly."
>
> I see no ground for concluding that the omission of the words 'without the consent of the owner' was inadvertent and not deliberate, and to read the subsection as if they were included is, in my opinion, wholly unwarranted. Parliament by the omission of these words has relieved the prosecution of the burden of establishing that the taking was without the owner's consent. That is no longer an ingredient of the offence.
>
> Belief or the absence of belief that the owner had . . . consented to the appropriation is relevant to the issue of dishonesty, not to the question whether or not there has been an appropriation. That may occur even though the owner has permitted or consented to the property being taken."

There is some uncertainty as to whether Viscount Dilhome's pronouncement that appropriation may occur even though the owner has permitted or consented to the property being taken is part of the ratio of the case or is merely obiter. It might be regarded as no more than obiter, since, if the evidence fell short of establishing consent on the part of Mr Occhi (as Viscount Dilhome thought it did), whether or not there could be an appropriation where there was consent was not a matter that the court had to decide. On the other hand, Viscount Dilhorne's pronouncement was in line with the answer given by his Lordship to the first certified question, of whether s.1(1) of the Act was to be construed as though it contained the words "without the consent of the owner" or words to that effect. Thus, even though Viscount Dilhorne was of the opinion that the evidence fell short of establishing consent to the taking, it could be said to be an element of the decision that it made no difference whether or not there was consent to the taking and accordingly part of the ratio of the case. As to whether the pronouncement was part of the ratio or whether it was obiter, differing views have been expressed in subsequent cases (see Bingham L.J. in *Dobson v General Accident Fire and Life Assurance Corp Plc* [1990] 1 Q.B. 274 at 289 (*Dobson*) below, 17–005; Lord Keith in *Gomez* [1993] A.C. 442 at 457, below, 17–009; and Lord Lowry in *Gomez* [1993] A.C. 442 at 494, below, 17–009.)

▶ 3. The Court of Appeal Decision in *R. v Skipp*

Within a relatively short time of the House of Lords' decision in *Lawrence*, there **17–003** were cases decided by the Court of Appeal which appeared to suggest that "appropriates" required some unauthorised conduct on the part of the defendant. Conduct which is unauthorised would not seem to be conduct to which the owner has consented and this raised doubts as to how far these decisions were consistent with *Lawrence*. One such decision was *R. v Skipp* [1975] Crim. L.R. 114 (*Skipp*). In this case, the defendant, posing as a genuine haulage contractor, obtained instructions to collect three loads from different locations in London and deliver them to customers in Leicester. The defendant was charged in one count of an indictment with theft of all the goods and contended that the count was bad for duplicity in that there were three separate appropriations at different times and places. (Indictments set out criminal charges and are divided into paragraphs called counts and, if a defendant is charged with more than one offence in a count, objection maybe taken to the indictment on account of duplicity, or being double.) It was held, however, that, although the defendant may have intended to steal when he collected each load, he had not done anything inconsistent with the owner's rights by loading the goods. The court thought it was probably only when he diverted the goods from their intended destination that he acted inconsistently with the rights of the owner. At this point, he had gone beyond what he was authorised to do. If a person does not appropriate property when he is doing what he is authorised to do, this appears to cast doubt on whether there can be an appropriation where the owner consents to the taking: if there is consent to the taking, it is hard to see how a person can be said to be going beyond what he is authorised to do. However, the meaning of appropriation was not considered in any detail by the court nor was there any mention of the decision in *Lawrence*.

If the pronouncement of Viscount Dilhorne in *Lawrence* that there could be an appropriation whether or not the owner consented was only obiter, the pronouncement would not be binding on the Court of Appeal, which would be free not to follow it. No question would therefore arise as to the correctness of the decision in *Skipp*. If, on the other hand, the pronouncement in *Lawrence* formed part of the ratio of that case, this would be binding on the Court of Appeal in *Skipp*, which would be obliged to follow it. If *Skipp* had failed to follow *Lawrence* when obliged to do so, *Skipp* would have to be regarded as wrongly decided. However, if *Lawrence* could be considered distinguishable, the Court of Appeal in *Skipp* would not be obliged to follow it since the precedent would not have application. As will be seen, the question of whether *Lawrence* could be distinguished from *Skipp* was subsequently considered by Parker L.J. in *Dobson* (see below, 17–005).

▶ ## 4. The Decision in *R. v Morris*

17–004 The possible inconsistency between *Lawrence* and Court of Appeal decisions like *Skipp* was subsequently considered in *R. v Morris* [1984] A.C. 320 (*Morris*). This case involved price label switching in a supermarket, in which the defendant took goods from the shelves, replaced the price labels attached to them with labels showing a lesser price and paid the lesser price for the goods at the checkout. He was subsequently arrested. He was convicted of theft, following a direction by the trial judge that the changing of the price labels constituted an appropriation. He appealed, contending that this was a misdirection, but the conviction was upheld by the Court of Appeal. When considering the meaning of appropriation, the Court of Appeal (per Lord Lane C.J. at [1983] Q.B. 587 at 593) recognised that there were two schools of thought:

> "The first contends that the word "appropriate" has built into it a connotation that it is some action inconsistent with the owner's rights, something hostile to the interests of the owner or contrary to his wishes and intention or without his authority. The second school of thought contends that the word in this context means no more than to take possession of an article and that there is no requirement that the taking or appropriation should be in any way antagonistic to the rights of the owner."

Since *Lawrence* indicated that there could be an appropriation even if the owner consented, it clearly belonged to the second school of thought, whereas subsequent Court of Appeal cases like *Skipp*, which had suggested that appropriation required unauthorised conduct on the part of the defendant, belonged to the first school of thought. The Court of Appeal felt constrained to follow *Lawrence* and adopt the second school of thought. The Court of Appeal made no pronouncement whether it considered the statements in *Lawrence* to be ratio or obiter, but clearly regarded it as important that effect should be given to the House's views. Lord Lane C.J., having referred to the House's ruling in *Lawrence* that the words "without the consent of the owner" should not be read into s.1(1), stated (at 597):

> "That being the emphatic view of their Lordships, it would, we think, be quite wrong in effect to re-import into the offence the necessity of proving what amounts to absence of consent on the part of the owner by saying that the word "appropriates" necessarily means some action contrary to the authority or interests of the owner and that that is one of the requirements which the prosecution must prove."

The Court of Appeal accordingly held that taking the article from the shelf with a view to transporting it to the checkout was an appropriation, since removing it amounted to the assumption of one of the owner's rights (which the court held to be sufficient for an appropriation), that of removing the article from the shelf, notwithstanding that the taking would not have been without the consent of the owner at the time.

On appeal, the House of Lords upheld the convictions, but took a different view of the meaning of appropriation. Lord Roskill, with whose judgment all other members of the House agreed, was unable to accept Lord Lane C.J.'s interpretation of appropriation, stating ([1984] A.C. 320 at 332):

> "If one postulates an honest customer taking goods from a shelf to put in his or her trolley to take to the check-point there to pay the proper price, I am unable to see that any of these actions involves any assumption by the shopper of the rights of the supermarket. In the context of section 3(1), the concept of appropriation in my view involves not an act expressly or impliedly authorised by the owner but an act by way of adverse interference with or usurpation of those rights."

In Lord Roskill's view, an appropriation would not occur until there was a switching of the labels and a removal of the goods from the shelf with a view to transporting them to the checkout to pay the lower price.

By taking the view that appropriation involved unauthorised conduct, Lord Roskill, although not expressly approving the decision in *Skipp*, appeared to confirm the correctness of that decision. His Lordship, however, made no attempt to explain any possible conflict between his view of appropriation and the pronouncement of Viscount Dilhome in *Lawrence*. His Lordship merely contented himself with remarking (at 331):

> "That there was in that case *[Lawrence]* a dishonest appropriation was beyond question and the House did not have to consider the precise meaning of that word in section 3(1)".

If, in Lord Roskill's view, the House of Lords in *Lawrence* did not have to consider the precise meaning of the word "appropriation" in s.3(1), whereas the House did have to consider this in *Morris*, it might be questioned whether Lord Roskill could be said to have distinguished *Lawrence* (see Spencer [1984] Camb. L.J. 7, 9: "we must guess whether it *[Lawrence]* is distinguishable, right for the wrong reasons or impliedly overruled"). Further, it is likely that Lord Roskill's statement that "appropriation" involved "not an act expressly or impliedly authorised by the owner but an act by way of adverse interference with or usurpation of those rights" was not necessary to the decision in *Morris* and did not form part of the ratio of the case. The switching of the price labels in the case was unauthorised and it did not have to be decided whether acts which were authorised could constitute an appropriation.

▶ ## 5. Subsequent Court of Appeal Cases

17-005   In the period following *Morris*, the view of Lord Roskill gained acceptance in the Court of Appeal. It was applied by the Court of Appeal in *R. v Fritschy* [1985] Crim. L.R. 745 (*Fritschy*), where the defendant, following instructions, collected Krugerrands in England and took them to Switzerland where he departed from his instructions and dishonestly disposed of them for his own benefit. Whilst there was no doubt that the property was stolen in Switzerland, the Court of Appeal held that it was not stolen in England (and therefore fell outside the court's jurisdiction), even though the defendant had already decided to steal it before leaving for Switzerland, since he had done nothing within the jurisdiction that he was not authorised to do. In the later case of *R v McHugh* (1989) 88 Cr. App. R. 385 at 393, the Court of Appeal, without expressing approval of Lord Roskill's statement in *Morris*, but referring to several reported decisions which included *Lawrence* and *Morris*, stated that there were a number of propositions founded upon these cases. One of these propositions was that an act done with the authority of a company could not amount to an appropriation from the company, a proposition which is consistent with Lord Roskill's statement in *Morris*.

In later cases, however, notably *R. v Phillipou* (1989) 89 Cr. App. R. 290 and *Dobson* [1990] 1 Q.B. 274, a civil case involving an insurance claim for theft, the Court of Appeal expressed the view that there could be an appropriation even where there was consent on the part of the owner, which the court regarded as being in accordance with *Lawrence*. In *Dobson*, some attempt was made to reconcile the apparently conflicting views in *Lawrence* and *Morris*. Although the statements of Viscount Dilhorne in *Lawrence* and Lord Roskill in *Morris* appear to conflict, they could be said not to be *directly* contradictory since one mentions consent, whereas the other refers to an act not authorised. If a distinction can be drawn between consent and authorisation, the statements might be reconciled. An attempt to draw such a distinction was made by Parker L.J. in *Dobson* (at 285–286), his Lordship being of the view that there could be an appropriation where there was mere consent on the part of the owner, but not where there was express authorisation given by the owner. On this basis, although following and applying *Lawrence*, he approved two decisions widely thought to be consistent with *Morris*, *Skipp* and *Fritschy*:

> "That case *[Skipp]* can in my view only be reconciled with *Reg. v Lawrence (Alan)* [1972] A.C. 626 on the basis that there was much more than mere consent of the owner. There was express authority, indeed instruction to collect the goods. It could not therefore be said that the defendant was assuming any rights. Whatever his secret intentions he was, until he diverted *[from his route]*, exercising the owner's right on his instructions and on his behalf. *Reg. v Fritschy* was a somewhat similar case . . . *[where the]* defendant did collect the coins as instructed and went with them to Switzerland but then made off with them. He had a dishonest intention throughout. He was convicted of theft but on appeal his conviction was quashed by the Court of

Appeal. The ground of the decision is shortly stated in the judgment of the court which was delivered by Skinner J. He said:

"There was no evidence of any act by the appellant within the jurisdiction which was not expressly authorised by Mr. Hoedl. That, in the light of the decision of the House of Lords in *Reg. v Morris* [1984] A.C. 320, is fatal to the charge of theft. In those circumstances we are compelled to the conclusion that the learned judge's direction was wrong, and that this appeal must be allowed."

Here, as in *Reg. v Skipp* [1975] Crim.L.R. 114, what the defendant did was expressly authorised, i.e. there was more than mere consent. On this basis the decision can be reconciled with both *Reg. v Lawrence (Alan)* [1972] A.C. 626 and *Reg. v Morris (David)* [1984] A.C. 320."

Whilst *Skipp* and *Fritschy* might be reconciled with *Lawrence* on this basis, there may, however, be other decisions such as *Eddy v Niman* (1981) 73 Cr. App. R. 237 which cannot be (see Gardner, "Is Theft a Rip-Off?" (1990) 10 O.J.L.S. 441 at 443).

An alternative approach to reconciling *Lawrence* and *Morris* was adopted by Bingham L.J. in *Dobson* [1990] 1 Q.B. 274 at 289. His Lordship sought to reconcile the two decisions on the basis that the Italian student in *Lawrence* had not in fact consented to the taxi driver taking anything in excess of the correct fare. Since the student's consent had been procured by deceit, there was only apparent consent and not actual consent to the taking:

"I do not find it easy to reconcile this ruling of Viscount Dilhome, which was as I understand central to the answer which the House of Lords gave to the certified question, with the reasoning of the House in *Reg. v Morris (David)* [1984] A.C. 320. Since, however, the House in *Reg. v Morris* considered that there had plainly been an appropriation in *Reg. v Lawrence (Alan)* [1972] A.C. 626, this must (I think) have been because the Italian student, although he had permitted or allowed his money to be taken, had not in truth consented to the taxi driver taking anything in excess of the correct fare. This is not a wholly satisfactory reconciliation, since it might be said that a supermarket consents to customers taking goods from its shelves only when they honestly intend to pay and not otherwise."

As Bingham L.J. recognised, however, there are problems with this approach. It suggested that removal of goods from a shelf in a supermarket by a person with an intent not to pay might be an appropriation, since the supermarket would not in fact consent to the taking, but this would be contrary to the view expressed by Lord Roskill in *Morris* (see above, 17–004) that an appropriation would not occur until there was a switching of labels and removal of goods from the shelf with a view to transporting them to the checkout to pay the lower price.

These attempted reconciliations in *Dobson* of the decisions in *Lawrence* and *Morris*, and the correctness of the views expressed in those cases as to the meaning of "appropriation", were subsequently considered in *Gomez*. In this case, the House of Lords was ultimately able to review the law and decide which of the competing views as to the meaning of "appropriation" should prevail.

▶ ## 6. The Decision in *Director of Public Prosecutions v Gomez*

▷ ### (a) The decision of the Crown Court and the Court of Appeal

17-006 In *Gomez*, the defendant, the assistant manager of a shop, persuaded the shop manager to agree to sell goods to his accomplice and to accept payment by cheques which, to the knowledge of the defendant and his accomplice, were stolen and worthless. The defendant was charged with theft. At the defendant's trial in the Crown Court, it was contended that the manager had expressly authorised the goods to be removed and that, following *Morris*, there was no appropriation. The trial judge rejected this submission, whereupon the defendant pleaded guilty. On appeal, the Court of Appeal held that the trial judge had been wrong to reject the submission and the defendant's conviction was quashed. The Court of Appeal, after considering *Lawrence* and *Morris* and noting the difficulty of reconciling the two decisions, stated ([1991] 3 All E.R. 394 at 398):

> "Suffice it to say that if there is a difference between the two decisions, that was not the view taken by their Lordships in *R v Morris*, and that is the decision which we must follow".

It might be questioned whether the Court of Appeal was bound to follow the decision in *Morris*. This would depend on whether the statement by Lord Roskill in *Morris* as to the meaning of appropriation was part of the ratio of the case or only obiter.

In reaching its decision, the Court of Appeal made no reference to Bingham L.J.'s attempted reconciliation in *Dobson* of *Lawrence* and *Morris*, although it did comment unfavourably on the distinction drawn by Parker L.J. in that case between express authority and mere consent. Lord Lane C.J. stated (at 399):

> "We remark in passing that at least so far as the criminal law is concerned we find it difficult to draw a line between express authority and consent. Guilt or innocence should not depend upon so fine a distinction, if indeed the distinction be shown to exist."

Following *Morris*, the Court of Appeal concluded (at 400):

> ". . . that the transfer of the goods to him *[the accomplice]* was with the consent and express authority of the owner and that accordingly there was no lack of authorisation and no appropriation".

The Court of Appeal did, however, certify the following point of law of general public importance for the consideration of the House of Lords:

> "When theft is alleged and that which is alleged to be stolen passes to the defendant with the consent of the owner, but that consent has been by a false representation, has (a) an appropriation within the meaning of section 1(1) of the Theft Act 1968 taken place, or, (b) must such a passing of property necessarily involve an element of adverse *[interference]* with or usurpation of some right of the owner?"

In short, the question was whether there could be an appropriation where the owner consents to the taking of the property or whether some adverse interference, suggesting an absence of consent or authority, was needed.

▷ (b) The decision of the House of Lords

When the case went on appeal to the House of Lords, the House was unanimously **17–007** of the view that the decisions in *Lawrence* and *Morris* could not be reconciled. Most forthright was Lord Lowry who, without referring to the attempts at reconciliation of Parker and Bingham L.JJ. in *Dobson*, stated ([1993] A.C. 442 at 494): "In my opinion, any attempt to reconcile the statements of principle in *Lawrence* and *Morris* is a complete waste of time". Similarly, Lord Browne-Wilkinson (at 495–496), again without reference to the attempts at reconciliation in *Dobson*, felt that "it is impossible to reconcile the decision in *Lawrence* . . . with the views expressed in *Morris*". The only judgment in which reference was made to the attempts at reconciliation in *Dobson* was that of Lord Keith; the remaining two members of the House, Lords Jauncey and Slynn, did not deliver judgments, but confined themselves to expressing agreement with Lord Keith. Lord Keith (at 463–464) firmly rejected Bingham L.J.'s attempted reconciliation:

> "As regards the attempted reconciliation by Bingham L.J. of the reasoning in *Reg. v Morris* [1984] A.C. 320 with the ruling in *Reg. v Lawrence* [1972] A.C. 626 it appears to me that the suggested basis of the reconciliation, which is essentially speculative, is unsound".

The attempted reconciliation of Parker L.J. was not expressly rejected by Lord Keith, although it appeared to be impliedly rejected in the light of his Lordship's remarks (at 460) when commenting on *Morris* and its potential conflict with Lawrence: "It does not appear to me that any sensible distinction can be made in this context between consent and authorisation".

Although unanimous in the view that the decisions in *Lawrence* and *Morris* could not be reconciled, the House was not unanimous in its view as to the answers to be given to the certified questions. The House, by a 4–1 majority (Lord Lowry dissenting), answered the questions respectively in the affirmative and in the negative. The approach taken by the majority contrasted sharply with that of Lord Lowry in his dissenting judgment. Although the appeal turned on the proper construction to be given to the word "appropriates" in s.1(1), only Lord Lowry focused on ascertaining the intention of Parliament when enacting the legislation. His Lordship gave detailed consideration to the legal meaning to be ascribed to the word, having regard, inter alia, to the ordinary dictionary definition of the word, the use of the word in various sections of the Theft Act 1968 other than s.1(1), and the Eighth Report of the Criminal Law Revision Committee (Cmnd.2977 (1966)) together with the draft Bill annexed to the Report. The majority, in contrast, considered the matter more from a precedent standpoint, referring back to the examination of the issue in previous cases, notably *Lawrence* and *Morris*.

(i) Ascertaining the intention of Parliament when enacting the legislation

17–008   Lord Lowry (at 469) began his examination of the legal meaning to be attributed to "appropriates" by examining the dictionary definition of the term, which he considered to be confined to an act done without the consent or authority of the owner:

> "The ordinary and natural meaning of "appropriate" is to take for oneself, or to treat as one's own, property which belongs to someone else. The primary dictionary meaning is "take possession of, take to oneself, especially without authority," and that is in my opinion the meaning which the word bears in section 1(1). The act of appropriating property is a one-sided act, done without the consent or authority of the owner. And if the owner consents to transfer the property to the offender or to a third party, the offender does not appropriate the property, even if the owner's consent has been obtained by fraud."

However, if the dictionary definition is to "take possession of, take to oneself, *especially* without authority" (emphasis supplied), does this not recognise that there can be appropriations *with* authority (or consent)? In the light of this wording, it might be questioned whether the dictionary definition to which Lord Lowry refers does confine "appropriation" to acts done without the consent or authority of the owner.

In Lord Lowry's view, the ordinary dictionary meaning of the word (as comprising an act done without the consent or authority of the owner) was the meaning which Parliament intended the word to have. His Lordship justified his view that the ordinary meaning of "appropriation" was the legal meaning to be attributed to the word in its statutory context by reference both to intrinsic material within the statute and extrinsic material outside the statute, as well as making reference to a presumption as an aid to construction of the statutory provision. In the first instance, his Lordship had recourse to intrinsic material within the statute itself, namely, other sections of the Theft Act 1968, apart from s.1, in which the word in question appeared. The word appeared in ss.2, 3, 4 and 6 and, after reviewing these sections, Lord Lowry stated (at 470):

> ". . . reading sections 1 to 6 as a whole . . . the ordinary and natural meaning of "appropriates" in section 1(1) is confirmed. So clear is this conclusion to my mind that, notwithstanding anything which has been said in other cases, I would be very slow to concede that the word "appropriates" in section 1(1) is in its context ambiguous. But . . . the Crown case requires that there must be ambiguity and further requires that the ambiguity must be resolved against the ordinary meaning of the word and in favour of the neutral meaning preferred and required by the Crown's argument. Therefore, my Lords, I am willing for the purpose of argument to treat the word "appropriates" as ambiguous in its context . . ."

Lord Lowry subsequently went on to consider extrinsic material outside the statute, in this instance, the Eighth Report of the Criminal Law Revision Committee and the draft Bill annexed to the Report, "for such guidance as it may afford" for resolving the ambiguity. When Parliament enacted the Theft Act 1968, it adopted, substantially unchanged, the draft Bill annexed to the Committee's report and both the definitions of theft in s.1(1) and appropriation in s.3(1) were identical to those contained in the draft Bill. This, for Lord Lowry, was a clear indication that Parliament intended to implement the Committee's thinking:

> "While the report may not completely resolve the question for your Lordships, it provides in the first place a very useful summary of the state of the law in 1966. It also discusses in some detail the shortcomings of the law in regard to theft and kindred offences, as they appeared to the committee, and it proposes remedies. A reading of the 1968 Act, which was based on the draft Bill annexed to the report, leads me to the conclusion that, when using the very words of the draft, Parliament intended to implement the committee's thinking. Of course, if the words of the 1968 Act clearly achieve a different result from that which seemed to be intended by the committee, it is the words which must prevail and strained constructions must not be adopted in order to give effect to the report.
>
> In paragraph 15 the committee discuss the "chief defects in the existing law of larceny," including its failure to deal with certain kinds of dishonesty. In paragraph 16 they point out that the defects stem from regarding larceny as a violation of possession and not of rights of ownership, with the offence depending on a *taking* of the property *[at 470–471]*. . .
>
> The committee's proposed remedies for the defects of the law as they found it clearly appear from . . . paragraphs *[35 to 38]*. "Fraudulent conversion" is accepted as the starting point for the new and comprehensive definition of theft and "dishonest appropriation" is chosen as a synonym. Both expressions

embody the notion of an adverse unilateral act done to the prejudice of the owner and without his authority; indeed, fraudulent conversion can have no other meaning [*at 475*] . . .

. . . the report contains a great deal which confirms and nothing which contradicts the interpretation of the word "appropriates" which I have preferred, and a comparison of the Act with the draft Bill gives no support to the contrary view . . . The conclusion from this comparison of the draft Bill and the Act is that Parliament has in all material respects adopted the committee's approach and has thereby endorsed the committee's point of view [*at 476–477*]."

The extent to which a committee report preceding the introduction of legislation, and any draft Bill attached to it which forms the basis for the legislation, can be taken into account when seeking to ascertain the meaning of words used in a provision in the statute had been considered some years earlier by the House of Lords in *Black-Clawson Ltd v Papierwerke Waldhof-Aschaffenburg AG* [1975] A.C. 591, where different views had been expressed on this matter. Viscount Dilhorne (at 623) in that case was of the view that, where a draft Bill drawn up by a committee had been enacted without alteration, the committee's recommendations and observations on the draft Bill constituted a valuable aid to construction of the statute and Lord Lowry in *Gomez* (at 477) referred to this view with approval:

"While not forgetting the observations in *Black-Clawson Ltd v Papierwerke Waldhof-Aschaffenburg A.G.* [1975] A.C. 591 of Lord Reid, at p.614F, Lord Wilberforce, at p.629C–G, and Lord Diplock, at p.637D, where he wisely warned against departing from the plain and natural meaning in favour of a strained construction, I am much impressed by the more adventurous but very logical pronouncements of Viscount Dilhorne . . . [*who*] said, at p.623:

"While I respectfully agree that recommendations of a committee may not help much when there is a possibility that Parliament may have decided to do something different, where there is no such possibility, as where the draft Bill has been enacted without alteration, in my opinion it can safely be assumed that it was Parliament's intention to do what the committee recommended and to achieve the object the committee had in mind. Then, in my view the recommendations of the committee and their observations on the draft Bill may form a valuable aid to construction which the courts should not be inhibited from taking into account.""

Finally, Lord Lowry had regard to a presumption against alteration in the existing law when considering the meaning of "appropriates" in s.1(1). In his Lordship's opinion, this provided additional support for his view that "appropriates" had its ordinary meaning of a unilateral act done without the owner's consent or authority. Lord Lowry stated (at 488–489):

"My Lords, to sum up, every indication seems to me to point away from adopting a neutral meaning of the word "appropriation." I would reinforce that view by recalling that in *George Wimpey & Co. Ltd v B.O.A.C.* [1955] A.C. 169, 191, Lord Reid stated that if the arguments are fairly evenly balanced (not that I believe they are in this case), that interpretation should be chosen which involves the least alteration of the existing law. *Maxwell on Interpretation of Statutes*, 12th ed. (1969), states, at p.116:

"Few principles of statutory interpretation are applied as frequently as the presumption against alterations in the common law. It is presumed that the legislature does not intend to make any change in the existing law beyond that which is expressly stated in, or follows by necessary implication from, the language of the statute in question."

If the change in the law of theft which is signalled by decisions such as that reached in *Dobson v General Accident Fire and Life Assurance Corporation Plc.* [1990] 1 Q.B. 274 has in reality occurred, the position of insurers in that field has in the result been prejudiced by legislation the effect of which was far from clear."

The approach of Lord Lowry, of having recourse to various aids to ascertaining the legal meaning of "appropriates", was in stark contrast to that of Lord Keith, who delivered the leading judgment of the majority and with whose judgment Lords Browne-Wilkinson, Jauncey and Slynn expressed agreement. Lord Keith neither examined other sections of the Theft Act 1968 in which the word appeared nor made reference to any presumptions. Further, Lord Keith felt that little was to be gained by looking back to a committee report preceding the legislation, stating (at 464):

"In my opinion it serves no useful purpose at the present time to construe the relevant provisions of the Theft Act by reference to the report which preceded it, namely, the Eighth Report of the Criminal Law Revision Committee on Theft and Related Offences (1966) (Cmnd 2977)."

The majority's failure to have regard to the Committee's report has attracted strong criticism, as having led to a meaning being attributed to "appropriates" which is contrary to the intention of Parliament. Professor J.C. Smith (at [1993] Crim. LR. 304, 305–306) has remarked:

"The crux of this case was the decision of the majority not to refer to the Eighth Report of the CLRC. "In my opinion," said Lord Keith, "it serves no useful purpose at the present time to seek to construe the relevant provisions of the Theft Act by reference to [*the Eight Report*]." No useful purpose! Except of course that it demonstrated conclusively that the decision of the majority flatly contradicted the intention of Parliament—intention which was readily apparent from the fact that Parliament, having received the CLRC's clear exposition of the effect of their draft bill, enacted legislation identical in all material respects

> with it. Of course, the majority were in fact aware of all this. It is apparent, though only through Lord Lowry's dissent, that the case was very fully argued by counsel for the respondent. As for the dissent, one can only echo the editorial comment in *Archbold News* (Issue 1, January 20, 1993, p.4): "It is a mystery how the majority of their Lordships failed to be persuaded by the elaborate and scholarly dissenting speech delivered by Lord Lowry which they do not answer." Clearly, there was a decision to turn a blind eye to the intention of the framers of the legislation and of Parliament. This is all the more remarkable in the light of their Lordships' decision in *Pepper v Hart* [1993] 1 All E.R. 42 that, in appropriate cases, they may look not only at committee reports, but also at *Hansard* . . . In the present case, it was only necessary to look at the report."

The decision in *Gomez* was delivered by the House on December 3, 1992, one week after the decision in *Pepper v Hart*, which was delivered on November 26, 1992, and which was considered above, 1–084. It is inconceivable that the House was not aware of the decision in *Pepper v Hart* when considering the appeal in *Gomez*, not least since two members of the House, Lords Keith and Browne-Wilkinson, sat in both cases!

(ii) The view taken of Lawrence

17–009   For the majority, how "appropriates" should be construed was a matter which had already been resolved, for the issue had previously been considered and essentially determined in *Lawrence*. In the view of Lord Keith (at 457), Viscount Dilhorne's speech in *Lawrence* contained two clear pronouncements:

> "First that it is no longer an ingredient of the offence of theft that the taking should be without the owner's consent and second, that an appropriation may occur even though the owner has permitted or consented to the property being taken. The answer given to the first certified question was in line with those pronouncements, so even though Viscount Dilhorne was of opinion that the evidence fell short of establishing that Mr. Occhi had consented to the taking of the £6 it was a matter of decision that it made no difference whether or not he had so consented."

By stating that these pronouncements were in line with the answer given to the certified question and that it was a matter of decision that the defendant was liable whether or not Mr Occhi consented, notwithstanding that the evidence seemed to fall short of establishing consent, Lord Keith seemed to regard these pronouncements as having been part of the ratio of the case. This was reinforced when his Lordship, at a later point in his judgment, stated (at 464):

> "The decision in *Lawrence* was a clear decision of this House upon the construction of the word "appropriate" in section 1(1) of the Act, which had stood for 12 years when doubt was thrown upon it by obiter dicta in *Morris*. *Lawrence*

> must be regarded as authoritative and correct, and there is no question of it now being right to depart from it."

The pronouncements of Viscount Dilhorne in *Lawrence* might, however, be regarded as no more than obiter. As has been stated above (see 17–002), the view might be taken that, if the evidence fell short of establishing consent on the part of Mr Occhi, whether or not there could be an appropriation where there was consent was not a matter the court had to decide. As such, the pronouncements would not be capable of forming a binding precedent. Accordingly, the House in *Gomez*, like any other court, would be free to depart from them. This course of action was advocated by Lord Lowry (at 494):

> "If my submissions are correct [*that appropriation requires an act done without the consent or authority of the owner*], the question finally remains whether your Lordships are bound by the doctrine of precedent to follow and apply the statements in *Reg. v Lawrence* [1972] A.C. 626, 632 that Parliament, by omitting the words "without the consent of the owner" from section 1(1) of the Act of 1968, has "relieved the prosecution of the burden of establishing that the taking was without the owner's consent" and that "[*appropriation*] may occur even though the owner has permitted or consented to the property being taken." I suggest not . . . Viscount Dilhorne had already expressed the opinion that the facts of the case fell far short of establishing that the victim had consented to the acquisition by the appellant of the money he was alleged to have stolen. This line of reasoning . . . supports a conviction for theft under section 1(1) on any view of the law and enables your Lordships to regard the statements at p.632 as obiter dicta."

Even if the pronouncements of Viscount Dilhorne in *Lawrence* were to be regarded not as obiter but as part of the ratio, however, they would not be binding on the House of Lords, although they would be on lower courts. The House is not bound by its previous decisions and can depart from them in accordance with its *Practice Statement (Judicial Precedent)* issued in 1966. By this statement, the House pronounced its willingness "while treating former decisions of this House as normally binding, to depart from a previous decision when it appears right to do so" and in this connection indicated that it "will bear in mind . . . the especial need for certainty in the criminal law" ([1966] 1 W.L.R. 1234). Lord Lowry (at 494–495), had he not regarded Viscount Dilhorne's pronouncements as obiter, would have been prepared to have departed from them under the *Practice Statement*:

> ". . . let me assume that Viscount Dilhorne's statements have the character of a "decision" as that word is used in the *Practice Statement (Judicial Precedent)* [1966] 1 W.L.R. 1234, which intimated that this House would depart from a previous decision "when it appears right to do so." Your Lordships might then so elect. The Practice Statement referred to "the especial need for certainty as to the criminal law," but there is ample proof that both before and after *Morris* certainty has been lacking. The cases on the *Practice Statement* are

conveniently found in *Halsbury's Laws of England*, 4th ed., vol. 26 (1979), p.296, para. 577. A previous decision should not be departed from merely because the House considers it to be wrong and only rarely should questions of construction be reconsidered. But the precise *meaning* of section 1(1) has not received serious judicial attention before."

The precise meaning of s.1(1) had not, according to Lord Lowry, received serious judicial attention in *Lawrence* because, as his Lordship had remarked earlier in his judgment, both the Court of Appeal and the House of Lords had been concerned with whether the words "without the consent of the owner" should be read into s.1(1):

"Both the contention of the defence [*in Lawrence*] and the court's refutation of it were misconceived: the absence of consent on the part of the owner is already inherent in the word "appropriates," properly understood, and therefore the argument for the defence got off on the wrong foot and the counter-argument that the words specified by the defence cannot be read into section 1(1) did not assist the prosecution. And the observation, without further discussion, that the omission of the words "without the consent of the owner" is deliberate seems to have led directly to the erroneous conclusion that a supposed appropriation with consent of the owner is one of the four ingredients which are required (and which suffice) to constitute theft . . . [*at 479*]

. . . the defence argument was primarily directed towards implying words into section 1(1), a difficult task at best, and only secondarily towards the meaning of "appropriates:" see [[1972] A.C.] p.631A. But the only speech delivered did not consider this second point and the summary treatment of the appellant's argument is reflected in the opinion expressed, at p.633, that the point certified and argued was scarcely worthy of their Lordships' attention. [*at 483*]"

(iii) The view taken of Morris

17–010 In *Gomez*, Lord Keith sought to dismiss Lord Roskill's remarks in *Morris* as to the meaning of appropriation as unnecessary for the decision in that case and accordingly as only having the status of obiter dicta. His Lordship (at 464) regarded the remarks as erroneous and as wrongly throwing doubt on the decision in *Lawrence*:

"The actual decision in *Morris* was correct, but it was erroneous, in addition to being unnecessary for the decision, to indicate that an act expressly or impliedly authorised by the owner could never amount to an appropriation . . .

The decision in *Lawrence* was a clear decision of this House upon the construction of the word "appropriates" in section 1(1) of the Act, which had stood for 12 years when doubt was thrown upon it by obiter dicta in *Morris*. *Lawrence* must be regarded as authoritative and correct, and there is no question of it now being right to depart from it."

Lord Lowry, on the other hand, did not regard *Lawrence* as authoritative, considering Viscount Dilhorne's pronouncements in that case only to have the status of obiter dicta (see above, 17–009). As such the pronouncements had no greater authority than the remarks of Lord Roskill in *Morris*, which, as Lord Lowry recognised (at 494), were also obiter. Both statements, which are by the same court in different cases, will carry equal weight in terms of precedent and either statement may be followed. As the remarks of Lord Roskill in *Morris* accorded with Lord Lowry's interpretation as to the meaning of appropriation, Lord Lowry (at 484) not surprisingly expressed himself to be in agreement with Lord Roskill's views:

> "I would respectfully agree with his description, in relation to dishonest actions, of appropriation as involving an act by way of adverse interference with or usurpation of the owner's rights, but I believe that the less aggressive definition of appropriation which I have put forward [i.e. to take possession of, take to oneself, especially without authority] fits the word as used in an honest sense in section 2(1) as well as elsewhere in the Act. The important feature, of course, which our definitions have in common is that the appropriation must be an act done without the authority or consent, express or implied, of the owner."

(iv) Academic opinion

17–011

Although no mention was made by Lord Keith in his judgment of academic discussion or comment on the meaning of appropriation, Lord Lowry did make reference to this at various points in the course of his dissenting judgment. The assistance derived from this was acknowledged and there was a recognition (at 489) of the increasing willingness of the courts to entertain submissions from counsel based on such discussion or comment:

> "Not only *Reg. v Lawrence* [1972] A.C. 626 and *Reg. v Morris* [1984] A.C. 320, but a large number of cases on section 1(1) have furnished the material for animated and often penetrating academic discussion. I am encouraged to have seen that submissions based on such discussion are increasingly made by counsel and entertained by the courts and your Lordships have in the present appeal benefited from counsel's industry in this respect. I could not possibly do justice in this speech to all that has been written on the subject, but I hope that I have profited from the many articles which I have read since the hearing."

(v) Summary

17–012

With the majority of the House approving the *Lawrence* view of appropriation and not that expressed in *Morris*, the House answered the question certified by the Court of Appeal (see above, 17–006) in the affirmative on the first part and in the negative on the second part. Thus, where property passes to the defendant with the consent of the owner, an appropriation within the meaning of s.1(1) of the Theft Act 1968 will have taken place (the affirmative answer to the first part of the question) and the passing of the property need not necessarily involve an element of adverse interference with or usurpation of some right of the owner (the negative answer to the second part of the question). It will also be seen that the certified question was expressed with regard to cases where the consent had been obtained by a false representation, that is, by a deception. It might therefore be asked whether the ratio of *Gomez* is that there can be an appropriation where property passes to the defendant with the consent of the owner and no element of adverse interference is necessary only in cases where the consent has been obtained by deception. It was stated in the headnote to the case, both in the Appeal Cases report (see [1993] A.C. 442) and in other reports of the case (see [1992] 3 W.L.R. 1067; [1993] 1 All E.R. 1; and (1996) 96 Cr. App. R. 359), that:

> ". . . an act expressly or impliedly authorised by the owner of goods or con-sented to by him could amount to an appropriation of the goods within section 1(1) of the Theft Act 1968 where such authority or consent had been obtained by deception."

This suggests that the ratio might be confined to cases where consent has been obtained by deception, although (as with all cases) the statement in the headnote can be no more than a tentative statement of the ratio. A more definitive view of the ratio is possible only when later courts have subsequently considered a case. Would later courts confine the ratio to cases where consent was obtained by deception or would they take a broader view? Would the ratio extend to *any* case where consent has been obtained, or, even if a broader view was taken, would there be qualifications to and restrictions in respect of it?

▶ 7. Court of Appeal Cases Subsequent to *Gomez*

▷ (a) R. v Gallasso

17–013 An opportunity to consider *Gomez* was not long in coming, for the Court of Appeal in *R. v Gallasso* (1992) 98 Cr. App. R. 284 (*Gallasso*) heard an appeal on the very day that the House of Lords gave judgment in *Gomez*. In this case, the defendant, a nurse who was responsible for the care of mentally handicapped patients and their finances, received cheques on behalf of one patient and properly paid them into trust accounts (with the patient as beneficiary) at a building society. Two accounts had been opened, followed by a third account, which had access with a cashcard and into which a cheque was paid. The prosecution case was that this cashcard account had been opened in order to facilitate unauthorised withdrawals and that the paying in of the cheque, done dishonestly and with the intention of permanently depriving, amounted to theft. A submission of no case to answer was made at trial on behalf of the defendant, on the basis that the paying in of the cheque, even with dishonest intent, did not constitute an appropriation as there was no assumption by the defendant of any of the patient's rights in relation to the cheque. Particular reliance was placed on Lord Roskill's statement in *Morris* that an act of adverse interference with or usurpation of the owner's rights was needed and, it was contended, there was no such act here. The submission was rejected by the trial judge and, on appeal, it was contended that the trial judge had been wrong in doing so. That the House of Lords in *Gomez* had disapproved Lord Roskill's statement in *Morris* did not, however, affect the basis of the appellant's contention that there had been no assumption of the right of an owner. As Lloyd L.J. stated (at 287–288):

> "We offered Mr. Saggerson [*counsel for the defendant*] an opportunity to reconsider his position in the light of *Gomez*. He said that he could proceed at once with his appeal. The decision did not affect his basic argument in any way. It only removed an unnecessary plank. *Gomez* makes clear that a taking with consent may amount to an appropriation. But there must still be a taking. The applicant's [*defendant's*] argument, we were told, did not depend on showing that Mr. Jeakins [*the patient*] had consented, either expressly or impliedly, to the cheque being paid into the cash card account. It depended on showing that the paying-in was not a taking at all. By paying in the cheques, the applicant was not assuming the rights of the owner. On the contrary, she was affirming those rights, by placing the cheque in trust accounts of which he was the named beneficiary."

The Court of Appeal found this argument "convincing" and allowed the appeal. The reference to the need for a "taking" suggests that this was one of the material facts in *Gomez* and thus part of the ratio of the case. If this is correct, this would make the ratio of *Gomez* a narrow one, since it would exclude those cases where the appropriation was with the consent of the owner, but did not take the form of taking. It seems highly unlikely, however, that a taking would have been seen as a material fact by the House of Lords when it was deciding the case of *Gomez*. The certified questions for the House of Lords were expressed, and answered, in terms of where property passes to the defendant with the consent of the owner and not in terms of whether the defendant has taken it. Although Lord Keith, delivering the main judgment in *Gomez*, referred to taking with or without consent when considering cases such as *Lawrence* (where taking was the form of appropriation), his remarks cannot be regarded as having application only in respect of cases of taking. There is nothing in *Gomez* to indicate that "there must still be a taking" and, indeed, evidence to indicate that there need not be, since Lord Keith's opinion that mere label swapping with intent could be theft is inconsistent with any requirement of taking. To the extent that *Gallasso* regards *Gomez* as establishing the need for a taking, the decision has been, and continues to be, widely criticised and regarded as incorrect (see, for example, Edward Griew, *The Theft Acts 1968 and 1978*, 7th edn (1995), where it was stated to be a "strange judgment" (para.2–89) "which may defy rationalisation" (para.2–91); A.T.H. Smith, *Property Offences* (1994), para.5–56, who concluded that it is "simply wrong"; and, more recently, Smith & Hogan, *Criminal Law*, 11th edn (2005), p.656, where it is described as "an untenable opinion").

▷ **(b) R. v Mazo; R. v Kendrick and Hopkins; and R. v Hinks**

17–014 Further consideration was given to *Gomez* by the Court of Appeal in three cases involving defendants who were the recipients of gifts made by elderly persons of failing powers.

(i) R. v Mazo (1997) 2 Cr. App. R. 518 (Mazo)

17–015 In this case, the defendant, a maid employed to look after an elderly lady, was charged with theft of large sums of money that the lady had given to her. The prosecution case was that the defendant had taken dishonest advantage of the lady's mental incapacity and the defence case was that the sums were valid gifts made to her. The defendant was convicted and appealed on the ground that the trial judge had not directed the jury to consider whether a valid gift had been made and whether the lady had the mental capacity to make a valid gift. The Court of Appeal allowed the appeal, accepting that such a direction should have been given. Pill L.J., delivering the judgment of the court, stated (at 520–521):

> "On behalf of the appellant, Mr Webber submits that the directions in the summing-up were, in the circumstances, deficient. He submits that there was an issue as to Lady S's ability to manage her affairs as well as an issue as to the honesty of the appellant. His central submission is that no sufficient direction was given to the jury upon one element of the offence which needed in the circumstances to be proved, namely that the transfers to the appellant, the gifts, *inter vivos*, were not valid gifts.
>
> Counsel agree that there were two issues in the case. Mr Oldland [*counsel for the prosecution*] accepts that if there were valid gifts, *inter vivos*, there could be no theft. He accepts too that the jury required a direction as to the validity of the gifts, as well as a direction upon the state of mind of the appellant in receiving them.
>
> Clearly the circumstances of the transfers needed to be considered; on the one hand the state of mind of the donor and on the other the conduct of the appellant and her state of mind in receiving and cashing the cheques.
>
> It is clear that a transaction may be a theft for the purpose of section 1(1) of the Theft Act 1968 notwithstanding that it was done with the owner's consent if it was induced by fraud, deception or a false representation: see *Director of Public Prosecution v Gomez* (1993) 96 Cr. App. R. 359, [1993] A.C. 442. It is also common ground that the receiver of a valid gift, *inter vivos*, could not be the subject of a conviction for theft. In *Gomez*, reference was made to the speech of Viscount Dilhorne in *Lawrence v Metropolitan Police Commissioner* (1971) 55 Cr. App. R. 471, [1972] A.C. 626. In the course of his speech, with which the other members of the House agreed, Lord [*sic*] Dilhorne stated at p.475 and p.632 respectively:

> "*A fortiori*, a person is not to be regarded as acting dishonestly if he appropriates another's property believing that, with full knowledge of the circumstances, that other person has in fact agreed to the appropriation."
>
> It is implicit in that statement that if in all the circumstances there is held to be a valid gift there can be no theft."

The court appeared to distinguish *Gomez* on the ground that in that case there had been no valid gift but a transaction induced by fraud, deception or a false representation. Where there was a valid gift, the recipient would acquire an absolute and indefeasible (cannot be defeated) title to the property, but where there was a transaction induced by deception, as in *Gomez*, the recipient would acquire only a voidable title to the property. The voidable title would be defeasible, for the victim of the deception could avoid the transaction and might obtain the return of his property. This appears to confine the ratio of *Gomez* to cases where there is a defeasible title. Such cases will include, but will not be limited to, transactions induced by deception, for transactions may be rendered voidable by other factors, e.g. duress. Presumably the ratio would also extend to cases where a transaction is rendered void for some reason, e.g. fundamental mistake, since here the recipient will not acquire even a defeasible title, but will acquire no title at all.

Whether the court's views on the ratio of *Gomez* were part of the ratio of the case (*Mazo*) itself or whether they were merely obiter is not entirely clear. The point of law that the court had to decide was whether the trial judge ought to have directed the jury to consider whether the victim was capable of making the gifts concerned. It decided that he ought to have done so and this was based on acceptance of the proposition that there could be no appropriation if there was a valid gift. Pill L.J. stated (at 523):

> "It is, in the judgment of the Court, as important upon the present criminal charge as it is in a civil case involving a transfer *inter vivos* to consider the state of mind of the donor and whether a valid gift can be and is made.
>
> The direction that an element of the offence is that the donor gave the cheques "as a result of her reduced mental state" does not, in the judgment of the Court, sufficiently confront the jury with this issue or direct them upon it . . .
>
> It did not direct the jury to consider whether Lady S was capable of making the gifts concerned."

Acceptance of the proposition thus appears to be a material fact in the making of the decision about the trial judge's direction, for the court could not have made the decision it did *without* accepting that there could be no appropriation if there was a valid gift. Accepting this proposition was therefore a necessary pre-condition to deciding that the jury should be directed to consider whether the victim was capable of making the gifts concerned. There would be no point in the jury considering this if there could be an appropriation whether or not there was a valid gift.

It is true that the court did not decide whether there could be no appropriation if there was a valid gift, in the sense of adjudicating between competing arguments on this point. Nevertheless, the court did decide the point in the sense that it accepted the agreement reached by counsel in the case in respect of this issue, which it need not have done. Although acceptance of the agreement, without detailed consideration of any arguments on that point, weakens the strength of the case as a precedent, it would not seem to prevent the proposition from being a material fact to the decision that a direction should have been given on the victim's capability to make a gift. If so, it would seem not to be obiter but part of the ratio of the case.

(ii) R. v Kendrick and Hopkins [1997] 2 Cr. App. R. 524 (Kendrick and Hopkins)

17–016 In this case, the defendants ran a residential home and were charged with theft of large sums of money that one of the occupants, Mrs Clare, had given to them, which they contended were valid gifts. The trial judge, when directing the jury, did make reference to the question of gifts and Mrs Clare's mental capacity to make gifts, but only in respect of the issue of the defendants' dishonesty, stating (at 534):

> "If they were gifts then you would have to consider whether the defendants were dishonest in accepting them. The relevant question in relation to each gift would be this: was Mrs Clare so mentally incapable that the defendants realised that ordinary people would regard it as dishonest to accept that gift from her?"

No reference was made to these matters in respect of appropriation, the trial having taken place shortly before the Court of Appeal's decision in *Mazo*. The defendants were convicted and sought leave to appeal. The Court of Appeal, when considering whether to grant leave, felt that the trial judge's direction was in accordance with the law as it was understood prior to *Mazo*, i.e. that the making of a valid gift and whether a person had the capacity to make the gift might affect whether the defendants were dishonest when receiving the gift, but would not be relevant to whether there was an appropriation. (It would not, as so understood, be relevant to appropriation, since the defendants had received the gifts from Mrs Clare with her consent, but *Gomez* had established that there could be an appropriation even with consent.) Nevertheless, the court felt that, in the light of the decision in *Mazo*, there may be an arguable point as to whether the directions were unsafe and accordingly gave leave to appeal.

When the appeal was heard, the appellants contended that, following *Mazo*, where an alleged gift was made, consent *was* relevant to the appropriation and not simply to the dishonesty of the appropriation. Accordingly, the judge should have directed the jury that, in considering whether or not the alleged gifts were appropriated, the consent of the donor would preclude theft where the donor's mind was not incapacitated, and he should have gone on to indicate the level of mental incapacity that would be necessary to render the actions of the appellant theft. The Court of Appeal, when summarising the appellants' arguments, regarded them as "bold" and not in accordance with the decision in *Gomez*. Ebsworth J., delivering the only judgment, stated (at 534–535):

> "Counsel on behalf of the appellants before us seeks to say . . . that, first of all, it is necessary to look at appropriation and, secondly, it is necessary to look at whether or not such an appropriation is dishonest. He argues that when one is looking at whether or not there is an appropriation the consent of the donor negates theft and, therefore, the state of the donor's mind is relevant to the question of whether or not there has been an appropriation, because if the donor's mind is such that the donor has the capacity to make a gift or to consent to the transfer of property, then there is no appropriation and no theft. The state of mind of the donee is another and separate matter.
>
> That seems to us to be a bold and perhaps surprising submission, and counsel conceded its boldness because it is difficult to square it with the decisions of the House of Lords in *Lawrence* and *Gomez*."

The court, going on to consider these decisions, referred (at 535–536) to Lord Browne-Wilkinson's view in *Gomez* that "I regard the word 'appropriation' in isolation as being an objective description of the act done irrespective of the mental state of either the owner or the accused" and emphasised (at 536) that "what this jury needed to be directed about was whether or not there was a dishonest appropriation".

Referring, at an earlier point in his judgment, to the reliance that had been placed upon *Mazo*, Ebsworth J. confined himself to observing (at 531):

> "It is not for these purposes, we find, necessary to consider whether or not that apparent gloss on *Gomez* [*that if there is a valid gift there can be no theft*] is well-founded. What we are concerned with is whether the directions given to this jury on the issues that were before them in this case were appropriate."

The court accordingly focused only on the question of the adequacy of the directions on dishonest appropriation and whether the directions in respect of Mrs Clare's mental capacity to make a gift might have caused the jury to be confused as to the true nature of dishonesty. It did not find it necessary to consider what effect Mrs Clare's mental capacity might have had on her ability to make a valid gift and whether, if such a gift were made, there could be an appropriation and a theft. Unlike in *Mazo*, the court thought that the directions given on dishonest appropriation were correct and that the present case was "very different on its facts". Ebsworth J. stated (at 538):

> "It was, in our judgment, a case in relation to Mrs Clare's mental capacity, very different on its facts from *Mazo* and the judge in summing-up, in our view, made it wholly clear to the jury, for the purposes of the law, what the evidence was in relation to the level of mental capacity.

> There is nothing in the summing-up, and nothing in the evidence, as it appears from the summing-up, which could have resulted in a jury being confused as to whether Mrs Clare was somebody who is just "not quite up to it", with reduced mental capacity, which was what was said of Lady S, or lacking the capacity to manage her affairs."

By regarding the present case as "very different on its facts", the court thus proceeded to distinguish *Mazo*. The decision was not disapproved, although doubt on it was cast with the court's reference (obiter) to whether the "apparent gloss" on *Gomez* was "well-founded".

▶ 8. The Decision in *R. v Hinks*

17-017 In *R. v Hinks* (*Hinks*), the defendant had befriended a man who was naïve, gullible and of limited intelligence and sums of money belonging to him had subsequently been withdrawn from his building society account and given to the defendant. The defence case was that the sums were loans or gifts and a submission was made that the case should not be left to the jury. There was no evidence, it was contended, that the money had been parted with unwillingly or by reason of duress or deception and, if the money had been a valid gift, there could be no appropriation. The trial judge rejected this submission, the defendant was convicted and appealed on the ground that the judge had been wrong to allow the case to go to the jury. The recipient of a valid gift could not, it was submitted, relying on *Mazo*, be convicted of theft. This submission advocated a narrow view of the ratio of *Gomez*, that there could be appropriation with consent only where the consent was obtained by deception or duress. The prosecution essentially advocated a broad view, that there could be appropriation in *any* case where consent had been obtained, for appropriation did not depend on the consent of the owner. The Court of Appeal considered the differing views expressed in *Mazo* and in *Kendrick and Hopkins* and Rose L.J., delivering the only judgment, stated (at [2000] 1 Cr. App. R. 1, 8):

> "Mr Lowe's [*counsel for the appellant's*] submission is that, although the Court is bound by *Lawrence* and *Gomez*, it should construe them narrowly as not applying to gifts or to cases where property has been obtained with the consent of the owner and that consent was not induced by deception or duress. He sought comfort in that submission from a number of articles by Professor Sir John Smith Q.C., in particular one at [1996] Crim. L.R. 435.
>
> On behalf of the Crown, Mr Morse succinctly submitted that the Theft Act 1968 created a new form of theft, and that Mr Lowe's submission could only succeed if that crucial history was ignored. Appropriation is a matter independent of the consent of the owner as *Lawrence* and *Gomez* unequivocally asserted and as a differently constituted division of this Court in *Kendrick and Hopkins* [1997] 2 Cr. App. R. 524 plainly recognised."

The court rejected an invitation to consider the Eighth Report of the Criminal Law Revision Committee, which preceded the Theft Act 1968 (see above, 17–008), when approaching its interpretation of the Act—"That is an invitation which we unhesitatingly rejected, having regard to what Lord Keith said . . . in *Lawrence* [*sic*]" [*i.e. that no useful purpose would be served by construing the relevant provisions of the Theft Act by reference to the report which preceded it*]—and proceeded to reject the appellant's contention for a narrow view of the ratio of *Gomez*. Rose L.J. stated (at 9–10):

"In our judgment, it is clear beyond peradventure, on the authorities, that appropriation for the purpose of the Theft Act 1968 does not depend on the consent of the owner. That point was central to the House of the Lords' decision in *Lawrence* . . . That position was made plain in *Dobson v General Accident*, in particular, by Parker L.J. . . . and *Dobson v General Accident* was approved in *Gomez*, by Lord Keith . . . Furthermore, as is plain, *Gomez* ambiguously [*sic*] reaffirmed the *Lawrence* approach. . .

In our judgment, in relation to theft, one of the ingredients for a jury to consider is not whether there has been a gift, valid or otherwise, but whether there has been appropriation. A gift may be clear evidence of appropriation. But a jury should not, in our view, be asked to consider whether a gift has been validly made because, first, that is not what section 1 of the Theft Act requires; secondly, such an approach is inconsistent with *Lawrence* and *Gomez*, and thirdly, the state of mind of a donor is irrelevant to appropriation: see, in particular, the speech of Lord Browne-Wilkinson, with which Lord Jauncey agreed, in *Gomez* at 396 and 495H respectively:

". . . I regard the word "appropriation" in isolation as being an objective description of the act done irrespective of the mental state of either the owner or the accused. It is impossible to reconcile the decision in *Lawrence* (that the question of consent is irrelevant in considering whether there has been an appropriation) with the views expressed in *Morris*, which latter views in my judgment were incorrect."

Accordingly, as it seems to us, the two concessions made by prosecuting counsel during the hearing of the appeal in *Mazo*, namely that there cannot be theft if there was a valid gift, and that a direction to the jury is necessary as to the validity of gifts were wrongly made and led that Court into error. At page 521C, where the Court cites the passage from Lord Dilhorne's speech in *Lawrence*, relating to dishonesty, it does so as impliedly excluding valid gifts from the ambit of theft. For our part, we are unable to read that passage in Lord Dilhorne's speech as bearing that implication. The authorities, as it seems to us, make clear the importance of maintaining a distinction in relation to theft between the two quite separate ingredients of appropriation and dishonesty. Belief or lack of belief that the owner consented to the appropriation is relevant to dishonesty. But appropriation may occur even though the owner has consented to the property being taken.

> In the present case, the jury were so directed. The direction was, in our judgment, an entirely appropriate and accurate direction as to dishonesty. Despite the strictures of Professor Sir John Smith Q.C. in [1997] Crim. L.R. 359, we respectfully agree with the approach of the differently constituted division of this Court in *Kendrick and Hopkins* [1997] 2 Cr. App. R. 524. Civil unlawfulness is not a constituent of the offence of theft . . ."

The reference to civil unlawfulness not being a constituent of the offence of theft appears to be an alternative way of saying that it is not necessary, where property is obtained by consent, for the consent to have been obtained by deception or duress. Obtaining consent by deception or duress would be civilly unlawful and would render the transaction by which the property was obtained voidable. However, this is not a constituent of theft, according to the court, because there can be theft, even in the case of a valid gift. There can be an appropriation in such cases, even though, with a valid gift, there will be no civil unlawfulness.

The court in *Hinks* thus took a broad view of the ratio of *Gomez*, approving *Kendrick and Hopkins* and disapproving, if not overruling, *Mazo*. Certainly *Mazo* was disapproved, for the court in *Hinks* appeared to regard it as wrong. It stated that the concessions in that case, that there could be no theft if there was a valid gift and that the jury needed to be directed as to validity of the gift, were wrongly made and had led the court in *Mazo* into error. It is less clear, however, whether *Mazo* was overruled. The Court of Appeal cannot generally overrule its previous decisions and the case appears not to fall within any of the recognised exceptions in *Young v Bristol Aeroplane Co Ltd* (see Chapter 1, 1–021). It did not fall within the first exception, as it was not in conflict with a previous Court of Appeal decision (in which case the decision that is not followed is deemed to be overruled). *Mazo* was not followed in *Hinks*, but there was no conflict with the earlier Court of Appeal decision in *Kendrick and Hopkins*, because *Mazo* was distinguished in that case. It did not fall within the second exception because there was no subsequent House of Lords' decision with which it could not stand. There were only earlier House of Lords' decisions, *Lawrence* and *Gomez*, with which it could not, as those decisions were interpreted in *Hinks*, stand. Nor would it appear to fall within the third exception because it is hard to say that the decision in *Mazo* was reached per incuriam. There was no want of care, as where a relevant authority was not considered. Relevant authorities such as *Lawrence* and *Gomez* were considered but were interpreted differently from the court in *Hinks*. Other exceptions have, however, subsequently been recognised, including where a proposition of law, although part of the ratio of an earlier decision, has been assumed to be correct by the earlier court, but has not been the subject of argument before, or consideration by, that court (see Chapter 1, 1–021).

Thus, if it was part of the ratio of *Mazo* that there could be no appropriation if there was a valid gift, as suggested above (see 17–015), the Court of Appeal in *Hinks* might have been justified in not following *Mazo* on the basis of this exception. However, the question of whether the court in *Hinks* was bound by *Mazo* or whether any recognised exception applied was not a matter addressed by the court. Further, no reason can be ascertained for not following its previous decision in *Mazo* other than that it thought the court in that case had incorrectly interpreted the earlier House of Lords' decisions in *Lawrence* and *Gomez*. A previous Court of Appeal case that has interpreted an earlier House of Lords' decision is, however, as a matter precedent, binding on the Court of Appeal and it is not generally open to the Court of Appeal to reinterpret the earlier House of Lords' decision.

The Appeal Committee of the House of Lords granted the defendant leave to appeal on the following certified question on a point of law of general public importance:

> "Whether the acquisition of an indefeasible title to property is capable of amounting to an appropriation of property belonging to another for the purposes of section 1(1) of the Theft Act 1968".

The House, by a 4–1 majority, held that it was, rejecting submissions that: (i) a person does not appropriate property belonging to another unless the other retains, beyond the instant of the alleged theft, some proprietary interest or the right to resume or recover some proprietary interest; and (ii) the word "appropriates" should be interpreted as if the word "unlawfully" preceded it so that only an act which is unlawful (civilly) under the general law can be an appropriation. Lord Steyn, delivering the judgment of the majority, regarded the former submission as "directly contrary" to the holdings in *Lawrence* and *Gomez*, taking the view that an indefeasible gift of property fell within the ratio of *Gomez*. His Lordship stated (at [2001] 2 A.C. 241, 250–251):

> "In *Gomez* [1993] AC 442 the House was expressly invited to hold that "there is no appropriation where the entire proprietary interest passes": at p 448b. That submission was rejected. The leading judgment in *Gomez* was therefore in terms which unambiguously rule out the submission that section 3(1) does not apply to a case of a gift duly carried out because in such a case the entire proprietary interest will have passed. In a separate judgment (with which Lord Jauncey of Tullichettle expressed agreement) Lord Browne-Wilkinson observed, at pp 495–496:
>
>> ". . . I regard the word 'appropriation' in isolation as being an objective description of the act done irrespective of the mental state of either the owner or the accused. It is impossible to reconcile the decision in *Lawrence* (that the question of consent is irrelevant in considering whether there has been an appropriation) with the views expressed in *Morris*, which latter views in my judgment were incorrect."
>
> In other words it is immaterial whether the act was done with the owner's consent or authority. It is true of course that the certified question in *Gomez* referred to the situation where consent had been obtained by fraud. But the majority judgments do not differentiate between cases of consent induced by fraud and consent given in any other circumstances. The ratio involves a proposition of general application. *Gomez* therefore gives effect to section 3(1)

of the Act by treating "appropriation" as a neutral word comprehending "any assumption by a person of the rights of an owner". If the law is as held in *Gomez*, it destroys the argument advanced on the present appeal, namely that an indefeasible gift of property cannot amount to an appropriation."

Thus, *Gomez* was taken to have a broad ratio and the presence of fraud in inducing consent was not regarded as a material fact in the decision. The submission that the word "appropriates" should be interpreted as if the word "unlawfully" preceded it was also considered to be inconsistent with the ratio of *Gomez* and the House's earlier decision in *Lawrence*. This, Lord Steyn stated (at 253), involved "an invitation to interpolate a word in the carefully crafted language of the 1968 Act . . . [*which*] runs counter to the decisions in *Lawrence* and *Gomez*". Although no overt reference is made by his Lordship to policy considerations in the course of his judgment, it seems that he had regard to the perceived social consequences of taking a broad view of the ratio of *Gomez*, for he stated (at 252–253):

"If the law is restated by adopting a narrower definition of appropriation, the outcome is likely to place beyond the reach of the criminal law dishonest persons who should be found guilty of theft. The suggested revisions would unwarrantably restrict the scope of the law of theft and complicate the fair and effective prosecution of theft . . . My Lords, if it had been demonstrated that in practice *Lawrence* and *Gomez* were calculated to produce injustice that would have been a compelling reason to revisit the merits of the holdings in those decisions. That is however, not the case. In practice the mental requirements of theft are an adequate protection against injustice. In these circumstances I would not be willing to depart from the clear decisions of the House in *Lawrence* and *Gomez*."

Although agreeing with Lord Steyn on the answer to the certified question, Lord Hutton dissented from the decision to dismiss the appeal on grounds of misdirection by the trial judge on the issue of dishonesty, which included a failure to make it clear to the jury that if there was a valid gift the defendant could not be found to be dishonest, no matter how much the jury thought her conduct morally reprehensible. In contrast, Lord Hobhouse's dissent from the decision to dismiss the appeal was based on a negative answer to the certified question. His Lordship stated (at 274–275):

"Does the primary question in *Gomez* receive the same answer if one deletes the words "obtained by false representation?" The Court of Appeal in the present case held that it should. Two strands of reasoning led them to this conclusion. The first was that section 3(1) should be construed in isolation from the remainder of sections 1 to 6. In this they followed the lead given by Lord Browne-Wilkinson and the Court of Appeal judgment in *Kendrick and Hopkins* [1997] 2 Cr App R 524 . . . I consider that this is wrong.

The second was the view that Lord Keith of Kinkel [*in Gomez*] and Parker LJ [*in Dobson*] had ruled that consent of the owner is always wholly irrelevant to what acts amount to appropriation. They achieved this position only by standing on its head what Lord Keith and Parker LJ had said. What Lord Keith and Parker LJ confirmed was that "consent" (in the Larceny Act 1916 sense) will not necessarily negative appropriation. What Rose LJ [*in the Court of Appeal in the present case*] has derived from this is that consent can never negative appropriation . . . This leads Rose LJ directly to the position that a valid gift is fully consistent with theft, a proposition which is seriously inconsistent with the scheme of sections 1 to 6 and with other parts of the 1968 Act and which is not a proposition to be derived from any of the House of Lords decisions (with the possible exception of the speech of Lord Browne-Wilkinson in *Gomez* [1993] AC 442).

To say, as does Rose LJ [2000] 1 Cr App R 1, 10, that "civil unlawfulness is not a constituent of the offence of theft" is of course true. That expression does not occur in section 1(1) and it is anyway not clear what it encompasses. But to proceed from there to the proposition that the civil law of property is irrelevant is . . . a far greater error . . .

My Lords, the relevant law is contained in sections 1 to 6 of the Act. They should be construed as a whole and applied in a manner which presents a consistent scheme both internally and with the remainder of the Act. The phrase "dishonestly appropriates" should be construed as a composite phrase. It does not include acts done in relation to the relevant property which are done in accordance with the actual wishes or actual authority of the person to whom the property belongs. This is because such acts do not involve any assumption of the rights of that person within section 3(1) or because, by necessary implication from section 2(1), they are not to be regarded as dishonest appropriations of property belonging to another. Actual authority, wishes, consent (or similar words) mean, both as a matter of language and on the authority of the three House of Lords cases, authorisation not obtained by fraud or misrepresentation."

Unlike the majority, Lord Hobhouse thus focused on the importance of having regard to other sections in the Act as an intrinsic aid to ascertaining meaning (see Chapter 1, 1–076) and looking at the statute as a whole when interpreting the word "appropriates". This might be contrasted with the view expressed by Lord Browne-Wilkinson in *Gomez*, to which Lord Steyn refers with approval in the present case, that:

"I regard the word 'appropriation' in isolation as being an objective description of the act done irrespective of the mental state of either the owner or the accused".

▶ ## 9. Conclusion

17–018 The courts' interpretation of the requirement of "appropriation" in the offence of theft provides something of a contrast with the other case studies considered in this final part of the book. In the other case studies, the law has developed through a series of cases or through a series of cases and statutory provisions to move from one particular position to another. This is not the case in the present study, which provides an illustration of where the development of the law has been characterised by a "yo-yo" or "pendulum" effect, with the law oscillating between two opposing positions. At different periods of time, different viewpoints have prevailed, but in the end the "yo-yo" or "pendulum" seems to have returned to its starting point that there can be an appropriation even where there is the consent of the owner. The law ultimately appears to have come a full circle so as to return, via *Gomez*, to the position initially adopted in *Lawrence*. Whether it has gone beyond this with the decision in *Hinks*, by deciding that there can be an appropriation with the consent of the owner even in the case of a valid gift made, is open to question. Such a case may be seen as falling within the ratio of *Lawrence* and *Gomez* or, as observed by Professor J.C. Smith when commenting on the Court of Appeal decision in *Hinks* (at 1998] Crim. L.R. 905–906), as a completely new development from those cases which are readily distinguishable:

> "In *Lawrence* and in *Gomez* there was no doubt that the defendant was guilty of a crime . . . under the 1968 Act, s. 15, of obtaining by deception . . . The only issue necessary for decision was whether the definition of theft embraced the offence under section 15. The House in *Gomez* (in my opinion, wrongly) decided, Lord Lowry dissenting, that it did. But the conviction of a donee for receiving a perfectly valid gift is, I believe, a completely new departure. *Lawrence* and in *Gomez* are easily distinguishable on the facts because in both cases there was a deception and the offender was certainly not entitled to keep the property he obtained . . .
>
> . . . No court before *Kendrick* has ever decided that the recipient of an indefeasible gift can be guilty of stealing it; and the court in *Mazo* thought it self-evident that there could be no such theft."

The House of Lords in *Hinks*, however, did not think it self-evident that there could be no theft and, indeed, decided that the recipient of an indefeasible gift could be guilty of the offence. In consequence, a person can be guilty of stealing property which is his and in which no other person has any legal interest at all, a proposition described by Professor J.C. Smith, when commenting on the House of Lords in *Hinks* (at [2001] Crim. L.R. 162, 164), as "absurd" and "contrary to common sense".

Further Reading

Clarkson, "Authorised acts and appropriation" (1992) 55 M.L.R. 265

Gardner, "Appropriation in theft: the last word?" (1993) 109 L.Q.R. 194

Halpin, "The appropriate appropriation" [1991] Crim. L.R. 426

Melissaris, "The concept of appropriation and the offence of theft" (2007) 70 M.L.R. 581

Shute, "Appropriation and the law of theft" [2002] Crim. L.R. 445

Smith, "Theft: appropriation" [2001] Crim. L.R. 162

Spencer, "Theft—appropriation and consent" [1990] C.L.J. 200

INDEX

Abortion regulation, 11–001—11–016
  Bourne, 1–005, 11–001—11–002
    common law view, 11–002—11–003
    precedential strength, 1–046
    statutory interpretation, 11–002
    textbooks, 11–002
  circulars, 1–059
  common law, 11–002
  distinguishing cases, 11–017
  policy considerations, 11–009—11–017
  precedential strength, 1–048
  Royal College, 1–004—1–006, 11–001,
    11–003—11–017
    circulars, 1–059
    Court of Appeal decision, 11–007
    distinguishing cases, 11–017
    High Court decision, 11–007
    House of Lords decision, 11–008, 11–017
    policy considerations, 11–009—11–017
    precedential strength, 1–046
    statutory interpretation, 1–059, 1–070,
      1–081, 1–093, 11–002—11–017
    textbooks, 11–002
Absence of argument, 1–051—1–052
Academic opinion *See* **Textbooks and articles**
Aids to statutory interpretation, 1–056, 1–075—
  1–091
Appeals, 1–015—1–016, 1–031, 1–037—1–039
  See also **Court of Appeal**
Appropriation in theft, 17–001—17–018
  academic opinion, 1–037, 17–010
  'appropriates', meaning of, 17–002, 17–009,
    17–010—17–018
  authors, views of, 1–037, 17–010, 17–017
  binding precedents, 1–019, 1–023, 17–009,
    17–016
  consent, 17–001, 17–002—17–003, 17–005—
    17–008, 17–009—17–013, 17–016—17–017
  Court of Appeal cases, 17–002—17–003,
    17–005—17–007, 17–013—17–016
  definition, 1–037
  distinguishing precedents, 1–068, 17–007,
    17–017—17–018
  Gallasso, 17–013—17–017
  gifts, 17–017—17–018
  Gomez, 17–006—17–013
    academic opinion, 17–010
    Court of Appeal, 17–006—17–007
    Crown Court, 17–006—17–007
    distinguishing precedents, 1–068
    House of Lords, 17–007—17–013
    obiter dicta, 17–006, 17–009, 17–015
    persuasive precedents, 1–029, 1–037

  ratio decidendi, 1–009, 1–012, 17–006,
    17–007, 17–009, 17–013—17–015,
    17–018
  statutory interpretation, 1–068, 1–070,
    1–088, 1–090, 17–007—17–013
  Hinks, 17–017
    binding precedents, 1–023
    Court of Appeal, 17–017
    disapproval of *Mazo*, 17–017
    House of Lords, 17–017
    precedential strength, 1–051
    ratio decidendi, 1–010, 17–017
  Kendrick and Hopkins, distinguishing
    precedents, 1–068
  Lawrence, 17–002, 17–004—17–005, 17–007,
    17–016
    dissenting judgments, 1–002
    House of Lords' view of in *Gomez*, 17–009,
      17–013
    obiter dicta, 17–002, 17–009
    persuasive precedents, 1–026
    ratio decidendi, 17–002, 17–009
    statutory interpretation, 17–001—17–002
  Mazo, 1–002, 17–016—17–017
    binding precedents, 1–023
    disapproval of, 17–017
    distinguishing precedents, 1–068, 17–017
    obiter dicta, 17–016
    overruling decisions, 17–016—17–017
    precedential strength, 1–051
    ratio decidendi, 1–009, 17–016
  Morris, 17–003—17–004, 17–007
    binding precedents, 1–019
    House of Lords' view of in *Gomez*, 17–009—
      17–013
    obiter dicta, 17–003, 17–009—17–010
    persuasive precedents, 1–029
    ratio decidendi, 1–012, 17–003—17–004
  obiter dicta, 17–002—17–003, 17–006,
    17–009—17–010, 17–015—17–016
  overruling decisions, 17–016—17–017
  persuasive precedents, 1–026, 1–029, 1–037
  precedential strength, 1–051
  ratio decidendi, 1–009, 1–012, 17–002—17–
    004, 17–006, 17–009, 17–013—17–018
  Skipp, 17–002—17–003, 17–005
    obiter dicta, 17–002—17–003
    ratio decidendi, 17–002—17–003
  statutory interpretation, 1–068, 1–070, 1–088,
    1–090, 17–001—17–002, 17–008—17–013
Assizes, 2–019
Authors *See* **Textbooks and articles**

Binding precedents, 1–007

appropriation in theft, 1–019, 1–023, 17–009, 17–017
contractual obligations arising out of invitations to tender, 6–010
Court of Appeal, 1–019, 1–021–1–022
court hierarchy, 1–014–1–022, 2–002
Crown Court, 1–016, 1–022
Divisional Court, 1–019–1–022
equal pay, 1–022–1–023
(European) Court of Justice, 1–005, 1–014, 1–016–1–021
High Court, 1–016, 1–022
Human Rights Act 1998, 5–016–5–017
legal rules, formulation of, 1–001
magistrates' courts, 1–019
marital rape, 16–006
overruling, 1–021
per incuriam, 1–021
policy considerations, 1–057
private nuisance, 1–022
ratio decidendi, 1–001, 1–011, 1–014
  higher courts of, 1–019
  same courts of, 1–019–1–023
res judicata, 1–001
rulings on EU law, 4–040
stare decisis, 1–014, 1–019, 1–021
Supreme Court, 1–019
tribunals, 1–026–1–037

Case law and precedent, 1–001–1–058
binding precedents, 1–016–1–023
distinguishing precedents, 1–051–1–068
(European) Court of Justice, 1–005–1–007
European Union, membership of, 1–005–1–007
legal rules, formulation of, 1–001–1–005
obiter dicta, 1–001, 1–007–1–014
persuasive precedents, 1–023–1–037
policy considerations, 1–058
precedential strength, 1–026–1–051
ratio decidendi, 1–001, 1–007–1–014
sources of English law, 1–001
tribunals, 1–026–1–037
Cases of first impression, 1–003
Central Criminal Court, 2–019
Circulars, 1–059
Codes of practice, 1–059
Codification, 4–004
Common law
abortion regulation, 11–002–11–003
Human Rights Act 1998, 5–018
sources of law, 1–001
spouses as prosecution witnesses, 12–004, 12–006
statutory interpretation, 1–068
Constitutions, 4–002–4–004
Continental legal tradition
codification, 4–004–4–007
European Convention on Human Rights, 5–002
European Court of Human Rights, 5–007

European Union legal order, 4–001–4–007, 4–018
general principles of law, 4–005, 4–007
judicial function, 4–004–4–005
  techniques, 4–005–4–007
key features, 4–002–4–005
precedent, 4–006–4–007
previous cases, using, 4–006–4–007
statutory interpretation, 4–001–4–003, 4–005–4–006
Contractual obligations arising out of an invitation to tender, 6–001–6–010
binding precedents, 6–010
Blackpool and Fylde Aero Club
  Court of Appeal's view, 6–003–6–004
  judicial approaches, differing, 6–004
  ratio decidendi, 1–008, 1–011, 6–005–6–006
  tort claims, 6–009–6–010
distinguishing cases, 6–010
expressio unius exclusio alterius, 6–006–6–007
implying a contract, 6–007–6–008
invitations to tender as invitations to treat, 6–002–6–007
  supporting authority, 6–002–6–003
obiter dicta, 6–005
precedent, 6–001–6–002, 6–007–6–008
ratio decidendi, 1–008, 1–011, 1–012, 6–004, 6–005–6–006
  dual, 6–006
  single, 6–006
reasonable expectations, 6–008
statutory interpretation, 1–089–1–090, 6–007
Conventions, 1–037, 1–088–1–089, 4–009–4–020, 4–036–4–037
See also **European Convention on Human Rights**
Council of Europe, 5–001–5–002
County courts, 2–008
binding precedents, 1–019
persuasive precedents, 1–026
Court of Appeal, 2–005
binding precedents, 1–019–1–021
criminal appeals, 2–013
Court of Chancery, 2–018
Court of Common Pleas, 2–016
Court for Crown Cases Reserved, 2–014
Court of Exchequer, 2–017
Court of First Instance, 2–003, 3–001, 4–016, 4–019
see also **General Court**
Court of Justice *See* **(European) Court of Justice**
Court of King's (or Queen's) Bench, 2–015
Courts
See also types of court e.g. **Magistrates' courts**
appeals, 1–014–1–016
binding precedents, 1–014–1–016
composition, 1–026–1–048, 1–068, 2–003
foreign, 1–032–1–034
hierarchy, 1–014–1–032, 2–002

public authorities, as, 5–010
Crown Court, 2–007
  binding precedents, 1–016, 1–022
  persuasive precedents, 1–026

Declarations of incompatibility, 1–074, 5–010,
  5–013, 5–018
Delegated legislation, 1–059, 1–070
Dictionaries, 1–067, 1–068, 8–006, 9–003,
  17–008
Direct effect, 4–018, 4–023—4–024, 4–032,
  5–013, 14–005, 14–018—14–020
Disapproving precedents, 1–001—1–002
Discrimination
  EU law, 4–036
  sex, 4–036—4–037
Dissenting judgments, 1–002, 1–048, 1–049
  precedential strength, 1–048, 1–049
Distinguishing precedents, 1–002, 1–054—
  1–055
  abortion regulation, 11–016
  appropriation in theft, 1–068, 17–007, 17–017—
    17–018
  case law and precedent, 1–054—1–056
  contractual obligations arising out of
    invitations to tender, 6–010
  (European) Court of Justice, 1–005
  existing obligations as consideration in
    contract, 1–054, 7–006
  false imprisonment, "detention" and the MHA
    1983, 1–055, 9–010
  headnotes, 1–055
  marital rape, 16–011
  material facts, 1–054
  nervous shock, 1–055, 15–006, 15–007—
    15–008, 15–011, 15–020
  ratio decidendi, 1–054
  spouses as prosecution witnesses, 1–055,
    12–003
Divisional Court, 2–006
  binding precedents, 1–019—1–022

Ejusdem generis principle, 1–089, 10–001—
  10–002, 10–003
Employment Appeal Tribunal, 1–016, 1–039,
  2–010
Employment tribunals, 1–016, 1–039, 2–010
Equal pay, 14–001—14–020
  binding precedents, 1–022—1–023
  compliance gaps, 14–002
  direct effect, 14–005, 14–018—14–020
  directives, 14–001—14–002
  EU law, 1–059, 1–070, 14–002, 14–005—
    14–021
  (European) Court of Justice, 1–016, 14–001—
    14–021
  European Union legal order, 4–013, 4–016,
    4–026, 14–001—14–021
  Garland, 14–008—14–013
    binding precedents, 1–016
    Court of Appeal, 14–010—14–011

Employment Appeal Tribunal, 14–009—
  14–010
European Court of Justice, 14–011—14–013
House of Lords, 14–013
industrial tribunal, 14–009
statutory interpretation, 4–031, 14–008—
  14–011
interpretation, 4–016, 4–028—4–030,
  4–032—4–033, 4–040
legislative framework, 14–001—14–002
Macarthys, 14–002—14–008
  binding precedents, 1–016
  Court of Appeal, 14–007—14–008
  Employment Appeal Tribunal, 14–004—
    14–005
  European Court of Justice, 14–006—14–008
  industrial tribunal, 14–004—14–005
  interpretation, 4–032, 4–040, 14–016
  rulings on EU law, 4–027—4–028,
    14–005—14–006
  statutory interpretation, 4–031, 4–033,
    4–035, 14–002—14–008
O'Brien
  binding precedents, 1–022—1–023
Pickstone, 14–013—14–021
  binding precedents, 1–022
  Court of Appeal, 14–016—14–021
  direct effect, 14–018—14–020
  Employment Appeal Tribunal, 14–015—
    14–016
  House of Lords, 14–021
  industrial tribunal, 14–015—14–016
  interpretation techniques, 4–028—4–032,
    4–033, 4–035, 4–040
  stare decisis, 14–018—14–019
  statutory interpretation, 1–070, 1–086,
    4–028, 4–033, 4–035, 14–014—
    14–021
  tribunals, 1–039
precedent, 14–001
rulings on EU law, 4–027—4–028, 4–039,
  4–040, 14–005—14–006
stare decisis, 14–018—14–019
statutory interpretation, 1–059, 1–070, 1–086,
  4–028, 4–029, 4–033, 4–035, 4–040,
  14–001—14–021
supremacy of EU law, 14–005
textbooks, 14–002
Treaty articles, 14–001—14–004, 14–005—
  14–021
  renumbering of, 14–001
tribunals, 1–040, 14–004—14–005, 14–009—
  14–010, 14–015—14–016
EU law
  See also **European Union, (European) Court**
    of Justice
  Court of First Instance, 3–001—3–002, 4–016,
    4–019 *See also* **General Court**
  effect of, 4–028—4–030
  equal pay, 1–059, 1–070, 14–002, 14–005—
    14–020

European Convention on Human Rights, 5–002
Human Rights Act 1998, 5–013
interpretation, 4–028—4–038, 5–019
key features, 4–010—4–016
legal order, development of, 3–001—3–002
legislation, forms of, 1–059
precedent, 3–001—3–002
statutory interpretation, 1–059, 1–063—1–065, 1–074—1–075, 1–094, 3–001—3–002, 4–030—4–038
supremacy, 4—023, 4—039, 4–032—4–034, 14–005
European Commission on Human Rights, 2–023, 5–005, 14–002, 16–010
European Communities Act 1972, 3–002, 4–016
drafting, 4–024
(European) Court of Justice, 4–024—4–030, 4–038—4–040
implied repeal doctrine, 4–024
interpretation, 4–024—4–028, 4–030—4–038
judiciary, 4–025—4–040
Parliamentary sovereignty, 4–024
precedent, 4–025—4–040
rulings on EU law, 4–024
statutory interpretation, 4–025—4–040
supremacy of EU law, 4–032
European Convention on Human Rights
See also **European Commission on Human Rights, European Court of Human Rights, Human Rights Act 1998**
applications, 5–002
articles of, 5–010
renumbering, 5–001
Committee of Ministers, 5–002, 5–006
'Constitution' of, 5–005
Continental legal tradition, 5–005
Convention rights, giving further effect to, 5–001, 5–009—5–010
Council of Europe, 5–001—5–002
derogations, UK, 5–010
drafting style, 5–005
Eleventh Protocol, 5–001, 5–005—5–006
European Union legal order, 4–021, 5–002
false imprisonment, "detention" and the MHA 1983, 9–012
generally, 5–001—5–019
historical background, 5–009—5–010
home, right to respect for, 8–007
incorporation, 5–010
key features, 5–005—5–006
development of, 3–001—3–002
living instrument, as, 5–007
marital rape, 16–010
precedent, 5–007—5–008
private nuisance, 1–037
ratification, 5–009
remedies, 5–010
reservations on acceptance, 5–002

retrospectivity, 16–010
statutory interpretation, 1–074—1–075, 1–089, 1–094
succession rights under the Rent Act 1977, 13–002, 13–003, 13–004
Vienna Convention, 5–006
European Court of First Instance *See* **Court of First Instance**
European Court of Human Rights
applications to, 5–002
composition, 2–023
Continental legal tradition, 5–007
(European) Court of Justice, 5–005
false imprisonment, "detention" and the MHA 1983, 9–012
general principles, 5–008—5–009
Human Rights Act 1998, 5–010
judiciary
function, 5–006
techniques, 5–006—5–009
margin of appreciation, 5–009
marital rape, 16–010
persuasive precedents, 1–023
previous cases, using, 5–007—5–008
stare decisis, 5–007
(European) Court of Justice, 2–003
binding precedents, 1–005, 1–014, 1–016—1–021
case law and precedent, 1–005—1–007
'constitution', guardian of, 4–011
Court of First Instance/General Court, 4–018—4–019
decisions, consistency of, 4–018
equal pay, 1–016, 14–001—14–020
European Communities Act 1972, 4–024—4–030, 4–038—4–040
European Court of Human Rights, 5–005
general principles of law, 4–019
interpretation, 1–063—1–065, 3–002, 4–011, 4–016, 4–018, 4–028
jurisdiction, 5–005
legal rules, formulation of, 1–005
persuasive precedents, 4–018
precedent, 4–016—4–019, 4–038—4–040
principles, 4–024, 4–028—4–030, 4–033
ratio decidendi, 1–005, 4–038—4–039
references from national courts, 1–016
res judicata, 4–018
role of, 4–011
rulings on EU law, 1–016, 4–024, 4–027—4–028, 4–038—4–039, 14–005—14–006
sources of English law, 1–001, 1–005—1–007
supremacy of EU law, 4–023, 4–039
European Human Rights Convention *See* **European Convention on Human Rights**
European Union
See also **European Communities Act 1972, (European) Court of Justice**
binding precedent, 4–018
Charter of Fundamental Rights, 4–010
constitution of the EU, 4–010—4–011

Continental legal tradition, 4–001–4–007, 4–013, 4–018
Court of First Instance/General Court, 4–018–4–019
direct effect, 4–023–4–024, 4–032, 5–013, 14–005, 14–018–14–020
EC Treaty, renumbering of, 4–001
equal pay, 4–010, 4–013–4–016, 4–018, 14–001–14–020
European Convention on Human Rights, 4–020
general principles of law, 4–020
generally, 4–001–4–040
impact of membership, 1–006
indirect effect, 4–023, 4–033–4–036
institutions, 4–009
introduction into English legal system, 4–020
judiciary
  attitudes of, 4–021–4–023
  ECA 1972, approaches to, 4–025–4–040
  function, 4–013–4–016
  techniques of, 4–016–4–020
legislation, 4–001, 4–009–4–013
Parliamentary sovereignty, 4–024–4–025
precedent, impact on, 4–038, 4–040
previous cases, use of, 4–016–4–019
proportionality, 4–008, 4–020
res judicata, 4–038
statutory interpretation, 4–001–4–040
  schematic approach, 4–016
  textual approach, 4–016
supranational legal order, as, 4–023
supremacy of EU law, 4–023–4–025, 14–005
Treaty on Functioning of European Union, 4–001, 4–010–4–012, 4–016, 4–023, 4–025, 4–028, 4–029, 4–034, 4–035, 4–039, 4–041
Treaty of Lisbon, 4–001, 4–010
UK, relationship between EU and, 4–024–4–025
Existing obligations as consideration in contract, 7–001–7–006
Anangel, 7–001, 7–006
  distinguishing precedents, 1–054
distinguishing precedents, 1–054, 7–006
Foakes v Beer, 7–006
Harris v Watson
  overruling decisions, 7–002–7–003
  precedential strength, 1–048, 7–002
overruling decisions, 7–002
  persuasive precedents, 1–023, 1–029
precedents, 7–001–7–002
  strength, 1–026, 1–048, 7–002
Selectmove, 7–001, 7–006
Stilk v Myrick, 7–001–7–005
  overruling decisions, 7–002–7–003
  persuasive precedents, 1–023
  precedential strength, 1–026, 1–048, 7–002
Williams v Roffey, 7–001–7–006
  application in *Adam Opel GmbH, Renault S.A*, 7–006

Court of Appeal's decision, 7–001–7–002
  distinguishing precedents, 1–054, 7–006
  persuasive precedents, 1–023
  precedential strength, 1–026
Woodhouse
  persuasive precedents, 1–029
Expressio unius exclusio alterius, 1–089–1–090, 6–006–6–007

False imprisonment, "detention" and the MHA 1983, 9–001–9–012
Bournewood
  analogous area of law, 1–003, 9–003–9–004
  Court of Appeal decision, 9–005–9–007
  distinguishing precedents, 1–068
  European Court of Human Rights, 9–012
  High Court decision, 9–002–9–004
  House of Lords decision, 9–008–9–011
  policy considerations, 1–093, 9–011–9–012
  ratio decidendi, 1–009, 1–032, 9–006–9–007, 9–010
  statutory interpretation, 1–068, 1–070, 1–081, 1–086, 1–090, 1–093, 9–002, 9–007, 9–010
  textbooks, 1–035
definition of detention, 9–003–9–004, 9–006–9–007, 9–008–9–010
dictionaries, 9–003–9–004
distinguishing precedents, 1–068
European Convention on Human Rights, 9–012
Forsey
  distinguishing precedents, 1–068
  ratio decidendi, 1–009, 1–032
Human Rights Act 1998, 9–012
obiter dicta, 9–007
policy considerations, 9–011–9–012
procedural safeguards, 9–012
ratio decidendi, 1–009, 1–032, 9–006–9–007, 9–010
reform, 9–012
Royal Commission Report, 9–010
statutory interpretation, 1–068, 1–070, 1–081, 1–086, 1–090, 1–093, 9–002, 9–007, 9–010
textbooks, 1–035, 9–007
White Papers, 9–010, 9–012

General Court, 2–003, 3–001, 4–016, 4–019 *See also* **European Court of First Instance**
General principles of law
Continental legal tradition, 4–005, 4–007
contractual obligations arising out of invitations to tender, 6–002–6–003
European Court of Human Rights, 5–008–5–009
European Union legal order, 4–020
proportionality, 4–025

Hansard, 1–081

Headnotes, 1–007, 1–068
High Court, 2–006
  see also **Dvisional Court**
  binding precedents, 1–016, 1–022
  persuasive precedents, 1–026
  ratio decidendi, 1–026
House of Lords, 2–012
  see also **Supreme Court**
  binding precedents, 1–019
  persuasive precedents, 1–023–1–026
Human Rights Act 1998
  binding precedents, 5–016–5–018
  coming into force, 5–010
  common law, 5–018
  Convention rights, giving further effect to, 5–001, 5–009–5–010
  declarations of incompatibility, 1–074, 5–010, 5–013, 5–018
  EU law, 5–013
  European Court of Human Rights, 5–010
  false imprisonment, "detention" and the MHA 1983, 9–012
  freedom of expression, 5–010–5–012
  general principles, 5–018
  incorporation of ECHR, 3–002
  legislation, compatibility of, 5–012–5–016
  precedent, impact on, 5–016–5–018
  private nuisance, 8–007
  proceedings against, 5–017–5–018
  public authorities, 5–010, 5–018
  remedy, right to an effective, 5–010
  statutory interpretation, 1–074, 1–089, 5–001–5–018
  succession rights under the Rent Act 1977, 13–002
Human rights *See* **European Convention on Human Rights, Human Rights Act 1998**

Implied repeal doctrine, 4–024
Indirect effect, 4–023, 4–033–4–036
Industrial tribunals *See* **Employment Appeal Tribunal, Employment tribunals**
International standards, 1–037
International treaties and conventions, 1–037, 1–088–1–089, 4–021, 4–036–4–037, 13–004
  See also **European Convention on Human Rights**
Interpretation
  See also **Statutory interpretation**
  ambiguity approach, 4–030–4–032, 4–039, 5–012, 14–004, 14–020
  Continental legal tradition, 4–013
  equal pay, 4–019, 4–028–4–030, 4–032–4–033, 4–040
  EU law, 4–028–4–038, 5–019
  European Court of Human Rights, 5–006–5–007, 5–008–5–009
  (European) Court of Justice, 3–002, 4–011, 4–016, 4–018, 4–028

  gap, filling in, 4–016, 4–032–4–033, 4–037, 14–001–14–002, 14–005, 14–021
  general interpretation approach, 4–034–4–038, 4–039, 5–013, 14–005, 14–020
  priority approach, 4–032–4–033, 4–040, 14–005, 14–008, 14–020
  reading words into statutes, 1–062, 1–063, 1–070, 13–004
  rulings on EU law, 4–027
  schematic approach, 4–016, 4–028, 4–030, 4–032, 5–013, 14–007, 14–018
  teleological approach, 4–016, 4–028, 4–030, 4–032, 5–013, 14–007
  textual approach, 4–016

Judicial Committee of the Privy Council *See* **Privy Council**

Legal rules, formulation of, 1–001–1–005
Legislation
  See also **European Communities Act 1972, European Convention on Human Rights, Human Rights Act 1998, Statutory interpretation**
  delegated legislation, 1–059, 1–070
  European Union legal order, 4–001, 4–009–4–013, 4–021
  treaties and conventions, 1–037, 1–088–1–089, 4–021, 4–036–4–037

Magistrates' courts, 1–019, 1–026, 2–009
Margin of appreciation, 5–009
Marital rape, 16–001–16–011
  authors, view of, 16–002–16–005, 16–006
  binding precedents, 16–006
  Clarence, 16–003–16–005
    obiter dicta, 16–003
    textbooks, 16–003
  Clarke, 16–004
    obiter dicta, 16–004
    persuasive authorities, 16–004
    ratio decidendi, 1–009, 16–004
  distinguishing cases, 16–011
  European Convention on Human Rights, 16–001, 16–010
  extra-judicial lawmaking, 16–002–16.003
  Miller
    ratio decidendi, 1–009
  obiter dicta, 16–003, 16–004, 16–005, 16–006
    persuasive precedents, 1–034, 1–035–1–037, 16–004
    policy considerations, 1–058, 16–008
    precedential strength, 1–026
  R v R
    binding precedents, 16–006
    distinguishing cases, 16–011
    foreseeability, 16–010
    obiter dicta, 16–006
    persuasive precedents, 1–034, 1–035–1–037
    policy considerations, 1–058

precedential strength, 1–026
ratio decidendi, 16–006
retrospectivity, 16–010
statutory interpretation, 1–081, 1–094,
    16–006–16–010
textbooks, 1–035, 16–002–16–003
ratio decidendi, 1–009, 16–004, 16–006
Scottish decision, 16–005
statutory interpretation, 1–081, 1–094,
    16–001–16–002, 16–005, 16–006–
    16–010
SW v UK, 16–010
textbooks, 1–035, 16–002–16–005, 16–006
"unlawful" sexual intercourse, 16–005,
    16–008–16–009
Ministerial circulars, 1–059, 11–008

Nervous shock, 15–001–15–021
Alcock, 1–008–1–009, 15–010–15–011
    persuasive precedents, 1–029
    policy considerations, 1–057, 15–010–
        15–011
    ratio decidendi, 1–008–1–009, 15–011
Bell
    persuasive precedents, 1–034
    precedential strength, 1–050
Boardman, 15–008–15–009
    distinguishing precedents, 1–055, 15–008
    obiter dicta, 15–009
    ratio decidendi, 15–009
Bourhill, 15–006–15–007
    distinguishing precedents, 1–055, 15–007,
        15–011
    obiter dicta, 15–007
    precedential strength, 1–050
Coultas, 1–032, 1–035
dissenting judgments, 1–050, 15–016–15–017
distinguishing precedents, 1–055, 15–006,
    15–007–15–008, 15–011
Dulieu, 15–002–15–005
    obiter dicta, 15–003
    persuasive precedents, 1–029, 1–032, 1–034
    physical injury, fear of, 15–002–15–004
    ratio decidendi, 1–014, 15–003–15–004
    remoteness, 15–004–15–005
floodgates argument, 15–009, 15–016, 15–019
Grieves, 15–020
    distinguishing precedents, 1–055, 15–020
Hambrook case, 15–005–15–006
    distinguishing precedents, 1–068, 15–006
    persuasive precedents, 1–029
    precedential strength, 1–050
King v Phillips, 15–007–15–008
    distinguishing precedents, 1–068
McLoughlin, 1–008–1–009, 15–009–15–010
    floodgates argument, 15–009
    foreseeability, 15–009–15–010
    policy considerations, 1–057, 15–009–
        15–010
    ratio decidendi, 1–008–1–009, 15–010
obiter dicta, 15–003, 15–007, 15–009

Page v Smith, 15–011–15–012
    distinguishing precedents, 1–068, 15–011
    foreseeability, 15–011
    persuasive precedents, 1–032, 1–035
    policy considerations, 1–057
    ratio decidendi, 1–009, 1–012, 1–014,
        15–011–15–012
persuasive precedents, 1–029, 1–032, 1–034,
    1–035, 15–014
physical injury, fear of, 15–002, 15–004
policy considerations, 1–057, 15–009, 15–013,
    15–015–15–017, 15–019, 15–021
precedential strength, 1–050
primary victims, 15–01, 15–012–15–017
proximity, 15–007, 15–010–15–011, 15–021
ratio decidendi, 1–008–1–009, 1–012, 1–014,
    15–003–15–004, 15–009, 15–010,
    15–011–15–012, 15–014
remoteness, 15–002, 15–004–15–005,
    15–010
rescuers, 15–012, 15–017–15–019
reserving judgments, 1–051
secondary victims, 15–011, 15–012, 15–014
stress at work, 15–021
textbooks, 1–035, 15–004–15–005, 15–011,
    15–013–15–014
Wagon Mound
    persuasive precedents, 1–032, 15–011
White, 15–012–15–020
    Court of Appeal decision, 15–012
    employment argument, 15–013–15–017
    floodgates argument, 15–016, 15–019
    foreseeability, 15–016–15–019
    persuasive precedents, 1–029, 1–034,
        15–014
    policy considerations, 15–013, 15–015–
        15–017, 15–019, 15–021
    precedential strength, 1–051
    ratio decidendi, 15–014
    rescuers, 15–012, 15–017–15–019
Novel cases, 1–003

Obiter dicta
appropriation in theft, 17–002–17.003,
    17–006, 17–009–17–010, 17–015–17–016
case law and precedent, 1–001, 1–007–1–014
contractual obligations arising out of
    invitations to tender, 6–005
false imprisonment, "detention" and the MHA
    1983, 9–007
marital rape, 16–003, 16–004, 16–005,
    16–006
nervous shock, 15–003, 15–007, 15–009
persuasive precedents, 1–026, 1–029
Privy Council, 1–029–1–032
ratio decidendi, 1–011, 1–012
spouses as prosecution witnesses, 12–004
Old Bailey, 2–019
Overruling precedents 1–001–1–002
appropriation in theft, 1–002, 17–016–17–017
binding precedents, 1–021

private nuisance, 1–002, 8–004—8–005,
8–006
wives as prosecution witnesses, 12–005

Parliament
intention of, 1–065–1–094, 10–002–10–003,
11–005, 11–007
materials, 1–084—1–085
statutory interpretation, 1–065–1–094
Pepper v Hart, 1–079, 1–084
Per incuriam
binding precedents, 1–021
statutory interpretation, 2–003
video cassettes as obscene articles, 10–003
Persuasive precedents, 1–007
appropriation in theft, 1–026, 1–029, 1–037
authors, views of, 1–034—1–037
case law and precedent, 1–023—1–037
Continental legal tradition, 4–007
county courts, 1–026, 2–008
courts of other jurisdictions, 1–032–1–034,
12–006
Crown Court, 1–026
(European) Court of Justice, 1–023, 4–018
existing obligations as consideration in
contract, 1–023, 1–029
false imprisonment, "detention" and the MHA
1983, 1–032, 1–035
foreign courts, 1–032–1–034, 12–006
High Court, 1–026
House of Lords, 1–026
international standards, 1–036
Law Commission, 1–034
law reform bodies, 1–034—1–037
magistrates' courts, 1–026
marital rape, 1–035, 16–004
nervous shock, 1–029, 1–032, 1–034, 1–035,
15–014
obiter dicta, 1–028–1–029
private nuisance, 1–022, 1–025, 1–033, 1–035,
1–037
Privy Council, 1–030–1–031
ratio decidendi, 1–001, 1–023–1–032
lower courts, 1–024—1–025
Privy Council, 1–030–1–031, 2–022
same courts of, 1–026–1–027
spouses as prosecution witnesses, 1–025,
1–027, 1–029, 1–035, 11–016, 12–003,
12–006
Supreme Court, 1–026
textbooks, 1–034–1–035
Persuasive precendents
treaties, 1–036–1–037
Policy considerations
abortion regulation, 1–092, 11–010, 11–013
appropriation in theft, 1–092, 17–017
case law and precedent, 1–057
false imprisonment, "detention" and the MHA
1983, 1–092, 9–011
marital rape, 1–057, 1–092, 16–008

nervous shock, 1–057, 15–009, 15–010, 15–011,
15–015, 15–016, 15–019
private nuisance, 1–057, 8–005, 8–006
spouses as prosecution witnesses, 12–007
statutory interpretation, 1–092
succession rights under the Rent Act 1977,
1–092, 13–003, 13–004
succession rights under the Rent Act, 1–092,
13–003, 13–004
video cassettes as obscene articles, 1–092,
10–003
Precedent
See also **Binding precedents**, **Case law and
precedent**, **Persuasive precedents**
absence of argument, 1–051
age of, 1–026
cases of first impression, 1–003
Continental legal tradition, 4–006—4–007
Court of First Instance
/General Court, 4–018—4–019
courts, composition of, 1–045–1–047,
2–003–2–023
disapproving, 1–001–1–002
dissent, existence of, 1–048–1–050
dissenting judgments, 1–002–1–003
distinguishing, 1–002
EU law, 3–001–3–002
European Communities Act 1972, 4–025—
4–040
European Communities Act, 4–025—4–040
European Convention on Human Rights,
5–001—5–018
European Court of Human Rights, 5–007—
5–008
(European) Court of Justice, 4–016—4–019,
4–038—4–040
European Union legal order, 4–016—4–019
exclusionary rule, 1–084
Human Rights Act 1998, 5–016—5–018
legal rules, formulation of, 1–001–1–002
non binding, 1–001
novel cases, 1–003
obiter dicta, 1–001, 1–007
overruling, 1–001–1–002
Pinochet case, 1–001
precedential strength, 1–042–1–053
private nuisance, 8–002
ratio decidendi, 1–001, 1–007
relevancy, 1–002
reliance on, 1–003, 1–005
reserving of decisions, 1–050–1–051
strength of, 1–042–1–053, 7–002
Private nuisance, 8–001—8–007
academic opinion, 8–007
binding precedents, 1–022, 8–002
Dobson v Thames Water Utilities, 8–007
European Convention on Human Rights, 1–037
Human Rights Act 1998, 8–007
Hunter
House of Lords decision, 8–002—8–007
majority judgments, 8–003, 8.006

minority judgments, 8–006—8–007
persuasive precedents, 1–023, 1–032,
    1–035, 1–037
policy considerations, 1–057
rationale for the decision, 8–003—8–004
standing, 8–001—8–007
statutory interpretation, 1–063
international standards, 8–006—8–007
Khorasandjian, 8–004—8–005, 8–007
    binding precedents, 1–022
    gap, filling in, 1–063
    overruling decisions, 8–005
    persuasive precedents, 1–023
    ratio decidendi, 1–008, 1–011
Malone, 8–004—8–005
    binding precedents, 1–022, 8–002
    persuasive precedents, 1–023
    ratio decidendi, 1–008, 1–011
modernisation of the law, resistance to,
    8–005—8–006
overruling decisions, 8–005
persuasive precedents, 1–023, 1–032, 1–035
policy considerations, 1–057
ratio decidendi, 1–011
textbooks, 1–037
United States cases, 8–007
Privy Council, 2–022
    appeals, 1–016, 1–031—1–032,
    persuasive precedents, 1–031—1–032
Proportionality, 4–007, 4–020, 5–008, 5–018
Psychiatric injury, *See* Nervous shock

Quarter Sessions, 2–019

Rape, See Marital rape
Ratio decidendi
    appropriation in theft, 1–009, 1–012, 17–002—
        17–004, 17–006, 17–009, 17–013—17–016,
        17–017, 17–018
    ascertaining, 1–007
    binding precedents, 1–001, 1–011, 1–014,
        1–019—1–023
    broad or narrow, 1–009—1–011
    case law and precedent, 1–001, 1–007—1–014
    cases where no ratio, 1–008
    competing, 1–008—1–009
    contractual obligations arising out of invitation
        to tender, 1–008, 1–011, 1–012, 6–004,
        6–005—6–006
    definition, 1–001, 1–094
    discretion, 1–009—1–011
    distinguishing precedents, 1–054—1–056
    (European) Court of Justice, 1–005, 4–038—
        4–039
    false imprisonment, "detention" and the MHA
        1983, 1–009, 1–032, 9–006—9–007,
        9–010
    headnotes, 1–007
    High Court, 1–026
    Human Rights Act 1998, 5–017—5–018
    legal rules, formulation of, 1–001

marital rape, 1–009, 16–004, 16–006
material facts, 1–009—1–010
nervous shock, 1–008—1–009, 1–012, 1–014,
    15–003—15–004, 15–009, 15–010,
    15–011—15–012, 15–014
obiter dicta, 1–011—1–012
persuasive precedents, 1–001, 1–023—1–032
policy considerations, 1–011
private nuisance, 1–008, 1–011
Privy Council, 1–016, 1–031—1–032
rulings on EU law, 4–038—4–039
spouses as prosecution witnesses, 1–009,
    1–012, 12–002—12–003, 12–004
stare decisis, 1–014, 1–019, 1–021
tribunals, 1–037—1–039
video cassettes as obscene articles, 1–012,
    10–003—10–004
Res judicata
    binding precedents, 1–001
    (European) Court of Justice, 4–018
    European Union legal order, 4–038
Reserved decisions, 1–001, 1–050—1–051
Rules of interpretation, 1–063, 1–066—1–075,
    1–094
Rulings on EU law, 1–016, 4–024, 4–027—
    4–028, 4–038—4–039, 14–005—14–006

Sources of law
    common law, 1–001
    EU law, 1–001
    statute law, 1–001, 1–070
Spouses as prosecution witnesses, 12–001—
    12–008
    All Saints, Worcester, 12–002—12–004
        distinguishing precedents, 1–055, 12–003
        persuasive precedents, 1–025, 12–003
        precedential strength, 1–048
        ratio decidendi, 12–002—12–003
        textbooks, 12–003
    Criminal Law Revision Committee, 12–007—
        12–008
    dissenting judgments, 1–002
    distinguishing precedents, 1–068, 12–003
    foreign cases, 12–006
    Hoskyn, 12–001—12–008
        dissenting judgments, 1–002
        distinguishing precedents, 1–055
        persuasive precedents, 1–025, 1–029, 1–035
        policy considerations, 1–057
        precedential strength, 1–029, 1–044, 1–051
        ratio decidendi, 1–009, 1–012
        statutory reversal of, 12–008
    Lapworth, 12–005—12–006
        persuasive precedents, 1–023
        precedential strength, 1–026
    Leach, 12–004—12–005
        obiter dicta, 12–004
        persuasive precedents, 1–026
        precedential strength, 1–051
        ratio decidendi, 12–004
        statutory interpretation, 12–004

persuasive precedents, 1–023, 1–026, 1–029,
1–034, 1–035, 12–003, 12–006
policy considerations, 1–057, 12–006—12–008
precedential strength, 1–026, 1–048, 1–051
R v L, 12–008
ratio decidendi, 1–009, 1–012, 12–002—
12–003, 12–004
reserving judgments, 1–051
statutory interpretation, 12–004
textbooks, 1–035, 12–003
Stare decisis
binding precedents, 1–014, 1–019, 1–021
equal pay, 14–018—14–019
European Court of Human Rights, 5–007
Statute law, 1–001, 1–059
Statutory instruments, 1–059
Statutory interpretation, 1–059–1–094
abortion regulation, 1–059, 1–070, 1–081,
1–093
absurdity, 2–007—2–009
aids, 1–063, 1–075–1–090, 5–018, 9–007
ambiguity, 1–066, 1–070, 1–084, 4–030—
4–032, 4–039–4–040, 5–010, 5–013,
14–004, 14–020
ambulatory, 1–073, 5–007
appropriation in theft, 1–068, 1–070, 1–088,
1–090, 17–001–17–002, 17–008–17–013
circulars, 1–059
codes of practice, 1–059
codification, 4–005–4–006
constitutional principle, 1–084
Continental legal tradition, 4–001—4–003,
4–005—4–006
delegated legislation, 1–059, 1–070
dictionaries, 1–066–1–068, 9–003–9–004
ejusdem generis, 1–089, 10–001–10–002,
10–003
equal pay, 1–059, 1–070, 1–086, 4–028,
4–030, 4–031, 4–034, 4–040, 14–001–
14–021
EU law, 1–059, 1–063–1–065, 1–074–1–075,
1–089, 1–094, 3–001–3–002, 4–030—
4–038
European Communities Act 1972, 4–025—
4–040
European Communities Act, 4–025–4–040
European Convention on Human Rights,
1–089, 1–094, 5–001–5–018
European Union legal order, 4–001–4–040
exclusionary rule on Parliamentary
statements, 1–084
Explanatory Notes, 1–079
expressio unius exclusio alterius, 6–007
extrinsic material, 1–070—1–079
false imprisonment, "detention" and the MHA
1983, 1–068, 1–070, 1–081, 1–086, 1–090,
1–093, 9–002, 9–007, 9–010
form and substance, presumptions of, 1–089—
1–090
general interpretation approach, 4–034—
4–038, 4–040, 5–013, 14–005, 14–020
golden rule, 1–066—1–069, 1–070
Hansard, 1–084
Human Rights Act 1998, 1–074–1–075,
1–089, 5–001–5–018
intention of Parliament, 1–065–1–094,
10–002, 10–003, 11–005, 11–007
intrinsic material, 1–076, 1–077
legislative history, 13–004
literal rule, 1–066—1–069, 1–070–1–073
marital rape, 1–081, 1–094, 16–001–16–002,
16–005, 16–006–16–010
meaning of words, 1–065—1–066, 1–070,
1–081, 1–094
ministerial circulars, 1–059
ministerial statements, 1–084
mischief rule, 1–068–1–074
modification of traditional, 1–074–1–075,
4–030–4–038, 5–013–5–016
obscurity, 1–084
ordinary meaning, 1–068, 10–003, 11–008,
14–005, 14–017
Parliament
intention, 1–065–1–094, 10–002—10–003,
11–005, 11–007
materials, 1–076–1–088
Pepper v Hart, 1–079, 1–084, 1–085
policy considerations, 1–090–1–094
pre-Parliamentary publications, 1–086–1–088
presumptions, 1–089–1–090
primary legislation, 1–059
priority approach, 4–032–4–033, 4–040,
14–005, 14–008, 14–020
purposive approach, 1–068–1–074
reading words into statutes, 1–062, 1–063,
1–070, 13–004
rules, 1–063, 1–066–1–075, 1–094
spouses as prosecution witnesses, 12–004
statute law, 1–001, 1–059
statutory instruments, 1–059
succession rights under the Rent Act 1977,
13–002, 13–004
succession rights under the Rent Act, 13–002,
13–004
surplusage, 16–009
travaux preparatoires, 1–088, 4–006
treaties and conventions, 1–088–1–089,
4–036–4–037
video cassettes as obscene articles, 1–073—
1–074, 1–090, 1–093, 10–001–10–004
Strasbourg Court *See* **European Court of
Human Rights**
Subordinate legislation, 1–059, 1–070
Succession rights under the Rent Act 1977
Human Rights Act 1998, 13–002
international treaties, 13–004
legislative history, 13–004
policy considerations, 13–003, 13–004
reading words into a statute, 13–004
Supremacy of EU law, 4–023, 4–032–4–033,
4–039, 14–005
Supreme Court, 2–004

see also **House of Lords**
binding precedents, 1–019
persuasive precedents, 1–023—1–026

Textbooks and articles
abortion regulation, 11–003
appropriation in theft, 1–037, 17–010
false imprisonment, "detention" and the MHA
1983, 1–035, 9–007, 9–011
marital rape, 1–035, 16–002—16–005, 16–006
nervous shock, 1–035, 15–004—15–005,
15–011, 15–013—15–014
persuasive precedents, 1–034—1–035
private nuisance, 1–035, 8–003
spouses as prosecution witnesses, 1–035,
12–003
Travaux preparatoires, 1–088, 4–006
Treaties, 1–037, 1–088—1–089, 4–021, 4–036—
4–037
See also **European Convention on Human
Rights, European Union**
Tribunals
See also **Employment Appeal Tribunal,
Employment tribunals**

binding precedent, 1–039—1–041
case law and precedent, 1–038, 2–001
court hierarchy, 1–016
First-tier Tribunal, 2–010
new structure, 2–020
two-tier structure, 1–016
Upper Tribunal, 2–010

Video cassettes as obscene articles, 10–001–
10–004
Attorney-General's Ref (No 5 of 1980)
Court of Appeal decision, 10–002—10–004
Crown Court decision, 10–002
obiter dicta, 10–004
per incuriam, 10–003
ratio decidendi, 1–012, 10–003—10–004
statutory interpretation, 1–073—1–074,
1–090, 1–093, 10–001—10–004
ejusdem generis, 10–001—10–002, 10–003
obiter dicta, 10–004
per incuriam, 10–003
ratio decidendi, 1–012, 10–003—10–004
statutory interpretation, 1–073—1–074, 1–090,
1–093, 10–001—10–004